Footprint Handbook

Ecuador & Galápagos

ROBERT & DAISY KUNSTAETTER

This is
Ecuador &
Galápagos

Ecuador is compact by South American standards, compact enough for you to have breakfast as you watch dawn break over the Amazon jungle canopy, lunch at the foot of a smoking snow-capped volcano and dinner amid the last rays of sunset over the Pacific ocean. Within this small area, it boasts extraordinary diversity: geographical diversity ranging from an avenue of volcanoes straddling the Equator, to rainforest, beaches and tropical islands; biological diversity, amongst the highest in the world, protected by 50 national parks and reserves; and cultural diversity, with 17 ethnically distinct indigenous groups.

With so much variety, Ecuador has something for everyone. Birdwatching, trekking, mountaineering, mountain biking, whitewater rafting, paragliding and surfing are among the country's many privileged outdoor activities. Yet the draw is not only about hiking boots and adrenalin. Archaeology, art and local culture are also abundant and varied. The capital, Quito, and the southern highland city of Cuenca, have two of the finest colonial districts in South America, an excellent selection of museums and a lively tourist scene.

The smaller towns and villages of Ecuador offer the most authentic experience as well as the opportunity to share their traditions at fiestas and through community tourism. Indulge your senses at one of their many markets, with dizzying arrays of textiles, ceramics, carvings and other crafts, not to mention the plethora of domestic animals and cornucopia of fresh produce. They are all there for the local people but tourists are very welcome.

The Galápagos Islands, cradle and showcase of Darwin's theory of evolution, are the rich icing on the Ecuadorean cake. Fragile and expensive, the Galápagos are not for everyone, but if you are passionate about nature, they offer a once-in-a-lifetime experience worth saving for.

Ecuador is your oyster and it is also our home. We are proud of its many wonders and concerned about their future. We warmly welcome you to share the sense of wonder that Ecuador can inspire and we ask you to please tread lightly here, so that the traveller's dream may continue.

Robert and Daisy Kunstaetter

Best of
Ecuador &
Galápagos

top things to do and see

❶ Colonial Quito and around

The capital's treasure trove of religious art and architecture is the heart of a vibrant city, offering many urban delights. It also provides access to outstanding natural areas nearby, such as Mindo and the cloudforests of Pichincha volcano, a nature lover's paradise. Pages 41 and 85.

❷ Otavalo

Best known for the largest craft market in South America, this town is also home to a proud and prosperous indigenous people. They have made their name not only as successful weavers and traders, but also as symbols of cultural fortitude. Page 112.

❸ Parque Nacional Cotopaxi

Cotopaxi (5897 m) is one of the world's highest active volcanoes and it resumed activity in 2015. The surrounding national park is closed to visitors until volcanic activity subsides but the mountain's perfect snow-covered cone and impressive plume of ash can be admired from Quito and surrounding areas. Page 148.

❺ Baños

A traditional Ecuadorean highland resort known for its thermal baths, Baños offers adventure and relaxation at the foot of active Volcán Tungurahua. It is a good base for trekking, horse riding, mountain biking, waterfall watching and watching the world go by. Page 169.

❻ Cuenca

A UNESCO World Heritage Site and the most congenial city in Ecuador, Cuenca's cobblestone streets, flowering plazas and pastel-coloured buildings make it a pleasure to explore. Its many charms have attracted the largest expat community in the country. Page 195.

❹ Quilotoa Circuit

This 200-km loop includes an emerald-green crater lake and many indigenous villages known for their authentic markets and distinctive crafts. Depending on your time and stamina, the circuit can be done by bus, bike or on foot. Page 157.

❼ Vilcabamba

Once a fabled fountain of youth, this small town is the rainbow at the south end of Ecuador's gringo trail. It offers access to the hinterlands of Parque Nacional Podocarpus and everything from great horse riding to a colourful café scene. Page 221.

❽ Montañita

Famed for its surf and scene, this seaside-village-turned-resort attracts many Ecuadoreans and foreigners. Easily reached from Guayaquil, it is packed with hotels, restaurants, surf shops, tattoo parlours and craft and jewellery vendors. There are also more tranquil beaches nearby. Page 256.

❾ Puerto López

A very popular base for whale watching from June to September, this seaside town provides year-round access to the gorgeous Los Frailes beach and Parque Nacional Machalilla, which protects tropical forests, a marine ecosystem and Isla de la Plata. Page 258.

⑩ Tena

Relaxed and friendly, Tena is Ecuador's most important centre for whitewater rafting. It also offers ethno-tourism, with visits to indigenous communities, as well as jungle tours. It also makes a good stop when travelling overland between the highlands and Oriente jungle. Page 306.

⑪ Reserva Faunística Cuyabeno

This 603,000 ha wildlife reserve is filled with jungle rivers, lagoons and an extraordinary variety of Amazon wildlife. Paddle your canoe beneath the canopy to take in one of the finest protected natural areas in the country. Page 297.

⑫ Galápagos Islands

Here, in one of the world's foremost wildlife sanctuaries, you can snorkel with penguins and sea lions, watch 200-kg tortoises lumbering through giant cactus forest, and enjoy the courtship display of the blue-footed booby and frigate bird, all in startling close-up. Page 322.

COLOMBIA

Río Putumayo

SUCUMBIOS · Reserva
Faunística
Cuyabeno

11

Río Aguarico

Parque
Nacional ♦
Yasuní

Río Napo

Nuevo
Rocafuerte ○

PERU

Route planner
Ecuador & Galápagos

putting it all together

Ecuador is small enough to make travelling around easy, and varied enough to make almost any itinerary worthwhile. The following are but a few suggestions and you are heartily encouraged to venture further afield.

One week

explore sights around Quito and the central highlands

Seven days is a bit rushed but feasible. You could fly to any one of the following regions – southern highlands, Pacific coast, Oriente jungle or Galápagos – and make visiting that one area your entire trip. Or stay close to Quito and visit places within easy reach of the capital. Acclimatize to the altitude while you get to know Colonial Quito, play tourist at Mitad del Mundo or visit a museum; then ride the Teleférico high above the city. Head north to Otavalo, perhaps for the Saturday market. From Otavalo visit Lago San Pablo or Cuicocha crater lake, and one of the nearby craft towns. You could also visit Cotopaxi National Park, or the town of Mindo surrounded by cloudforest and birdwatching opportunities, followed by a visit to Papallacta thermal baths.

Right: Tungurahua volcano, near Baños
Opposite page: Marine iguana, Galápagos Islands

• 11

For most people, this is the ideal length of a visit to Ecuador. The following are all overland routes but you can take shortcuts by flying one way, such as travelling by bus as far as Cuenca and returning to Quito by plane.

Highlands and Oriente jungle Head south by road from Quito to Latacunga, then to Quilotoa's emerald-green crater lake. Spend a night in the traditional villages along the Quilotoa circuit before continuing to Baños, where nearby 'Mama' Tungurahua, an active volcano, might welcome you with a bang. Trekking, biking and horse riding, thermal baths, cafés and nightlife are the main draws in Baños. Tear yourself away to continue along the spectacular Río Pastaza valley with its plethora of waterfalls, to Puyo, then north to Misahuallí or Tena. Although not primary, nearby rainforest is easy to visit. Tena also has whitewater rafting and kayaking, as does Quijos valley along the road back toward Quito. Don't miss Papallacta hot springs before returning to the capital.

Right: Whitewater rafting
Below: Plaza de la Independencia, Quito
Opposite page: Riobamba train

Highlands and Pacific coast From Quito travel to Baños as above, then continue south to Riobamba. The city and its surroundings has the famous Devil's Nose train ride, as well as excellent climbing, trekking, mountain biking and highland indigenous culture. From Riobamba take a bus down to the city of Guayaquil. Spend a day here and stroll the riverside promenade, or just change buses and continue north to Montañita, a lively party/surfing beach, or the more tranquil Olón or Ayampe nearby. Continue north to Puerto López,
where whale watching is a must from June to September, and a visit to Isla de la Plata and the Parque Nacional Machalilla is worthwhile year round. Further north is the friendly resort of Bahía de Caráquez and the popular beach at Canoa. Return to Quito from Bahía or continue beachcombing your way north, stopping at another great surfing beach at Mompiche.

El Austro The attractive city of Cuenca is easy to reach by road or air, and is worth visiting for a few days. It's also the ideal base for exploring this geographically and culturally distinct region of Ecuador. Not far away is Ingapirca, Ecuador's premiere archaeological site, and *páramo*-clad Parque Nacional Cajas, both good for either a day trip or over-nighter. Take the bus south from Cuenca to Loja and on to Vilcabamba, next to the Parque Nacional Podocarpus with good trekking. On one side of Podocarpus is high jungle accessed from the city of Zamora, a short bus ride from Loja. On the other side is a delightful backwater: the colonial gold mining town of Zaruma. You can loop back to Cuenca from either Zaruma or Zamora, the latter route taking you along back roads through Gualaquiza in the seldom-visited southern Oriente.

One month or more

head deeper into the jungle for wildlife and activities

Given sufficient time, any of the above can be combined into longer routes and circuits. You can also widen the scope by heading downriver to the Amazon. Start by riding from Quito to Lago Agrio via Baeza, visiting the active Reventador volcano and Cascada San Rafael, Ecuador's highest waterfall, along the way. From Lago Agrio visit the Cuyabeno Wildlife Reserve, with some of the best jungle wildlife in Ecuador. Head south to Coca on the lower Río Napo, the jumping off point for several world-class jungle lodges and community-based jungle tours in Parque Nacional Yasuní. The truly adventurous can sail down the Río Napo from Coca to the frontier at Nuevo Rocafuerte, then to Iquitos (Peru) and beyond.

Best
markets
& crafts

Otavalo market

Home to what may be the largest and most visited indigenous craft market in all South America, Otavalo on a Saturday morning is an unforgettable experience. The cornucopia of crafts fills the streets: paintings, jewellery, weavings, baskets, leather goods, hats, wood carvings, ceramics, antiques and almost anything else you can think of. Market traders come from all over Ecuador, and beyond. It's worth arriving early, so consider staying in Otavalo on Friday night. Page 112.

Saquisilí market

Fewer visitors make it to Saquisilí than to Otavalo, and the Thursday market here is primarily for the indigenous locals. The streets throng with colourfully dressed highlanders from surrounding communities, with their red ponchos and felt hats. In addition to produce, most goods for sale here are utilitarian but you can also find *shigras* (crocheted shoulder bags), shawls, blankets and other textiles and ornamental crafts. Page 161.

Left: Otavalo market
Above: Saquisilí market
Opposite top left: Guamote market
Opposite top right: Tagua beads
Opposite bottom left: Panama hats
Opposite bottom right: Bread figurines

Guamote market

The Thursday market in the central highlands town of Guamote is even further off the beaten path and sees few outside visitors. Animals and local produce, including an impressive selection of local potatoes, are the main items here. The indigenous highland atmosphere is thoroughly authentic. Page 184.

Sombreros de paja toquilla

These most typical of Ecuadorean crafts are ironically known around the world as *Panama* hats. Montecristi, near Manta, is famous for the outstanding quality of its hats. They are also woven in the highlands, especially the provinces of Azuay and Cañar, near Cuenca, which is the main site of factories producing the hats and home to numerous shops selling them. Page 388.

Tagua

The tagua or ivory nut is a palm which grows below 1200 m on both the eastern and western slopes of the Andes. During the late 1800s, its very hard creamy-white seeds, known as vegetable ivory, were used to make buttons and toys. Toward the end of the 20th century, the tagua tradition was revived and Ecuador produces a wonderful variety of tagua crafts. Pages 26 and 256.

Bread figurines

Calderón, just north of Quito, is the place where figurines are made of bread dough. The original edible *guaguas de pan* ('bread kids') were placed in cemeteries on *Finados* (Day of the Dead) as offerings to hungry souls of the departed. Today they include a variety of themes, the Nativity collection is especially popular and attractive. Pages 109 and 390.

When to go

...and when not to

Climate

Ecuador is a year-round destination and the climate is unpredictable. As a general rule, however, in the **Sierra**, there is little variation by day or by season in the temperature, this depends on altitude. The range of shade temperature is from 6°C to 10°C in the morning, to 19°C to 23°C in the afternoon, though it can get considerably hotter in the lower basins. The day length (sunrise to sunset) is almost constant throughout the year.

Rainfall patterns depend on whether a particular area is closer to the eastern or western slopes of the Andes. To the west, June to September are dry and October to May are wet (but there is a short dry spell in December or January). To the east, October to February are dry and March to September are wet. There is also variation in annual rainfall from north to south, with the southern highlands being drier.

Along the **Pacific coast**, rainfall also decreases from north to south, so that it can rain throughout the year in northern Esmeraldas and seldom at all near the Peruvian border. The coast, however, can also be enjoyed year-round, although it may be a bit cool from June to November, when mornings are often grey with the *garúa* mists. January to May is the hottest and rainiest time of the year. Like the coast the **Galápagos** may receive *garúa* from May to December; from January to April the islands are hottest and brief but heavy showers can fall. In the **Oriente**, heavy rain can fall at any time, but it is usually wettest from March to September.

Ecuador's **high season** is from June to early September, which is also the best time for climbing and trekking. There is also a shorter tourist season in December and January. At major fiestas (see below), especially **Carnival**, **Semana Santa** (Easter), **Finados** (2 November) and over **New Year**, accommodation can be hard to find. Hotels will be full in individual towns during their particular festivals and resorts may be busy at weekends year-round.

Festivals are an intrinsic part of Ecuadorean life. In prehispanic times they were organized around the solar cycle and agricultural calendar. After the conquest, the church integrated the indigenous festivals with their own feast days and so today's festivals are a complex mixture of Roman Catholicism and indigenous traditions. Every community in every part of the country celebrates their own particular festival in honour of their patron saint and there are many more that are celebrated in common up and down the country, particularly in the Sierra. The exact dates of many fiestas vary from year to year, either with the ecclesiastic calendar or for other reasons; enquire locally to confirm current dates.

Outsiders are usually welcome at all but the most intimate and spiritual of celebrations and, as a gringo, you might even be a guest of honour. Ecuadoreans can be very sensitive, however, and you should make every effort not to offend (for example, by not taking a ceremony seriously or by refusing food, drink or an invitation to dance). At the same time, you should keep in mind that the resulting disinhibition is seldom pleasant.

January One of the least-known and least-understood fiestas in Ecuador is the **Diablada** or dance of the devils which takes place in Píllaro, in the province of Tungurahua, during the first six days of the year. Thousands of people from the town and nearby indigenous communities parade dressed as devils wearing elaborate masks. The event is unique in Ecuador and apparently unrelated to the larger and more famous *diablada* held each year for Carnaval in Oruro, Bolivia.

February-March Carnaval The four days before Ash Wednesday is when Ecuador runs riot. Children begin to play with water pistols and throw water-filled balloons soon after New Year, but the fun begins in earnest a week or two before the holiday. In a few places, flour and ink add to the mayhem and the mess. Loud music and free-flowing alcohol are also the rule in most places, and Guaranda is known for its especially wild carnival. One island of sanity is Ambato, where water-throwing is banned and flour is replaced by flowers at the city's **Fiesta de las Frutas y Flores**. Here colourful parades featuring elaborate floats are the main attraction.

March-April Semana Santa (Holy Week) is held the week before Easter and begins on **Palm Sunday** (Domingo de Ramos). This is celebrated throughout the country, but is especially dramatic in Quito, with a spectacularly solemn procession through the streets on **Good Friday**; also in Riobamba on Tue.

A particularly important part of Holy Week is the tradition of eating *fanesca* with family and friends. *Fanesca* is a soup made with salt fish and many different grains, and a good example of the syncretism of Catholic and earlier beliefs. In this case the Catholic component is the lack of meat, which was not consumed during Lent, while the many grains came from native traditions to celebrate the beginning of the harvest at this time of year. The original native version might have been made with *cuy* (guinea pig).

May-June **Corpus Cristi** is celebrated on the Thursday and weekend after Trinity Sunday. This festival is especially impressive in the towns of Pujilí, Saquisilí and Píllaro, as well as surrounding indigenous villages in the highlands of Cotopaxi and Tungurahua. Most notable are the *danzantes*, masked dancers with elaborate and very tall headdresses who parade through the streets. In Pujilí the festival includes *castillos*, 20-m-high poles which people climb to get prizes suspended from the top, including sacks of potatoes and live sheep. Different, but equally colourful, Corpus Cristi celebrations take place in Cuenca.

21-24 June **Inti Raymi** The solstice has been celebrated throughout the Andes since time immemorial. It overlapped and blended with Catholic festivals following the Spanish conquest and, in recent years, has experienced a revival in the highlands of Ecuador. In Otavalo the solstice *per se* and the **San Juan** festival (21 and 24 June, respectively) merge to create a week-long celebration. This usually begins with a ritual bath in a stream or pond and is followed by house to house dancing to the tune of native instruments. In Cayambe, **San Pedro y San Pablo** (29 June) is the preferred fiesta, when bonfires are lit and people jump over them. San Pedro is also celebrated in southern Chimborazo (Alausí and Achupallas) and among fishermen along the coast, where an image of St Peter is traditionally taken out in a boat.

23-25 September **Mama Negra** Held in Latacunga, once in September and again on the weekend before 11 November, Mama Negra is as unusual as festivals get in Ecuador. There is a tumultuous parade in which a man dressed as a black woman, the *Mama Negra*, is the focus of the celebrations. He/she rides a horse, carries a doll and changes kerchiefs at every corner. Another prominent character is the *Shanga*, also painted black and carrying a pig. The symbolism behind all this confusing choreography, which combines homage to the Virgen de las Mercedes with traditions of black slaves of colonial times, is all but inscrutable. Market vendors and other humble tradespeople are among the most enthusiastic participants in the September event, which is reputed to be the more authentic of the two.

2 November   Día de los Difuntos or **Finados** (Day of the Dead) is an important holiday nationwide. This tradition has been practised since time immemorial. In the Incaic calendar, Nov was the eighth month and represented *Ayamarca*, or land of the dead. *Colada morada*, a sweet drink made from various fruits and purple corn is prepared, as are *guaguas de pan* (bread dolls). In a few places, native families may build a special altar in their homes or take their departed relatives' favourite food and drink to the cemetery. Most Ecuadoreans commemorate *Día de los Difuntos* in more prosaic fashion, by placing flowers at the graveside of their deceased relatives.

December   Navidad (Christmas) is an intimate family celebration, starting with *Misa del Gallo* (Midnight Mass) followed by a festive meal. *Pases del Niño* (processions of the Christ child), take place through the country on various dates around Christmas time. Families who possess a statue of the baby Jesus carry them in procession to the local church, where they are blessed during a special Mass. The most famous *Pase del Niño* is in Cuenca on the morning of 24 December. Other notable celebrations take place in Saraguro, in Loja province, in Pujilí and Tanicuchí in Cotopaxi province and throughout the province of Cañar.

31 December   Año Viejo (New Year's Eve) Life-size puppets or effigies are built and displayed throughout the country, depicting important events of the year gone by. Children dressed in black are the old year's widows, and beg for alms in the form of sweets or coins. Just before midnight the will of the *Año Viejo* is read, full of bawdy humour and satire, and at the stroke of midnight the effigies are doused with gasoline and burned, thus wiping out the old year and all that it had brought with it. In addition to sawdust, the puppets usually contain a few firecrackers making for an exciting finale.

What to do

Birdwatching and nature tourism

With over 1600 known species, Ecuador is one of the richest places in the world for birds (see www.avesecuador.com and www. birdsinecuador.com). Some of the planet's most beautiful birds can be found here and birdwatching has gained recognition as an important tourist activity. The lowlands excel in cotingas, manakins, toucans, antbirds and spectacular birds of prey, while the cloudforests are noted for their abundance of hummingbirds, tanagers, mountain toucans and cock-of-the-rock.

Ecuador has an excellent network of lodges and reserves specializing in this wonderful avian diversity. These are a great asset not only for birdwatchers, but also for hikers, as well as orchid, bromeliad, frog, beetle and butterfly enthusiasts; indeed, for anyone who enjoys nature. See also page 400 for more on Ecuador's wildlife.

There is great pleasure in coming to grips with tropical birds on your own, but a good professional bird guide can show you many more species than you will find by yourself. There are some highly regarded Ecuadorean companies which specialize in bird tours, see page 72. Price is usually a good indicator of quality.

Sadly, natural habitat is quickly being destroyed in Ecuador, and many birds are threatened with extinction. Responsible ecotourism is one way to fight this trend; by visiting the lodges you are making it economically feasible for the owners to protect their land instead of farming or logging it. Another way you can help protect important Ecuadorean forest tracts is by donating to foundations that buy land for nature reserves; among these are the **Jocotoco Foundation** (www. fjocotoco.org) and the **Ecominga Foundation** (www.ecominga.com). You can also help by observing the guidelines outlined in www.responsibletravel.org.

For a comprehensive list and map of national parks and reserves, pages 406 and 404.

Climbing

Ecuador's mountains are one of its special attractions and there are 10 summits over 5000 m, of which six have glaciers. Many of the sub-5000-m mountains are enjoyable walk-ups and some of the big 10 are suitable for beginners, while others are only for experienced mountaineers.

Along with the exotic beauty of its mountains, outrageously easy access makes Ecuador a fantastic place to get some high-altitude climbing experience. From Quito, using public transport, you could theoretically arrive at the base of seven of the country's big 10 mountains the same day and summit the next day, after you have acclimatized to the altitude. Acclimatization is very important in Ecuador, as is preventing sunburn and snowblindness.

There are two climbing seasons in Ecuador: June to August and November to January, but the weather can be good or bad on any day of the year. More important than the time of year is the time of day. You should aim to reach the summit of any of the snow capped peaks at 0700 so that descent is completed well before midday. As the equatorial sun warms the snow it makes for difficult going and is prone to avalanches. Nights and early mornings are generally clear but cloud can roll in after sunrise, often reducing visibility to zero.

Due to deglaciation, conditions and routes are constantly changing. Neither the general descriptions provided in this book nor those in specialized climbing guides can be assumed to remain correct.

Government regulations state that no one may climb in Ecuador without a licensed guide from an authorized agency. Independent climbers and guides may be refused entry to national parks but exceptions might be made for internationally (UIAA) certified guides and members of Ecuadorian climbing clubs. The situation continues to evolve, so confirm current details locally.

There are mountain shelters on Cotopaxi, Chimborazo, Cayambe, Guagua Pichincha and the Ilinizas. Some have been recently refurbished; prices and access information are given in the main text. Equipment can be bought or rented from Quito's climbing and outdoor shops, but selection may be limited. Always check the condition of rented equipment before you take it out. Mountain rescue facilities in Ecuador are rudimentary but gradually improving. Report all emergencies first to T911. The most up-to-date climbing guide to Ecuador is *Berführer Ecuador* by Günther Schmudlach (Panico Alpinverlag, 2009, in German). Climbing agencies are listed in the relevant chapters throughout this book. Rock climbing information and equipment is available from the **Mono Dedo** shop, see page 71.

Diving and snorkelling

The coast of Ecuador is a paradise for divers, combining both cool- and warm-water dive sites in one of the most biologically diverse marine environments on Earth. The Galápagos Islands are undoubtedly the most popular destination, but diving in lesser-known waters such as those off the central coast of Ecuador is also worthwhile. The secluded coves of Isla de la Plata, 24 km offshore and part of Parque Nacional Machalilla, contain an abundance of multicoloured tropical fish which make diving and snorkelling a great experience. Access is from Puerto López, see page 258.

The Galápagos Islands are well known for their distinctive marine environments and offer more than 20 dive sites including opportunities for night diving. Each island contains its own unique environment and many are home to underwater life forms endemic to this part of theworld. For a detailed description of diving in Galápagos, see page 368. Dive operators in other parts of Ecuador are given in the main text.

The cost of doing a PADI course in Ecuador is relatively low by international standards. Equipment can be hired, but it is advisable to check everything thoroughly. The larger bookshops stock diving books and identification guides for fish and other marine life. There is only one decompression chamber on the Galápagos Islands, and possibly another operated by the navy in Guayaquil.

Horse riding
The horse was only introduced to South America during the Spanish conquest but it has become an important part of rural life throughout Ecuador. Horse riding, whether for a brief excursion or a multi-day trek, is an excellent way to get to know the countryside, its people and local equestrian traditions. Haciendas throughout the country (see page 30) generally offer horse riding. There are good riding opportunities in Otavalo, Machachi, Parque Nacional Cotopaxi, Baños and especially Vilcabamba; for details, see What to do in the listings of the corresponding towns.

Mountain biking
Ecuador offers excellent biking opportunities through spectacular mountain scenery or along rugged back roads throughout the country. You can rent bikes or sign up for day tours in many places; the most popular are Quito, Baños and Riobamba (see What to do in the listings for these cities). The tours are mostly downhill; you are driven up to a high point and ride down accompanied by a support vehicle. It's exhilarating and good fun.

Those seeking a longer cycling experience can either bring their own bike or purchase one locally, although the price, selection and quality of locally available models may not be as good as in other parts of the world.

What many people don't take into account is the frequently extreme conditions in which they find themselves cycling. Dehydration can be a very real issue when cycling at high altitudes or in the hot tropical lowlands. Always carry water; a water pump or other means of purification are useful away from towns. Sunscreen is essential at high altitudes even on cloudy days. Wraparound sunglasses help to restrict the amount of dust which gets into the eyes.

When planning routes you can use IGM 1:50,000 topographical maps (see page 422). You should in addition seek local knowledge, as the road network has changed substantially since these maps were made. In general, for biking as for hiking, the further from the main tourist trail, the safer you are. See advice about camping on page 31.

Paragliding and hang-gliding

These are pretty specialized and special activities, be it amid the high mountains or along the Pacific shoreline. They have a following in Ecuador and devotees can sometimes be seen in the rays of the afternoon sun drifting off toward a valley or the beach. The air sports are especially popular in the oceanside town of Crucita and to a lesser extent in Canoa, as well as highland locations including Ibarra and Ambato. Tandem flights and courses are available for beginners. See www.parapentecrucita.com and www.flyecuador.com.ec.

Rafting and kayaking

In Ecuador, the perfect storm of geological accidents and climatic conditions has resulted in high rainfall and year-round mostly warm whitewater. These factors combined with dozens of accessible rivers – ranging from easy to challenging – make the country an exceptional destination for rafters and kayakers, from beginner to expert.

Commercial river running, particularly rafting, has blossomed in recent years. About two dozen operators based out of Quito, Tena, Baños and the Quijos valley offer all-inclusive day trips. Multi-day trips involve either remote riverside camping or are based at lodges in more accessible areas. No previous rafting experience is needed to join most trips although participants should have a spirit of adventure and be able to swim.

Although more specialized than rafting, kayaking is becoming increasingly popular in Ecuador. Several operators offer guided trips for kayakers and rental kayaks are available for those with the experience and confidence to go it alone. Kayaking courses are likewise available.

There are various grades of rivers in Ecuador. Plunging off the Andes are very steep creeks offering, if they're runnable at all, serious technical grade V, suitable for expert kayakers only. As the creeks join on the lower slopes they form rivers navigable by both raft and kayak. Some of these rivers offer up to 100 km of continuous grade III-IV whitewater before flattening out in the jungle or coastal alluvial plain.

The most popular rivers for commercial rafting include: the Jatunyacu and the Lower Jondachi (an incredible raft run), both accessed from Tena; the Quijos and its tributaries, accessed from Baeza; and the Toachi/Blanco, usually reached from Quito. Rafting is also offered in Baños. Operators are listed in the What to do sections for these places.

Although guiding and safety standards are generally improving, it is wise to ask a few questions before booking a trip. The most important things to look for are experienced guides and top-notch equipment. Ask about guides' licenses; their rafting, river rescue and first aid training; whether they carry first aid, raft repair and river rescue kits; whether they use safety kayakers and have emergency communications. Since some of Ecuador's rivers are badly polluted, also ask about water quality before signing up for a trip.

A useful book is *The Kayakers' Guide to Ecuador*, www.kayakersguideto ecuador.wordpress.com.

Surfing

Ecuador has a few select surfing spots which are popular for both their waves and scene. On the mainland, from north to south, are: Mompiche, south of Muisne; San Mateo, south of Manta; Montañita, between Olón and Manglaralto; and Playas near Guayaquil. In Galápagos, there is surfing at Playa Punta Carola, outside Puerto Baquerizo Moreno on San Cristóbal Island. Details are given in the relevant chapter. Waves are best from December to March, except at Playas where the surfing season is from June to September. For more information contact the **Federación Ecuatorian de Surf**, http://fesurf.website.

Trekking

Ecuador's varied landscape, diverse ecological environment and friendly villagers make travelling on foot a delight. Although the most commonly travelled routes are in the Sierra, there are also a few good trekking opportunities that take you from the highlands to the coast or Oriente. You can descend east or west from the windswept *páramo* through cloudforest to tropical rainforest on either side of the Andes, and observe many of the ecosystems of Ecuador during a single excursion. Many hikes pass through protected natural areas (see box, page 406) but it is ruggedness and isolation, more than legislation, that protects most of these and makes them so appealing to wilderness travellers. There are not nearly as many well-marked trails and facilities as you might find in national parks in other parts of the world. In some places routes have been used for hundreds of years and are relatively easy to follow. In other areas you may have to make your own trail.

Reasonable fitness, strong navigation skills (using a map, compass and GPS) and a basic knowledge of Spanish are the most important prerequisites for independent trekking.

It is also possible to join a group or hire guides from tour operators. Many Quito companies offer trekking tours; see page 73. Guides and gear can also be hired through agencies in Otavalo, Latacunga, Baños, Riobamba and Cuenca.

It is best to bring trekking equipment from home, but some gear can be purchased or hired at outfitters in Quito and elsewhere. Check rented

Shopping tips

Almost everyone who visits Ecuador will end up buying a souvenir of some sort from the vast array of arts and crafts (*artesanías*) on offer. The most colourful places to shop for souvenirs, and pretty much anything else in Ecuador, are the many markets which can be found everywhere. The country also has more than its share of shiny, modern shopping centres, but remember that the high overheads are reflected in the prices.

Otavalo's massive market is the best-known place for buying wall-hangings and sweaters. Another market, at **Saquisilí**, south of Quito, is renowned for shawls, blankets and embroidered garments. Fewer handicrafts can be found on the coast, but this is where you can buy an authentic Panama hat at a fraction of the international price. The best, called *superfinos*, are reputed to be made in the little town of **Montecristi** near Manta, but the villages around Cuenca claim to produce superior models. **Cuenca** is a good place to buy Panama hats, and other types of hats can be bought throughout the highlands. Ecuador also produces fine silver jewellery, ceramics and brightly painted carvings. Particularly good buys are the many beautiful items fashioned from tagua, or vegetable ivory. By purchasing these you are promoting valuable conservation of the rainforests where the tagua palm grows.

All manner of *artesanías* can be bought in **Quito**, either at the Mercado Artesanal La Mariscal (see page 71) or in any of the many craft shops. An advantage of buying your souvenirs in a shop is that they'll usually package your gifts well enough to prevent damage on the flight home. Craft cooperatives are also a good place to shop, since there is a better chance that a fair share of the price will go to the artisan.

Stall holders in markets expect you to bargain, so don't disappoint them. Many tourists enjoy the satisfaction of beating down the seller's original price and finding a real 'bargain', but don't take it too far. Always remain good natured, even if things are not going your way (remember that you're on holiday and they're working). And don't make a fool of yourself by arguing for hours over a few cents. See also Best markets and crafts (page 14), and Arts and crafts (page 388). For local markets and shops see the Shopping lisings of the relevant town, city or village.

gear carefully. Topographic maps can only be purchased at the IGM in Quito (see page 422). The 1:50,000 scale maps are most useful, but their coverage of roads and trails is dated. The standard hiking shoe for Ecuador is the calf- to knee-high rubber boot, which is worn by most *campesinos* (rural dwellers) and costs about US$10. When combined with a good pair of wool socks, they keep feet warm and dry on the often muddy terrain. Note, however, that very large sizes may be hard to find.

On the trail and elsewhere, all water must be boiled or otherwise purified before drinking. The most common stove fuel available in Ecuador is the screw-on *camping gaz* canister; white gas is not available. Although dirty, all gasoline in Ecuador is unleaded and may be burnt by some stoves.

Ecuador's climate is inherently unpredictable and, as a trekker, you must be prepared for all conditions at any time of the year. Acclimatization to altitude and preventing sunburn are both important precautions. It is worth carrying a mobile phone on the trail (report all emergencies on T911) but self-sufficiency is very important, in the event of an accident self-evacuation may be your only option. In terms of public safety, the further off the tourist track you go the safer you are. See advice about camping on page 31. Enquire locally about safety before starting any trek.

For further information see www.trekkinginecuador.com. For trekking guidebooks, see page 413.

Yachting

Several hundred private yachts call on the Galápagos Islands every year, mainly en route from Panama to the Marquesas Islands and Tahiti. All yachts calling on Galápagos must use an agent and regulations are strictly enforced; see www.gos.ec and www.naugala.com.

The Pacific coast ports of mainland Ecuador also have their following. There are yacht clubs in Salinas (the most traditional), La Libertad/Puerto Lucía and Punta Blanca, all in Santa Elena; and Casa Blanca in Esmeraldas. All these are playgrounds of the Ecuadorean elite. Bahía de Caráquez, in Manabí, is the most low-key option for international boaters but due to silting of the Río Chone estuary it can't easily admit vessels with a draught greater than 2 m. A pilot is available.

You may also be able to arrange a secure berthing in commercial ports like Esmeraldas and Manta. If your vessel needs repairs or maintenance, or you just want some time to go travelling ashore, then the mainland may have more facilities and lower prices than Galápagos.

Where to stay

from haciendas to homestays

There are a great many hotels in Ecuador, with something to suit every taste and budget. The greatest selection and most upscale establishments are found in the largest cities and more popular resorts. In less visited places the choice of better-class hotels may be limited, but friendly and functional family-run lodgings can be had almost everywhere.

The following terms are loosely applied. *Hotel* is generic, much as it is in English. A *hostal* or *posada* (inn) may be an elegant expensive place, while the terms *pensión*, *residencial*, *hospedaje* and *alojamiento* often refer to more modest, economical establishments. *Hosterías* and *haciendas* (see page 30) usually offer upmarket rural lodgings. *Turismo comunitario* is another option, community tourism whereby visitors are offered accommodation as well as meals and activities by a local family (see www.turismocomunitario.ec). A *motel* is not a 'motor hotel' as it is in North America, rather it is a place where couples go for a few hours of privacy.

'Boutique hotel' as used in Ecuador is a buzz-word which does not necessarily mean anything except that a place is expensive. There is nonetheless a handful of very special lodgings in Ecuador which genuinely deserve distinction: exquisitely renovated old homes with a few beautifully appointed rooms or suites and personalized service from the owners or manager; all at the top end of the price range.

Price codes

Where to stay

$$$$ over US$150
$$$ US$66-150
$$ US$30-65
$ under US$30

Price of a double room in high season, including taxes.

Restaurants

$$$ over US$12
$$ US$7-12
$ under US$7 and under

Price of a two-course meal for one person, excluding drinks or service charge.

During major holidays accommodation is hard to find and prices rise. It is advisable to book in advance at these times, as well as during school holidays and local festivals, and even on ordinary weekends in popular areas.

Hotel owners may try to let their less attractive rooms first, but they are not insulted if you ask for a bigger room, better beds or a quieter area. In cities, remember that rooms away from the street will usually be less noisy. Likewise, if you feel a place is overpriced then do not hesitate to bargain politely. Always take a look at the rooms and facilities before you check in; there are usually several nearby hotels to choose from and a few minutes spent selecting among them can make the difference between a pleasant stay and miserable one.

In cheaper places, do not merely ask about hot water; open the tap and check for yourself. Tall travellers (above 180 cm) should note that many cheaper hotels, especially in the highlands, are built with the modest stature of local residents in mind. Make sure you fit in the bed and remember to duck for doorways.

Air conditioning is only of interest in the lowlands of the coast and Oriente. If you want an air-conditioned room expect to pay around 30% extra, otherwise look for a place with a good fan or sea breeze, and mosquito net. Conversely, hot water is only necessary in the highlands, where almost all places have it. A cool shower feels refreshing in the steamy climate of the coast and jungle. The electric showers sometimes used in cheaper hotels should be treated with respect. If you do not know how to use them, then ask someone to show you, and always wear rubber sandals or flip-flops.

Most of the better hotels have their own restaurants serving all meals. Few budget places have this facility, though some may serve a simple breakfast. Better hotels will often have their own secure parking but even more modest ones can usually recommend a nearby public car park. Most places have sufficient room to safely park a bicycle or motorcycle.

Some hotels charge per person or per bed, while others have a set rate per room regardless of the number of occupants. If travelling alone, it is usually cheaper to share with others in a room with three or four beds, or in a larger dormitory.

Even cheaper hotels may charge 12% *IVA* (VAT or sales tax), but enquire beforehand if this is included in their price. At the higher end of the scale 22% (12% tax + 10% service) is usually added to the bill.

The cheapest (and often nastiest) hotels can be found around markets and bus stations. If you're just passing through and need a bed for the night, they may be OK. In small towns, better accommodation may be found around the main plaza.

Many hotels in Ecuador can be booked online, either through their own websites or one of the many e-businesses which offer this service. Remember that the latter charge a commission which inflates the price and that you will generally pay more online than if you show up in person and bargain politely, although there are exceptions. Some cheaper hotels may offer online booking but do not always take such bookings seriously. You might turn up with your neatly printed reservation sheet only to be greeted with a puzzled stare. Also keep in mind that all hotels look good on their websites.

When booking a hotel from an airport or bus station by phone, try to talk to the hotel yourself rather than having someone do it for you. You may be told the hotel of your choice is full and be directed to one which pays a higher commission. Likewise, make sure that taxi drivers take you to the hotel you want, rather the one they say is best; they may be touting for a commission.

Almost without exception used toilet paper should not be flushed, but placed in the receptacle provided. This is also the case in most Ecuadorean homes and may apply even in some upmarket places; when in doubt ask. Tampons and sanitary towels should likewise be disposed of in the rubbish bin. See also Choosing a hotel in Quito (page 59) and Guayaquil (page 239).

Haciendas

The great haciendas of Ecuador were founded shortly after the Spanish conquest, either as Jesuit *obrajes* (slave workshops) or land grants to the conquistadors. When the Jesuits fell from favour and were expelled from South America, these huge land holdings passed to important families close to the Spanish royalty. They were enormous properties covering entire watersheds; most of the owners never even laid eyes on all their land. The earliest visitors to Ecuador, people like La Condamine and Humboldt, were guests at these haciendas.

The hacienda system lasted until agrarian reform in the 1960s. The much-reduced land holdings which remained in the hands of wealthy families, frequently surrounding beautiful historic homes, were then gradually converted to receive paying guests. Among the first to take in tourists were **Chorlaví**, near Ibarra; **Cusín**, by Lago San Pablo; **La Ciénega**, near Lasso; **La Andaluza**, outside Riobamba; and **Uzhupud**, between Gualaceo and Paute. They have since become successful upscale *hosterías* and are listed under the corresponding geographic locations in the text. They are no longer working haciendas but are nonetheless pleasant and comfortable places to stay.

Encouraged by the success of these first tourist haciendas, a few more opened to the public in the 1990s: **Pinsaquí**, north of Otavalo, and **Yanahurco**, near the Parque Nacional Cotopaxi. They offer accommodation attached to working farms, and feature activities like horse riding and cattle roundups. More recently, some of the most historic haciendas have also opened their doors to a few well-heeled guests. These are truly ancestral homes and a gateway to the country's past, to a time when *hacendados* (wealthy landowners) ruled supreme in their own little fiefdoms. Their descendants remain among Ecuador's economic and social elite and, even today, they and their servants welcome outsiders with the slightest hint of aloof condescension.

Some of the best-known haciendas open to visitors include: **Hacienda Chillo-Jijón**, outside Quito, www.hacienda-ecuador.com; **Hacienda Leito**, near Patate, www.hacienda leito.com; **Hacienda Zuleta**, between Ibarra and Cayambe, www.zuleta.com; **La Carriona**, outside Quito, www.lacarriona.com; **San Agustín de Callo**, near Parque Nacional Cotopaxi, www.incahacienda. com. These and others are described in the relevant chapters of this book. With a few exceptions, prices are in our $$$$ range and up.

Homestays

Homestays are especially popular with travellers attending Spanish schools in Quito and Cuenca. The schools can make these arrangements as part of your programme. You can live with a local family for weeks or months, which is a good way to practise your Spanish and learn about the local culture. Do not be shy to change families, however, if you feel uncomfortable with the one you have been assigned. Look for people who are genuinely interested in sharing (as you should also be), rather than merely providing room and board. Try a new place for a week or so, before signing up for an extended period.

Camping

Camping in protected natural areas can be one of the most satisfying experiences during a visit to Ecuador – see Trekking, page 25. Organized campsites, car or trailer camping on the other hand are very rare. The most frugal travellers may want to camp to keep costs down, and long-distance cyclists will sometimes need to camp between towns. In this case the best strategy is to ask permission to camp on someone's private land, preferably within sight of their home for safety. It is not safe to pitch your tent at random near villages and even less so on beaches. Those travelling with their own trailer or campervan can also ask permission to park overnight on private property, in a guarded car park or at a 24-hour petrol station (although this will be noisy). It is unsafe to sleep in your vehicle on the street or roadside.

Food
& drink

Ecuadoreans take their meals pretty seriously, not only for nutrition but also as a social experience. In smaller towns, most families still gather around the lunch table at home to eat and discuss the day's events. Sharing food is also a very important part of traditional celebrations and hospitality. A poor family, who generally must get by on a very basic diet, might prepare a feast for a baptism, wedding or high school graduation.

In many Ecuadorean homes, *desayuno* (breakfast) is fresh fruit juice, coffee, bread, margarine, and perhaps a little jam or white cheese. On the coast, a mid-morning *ceviche* may be enjoyed with a cold drink. *Almuerzo* (lunch) is by far the most important meal of the day. It may begin with a small appetizer, such as an *empanada*, followed by soup – compulsory and often the most filling course. Then comes a large serving of white rice, accompanied by modest quantities of meat, chicken or fish and some cooked vegetables or salad. Dessert, if served at all, might be a small portion of fruit or sweets. Lunch is also accompanied by fruit juice or a soft drink. *Merienda* or *cena* (supper) is either a smaller repetition of lunch or a warm drink with bread, cheese, perhaps cold cuts, *humitas* or *quimbolitos*.

Typical dishes
The details of the above vary extensively with each region based on custom and traditionally available ingredients. The following are some typical dishes worth trying. A recommended cookbook is *Comidas del Ecuador* by Michelle Fried.

In the highlands *Locro de papas* is a potato and cheese soup. *Mote* (white hominy) is a staple in the region around Cuenca, but used in a variety of dishes throughout the Sierra. *Caldo de patas* is cow heel soup with *mote*. *Llapingachos* (fried potato and cheese patties) and *empanadas de morocho* (a ground corn shell filled with meat) are popular side dishes and snacks. *Morocho*, on the other hand, is a thick drink or porridge made from the same white corn, milk, sugar and cinnamon. *Sancocho de yuca* is a meat and vegetable soup with manioc root. The more adventurous may want to try the delicious roast *cuy* (guinea pig), most typical of highland dishes. Also good is *fritada* (fried pork) and *hornado* (roast pork). Vegetarians can partake of such typically Andean specialities as *chochos* (lupins) and *quinua* (quinoa). *Humitas* are made of tender ground corn steamed in corn leaves, and similar are *quimbolitos*, which are sweet and prepared with white cornflour and steamed in achira leaves.

On the coast Seafood is excellent and popular everywhere. *Ceviche* is marinated fish or seafood which is usually served with popcorn, *tostado* (roasted maize) or *chifles* (plantain chips). *Langosta* (lobster) is an increasingly endangered species but continues to be illegally fished; so please be conscientious. Other coastal dishes include *empanadas de verde* which are fried snacks: a ground plantain shell filled with cheese, meat or shrimp. *Sopa de bola de verde* is plantain dumpling soup. *Encebollado* is a tasty fish and *yuca* chowder served with pickled onions, especially popular in Guayaquil. *Encocadas* are dishes prepared with coconut milk and fish or seafood, which are very popular in the province of Esmeraldas. *Cocadas*, on the other hand, are sweets made with coconut. *Viche* is fish or seafood soup made with ground peanuts, while *corviche* is fish or seafood deep fried in a plantain dumpling. *Patacones* are thick fried plantain slices served as a ubiquitous side dish. Only *ceviche de pescado* (fish) and *ceviche de concha* (clams), which are marinated raw, potentially pose a health hazard. Other varieties of *ceviche* such as *camarón* (shrimp/prawn), and *langostino* (jumbo shrimp/king prawn) are cooked before being marinated, so are generally safe.

In the Oriente Many dishes are prepared with *yuca* (manioc or cassava root) and a wide variety of river fish. *Maitos* (in northern Oriente) and *ayampacos* (in the south) are spiced meat, chicken, fish or palm hearts wrapped in special leaves and roasted over the coals. A traditional treat for jungle natives which has become increasingly popular with the population at large, is *chontacuro*, the larva of a large beetle roasted on a skewer; it makes *cuy* seem tame.

Special foods
Fanesca is a fish soup with beans, many grains, ground peanuts and more, sold during Easter Week throughout the country. *Colada morada* (a thick dark purple fruit drink) and *guaguas de pan* (bread dolls) are made around the time of Finados, the Day of the Dead, at the beginning of November. Special *tamales* and sweet and sticky *pristiños* are Christmas specialities.

Ecuadorean food is not particularly spicy. However, in most homes and restaurants, the meal is accompanied by a small bowl of *ají* (hot pepper

FOOD

Fruit salad

Treat your palate to some of Ecuador's exquisite and exotic fruits. They are great on their own, as *ensalada de frutas*, or make delicious juices (*jugos*), smoothies (*batidos*) and ice creams (*helados*). Always make sure these are prepared with purified water and pasteurized milk.

Babaco, highland papaya. Great for juice.

Chirimoya, custard apple. A very special treat, soft when ripe but check for tiny holes in the skin which usually mean worms inside.

Granadilla, golden passion fruit. Slurp it from the shell without chewing the seeds.

Guanábana, soursop. Makes excellent juice and ice cream.

Guava, ice cream bean. Large pod with sweet white pulp around hard black seeds. Not to be confused with guayaba, below.

Guayaba, guava (in English). Good plain or in syrup, also makes nice jam and juice.

Mango, the season is short: December and January. Try the little mangos de chupar, for sucking rather than slicing.

Maracuyá, yellow passion fruit. Makes a very refreshing juice and ice cream.

Mora, raspberry or blackberry. Not all that exotic but makes an excellent and popular juice and ice cream.

Naranjilla, very popular juice, often cooked with a dash of oatmeal to make it less tart.

Orito, baby banana. Thumb-sized banana, thin skinned and very sweet.

Papaya, great plain or as juice.

Piña, pineapple. A popular juice.

Taxo, banana passion fruit. Peel open the thin skin and slurp the fruit without chewing the seeds.

Tomate de arbol, tamarillo or tree tomato. Popular as juice but also good plain or in syrup. The secret ingredient of Ecuadorean *ají*.

Tuna, prickly pear. Sweet and tasty but never pick them yourself. Tiny blond spines hurt your hands and mouth unless they are carefully removed first.

Zapote or sapote. Fleshy and sweet, get some dental floss for the fibres that get stuck between your teeth.

sauce) which may vary greatly in potency. *Colada* is a generic name which can refer to cream soups or sweet beverages. In addition to the prepared foods mentioned above, Ecuador offers a huge variety of delicious temperate and tropical fruits, some of which are unique to South America (see box, above).

Drink

The usual soft drinks, known as *colas*, are widely available. Much better and more interesting is the bewildering array of freshly made fruit juices. Bottled water (*agua mineral*) is available everywhere, either still or carbonated.

The main beers include Pilsener and Club, both of which are reasonable. Some places have good microbrews and upmarket bars offer a wide selection of foreign beers. Quality imported wines are available but are not cheap, whilst imported liquor is even more expensive. *Aguardiente* ('fire-water') is the local potent sugar cane liquor, also known as *paico* and *trago de caña*, or just *trago*. *Chicha*, a native beverage fermented from corn in the highlands (*chicha de jora*) and from *yuca* (manioc root) or *chonta* (palm fruit) in Oriente, is not for those with a delicate stomach. Alcoholic beverages may not be sold or served on Sunday or the final day of a holiday (for example, on the Tuesday of carnival).

Dining out

The simplest and most common eateries found throughout Ecuador are small family-run *comedores* or *salones* serving only set meals: *almuerzos* and *meriendas* of the type described above. These cost US$2.50-5 and are easiest to find at midday. As long as the establishment is clean, you are unlikely to go wrong at one of these places, but you are unlikely to discover a hidden gastronomic treasure either. One step up, and available in provincial capitals, arRestaurants which serve both set meals (perhaps an *almuerzo ejecutivo* for lunch) and à la carte at night. They may feature Ecuadorean or international food, more swanky surroundings, and can be good for around US$10-12. Outside main cities and resorts, the above are seldom supplemented by more than *chifas* (Chinese restaurants, some quite good, others terrible) and Italian or pizza places, which are usually a safe bet. Vegetarians must be adaptable in small towns, but can count on the goodwill and ingenuity of local cooks.

In Quito, Guayaquil, Cuenca and the more popular tourist resorts, the sky is the limit for variety, quality, elegance and price of restaurant dining. You can find anything from gourmet French cuisine to sushi or tapas, very upscale Ecuadorean *comida típica*, plush cafés, and neon-on-plastic fast food chains. On the periphery of cities are many *paradores*, places where Ecuadorean families go at weekends to enjoy traditional fare or grilled meat. Some are very good.

At the lowest end of the price range, every market in Ecuador has a section set aside for prepared foods. You always take a chance eating in a market, but if a place is clean then you might still find a tasty nourishing meal for about US$2. Food vendors in the street, however, who have no way to properly wash their hands or utensils, should be avoided.

Aguado de pollo Chicken broth with rice.

Ají Hot pepper sauce, found on every table. It can be very tasty but also very strong. Try a little before applying dollops to your food.

Almuerzo The midday meal. It also refers to an economical set lunch.

Arroz Rice, served with most meals throughout Ecuador.

Bolón de verde Fried plantain dumpling served for breakfast in the lowlands.

Caldo de gallina con presa Chicken soup with a large piece of chicken.

Caldo de patas Cow-heel soup with mote. A popular hangover remedy.

Ceviche or **cebiche** Marinated fish or seafood which is usually served mid-morning with *canguil* (popcorn), *tostado* (roasted maize) or *chifles* (plantain chips). Varieties include *pescado* (fish), *camarón* (shrimp/prawn), *langostino* (jumbo shrimp/king prawn) and *concha* (shellfish).

Chaulafán Rice mixed with vegetables and bits of chicken or meat, served mostly in *chifas* (Chinese restaurants).

Choclo Fresh young corn, often served on the cob.

Chupé Fish soup.

Cocada Coconut macaroon, typical of the province of Esmeraldas.

Cola Any soft drink.

Colada Can refer to cream soups or sweet warm or cold beverages.

Colada morada Thick purple spicy fruit drink, served warm or cold around the time of Finados, the Day of the Dead (2 Nov).

Cuy Guinea pig roast on the spit, served with potatoes and a peanut sauce. The most typical and prized of all highland dishes.

Desayuno Breakfast.

Dulce de leche Spreadable soft toffee.

Empanada Any of several sweet or savoury, fried or baked, snacks in a pastry shell.

Encebollado Fish or seafood served with its broth on boiled *yuca* (manioc root) and pickled onions. Typical of the coast.

Encocado Savoury fish, seafood or chicken prepared in coconut milk, typical of the province of Esmeraldas.

Estofado Stew, may be de *res* (beef), *pollo* (chicken) or *pescado* (fish).

Fanesca Special soup made with salt fish, many different grains, beans, ground peanuts and more. Served during Easter Week throughout the country.

Fritada Deep-fried pork. Very popular with Ecuadoreans, especially in the highlands.

Guatita Tripe prepared with ground peanuts and potatoes.

Hornado Baked pork, the whole hog with a tomato in its mouth.

Humitas Sweet or savoury tender ground corn steamed in corn leaves.

Llapingachos or **tortillas** Fried potato and cheese patties.

Locro de papas A warming potato and cheese soup, served with slices of avocado.

Menestra Bean or lentil stew served as a side dish.

Merienda Supper. Also refers to an economical set meal served in the evening.

Mote White hominy. Soft corn kernels burst with alkali, common in Cuenca and the southern highlands.

Patacones Thick fried plantain chips.

Quaker A tangy drink made with *naranjilla* or other fruit and a dash of oatmeal (hence the name). May be served warm or cold.

Quimbolitos A sweet made with wheat or other flour steamed in achira leaves.

Refresco or **fresco** Slightly watered-down fresh fruit drink, often served with a set meal.

Sancocho Hearty meat and vegetable soup containing *yuca* (manioc root) and corn.

Seco Generic for second or main course, usually served with rice.

Seco de chivo Goat stew.

Sopa de bola de verde Hearty soup with plantain dumplings, typical of the coast.

Viche Hearty fish or seafood soup, with peanuts, typical of the province of Manabí.

Quito
& around

spectacular setting and handsome architecture

Few cities have a setting to match that of Quito, the second highest capital in Latin America. It sits in a narrow valley at the foot of the volcano Pichincha. From El Panecillo hill there are fine views of the city and the encircling volcano cones.

Quito is a city of many faces. The first UNESCO World Heritage Site city in the world, Quito's charm lies in its colonial centre, the Centro Histórico. Here, pastel-coloured houses and ornate churches line a warren of steep and narrow streets. Modern Quito is an altogether different place, with busy avenues lined with office towers, shopping malls, restaurants and bars, and a huge variety of hotels.

Quito is surrounded by scenic countryside which is well worth visiting. Within easy reach of the city are nature reserves, wonderful thermal baths, mountains to climb, quaint villages and the monument to the equator. The western slopes of Pichincha, also nearby, are covered in beautiful cloudforest where nature lovers can indulge their taste for adventure.

Best for
Churches ■ Mountains ■ Museums ■ Nightlife

Footprint
picks

★ **La Compañía**, page 45

Among Quito's 86 churches, La Compañía has the most ornate and richly sculptured façade and interior.

★ **Museo Nacional**, page 50

This is the most comprehensive of Quito's many excellent museums.

★ **El Teleférico**, page 56

This cable car climbs to 4050 m on the flanks of Pichincha, with gorgeous view along the way.

★ **Mitad del Mundo**, page 56

Every tourist knows that this is the place to straddle the equator. The ethnographic museum and Museo Inti-Ñan here are worth visiting.

★ **Papallacta**, page 88

There is nowhere to soak like Papallacta, the best developed thermal baths in Ecuador.

★ **Mindo**, page 97

Not far from Quito, Mindo and the cloudforests of the western slopes of Pichincha are a nature lover's paradise.

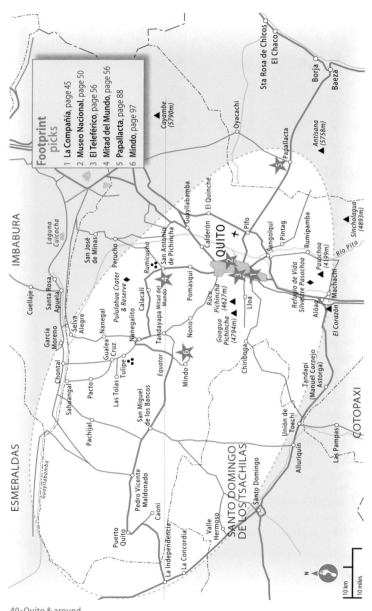

Footprint
picks

1 La Compañía, page 45
2 Museo Nacional, page 50
3 El Teleférico, page 56
4 Mitad del Mundo, page 56
5 Papallacta, page 88
6 Mindo, page 97

IMBABURA

Laguna
Cuicocha

Cuellaje
Santa Rosa
Apuela
García
Moreno
San José
de Minas
Perucho
Rumicucho
San Antonio
de Pichincha

Cayambe
(5790m)

Oyacachi

Sta Rosa de Chicos
El Chaco

Borja

Baeza

Antisana
(5758m)

Papallacta

Guyllabamba
El Quinche

Calderón
Pifo

QUITO

Sangolquí
Pintag
Rumipamba
Río Pita
Sincholagua
(4893m)

ESMERALDAS

Chontal
Selva
Alegre
Nanegal
Gualea
Cruz
Nanegalito
Tandayapa
Equator
Mindo

Pululahua Crater
& Reserve
Calacali
Mitad del
Mundo
Pomasqui
Nono

Lloa
Rucu
Pichincha
(4627m)

Guagua
Pichincha
(4794m)

Refugio de Vida
Silvestre Pasochoa
Machachi
Pasochoa
(4199m)

Alóag
El Corazón

COTOPAXI

Guayllabamba
Tulipe
Las Tolas
San Miguel
de los Bancos
Chiriboga

Pachijal
Pacto
Sahuangal

Pedro Vicente
Maldonado
Caoni

Puerto Quito

La Independencia
La Concordia

Valle
Hermoso

Santo Domingo

SANTO DOMINGO
DE LOS TSÁCHILAS

Unión de
Toachi

Alluriquín

Las Pampas

Tandapi
(Manuel Cornejo
Astorga)

N

10 km

10 miles

Quito

The city's main attraction is its colonial centre, where cobbled streets are steep and narrow, dipping to deep ravines. Modern Quito has broad avenues lined with contemporary office buildings, fine private residences, parks, embassies and villas. Here you'll find Quito's main tourist area in the district known as La Mariscal, bordered by Avenidas Amazonas, Patria, 12 de Octubre and Orellana. Beyond lie Quito's upmarket residential areas.

Colonial Quito *Colour map 1, C4.*

a pleasant place to stroll and admire architecture, monuments and art

The revitalized colonial district of Quito (altitude 2850 m) has a lot of movement in the streets and plazas and is particularly nice on Sunday when it is closed to vehicles. At night, the illuminated plazas and churches are very beautiful. The area's artistic treasures include many fine examples of the Quito School of Art (see page 393).

Plaza de la Independencia and around

The heart of the old city is **Plaza de la Independencia** or **Plaza Grande**, whose pink-flowered arupo trees bloom in September. It is dominated by a somewhat grim **Cathedral** ① *entry through museum, Venezuela N3-117, T02-257 0371, Tue-Sat, 0900-1730, no visits during Mass 0600-0900, US$4 for the museum, night visits to church and cupolas on request,* built 1550-1562, with grey stone porticos and green tile cupolas. On its outer walls are plaques listing the names of the founding fathers of Quito, and inside are the tomb of Sucre and a famous Descent from the Cross by the indigenous painter Caspicara. There are many other 17th- and 18th-century paintings; the interior decoration shows Moorish influence. Facing the Cathedral is the **Palacio Arzobispal**, part of which now houses shops, restaurants and a post office. Next to it, in the northwest corner, is the **Hotel Plaza Grande** (1930), with a baroque façade, the first building in the old city with more than two storeys. On the northeast side is the concrete **Municipio**, which fits in quite well. The low colonial Palacio de Gobierno or **Palacio de Carondelet**, silhouetted against the flank of Pichincha, is on the northwest side of the Plaza. On the first floor is a gigantic mosaic mural of Orellana navigating the Amazon and a painting by 20th-century artist Oswaldo Guayasamín, depicting milestones in Latin American

Essential Quito

Finding your feet

Mariscal Sucre airport is about 30 km northeast of the city. Long-distance bus services arrive at terminals at the extreme edges of the city: Quitumbe in the south and Carcelén in the north.

Quito is a long city stretching from north to south, with Pichincha rising to the west. Its main arteries run the length of the city and traffic congestion along them is a serious problem. Avenida Occidental or Mariscal Sucre is a less congested road to the west of the city. The Corredor Periférico Oriental or Simón Bolívar is a bypass to the east of the city running 44 km between Santa Rosa in the south and Calderón in the north. Roads through the eastern suburbs in the Valle de los Chillos and Tumbaco can be taken to avoid the city proper. Most places of historical interest are in colonial Quito, while the majority of the hotels, restaurants, tour operators and facilities for visitors are in the modern city to the north.

Tip...
Take it easy for the first 48 hours because of the altitude, which may make you feel some discomfort. The city has a serious air pollution problem.

Tip...
A number of museums are closed on Monday.

The street numbering system is based on N (Norte), E (Este), S (Sur) and Oe (Oeste), plus a number for each street and a number for each building; however, an older system of street numbers is also still in use.

Getting around

Both colonial Quito and La Mariscal in modern Quito can be explored on foot, but getting between the two requires some form of public transport; using taxis is the best option. There is plenty of public transport but it's not safe when crowded. Taxis are cheap and abundant. See also Safety, page 430, and Transport, page 80.

When to go

Quito is within 25 km of the equator, but its altitude makes its climate similar to spring in England, with pleasantly warm days and cool nights. The rainy season is October to May with a lull in December and the heaviest rainfall in April. Rain usually falls in the afternoon.

Time required

Allow two to three days to acclimatize to the altitude and see the city's highlights, and one week or more for day trips.

Weather Quito

January	February	March	April	May	June
19°C 10°C 59mm	19°C 10°C 61mm	19°C 10°C 83mm	19°C 10°C 58mm	19°C 10°C 52mm	20°C 9°C 16mm

July	August	September	October	November	December
29°C 10°C 11mm	20°C 9°C 15mm	20°C 9°C 50mm	20°C 10°C 61mm	19°C 10°C 60mm	19°C 10°C 47mm

ON THE ROAD

Flying into Quito at night

Several flights from North America, Central America, Colombia and Guayaquil arrive at night. Quito airport operates 24 hours, including the information desk at arrivals, restaurants, cafés, cyber café, phone office, currency exchange and pharmacy. If you have an early morning connection and want to stay at the airport, you can do so. The VIP lounges are open to the public for a fee (US$26 at international departures, US$17 at domestic departures), but only available after you have checked in for your next flight. There are several hotels 10-20 minutes away by taxi.

If your destination is Quito and you have not booked a hotel, ask for assistance at the information desk before leaving the airport. Taxis are available 24 hours and Aero Servicios express buses run to the city every hour from 2400 to 0600 and every 30 minutes the rest of the day. They also offer transport from their terminus in Quito to any hotel. Use this transfer service or a taxi to your hotel. Taking a city bus or walking is not safe.

If your destination is outside Quito, wait until the morning, then take a taxi to the roundabout on highway E-35 and a bus which bypasses Quito going north or south, or a bus coming from Quito and heading east. Another alternative in daylight is to take a city bus from the airport to one of the long-distance bus terminals: Quitumbe for the south and Carcelén for points north.

history. The ironwork on the balconies looking over the main plaza is from the Tuilleries in Paris. Visitors can take **tours** ⓘ *T02-382 7700, www.presidencia.gob.ec Tue-Fri 0900-1900, Sat 0900-2200, Sun 0900-1600, take passport or copy.*

From Plaza de la Independencia two main streets, Venezuela and García Moreno, lead straight towards the Panecillo. Parallel with Venezuela is Calle Guayaquil, the main shopping street. These streets all run south from the main plaza to meet Calle Morales, better known as **La Ronda**, one of the oldest streets in the city. This narrow cobbled pedestrian way and its colonial homes with wrought iron balconies have been refurbished and house hotels, restaurants, bars, artisans' workshops, cultural centres, galleries and shops. It is a quaint corner of the city growing in popularity for a night out or an afternoon stroll. Typical Ecuadorean children's toys are sometimes on display here.

Around the corner from the Cathedral on García Moreno N3-94 is the beautiful **El Sagrario** ⓘ *Mon-Fri, 0800-1800, Sat-Sun 1000-1400, no entry during Mass, free*, church with a gilded door. Opposite, the **Centro Cultural Metropolitano** is at the corner of Espejo, housing the municipal library, a museum for the visually impaired, temporary art exhibits and the **Museo Alberto Mena Caamaño** ⓘ *entry on C Espejo, T02-395 2300, ext 155, www.centrocultural-quito.com, Tue-Sat 0900-1730, Sun 1000-1600, US$1.50.* This wax museum depicts scenes of Ecuadorean colonial history. The scene of the execution of the revolutionaries of 1809 in the original cell is particularly vivid.

⬜ 1 Quito orientation

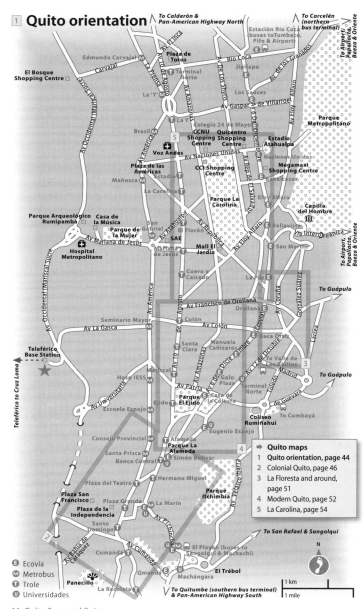

To Calderón &
Pan-American Highway North

To Carcelén
(northern
bus terminal)

To Airport,
Papallacta,
Baeza & Oriente

Estación Río Coca
buses toTumbaco,
Pifo & Airport

El Bosque
Shopping Centre ⬜

Edmundo Carvajal Ⓜ

Carvajal

Av El Inca

Plaza de
Toros

Ⓣ Terminal
Norte

Río Coca

Jipijapa

Av De los Shyris

Av De los Granados

Los Sauces

Av Gaspar de Villarroel

La 'Y' Ⓣ

Av Eloy Alfaro

La 'Y'

Colegio 24 de Mayo

Brasil Ⓜ

CCNU   Quicentro
Shopping   Shopping
Centre   Centre

5

Voz Andes ✚

Estadio
Atahualpa

Parque
Metropolitano

Plaza de las
Américas

Av Naciones Unidas

CCI Shopping
Centre

Mégamaxi
Shopping Centre

Estadio Ⓣ

Naciones Unidas Ⓔ

Mañosca

La Carolina Ⓣ

Av República de El Salvador

Parque La
Carolina

Av Eloy Alfaro

Banalcázar

Eloy Alfaro Ⓔ

Capilla
del Hombre 🏛

Parque Arqueológico
Rumipamba ⬜

Casa de
la Música

Parque de
la Mujer

San
Gabriel Ⓣ

El Florón Ⓣ

Bellavista Ⓔ

Vía Interoceánica

Hospital
Metropolitano ✚

Av Mariana de Jesús

SAE Ⓣ

Mall El
Jardín

San Martín Ⓔ

To Airport,
Papallacta,
Baeza & Oriente

Mariana
de Jesús Ⓣ

Cuero y
Caicedo Ⓣ

La Paz Ⓔ

Av América

Av Atahualpa

Av República

Av Eloy Alfaro

González Suárez

To Guápulo

Av Francisco de Orellana

Orellana Ⓔ

Seminario Mayor Ⓜ

Av La Gasca

Colón Ⓣ

Av Colón

Av 10 de Agosto

Av Amazonas

Baca Ortiz Ⓔ

Santa
Clara Ⓣ

Manuela
Cañizares

Av 6 de Diciembre

Av 12 de Octubre

Mariscal Ⓣ

Hosp IESS Ⓣ

Galo
Plaza Ⓣ

La Coruña

Ecovía

Madrid Ⓔ

To Valle de
Los Chillos

3

To Guápulo

Av Universitaria

Av Patria

Toledo

Terminal
Norte

de Guevara

To Cumbayá

Av 6 de Diciembre

Casa de
la Cultura

Parque
El Ejido

Coliseo
Rumiñahui

Ejido Ⓤ

Escuela Espejo Ⓜ

Eugenio Espejo Ⓤ

Consejo Provincial Ⓜ

Alameda Ⓣ
Parque La
Alameda

Santa Prisca Ⓜ

Simón Bolívar Ⓣ

Banco Central Ⓜ

Hermano Miguel Ⓣ

Plaza del Teatro Ⓣ

Parque
Itchimbía

Plaza San
Francisco ⬜

Plaza Grande ⬜

La Marín Ⓣ

Plaza de la
Independencia

Santo
Domingo Ⓣ

Av Pichincha

⬛ Ecovía
Ⓜ Metrobus
Ⓣ Trole
Ⓤ Universidades

Cumandá Ⓣ

Av Bahía de Caráquez

Av Cumandá

Panecillo ☀

Qmandá Ⓣ

La Recoleta Ⓣ

Machángara

El Plavón (buses to
Sangolqui & Machachi)

El Trébol

To San Rafael & Sangolqui

To Quitumbe (southern bus terminal)
& Pan-American Highway South

N

⮕ Quito maps
1 Quito orientation, page 44
2 Colonial Quito, page 46
3 La Floresta and around,
  page 51
4 Modern Quito, page 52
5 La Carolina, page 54

Teleférico to Cruz Loma

Teleférico
Base Station ★

Av Occidental Mariscal Sucre

Av Occidental Mariscal Sucre

1 km
1 mile

ON THE ROAD

El chulla quiteño

Quito's spectacular location and its beautifully restored colonial centre are matched only by the complex charm of the capital's people, the *'chullas quiteños'* as they call themselves; the term defies translation but is akin to 'real Quitonians'. These are not the colourfully dressed inhabitants of highland villages, tending crops and haggling with tourists to sell their crafts. They are young professionals, office workers and government bureaucrats, conservatively attired and courteous to a fault, and they form the backbone of a very urban society. You will see them going out for lunch with colleagues during the week, making even a cheap *almuerzo* seem like a formal occasion. You will also find them in the city's bars and clubs at weekends, letting their hair down with such gusto that they seem like entirely different people. When you hear them singing : "yo soy el chullita quiteño...", you will know what it is all about.

The fine Jesuit church of ★ **La Compañía** ⓘ *García Moreno N3-117 y Sucre, T02-258 1895, Mon-Thu 0930-1830, Fri 0930-1730, Sat and holidays 0930-1600, Sun 1230-1600, US$4, students US$2,* has the most ornate and richly sculptured façade and interior. Replicas of paintings of hell and the final judgement by Hernando de la Cruz can be seen at the entrance and are most striking. Behind the church, on Calle Benalcázar, is **Capilla del Milagro** ⓘ *free,* with a painting of the much venerated Virgen la Dolorosa. Diagonally opposite La Compañía is the **Casa Museo María Augusta Urrutia** ⓘ *García Moreno N2-60 y Sucre, T02-258 0103, Tue-Fri 1000-1800, Sat-Sun 0930-1730, US$2,* the home of a Quiteña who devoted her life to charity, showing the lifestyle of 20th-century aristocracy. Colonial and republican era furniture and paintings by Victor Mideros are on display.

Two blocks west of Plaza de la Independencia is the church of **La Merced** ⓘ *Chile y Cuenca, 0630-1200, 1300-1800, free,* with many splendidly elaborate styles. Nearby is the **Museo de Arte Colonial** ⓘ *Cuenca N6-15 y Mejía, T02-228 2297, Tue-Sat 0900-1630, US$2,* housed in a 17th-century mansion, it features a collection of colonial sculpture and painting and temporary exhibits (free).

A block away is **Museo Casa de Sucre** ⓘ *Venezuela N4-71 y Sucre, T02-295 2860, daily 0930-1730, free,* in the beautiful restored house of Sucre, with a pleasant patio and fountain. This historical museum has displays about life in the 19th century and Sucre's role in Ecuador's Independence.

South of Plaza de la Independencia

South of Museo Casa de Sucre and housed in the restored 16th-century Hospital San Juan de Dios is the **Museo de la Ciudad** ⓘ *García Moreno S1-47 y Rocafuerte, T02-228 3883, www.museociudadquito.gob.ec, Tue-Sun 0930-1730 (last group in 1630), US$3, free entry on the last Sat of each month, English guide service US$4 per group (request ahead).* This is a very good museum which takes you through Quito's history from prehispanic times to the 19th century, and has imaginative

2 Colonial Quito

Where to stay

1 Casa Gangotena C2
2 Casa Gardenia B2
3 Catedral Internacional B2
4 Chicago Hostal A3
5 Community Hostel B3
6 Guayunga A3
7 Huasi Continental C3
8 La Casona de La Ronda C3
9 Patio Andaluz B2
10 Plaza Grande B2
11 Quito Cultural B3
12 Relicario del Carmen B2
13 San Francisco
   de Quito C2
14 Secret Garden A3

Restaurants

1 Caffeto B3
2 El Ventanal A1
3 Govinda B2
4 Hasta la vuelta, Señor B2
5 Heladería San Agustín B2
6 Los Geranios C3
7 Plaza Chica B2
8 San Ignacio C2
9 Tianguez C1
10 Vista Hermosa B2

E Ecovía
M Metrobus
T Trole
U Universidades

BACKGROUND

Quito

Archaeological finds suggest that the valley of Quito and surrounding areas have been occupied for some 10,000 years. The city gets its name from the Quitus, who lived here during the period AD 500-1500. By the end of the 15th century, the northern highlands of Ecuador were conquered by the Incas and Quito became the capital of the northern half of their empire under the rule of Huayna Capac and later his son Atahualpa. As the Spanish conquest approached, Rumiñahui, Atahualpa's general, razed the city, to prevent it from falling into the invaders' hands.

The colonial city of Quito was founded by Sebastián de Benalcázar, Pizarro's lieutenant, on 6 December 1534. It was built at the foot of El Panecillo on the ruins of the ancient city, using the rubble as construction material. Examples of Inca stonework can be seen in the façades and floors of some colonial buildings such as the Cathedral and the church of San Francisco. Following the conquest, Quito became the seat of government of the Real Audiencia de Quito, the crown colony, which governed current day Ecuador as well as parts of southern Colombia and northern Peru. Beautifully refurbished, colonial Quito is today the city's most attractive district. In 1978, Quito was the first city to be declared a UNESCO World Heritage Site.

The 20th century saw the expansion of the city to the north and south, and later to the valleys to the east. The commercial, banking and government centres moved north of the colonial centre and residential and industrial neighbourhoods sprawled in the periphery. These make up the Distrito Metropolitano, which stretches for almost 50 km from north to south. The current population of Quito is estimated at 1,670,000.

displays; the café by the entrance overlooks La Ronda. Almost opposite on García Moreno are the convent and museum of **El Carmen Alto** ⓘ *T02-295 5817, Wed-Sun 0930-1630, US$3, request ahead for guiding in English*. In 2013, this beautifully refurbished cloister opened its doors to the public for the first time since 1652. It has a good collection of altarpieces with carved frames and gives a vivid indication of cloistered life. Products prepared by the nuns are available at the museum.

El Panecillo and around

On **El Panecillo** ⓘ *Mon-Thu 0900-1700, Fri-Sun 0900-2100, US$1 per vehicle or US$0.25 per person if walking, for the neighbourhood brigade; entry to the interior of the monument US$2*, a hill to the south of the colonial city, is a statue of the Virgen de Quito and a good view from the observation platform. Although the neighbourhood brigade patrols the area, it is safer to take a taxi (US$6 return from the colonial city, US$10 from La Mariscal, with a short wait). In the museum of the monastery of **San Diego** ⓘ *Calicuchima 117 y Farfán, entrance to the right of the church, T02-317 3185, Tue-Sat 1000-1300, 1400-1700, Sun 1000-1400, US$2*, by the cemetery of the same name, just west of Panecillo, guided tours (Spanish only) take you around four colonial patios where sculpture and painting are shown. Of special interest are the gilded pulpit by Juan Bautista Menacho and the Last Supper painting in the refectory, in which a *cuy* and *humitas* have taken the place of the paschal lamb.

Plaza de San Francisco and around

Plaza de San Francisco (or Bolívar) is southwest of Plaza de la Independencia; here are the great church and monastery of the patron saint of Quito, **San Francisco** ⓘ *daily 0800-1200, 1500-1800*. The church was constructed by the Spanish in 1553 and is rich in art treasures. A modest statue of the founder, Fray Jodoco Ricke, the Flemish Franciscan who sowed the first wheat in Ecuador, stands nearby. See the fine wood carvings in the choir, a high altar of gold and an exquisite carved ceiling. There are some paintings in the aisles by Miguel de Santiago, the colonial *mestizo* painter. The **Museo Franciscano Fray Pedro Gocial** ⓘ *in the church cloisters to the right of the main entrance, T02-295 2911, Mon-Sat 0900-1730, Sun 0900-1300, US$2*, has a beautiful collection of religious art. The pieces are gradually being restored, so expect a few empty displays. Also adjoining San Francisco is the **Cantuña Chapel** ⓘ *Cuenca y Bolívar, T02-295 2911, Tue and Thu 0800-0900, Sun 0900-1000, free*, with sculptures.

Not far to the south along Calle Cuenca is the excellent archaeological museum **Museo Casa del Alabado** ⓘ *Cuenca 335 y Rocafuerte, T02-228 0940, daily 0900-1730, US$4, guides extra, excellent art shop*. An impressive display of pre-Columbian art from all regions of Ecuador, amongst the best in the city, housed in a beautifully restored colonial building.

Plaza de Santo Domingo and around

At **Plaza de Santo Domingo** (or Sucre), southeast of Plaza de la Independencia, is the church and monastery of **Santo Domingo** ⓘ *daily 0700-1300, 1700-1845*, with its rich wood-carvings and an impressive silver throne in the main altar, weighing around 100 kg. To the right of this altar is the remarkable Capilla del Rosario, built on top of the arch of the same name. In the monastery is the **Museo Dominicano Fray Pedro Bedón** ⓘ *T02-228 0518, Mon-Sat 0915-1330, 1500-1700, US$2, English speaking guides available, tour includes Capilla del Rosario*, another fine collection of religious art. In the centre of the plaza is a statue of Sucre, facing the slopes of Pichincha where he won his battle against the Royalists. Going through the Capilla del Rosario arch you enter **La Mama Cuchara** (the 'great big spoon'), a street which ends on a circle, in the authentic residential neighbourhood of La Loma Grande, with the **Centro Cultural Mama Cuchara**, where concerts are held.

Just south of Santo Domingo, in the old bus station, is **Parque Cumanadá** ⓘ *Tue-Sun 0900-1300, 1500-1800, busy on weekends*, with a pool, sport fields, climbing wall, gym and activities.

Northeast of Plaza de Santo Domingo is **Museo Manuela Sáenz** ⓘ *Junín Oe 1-13 y Montúfar, T02-228 3908, www.museomanuelasaenz.com, Mon-Fri 1000-1200, 1400-1700, US$4*, a tribute to a legendary Quiteña, Simón Bolívar's lover, who played an important role in the struggle for independence. Some of her personal belongings, letters, as well as works of art and weapons, are on display.

ON THE ROAD

Museo Monacal Santa Catalina ① *Espejo 779 y Flores, T02-228 4000, Mon-Fri 0900-1700, Sat 0900-1200, US$2.50*, said to have been built on the ruins of the Inca House of the Virgins, depicts the history of cloistered life.

Many of the heroes of Ecuador's struggle for independence are buried in the monastery of **San Agustín** ① *Chile y Guayaquil, Mon-Sat 0700-1200, 1500-1700, Sun 0715-1315*, which has beautiful cloisters on three sides where the first act of independence from Spain was signed on 10 August 1809. Here is the **Museo Miguel de Santiago** ① *Chile 924 y Guayaquil, T02-295 1001, Mon-Fri 0900-1230, 1400-1700, Sat 0900-1230, US$2*, with religious art.

North of Plaza de la Independencia

To the northeast of Plaza de la Independencia is **Plaza del Teatro** where open-air cultural events are held. Here stand the lovely neoclassical 19th-century **Teatro Sucre** ① *Manabí N8-131 y Guayaquil, T02-295 1661*, and the smaller **Teatro Variedades Ernesto Albán**, both beautifully restored. Nearby is **Museo Camilo Egas** ① *Venezuela N9-02 y Esmeraldas, T02-257 2012, www.museos.gob.ec, Tue-Fri 0830-1700, Sat 1000-1600, free*, housed in a restored 18th-century home. It exhibits the work of the Ecuadorean artist Camilo Egas (1889-1962) and has a good video about his life. He was the first painter to portray the life of the Ecuadorean *indígena*. It is interesting to see the evolution of style in his art.

Further north, on Parque García Moreno, the **Basílica** ① *Carchi 122 y Venezuela, T02-228 9428, visits 0600-1900 daily, US$2, Mass at 0700, 1200 and 1800 (please be respectful); clock tower open 0900-1630 daily, US$2*, is very large, has many gargoyles (some in the shape of Ecuadorean fauna), stained glass windows and fine, bas relief bronze doors (begun in 1926; some final details remain unfinished due to lack of funding). Climb above the coffee shop to the top of the clock tower for stunning views. The **Centro de Arte Contemporáneo** ① *Luis Dávila y Venezuela, San Juan, T02-398 8800, Tue-Sun 0900-1700, free*, in the beautifully restored Antiguo Hospital Militar, built in the early 1900s, has rotating art exhibits.

West of the colonial centre

To the west of the city, the **Yaku Museo del Agua** ⓘ *El Placer Oe11-271, T02-251 1100, www.yakumuseoagua.gob.ec, Tue-Sun 0900-1700, US$3, take a taxi to main entrance or enter through the parking lot at the top of C Bolívar and take the lift up,* has lovely views. This interactive museum is great for kids of all ages. Its main themes are water and climate, and there's also a self-guided trail: *eco-ruta*.

South of the colonial centre

Another must for children, in Chimbacalle south of the colonial city, is the **Museo Interactivo de Ciencia** ⓘ *Tababela Oe1-60 y Latorre, T02-264 7834, Wed-Sun 0900-1630, US$3, children US$1.* Nearby are Quito's train station (see page 79), with a museum and concert hall, and **Teatro México** ⓘ *Tomebamba y Antisana, west of Av Maldonado, T02-265 0660,* the largest theatre in the city.

East of the colonial centre

East of the colonial city is **Parque Itchimbía** ⓘ *T02-228 2017, park open daily 0600-1800, exhibits 0900-1630*; a natural lookout over the city with walking and cycle trails and a cultural centre housed in a 19th-century 'crystal palace' which came from Europe, and which once housed the Santa Clara market.

Modern Quito

the capital's main tourist and business area

North of the colonial centre is modern Quito, with a big city feel, congested avenues, tall buildings, shopping centres and a wide selection of hotels, restaurants, bars, tour agencies and other services. Several large parks provide a welcome relief from the bustle.

Parque La Alameda has the oldest **astronomical observatory** ⓘ *T02-257 0765, ext 101, http://oaq.epn.edu.ec, museum Mon-Fri 1000-1700, US$3, night observations Wed and Thu 1830-1930 weather permitting,* in South America dating to 1873 (native people had observatories long before the arrival of the Europeans). There is also a splendid monument to Simón Bolívar, lakes, and in the northwest corner a spiral lookout tower with a good view.

A short distance north of Parque La Alameda, opposite Parque El Ejido and bound by 6 de Diciembre, Patria, 12 de Octubre and Parque El Arbolito, is the **Casa de la Cultura**, a large cultural and museum complex. The ★ **Museo Nacional** ⓘ *entrance on Patria, T02-222 3258, www.museos.gob.ec, Tue-Fri 0900-1700, Sat-Sun 1000-1600, free, guided tours in English by appointment,* housed in the north side of the Casa de la Cultura, is the most comprehensive museum in the city. If you only have time to visit one museum in Quito, it should be this. The **Sala de Arqueología** is particularly impressive with beautiful pre-Columbian ceramics. The **Sala de Oro** has a good collection of prehispanic gold objects, and the **Sala de Arte Colonial** has religious art from the Quito School. On the east side of the complex are the museums administered by the **Casa de la Cultura** ⓘ *entrance on 12 de Octubre,*

T02-290 2272, ext 420, Tue-Sat 0900-1300, 1400-1645, US$2: The **Museo de Arte Moderno** has paintings and sculpture since 1830 and also rotating exhibits, and the **Museo de Instrumentos Musicales displays** an impressive collection of musical instruments, said to be the second in importance in the world. Also on the east side are an art gallery for temporary exhibits and the **Agora**, a large open space used for concerts. On the west side are halls for temporary art exhibits,

3 La Floresta & around

in the original old building, and the entrance to the **Teatro Nacional**, with free evening performances. On the south side are the **Teatro Demetrio Aguilera Malta** and other areas devoted to dance and theatre.

Near the Casa de la Cultura, in the Catholic university's **cultural centre** ① *12 de Octubre y Roca,* is the superb **Museo Jijón y Caamaño** ① *T02-299 1700, ext 1078, Mon-Fri 0900-1600, free*, with a private collection of archaeological objects, historical documents and art. The interactive displays and narration in Spanish are excellent. Here too are temporary exhibits and the **Museo Weilbauer** ① *T02-299 1700 ext1681, being restored in 2015*, with archaeological and photo collections.

North of Universidad Católica, at the Politécnica Salesiana, is the **Museo Abya-Yala** ① *12 de Octubre N23-116 y Wilson, T02-396 2800, ext 2165, Mon-Fri 0930-1300, 1400-1730, US$2, Spanish guides only*, with interesting displays of Amazonian flora and fauna, tribal culture and the impact of the oil exploration. Next door is a bookshop (selling mostly Spanish titles).

In La Floresta further northeast is **Casa Cultural Trude Sojka** ① *Toledo N24-569 y Coruña, entrance from Pje Moeller, T02-222 4072, www.trudesojka. com, Mon-Fri 1000-1300, 1500-1700, US$2*, a cultural centre which promotes peace, tolerance and art. It exhibits the works of Trude Sojka (1909-2007), a Czech-born painter and sculptor,

Where to stay 🛏
1 Casona de Mario
2 Villa Nancy

Restaurants 🍴
1 Chez Jérôme
2 La Briciola
3 La Choza
4 La Gloria
5 Mr Bagel
6 Pekín

Bars & clubs 🍸
7 El Pobre Diablo
8 La Juliana

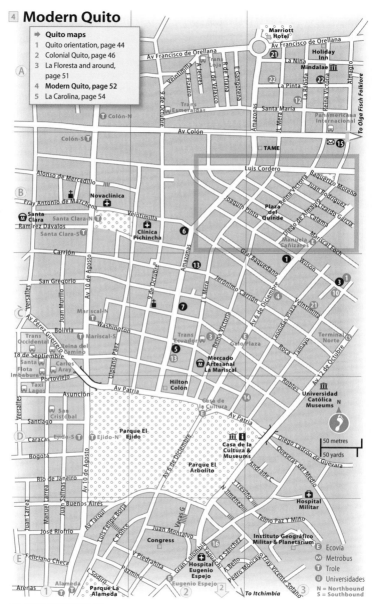

Av Francisco de Orellana

Marriott Hotel

Av Francisco de Orellana

Holiday Inn

Mindalae

Trans Loja

La Nina

La Pinta

Santa María

Panamericana Internacional

To Olga Fisch Folklore

Veintimilla

Pinzón

R de Villalengua

E Gangotena

La Niña

Reina Victoria

Amagasí

Trans Esmeraldas

Colón-N

Av Colón

TAME

Colón-S

Luis Cordero

Baquerizo Moreno

Alonso de Mercadillo

Joaquín Pinto

Plaza del Quinde

Reina Victoria

Juan Rodríguez

Eduardo García

Novaclínica

Fray Antonio de Marchena

Veintimilla

Diego de Almagro

Calama

Mariscal Foch

Santa Clara

Santa Clara-N

Ramírez Dávalos

Santa Clara-S

Clínica Pichincha

Manuela Cañizares

Carrión

Gral Baquedano

Wilson

San Gregorio

Jerónimo Carrión

Leonidas Plaza

Veintimilla

Juan Murillo

Mariscal-N

Washington

Av 6 de Diciembre

Roca

Tamayo

Terminal Norte

Bolívia

Mariscal-S

Reina del Camino

Reina Victoria

Galo Plaza

Trans Ecuador

Av Pérez Guerrero

Trans Occidental

18 de Septiembre

Santa Flota Imbabura

Carlos Aray

Portoviejo

Av Patria

Mercado Artesanal La Mariscal

Robles

Av 12 de Octubre

Taxi Lagos

Asunción

Hilton Colón

Casa de la Cultura

Universidad Católica Museums

San Cristóbal

Santiago

Ejido-S

Av Patria

Av 10 de Agosto

Ejido-N

Parque El Ejido

Diego Ladrón de Guevara

Caracas

Bogotá

Río de Janeiro

Buenos Aires

Parque El Arbolito

Casa de la Cultura & Museums

Andrade C

Queseras del Medio

50 metres

50 yards

Juan Larrea

Manuel Larrea

Av Tarqui

Luis Felipe Borja

Ponce

Vargas G

Trévijo

Jiménez

Hospital Militar

Av 10 de Diciembre

Av 10 de Diciembre

José Riofrío

Juan Salinas

Congress

Juan Montalvo

Gran Colombia

Yaguachi

O Sánchez

A Bello

Telmo Paz Y Miño

Instituto Geográfico Militar & Planetarium

Feliciano Checa

Sodiro

V Piedrahita

Pazmiño

Hospital Eugenio Espejo

Eugenio Espejo

Pedro Moncayo

Fray Vicente Solano

Arenas

Alameda

Parque La Alameda

To Itchimbia

E Ecovía
M Metrobus
T Trole
U Universidades
N = Northbound
S = Southbound

and a Jewish survivor of the Holocaust who emigrated to Ecuador. The centre also includes a Holocaust memorial, temporary exhibits and a library, and offers art workshops.

Extending north of Parque El Ejido, the district of **La Mariscal**, bordered by Avenidas Patria, Amazonas, 12 de Octubre and Orellana, is the heart of Quito's nightlife, with a multitude of restaurants, bars and clubs. It is also an important tourist area with many hotels and hostels. A focal point in La Mariscal is **Plaza Foch** (Reina Victoria y Foch), also called **Plaza del Quinde**, a popular meeting place surrounded by cafés and restaurants. Further north, at the corner of Reina Victoria and La Niña, is the excellent **Museo Mindalae** ⓘ *T02-223 0609, ext 101, www.mindalae.com, Mon-Sat 0900-1730, US$3*, which exhibits Ecuadorean crafts and places them in their historical and cultural context, as well as temporary exhibits and a good fairtrade non-profit shop. **Olga Fisch Folklore** ⓘ *Colón E10-53 y Caamaño, T02-254 1315, www.olgafisch.com, Mon-Fri 0900-1900, Sat 1000-1800, museum until 1700 daily, donations welcome*, is an exclusive crafts shop with an

La Mariscal detail

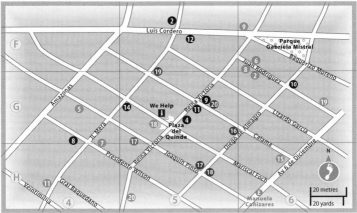

Where to stay 🛏	13 Hothello *C2*	Restaurants 🍴	13 Sakti *C2*
1 Anahi *C3*	14 La Cartuja *D3*	1 Baalbek *C3*	14 The Magic Bean *G5*
2 Backpackers Inn *G6*	15 La Casa Sol *H6*	2 Chandani Tandoori *F5*	15 Yu Su *B3*
3 Café Cultura *C2*	16 L'Auberge Inn *E2*	3 Chez Alain *C3*	
4 Casa Helbling *C3*	17 Mansión del Angel *G5*	4 Coffee Bar *G5*	Bars & clubs 🍸
5 Casa Joaquín *G4*	18 Nü House *G5*	5 Coffee Tree *C2*	16 Bungalow Six *G5*
6 Cayman *F6*	19 Posada del Maple *G6*	6 El Hornero *B2*	17 Cherusker *H5*
7 City Art Hotel Silberstein *G4*	20 Queen's Hostel *H5*	7 Ethnic Coffee *C2*	18 Finn McCool's *H5*
8 El Arupo *F6*	21 Sierra Madre *C3*	8 Kallari *G4*	19 No Bar *F5*
9 El Cafecito *F6*	22 Travellers Inn *A3*	9 La Boca del Lobo *G5*	20 Selfie *G5*
10 Fuente de Piedra I *C3*		10 La Petite Mariscal *G6*	21 Turtle's Head *A3*
11 Fuente de Piedra II *H4*		11 Mama Clorinda *G5*	22 Varadero *A3*
12 Hostal de la Rábida *A3*		12 Paléo *F5*	

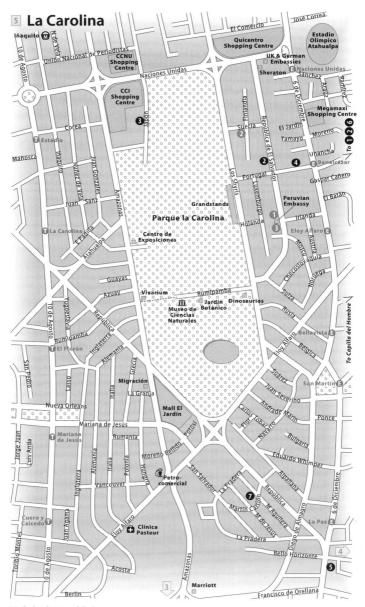

⑤ La Carolina

Iñaquito Ⓜ
N de Vera
10 de Agosto
Unión Nacional de Periodistas
CCNU Shopping Centre
Naciones Unidas
El Comercio
José Correa
Quicentro Shopping Centre
Estadio Olímpico Atahualpa
UK & German Embassies
Naciones Unidas
Sánchez
Sheraton
6 de Diciembre
Araiz
Ramírez
CCI Shopping Centre
❸
Jabón
Corea
Finlandia
Suecia
❷
República de El Salvador
El Jardín
Tamayo
Moreno
Megamaxi Shopping Centre
To ❶❷❻
Ⓣ Estado
Mañosca
Iñaquito
Juan González
Nuñez de Vela
Juan Sanz
Amazonas
Portugal
Luxemburgo
Los Shyris
Unanchu
Benalcázar Ⓔ
Gaspar Cañero
El Batán
❷
❹
Ⓣ La Carolina
F Padilla
Atahualpa
Guayas
Azuay
Grandstands
Parque la Carolina
Centro de Exposiciones
Peruvian Embassy
Irlanda
Eloy Alfaro Ⓔ
❶
❸
Holanda
República
Rumipamba
Ⓣ El Florón
Vivárium
Rumipamba
Jardín Botánico
Dinosaurios
Museo de Ciencias Naturales
Sucre
Rusia
Chvcrostov aquila
Nórtega
Eloy Alfaro
Bélgica
Bellavista Ⓔ
To Capilla del Hombre
10 de Agosto
Yugoslavia
Inglaterra
Alemania
Grecia
Italia
Lasso
San Pedro
Migración
La Granja
Mall El Jardín
Stéfer
Juan Severino
Andrade Marín
San Martín Ⓔ
Ponce
Nueva Orleans
Mariana de Jesús
Ⓣ Mariana de Jesús
Rumanía
Alemania
Italia
Polonia
Humana
Moreno Bellido
Porotó
Vancouver
Carlos Tobar
Flor
Navarro
Bulgaria
Eduardo Whimper
Alpallana
6 de Diciembre
Jorge Juan
Luis Anda
Cuero y Caicedo Ⓣ
Juan Agama
Tomás Montes
10 de Agosto
Eloy Alfaro
Ⓗ Clínica Pasteur
Acosta
Berlín
❸
Petrocomercial
San Salvador
La Pradera
❼
Martín Ca. de Jesús
República
M Aguilera
Diego de Almagro
La Pradera
Martín Ca. de Jesús
La Paz Ⓔ
Bello Horizonte
❹
❺
Marriott
Francisco de Orellana

excellent small museum with crafts and archaeological pieces. Housed in Olga Fisch's home, it honours the memory of a special lady, an immigrant to Ecuador who for five decades worked side-by-side with Ecuadorean artisans to encourage them to excel and rescue native designs and techniques.

North of La Mariscal is the large **Parque La Carolina**, a favourite recreational spot at weekends. Around it is the banking district, several shopping malls, hotels and restaurants. In the park is the **Jardín Botánico** ⓘ *T02-333 2516, www. jardinbotanicoquito.com, Mon-Fri 1000-1700, Sat-Sun 0900-1700, US$3.50*, which has a good cross section of Andean flora. Also here is the **Vivarium** ⓘ *T02-227 1799, www.vivarium.org.ec, Tue-Sun 0930-1300, 1330-1730, US$3.25*, dedicated to protect endangered snakes, reptiles and amphibians, and the **Museo de Ciencias Naturales** ⓘ *T02-244 9824, http://inb.ambiente.gob.ec, Mon-Fri 0800-1300,1345-1630, US$2*. Beyond La Carolina, on the grounds of Quito's former airport, is **Parque Bicentenario** ⓘ *daily 0430-1800*, with sports fields and a great cycling track, right on the old tarmac. To the east of La Carolina is the large **Parque Metropolitano**, with trails in a eucalyptus forest.

Quito suburbs

East To the east of Quito lie the valleys of the Machángara, San Pedro, Pita and Huambi rivers. Formerly Quito's market garden, the area is rapidly filling with suburbs and the towns are now part of the city's metropolitan area. With a milder climate the valleys and their thermal pools attract inner city dwellers at weekends.

The beautiful district of **Guápulo**, a colonial town, is perched on the edge of a ravine on the eastern fringe of Quito, overlooking the Río Machángara. It is popular with Quito's bohemian community and a worthwhile place to visit. Built by Indian slaves in 1693, the **Santuario de Guápulo** ⓘ *Mass Mon-Fri 1900, Sat 0700, Sun 0700-1200, 1600-1700*, perched on the edge of a ravine east of the city, is well worth seeing for its many paintings, gilded altars, stone carvings and the marvellously carved pulpit. The **Museo Fray Antonio Rodríguez** ⓘ *Plaza de Guápulo N27-138, T02-256 5652, Mon-Fri 0800-1200, 1400-1800, US$1.50*, has religious art and furniture, from the 16th to the 20th centuries. Guided tours (Spanish only) include a visit to the beautiful Santuario.

In the neighbourhood of Bellavista, overlooking the city from the northeast is the grandiose **Capilla del Hombre** ⓘ *Lorenzo Chávez E18-143 y Mariano Calvache, Bellavista, T02-244 8492, www.capilladelhombre.com, Tue-Sun 1000-1700, US$8, take a taxi or Batan-Colmena bus*, a monument to Latin America conceived by the internationally famous Ecuadorean artist Oswaldo Guayasamín (1919-1999) and completed after his death. This highly recommended

N

300 metres
300 yards

museum includes a collection of murals depicting the fate of Latin America from pre-Columbian to modern times and, in Guayasamín's home and studio, his works, as well as pre-Columbian, colonial and contemporary art collections. Works of art, jewellery and clothing decorated with Guayasamín's art are for sale.

The **Valle de los Chillos** lies southeast of the centre of Quito. It is accessed via the Autopista General Rumiñahui, which starts at El Trébol east of Parque Qmandá. **Sangolquí** (population 82,600) is the largest city in Los Chillos. It has a pleasant park, an attractive church and an impressive statue of Rumiñahui by Guayasamím. There is a busy Sunday market (and a smaller one on Thursday) and few tourists. On two roundabouts east of town are lovely mosaic sculptures by 20th-century artist Gonzalo Endara Crow: an ear of corn, the main crop of the valley, and a hummingbird. South of Sangolquí is the Río Pita canyon, see page 86. North of Los Chillos is the extinct volcano Ilaló, which can be climbed, and beyond, east of the centre of Quito, the **Valle de Tumbaco**, accessed by the Vía Interoceánica, the road leading to the airport, Papallacta, Baeza and the northern Oriente.

West Several Quito neighbourhoods climb along Pichincha's steep slopes which have good views of the city and surrounding mountains. Above these are **Bosque Protector Pichincha**, a belt of eucalyptus forest and some private reserves in old haciendas protecting *páramo* and the last native forest remnants close to the city. The latter also has places to stay; see Where to stay, page 63.

For spectacular views ride the ★ **Teleférico** ⓘ *Av Occidental above La Gasca, T02-222 4424, daily 0800-1930, US$8.50, children and seniors US$6.50, the area below is not safe, it's best to take a taxi (US$1.50 from América y Colón).* The cable car is part of a complex with an amusement park, shops and food courts. It climbs to 4050 m on the flanks of Pichincha, where there are walking trails, including one to the summit of Rucu Pichincha, and horse riding just past the fence.

Parque Arqueológico y Ecológico Rumipamba ⓘ *east side of Av Occidental just north of Mariana de Jesús, T02-224 2313, Wed-Sun 0830-1700, free, some English speaking guides*, is a 32-ha park on the slopes of Pichincha, where vestiges of human occupation of several pre-Inca periods, dating from 1500 BC to AD 1500, have been found. There are walking trails in some pockets of native vegetation. Northwest of Rumipamba, in the neighbourhood of San Vicente de la Florida is the excellent **Museo de Sitio La Florida** ⓘ *C Antonio Costas y Villacrés, T02-380 3043, Wed-Sun 0800-1600, free, some English speaking guides, at north end of El Ejido-San Vicente bus line*. At this necropolis of the Quitus people, 10 17-m deep burial chambers, dating to AD 220-640, have been excavated. The elaborate dress and jewellery found in the tombs suggests most were prominent citizens.

★ **Mitad del Mundo and around**
The location of the equatorial line here (23 km north of central Quito) was determined by Charles-Marie de la Condamine and his French expedition in 1736, and agrees to within 150 m with modern GPS measurements. The monument forms the focal point of the **Ciudad Mitad del Mundo** ⓘ *T02-239 4806, ext 115, daily 0900-1700 (very crowded on Sun); entry to complex and pavilions US$3.50,*

pavilions and planetariun US$5.50, pavilions and ethnographic museum US$6.50 (includes guided tour in Spanish or English), all the facilities US$7.50, a leisure park built as a typical colonial town, with restaurants, gift shops, post office and travel agency. In the interior of the equatorial monument is the very interesting **Museo Etnográfico**, refurbished in 2015, with displays about Ecuador's indigenous cultures. Each of the nations which participated in the 18th-century expedition has a pavilion with exhibits including an interesting **model of old Quito**, about 10 sq m, with artificial day and night and an **insectarium**. The **Museo Inti-Ñan** ① *200 m north of the monument, T02-239 5122, www.museointinan.com.ec, daily 0930-1700, US$4*, is eclectic, very interesting, has lots of fun activities and gives equator certificates for visitors. Research about the equator and its importance to prehistoric cultures is carried out near Cayambe, by an organization called **Quitsato** ① *www.quitsato.org, daily 0800-1700, US$2*. On weekends, **Quito Tour Bus**, see page 72, offers tours to Mitad del Mundo and Pululahua.

Pululahua ① *park office by the rim lookout, T02-239 6543, 0800-1700*, is a geobotanical reserve in an inhabited, farmed volcanic caldera. Four kilometres beyond Mitad del Mundo, off the road to Calacalí, Mirador Ventanillas – a lookout on the rim of Pululahua – gives a great view, but go in the morning, as the cloud usually descends around 1300. You can go down to the reserve and experience the rich vegetation and warm microclimate inside. From the mirador: walk down 30 minutes to the agricultural zone then turn left. There are picnic and camping areas. A longer road allows you to drive into the crater via Moraspungo. To walk out this way, starting at the mirador, continue past the village in the crater, turn left and follow the unimproved road up to the rim and back to the main road, a 15- to 20-km round trip.

Listings Quito maps p44, p46, p52, p51 and p54

Tourist information

General information about Quito is found on www.in-quito.com, information about museums on www.museosquito.gob.ec and http://museos.arqueo-ecuatoriana.ec; city photos in www.quitoenfotos.com. To file a complaint about services contact the Quito Visitor's Bureau headquarters (see below).

Empresa Metropolitana Quito Turismo/Quito Visitor's Bureau
HQ at Parque Bicentenario (old airport), T02-299 3300, www.quito.com.ec. Information offices with English-speaking personnel, brochures and maps, and an excellent website. They also run walking tours of the colonial city, see **Rutas Turísticas**, page 73. There are also offices at the airport (Arrivals area, T02-395 4200, ext 2008, daily 0600-2200), the bus station (Terminal Quitumbe, T02-382 4815, daily 0800-1800), train station (T02-261 7661, Mon-Fri 0800-1630), colonial Quito (Plaza de la Independencia, El Quinde craft shop at Palacio Municipal, Venezuela y Espejo, T02-257 2445, Mon-Fri 0900-1800, Sat 0900-1900, Sun 1000-1700), and La Mariscal (Foch E6-11 y Reina Victoria, T02-255 1566, daily 0900-1800), which

also sell tickets for the double decker bus tours, see page 72.

Ministerio de Turismo
Av Gran Colombia y Briceño,
T02-399 9333 or T1-800-887476,
www.turismo.gob.ec. Mon-Fri 0815-1700.
Offers information at their reception desk.

Servicio de Seguridad Turística
HQ at Reina Victoria N21-208 y
Roca, La Mariscal, T02-254 3983,
ssturistica98@gmail.com. Open
0800-1800 for information, 24 hrs for
emergencies. Other offices at: Plaza de
la Independencia, Casa de los Alcaldes,
Chile Oe4-66 y García Moreno, T02-295
5785, 0800-2400; La Ronda, Casa de las
Artes, Morales y Guayaquil, T02-295 6010,
Sun-Tue 0800-2300, Wed-Sat 0800-0400;
airport, T02-394 5000, ext 3023, Mon-Fri
0600-2400, Sat-Sun 0600-1800; Terminal
Quitumbe, Tue-Fri 0800-0000, Sat-Mon
0730-1800; and Mitad del Mundo, daily
0800-1800.
Offers information and is the place to obtain a police report in case of theft.

South American Explorers
Mariana de Jesús Oe3-32 y Ulloa,
T02-222 7235, quitoclub@saexplorers.
org. Mon-Fri 0930-1700, Sat 0900-1200.
Offers information, has rooms for rent, a hiking club and members may store gear. Local discounts with SAE card.

We help
Same premises as La Mariscal tourist
information (see under Empresa
Metropolitana Quito Turismo, above),
T02-252 2838. Mon-Sat 0930-2400,
Sun 1000-1600.
Airport transfers, travel insurance, storage lockers (free during the day, US$5 overnight) and booking for several tourist services.

Where to stay

For websites with extensive lists of hotels see Practicalities, page 436. For lodgings near the airport, see Quito suburbs below. Near the Quitumbe bus terminal are a few simple establisments catering to short stay customers and there is one simple *hostal* (**$ Madrid**) opposite the Carcelén bus terminal, along busy Av Eloy Alfaro. Large international chain hotels are represented in the city and meet their international standards.

Colonial Quito

$$$$ Casa Gangotena
Bolívar y Cuenca, T02-400 8000,
www.casagangotena.com.
Superb location by Plaza San Francisco, luxury accommodation in a beautifully refurbished classic family home with 31 rooms and suites, and a fine restaurant.

$$$$ La Casona de La Ronda
Morales Oe1-160 y Guayaquil, T02-228
7538, www.lacasonadelaronda.com.
Tastefully renovated colonial house in the heart of La Ronda, comfortable rooms and suite. Rates include buffet breakfast, and the restaurant serves Ecuadorean specialities and some international dishes.

$$$$ Patio Andaluz
García Moreno N6-52 y Olmedo, T02-228
0830, www.hotelpatioandaluz.com.
Beautifully reconstructed 16th-century mansion with large arches, balconies and patios. There's an upmarket restaurant serving Ecuadorean and Spanish cuisine, as well as a library and a gift shop. Breakfast extra.

Choosing a hotel in Quito

There are a great many hotels in Quito, of which we list a small fraction. With so much accommodation being offered, you can find a good place to stay regardless of your taste or budget, but the large selection can be bewildering. So narrow your search by reading up on the city, its neighbourhoods and hotels before you arrive.

Modern Quito has the greatest number of hotels. Many are concentrated in **La Mariscal**, Quito's tourist neighbourhood par excellence, the place for those who want to be in the heart of the action. Here you will be surrounded by restaurants, bars, nightlife, tour agencies, craft shops, Spanish schools, and even launderettes. Many budget hotels are in this area. With so much going on, it is not surprising that parts of La Mariscal are noisy, nor that this is where thieves and drug dealers can find the highest concentration of tourists.

La Floresta and other neighbourhoods to the east of La Mariscal, as well as **La Carolina** to the north, offer a variety of good accommodation in more relaxed residential surroundings. This is also where a number of the international hotels are located, while in the suburbs and to the west along the flanks of Pichincha are a handful of stylish hotels in rural settings not far from the city.

For those who prefer to stay in the historical heart of the city, there are a number of hotels in restored buildings in **colonial Quito**. Several posh places are by the main plazas and this area has some good mid-range hotels and B&Bs as well. The cheap hotels in this district tend to cater to short-stay couples and are not recommended.

Between colonial and modern Quito are ageing residential neighbourhoods with neither the charm of the old city, nor the vibrant scene of La Mariscal. The sector is nonetheless conveniently located and has some good-value accommodation.

Staying near the **airport** is handy if you are just stopping overnight. There is a choice of hotels in the mid-range price categories located in rural areas about 10- to 20-mins' drive from the airport. Some are in small towns where there are also simple restaurants, but others are off on their own, with no other services nearby. There are some simple hotels near Quito's long-distance **bus stations** in the extreme south and north of the city. There is not much of interest here, so it's only worth staying if you are taking another bus early the next day.

$$$$ Plaza Grande
García Moreno N5-16, Plaza de la Independencia, T02-251 0777, www.plazagrandequito.com.
Exclusive top-of-the-line hotel with an exceptional location, 15 suites including a presidential suite for US$2000, jacuzzi in all rooms, climate control, 3 restaurants including **La Belle Epoque**, gourmet French cuisine and a wine cellar, mini-spa and 110/220V outlets.

$$$ Casa Gardenia
Benalcázar N9-42 y Oriente, T02-295 7936.
Pleasant 9-room hotel in a quiet location with lovely views from the terrace. Price includes a buffet breakfast.

$$$ Catedral Internacional
Mejía Oe6-36 y Cuenca, T02-295 5438, www.hotelcatedral.ec.
Well-restored colonial house with 15 carpeted rooms, heaters, small patio, popular restaurant and a spa.

$$$ Relicario del Carmen
Venezuela N6-43 y Olmedo, T02-228 9120, www.hotelrelicariodelcarmen.com.
Attractive colonial house, with a good restaurant, cafeteria and pleasant rooms and service. No smoking.

$$ Quito Cultural
Flores N4-160 y Chile, T02-228 8084, www.hostalquitocultural.com.
Bright colonial house, with good views from its rooftop terrace and an appealing patio with plants. A bit pricey.

$$ San Francisco de Quito
Sucre Oe3-17 y Guayaquil, T02-295 1241, www.sanfranciscodequito.com.ec.
Well-run hotel in a converted colonial building. Breakfast is served in an attractive patio or underground cloisters, and there's also a restaurant. Suites are particularly good value.

$$-$ Community Hostel
Cevallos N6-78 y Olmedo, T02-228 5108, www.communityhostel.com.
Popular hostel offering 2 doubles and dorms for 4-6 (US$10 pp), with comfy beds. Shared bath (you may have to wait for the toilet in the morning), with good showers. The place is very clean and efficient and has an attractive sitting area, kitchen facilities and helpful staff. Breakfast is extra.

$$-$ Huasi Continental
Flores N3-08 y Sucre, T02-295 7327.
Slightly dark colonial house. The restaurant serves good breakfast and lunch (both extra). There's a choice of private or shared bath, and parking; good service and value.

In between the colonial and modern cities

$$$$ Mansión del Angel
Los Ríos N13-134 y Pasaje Gándara, T02-254 0293, www.mansiondelangel.com.ec.
Luxurious hotel decorated with antiques in a handsomely renovated mansion, with 14 ample rooms and a palatial suite. Lovely atmosphere, fine gardens and a spa. Dinner is available.

$$-$ Guayunga
Antepara E4-27 y León, T02-228 3127.
Good hostel with a few double rooms with and without bath and dorms for 3-9 (US$14 pp), an interior patio, an attractive rooftop terrace with great views, and parking. Breakfast is extra.

$$-$ L'Auberge Inn
Gran Colombia N15-200 y Yaguachi, T02-255 2912, www.auberge-inn-hostal.com.
Good spacious rooms, duvets, private or shared bath, excellent hot water, buffet breakfast and dinner available, grill next door for lunch, spa, cooking facilities, parking, lovely garden, terrace and communal area, helpful, good atmosphere. Highly recommended.

$$-$ Secret Garden
Antepara E4-60 y Los Ríos, T02-295 6704, www.secretgardenquito.com.
Renovated in 2015, this well-decorated house, has rooms (some of which are small and dark) with a choice of private or shared bath; US$12 pp in a dorm. There's a lovely rooftop terrace

restaurant, a pleasant atmosphere, and it's a very popular meeting place. Breakfast is extra. Its Ecuadorean-Australian owners also run a rustic lodge between Pasochoa and Cotopaxi, www.secretgardencotopaxi.com.

$ Chicago Hostal
Los Ríos N11-142 y Briceño, T02-228 1695, www.chicagohostalecuador.com.
This popular family-run hostel is a good economy option with small rooms, US$11 pp in dorm, and cooking facilities.

Modern Quito

$$$$ Le Parc
República de El Salvador N34-349 e Irlanda, T02-227 6800, www.leparc.com.ec.
Modern hotel with 30 executive suites, full luxury facilities and service, restaurant, spa, gym and parking.

$$$$ Nü House
Foch E6-12 y Reina Victoria, T02-255 7845, www.nuhousehotels.com.
Modern luxury hotel with minimalist decor, a restaurant, some suites with jacuzzi, and parking. All furnishings and works of art are for sale.

$$$ Anahi
Tamayo N23-95 y Wilson, T02-250 8403, www.anahihotelquito.com.
Tastefully and individually decorated suites, with ample bathrooms, safety box, fridge and terrace with attractive views. Good value. Buffet breakfast.

$$$ Café Cultura
Robles E6-62, T02-250 4078, www.cafecultura.com.
A well-established hotel with large suites, social areas including a wood-panelled library with a fireplace, a restaurant and attentive service.

They're planning to relocate to Calle Washington y Páez soon.

$$$ Casa Joaquín
Pinto E4-376 y JL Mera, T02-222 4791, www.hotelcasajoaquin.com.
Attractively refurbished Belgian-run hotel in the heart of La Mariscal. The covered patio makes it warm. Good service, but a bit pricey.

$$$ Cayman
Rodríguez E7-29 y Reina Victoria, T02-256 7616, www.hotelcaymanquito.com.
A pleasant hotel with a lovely dining room, a cafeteria, a sitting room with a fireplace, parking and a garden. Rooms are a bit small.

$$$ City Art Hotel Silberstein
Wilson E5-29 y JL Mera, T02-603 2213, www.cityartsilberstein.com.
10 comfortable rooms and suites in an attractively renovated building. Price includes buffet breakfast.

$$$ Finlandia
Finlandia N32-129 y Suecia, T02-224 4288, www.hotelfinlandia.com.ec.
A pleasant small hotel in a residential area, with spacious rooms, a restaurant, sitting room with fireplace, small garden, parking and helpful staff. Buffet breakfast.

$$$ Fuente de Piedra I & II
Wilson E9-80 y Tamayo, T02-255 9775 and JL Mera N23-21 y Baquedano, T02-252 5314, www.ecuahotel.com.
Well-decorated comfortable, modern hotels with attractive sitting areas. Some rooms are small.

$$$ Hostal de la Rábida
La Rábida 227 y Santa María, T02-222 2169, www.hostalrabida.com.
Lovely converted home, run by an Ecuadorean and an Italian, with bright

and comfortable rooms, a good restaurant for breakfast and dinner (both extra) and parking. Recommended.

$$$ La Cartuja
Plaza N20-08 y 18 de Septiembre, T02-252 3577, www.hotelacartuja.com.
In the former British Embassy, beautifully decorated, spacious comfortable rooms, cafeteria, parking, lovely garden, very helpful and hospitable. Highly recommended.

$$$ La Casa Sol
Calama 127 y 6 de Diciembre, T02-223 0798, www.lacasasol.com.
Lovely small hotel with a courtyard and very helpful staff. English and French spoken. They also run Casa Sol in Otavalo. Recommended.

$$$ Sierra Madre
Veintimilla E9-33 y Tamayo, T02-250 5687, www.hotelsierramadre.com.
Fully renovated villa with comfortable rooms, restaurant and an appealing sun roof. English spoken. Rates include buffet breakfast.

$$$ Villa Nancy
Muros N27-94 y 12 de Octubre, T02-256 2483, www.hotelvillanancy.com.
Quaint hotel in a quiet residential area, with helpful multilingual staff, buffet breakfast and parking. Homely and comfortable atmosphere. Recommended.

$$ El Arupo
Rodríguez E7-22 y Reina Victoria, T02-255 7543, www.hostalelarupo.com.
Good hotel with cooking facilities. English and French spoken. Recommended.

$$ Hothello
Amazonas N20-20 y 18 de Septiembre, T02-256 5835, www.hotelothello.com.

Small bright hotel with tastefully decorated rooms, heating and helpful multilingual staff.

$$ Queen's Hostel/Hostal de la Reina
Reina Victoria N23-70 y Wilson, T02-255 1844.
Pleasant small hotel, popular among travellers and Ecuadoreans, with a cafeteria, cooking facilities and a sitting room with a fireplace. Breakfast is extra.

$$ Travellers Inn
La Pinta E4-435 y Amazonas, T02-255 6985, www.travellersecuador.com.
In an attractively converted home, includes good breakfast, private or shared bath, parking, good common area and bike rentals. Recommended.

$$-$ Casa Helbling
Veintimilla E8-152 y 6 de Diciembre, T02-256 5740, www.casahelbling.de.
Excellent popular hostel, offering spotless rooms with private or shared bath. Thereh's also a 6-bed dorm (US$12 pp), laundry and cooking facilities, English and German spoken, a pleasant atmosphere, reliable information, luggage storage and parking. Breakfast is extra. Highly recommended.

$$-$ Posada del Maple
Rodríguez E8-49 y 6 de Diciembre, T02-254 4507, www.posadadelmaple.com.
Popular hostel, private or shared bath, also 8-bed dorm (US$7 pp), cooking facilities, warm atmosphere and free tea and coffee.

$ Backpackers Inn
Rodríguez E7-48 y Reina Victoria, T02-250 9669, www.backpackersinn.net.
Popular hostel, with private or shared bath, adequate dorms (US$8 pp), laundry and cooking facilities. Breakfast is extra.

$ Casona de Mario
Andalucía N24-115 y Galicia, La Floresta,
T02-254 4036, www.casonademario.com.
Busy Argentine-owned hostel, offering
rooms with shared bath, laundry
facilities, well-equipped kitchen, parking,
sitting room, pretty garden, book
exchange and long stay discounts. No
breakfast. Repeatedly recommended.

$ El Cafecito
Cordero E6-43 y Reina Victoria,
T02-223 4862, www.cafecito.net.
Good Canadian-owned backpacker place
with a decent café offering vegetarian
and vegan options. Rates are cheaper in
a dorm (US$8); 1 room with bath. There's
a relaxed atmosphere but it can get noisy
until 2200. Breakfast is extra.

Quito suburbs

$$$$ Hacienda Rumiloma
Obispo Díaz de La Madrid, T02-254 8206,
www.haciendarumiloma.com.
Luxurious hotel in a 40-ha hacienda
on the slopes of Pichincha. Sumptuous
suites with lots of attention to detail,
lounges with antiques, good pricey
restaurant, bar with fireplace, and great
views. There's personalized attention
from the owners and it's ideal for a
luxurious escape close to the city.

$$$ Hostería San Jorge
Km 4 vía antigua Quito-Nono, to the
west of Av Mariscal Sucre, T02-339 0403,
sanjorgeecolodges.com.
Converted 18th-century hacienda on
a 80-ha private reserve on the slopes
of Pichincha, with an expensive but
excellent restaurant, heating, pool, sauna,
jacuzzi, horse riding and birdwatching.
Full board available. Operates several
nature reserves, see page 96.

Quito airport

2 luxury hotels by the airport were
under construction in 2015. Note that
taxi drivers may not be familiar with the
hotels in towns near the airport, so print
the hotel's map before travelling. Many
hotels here are in rural settings where
there are no restaurants. There's a food
court in the shopping area opposite
the airport.

Towns near the airport with
accommodation include: **Tababela**,
off highway E-35, 10 mins from the
airport towards Quito (airport taxi
US$10). Nearby, by the junction of E-35
and the Vía Interoceánica, is **Pifo**, also
about 10 mins from the airport (taxi
US$10). From Pifo you can go northwest
to Quito, southwest to Sangolquí and
points south or east to Papallacta
and Oriente. **Puembo**, past Pifo on
the Vía Interoceánica, is 20 mins from
the airport (taxi US$15-20) and closer
to Quito. **Oyambarillo**, north of the
airport off E-35, is 10 mins away (taxi
US$10). On E-35 to the north are **Checa**,
about 15 mins away (taxi US$12-15),
and **El Quinche**, about 20 mins from
the airport (taxi US$15-20). The latter 2
are convenient if going to Otavalo and
points north, without going to Quito

$$$ Garden Hotel San José
Manuel Burbano s/n, Barrio San José,
Puembo, T02-239 0276, T1-800-180180,
www.hosteriasanjose.com.
An 18th-century hacienda set in
4-ha grounds, with modern rooms,
restaurant, pool and spa. Airport
transfers are US$10 pp.

$$$ Hostal Su Merced
Julio Tobar Donoso, Puembo, T02-239
0251, www.sumerced.com.
Attractively refurbished 18th-century
hacienda house, well-appointed rooms

with bathtubs, restaurant, sauna and gardens and a traditional breakfast. Airport transfers cost US$15 per vehicle.

$$$ Posada Mirolindo
Vía Oyambarillo, T02-215 0363, www.posadamirolindo.com.
Pleasant rooms and cottages. The price includes transfers to and from the airport. Breakfast is provided, other meals are available on request.

$$ Hostal El Parque
29 de Abril y 24 de Septiembre, opposite the main park in Tababela, T02-239 1280, patriciogarzon70@hotmail.com.
Rooms with private or shared bath, gardens and meals available. Airport transfers US$5 per vehicle.

$$ Hostería San Carlos
Justo Cuello y Maldonado, Tababela, T02-359 9057, www.hosteriasancarlostababela.com.
Hacienda-style inn with ample grounds, restaurant, pool, jacuzzi, rooms with bath and dorms (US$20 pp). Airport transfers US$5 per person.

$$ Quito Airport Suites
Alfonso Tobar 971 y Tulio Guzmán, Tababela, 1 block from the plaza, T02-359 9110 or T09-8889 9774, airporthotelquito.com.
Rooms are available for day use between flights ($); luggage storage US$1 per case, per day, available to non guests. The room price includes breakfast which can be a box breakfast in case of an early departure; dinner is extra. English spoken. Long-term parking; airport transfers are US$8 per vehicle.

$$-$ Hostal Colibrí
Pje Tobías Trujillo, 3 blocks downhill from the Tababela park, T02-215 0100, www. hostalcolibriaeropuerto.com.

Hacienda-style hotel with private rooms and dorm for 12 (US$15 pp), a garden with a pool and a jacuzzi. They can offer plenty of information and also arrange excursions. Rates include breakfast; dinner is extra. Airport transfers are US$10 for 2 passengers. Recommended.

$ Nevada
E-35 Km 26, outside Pifo, near the turn-off for Sangolquí, T02-238 0074.
Simple economical rooms, with traffic noise.

Restaurants

Eating out in Quito is excellent, varied, upmarket and increasingly cosmopolitan. There are many elegant restaurants offering Ecuadorean and international food, as well as small simple places serving set meals for US$2.50-5, the latter closing by early evening and on Sun.

Colonial Quito

$$$ El Ventanal
Carchi y Nicaragua, west of the Basílica, in Parque San Juan, take a taxi to the parking area and a staff member will accompany you along a footpath to the restaurant, T02-257 2232, www.elventanal.ec. Tue-Sat 1300-1500, 1800-2230, Sun 1200-1600.
International nouvelle cuisine with a varied menu including a number of seafood dishes. Fantastic views over the city.

$$$ Los Geranios
Morales Oe1-134, T02-295 6035. Mon-Thu 0900-0000, Fri-Sat 0900-0200, Sun 1000-2200.
Upscale *comida típica*, in a well-restored La Ronda house.

ON THE ROAD

Dining out

Quito offers excellent, varied, cosmopolitan and upmarket dining, which is reasonable by international standards. The majority of restaurants are in modern Quito, where there is almost any type of cuisine. At Plaza Foch there are some 25 restaurants, cafés and many bars. A number of upscale restaurants are found in La Floresta neighbourhood, near Swissôtel, east of La Mariscal, near Parque La Carolina and along Avenida Eloy Alfaro. Colonial Quito also has some very elegant expensive establishments serving international and Ecuadorean food.

If you are on a tight budget, there are also a great many simple little places throughout the city serving cheap and adequate set meals, *almuerzos* and *meriendas* from US$2.50-5. With so much else on offer we list just a few of these but they are everywhere. There are also reasonable restaurants in the food courts of shopping malls.

Many restaurants close on Sun evenings. Those with stickers indicating acceptance of credit cards do not necessarily do so, so ask first. In many expensive restaurants 12% tax and 10% service is added to the bill.

$$$ Theatrum
Plaza del Teatro, 2nd floor of Teatro Sucre, T02-228 9669, www.theatrum.com.ec. Mon-Fri 1230-1500, 1900-2200, Sat-Sun 1900-2200.
Excellent creative gourmet cuisine in the city's most important theatre. The wide selection of fruit desserts come with an explanatory card.

$$$-$$ Hasta la Vuelta Señor
Pasaje Arzobispal, 3rd floor. Mon-Sat 1100-2300, Sun 1100-2100.
A *fonda quiteña* perched on an indoor balcony with *comida típica* and snacks; try the *empanadas* (pasties) or a *seco de chivo* (goat stew).

$$ Tianguez
Plaza de San Francisco under the portico of the church. Mon-Wed 0900-1900, Thu 0900-2200, Fri-Sat 0800-2300.
Popular place serving international and local dishes, good coffee, snacks and sandwiches. There's also a craft

shop (closes 1830), run by Fundación Sinchi Sacha.

$$ Vista Hermosa
Mejía 453 y García Moreno. Mon-Sat 1300-2400.
With lovely terrace-top views of the colonial centre, this place offers good meals and pizza, with live music on weekends.

$$-$ San Ignacio
García Moreno N2-60, at the Museo María Agusta Urrutia. Mon-Sat 0800-2200, Sun 0800-1600.
Good popular set lunch (US$4-4.50) with a choice of dishes and buffet salad bar; à la carte in the evening.

$ Govinda
Esmeraldas Oe3-115 y Venezuela. Mon-Sat 0800-1800.
Vegetarian dishes, good value economical set lunch and à la carte snacks; also breakfast.

$ Plaza Chica
Between Venezuela and Guayaquil, on an interior patio behind the Municipio. Mon-Fri 0830-1600.
An excellent choice for an elegant set lunch with a choice of dishes, also coffee and pastries. It's very busy so be prepared to wait.

Cafés

Caffeto
Chile 930 y Flores. Mon-Sat 0800-1900, Sun 0815-1600.
Variety of coffees, snacks, sandwiches and sweets.

Heladería San Agustín
Guayaquil N5-59 y Chile. Mon-Fri 1000-1630, Sat-Sun 1030-1530.
A Quito tradition since 1858, this ice cream parlour serves traditional homemade cakes, ices and lunch.

Modern Quito
There are at least 25 restaurants ($$$-$$) and cafés within a block of Plaza Foch. There are many restaurants serving good economical set lunches along both Pinto and Foch, between Amazonas and Cordero.

$$$ Carmine
Catalina Aldaz N34-208 y Portugal, T02-333 2829, www.carmineristorante.com. Mon-Sat 1200-2300, Sun 1200-1800.
Creative international and Italian cuisine.

$$$ Chez Jérôme
Whymper N30-96 y Coruña, T02-223 4067, www.chezjeromerestaurante.com. Mon-Fri 1230-1500, 1930-2300.
Excellent French cuisine, traditional and modern dishes with a touch of local ingredients, good ambiance and service.

$$$ Il Risotto
Eloy Alfaro N34-447 y Portugal, T02-224 6850 and República de El Salvador N35-79 y Portugal, near Parque La Carolina, T02-224 8487. Mon-Fri 1130-1530, 1830-2300, Sat 1130-2300, Sun 1130-2200 (Eloy Alfaro); Mon-Sat 1200-2300, Sun 1200-2200 (Rep ES).
Very popular and excellent Italian cooking; prices on Eloy Alfaro are somewhat higher. A Quito tradition.

$$$ La Boca del Lobo
Calama 284 y Reina Victoria, T02-223 4083, wwwlabocadellobo.com.ec. Sun-Wed 1700-2330, Thu-Sat 1700-0100.
Busy, stylish bar-restaurant with eclectic food, drink, decor, and atmosphere, good food and cocktails. A good meeting place.

$$$ La Briciola
Isabel la Católica y Salazar esquina, La Floresta, T254 5157, www.labriciola.com.ec. Daily 1200-2400.
Extensive Italian menu, excellent food, homely atmosphere and very good personal service.

$$$ La Choza
12 de Octubre N24-551 y Cordero, La Floresta, T02-223 0839. Mon-Sat 1200-1600, 1800-2130, Sun 1200-1600.
Traditional Ecuadorean cuisine, with good music and decor.

$$$ La Gloria
Valladolid N24-519 y Salazar, La Floresta, T02-252 7855, www.lagloria.com.ec. Daily 1200-1530, 1900-2200.
Innovative Peruvian and international cuisine, excellent food and service. Under the same ownership as **Theatrum** (see above).

$$$ La Petite Mariscal
Almagro N24-304 y Rodríguez, T02-604 3303, www.lapetitemariscal.com. Tue-Fri 1200-1500, 1800-2200, Sat 1800-2200.
Upmarket European cuisine with an Ecuadorean touch. They also serve a good set lunch.

$$$ San Telmo
Portugal 440 y Casanova, T02-225 6946. Mon-Sat 1200-2300, Sun until 2100.
Good Argentine grill, seafood and pasta, served in a pleasant atmosphere with great service.

$$$ Zazu
Mariano Aguilera 331 y La Pradera, T254 3559, www.zazuquito.com. Mon-Fri 1230-1500, 1900-2300, Sat 1900-2300.
South of Parque La Carolina, this elegant and exclusive restaurant serves international and Peruvian specialities, and has an extensive wine list and attentive service. Reservations required.

$$$-$$ Baalbek
6 de Diciembre N23-123 y Wilson, T02-255 2766. Sun-Tue 1200-1700, Wed-Sat 1200-2230.
Authentic Lebanese cuisine, great food and atmosphere, and friendly service.

$$ Chez Alain
Wilson E9-68 y Tamayo. Mon-Sat 1200-1530.
Choice of good 4-course set lunches, served in a pleasant relaxed atmosphere. Recommended.

$$ The Magic Bean
Foch E5-08 y JL Mera. Daily 0800-2200 and Portugal y Los Shyris, daily 0800-1730.
Fine coffees and natural food, more than 20 varieties of pancakes, good salads, large portions and outdoor seating. Also has popular lodging ($).

$$ Mama Clorinda
Reina Victoria N24-150 (11-44) y Calama. Daily 1100-2300.
Ecuadorean à la carte and set meals, which are filling and good value.

$$ Mr Bagel
Portugal 546 y 6 de Diciembre and Cordero E10-55 y 12 de Octubre, near Parque La Carolina. Mon-Fri 0700-1500, Sat-Sun 0730-1500 (Portugal); Mon-Fri 0730-1830, Sat-Sun 0800-1300 (Cordero).
Very popular breakfast and lunch restaurant, with 17 varieties of bagels and many spreads, sandwiches, soups, salads and desserts. Also takeaway options, Wi-Fi and book exchange.

$$ Paléo
Cordero E5-36 y JL Mera. Mon-Tue 1200-1600, Wed-Sat 1200-1530, 1830-2300.
Authentic Swiss specialities such as rösti and raclette. Also offers a good economical set lunch. Recommended.

$$ Pekín
Whymper N26-42 y Orellana, www.restaurante-pekin.com. Mon-Sat 1200-1530, 1800-2230, Sun 1200-2000.
Excellent Chinese food, served in a pleasant atmosphere.

$$-$ El Hornero
Veintimilla y Amazonas, República de El Salvador N36-149 y Naciones Unidas and on González Suárez. Daily 1200-2300.
Very good wood-oven pizzas; try one with *choclo* (fresh corn). Recommended.

$$-$ Las Palmeras
Japón N36-87 y Naciones Unidas, opposite Parque la Carolina. Daily 0900-1700.
Excellent, good-value *comida Esmeraldeña*; try their hearty *viche* soup at this busy restaurant, with outdoor tables. Recommended.

$$-$ Rincón Ecuatoriano Chileno
6 de Diciembre N28-30 y Belo Horizonte.
Mon 1200-1800, Tue-Sat 1200-2000,
Sun 1200-1700.
Good tasty home cooking, including
Chilean specialities such as *empanadas*,
with large portions and efficient service.
Some tables are in the garden.

$$-$ Sakti
Carrión E4-144 y Amazonas.
Mon-Fri 0830-1730.
Good quality vegetarian food, tasty
healthy breakfast, daily specials,
fruit juices and great desserts. Also
rooms around a small garden ($$-$).
Recommended.

$ Chandani Tandoori
JL Mera 1312 y Cordero. Mon-Sat
1200-2130, Sun 1200-1530.
Excellent authentic Indian cuisine,
including inexpensive, good-value set
meals. Recommended.

$ Yu Su
Almagro y Colón, edif Torres de Almagro.
Mon-Fri 1230-1600, 1800-2000,
Sat 1230-1600.
Great Korean-run sushi bar, with
a pleasant atmosphere and a
takeaway service.

Cafés

Coffee Bar
Reina Victoria y Foch. Open 24 hrs.
Popular café serving snacks, pasta,
burgers and coffee. Wi-Fi. Very
similar are **Coffee Tree** (Amazonas y
Washington), and **Coffee Tov** (next to
Museo Mindalae, Reina Victoria).

Ethnic Coffee
Amazonas y Roca, Edif Hotel Mercure,
local 3, www.ethniccollection.com.
Mon-Fri 1000-2030.

Appealing café with gourmet coffee as
well as a wide range of desserts, meals
($$) and drinks.

Kallari
Wilson y JL Mera, www.kallari.com.
Mon-Fri 0900-1830, Sat 0900-1400.
Fairtrade café, serving breakfast, snacks,
salad and sandwich set lunches, organic
coffee and chocolate and crafts. It's run
by an association of farmers and artisans
from the Province of Napo working on
rainforest and cultural conservation.

Bars and clubs

Note that the sale and consumption of
alcohol is not permitted on Sun or the
final day of a holiday (eg on the Tue of
carnival). In Colonial Quito, nightlife is
concentrated along La Ronda.

Modern Quito

Bungalow Six
Almagro N24-139 y Calama. Tue-Sat
1900-0200, Sun 1200-1900.
US-style sports bar and club. A great
place to hang out and watch a game or a
film, with dancing later on, varied music.
Cover US$5 (Thu free), ladies' night on
Wed, happy hour 2000-2200.

Cherusker
Pinto y Diego de Almagro esquina.
Mon-Fri 1500-2330, Fri-Sat 1500-0130.
Various microbrews and German food.

El Pobre Diablo
Isabel La Católica N24-224 y Galavis,
La Floresta, www.elpobrediablo.com.
Mon-Sat 1230-0200.
A popular place to hang out and chill,
with a relaxed, friendly atmosphere, jazz,
sandwiches, snacks and good meals and
set lunches. Live music Wed, Thu and Sat.

Finn McCool's
Almagro N24-64 y Pinto. Daily 1100-0200.
Irish-run pub, Irish and international food, darts, pool, table football, sports on TV, Wi-Fi; a popular meeting place.

La Juliana
12 de Octubre N24-722 y Coruña. Thu-Sat 2130-0300.
Busy club playing live 1990s Latin music, cover US$12.

No Bar
Calama E5-01 y JL Mera. Mon-Sat 1900-0300.
Good mix of Latin and Euro dance music, packed at weekends. Free drinks for women until 2200, Thu-Sat after 2200 entry US$5 with 1 free drink.

Selfie
Calama E7-35 y Reina Victoria. Wed-Thu 1500-2400, Fri 1200-0200, Sat 1200-2400.
Popular disco attracting a young crowd, entry US$3.

Turtle's Head
La Niña E4-451 y JL Mera. Mon-Thu 1600-2400, Fri-Sat 1600-0200.
Microbrews, fish and chips, curry, pool table and darts, in a fun atmosphere.

Varadero
Reina Victoria N26-99 y La Pinta. Fri-Sat 2000-0300.
Bar-restaurant, with live Cuban music, attached to **La Bodeguita de Cuba** restaurant, attracting a mixed crowd.

Entertainment

There are always many cultural events taking place in Quito, often free of charge. Films are listed daily in *El Comercio*, www.elcomercio.com.

Cinema
There are several multiplexes, eg **Cinemark** (www.cinemark.com.ec), and **Multicines** (www.multicines.com.ec).
Casa de la Cultura, *Patria y 6 de Diciembre, T02-290 2272.* Shows foreign films and often has documentaries and film festivals, which are all free.
Ocho y Medio, *Valladolid N24-353 y Guipuzcoa, La Floresta, T02-290 4720.* Cinema and café, good for art films; a programme is available at **Libri Mundi** and elsewhere.

Dance
Casa de la Danza, *Junín E2-186 y Javier Gutiérrez, Parque San Marcos in the colonial city, T02-295 5445, www. casadeladanza.org.* Run by the well-known Ecuadorean dancer Susana Reyes, this is the venue for dance festivals and events. It also has exhibits and hosts the Saruymanda ballet (see below). There's an Italian restaurant on the premises.

Ecuadorean folk ballet Ballet Andino Humanizarte, *at Casa 707, Morales 707, La Ronda, T02-257 3486. Thu 2100, Fri-Sat 2130. Tickets US$5.* Plays and comedies are also often in their repertoire, and there's a restaurant on the premises.
Jacchigua, *at Teatro Demetrio Aguilera Malta, Casa de la Cultura, 6 de Diciembre y Patria, T02-295 2025, www. jacchiguaesecuador.com. Wed at 1930.* Entertaining, colourful and touristy, reserve ahead, US$30.
Saruymanda, *at Casa de la Danza, T09-8414 3747, www.saruymanda.com. Sat at 1930. Minimum donation US$5.* Performances draw on Ecuadorean traditions and folklore.

Music

Classical Casa de la Música, *Valderrama s/n y Mariana de Jesús, T02-226 7093, www.casadelamusica.ec.* Concerts by the Orquesta Sinfónica Nacional, Orquesta Filarmónica del Ecuador, Orquesta de Instrumentos Andinos and invited performers. Excellent acoustics.

Orquesta Sinfónica Nacional, *T02-250 2815.* Performs at **Teatro Sucre, Casa de la Música, Teatro Escuela Politécnica Nacional, Teatro México**, in the colonial churches and regionally.

Folk Folk music is popular in *peñas* which come alive after 2230. Below is a selection.

Noches de Quito, *Washington E5-29 y JL Mera, T02-223 4855. Thu-Sat 2000-0300, show starts 2130.* Varied music, entry US$6. Being remodelled in 2015.

Ñucanchi, *Av Universitaria Oe5-188 y Armero, T02-254 0967. Thu-Sat 2000-0300, show starts at 2130. Entry US$8-10.* Ecuadorean and other music, including Latin dance later in the night.

Theatre

Agora (open-air theatre), **Teatro Nacional** (large) and **Prometeo** (informal), all at Casa de la Cultura, stage plays and concerts.

Teatro Bolívar, *Espejo 847 y Guayaquil, T02-258 2486, www.teatrobolivar.org.* Despite restoration work you can have a tour.

Teatro Sucre, *at Plaza del Teatro, T02-295 1661.* Beautifully restored 19th-century building, the city's classical theatre.

Festivals

New Year Años Viejos, life-size puppets satirize politicians and others. At midnight on 31 Dec a will is read, the legacy of the outgoing year, and the puppets are burnt; it's good at Av Amazonas, where a competition is held; very entertaining and good humoured. On New Year's Day everything is shut.

6 Jan (may be moved to the weekend) **Inocentes**, a colourful procession from Plaza de Santo Domingo at 1700.

8 Mar International Women's Day marks the start of **Mujeres en la Danza**, a week-long international dance festival organized by Casa de la Danza, www.casadeladanza.org.

Easter Palm Sunday, colourful procession from the Basílica, 0800-1000. **Good Friday**, the solemn processions are most impressive.

24 May Independence commemorating the Battle of Pichincha in 1822 with early morning cannon-fire and parades; everything closes.

Aug Agosto Arte y Cultura, organized by the municipality, cultural events, dance and music in different places throughout the city.

1-6 Dec Día de Quito is the city's main festival and commemorates the foundation of the city with elaborate parades, bullfights, performances and music in the streets; very lively. Hotels charge extra, everything except a few restaurants shuts on 6 Dec.

24-25 Dec Christmas, foremost among **the festive** celebrations is the **Misa del Gallo** (Midnight Mass). Nativity scenes can be admired in many public places. Over Christmas, Quito is crowded, hotels are full and the streets are packed with vendors and shoppers.

Shopping

Shops generally open 0900-1900 on weekdays, some close at midday and most shut Sat afternoon and Sun. Shopping centres are open at weekends.

In modern Quito much of the shopping is done in malls. For maps see page 422.

Bookshops
The following have a selection of books in English:
Confederate Books, *Amazonas N24-155 y Calama*. Used books.
The English Bookshop, *Calama 217 y Almagro*. Used books sales and exchange.
Libri Mundi, *JL Mera N23-83 y Veintimilla, Quicentro Shopping, other malls and the airport, www.librimundi.com*.
Mr Books, *Mall El Jardín, p3 and Scala and El Condado shopping centres, www. mrbooks.com*.

Camping
Camping gas is available in many of the shops listed below, white gas is not.
Aventura Sport, *Quicentro Shopping, 2nd level*. Tents, a good selection of glacier sunglasses, and Ecuadorean and imported outdoor clothing and gear. The following 2 shops stock the same products.
Camping Sports, *Colón E6-39 y Reina Victoria*.
Equipos Cotopaxi, *6 de Diciembre N20-36 y Patria*.
Explorer, *Plaza Foch and all main shopping centres in the city*. Clothing and equipment for adventure sports. Also have noticeboards for travellers.
Mono Dedo, *Rafael León Larrea N24-36 y Coruña, La Floresta, www. monodedoecuador.com*. Climbing equipment. Part of a rock climbing club, with lessons available.
Tatoo, *Av de los Granados y 6 de Diciembre and CC Scala in Cumbayá, www.tatoo.ws*. Quality backpacks and outdoor clothing.

Chocolate
Ecuador has exported its fine cacao to the most prestigious chocolatiers around the world for over 100 years. Today, quality chocolate is on offer in specialized shops and food stores.
Galería Ecuador, *Reina Victoria N24-263 y García*. Shop and café featuring Ecuadorean gourmet organic coffee and chocolate as well as some crafts.
Pacari, *Zaldumbide N24-676 y Miravalle, www.pacarichocolate.com*. Factory outlet for one of the most highly regarded manufacturers. They have won more international chocolate awards than any other company in the world. Also have an organic products market on Tue.
República del Cacao, *Reina Victoria y Pinto, Plaza Foch; Morales Oe1-166, La Ronda, Plaza de las Américas and at the airport*. Chocolate boutique and café; also sell Panama hats.

Handicrafts
Note that there are controls on export of arts and crafts. Unless they are obviously new handicrafts, you may have to get a permit from the **Instituto Nacional de Patrimonio Cultural** (Colón Oe1-93 y 10 de Agosto, T02-254 3527, offices also in other cities), before take things home. Permits cost US$5 and take time.

A wide selection can be found at the following craft markets: **Mercado Artesanal La Mariscal** (Jorge Washington, between Reina Victoria and JL Mera, daily 1000-1800), interesting and worthwhile; **El Indio** (Roca E4-35 y Amazonas, daily 0900-1900); and **Centro de Artesanías CEFA** (12 de Octubre1738 y Madrid, Mon-Sat 0930-1830).

On weekends, crafts are sold in stalls at **Parque El Ejido** and along the Av Patria side of this park, and artists sell their paintings. There are crafts and art shops along La Ronda and souvenir shops on García Moreno in front of the Palacio Presidencial.

Recommended shops with an ample selection are:

Camari, *Marchena 260 y Versalles*. Fairtrade shop run by an artisan organization.

EBD Carmal, *Amazonas N24-126 y Foch, ebdcarmal.com*. Pan*ama and fedora hats. Ethnic Collection, Amazonas y Roca, Edif Hotel Mercure, www.ethniccollection.com*. Wide variety of clothing, leather, bags, jewellery and ceramic items. There's also a café 2 doors south.

Folklore, *Colón E10-53 y Caamaño*. The store of the late Olga Fisch, who for decades encouraged craftspeople to excel. Attractive selection of top quality, pricey handicrafts and rugs. A small museum upstairs includes a very good collection of pre-Columbian ceramics.

Galería Latina, *JL Mera 823 y Veintimilla. Daily*. Fine selection of alpaca and other handicrafts from Ecuador, Peru and Bolivia; visiting artists sometimes demonstrate their work.

Hilana, *6 de Diciembre N23-10 y Veintimilla*. Beautiful 100% wool blankets, ponchos and clothing with Ecuadorean motifs, also cotton garments; excellent quality.

Kallari, *see page 68*. Crafts from the Oriente sold in the café.

K Dorfzaun, *República del Cacao shops, see page 71*. Fine Panama hats.

La Bodega, *JL Mera 614 y Carrión*. Recommended for antiques and handicrafts.

Mindalae, *see page 53*. Good crafts are sold at this museum.

Productos Andinos, *Urbina 111 y Cordero*. Artisan's coop, with a good selection, including unusual items.

Saucisa, *Amazonas N22-18 y Veintimilla,*

and a couple other locations in La Mariscal. Excellent place to buy Andean music and instruments.

Jewellery

Argentum, *JL Mera 614*. Excellent selection, reasonably priced.

Ari Gallery, *Bolívar Oe6-23, Plaza San Francisco*. Fine silver with ancestral motifs.

Taller Guayasamín, *at Capilla del Hombre, see page 55*. Jewellery with native designs.

What to do

Birdwatching and nature

The following are specialized operators: **Andean Birding**, www.andeanbirding. com; **BirdEcuador**, www.birdecuador. com; **Ecuador Experience**, www. ecuador-experience.com (in French); **Mindo Bird Tours**, www. mindobirdtours.com; **Neblina Forest**, www.neblinaforest.com; **Pluma Verde**, www.plumaverdetours.com; Tropical Birding, www.tropicalbirding.com. Local birding guides are also available in Mindo.

City tours

Quito Tour Bus, *T02-245 8010, www. quitotourbus.com*. Tours on double-decker bus, stops at 11 places of interest. It starts and ends at Av Naciones Unidas, on the south side. You can alight at a site and continue later on another bus. Hourly, 0900-1600, 3-hr ride, US$15, children and seniors US$7.50, ticket valid all day. Night tour Fri, Sat and holidays at 1900, US$15, with a 1½-hr stop at La Ronda. Mitad del Mundo and Pululahua tour, Sat and Sun at 1100, US$30, children and seniors US$20, includes museum entrance fees, 7 hrs.

Rutas Turísticas, *tours start at the Plaza de la Independencia tourist information office, Venezuela y Espejo, T02-257 2445.* Walking tours of the colonial city led by English- or French-speaking officers of the Policía Metropolitana. Advanced reservation and a minimum of 2 people required. There are 2 choices: **Ruta Patrimonial**, Tue-Sat at 0900, 1000 and 1400, Sun at 1100, 2½ hrs, US$15, children and seniors US$7.70, includes museum entrance fees for La Compañía, San Francisco and Museo de la Ciudad; and **Fachadas**, a daily historic buildings walking tour, at the same times, 1½ hrs, US$8; also an evening tour at 1800, US$10.

Climbing, trekking and walking

The following Quito operators specialize in this area; most also offer conventional tours and sell Galápagos and jungle tours. Note that no one may climb without a licensed guide employed by an authorized agency. Independent climbers and guides are refused entry to national parks but exceptions may be made for internationally (UIAA) certified guides and members of Ecuadorian climbing clubs.

Andes Explorer, *Tamayo N24-96 y Foch, of 801, T02-290 1493, www.andes-explorer. com.* Good-value budget mountain and jungle trips.

Campus Adventures, *T02-234 0601, www.campustrekking.com.ec.* Good-value trekking, climbing and cultural tours, 8- to 15-day biking trips, tailor-made itineraries. Also run **Hostería Pantaví** near Ibarra; 8 languages spoken.

Climbing Tours, *Amazonas N21-221 y Roca, T02-254 4358, www.climbingtour. com.* Climbing, trekking and other adventure sports and tours to regional attractions. Also sell Galápagos and jungle tours. Well-established operator.

Compañía de Guías, *Valladolid N24-70 y Madrid, T02-290 1551, www. companiadeguias.com.* Climbing and trekking specialists. Speak English, German, French and Italian.

Condor Trekk, *Reina Victoria N24-295 y Cordero, T02-222 6004, www. condortrekkexpeditions.com.* Climbing, trekking and fishing trips, 4WD transport, equipment rentals and sales.

Cotopaxi Cara Sur, *contact Eduardo Agama, T09-9800 2681, www. cotopaxicarasur.com.* Offers climbing and trekking tours, and runs Albergue Cara Sur on Cotopaxi.

Gulliver, *JL Mera N24-156 y Calama, T02-290 5036, www.gulliver.com.ec.* Climbing and trekking and a wide range of economical adventure and traditional

tours. Operates **Hostería Papagayo** south of Quito.

High Summits, *Pinto E5-29 y JL Mera, p2, T02-254 9358, www.climbing-ecuador. com*. Climbing specialists for over 40 years, Swiss/Ecuadorean-run.

Latitud 0°, *Mallorca N24-500 y Coruña, La Floresta, T02-254 7921, www.latitud0. com*. Climbing specialists, French spoken.

Original Ecuador, *La Tolita E18-195 y Pasaje Ninahualpa, p2, Guápulo, T02-255 9339, www.originalecuador.com*. Runs 1- to 7-day highland tours which involve walking several hours daily, also custom-made itineraries.

TribuTrek, *T09-9282 5404, www.tributrek. com*. Hiking and trekking, cultural and budget tours.

Cycling and mountain biking

Quito has many bike paths and bike lanes on city streets, but mind the traffic and aggressive drivers. The city organizes a *ciclopaseo*, a cycle day, every Sun 0800-1400. Key avenues are closed to vehicular traffic and thousands of cyclists cross the city in 29 km from north to south. This and other cycle events are run by **Fundación Ciclópolis** (Equinoccio N17-171 y Queseras del Medio, T02-322 6502, www.ciclopolis.ec); they also hire bikes, US$5.60 per *ciclopaseo* (must book Mon-Fri), US$11.20 per day on other days. Rentals also from **La Casa del Ciclista** (Eloy Alfaro 1138 y República, near the *ciclopaseo* route, T02-254 0339, US$3 per hr, US$12 per day). If staying a long time in the city, sign up with **BiciQ**, to use their bikes stationed throughout town. **Biciacción** (www.biciaccion.org), has information about routes in the city and organizes trips outside Quito.

Mountain bike tours Many operators offer bike tours. The following are specialists:

Aries, *T09-9981 6603, www. ariesbikecompany.com*. 1- to 3-day tours, all equipment provided.

Biking Dutchman, *La Pinta E7-31 y Reina Victoria, T02-256 8323, after hours T09-9420 5349, www.biking-dutchman.com*. Tours of between 1 and several days, which are great fun and well organized, with good food, run by pioneers in mountain biking in Ecuador. English, German and Dutch spoken.

Dance classes

One-to-one or group lessons are offered for US$4-6 per hr.

Ritmo Tropical, *Amazonas N24-155 y Calama, T02-255 7094, www. ritmotropicalsalsa.com*. Classes in salsa, capoeira, merengue, tango and more.

Salsa y Merengue School, *Foch E4-256 y Amazonas, T02-222 0427*. Also offers cumbia.

Horse riding

Horse riding tours are offered on Pichincha above the gate of the *teleférico*; see page 56.

Green Horse Ranch, *see page 80*.

Ride Andes, *T09-9973 8221, www. rideandes.com*. Private and set date tours in the highlands including stays in haciendas, also in other South American countries.

Motorbiking

Freedom Bike Rental, *Juan de Velasco N26-128, T02-600 4459, www.freedom bikerental.com*. Motorcycle rentals US$75-200 per day, scooter US$25, good equipment including mountain bikes, GPS, route planning, also tours.

Language schools

Quito is one of the most important centres for Spanish language study in Latin America with some 80 schools operating. There is a great variety to choose from. Identify your budget and goals for the course: rigorous grammatical and technical training, fluent conversation skills, getting to know Ecuadoreans or just enough basic Spanish to get you through your trip.

Visit a few places to get a feel for what they charge and offer. Prices vary greatly, from US$6 to US$12 per hour. There is also tremendous variation in teacher qualifications, infrastructure and resource materials. **Internacional de Español (IE)**, www.diplomaie.com, trains teachers who offer tuition in Spanish as a second language and maintains a list of qualified schools and teachers. Schools usually offer courses of four to seven hours per day. Many readers suggest that four hours is enough. Some schools have packages which combine teaching in the morning and tours in the afternoon, others combine teaching with travel throughout the country. A great deal of emphasis has traditionally been placed on one-to-one teaching, but a well-structured small classroom setting is also recommended.

The quality of homestays offered as part of language study packages likewise varies. The cost including half board is US$16-20 per day (more for full board). Try to book just one week at first to see how a place suits you. For language courses as well as homestays, deal directly with the people who will provide services to you, avoid intermediaries and always get a detailed receipt.

If you are short on time it can be a good idea to make your arrangements from home, either directly with one of the schools or through an agency, who can offer you a wide variety of options. If you have more time and less money, then it may be more economical to organize your own studies after you arrive. **South American Explorers** provides a list (free to members) of recommended schools and these may give club members discounts.

We have received positive recommendations for the following schools, but the list is not exhaustive:
Amazonas, www.eduamazonas.com.
Andean Global Studies, www.andeanglobalstudies.org.
Beraca, www.beraca.net.
Bipo & Toni's, www.bipo.net.
Cristóbal Colón, www.colonspanishschool.com.
Equinox, www.ecuadorspanish.com.
Instituto Superior, www.instituto-superior.net.
La Lengua, www.la-lengua.com.
Mitad del Mundo, www.mitadmundo.com.ec.
Sintaxis, www.sintaxis.net.
South American, www.southamerican.edu.ec.
Universidad Católica, T02-299 1700 ext 1388, idiomas@puce.edu.ec.
Group lessons.
Vida Verde, www.vidaverde.com.

Paragliding

Escuela Pichincha de Vuelo Libre, *Carlos Endara Oe3-60 y Amazonas, T02-225 6592 (office hours), T09-9993 1206, parapent@uio.satnet.net*. Offers complete courses for US$450 and tandem flights for US$65-US$105 (Pichincha).

Tour operators

Most operators also sell Galápagos cruises and jungle tours.

Advantage Travel, *Gaspar de Villarroel 1100 y 6 de Diciembre, T02-336 0887, www.advantagecuador.com*. Tours on the **Manatee** floating hotel on Río Napo and to Machalilla.

Andando Tours-Angermeyer Cruises, *Moreno Bellido E6-167 y Amazonas, T02-323 8631, www.andandotours.com*. Operate the *Mary Anne* sailing vessel, *Anahi* catamaran and *Passion* motor yacht, as well as land-based highland tours, see www.humboltexpeditions.com.

Andean Travel Company, *Amazonas N24-03 y Wilson, p 3, T02-222 8385, www.andeantc.com*. Dutch/Ecuadorean-owned operator, wide range of tours including trekking and cruises on the *Nemo I* catamaran and *San José* yacht.

Andes Overland, *Muro N27-94 y González Suárez, T02-512 3358, www.andesoverland.com*. New guaranteed-departure group tour passing through 4 different countries (Bolivia, Peru, Ecuador and Colombia), 6 shorter itineraries can be combined as a 72-day tour. 2 levels: Adventure and Comfort, to suit both organized backpackers and concerned travellers.

Creter Tours, *Pinto E5-29 y JL Mera, T02-254 5491, www.cretertours.com.ec*. Operate the *Treasure of Galapagos* catamaran, day tours on the *Freewind* and *Solmar* vessels and sell island-hopping tours.

Dracaena, *Pinto E4-375 y Amazonas, T02-290 6644, www.amazondracaena.com*. Runs good budget jungle tours to **Nicky Lodge** in Cuyabeno and trekking trips, popular.

EcoAndes/Unigalapagos, *Baquedano E5-27 y JL Mera, T02-222 0892, www.ecoandestravel.com*. Classic and adventure tours, and volunteer opportunities. Also operate hotels in Quito.

Ecoventura, *La Niña E8-52 y Almagro, T02-323 7393, www.ecoventura.com*. Operate first-class Galápagos cruises on the *Eric*, *Flamingo I* and *Letty* motor yachts and organize mainland tours.

Ecuador Galápagos Travels (EGT), *Veintimilla E10-78 y 12 de Octubre, Edif El Girón, Torre E, of 104, T02-254 7286, www.galapagos-cruises.ec*,

www.ecuadortravels.ec. Wide range of traditional and adventure tours throughout Ecuador; tailor-made itineraries.

Ecuador Journeys, *T02-603 5548, www.ecuadorexpatjourneys.com*. Adventure tours to off-the-beaten-path destinations, day tours, treks to volcanoes, and tours to expat hotspots.

Ecuador Nature, *Jiménez de la Espada N32-156 y González Suárez, T02-222 2341, www.ecuadornature.com*. Offers a variety of mainland and Galápagos tours, and can arrange kosher food.

Ecuador Treasure, *Wilson E4-269 y JL Mera, T02-222 6407, T09-8901 6638, www.ecuadortreasure.ec*. Daily tours, climbing, hiking, biking, trekking, horse riding and transport. Run **Chuquiragua Lodge**, near Reserva Los Ilinizas.

Enchanted Expeditions, *de las Alondras N45-102 y de los Lirios, T02-334 0525, www.enchantedexpeditions.com*. Operate the *Cachalote* and *Beluga* Galápagos vessels and sell jungle trips to Cuyabeno and highland tours. Very experienced.

Equateur Voyages Passion, *Gran Colombia N15-220 y Yaguachi, next to L'Auberge Inn, T02-322 7605, www.magical-ecuador.com*. Full range of adventure tours, run in highlands, coast and jungle. Also custom-made itineraries.

Galacruises Expeditions, *9 de Octubre N22-118 y Veintimilla, pb, T02-252 3324, www.islasgalapagos.travel*. Galápagos cruises on the *Archipel I and II* vessels and diving tours on the *Pingüino Explorer*. Also island hopping and land tours on Isabela, where they operate **Casa Isabela on the Beach**.

Galápagos Natural Life Tour Operator, *Joaquín Pinto E8-64 y Diciembre, La Mariscal, T02-252 0575, www.galapagoslastminute.net*. Arranges last-minute tours to Galápagos and also land-based tours all year around.

Galasam, *Amazonas N24-214 y Cordero, T02-290 3909, www.galasam.net*. Has a fleet of boats in different categories for Galápagos cruises, including the *Humboldt Explorer* diving yacht. City tours, full range of highland tours and jungle trips to **Siona Lodge** in Cuyabeno.

Galextur, *De los Motilones E14-58 y Charapa, T02-292 1739*. Run land-based Galápagos tours with daily sailings. Sell liveaboard and diving tours on the *Astrea* motor yacht. Operate **Hotel Silberstein** in Puerto Ayora and **City Art Hotel Silberstein** in Quito. Good service.

Geo Reisen, *Shyris N36-46 y Suecia, T02-243 6081, www.georeisen-ecuador.com*. Specializing in cultural, adventure and nature tours adapted for individuals, groups or families.

Happy Gringo, *Catalina Aldaz N34-155 y Portugal, Edif Catalina Plaza, of 207, T02-512 3486, www.happygringo.com.* Tailor-made tours throughout Ecuador, Quito city tours and Otavalo. Sell Galápagos, jungle and other destinations; good service. Recommended.

Klein Tours, *Eloy Alfaro N34-151 y Catalina Aldaz, also Shyris N34-280 y Holanda, T02-226 7000, www.kleintours.com.* Operate the *Galapagos Legend* and *Coral I* and *II* cruise ships. Also run community-based tours in Imbabura and highland tours with tailor-made itineraries. English, French and German spoken.

Latin Trails, *T02-286 7377, www.latintrails.com.* Run cruises in various Galápagos vessels including the *Seaman Journey*, *Sea Star Journey* and *Odyssey*; offer a variety of land trips in several countries and operate **Hakuna Matata Lodge** in Archidona.

Metropolitan Touring, *Av de las Palmeras N45-74 y de las Orquídeas; Amazonas N20-39 y 18 de Septiembre; Amazonas N40-80 y Naciones Unidas; and at shopping centres; T1800-115115, T02-298 8200, www.metropolitan-touring.com.* Ecuador's top travel operator, runs a trio of Galápagos vessels (*Santa Cruz Galápagos Cruise, Yacht La Pinta Galápagos Cruise* and *Isabela II Galápagos Cruise*), and hotels (**Casa Gangotena**) in Quito, (**Mashpi Lodge**) west of Quito and (**Finch Bay**) in Puerto Ayora. Also runs adventure, cultural and gastronomy tours.

Positiv Turismo, *Jorge Juan N33-38 y Atahualpa, T02-600 9401, www.positivturismo.com.* Cultural trips, Cuyabeno, trekking and special interest tours; Swiss-run.

Pure! Ecuador, *Muros N27-94 y González Suárez, T02-512 3358, www.pure-ecuador.com.* A Dutch/Ecuadorean operator offering tours throughout Ecuador and the Galápagos, trips to **Cotococha Amazon Lodge**, and tailor-made tours.

Quasar Náutica, *T02-244 6996, T1-800 247 2925 (USA), www.quasarnautica.com.* Offer 7- to 10-day naturalist and diving Galápagos cruises on 8- to 16-berth yachts.

Rolf Wittmer Turismo/Tip Top Travel, *Foch E7-81 y Almagro, T02-256 3181, www.rwittmer.com.* Run first class yachts: *Tip Top-III* and *IV*. Also tailor-made tours throughout Ecuador.

Safari Tours, *Colón y Reina Victoria N25- 33, Banco de Guayaquil, 13th floor, T02-255 2505, www.safari.com.ec. Daily 0930-1830.* Adventure travel, personalized itineraries, mountain climbing, cycling, rafting, trekking and cultural tours. Also book Galápagos tours. Recommended.

South America for All, *T02-237 7430, www.southamericaforall.com*. Specialized tours to all regions of Ecuador for the mobility and hearing impaired traveller. Also operate in Peru and Argentina and run the **Huasquila Amazon Lodge** near Tena.

Surtrek, *San Ignacio E10-114 y Caamaño, T02-250 0660, T1-866-978 7398 in the US, www.surtrek.com*. Wide range of tours in all regions, helicopter and ballon flights, birdwatching, rafting, horse riding, mountain biking and jungle tours, arrange last-minute Galápagos tours, also sell domestic flights and run **Las Cascadas Lodge**.

Tierra de Fuego, *Amazonas N23-23 y Veintimilla, T02-250 1418, www.ecuadortierradefuego.com*. Provide transport and tours throughout the country, domestic flight tickets, Galápagos bookings, and own and operate the *Guantanamera* yacht.

Tropic Journeys in Nature, *Pasaje Sánchez Melo Oe1-37 y Av Galo Plaza, T02-240 8741, www.destinationecuador.com*. Environmental and cultural jungle tours to the **Huaorani Ecolodge**, see page 303. Also private day tours in Quito, coast, highlands, lodge-to-lodge mountain treks, Amazon lodges and Galápagos land-based and multisport tours. Community-based tourism

working with and donating a percentage of all profits to **Conservation in Action**. Winner of awards for responsible tourism.

Yacu Amu Experiences, *Checoslovaquia E10-137 y 6 de Diciembre, T02-246 1511, www.yacuamu.com*. Tailor-made adventure, nature and cultural trips for active couples, families and small groups.

Zenith Travel, *JL Mera N24-264 y Cordero, T02-252 9993, www.zenithecuador.com*. Good-value Galápagos cruises as well as various land tours in Ecuador and Peru. All-gay Galápagos cruises available. Multilingual service, knowledgeable helpful staff, good value.

Train rides

Estación Eloy Alfaro (Chimbacalle), *2 km south of the colonial city at Maldonado y Sincholagua, T1-800-873637, T02-265 6142, www.trenecuador.com*. Mon-Fri 0800-1630. This lovely refurbished train station, with a railway museum and working concert hall, is the starting point of journeys on a luxury tourist train, *Tren Crucero*, which runs about twice per month (but not every month) in either direction between Quito and Durán, outside Guayaquil. Part of the route is run with a historic steam locomotive. The complete route takes 4 days and costs US$1393 one way; you

can also take it for segments from 1 to 3 days. The tour includes visits to places of interest and accommodation in luxury inns. See www.trenecuador.com/crucero for details.

Tourist trains run Thu-Sun and holidays from Quito to **Machachi** and **El Boliche** (0800, US$39-44 includes lunch), combined transport by train one way and by bus the other. A farm is visited in Machachi. At El Boliche station is **Restaurante Nuna**, and nearby, **Area Nacional de Recreación El Boliche**, a protected area bordering Parque Nacional Cotopaxi, where the tour includes a walk. There are lovely views of Cotopaxi and Los Ilinizas. Purchase tickets in advance by phone, internet, at the station or **El Quinde craft shop**, Palacio Municipal, Venezuela y Espejo. You need each passenger's passport number and age to purchase tickets. Boarding 30 mins before departure, you can visit to the railway museum before boarding.

Whitewater rafting
Río Blanco/Toachi tours cost US$87. **Ríos Ecuador** *(see Tour operators, page 319)*, T02-260 5828 in Quito, www.riosecuador.com. Very professional, rafting and kayaking trips of 1-6 days, also kayak courses. Highly recommended.

Mitad del Mundo
On weekends, **Quito Tour Bus**, see City tours above, offers tours to Mitad del Mundo and Pululahua.
Calimatours, *30 m east of monument, Mitad del Mundo local 92*, T02-239 4796, *www.mitaddelmundotour.com*. Tours to Pululahua and other sites in the vicinity such as Rumicucho and Kati Killa; also tours for special events such as the solstice. Very helpful.

Pululahua
Green Horse Ranch, *Astrid Muller, T09-8612 5433, www.horseranch.de*. 1- to 9-day rides; including a 3-day ride to Bellavista.

Transport

Air
Details of internal air service are given under the respective destinations. Quito's **Mariscal Sucre Airport** (T02-395 4200, www.quitoairport.aero for information about current arrival and departures, airport services and airlines) is in Tababela, off Highway E-35, about 30 km northeast of the city, at 2134 m above sea level. There are ATMs and a *casa de cambio* for exchange in the arrivals level and banks and ATMs in the shopping mall across the street. Luggage storage and lockers downstairs at arrivals, www.bagparkingquito.com, US$7-15 per case per day; see also **Quito Airport Suites** hotel, page 64. The information office (arrivals level, T02-395 4200, ext 2008, open 24 hrs), will assist with hotel bookings. The airport taxi cooperative (T02-281 8008, www.taxienquitoecuador.com) has set rates to different zones of the city; these are posted by arrivals (US$25 to La Mariscal, US$26 to colonial Quito, US$33 to Quitumbe bus station, US$26.50 to Carcelén station); taxi rates from the city to the airport are about 10% cheaper. **Aero Servicios** express bus (T02-604 3500, T1-800-237673) runs 24 hrs per day, between the new airport and the old airport in northern Quito (Parque Bicentenario); US$8, US$4 seniors and children. From Tababela, departures are hourly from 2400 to 0600 and every 30 mins the rest of the day; from Quito, departures are hourly from1800 to 0300

and every 30 mins the rest of the day. They also offer transfers between the old airport and other locations in the city (eg.US$3.50 to/from the Mariscal, US$4 to/from the colonial city). Taking a transfer service or a taxi from the old airport to your hotel is recommended. **HATS** (T223 1824 or T09-8336 1518) is a shuttle bus to/from hotels in La Mariscal, US$10 pp, minimum 4 passengers. Regional buses with limited stops run every 15 mins, 0600-2145, between the airport and Terminal Quitumbe in the south and Terminal Río Coca in the north, US$2. Private van services are good value for groups, but require advanced arrangements: **Trans-Rabbit** (T02-290 2690, www.transrabbit.com. ec), US$30 for 2 passengers, US$5 per additional person.

Note It takes at least 45 mins to reach the airport from Quito, but with traffic it can be much longer, so allow enough time. There are 3 access roads to the airport: the most direct from the city centre is the Ruta Viva which starts on Av Simón Bolívar; the Vía Interoceánica originates in Plaza Argentina, northeast of La Mariscal, and goes through the suburbs of Cumbaya, Tumbaco and Puembo; and the Vía Collas, which starts in Oyacoto, past the toll both along the Panamericana, north of the city. If going to the airport from other cities, take a bus that bypasses Quito along highway E-35 (available from Baños, Ambato and Ibarra), get off at the airport roundabout and take the regional bus; 4.5 km from there. If coming from the east (Papallacta, Baeza or Oriente), go as far as Pifo and transfer to the regional bus there.

Bus

Local Quito has 5 parallel mass transit lines running from north to south, mostly on exclusive lanes, covering almost the length of the city. There are several transfer stations where you can switch from one line to another without cost. At rush hour there are express buses with limited stops. Feeder bus lines (*alimentadores*) go from the terminals to outer suburbs. Within the city the fare is US$0.25; the combined fare to some suburbs is US$0.40. Public transit is not designed for carrying heavy luggage and is often crowded.

Trole (T02-266 5016, Mon-Fri 0500-2345, weekends and holidays 0600-2145, plus hourly overnight service with limited stops) is a system of trolley buses which runs along Av 10 de Agosto in the north of the city, C Guayaquil (southbound) and C Flores (northbound) in colonial Quito, and mainly along Av Maldonado and Av Teniente Ortiz in the south. The northern terminus is north of 'La Y', the junction of 10 de Agosto, Av América and Av de la Prensa; south of the colonial city are important transfer stations at El Recreo and Morán Valverde; the southern terminus is at the Quitumbe bus station. Trolleys do not necessarily run the full length of the line; the destination is marked in front of the vehicle. Trolleys have a special entrance for wheelchairs. **Ecovía** (T02-243 0726, Mon-Sat 0500-2200, Sun and holidays 0600-2200) articulated buses run along Av 6 de Diciembre from Estación Río Coca, at Calle Río Coca east of 6 de Diciembre, in the north, to La Marín transfer station and on to Cumandá, east of colonial Quito. **Metrobus** (T02-346 5149, Mon-Fri 0530-2230, weekends and holidays 0600-2100) also runs articulated buses along Av de la Prensa and Av América from Terminal La Ofelia in the north to La Marín in the south. **Corredor Sur** buses run from the Seminario Mayor interchange (Av América y Colón) in the north, along Av América, Av Universitaria and Av Occidental to Terminal Quitumbe in the south; interchanges on this route are at Av Universitaria and the El Tejar and San Roque tunnels on Av Occidental. **Universidades** articulated buses run from 12 de Octubre y Veintimilla in the north to Quitumbe bus terminal. There are also 2 types of **city buses**: *Selectivos* are red, and *Bus Tipo* are royal blue; both cost US$0.25. Many bus lines go through La Marín and El Playón Ecovía/Metrobus stations. Extra caution is advised here: pickpockets abound and it is best avoided at night. For **Quito Tour Bus**, see page 72.

Regional Outer suburbs are served by green *Interparroquial* buses. Those running east to the valleys of Cumbayá, Tumbaco and the airport leave from the Estación Río Coca (see Ecovía, above). Buses southeast to Valle de los Chillos leave from El Playón Ecovía/Metrobus station, from Isabel la Católica y Mena Caamaño, behind Universidad Católica and from Alonso de Mercadillo by the Universidad Central. Buses going north (ie Calderón, Mitad del Mundo) leave from La Ofelia Metrobus station. Regional destinations to the north (ie Cayambe) and northwest (ie Mindo) leave from a regional station adjacent to La Ofelia Metrobus station. Buses west to Nono from the Plaza de Cotocollao, to Lloa from C Angamarca in Mena 2 neighbourhood. Buses south to Machachi from El Playón, La Villaflora and Quitumbe. Buses to Papallacta, Baeza and El Chaco leave from Chile E3-22 y Pedro Fermín Cevallos, near La Marín.

Long distance Quito has 2 main bus terminals: **Terminal Quitumbe** in the southwest of the city, T02-398 8200,

serves destinations south, the coast via Santo Domingo, Oriente and Tulcán (in the north). It is served by the Trole (line 4: El Ejido–Quitumbe, best taken at El Ejido) and the Corredor Sur and Universidades buses; however, it is advisable to take a taxi, about US$6, 30-45 mins to the colonial city, US$8-10, 45 mins-1 hr to La Mariscal. Arrivals and tourist information are on the ground floor. Ticket counters (destinations grouped and colour coded by region), and departures in the upper level. Left luggage (US$0.90 per day) and food stalls are at the adjoining shopping area. The terminal is large, so allow extra time to reach your bus. Terminal use fee US$0.20. Watch your belongings at all times. There have been reports of scams on long-distance buses leaving Quito, especially to Baños; do not give your hand luggage to anyone and always keep your things on your lap, not in the overhead rack nor on the floor. On holiday weekends it is advisable to reserve the day before.

The smaller **Terminal Carcelén**, Av Eloy Alfaro, where it meets the Panamericana Norte, serves destinations to the north (including Otavalo) and the coast via the Calacalí–La Independencia road. It is served by feeder bus lines from the northern terminals of the Trole, Ecovía and Metrobus, a taxi costs about US$5, 30-45 mins to La Mariscal, US$7, 45 mins-1 hr to colonial Quito. Ticket counters are organized by destination. See under destinations for fares and schedules; these are also listed in www.latinbus.com, where for US$3 you can also purchase tickets online for buses departing Quito. A convenient way to travel between Quitumbe and Carcelén is to take a bus bound for Tulcán, **Trans Vencedores** or **Unión del Carchi**

(Booth 12), every 30 mins during the day, hourly at night, US$1, 1 hr; from Carcelén to Quitumbe, wait for a through bus arriving from the north; taxi between terminals, US$15.

All long-distance buses depart from either Quitumbe or Carcelén; the following companies also have ticket sales points in modern Quito: **Flota Imbabura**, Larrea 1211 y Portoviejo, T02-256 9628, for **Cuenca**, **Guayaquil** and **Manta**; **Transportes Ecuador**, JL Mera N21-44 y Washington, T02-250 3842, hourly to **Guayaquil**; **Transportes Esmeraldas**, Santa María 870 y Amazonas, T02-250 9517, for **Esmeraldas**, **Atacames**, **Coca**, **Lago Agrio**, **Manta** and **Huaquillas**. Reina del Camino, Larrea y 18 de Septiembre, T02-321 6633, for **Bahía**, **Puerto López** and **Manta**; **Carlos Aray** Larrea y Portoviejo, T02-256 4406, for **Manta** and **Puerto López**; **Transportes Loja**, Orellana y Jerves, T02-222 4306, for **Loja** and **Lago Agrio**; **Transportes Baños**, Santa María y JL Mera, T02-223 2752, for **Baños** and **Oriente** destinations. **Panamericana Internacional**, Colón E7-31 y Reina Victoria, T02-255 7133, ext 131 for national routes, ext 125 for international, for **Huaquillas**, **Machala**, **Cuenca**, **Loja**, **Manta**, **Guayaquil** and **Esmeraldas**.

International Buses depart from private stations; prices vary according to demand (higher in Jul-Aug and Dec); reserve ahead. **Ormeño Internacional**, from Perú, Shyris N35-52 y Portugal, of 3B, T02-245 6632, Tue, Thu and Sun to **Máncora**, US$50, 16 hrs and **Lima**, US$100, 36 hrs, with connections to other countries; Tue, Thu and Sat to **Cali**, US$80, 17 hrs and **Bogotá**, US$100, 30 hrs; every 2 weeks on Tue to **Medellín**, US$100, 30 hrs; Tue to **Caracas**, US$180-200, 2½ days. **Panamericana Internacional**, see above, to **Caracas**, on Mon; does not go into Colombian cities, but will let passengers off by the roadside (eg Popayán, Palmira for Cali, or Ibagué for Bogotá), **Rutas de América**, Selva Alegre Oe1-72 y 10 de Agosto, T02-250 3611, www.rutasenbus.com, to **Lima**, Thu and Sun; same days to **Cali**, US$60, 17 hrs, **Ibagué**, US$85, 28 hrs and **Caracas**. The route to **Peru** via Loja and Macará takes much longer than the Huaquillas route, but is more relaxed. Don't buy Peruvian bus tickets (or any other country's) here, because they're cheaper outside Ecuador.

Long-distance taxis and vans
Shared taxis and vans offer door-to-door service to some cities and avoid the hassle of reaching Quito's bus terminals. Some companies have set departures, others travel according to demand; on weekends there are fewer departures. Reserve at least 2 days ahead. There is service between Quito and Otavalo, Ibarra, Latacunga, Ambato, Riobamba, Cuenca, Baños, Puyo, Santo Domingo and Esmeraldas. For details, see Transport under the corresponding destination.

Car hire
There are vehicular restrictions Mon-Fri 0700-0930 and 1600-1930, based on the last digit of the licence plate; seniors are exempt. Colonial Quito is closed to vehicles Sun 0900-1600 and some main avenues across the city close Sun 0800-1400 for the *ciclopaseo* (see page 74). All the main international car rental companies are at the airport. For rental procedures see Driving in Ecuador, page 419. A local company is: **Simon Car Rental**, Los Shyris N41-160 e Isla Floreana, T02-243 1019,

www.simoncarrental.com, good rates and service. **Trans-Rabbit**, T02-290 2690, www.transrabbit.com.ec, rent vans for 8-14 passengers, with driver, for trips in Quito and out of town.

Taxi

Taxis are a cheap and efficient way to get around the city, but for safety it is important to know how to select a cab. Authorized taxis have orange licence plates or white plates with an orange stripe on the upper edge; they display stickers with a unit number on the windscreen, the front doors and back side windows; the name of the company should be displayed on the back doors, the driver's photograph in the interior and they should have a working meter. Taxis with a red and blue 'Transporte Seguro' sticker on the windscreen and back doors should have cameras and red panic buttons linked to the 911 emergency system. At night it is safer to use a radio taxi (*taxi ejecutivo*), ie: **City Taxi**, T02-263 3333; **Hot Line**, T02-222 2222; **Taxi Americano**, T02-222 2333. Make sure they give you the taxi number and description so that you get the correct vehicle, because some radio taxis are unmarked. All taxis should use a meter; negotiate the price ahead if they refuse to use it. The minimum daytime fare is US$1.45, US$1.75 after 1900. Note the registration and the licence plate numbers if you feel you have been seriously overcharged or mistreated. You may then complain to the municipal police or tourist office. To hire a taxi by the hour costs from US$8 in the city, more out of town. For trips outside Quito, agree the fare beforehand: US$70-85 a day. Outside luxury hotels cooperative taxi drivers have a list of agreed excursion prices and most drivers are knowledgeable.

Train

There is no regular passenger service. For tourist rides, see Train rides, page 79.

Mitad del Mundo and around

Bus From Quito take a 'Mitad del Mundo' feeder bus from La Ofelia station on the Metrobus (transfer ticket US$0.15), or from the corner of Bolivia y Av América (US$0.40). Some buses continue to the turnoff for **Pululahua** (it is a 30-min walk from the turn to the Mirador) or Calacalí beyond. An excursion by **taxi** to Mitad del Mundo (with a 1 hr-wait) is US$25, or US$30 to include Pululahua. Just a ride from La Mariscal costs about US$15.

Around
Quito

Despite Quito's bustling big city atmosphere, it is surrounded by pretty and surprisingly tranquil countryside, with many opportunities for day trips as well as longer excursions. A combination of city and regional buses and pickup trucks will get you to most destinations. Excursions are also offered by Quito tour operators. The monument on the equator (see Mitad del Mundo, page 56) is just a few minutes away; there are nature reserves, craft-producing towns, excellent thermal swimming pools, walking and climbing routes and scenic train rides (see page 79). To the west of Quito on the slopes of Pichincha is a region of spectacular natural beauty with many crystal-clear rivers and waterfalls, worth taking several days to explore. Visit www.pichincha.gob.ec (click on 'Turismo en Pichincha') for some attractions near Quito.

Refugio de Vida Silvestre Pasochoa

45 mins southeast of Quito by car, very busy at weekends; park office at El Ejido de Amaguaña, T09-9894 5704.

Located towards the south end of Valle de los Chillos and accessed from Amaguaña, this natural park is set in humid Andean forest between 2700 m and 4200 m, on the slopes of Volcán Pasochoa. The reserve has more than 120 species of birds (unfortunately some of the fauna has been frightened away by the noise of the visitors) and 50 species of trees. There are walks of 30 minutes to eight hours, good for acclimatization. There are picnic and camping areas. Take a good sleeping bag, food and water.

Río Pita

To the southeast of Quito in the Valle de los Chillos is the Río Pita. Its ice-cold water, fed by the snow melt from Cotopaxi, runs through a scenic rocky canyon surrounded by remnants of Andean forest. There are 18 waterfalls along its course, and the trails are signposted. **Chorrera de Molinuco** ⓘ *access 3.5 km south of Loreto, US$1*, is a small waterfall, 20 minutes' walk from the road. Upstream (south) is the larger **Chorrera del Pita** ⓘ *access 3.25 km south of Loreto, US$2*, one hour's walk from the road. Further upstream along the banks of the river is a **municipal park** ⓘ *access 3.5 km south of Rumipamba, free*, with a swimming hole and trails leading south (three hours) to **Cóndor Machay**, the most impressive of the waterfalls, and north (two hours) to **Vilatuña**, a lookout above the Chorrera del Pita. The latter trail crosses the river seven times, and there are bridges and cables to assist you wading across and climbing rock faces.

The area is reached from **Sangolquí**, see page 56. The access to the falls is from the neighbourhood of **Loreto** for the first two falls and the village of **Rumipamba** for the latter, all south of Sangolquí. There are a couple of lodges in the area and **Hacienda Santa Rita** ⓘ *www.volcanoland.com, entry US$6.75*, with a forest reserve with trails and camping (US$5.60 per person). Continuing beyond Rumipamba you can approach **Sincholagua**, **Pasochoa** and **Cotopaxi** volcanoes; be prepared for cold and wet conditions. For more information, see www.ruminahui.gob.ec.

Reserva Ecológica Antisana

Pintag office: Antisana 1580, T02-238 4641, pablo.grados@ambiente.gob.ec, open for day visits only: 0700-1400, register at La Mica's rangers station, taxi Pintag–La Mica, US$25.

The magnificent **Volcán Antisana** (5758 m) tempts visitors when its veil of mist dissipates and it can be seen in the distance from Quito. It is part of the 120,000 ha Reserva Ecológica Antisana, ranging in altitude from 1400 to 5758 m. It spans the Cordillera Oriental from the highlands east to the jungle and is a magnificent area for hiking, where condors may be seen. There are no services and the area is quite rugged, so visitors must be self sufficient.

Access to the reserve is through Píntag, 22 km southeast of Sangolquí. In 24 km the road divides; the right fork goes to the base of Sincholagua (4898 m), the left fork to Laguna La Mica, the water source for southern Quito, around which are walking trails. Beyond is the base of Antisana. The reserve can also be accessed from Papallacta and from below Baeza. The **Trek of the Condor**, a three- to four-day strenuous walk through *páramo*, starts in El Tambo, west of Papallacta, goes through Reserva Antisana and on to Parque Nacional Cotopaxi. Arrange ahead with a Quito operator or Sr Carlos Tandayama at **Paradero Don Carlos** in **El Tambo** (T09-8566 2506). Native guides cost US$25 per day, horses US$20 per day. The **Cooperativa Agrícola El Tambo** charges trekkers US$5 per person.

In the reserve's buffer zone to the north of La Mica and 21 km from Pintag via Santa Rosa is **Laguna Muertepungo** ⓘ *T02-287 0021, T09-9335 5096, muertepungo@hotmail. com, US$5 includes guided walk to 4200 m, 4WD required*, a lake formed by a lava flow of Volcán Antisanilla, surrounded by attractive *páramo* and native vegetation; condors and other native fauna may be seen. There are walking trails, horse riding, fishing and a shelter at 4020 m (US$20 per person, take a sleeping bag, three meals cost US$30 per person). It is run by a local association that can arrange transport. Bridging the gap between Reserva Antisana and Parque Nacional Llanganates (see page 164) is the 93,246-ha **Reserva Biológica Colonso Chalupas**, created in 2014.

Parque Nacional Cayambe Coca
Headquarters in Cayambe, T02-211 0370, werner.barrera@ambiente.gob.ec. For details of climbing Volcán Cayambe, see page 110.

This 403,103-ha park, spread over four provinces, spans the Cordillera Oriental from the glaciated summit of Cayambe (5790 m) to the Amazon lowlands (600 m). It is easily reached from Quito. Going north of the city, the highland region around Nevado Cayambe is accessed from the town of the same name, see page 110. To the east of Quito, the Vía Interoceánica leading to Oriente gives access to the park at **La Virgen**, just at the pass before descending to the eastern slopes. There is a ranger's station and a side road headed north to the antennas gives access to an area of strikingly beautiful *páramo* dotted with lakes, popular among fishermen. There are several walking trails.

Past La Virgen is the hamlet of **El Tambo**, the start of **Trek of the Condor**, through Reserva Antisana (see above). Further east along the river canyon are a couple of thermal springs, including the community-run **Jamanco** ⓘ *US$3, daily until 1700*, with four pools, they adjust the water temperature on request; **El Pantanal** ⓘ *US$3, 150 m from the Interoceánica*, is in a pretty setting surrounded by forest; and **Sachayacu** ⓘ *T02-237 5817, on Facebook, advanced reservation required, pools only US$8, packages including lunch and massage from US$35*, with three pools in a forest setting, trails and waterfalls.

Further along is **Laguna Papallacta**, formed by a lava flow. Past the lake, the Interoceánica descends to El Triángulo, just east of the town of Papallacta. An older road goes from the lake directly to the village, and rejoins the main road at El Triángulo.

Abutting the national park (access from Termas de Papallacta) is the 250- ha **Rancho del Cañón private reserve** ⓘ *US$2 for use of a short trail; to go on longer walks you are required to take a guide for US$8 per person*. It follows the Río Papallacta upstream to cloudforest, where there are well-maintained trails. A road goes from Papallacta (behind the Termas) north to **Oyacachi**, another town with hot springs, see page 110, also within the park. It traverses both protected areas. A permit from Parque Nacional Cayambe Coca headquarters, which can be requested by email, is necessary to travel this road, even on foot. The walk through lovely scenery takes one to two days. The Baños ranger's station and camping area are a 1½-hour walk from Papallacta. Volcán Reventador and Cascada San Rafael, see page 289, to the northeast of Papallacta are also withing the national park.

★ **Papallacta** *Colour map 1, C5.*

Perched on the eastern slopes of the Cordillera Oriental is the village of Papallacta (population 950, altitude 3200 m), 64 km east of Quito just off the Vía Interoceánica, the road linking Quito and Oriente. It is an attractive area in the transition between *páramo* and cloudforest. The region has wonderful thermal baths and offers good walking and nature observation. At the **Termas de Papallacta** ⓘ *2 km from the town of Papallacta, T02-250 4787 (Quito), www.termaspapallacta.com*, the best developed hot springs in the country, are eight thermal pools, three large enough for swimming, and four cold plunge pools. There are two public complexes of springs: the regular **pools** ⓘ *daily 0600-2100, US$8.50*, and the **spa centre** ⓘ *Mon-Fri 1000-1800, Sat-Sun 0900-1800, US$22 (massage and other special treatments extra)*. There are additional pools at the Termas' hotel and cabins (see Where to stay) for the exclusive use of their guests. The complex is tastefully done and recommended. In addition to the Termas, just down the road from the complex are the simpler pools of **Jamanco** ⓘ *daily 0600-1800, US$4*, and in the village of Papallacta the good municipal pools of **Santa Catalina** ⓘ *daily 0800-1800, US$3*. There are also several more economical places to stay (some with pools) on the road to the Termas and in the village. On weekends and holidays all the pools and hotels are busy. The view, on a clear day, of Antisana while enjoying the thermal waters is superb. Near El Tambo (see above), along the highway to Quito, are several additional thermal pools. Note that Quito airport is between Quito and Papallacta.

Listings South and east of Quito

Where to stay

Río Pita

$$$ Cotopaxi Pungo
Past Rumipamba and El Vallecito access to the waterfalls, 15 km from Sangolquí and 14 km from the northern access to Cotopaxi, T09-9955 1215, www. cotopaxipungo.com.
Hacienda-style adobe house in a 7-ha property with trails, comfortable rooms with fireplace and excellent views of Cotopaxi, and a restaurant (meals extra).

$$ Campo Base
At La Moca, 2 km before reaching Rumipamba, T02-253 5510, T09-9936 5683 (Quito), www.campobaseecuador.com.
Run by experienced mountaineers Manuel and Diego Jácome, this 4-bedroom country lodge at 3050 m is a good place for acclimatization. Rooms have a shared bath and hot water, and there's a restaurant. Breakfast and dinner included. Reservations required. They can arrange trekking, cycling and climbing tours.

Papallacta

$$$$ Hotel Termas Papallacta
At the Termas complex, T06-289 5060.
Comfortable heated rooms and suites, some rooms with private jacuzzi; also cabins for up to 6. There's a good expensive restaurant, thermal pools set in a lovely garden, and a pleasant lounge with a fireplace. Guests have access to all areas in the complex and get discounts at the spa. Transport from Quito is extra. For weekends and holidays book a month in advance. Recommended.

$$$-$$ Hostería Pampallacta
On the road to Termas, T06-289 5022, www.pampallactatermales.com.
A variety of rooms with bathtubs, pools for exclusive use by guests and a restaurant. Prices are higher at the weekend.

$$$-$$ La Choza de Don Wilson
At the turn-off for Termas, T06-289 5027, www.hosteriachozapapallacta.com.
Rooms have good views of the valley. Fancier rooms have hot tubs and heaters, cheaper rooms are small and heaters extra. There's a good popular restaurant,

pools (US$5 for non-residents) and attentive service.

$$ Coturpa
Next to the Santa Catalina baths in Papallacta town, T06-289 5040, www.hostalcoturpa.com.
This place has a variety of rooms, some with hot tubs and heaters, and there's a restaurant.

$$-$ El Leñador
By entrance to Termas, T06-289 5003.
Opened in 2015, simple rooms with electric showers; skylights make it bright and warm. Restaurant, with breakfast extra.

East of Papallacta

$$$$ Guango Lodge
Near Cuyuja, 9 km east of Papallacta, T02-289 1880 (Quito), www.guangolodge.com.
Set in a 350-ha temperate forest reserve along the Río Papallacta, this lodge has good facilities and excellent birdwatching. Rates include 3 decent meals. Day visits cost US$5 and includes a snack. Reserve ahead. Taxi from Papallacta US$10.

Transport

Refugio de Vida Silvestre Pasochoa
Bus From Quito buses run from El Playón to **Amaguaña**, US$0.50 (ask the driver to let you off at the 'Ejido de Amaguaña'); from there follow the signs. It's about 8-km walk, with not much traffic except at weekends, or book a pick-up from Amaguaña, **Cooperativa Pacheco Jr**, T02-287 7047, about US$6.

Río Pita

Bus From Quito take a bus from Playón de La Marín or El Trébol to **Sangolquí**. For **Chorreras Molinuco** and **Pita**, from the Monumento a Rumiñahui in Sangolquí, a bus goes at 0800 to **Selva Alegre**, **Loreto** and the **trailheads** (return at 1400). For **Rumipamba**, the municipal park and the lodges, **Calsig Express** buses go from behind the Municipio in Sangolquí at 0700, 1000 (school days only), 1300 and 1900 (Mon-Sat), US$0.60, 1½ hrs. They turn back (2 hrs after departure) beyond Rumipamba and El Vallecito, near the municipal park.

Papallacta

Bus From Quito, buses bound for **Tena** or **Lago Agrio** from Terminal Quitumbe, or buses to **Baeza** from near La Marín (see page 305), 2 hrs, US$2.50. The bus stop is at El Triángulo, east of (below) the village, at the junction of the main highway and the old road through town. A **taxi** to **Termas** costs US$1 pp shared or US$2.50 private. The access to the Termas is uphill from the village, off the old road. The complex is a 40-min walk from town. To return to **Quito**, most buses pass in the afternoon; travelling back at night is not recommended. Taxi to Quito starts at US$50, from the airport US$40. **Transporte Santa Catalina** taxis in Papallacta, T09-8510 2556.

West of Quito

impressive volcanic peak

Climbing Pichincha

Pichincha has several peaks. Overlooking Quito from the west are two low antenna-topped peaks, Cruz Loma to the south and Las Antenas to the north. Rucu Pichincha (Old Pichincha, 4698 m), closest to the city and sometimes sprinkled with snow, can be seen from some parts of Quito. The highest of Pichincha's summits is that of Guagua Pichincha (Baby Pichincha, 4776 m), at the southwestern side of the massif; between it and Rucu are a couple of lesser peaks including Padre Encantado.

To climb **Rucu Pichincha,** take the Teleférico (see page 56) to Cruz Loma, from where a trail leads to the summit. After leaving the Teleférico, it takes about three hours to the summit and the views are magnificent. Be sure to go early in order to have enough time to catch the Teleférico down. Do not take valuables and enquire about safety at the Teleférico before climbing. There are many people on the trail on Sundays. Walking down to the city from either Cruz Loma or Las Antenas is dangerous; many armed robberies have occurred in the past.

After almost 350 years of dormancy, **Guagua Pichincha** renewed its volcanic activity in 1999. The level of activity subsequently diminished, but increased again in 2015 and descent into the crater remains dangerous. The caretakers at the *refugio* (shelter) can give you firsthand up-to-date information concerning conditions.

It is possible to reach Guagua Pichincha's *refugio* by road and to climb to the crater rim and summit from there. Access is from **Lloa**, a friendly village set in beautiful surroundings; outside town is a hacienda for lodging. From Lloa a 4WD track goes almost to the *refugio* at 4560 m, near the rim of the crater, just below the summit. Depending on road conditions you might be able to get a pickup from Lloa to the *refugio*. If walking you will need up to eight hours to climb, so set off early. The road to the summit is signposted from the right-hand corner of the main plaza as you face the volcano, and is easy to follow. There are a couple of forks, but head straight for the peak each time.

The *refugio*, run by the **Secretaría de Gestión de Riezgos** ① *T02-246 9009*, will provide a bunk and water for free. The warden has his own cooking facilities which he may share with you. It gets very cold at night and there is no heating or blankets.

The climb from the *refugio* to the summit is short and somewhat tricky, but is worth it for the views; many other volcanoes can be seen on a clear morning. The descent back to Lloa is faster, but is hard on the knees. The last bus for Quito leaves Lloa around 1830, or walk a few hundred metres past Lloa down the main road until you reach a fork. Wait here for a truck, which may take you to the outskirts of the city for around US$1. There are also **rock climbing** walls behind the *refugio* on Guagua Pichincha, see www.monodedoecuador.com.

From Lloa a road leads west 12.5 km to the basic **Palmira thermal baths** ① *daily until 1800, US$1*, water at 24°C, pickup from southern Quito US$15; 3.5 km beyond is a hacienda offering lodging, past which the road ends. This is the starting point for a two- to three-day **trek to Mindo**. It is a demanding walk and navigation is challenging, take care when crossing rivers.

Listings West of Quito

Transport

Climbing Pichincha

Bus Between Quito and Lloa, every 30 mins, 0600-1900, US$0.70, 30 mins. In Quito it departs from Calle Angamarca, at the entrance to the neighbourhood called Mena 2 in southwestern Quito. To get there, take an *alimentador* bus from El Recreo stop on the Trole, or any **Chillogallo**-bound bus; 1 goes along 12 de Octubre in modern Quito. Ask to be let off at El Triángulo, the intersection of Av Mariscal Sucre and the road to Lloa. Walk 1 block west (up) to where the Lloa bus stops.

Taxi From Quito to Lloa costs around US$20. A pickup from Lloa to the Pichincha shelter costs about US$40.

scenic area with lovely cloudforests and many bird-rich nature reserves

Despite their proximity to the capital (two hours from Quito), the western slopes of Volcán Pichincha (altitude: 1200-2800 m) and its surroundings are surprisingly wild, with fine opportunities for walking and birdwatching. Walking trails include portions of pre-Inca roads known as Caminos de los Yumbos. The area to the northwest is known as Noroccidente; the main tourist town in this region is Mindo. To the west of Mindo is a warm subtropical area of clear rivers and waterfalls, with a number of reserves, resorts and lodges. From the Noroccidente, three roads go northeast to the Río Guayllabamba and beyond to the Intag region (page 125).

Four roads drop into the western lowlands from Quito. In the **Noroccidente** (the northwest) is a very scenic old road, the **Ecoruta** or **Quito–Nono–Mindo** road, famous for its excellent birdwatching. It begins towards the northern end off Avenida Mariscal Sucre or Occidental, Quito's western ring road, at the intersection with Calle Machala. Also to the northwest and parallel to the Ecoruta is the **Calacalí– La Independencia** road or the **new route** starts at El Condado roundabout on Avenida Occidental, then goes by the Mitad del Mundo monument, Calacalí, Nanegalito, San Miguel de los Bancos, Pedro Vicente Maldonado and Puerto Quito, before joining the Santo Domingo–Esmeraldas road at La Independencia. Note that markers along the road refer to the distance from El Condado roundabout. This is the most direct route from Quito to the northern coast. There are connections between these two roads at Km 15, 52, 57 and 77 along the new road. This makes it possible to drive on the faster new route most of the way, even if your destination is one of the lodges on the Ecoruta. There is a regular bus service along the new route, which provides the most direct access to Mindo.

In the **Suroccidente** (the southwest) are two roads to the western lowlands, the unpaved Chiriboga road and the main Alóag–Santo Domingo road. The **Chiriboga road** is little used, prone to landslides and complicated to find; it starts in Quito's southern neighbourhood San Juan de Chillogallo. There is an irregular bus service on the first half of this road out of Quito; it is often muddy and difficult, especially November to April, when a 4WD is needed. The **Alóag–Santo Domingo** road is the main connection between Quito and Guayaquil and is served by buses from Terminal Quitumbe in Quito.

Ecoruta

With increased awareness of the need to conserve the cloudforests of the northwest slopes of Pichincha and of their potential for tourism, the number of reserves here is steadily growing. Keen birdwatchers are no longer the only visitors, and the region has much to offer all nature lovers. Infrastructure at reserves varies considerably. Some have comfortable upmarket lodges offering accommodation, meals, guides and transport. Others may require taking your own camping gear, food, and obtaining a permit.

The Ecoruta gives access to bird-rich cloudforest and has been dubbed the Paseo del Quinde or Route of the Hummingbird; indeed, many hummingbirds can be seen in this area. This paved road winds its way over the shoulder of Pichincha offering lovely views.The only town of any size along this route, **Nono** (altitude 2750 m) is just 18 km from Quito but seems like another world; a forgotten little village surrounded by lush pastures. **Cascada Guagrapamba** is 5 km from town. From Nono a side road goes to Calacalí on the new road. The Ecoruta continues to the hamlet of **Tandayapa**, around which many reserves are clustered, and nearby is **Cascada Los Yumbos**, a waterfall. From Tandayapa, another side road goes to the new route at Km 52, east of Nanegalito. The old road continues to **San Tadeo**, another hamlet, and then on to join the new route at Km 77, before the intersection for Mindo.

The new route From the Mitad del Mundo monument the road goes past the access to Pululahua (see page 57) and **Calacalí**, also on the equator, whose plaza has an older monument to the Mitad del Mundo. Beyond Calacalí at Km 15 a road turns south to Nono and north to **Yunguilla** (5.5 km), with a community tourism project; see www.yunguilla.org.ec and Where to stay, page 100.

At Km 56, **Nanegalito** (altitude 1533 m), a supply town and transport hub for this area, is the turn-off to Nanegal, with access to Maquipucuna and Santa Lucía reserves, see pages 94 and 96. From Nanegal, an unpaved road continues northeast to **Selva Alegre** in the Intag region, see page 125.

At Armenia (Km 60), a few kilometres beyond Nanegalito, a road heads northwest through Santa Elena, with a handicrafts market on Sunday, to the village and archaeological site of **Tulipe** (14 km; 1450 m). The site consists of several stone man-made 'pools' linked by water channels; they are unique in Ecuador. The stonework in one area suggests a later Inca occupation, however the material recovered in excavations is pre-Inca. They could have been ceremonial pools, bathing pools, mirrors to study the stars, or perhaps even a well-designed fish farm. A trail leads to a *mirador* overlooking the site as well as an orchid garden and a restaurant. Another path leads beside the Río Tulipe in about 15 minutes to a circular pool amid trees. The site **museum** ⓘ *T02-362 9605, www.museodesitiotulipe.com, US$3, Wed-Sun 0900-1600, guided tours (arrange ahead for English),* has exhibits in Spanish on the Yumbos culture and the *colonos* (contemporary settlers).

The Yumbos were traders who linked the Quitus with coastal and jungle peoples between AD 800-1600. Their trails are called *culuncos*, 1 m wide and 3 m deep, covered in vegetation for coolness. Several treks in the area follow them. Also to be seen are *tolas*, raised earth platforms (see Cochasquí, page 109); there are some 1500 around Tulipe. **Turismo Comunitario Las Tolas** ⓘ *6 km from Tulipe* offers lodging, food, craft workshops and guides to *tolas* and *culuncos*.

To the northwest of Tulipe are **Gualea** (7 km) and **Pacto** (4 km) beyond. Just before Pacto is the **Río Chirapi**. A trail along its left bank (heading upstream) leads, in about one hour, to a waterfall and swimming holes (US$1 entry). Just before a second waterfall, on rocks on the left side of the river, are **petroglyphs**. Beyond Pacto, the road divides, one branch goes west to **Mashpi**, the main branch northwest to **Sahuangal** by the Río Guayllabamba, where on the opposite side of the river runs the road coming from Otavalo via lthe lntag region. Both these roads are good for cycling.

The lower Guayllabamba is a lush subtropical area at altitudes around 500 m, where tourism is slowly developing. From Gualea Cruz a road branches north to the Río Guayllabamba and beyond to **Chontal** and **Magdalena Alto**, the access to **Los Cedros Research Station and Reserve**, see page 127. Back along the new route, past Nanegalito, at Km 79 is the turn-off for Mindo.

Noroccidente nature reserves

A number of private reserves, more than can be listed here, protect the region's lovely cloudforests. Those with lodges arrange transport from Quito or Mindo, if going independently, taxis can be hired in Nanegalito and Mindo. For details of accommodation at the following reserves and additional contact information, see Where to stay, below.

Bellavista Cloud Forest Reserve ⓘ *on the Ecoruta above Tandayapa, T02-223 2313 (Quito), T09-9416 5868 (lodge), www.bellavistacloudforest.com*, is a 700-ha reserve at about 2200 m, rich in botany and fauna, including the Olinguito (*Bassaricyon neblina*), a mammal new to science, first identified in 2013 (you can see it near the lodge most evenings). There is excellent birdwatching (it's the easiest place to see the plate-billed mountain toucan), good guides and lovely scenery, including waterfalls. There are 10 km of well-maintained trails ranging from easy to slippery/suicidal. Day visits including transport from Quito, two meals and guided walks are arranged. There are several access routes; from Quito, the fastest is to take the new route to Km 52, from where it is 12 km uphill to Bellavista, and from Mindo, take the new route towards Quito for 2 km and then the Ecoruta.

Intillacta/Tucanopy ⓘ *by the community of Miraflores, 2 km north of the new route, turn-off at Km 63.5, www.tucanopy.com, day visit US$5, open 0900-1600, closed Wed,* is a 100-ha reserve at 1700 m, with trails including Camino de los Yumbos, 2150 m of canopy ziplines (US$18), 500 m of canopy walkways (US$7 extra) and accommodation. They are involved with conservation projects and offer volunteer opportunities.

Maquipucuna ⓘ *www.maqui.org, entry US$10, guide US$15 pp (Spanish) US$150 (English) per day for group of 10,* has 6000 ha, surrounded by an additional 14,000 ha of protected forest. The cloudforest at 1200-2800 m contains a tremendous diversity of flora and fauna, including spectacled bears which can be seen when the aguacatillo trees are in fruit (around January) and about 350 species of bird. Especially noteworthy are the colourful tanager flocks, mountain toucans, parrots and quetzals. The reserve has 32 km of trails ranging in length from 15 minutes to all day. There is also a lodge, research station, experimental organic garden, organic coffee orchard and reforestation project. To get there, turn right at Nanegalito, follow the road to Nanegal for 12 km and turn right again (before

Nanegal). Pass through the village of Marianitas and it's another 4 km to the reserve. Past the turn-off the road is poor, especially in the January-to-May wet season; 4WD vehicles are recommended.

Mashpi ① *www.mashpilodge.com, open to lodge guests only.* Bosque Protector Mashpi is a 1300-ha cloudforest and montane rainforest reserve with an upmarket lodge at 900 m. There is a 26 m-high observation tower and two trails. It is a rich natural area, and the bird list is estimated at 500 species.

Milpe, Oreothraupis and Río Silanche ① *www.mindocloudforest.org, combined entry ticket available at Milpe*, are several bird-rich reserves owned by the **Mindo Cloudforest Foundation** to protect the habitat of important Chocó-endemic species. **Santuario de Aves Milpe**, 700 m north of the new route (turn-off at Km 91), is a 62-ha reserve (1020-1150 m) with basic facilities for four researchers. **Reserva Oreothraupis**, a 150-ha reserve between the Ecoruta and the Río Mindo at about 2400 m is part of the Bosque Protector Mindo-Nambillo. **Santuario de Aves Río Silanche**, 7 km from the new route (turn-off at Km 127) below Pedro Vicente Maldonado, is a 80-ha reserve in the low foothills (300-350 m); it has a canopy tower and walking trails.

Pachijal ① *www.pachijalreserve.com*, is a 120-ha reserve, 3 km north of the new route at Km 72. It consists of bird-rich forest at 1600 m, with 30 km of trails and a lodge.

Reserva Orquideológica El Pahuma ① *T02-603 5904 (Quito), www.ceiba.org, day visits 0700-1700, US$4, guide US$1 per person,* at Km 43 on the new route, is a 600-ha cloudforest reserve, less than an hour from Quito, with easy access. It is an interesting collaboration between a local landowner and the **Ceiba Foundation for Tropical Conservation**. It features an orchid garden and an orchid propagation programme. Trails start at 1900 m and go to 2800 m. A five-hour walk takes you to the Ecoruta, following for 4 km the pre-Inca Camino de los Yumbos (guide compulsory, US$20). Birds such as mountain toucans, torrent ducks and tanagers are present, and spectacled bears have been seen. There's a visitor centre and hostel on the south side of the road, with parking and a restaurant on the north side. To get there, take any bus for Nanegalito or points west.

Refugio Paz de las Aves ① *T09-8403 9860, US$15 per person for guided visit and breakfast,* 4 km south of the new route along the road to Miraflores (turn-off at Km 66), is a 70-ha property with 40 ha of bird-rich forest. It has a cock-of-the-rock lek and is the best place to see the Giant Antpitta.

El Quinde ① *T02-225 7016 (Quito),* 2 km east of Tandayapa on the Nono–Mindo road, is a 2200-ha reserve run by **Fundación Bosques para la Conservación**. About half the area is primary forest and has walking trails.

San Jorge ⓘ *www.eco-lodgesanjorge.com,* runs a series of reserves in bird-rich areas. Just west of northern Quito, 4 km along the road to Nono is the 80-ha **Reserva Ecológica San Jorge**, a remnant of high-altitude native vegetation at 3100 m. It has a lodge (see page 63). **San Jorge de Tandayapa** is a 40-ha cloudforest reserve at 1500 m, just below Tandayapa, along the Ecoruta; it has good trails and a lodge. **San Jorge de Milpe** is a 55-ha upper lowland forest reserve at 900 m, to the north of the new route at Km 91. It has decent trails, waterfalls, and a lodge. They also have a reserve to the east of Quito in the Cosanga area.

Santa Lucía ⓘ *office in Nanegal, T02-215 7242, www.santaluciaecuador.com, day visit US$10,* is a community-based conservation and ecotourism project. It protects a beautiful 730-ha tract of cloudforest, between 1900 and 2500 m, to the east of Maquipucuna. The area is very rich in birds (there are cock-of-the-rock leks) and other wildlife. There are waterfalls and walking trails, including the ancient Camino de los Yumbos and lodging, as well as volunteer opportunities. The British organization **Rainforest Concern** (www.rainforestconcern.org) works with this reserve. Access to the reserve is 30 minutes by car from Nanegal and a walk from there. Day tours combining Pululahua, Yunguilla and Santa Lucía and four-day walking tours from Yunguilla to Santa Lucía are available.

Tandayapa Bird Lodge ⓘ *www.tandayapa.com,* is on the Nono–Mindo road. It's a small reserve with three trails owned by dedicated birders who strive to keep track of all rarities on the property; they can reliably show you practically any of 318 species, even such rare birds as the white-faced nunbird or the lyre-tailed nightjar. It's recommended for serious birders. Access is faster via the new route: take the signed turn-off to Tandayapa at Km 52; it is 6 km from there.

Tulipe-Pachijal ⓘ *T02-222 2564, www.tulipecloudforest.com,* by Las Tolas, 7 km from Tulipe, is a 80-ha cloudforest reserve surrounded by additional 480 ha of forest between 900 and 1600 m. There are trails and guided walks by **Tours Unlimited**, www.tours-unlimited.com.

Verdecocha ⓘ *T02-255 1508 (Quito), www.verdecocha.com,* is 2.6 km from the Ecoruta along a secondary road which branches off at La Sierra, 8.6 km west of Nono. It's a 750-ha reserve at 2200-3480 m, run by **Fundación Nube Sierra**. They offer horse riding, cycling, llama trekking and volunteering opportunities.

Yanacocha ⓘ *www.fjocotoco.org,* 10 km from the Ecoruta along a secondary road which branches off at Km 8.7, is a 964-ha reserve run by the **Jocotoco Foundation**. It was created to protect a remnant of elfin polylepis forest at 3500 m. It is the home of the black-breasted pufflegg, Quito's emblematic hummingbird.

Suroccidente nature reserves

On the opposite side of Picihincha's massif, to the south and west of Quito, are several more reserves. Some are difficult to access and, in general, this area sees less tourism than the noroccidente. For details of accommodation and contact information, see page 102.

Bosque Nublado de Otonga ⓘ *www.parks.it/world/EC/riserva.otonga/Spar.html,* is a 1500-ha reserve between 1000 and 2300 m, run by **Fundación Otonga** (T02-290 3876, Quito), which works on conservation, community education and development. Much of the forest is virgin and rich in unusual orchids, gesneriads and birds. Access is south of the Alóag–Santo Domingo road, one section near Unión del Toachi, another higher by Las Pampas on a road to Sigchos; call ahead to arrange a visit.

Bosque Protector Guajalito ⓘ *T09-9587 2237, birdsinecuador.com/en/chapter-2/, entry US$2, call in advance,* at Km 59 on the Chiriboga road, is an 890-ha reserve, between 1800 and 2200 m, two hours southwest of Quito. It has a wide variety of birds and the lodge is a good base for birdwatching along the road and for getting inside the forest, which is normally impossible elsewhere. It is accessible by bus from Avenida El Tránsito y Julián Estrella in Chillogallo.

Reserva Bombolí ⓘ *5.8 km from the Aloag–Santo Domingo road at Km 20, T09-9982 0511, marianoisbomboli51@gmail.com, on Facebook,* preserves cloudforest between 2495 and 3450 m, and is rich in orchids and with 150 species of bird. Of interest are stands of tree ferns and an orchid 'hospital', tended by the owners, Oswaldo and Mariana Haro. They have a lodge (no electricity) and share their home and knowledge with visitors. A day visit including guiding and lunch costs US$35 per person, two days' full board including lodging and guiding $$$$; reserve ahead. **Galacruises** ⓘ *T02-250 4002, www.bombolicloudforest.com,* offers one- and two-day tours from Quito.

Tinalandia Ecolodge, on the Aloag road, near Santo Domingo, is one of the best places to see many species of birds with minimal effort. For details, see page 274.

★ Mindo *Colour map 1, B4.*

Mindo (population 2500, altitude 1250 m), a small town surrounded by dairy farms and lush cloudforest climbing the western slopes of Pichincha, is the main access for the 19,500-ha Bosque Protector Mindo-Nambillo. It gets crowded with Quiteños at weekends and holidays

The reserve, which ranges in altitude from 1400 m to 4780 m, features beautiful flora (many orchids and bromeliads), fauna (butterflies, frogs, about 450 species of birds including the cock-of-the-rock, golden-headed quetzal and toucan-barbet) and spectacular cloudforest, rivers and waterfalls. The region's rich diversity is threatened by proposed mining in the area. Access to the reserve proper is restricted to scientists, but there is a buffer zone of private reserves, some of them with lodges, which offer many opportunities for exploring. **Amigos de la Naturaleza de Mindo** ⓘ *9 de Octubre opposite El Quetzal Café, T02-217 0086, luisnolbertoj@yahoo.com, Tue-Sat 0900-1200, 1330-1700, entry US$2, US$40 per group for guided walks,* runs the **Centro de Educación Ambiental** (**CEA**), 4 km from town, a 17-ha reserve, with a shelter for 30 people. Lodging costs US$25 per

ON THE ROAD
A day in Mindo

There is plenty to do in Mindo, enough to spend several relaxing days. But if you would like to capture the essence of this area in a single day, try the following.

Start really early in order to make the most of the dawn chorus of birds. After breakfast, visit a butterfly farm in time to see the butterflies emerge from their cocoons, before continuing with a walk to the waterfalls. If you are in the mood for some adventure along the way, ride one of the canopy zip-lines or the cable car. By the time you reach the waterfalls, you'll be ready for a refreshing dip in the river and a picnic lunch. You can visit more waterfalls on your return to town. Your appetite will be whet for dinner by the time you get back and you'll probably be tempted to stay a day longer in Mindo.

person, full board including excursion. Arrangements have to be made in advance. During the rainy season (October to May) access to the reserve can be rough.

It is easy to admire the area's rich diversity. For birdwatching, stroll along any of the roads out of town; the access road into town is particularly good, as are the private 'Yellow House Trail' at **Hacienda San Vicente** and the garden at **El Descanso**, see Where to stay, below.

Some 250 species of butterflies have been identified around Mindo, you can see them close up at butterfly farms where the stages of metamorphosis are displayed and explained; go around 0900 when they are just emerging from their cocoons. **Mariposas de Mindo** ⓘ *2 km from town on the road to CEA, T02-224 2712, www.mariposasdemindo. com, US$6,* is a good butterfly farm with restaurant and lodging. **Nathaly** ⓘ *100 m from the main park, US$5,* is a small simple butterfly farm and orchid garden.

A fine collection of the region's orchids can be seen at **Jardín de Orquídeas** ⓘ *Ruta al Cinto, 2 blocks from the church, by the stadium, T02-217 0131, www.birdingmindo. com, US$3,* which also has cabins and a restaurant. **Mindo Lago** ⓘ *300 m from town on the road to Quito, T02-217 0201, www.mindolago.com.ec, closed Sun and Tue, US$1 day visit, frog concert at 1830, US$5,* has trails and cabins around a pretty pond surrounded by vegetation, where you can listen to frogs around sunset.

Several waterfalls can be visited, all on private land. On the Río Nambillo is the **Cascada de Nambillo** ⓘ *US$3,* with natural swimming holes and slides on the river. Just nearby is **Santuario de Cascadas** ⓘ *T02-256 9312 (Quito), US$5,* where there are seven falls on a tributary of the Nambillo, with the added attraction of a 530-m-long *tarabita* (cable car) to cross the river; if you do not want to use the *tarabita,* you can still visit the falls crossing on a bridge. Canopy ziplines are available on the way to Santuario de Cascadas for US$20. **Mindo Canopy** ⓘ *T09-9453 0624, www.mindocanopy.com,* with 3500 m of lines. **Mindo Ropes & Canopy** ⓘ *T02-217 0131, www.portalmindo.com/canopy.php,* has 2650 m of lines. **Tucanopy,** see page 94, in a reserve near Nanegalito has 2150 m of lines.

A very popular activity in the Mindo area is *regattas,* the local name for inner-tubing, floating down a river on a raft made of several inner tubes tied together.

The number of tubes that can run together depends on the water level. Several local agencies and hotels offer this activity on the Río Mindo for US$5-6, but experts also run the Río Blanco, where competitions are held during local holidays. Tour operators also offer canyoning (US$15 plus transport), horse riding and bicycle rentals.

El **Quetzal** offers tours of its chocolate factory and microbrewery and **The Beehive** apiary tours; see Restaurants, below.

San Miguel de los Bancos *Colour map 1, C3.*

The Calacalí–La Independencia road or new route continues west beyond the turnoff to Mindo. At Km 94.5, Los Bancos (regional population 9800, altitude 1100 m), as the locals call it, is a pleasant market town surrounded by farms. It is perched on a ridge above the Río Blanco and has a pleasant climate. A road goes south from town and then splits right to Santo Domingo via Valle Hermoso and left to Alluriquín on the Alóag-Santo Domingo road.

A pleasant day excursion from Los Bancos is to **Cascada La Sucia**. Take local transport bound for Alluriquín and get off at the bridge over the Río Blanco, about 15 minutes from Los Bancos. Just after crossing the bridge, turn left on a small dirt road and walk 2 km past the hamlet of Río Blanco. At the end of the road, turn left and descend to ford a small river, a tributary of the Blanco. Just upstream is a lovely cascade which spills into a great swimming hole. Leave enough time to catch a vehicle back to Los Bancos; otherwise it is a hot 5-km walk uphill from the bridge to town.

At Km 91 on the new route, 3.5 km east of Los Bancos, a secondary road goes northwest to yet another scenic area known as **Milpe**. Here are a couple of bird-rich reserves on remnants of foothills forest, see page 95.

Pedro Vicente Maldonado

Pedro Vicente Maldonado is a small supply town in a subtropical cattle-ranching area (regional population 11,800, altitude 600 m). At Km 104, a paved road goes northwest to Cielo Verde and beyond to the Río Guayllabamba, Manduriacos hydroelectric station and beyond to Intag (see page 125). The main road bypasses town to the south. About 8 km west of PV Maldonado, at Km 124 along the main road, is **Finca San Carlos**. Within the farm, it's a 15-minute walk to **Laguna Azul** ① *US$1,* a lovely pool at the base of a striking 35-m waterfall on the Río Negro. Accessed from PV Maldonado is the **Río Silanche** reserve, see page 95.

Puerto Quito

On the shores of the lovely Río Caoni is Puerto Quito, a small town which was once intended to be the capital's port. The main road bypasses the centre of town to the south. Along the Caoni and other rivers in the region (population 20,300, altitude 150 m) are several reserves, resorts and Quiteños' holiday homes. This is a good area for birdwatching, swimming in rivers and natural pools, walking, kayaking, or simply relaxing in pleasant natural surroundings.

The new route meets the Santo Domingo–Esmeraldas road 28 km southwest of Puerto Quito. Just south of the junction, on the way to Santo Domingo, is the village of **La Independencia** and 5 km further south the town of **La Concordia**.

Tourist information

Mindo

Municipal tourist information
Quito y 9 de Octubre, next to the bus station, turismo.municipiosmb@ gmail.com. Tue-Fri and Sun 0730-1300, 1430-1700.
Plenty of local information and pamphlets, map, some English spoken, very helpful.

Where to stay

Ecoruta

$ Quinta Margarita
On the main road in Nono, just above town, T02-278 6118.
A refurbished hacienda house, part of a working ranch, some rooms with private bath, others shared, with hot water. Horse riding. Call ahead to make sure owners will be there. Nearby are a couple of eateries.

The new route

$$$ Hostería Sumak Pakari
Tulipe, 200 m from the village, T02-361 3121, www.hosteriasumakpakari.com.
Cabins with suites with jacuzzi and rooms set in gardens, terraces with hammocks, pools, a restaurant and sports fields. Rates include breakfast and museum fee.

$$ Urcu de Mindo
Near Las Tolas, T02-287 3170, www.cloudforestecuador.com.
Set in a 42-ha property with forest around 1800 m are these 2 fancy treehouses with jacuzzi and rustic wood and bamboo cabins. There's a pool and waterfalls. Price

includes breakfast; other meals available. Packages including transport from Quito. Note it is not in Mindo.

$$$ Yunguilla
5.5 km north of the new route, turn-off at Km 15, T09-9954 1537, www.yunguilla.org.ec.
A cabin with 3 rooms for 3 people, shared bath and electric shower; price includes full board. Also organize housing with families (same price), camping US$5 pp or US$28 pp using their tent and full board. From Yunguilla you can hike to Maquipucuna, Santa Lucía or Pululahua, with guiding US$50 per day for up to 10 passengers. Access by pickup from Calacalí (US$5).

$ Posada del Yumbo
Up a side street off the main road, Tulipe, T02-361 2801.
Cabins and simple rooms in a large property with a river view, a pool and horse riding. No meals available. Also run restaurant **La Aldea**, by the archaeological site.

Noroccidente nature reserves

$$$$ Mashpi
T02-400 4100, in Quito T02-400 8088, www.mashpilodge.com.
Modern luxurious lodge with panoramic windows, rooms and suites with minimalist decor, good views and spa. Transport from Quito US$20 pp.

$$$$ Tandayapa Bird Lodge
T02-244 7520 (Quito), www.tandayapa.com.
Designed and owned by birders. Full board, 12 comfortable rooms, some have a canopy platform for observation, large

common area; guide US$168 per day, packages including guide and transport from Quito. Book well in advance.

$$$$-$$$ Bellavista Cloud Forest
T02-211 6232 (lodge); office in Quito at Jorge Washington E7-25 y 6 de Diciembre, T02-223 2313, www.bellavistacloudforest.com.
A dramatic lodge perched in beautiful cloudforest, includes unique geodesic dome. A variety of comfortable rooms ranging from suites to rooms with shared bath, all include 3 excellent meals (with vegetarian options), heaters, 1 wheelchair accessible room. New luxury suites were due to be completed in 2015. A bilingual guide service is included in packages. Good research station with dorms and kitchen facilities is available (US$20 pp), camping US$8 pp. Package tours with guide and transport from Quito available. Guided tours to Mindo and other reserves in the area. Best booked in advance. Very good service. Recommended.

$$$$-$$$ Maquipucuna Lodge
T02-250 7200, 09-9237 1945, www.maqui.org.
Comfortable rustic lodge, with rooms ranging from shared to rooms with bath, hot water and electricity. A campsite is 20 mins' walk from the main lodge, US$10 per tent (food extra). On offer is a coffee tour and chocolate massages. Rates include full board with good meals using ingredients from own organic garden (vegetarian and vegan available). Packages including transport and guiding are also available.

$$$$-$$$ Santa Lucía
T02-215 7242 (office), 02-361 3214 (lodge), www.santaluciaecuador.com.
The lodge with panoramic views is a 1½-hr walk from the access to the reserve, but mules are available to carry luggage (US$20 each way). Price includes full board with good food. There are cabins with private bath, rooms with shared composting toilets and hot showers and dorms (US$35 pp). A guide costs US$50 per day for up to 7 passengers.

$$$ Pachijal
T09-9955 4560, www.pachijalreserve.com.
Small 6-room lodge with a restaurant for guests only, a rooftop terrace with views and horse riding. Price includes breakfast and guiding.

$$$ San Jorge
T02-339 0403, T02-224 7549 (Quito), sanjorgeecolodges.com.
A series of reserves with lodges in bird-rich areas. One is 4 km from Quito

(see **Hostería San Jorge**, page 63), 1 in Tandayapa at 1500 m and another in Milpe, off the new road, at 900 m. The wooden lodges have observation decks with hammocks; rooms with panoramic windows cost more. Price includes breakfast, other meals available, packages including circuits through several reserves. Book at least 3 days ahead.

$$ Intillacta/Tucanopy
T09-8479 8986, www.tucanopy.com.
Simple cabins with bath, US$20 pp in dorm for 6. The price includes breakfast and use of the facilities, and the restaurant uses produce from their own organic garden (request meals ahead). Camping US$6 pp.

$ El Pahuma
T09-8755 1580, www.ceiba.org.
Rooms in the visitor centre with shared bath, hot water, kitchen facilities and the restaurant across the road is open weekends or with advanced booking. Camping US$3 pp. They also have a very rustic cabin, 2 hrs' climb from the entrance, US$5 pp; take sleeping bag.

Suroccidente nature reserves

$$ Otonga
At Unión del Toachi, on the road to Sigchos, 600 m from the junction with the Alóag–Santo Domingo road, T02-361 6039, T09-8780 6229 (Queti Tapia).
5 basic rooms with bath, next to the environmental education centre. Full board option available. A 30-room lodge was under construction in 2015.

$ Guajalito
T09-9587 2237, T02-297 1700, ext 1435, on Facebook.
A rustic lodge at 1900 m, with 3 basic rooms with shared bath and a dorm for 12; it gets cold so take a sleeping bag, use of kitchen or simple meals on request. Reservations required.

Mindo
There are more than 50 places to stay in and around Mindo; however, it advisable to reserve ahead for weekends and holidays. Note that many Mindo hotels ask you to remove your shoes before entering.

$$$$ Casa Divina
1.2 km on the road to Cascada de Nambillo, T09-9172 5874, www.mindocasadivina.com.
Comfortable 2-storey cabins with bathtubs set in a lovely location surrounded by 2.7 forested ha. Price includes breakfast and dinner, guiding extra. US/Ecuadorean-run.

$$$$ El Monte
2 km from town on the road to CEA, then opposite Mariposas de Mindo, cross river on tarabita *(rustic cable car), T02-217 0102, T09-9308 4675, www.ecuadorcloudforest.com.*
Beautifully constructed lodge in 44-ha property. The newer cabins are spacious and very comfortable, but there's no electricity. Price includes 3 meals, some (but not all) excursions with a *guía nativo* and tubing, other adventure sports and horse riding are extra. Reserve in advance. Recommended.

$$$ Séptimo Paraíso
2 km from Calacalí–La Independencia road along Mindo access road, then 500 m right on a small side road, well signed, T09-9368 4417, www.septimoparaiso.com.
All wood comfortable lodge in a lovely 420-ha reserve, with an expensive restaurant, pool and jaccuzi,

parking, great birdwatching, and walking trails open to non-guests for US$10. Recommended.

$$ Caskaffesu
Sixto Durán Ballén (the street leading to the stadium) y Av Quito, T02-217 0100, caskaffesu@yahoo.com.
Pleasant US- and Ecuadorean-run *hostal* with an attractive courtyard, and a bar offering live music Wed-Sat.

$$ Dragonfly Inn
On Av Quito (main street), 1st block after bridge, T02-217 0319, www.mindo.biz.
Popular hotel and restaurant offering comfortable rooms and apiary tours, see **The Beehive Café** in Restaurants, below.

$$ Hacienda San Vicente (Yellow House)
500 m south of the park, T02-217 0124.
Family-run lodge set in 200 ha of very rich forest, with attractive good-value rooms and good walking trails open to non-guests for US$6. Price includes an excellent breakfast. Reservations required. Highly recommended for nature lovers.

$$ Mindo Real
Vía al Cinto (extension Av Sixto Durán) 500 m from town, T02-217 0120, www.mindoreal.com.
Cabins and rooms in ample gardens on the shores of the Río Mindo with a pool and trails. Camping US$5 pp.

$$-$ El Descanso
C Colibríes (1st right after Río Canchupi bridge at entrance to town), 5 blocks from Av Quito, T02-217 0213.
Pleasant house with comfortable rooms, cheaper in loft with shared bath. Good birdwatching in the garden, open to non-guests for US$3, and cafeteria

open to the public for breakfast. Ample parking. Recommended.

$$-$ Jardín de los Pájaros
C Colibríes, 2 blocks from Av Quitot, T02-217 0159.
Family-run hostel with several types of rooms, a small pool, parking and a large covered terrace with hammocks; good value. Rates include a good breakfast. Recommended.

$ Charito
C Colibríes, 1 block from Av Quito, T02-217 0093, hostal_charitodemindo@hotmail.com.
Family-run hostel in a wooden house with good-value rooms, the newer ones in the back overlooking the Río Canchupi.

$ Rubby
5 blocks past the park along C Quito, T09-9193 1853, rubbyhostal@yahoo.com.
Family-run *hostal* on the outskirts of town, with good rooms, a kitchen and laundry facilities. English is spoken, and the owner Marcelo Arias is a birding guide.

San Miguel de los Bancos

$$$ Sapos y Ranas
Km 15, Via a Las Mercedes, T02-225 1446, ext 113, www.saposyranas.com.
Lodge and botanical gardens on a 20-ha property, offering cabins and rooms, includes meals and tours, pool, sauna and massage (extra). Refurbished in 2015.

$$ Mirador Río Blanco
Main road, at the east end of town, T02-277 0307.
Popular hotel/restaurant serving tropical dishes ($$), with small rooms and ample suites overlooking the river, breakfast extra, parking, terrace with bird feeders

(many hummingbirds and tanagers) and magnificent views of the river.

$ San Sebastián
On the new route 2 km west of town, T02-277 0802.
Friendly place offering rooms with bath and electric shower; use of pool, sauna and jacuzzi US$5.

Pedro Vicente Maldonado

$$$$ Arashá
4 km west of PV Maldonado, Km 121, T02-390 0007, Quito T02-244 9881 for reservations, www.arasharesort.com.
Well-run upmarket resort and spa, popular with families, with pools, waterfalls (artificial and natural) and hiking trails. Comfortable thatched cabins. Price includes all meals (cooked by a world-class chef), the use of the facilities (spa extra) and tours. They can also arrange transport from Quito. Attentive staff.

$ Moncayo
29 de Junio 754 (main street), T02-239 2065.
Simple but adequate hostel. Rooms have private bath and electric showers.

Puerto Quito

$$$ Selva Virgen
At Km 132, east of Puerto Quito, T02-362 9626, Quito office T02-331 7986, www.selvavirgen.com.ec. Wed-Sun, Mon-Tue with advanced booking only.
Nice *hostería* in a 100-ha property owned by the Universidad Técnica Equinoccial (UTE) and staffed by students. There are rooms with ceiling fan and spacious, comfortable cabins for 4 people with fan, fridge, jacuzzi and pleasant porch. Also here are 3 pools and a restaurant, all set in lovely grounds. Part of the property is forested and has trails. The facilities are also open to restaurant patrons.

$$ Shishink
Turn-off at the village of Puerto Rico (Km 149, 9 km west of Puerto Quito), then 5 km southeast, www.shishink.ec.
A resort in a 37-ha reserve, with thatched-roof cabins, waterfalls, natural pools, caves and opportunities for outdoor activities. Rates include 4 meals and excursions.

$ Bambú
On the main street C 18 de Mayo, T02-215 6252.
Basic, adequate hostel, with a restaurant and parking. Rooms have private bath, cold water and fan. Friendly owner.

Restaurants

Mindo

$$$-$$ El Quetzal
9 de Octubre, 3 blocks from the park, T02-217 0034, wwwelquetzaldemindo.com. Daily 0800-2000.
Decent restaurant serving international food with vegetarian options. Microbrews, local chocolate and other sweets are also for sale. Chocolate tours daily 1100-1700, US$6.

$$ Fuera de Babilonia
9 de Octubre y Los Ríos, 2 blocks from the park. Daily 0800-2100.
À la carte international dishes, trout, pizza, pasta; good food and atmosphere.

$ La Sazón de Marcelo
Av Quito past the park, opposite the children's playground. Daily 0830-2100.
Set meals and à la carte; one of their specialities is *bandeja mindeña*, a dish for 2 people with trout and tilapia.

$ The Beehive
Av Quito opposite Dragonfly Inn, www. thebehivemindo.com. Daily 0800-1900.
Café and honey and crafts shop, selling coffee, snacks and sweets. Arrange the previous day for apiary tours US$25 pp.

$ Productos Guerrero
By the park.
Excellent dairy products and jams made with regional fruits such as *borojó* and *arazá*.

What to do

Mindo
Endemic Tours, *Av Quito y Gallo de la Peña, T09-9888 5801, romelly85@hotmail. com.* Bicycle rentals US$10 per half day, US$15 per full day, hiking, regattas and other adventure activities.
Julia Patiño, *T09-8616 2816, juliaguideofbirds@gmail.com.* An English-speaking birding guide.
La Isla, *Av Quito next to the bus station, T02-217 0230, www.laislamindo.com.* Tours to all local attractions, adventure sports and bike rentals.
Mindo Xtreme Birds, *Sector Saguambi, just out of town on the road to CEA, T02-217 0188, www.mindoxtreme.com.* Birdwatching, regattas, cycling, hiking, waterfalls and horse riding. English spoken, very helpful.
Tours El Buho, *Av Quito, T02-217 0456, miguel_paladines@hotmail.com.* Tours to all local attractions, cycling, regattas and adventure sports.
Vinicio Pérez, *T09-947 6867, www. birdwatchershouse.com.* A recommended birding guide who speaks some English.

Transport

Tulipe
Bus From **Quito**, Estación La Ofelia, from 0615, US$1.90, 1¾ hrs: **Transportes Otavalo**, 7 daily, continue to Pacto (US$2.50, 2 hrs) and **Transportes Minas** 5 daily, continue to **Chontal** (US$3.75, 3 hrs). To **Las Tolas**, **Transportes Minas**, daily at 1730, US$2.50, 2½ hrs or take pick-up from Tulipe, US$5.

Mindo
Bus From **Quito**, Estación La Ofelia, **Coop Flor del Valle**, T02-217 0171, Mon-Fri 0800, 0900, 1100, 1300, 1600, Sat and Sun 0740, 0820, 0920, 11, 1300, 1400, 1600 (last one on Sun at 1700 instead of 1600); Mindo–Quito: Mon-Fri 0630, 1100, 1345, 1500, Sat and Sun 0630, 1100 and hourly 1300-1700; US$3.10, 2 hrs; weekend buses fill quickly, buy ahead. You can also take any bus bound for Esmeraldas or San Miguel de los Bancos (see below) and get off at the turn-off for Mindo from where there are taxis until 1930, US$0.50 pp or US$3 without sharing. **Cooperativa Kennedy** to/from **Santo Domingo** 5 daily, US$5, 3½ hrs.

West of Mindo
Bus From **Quito**, Terminal Carcelén, departures every 30 mins (**Coop Kennedy** and associates) to Santo Domingo via: **Nanegalito** (US$1.90, 1½ hrs), **San Miguel de los Bancos** (US$3.15, 2½ hrs), **Pedro Vicente Maldonado** (US$3.75, 3 hrs) and **Puerto Quito** (US$4.70, 3½ hrs). **Trans Esmeraldas** frequent departures from Terminal Carcelén also serve these destinations along the Quito–Esmeraldas route.

Northern highlands

lakes and crafts

North from Quito to the border with Colombia is an area of great natural beauty and cultural interest. The landscape is mountainous, with views of Cotacachi, Imbabura and Chiles volcanoes, as well as the glacier-covered Cayambe, interspersed with lakes.

This is also a region renowned for its *artesanía*. Countless villages specialize in their own particular craft, be it textiles, hats, woodcarvings, bread figures or leather goods. And, of course, there is Otavalo, with its outstanding market, a must on everyone's itinerary.

The Pan-American Highway, fully paved, runs northeast from Quito to Otavalo (94 km), Ibarra (114 km) and Tulcán (240 km), from where it continues to Ipiales in Colombia. Secondary roads go west from all these cities, and descend to subtropical lowlands. From Ibarra a paved road runs northwest to the Pacific port of San Lorenzo and south of Tulcán a road goes east to Lago Agrio. Parque Nacional Cayambe Coca and Reservas Cotacachi Cayapas and El Angel protect this region's natural wonders.

Best for
Boat rides ▪ Climbing ▪ Indigenous crafts ▪ Trekking

Footprint
picks

★ **Parque Arqueológico Tolas de Cochasquí**, page 109

Among the many pre-Inca structures found in northern Ecuador, these pyramids are the most elaborate.

★ **Otavalo market**, page 112

Featuring a dazzling array of indigenous textiles and crafts, Otavalo's Saturday market is second to none.

★ **Laguna Cuicocha**, page 124

Walk around the rim of Cuicocha crater lake for fantastic views of the surrounding volcanoes and the lake's two islands.

★ **Helados de paila**, page 130

Enjoy the delicious fresh fruit sorbets made in a copper kettle, an Ibarra speciality.

★ **Reserva Ecológica El Angel**, page 138

Admire Ecuador's largest stand of velvety leaved *frailejón* plants in the high-altitude El Angel Reserve.

★ **Tulcán cemetery**, page 140

In Tulcán's cemetery, the art of topiary is taken to incredible extremes.

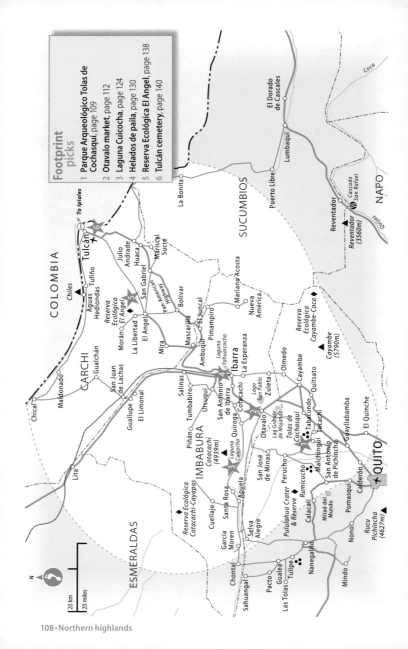

Footprint picks

1 Parque Arqueológico Tolas de Cochasquí, page 109
2 Otavalo market, page 112
3 Laguna Cuicocha, page 124
4 Helados de paila, page 130
5 Reserva Ecológica El Ángel, page 138
6 Tulcán cemetery, page 140

To Ipiales

COLOMBIA
Chiles
Aguas Hedionas
Tufiño
Tulcán ①⑥
Gualchán
Maldonado
Chical
Gualtal
San Juan de Lachas
CARCHI
Julio Andrade
Huaca
Mariscal Sucre
San Gabriel
Bolívar
Reserva Ecológica El Ángel ⑤
El Ángel
Morán
La Libertad
El Juncal
Mascarilla
Guallupe
El Limonal
Mira
Ambuquí
Pimampiro
Mariano Acosta
Nueva América
La Bonita
SUCUMBÍOS
Lita
Salinas
Tumbabiro
Urcuquí
San Antonio de Ibarra
Laguna Yahuarcocha
Ibarra
La Esperanza
Olmedo
Reserva Ecológica Cayambe-Coca
La Bonita
Puerto Libre
El Dorado de Cascales
Lumbaqui
Coca
NAPO
Quijos
Cascada San Rafael
Reventador
Reventador (3560m)
Piñán
Cotacachi
IMBABURA
Quiroga
Cotacachi (4939m)
Lago San Pablo
Zuleta
Cayambe
Cayambe (5790m)
Santa Rosa
Apuela
Laguna Cuicocha ③
San José de Minas
Otavalo ②
Lag Grande de Mojanda
Tabacundo
Quitsato
Reserva Ecológica Cotacachi-Cayapas
Cuellaje
García Moren
Selva Alegre
Perucho
Tolas de Cochasquí
Malchinguí
Tocachi
Guayllabamba
El Quinche
Chontal
Pululahua Crater & Reserve
Rumicucho
San Antonio de Pichincha
Calderón
QUITO
Sahuangal
Pacto
Gualea
Las Tolas
Tulipe
Nanegalito
Calacalí
Mitad del Mundo
Pomasqui
Nono
Rucu Pichincha (4627m)
Mindo
ESMERALDAS

N
20 km
20 miles

straddling the equator, a good area for crafts, trekking and pre-Inca pyramids

On the way from the capital to the main tourist centre in northern Ecuador, the landscape is dominated by the Cayambe volcano. The Panamericana (Pan-American Highway), an excellent toll road goes through arid valleys, followed by the country's main flower-growing area, before reaching the lake district in the province of Imbabura.

Quito to Cayambe

Calderón Some 32 km north of the centre of Quito, you can see the famous bread figurines being made at Calderón. Prices are lower than in Quito. On 1-2 November, the graves in the cemetery are decorated with flowers, drinks and food for the dead. The Corpus Christi processions are very colourful. Take a bus at La Ofelia Metrobus terminal. Beyond Calderón, at Oyacoto just past the toll booth, starts the Vía Collas which goes south to the airport.

Guayllabamba Valley The Pan-American Highway goes to the warm valley of Guayllabamba, home of the **Quito Zoo** (www.quitozoo.org) and a popular place for a Sunday outing among Quiteños. Here it branches, one road going through Cayambe and the second through Tabacundo before rejoining at Cajas.

★ **Parque Arqueológico Tolas de Cochasquí** ⓘ *T09-9822 0686, Quito T02-399 4405, www.pichincha.gob.ec/visita-cochasqui, http://parquecochasqui. blogspot.com, 0800-1600, US$3, entry only with a 1½-hr guided tour.* At 10 km past Guayllabamba on the road to Tabacundo, just north of the toll booth, a cobbled road to the left (signed Pirámides de Cochasquí) leads to Tocachi and further on to Cochasquí. The protected area contains 15 truncated clay pyramids (tolas), nine with long ramps, built between AD 950 and 1550 by the Cara or Cayambi-Caranqui people. Festivals with dancing are held on the equinoxes and solstices. There is a site museum and views from the pyramids, south to Quito, are marvellous.

Tolas are manmade structures built with adobe blocks or rammed earth, found throughout northern Ecuador. The smallest ones are rounded funerary mounds with a chamber in the centre. Larger rounded hills are thought to have served as the foundation for buildings. The large truncated pyramids, such as those excavated in Cochasquí, are thought to have served for ceremonial purposes. From Terminal Carcelén, be sure to take a bus that goes on the Tabacundo road and ask to be let off at the turnoff. From there it's a pleasant 8-km uphill walk. Alternatively, from Terminal La Ofelia, take a bus to Malchinguí (hourly, US$1.50, two hours) and a pickup to Cochasquí (US$3, 15 minutes) or a taxi (US$6). There are also buses between Malchiguí and Cayambe which go by Cochasquí. Opposite the park entrance is **Camping Cochasquí** ⓘ *T09-9491 9008, US$3 pp for camping, US$10 pp in cabins, meals available.*

Quitsato ① *T02-361 0908, www.quitsato.org, US$2.* On the other road, 8 km before Cayambe, a globe carved out of rock by the Pan-American Highway is at the spot where the French expedition marked the equator (small shops sell drinks and snacks). Just to the north is Quitsato, where studies about the equator and its importance to ancient cultures are carried out. There is a sun dial, 54 m in diameter, and a solar culture exhibit, with information about indigenous cultures and archaeological sites along the equator; here too there are special events for the solstices and equinoxes.

Cayambe *Colour map 1, B5.*

Cayambe (population 53,700), on the eastern (right-hand) branch of the highway, 25 km northeast of Guayllabamba, is overshadowed by the snow-capped volcano of the same name. The surrounding countryside consists of a few dairy farms and many flower plantations. The area is noted for its *bizcochos* (biscuits) served with *queso de hoja* (string cheese). At the Centro Cultural Espinoza-Jarrín, is the **Museo de la Ciudad** ① *Rocafuerte y Bolívar, Wed-Sun 0800-1700, free*, with displays about the Cayambi culture and ceramics found at **Puntiachil**, an important but poorly preserved archaeologic site at the edge of town. There is a *fiesta* in March for the equinox with plenty of local music; also Inti Raymi solstice and San Pedro celebrations in June. Market day is Sunday.

Climbing Volcán Cayambe

Cayambe, Ecuador's third highest peak, at 5790 m, lies within Parque Nacional Cayambe Coca (see page 87). It is the highest point in the world to lie so close to the equator (3.75 km north). The equator goes over the mountain's flanks. About 1 km south of the town of Cayambe is an unmarked cobbled road heading east via Juan Montalvo, leading in 26 km to the **Ruales-Oleas-Berge refuge** ① *T09-5955 9765, rooms for 4-10 people, take sleeping bag, US$14 pp with use of kitchen or US$30 with dinner and breakfast, rebuilt in 2015*, at 4600 m. The standard climbing route, from the west, uses the refuge as a base. There is a crevasse near the summit which can be very difficult to cross if there isn't enough snow, ask the refuge keeper about conditions. There are various acclimatization hikes around the refuge. Otavalo and Quito operators offer tours here. Further north, the Laguna Puruhanta sector of the park can be accessed from Pimampiro, past Ibarra, via Nueva América; to the south access is from Papallacta (page 88) and the lowland sector is reached from El Chaco and Reventador (page 289).

To the southeast of Cayambe, also within the park and surrounded by cloudforest at 3200 m is **Oyacachi** ① *T06-299 1842, oyacachi@gmail.com*, a traditional village of farmers and woodcarvers, with thermal baths (US$3), at 3100 m. Accommodation is in family *hospedajes*. There is good walking in the area, including a two-day walk to Papallacta and a three-day trek to El Chaco in the lowlands; these require a permit from the reserve, write ahead. The area is wet, so walking is best in the dry season, the route to El Chaco crosses several rivers.

Quito to Otavalo via San José de Minas

An alternative route from Quito to Otavalo is via **San José de Minas** (2400 m) reached on a paved road which starts just north of Guayllabamba along the road to Tabacundo or along another narrow paved road from San Antonio de Pichincha (**Mitad del Mundo**), past the ruins of **Rumicucho**. The scenery is magnificent and it is a great biking route since there is little traffic. In the valley below Minas, at Cubi, there are warm springs. After Minas the road is unpaved for the next climb to Tangalí, then paved again to join the Otavalo–Selva Alegre road about 15 km west from Otavalo.

Listings Quito to Otavalo

Where to stay

Cayambe

$$$ Hacienda Guachalá
South of Cayambe on the road to Cangahua, T02-361 0908, www. guachala.com.
The 1st hacienda in Ecuador, carefully restored, the chapel (1580) is built on top of an Inca structure. Simple but comfortable rooms in older section and fancier ones in newer area, fireplaces, delicious meals, covered swimming pool, parking, attentive service, good walking, horses for rent, excursions to nearby pre-Inca ruins, small museum.

$$$ Jatun Huasi
Panamericana Norte Km 1½, T02-236 3777, www.hosteriajatunhuasi.com.
US motel style, cabins with a sitting room with fireplace and frigo-bar and rooms, restaurant, indoor pool, spa, parking.

$$ Shungu Huasi
Camino a Granobles, 1 km northwest of town, T02-236 1847, www.shunguhuasi. com.
Comfortable cabins in a 6.5-ha ranch, excellent Italian restaurant with advanced reservation, heaters on request, pleasant setting, attentive service, offers horse riding excursions. Recommended.

$ La Gran Colombia
Panamericana y Calderón, T02-236 1238.
Modern multi-storey building, restaurant, parking, traffic noise in front rooms.

Restaurants

Cayambe

$$$ Casa de Fernando
Panamericana Norte Km 1.5. Closed Mon.
Varied menu, good international food.

$$-$ Aroma
Bolívar 404 y Ascázubi. Closed Wed.
Large choice of set lunches and à la carte, variety of desserts, very good.

Transport

Cayambe
Bus Flor del Valle, from La Ofelia, **Quito**, every 7 mins 0530-2100, US$1.50, 1½ hrs. Their Cayambe station is at Montalvo y Junín. To **Otavalo**, from traffic circle at Bolívar y Av N Jarrín, every 15 mins, US$0.95, 45 mins.

Parque Nacional Cayambe Coca

Road To **Volcán Cayambe**, most vehicles can go as far as the **Hacienda Piemonte El Hato** (at about 3500 m) from where it is a 3- to 4-hr walk, longer if heavily laden or if it is windy, but it is a beautiful walk. Regular pickups can often make it to 'la Z', a sharp curve on the road 30-mins' walk to the *refugio*. 4WDs can often make it to the *refugio*. Pickups can be hired by the market in Cayambe,

Junín y Ascázubi, US$45, 1½-2 hrs. Arrange ahead for return transport. A milk truck runs from Cayambe's hospital to the hacienda at 0600, returning between 1700 and 1900. To **Oyacachi**, from the north side of Cayambe, near the Mercado Mayorista, Mon, Wed, Sat at 1500, Sun at 0800, US$2.50, 1½ hrs; return to Cayambe Wed, Fri, Sat at 0400, Sun at 1400.

Otavalo and around *Colour map 1, B5.*

Otavalo's indigenous market is one of Ecuador's major attractions

Otavalo (population 55,000, altitude 2530 m), only a short distance from the capital, is a must on any tourist itinerary in Ecuador. The Tabacundo and Cayambe roads join at Cajas, then cross the *páramo* and suddenly descend into the land of the *Otavaleños*, a thriving, prosperous group, famous for their prodigious production of woollens. The town itself, consisting of rather functional modern buildings, is one of South America's most important centres of ethno-tourism and its enormous Saturday market, featuring a dazzling array of textiles and crafts, is second to none and not to be missed. Indigenous families speak Quichua at home, although it is losing some ground to Spanish with the younger generation. Otavalo is set in beautiful countryside, with mountains, lakes and small villages nearby. A visit to some of the nearby villages to learn how the crafts are made is recommended. The area is worth exploring for three or four days.

Sights

The ★ **Saturday market** comprises four different markets in various parts of the town with the central streets filled with vendors. The *artesanías* market is held 0700-1800, based around the Plaza de Ponchos (Plaza Centenario). The livestock section begins at 0500 until 0900, outside the centre, west of the Panamericana; go west on Calderón from the town centre. The produce market, at the old stadium, west of the centre, lasts from 0700 till 1400. The *artesanías* industry is so big that the Plaza de Ponchos is filled with vendors every day of the week. The selection is better on Saturday but prices are a little higher than other days when the atmosphere is more relaxed. Wednesday is also an important market day with more movement than other weekdays. Polite bargaining is appropriate in the market and shops. Otavaleños not only sell goods they weave and sew themselves, but they bring crafts from throughout Ecuador and from Peru and Bolivia. Indigenous people in the market respond better to photography if you buy something first, then ask politely.

While most visitors come to Otavalo to meet its native people and buy their crafts, you cannot escape the influence of the outside world here, a product of the city's very success in trade and tourism. The streets are lined not only with small kiosks selling homespun wares, but also with wholesale warehouses and international freight forwarders, as well as numerous hotels, cafés and restaurants catering to decidedly foreign tastes.

The **Museo Etnográfico Otavalango** ① *Vía a Selva Alegre Km 1, antigua Fábrica San Pedro, T09-8726 9827, Mon-Sat 0900-1700, must call ahead, US$5*, displays on all cultural aspects of Otavaleño life; live presentations of local traditions for groups.

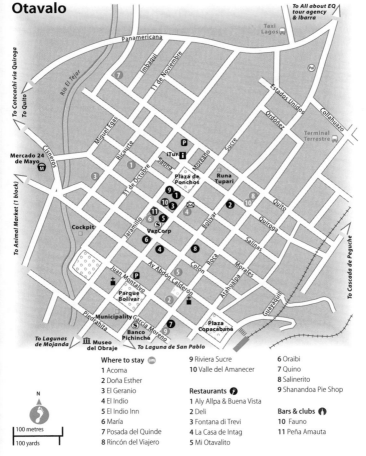

Otavalo

Where to stay 🛏️
1 Acoma
2 Doña Esther
3 El Geranio
4 El Indio
5 El Indio Inn
6 María
7 Posada del Quinde
8 Rincón del Viajero
9 Riviera Sucre
10 Valle del Amanecer

Restaurants 🍴
1 Aly Allpa & Buena Vista
2 Deli
3 Fontana di Trevi
4 La Casa de Intag
5 Mi Otavalito
6 Oraibi
7 Quino
8 Salinerito
9 Shanandoa Pie Shop

Bars & clubs 🍸
10 Fauno
11 Peña Amauta

N
100 metres
100 yards

The **Museo de Tejidos El Obraje** ⓘ *Sucre 6-08 y Olmedo, T06-292 0261, US$2, call ahead*, shows the process of traditional Otavalo weaving from shearing to final products. There are good views of town from **Centro de Exposiciones El Colibrí** ⓘ *C Morales past the railway line*.

Around Otavalo

Otavalo weavers come from dozens of communities. Many families weave and visitors should shop around as the less known weavers often have better prices and some of the most famous ones only sell from their homes, especially in Agato and Peguche. The easiest villages to visit are Ilumán (there are also many felt hatmakers in town and *yachacs*, or shamen, mostly north of the plaza – look for signs); Agato; Carabuela (many homes sell crafts including wool sweaters and alpargatas, local footwear); Peguche (musical instruments can also be found here). These villages are only 15-30 minutes away and have good bus service; buses

Around Otavalo

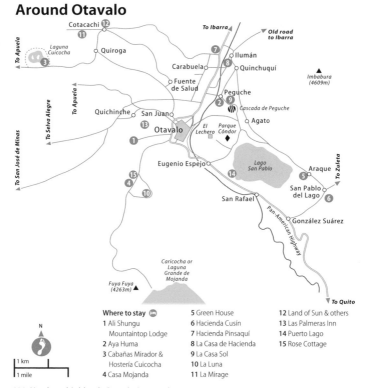

Where to stay
1 Ali Shungu Mountaintop Lodge
2 Aya Huma
3 Cabañas Mirador & Hostería Cuicocha
4 Casa Mojanda
5 Green House
6 Hacienda Cusín
7 Hacienda Pinsaquí
8 La Casa de Hacienda
9 La Casa Sol
10 La Luna
11 La Mirage
12 Land of Sun & others
13 Las Palmeras Inn
14 Puerto Lago
15 Rose Cottage

ON THE ROAD

The Otavaleños

The Otavaleños are a proud and prosperous people who have made their name not only as successful weavers and international business people, but also as unsurpassed symbols of cultural fortitude. Today, they make up the economic elite of their town and its surroundings and provide an example which other groups have followed. The Otavalo dialect of Quichua, the highland native tongue, has been adopted as the national standard.

There is considerable debate over the origin of the Otavaleños. In present-day Imbabura, pre-Inca people were Caranquis, or Imbaya, and, in Otavalo, the Cayambi. They were subjugated by the Caras who expanded into the highlands from the Manabí coast. The Caras resisted the Incas for 17 years, but the conquering Incas eventually moved the local population away to replace them with vassals from Peru and Bolivia. One theory is that the Otavaleños are descended from these forced migrants and also Chibcha salt traders from Colombia, while some current-day Otavaleños prefer to stress their local pre-Inca roots.

Otavalo men wear their hair long and plaited under a white trophy hat. They wear white, calf-length trousers and blue ponchos. The women's colourful costumes consist of embroidered blouses, shoulder wraps, a plethora of gold coloured necklace beads and red bead bracelets. Their ankle-length skirts, known as *anacos*, are fastened with an intricately woven cloth belt or *faja*. Traditional footwear for both genders is the *alpargata*, a sandal whose sole was originally made of coiled hemp rope, but today has been replaced by rubber.

Impeccable cleanliness is another striking aspect of many Otavaleños attire. Perhaps the most outstanding feature of the Otavaleños, however, is their profound sense of pride and self-assurance. This is aided not only by the group s economic success, but also by achievements in academic and cultural realms. In the words of one local elder: My grandfather was illiterate, my father completed primary school and I finished high school in Quito. My son has a PhD and has served as a cabinet minister!

leave from the terminal and stop at Plaza Copacabana (Atahualpa y Montalvo). You can also take a taxi (US$2).

To reach the lovely **Cascada de Peguche**, from Peguche's plaza, facing the church, head right and continue straight until the road forks. Take the lower fork to the right, but not the road that heads downhill. From the top of the falls (left side, excellent views) you can continue the walk to Lago San Pablo. The **Pawkar Raimi** festival is held in Peguche before carnival. At the falls there is a small information centre (contributions are appreciated).

The **Ciclovía** is a bicycle path which runs along the old rail line 21 km between Eugenio Espejo de Cajas and Otavalo. Because of the slope, starting in Cajas is recommended. You can take a tour or hire a bike and take a bus bound for Quito to the bike path. This and other cycling routes are described in www.visitotavalo.travel.

Lago San Pablo

To the southeast of Otavalo, at the foot of Cerro Imbabura and just off the Panamericana is the scenic Lago San Pablo, the largest natural lake in the country. A secondary road circumnavigates the lake. Along it are several native villages and a number of upmarket *hosterías* (inns). Reed mats and crafts are made with *totora* reeds from the lake. San Pablo is a popular weekend destination for wealthier Ecuadoreans looking for water sports, good food, or just a place to get away.

There is a network of old roads and trails between Otavalo and Lago San Pablo, none of which takes more than two hours to explore. It is worth walking either to or back from the lake for the views. Going in a group is recommended for safety. A nice half-day excursion is via Cascada de Peguche, **Parque Cóndor** ⓘ *on a hill called Curiloma, near the community of Pucará Alto, T06-304 9399, www.parquecondor. org, Wed-Sun 0930-1700, raptor flight demonstrations at 1130 and 1500, US$4.50, crowded on weekends*, a reserve and birds of prey rehabilitation centre, and back via **El Lechero**, a lookout by a tree considered sacred among indigenous people. From **San Pablo del Lago** it is possible to climb **Imbabura** volcano (4630 m, a serious climb and frequently under cloud), allow at least six hours to reach the summit and four hours for the descent. An alternative access is from La Esperanza or San Clemente (see page 131). Easier, and no less impressive, is the nearby Cerro Huarmi Imbabura, 3845 m, it is not signed but several paths lead there. Take a good map, food and warm clothing.

Lagunas de Mojanda

Southwest of Otavalo are the impressive Lagunas de Mojanda, accessed by cobbled roads from Otavalo or Tabacundo, or by a paths from Cochasquí or Tocachi. Otavalo agencies offer tours to the lakes.

Caricocha (or Laguna Grande de Mojanda), a crater lake is the largest of the Mojanda lakes. It is 18 km away from, and 1200 m higher than, Otavalo. About 25 minutes' walk above Caricocha is **Laguna Huarmicocha** and a further 25 minutes is **Laguna Yanacocha** (Laguna Negra). In 2015, the municipal government built a shelter between Caricocha and Yanacocha. At the time of writing it was not yet open to the public, but it is a recommended place to camp, as the bathrooms and cooking area are already open and there is always a guard there. The views on the descent are excellent. Take a warm jacket, food and drinks, a tent and warm sleeping bags if camping.

From Caricocha a trail continues south about 5 km before dividing: the left-hand path leads to **Tocachi**, the right-hand to **Cochasquí** (see page 109). Both are about 20 km from Caricocha and offer beautiful views of Quito and Cotopaxi (cloud permitting). You can climb **Fuya Fuya** (4263 m) and **Yanaurco** (4259 m).

Tourist information

The website www.visitotavalo.travel is a good multilingual site.

Dirección de Turismo
Corner of Plaza de Ponchos, Jaramillo y Quiroga, Otavalo, T06-292 7230. Mon-Sat 0800-1800.
For local and regional information, English spoken.

Where to stay

Otavalo
In town
Hotels may be full on Fri night before market.

$$$ Posada del Quinde
Quito y Miguel Egas, T06-292 0750, www.posadaquinde.com.
Good location, quiet but close to markets. Attractively decorated, all rooms around a lovely garden, also 2 suites, good restaurant, parking, US-run.

$$$-$$ El Indio Inn
Bolívar 9-04 y Calderón, T06-292 2922, www.hotelelindioinn.com.
Modern hotel, carpeted rooms and simple suites, restaurant, parking, spa.

$$ Acoma
Salinas 07-57 y 31 de Octubre, T06-292 6570, www.acomahotel.com.
Lovely re-built home in colonial style, parking, nice comfortable rooms, some

with balcony, 1 room with bathtub,
2 suites with kitchenette.

$$ Doña Esther
Montalvo 4-44 y Bolívar, T06-292 0739,
www.otavalohotel.com.
Carefully restored colonial house, a hotel
for over 100 years, very good restaurant,
rooms with nice wooden floors,
colourful decor, pleasant atmosphere,
transfers to Quito or airport.

$$ El Indio
Sucre 12-14 y Salinas, near Plaza
de Ponchos, T06-292 0060, www.
hostalelindio.com.
In a multi-storey building; ask for a room
with balcony. Simple restaurant, parking,
helpful service.

$$-$ Rincón del Viajero
Roca 11-07 y Quiroga, T06-292 1741,
www.hostalrincondelviajero.com.
Very pleasant hostel and meeting place.
Simple but nicely decorated rooms,
includes a choice of good breakfasts,
private or shared bath, cafeteria, small
parking, rooftop hammocks, sitting
room with fireplace, US/Ecuadorean-run,
good value. Recommended.

$$-$ Riviera Sucre
García Moreno 380 y Roca, T06-292 0241,
www.rivierasucre.com.
Traditional hotel with ample renovated
rooms, good breakfast available,
cafeteria, private or shared bath, kitchen
facilities, book exchange, bookshop with
good selection of English and German
titles, pleasant common areas, garden
and courtyard, good meeting place.
Recommended.

$$-$ Valle del Amanecer
Roca y Quiroga, T06-292 0990.
Small rooms, attractive courtyard with

hammocks, private or shared bath,
popular.

$ El Geranio
Ricaurte y Morales, T06-292 0185,
hgeranio@hotmail.com.
2 types of rooms, smaller ones with
electric shower and no TV are cheaper.
Laundry facilities and use of kitchen
to prepare cold foods, parking, quiet,
family-run, popular, runs trips. Good
value, recommended.

$ María
Jaramillo y Colón, T06-292 0672.
Bright rooms in multi-storey building,
parking for small car. Good value.

$ Santa Fé
Roca 7-34 y García Moreno, T06-292
3640, www.hotelsantafeotavalo.com.
Modern, pine decoration, restaurant, run
by indigenous Otavaleños, good value.

Out of town

$$$$ Ali Shungu Mountaintop Lodge
5 km west of Otavalo by the village
of Yambiro, T09-8950 9945, www.
alishungumountaintoplodge.com.
Country inn on a 16-ha private reserve.
4 comfortable nicely decorated
guesthouses for 4, each with living room,
woodstove and kitchenette. Includes
breakfast and dinner (vegetarian
available), horse riding, US-run.

$$$$ Casa Mojanda
Vía a Mojanda Km 3.5, T09-8033 5108,
www.casamojanda.com.
Comfortable cabins set in a beautiful
hillside. Includes breakfast and tasty
dinner prepared with ingredients from
own organic garden and short guided
hike to waterfall; each room is decorated
with its own elegant touch, outdoor hot

tub with great views, quiet, good library, horse riding. Recommended.

$$$ Hacienda Pinsaquí
Panamericana Norte Km 5, 300 m north of the turn-off for Cotacachi, T06-294 6116, www.haciendapinsaqui.com.
Converted hacienda dating to 1790, with 30 suites, one with jacuzzi, restaurant with lovely dining room, lounge with fireplace, beautiful antiques, colonial ambience, gardens, horse riding.

$$$ Las Palmeras Inn
Outside Quichinche, 15 mins by bus from Otavalo, T06-266 8067, www. laspalmerasinn.com.
Cabins with terrace and fireplace in a rural setting, restaurant, parking, nice grounds and views, pool table and ping-pong, British-owned.

$$ La Casa de Hacienda
Vía Ilumán, entrance at Panamericana Norte Km 3, then 300 m east, T06-269 0245.
Tasteful cabins with fireplace, restaurant, parking, horse riding, under new management in 2015.

$$ La Luna
On a side road going south off the Mojanda road at Km 4, T09-9315 6082, www.lalunaecuador.com.
Attractive hostel in nice surroundings, some rooms with fireplace, heater and private bath, others with shared bath, US$12 pp in dorm, camping US$8 pp, terrace with hammocks, pleasant dining room/lounge, transport information on hostel's website, excursions arranged, popular. Recommended.

$$ Rose Cottage
Vía a Mojanda Km 3, T09-9772 8115, www.rosecottageecuador.com.
Various rooms and prices in 7 separate houses, some with private bath, US$14 pp in dorm, camping US$6 pp (bring your own tent), restaurant, hammocks, good views.

Around Otavalo
Peguche

$$$ La Casa Sol
Near the Cascada de Peguche, T06-269 0500, www.lacasasol.com.
Comfortable rustic construction set on a hillside. Rooms and suites with balcony, some with fireplace, lovely attention to detail, restaurant.

$$ Aya Huma
On the railway line in Peguche, T06-269 0164, www.ayahuma.com.
In a country setting between the railway tracks and the river. Quiet, pleasant atmosphere, kitchen facilities, restaurant for breakfast and dinner, camping (US$4 pp), Dutch/Ecuadorean-run, popular. Recommended.

Lago San Pablo

$$$$-$$$ Puerto Lago
6 km from Otavalo, just off the Panamericana on the west side of the lake, T06-292 0920, www.puertolago.com.
Modern *hostería* in a lovely setting on the lakeshore, good expensive restaurant overlooking the lake, breakfast extra, rooms and suites with fireplace, very hospitable, a good place to watch the sunset, includes the use of row-boats, pedalos and kayaks for 30 mins, other watersports extra. Popular with *Quiteños*.

$$$ Hacienda Cusín
By the village of San Pablo del Lago to the southeast of the lake, T06-291 8013, www.haciendacusin.com.

A converted 17th-century hacienda with lovely courtyard and garden, fine expensive restaurant, rooms with fireplace, sports facilities (horses, bikes, squash court, games room), library, book in advance, British-run.

$$ Green House
C 24 de Junio, Comunidad Araque, by the east shore of the lake, northwest of San Pablo del Lago, T06-291 9298, www.araquebyb.hostel.com.
Family-run *hostal*, some rooms with bath, others with detached bath, dinner on request, sitting room with fireplace, rooftop terrace with views, transport.

Restaurants

Otavalo

$$ Quino
Roca 7-40 y Juan Montalvo.
Tue-Sun 1300-2300, Mon 1730-2300.
Traditional coastal cooking and some meat dishes, pleasant seating around patio.

$$-$ Buena Vista
Salinas entre Sucre y Jaramillo, p2, www.buenavistaotavalo.com. Open 1200-2200, Sat from 0900, closed Tue.
Bistro with balcony overlooking Plaza de Ponchos. Good international food, sandwiches, salads, vegetarian options, trout, good coffee, Wi-Fi.

$$-$ Deli
Quiroga 12-18 y Bolívar. Mon-Fri 1000-2100, Sat 0800-2200.
Good Mexican and international food, also pizza, good desserts, pleasant atmosphere, family-run, good value.

$$-$ Fontana di Trevi
Sucre 12-05 y Salinas, 2nd floor.
Daily 1300-2100.

Overlooking Calle Sucre, pizza and pasta, good juices, very friendly service.

$$-$ Mi Otavalito
Sucre y Morales.
Good for set lunch and international food à la carte.

$$-$ Oraibi
Sucre y Colón. Wed-Sat 0800-2000.
Vegetarian food in nice patio setting, pizza, salads, pasta, Mexican, breakfast, Swiss-owned.

$ Aly Allpa
Salinas 509 at Plaza de Ponchos.
Daily 0730-2030.
Good-value set meals, breakfast and à la carte including trout, vegetarian, meat. Recommended.

Cafés

La Casa de Intag
Colón 465 y Sucre. Mon-Sat 0800-1800.
Fair trade cafeteria/shop run by Intag coffee growers and artisans associations. Good organic coffee, breakfast, pancakes, sandwiches, sisal crafts, fruit pulp and more.

Salinerito
Bolívar 10-08 y Morales. Mon-Sat 0800-2200.
Café/deli run by the Salinas de Guaranda coop. Sandwiches, breakfast, coffee and juices. A good place to buy supplies such as cheese, cold cuts and chocolate.

Shanandoa Pie Shop
Salinas y Jaramillo. Open 1100-2100, Sat from 0900.
Good fruit pies, milk shakes and ice cream, popular meeting place, an Otavalo tradition.

Bars and clubs

Otavalo

Otavalo is generally safe but avoid deserted areas at night. Nightlife is concentrated at Morales y Jaramillo and C 31 de Octubre. Peñas are open Fri-Sat from 1930, entrance US$3.

Fauno
Morales y Jaramillo.
Café/bar, variety of cocktails, snacks.

Peña Amauta
Morales 5-11 y Jaramillo.
Good local bands, welcoming, mainly foreigners.

Festivals

Otavalo

Jun The end of Jun combines the **Inti Raymi** celebrations of the summer solstice (21 Jun), with the **Fiesta de San Juan** (24 Jun) and the **Fiesta de San Pedro y San Pablo** (29 Jun). These combined festivities are known as **Los San Juanes** and participants are mostly indigenous. Most of the action takes place in the smaller communities surrounding Otavalo, each one celebrates separately on different dates, some of them for a full week. The celebration begins with a ritual bath, the Peguche waterfall is used by Otavalo residents (a personal spiritual activity, best carried out without visitors and certainly without cameras). In Otavalo, indigenous families have costume parties, which at times spill over onto the streets. In the San Juan neighbourhood, near the Yanayacu baths, there is a week-long celebration with food, drink and music.

1st 2 weeks of Sep **Fiesta del Yamor** and **Colla Raimi**, feature local dishes,

amusement parks, bands in the plaza and sporting events.

Oct **Mes de la cultura**, cultural events throughout the month. Last Oct weekend, **Mojanda Arriba** is an annual full day hike from Malchinguí over Mojanda to reach Otavalo for the foundation celebrations.

What to do

Otavalo
Horse riding
Several operators offer riding tours. Half-day trips to nearby attractions cost US$25-35. Full-day trips, such as Cuicocha or Mojanda, cost US$40-50.

Language schools
Instituto Superior de Español, *Jaramillo 6-23 y Morales, T06-292 7354, www.instituto-superior.net.*
Mundo Andino Internacional, *Salinas 404 y Bolívar, T06-292 1864, www. mandinospanishschool.com.* Cooking classes and other activities included.
Otavalo Spanish Institute, *31 de Octubre 47-64 y Salinas, p 3, T06-292 1404, www.otavalospanish.com.* Also offers Quichua lessons.

Mountain biking
Several tour operators rent bikes and offer cycling tours for US$35-60 a day trip. See also **Ciclovía**, page 115. Rentals cost US$10-12 per day.
Taller Ciclo Primaxi, *Ricaurte y Morales and in Peguche.*

Tour operators
Most common tours are to indigenous communities, Cuicocha and Mojanda, US$20-30 pp.
All about EQ, *Los Corazas 433 y Albarracín, at the north end of town,*

Ecuadorean ball games

Like in all of Latin America, *fútbol* (football or soccer) is played by young and old throughout Ecuador. In addition, there are a number of traditional ball games which are part of the fabric of the country, either unique to Ecuador or shared with one of its neighbours. It is generally men who play and a fair bit of swearing accompanies the action. In many cases betting among the spectators make the game all the more exciting.

Walk by a park in any city or town in the late afternoon and you will see a crowd cheering around a volleyball court. If you pay close attention, you will see that there are only three players on either side of the court and that the ball is handled in a way not permitted in ordinary volleyball. This is *ecuavolley* or *voli*, Ecuador's very own sport.

A unique form of paddle ball most commonly played in the northern and central highlands is *pelota nacional* (the 'national' ball game), requiring considerable strength. It is also known as *pelota de tabla* (board ball) for its impressive paddles or *tablas*. A 1-m-long square wooden paddle with rubber spikes weighing about 1.5 kg is used for batting and another, up to 6 kg, for returning the heavy natural rubber ball. The paddle is secured to the forearm with a leather glove. There are five players on either side of the court and the rules are like those of tennis. *Pelota nacional* is played in the afternoons in the Yacucalle neighbourhood of Ibarra, south of the bus station, and in Quito on weekends at Parque La Carolina and in the southern neighbourhoods of Mena 2 and Quito Sur.

A similar game, also played in the north is *pelota de guante* (glove ball), where the 'glove' is really a wooden disk around 35 cm in diameter, covered in leather and studded with thick nails on one surface. Also similar is *pelota de mano* (hand ball), where a rubber or leather ball is struck with the hand.

Bolas is yet another popular game. The term refers to marbles, also known as *canicas*. These are placed inside a circle and each player tries to hit the opponent's pieces. In a similar fashion, large steel balls (*bolas de acero*) are propelled from about 50 m away to a court with an inner circle of small balls or palm fruits (*coquitos*). This game called *bolas* or *cocos*, is played in the central highlands and in Quito at Parque El Ejido.

T06-292 3633, www.all-about-ecuador. com. Interesting itineraries, trekking and horse riding tours, climbing, cycling, trips to Intag, Piñán, Cayambe, Oyacachi, volunteering on organic farms. English and French spoken. Recommended.
Ecomontes, *Sucre y Morales*, T06-292 6244, www.ecomontestour.com. A branch of a Quito operator, trekking, climbing, rafting, also sell tours to Cuyabeno and Galápagos.
Runa Tupari, *Sucre y Quito*, T06-292 2320, www.runatupari.com. Arranges indigenous homestays in the Cotacachi area, also the usual tours, trekking, horse riding and cycling trips and transport.

Train rides

Beautifully restored historic train station at Guayaquil y J Montalvo, T06-292 8172, www.trenecuador.com, Wed-Sat 0800-1300, 1400-1700, Sun 0800-1300. Combined train/bus day trips to Salinas 57 km away cost US$50.40. 2 similar itineraries include lunch. On Fri and Sat, departure by bus at 1015 and return by train ending at 1815, includes stops at Textil Imbabura, Lake Yahuarcocha, Salinas (brief) and San Antonio de Ibarra. Sat and Sun, departure by train at 0800, return by bus ending at 1615, stops at Textil Imbabura, Yachay, Salinas (including Museo de la Sal) and San Antonio de Ibarra. You can continue by bus from Salinas to **San Lorenzo**, see page 280.

Transport

Otavalo

Note Never leave anything in your car or taxi in the street. There are public car parks at Juan Montalvo y Sucre, by Parque Bolívar, and on Quito between 31 de Octubre and Jaramillo.

Bus Terminal at Atahualpa y Ordóñez (no departures after 1830). To **Quito** 2 hrs, US$2.50, every 10 mins; all depart from Terminal Carcelén in Quito, **Coop Otavalo** and **Coop Los Lagos** go into Otavalo, buses bound for Ibarra or Tulcán drop you off at the highway, this is inconvenient and not safe at night. From **Quito** or airport by taxi takes 1½ hrs, US$60 one way; shared taxis with **Taxis Lagos/Serviquito,** in Quito, Asunción Oe2-146 y Versalles, T02-256 5992; in Otavalo, Av Los Sarances y Panamericana, T06-292 3203, who run a hotel to hotel service (to/from modern Quito only) and will divert to resorts just off the highway; Mon-Sat hourly, 5 departures on Sun, 1½ hrs, US$15 pp, buy ticket at least 1 day before, they also go from Quito to Ibarra. Tour operators also offer transfers. Bus to **Ibarra**, every 4 mins, US$0.60, 40 mins. To **Peguche**, city bus on Av Atahualpa, every 10 mins, bus stops in front of the terminal and at Plaza Copacabana, US$0.25. To the **Intag region**, 5 daily.

Lago San Pablo

Bus From **Otavalo** to San Pablo del Lago every 25 mins, more often on Sat, US$0.25, 30 mins; taxi US$4. Also buses to many nearby communities.

Northwest of Otavalo is Cotacachi, a leatherworking town, from where a road goes west to the Cotacachi Cayapas reserve and the subtropical Intag region, with its lush cloudforested valleys, known for its coffee and its activism.

Cotacachi *Colour map 1, B5.*

West of the road between Otavalo and Ibarra is Cotacachi (population 17,700, altitude 2440 m), home to a growing expatriate community. Leather goods are made and sold here. There is also access along a secondary road from Otavalo through Quiroga. The **Casa de las Culturas** ① *Bolívar 1334 y 9 de Octubre*, a beautifully refurbished 19th-century building is a monument to peace. It houses the post office, a library, gallery and radio station. The **Museo de las Culturas** ① *García Moreno 13-41 y Bolívar, T06-255 4155, Mon-Fri 0800-1300, 1400-1700, Sat-Sun 0930-1400, free*, has good displays of early Ecuadorean history and regional crafts and traditions.

For information, contact **iTur Turec** ① *at Centro de Convenciones El Convento, García Moreno 13-66 y Sucre, T06-255 4122, Facebook: turecturismocotacachi for upcoming events, Mon-Fri 0900-1700, Sat 0900-1500*, run by an association of handicapped persons, offers a map, regional information, tours, rides on horse-drawn carriages and chivas (both with advanced reservations); also rents camping equipment and bicycles (US$2/hour). On the same premises are a restaurant and cafeteria. Additional tourist information in Spanish and a city map are found in www.cotacachi.gob.ec. Local festivals include **Inti Raymi/San Juan** in June and **Jora** during the September equinox.

Reserva Ecológica Cotacachi Cayapas

To the west of the town of Cotacachi is the scenic Cotacachi Cayapas reserve which extends from Laguna Cuicocha and the Cotacachi Volcano to the tropical lowlands on the Río Cayapas in Esmeraldas. The Cuicocha highland area of the reserve can be easily accessed along a paved road, via Quiroga, from either Cotacachi or Otavalo. The Piñán lakes region further north is accessed from Cuellaje, in the Intag region (see page 126) and Urcuquí, northwest of Ibarra (see page 132). The lowland area is reached from San Miguel (see page 279).

The lovely crater lake of ★ **Laguna Cuicocha** sits at the foot of Cotacachi Volcano at an altitude of 3070 m, and is a popular place for a Sunday outing. The visitors' centre has good natural history and cultural displays. The lake's two islands are closed to the public to protect the native species. There is a pier and a *hostería* on the east shore of the lake. Motor boat rides around the islands cost US$3.25 per person for a minimum of eight people.

There is a well-marked 8-km path around the lake, which takes four to five hours and provides spectacular views of the Cotacachi, Imbabura and, occasionally Cayambe peaks. The best views are to be had in the early morning, when condors can sometimes be seen. There is a lookout at Km 3, two hours from the start. It's best to do the route in an anticlockwise direction. Take water and a waterproof jacket. The trail ends above the southwest shore, from where you have to walk on the road 4 km back to the park entrance. There is a shorter trail near the entrance featuring sacred places around the lake, visited with community guides, contact Antonio Morales, T09-9763 1568. At **Cabañas Mirador** (above the pier) you can get a meal and transport back to Quiroga, Cotacachi or Otavalo. **Warnings** Do not eat the berries which grow near the lake, as some are poisonous. The path around the lake is not for vertigo sufferers.

The three-hour walk from the lake to the town of Cotacachi is beautiful. After 1 km on the road from the park entrance, turn left (at the first bend) on to a secondary road. You can also walk to Otavalo, following the paved road to Quiroga and the secondary road from there.

To the north of Laguna Cuicocha and also within the reserve is the ragged peak of **Cotacachi Volcano** (4944 m). This beautiful mountain, often sprinkled with snow, is best admired from the pier side of Cuicocha. The road at the entrance to the park continues from Cuicocha to some antennas on the eastern flank of the mountain; this side is often shrouded in mist. To climb, it is best approached from the ridge to the west. It is a demanding climb and at the top there is dangerous loose rock. Climbing tours to Cotacachi are available through Otavalo agencies.

Intag region

To the northwest of Otavalo lies the lush subtropical region of Intag, named after the Intag River. Beautiful cloudforest-clad ridges separated by rushing rivers drop from the slopes of Volcán Cotacachi towards the western lowlands. One access to this area is along the road that follows the southern edge of Cuicocha, crosses the Cordillera Occidental and gradually descends to the southwest. This road is being paved in 2015. The area is also accessed by the road which goes from Otavalo to **Selva Alegre**, paved as far as Km 30. These roads meet at Aguagrun, from where a road goes to Chontal and further to the Río Guayllabamba Valley, where it connects with roads going to the Noroccidente, northwest of Quito.

Several reserves were created in the area to protect its rich cloudforests. **Intag Tours** ⓘ *at the Nangulví baths (see below)*, T06-301 6135, www.intagtours.com, part of the Red de Ecoturismo de Intag (REI), offers tours, adventure sports and arranges lodging in several Intag communities.

Santa Rosa and around The hamlet of **Santa Rosa**, 35 km from Cuicocha, is at the heart of several reserves. There is a women's cooperative, their attractive *cabuya* (sisal) wares are sold in town, and lodging nearby. A trail goes from the village towards the south to the hamlet of **Plaza Gutiérrez** and beyond; along it are several reserves good for birdwatching and other nature observation. Less than 1 km from Santa Rosa along this trail is **El Refugio de Intag** ⓘ *www.elrefugiocloudforest.com*, a 30-ha property by the Río Toabunchi with forest at about 1800 m. There is lodging (see Where to stay) and trails along the river and through the forest to a lookout. Further along the main trail are the

350-ha **La Florida Reserve** and 120-ha **Intag Cloud Forest Reserve** ⓘ *1-hr walk from Santa Rosa, T06-304 8861, toisan06@gmail.com, www.intagcloudforest. com, advanced reservations required, day visit US$10*, with primary cloudforest at 1800-2800 m.

Just east of Santa Rosa, a poor road runs north. This is the access to the 2500-ha **Reserva Alto Chocó** ⓘ *1-km walk from the turn-off*, on the left, between 1800 m and 4000 m; and to **Reserva Siempre Verde** ⓘ *30 mins by 4WD from the turnoff, go right at the bifurcation, www.siempreverde.org, day visit US$10*, a 334-ha reserve between 1900 m and 3350 m, along the upper Río Toabunchí, which receives student groups. On the main road, about 10 minutes past Santa Rosa before reaching the hamlet of Pucará, a turn to the left leads to **Reserva Puranquí**.

Apuela to Cuellaje **Apuela** is a small town 46 km from Cuicocha. The region's cloudforest is threatened by proposed mining projects, vigorously opposed by local communities. See **Defensa y Conservación Ecológica de Intag (Decoin)** ⓘ *on the main street, T06-301 6208, www.decoin.org*, for local conservation and community development projects. The area's rivers will also be affected by an irrigation and hydroelectric scheme in the Piñán area, see Northwest of Ibarra, page 132. The **Asociación Agroartesanal de Café Río Intag (AACRI)** ⓘ *at the end of the street parallel to the main street, T06-256 6029, www.aacri.com*, a fair trade organic coffee growers' association, offers tours of coffee plantations and processing plants in the region, coffee tasting, and volunteer opportunities.

After crossing the Río Apuela, some 800 m beyond the town, a secondary road goes north to Pueblo Viejo (3 Km) and **Cuellaje** (5 km further); nearby farms offer tours and lodging (see Where to stay, below). From Cuellaje, the road continues north 14 km to El Rosario, from where a trail leads to Lagunas de Piñán in **Reserva Ecológica Cotacachi-Cayapas**. It is about five to six hours' walking to Laguna Donoso and a further two hours to the village of Piñán, see page 132.

Another secondary road starts 2 km further along the main road from Apuela and leads to Peñaherrera (2 km) and on to Cuellaje (7 km further). Near the start of this road is the access to the **Tolas de Gualimán archaeological site** ⓘ *25-min walk from the main road, T06-301 6226, www.turgw.com, entry US$2, 0800-1900 daily*, within an 87-ha farm, on a plateau above the Río Intag. The site has 38 *tolas* from the Cara culture, carbon dated to around 760 BC; the largest is a truncated pyramid with a ramp, similar to those found in Cochasquí (see page 109), 187 m long and 41 m high. There is an on-site museum, trails to waterfalls and lookouts, guided walks, restaurant, lodging, camping, lovely views and a 800-m-long canopy zipline which crosses the Intag River, 320 m above the canyon.

The main road from Apuela continues south to the pleasant thermal baths of **Nangulví** ⓘ *5 km from Apuela, daily 0630-2030, US$3*, busy at weekends. There are five hot pools and one large cold one for plunging and lodging. The area is relaxed and pleasant for walking, with a waterfall one hour away. Beyond Nangulví, the main road continues southwest to **Aguagrun**, where it meets the road Otavalo road coming from **García Moreno**.

Junín Cloud Forest Reserve ⓘ *T09-8887 1860 (Rosario Piedra), T06-305 0922 (Polivio Pérez), volunteer opportunities.* Beyond Aguagrun, Junín Cloud Forest Reserve is an 800-ha forest reserve at 1500-2000 m. The local community is trying ecotourism as an alternative to forest destruction and has a lodge ($$ full board), which includes a guided hike to waterfalls. It is reached from either García Moreno or Chontal Bajo, the roads can be poor in the rainy season (worst January to April), so buses go further in the dry. There are good walking possibilities, including a trail to Los Cedros (see below). The scenery is lovely, with forest and waterfalls. For 20 years, the community of Junín has been involved in an ongoing struggle to prevent a large scale open-pit copper mine in this area. Their ecotourism project helps protect this lovely region. In 2015, the Ecuadorean government company Enami, with the Chilean Codelco, have started exploration. For current information regarding the mining threat see www.decoin.org.

Los Cedros Research Station ⓘ *2 hrs' walk from the road, T02-361 2546, T09-9277 8878, www.reservaloscedros.org, reservations necessary, full board in $$$ range, volunteer programme, minimum stay 1 month.* On the southwest boundary of Reserva Ecológica Cotacachi-Cayapas, Los Cedros Research Station has 6400 ha of pristine cloudforest, famous for the number of new orchid species discovered there. Birdlife is also abundant and large species are more common and less shy than in other places. Access to the station is from **Chontal,** a one-hour drive from García Moreno, or Magdalena Alto (not on the main road). Near Chontal is the community-owned 6000-ha **Reserva El Chontal**; for their tourism programme contact T06-305 1108. Further on are Magdalena, Manduriacos, where a hydroelectric dam was completed in 2015, and Cielo Verde. These communities work together in sustainable agriculture and ecotourism, for information contact T06-305 1151. From Cielo Verde a road goes to Pedro Vicente Maldonado, see page 99.

Listings West of Otavalo

Where to stay

Cotacachi

$$$$ La Mirage
500 m west of town, T06-291 5237, www.mirage.com.ec (see map, page 114).
Luxurious converted hacienda with elegant suites and common areas, includes breakfast and dinner, excellent restaurant, pool, gym and spa (treatments extra), beautiful gardens, tours arranged.

$$$-$$ Land of Sun
García Moreno 1376 y Sucre, T06-291 6009 (see map, page 114).
Refurbished colonial house in the heart of town, rooms with balcony, internal ones are cheaper, breakfast served in lovely patio, local specialities in restaurant, request dinner in advance, sauna, parking. Recommended.

$$ Runa Tupari
A system of homestays in nearby villages.
Visitors experience life with an indigenous family by taking part in daily

activities. The comfortable rooms have space for 3, fireplace, bathroom and hot shower, and cost US$35 pp including breakfast, dinner and transport from Otavalo. Arrange with **Runa Tupari**, www.runatupari.com, or other Otavalo tour operators.

$$-$ La Cuadra
Peñaherrera 11-46 y González Suárez, T06-291 6015, www.lacuadra-hostal. com.
Modern comfortable rooms, good mattresses, private or shared bath, no breakfast, kitchen facilities.

$ Bachita
Sucre 16-82 y Peñaherrera, T06-291 5063.
Simple place, private or shared bath, no breakfast, quiet.

Reserva Ecológica Cotacachi Cayapas

$$$ Hostería Cuicocha
Laguna Cuicocha, by the pier, T06-301 7218, www.cuicocha.org (see map, page 114).
Rooms overlooking the lake, internal ones are cheaper, includes breakfast and dinner, restaurant.

$$-$ Cabañas Mirador
On a lookout above the Cuicocha pier, follow the trail or by car follow the road to the left of the park entrance, T09-9055 8367, miradordecuicocha@yahoo.com (see map, page 114).
Rustic cabins with fireplace and modern rooms overlooking the lake, good economical restaurant, trout is the speciality, parking, transport provided to Quiroga (US$5), Cotacachi (US$5), or Otavalo (US$10); owner Ernesto Cevillano is knowledgeable about the area and arranges trips.

Intag region

$$$ El Refugio de Intag
Near Santa Rosa (see reserve description), intagcloud@gmail.com, www.elrefugiocloudforest.com.
3 guesthouses with porches, sitting room and dining room, comfortable rooms, price includes breakfast, other meals extra, rooms upstairs have good views of Cotacachi Volcano. Good birdwatching.

$$ Cabañas Río Grande
In Nangulví, next to the baths, T06-301 5629.
Comfortable log cabins with 2 rooms for 4 each (price is per room), restaurant, private bath, small thermal pool and larger cold-water pool, discounts in low season, reserve ahead.

$$ Complejo Ecoturístico Nangulví
At the municipal baths, T06-305 2024.
Simple cabins for 3 or 4, includes entry to the baths, riverside restaurant, also packages with full board, 1 wheelchair accessible cabin.

$$ Finca Río Lindo
1 km from Cuellaje towards Pueblo Viejo, T06-305-1987 or T06-292 3883 (Otavalo), suarezivan@hotmail.com.
Lodge in a farm, double rooms with shared bath, full board included, lovely gardens, orchid trail, birdwatching, coffee plantation and organic garden tours, walks in cloudforest reserve, treks to Piñán Lakes, day visits possible, stay can be part of a longer tour in Ecuador. Reserve ahead.

$$-$ Cabañas Flor de la Montaña
3 km past Apuela, before the Peñaherrera turnoff, T06-301 5715 or T06-292 2086.
Cabins with bath and hot water,

breakfast and economical set meals available.

$ Pradera Tropical
In Apuela, near the school.
Rustic basic cabins for 3, private bath, hot water, friendly knowledgeable owner.

Restaurants

Cotacachi
A local speciality is *carne colorada* (spiced pork).

$$ D'Anita
10 de Agosto, y Moncayo.
Daily 0800-2100.
Good set meal of the day, local and international dishes à la carte, popular, English spoken, good value.

$$-$ La Marqueza
10 de Agosto y Bolívar. Daily 0730-2130.
Set lunches and à la carte.

Café Río Intag
On Plaza San Francisco. Mon-Fri 0800-2000, Sat 1000-2200, Sun 1000-1800.
The best coffee, snacks, meeting place.

Transport

Cotacachi
Bus Terminal at 10 de Agosto y Salinas by the market. Every 10 mins to/from Otavalo terminal, US$0.25, 25 mins; service alternates between the Panamericana and the Quiroga roads. To **Ibarra**, every 15 mins, US$0.50, 40 mins; service alternates between the Panamericana and Imantag roads.

Reserva Ecológica Cotacachi Cayapas
Pickups To Laguna Cuicocha from **Otavalo** US$10. From **Cotacachi**, US$5 one way, US$10 return with short wait.

From **Quiroga** US$5. Return service from the lake available from **Cabañas El Mirador**, same rates.

Intag region
Bus From **Otavalo**, **Trans Otavalo** to Apuela, García Moreno, Chontal and Magdalena Bajo, daily at 0730, 1000, 1400 and 1600; The 1000 and 1600 buses continue to Cielo Verde on a road to PV Maldonado. To **Apuela**, US$2.50, 2 hrs. To **Nangulví**, US$2.85, 2¼ hrs. To **García Moreno**, US$3.50, 4 hrs. To **Chontal** US$4.40, 4 hrs. To **Magdalena Bajo** US$4.70, 4½ hrs. To **Cielo Verde**, US$5.35, 6 hrs. There is also service to Chontal from Quito, see page 105. **Trans 6 de Julio** to **Barcelona** (turn-off past Nangulví) Tue, Thu, Sat, Sun at 1200, US$4, 3-4 hrs. To **Peñaherrera**, **Trans Otavalo** at 1300 and **Trans 6 de Julio** at 1500, US$2.85, 3 hrs; the 1300 continues to **Cuellaje**, US$3.25, 3½ hrs. For **Junín**, take a bus to García Moreno, from there, on weekdays during the school year, a *ranchera* goes to Junín at 1400, US$2; or take a pickup, US$20, 1 hr. Junín is also reached from Chontal, pick up US$25, 1½ hrs. For **Los Cedros**, the access to the reserve is near Magdalena Alto. From Quito, take a bus to Chontal, see above. It is a 20-min ride (US$8 by pickup) or 2-hr walk from Chontal to the station's access, from where it is a 2-hr walk to the lodge; arrange with the station for donkeys to ride or carry luggage up. If coming from Otavalo, get off at Chontal or from Magdalena Bajo, you might be able to get a pickup (about US$4) to Los Cedros access.

a good base for visiting craft villages and hot springs

From Otavalo, the main highway goes north to the city of Ibarra and beyond into the hot Chota Valley from where a branch road goes west to the subtropical valley of the Río Mira and the coastal town of San Lorenzo.

Ibarra

Ibarra (population 137,000, altitude 2225 m), the provincial capital, is the main commercial centre and transport hub of the northern highlands. The city has an interesting ethnic mix, with blacks from the Chota Valley and Esmeraldas alongside Otavaleños and other highland *indígenas*, mestizos and Colombian immigrants. The **Virgen del Carmen** festival is on 16 July and **Fiesta de los Lagos** is in the last weekend of September. A speciality of the town is ★ **helados de paila** – delicious fresh fruit sorbets made in a copper kettle.

Ibarra

Where to stay 🛏	Restaurants 🍴	8 La Casona Ibarreña
1 Fran's Hostal	1 Café Arte	9 Olor a Café
2 Hacienda Chorlaví	2 Café Pushkin	
3 Hacienda Pimán	3 Caribou	
4 La Estelita	4 Casa Blanca	
5 Las Garzas	5 El Argentino	
6 Montecarlo	6 El Quinde Café	
7 Royal Ruiz	7 Heladería Rosalía Suárez	

N

100 metres
100 yards

On **Parque Pedro Moncayo** stand the Cathedral, the Municipio and Gobernación. One block away, at Flores y Olmedo, is the smaller Parque 9 de Octubre or **Parque de la Merced** after its church. Beyond the railway station, to the south and west of the centre, is a busy commercial area with several markets beyond which is the bus terminal. At the Centro Cultural Ibarra, the **Museo Regional Sierra Norte** ⓘ *Sucre 7-21 y Oviedo, T06-260 2093, Tue-Fri, 0900-1630, Sat-Sun and holidays 1000-1600,* has interesting archaeological displays about cultures of northern Ecuador, colonial and contemporary art and temporary exhibits.

Bosque Protector Guayabillas ⓘ *Urbanización La Victoria, on the eastern outskirts of town, www.guayabillas.com, Tue-Sun 0900-1700,* is a 54-ha park on a hill overlooking the city, which offers great views. There are trails amid the **eucalyptus forest**.

Around Ibarra

Off the main road between Otavalo and Ibarra is **San Antonio de Ibarra**, well known for its woodcarvings. It is worth seeing the range of styles and techniques and shopping around in the galleries and workshops. Further west is the town of **Atuntaqui**. On the opposite side of the Panamericana and along the rail line is Andrade Marín, home of the **Museo Fábrica Textil Imbabura** ⓘ *T06-253 0240, Wed-Sun 0900-1600, US$3, knowledgeable guides,* a good display of machinery of the most important producer and employer in the area between1926 and1966; included in train tours.

East of town, **Laguna Yahuarcocha** is a popular weekend recreation spot for Ibarreños who go to paddle on the lake, ride a bike, eat tilapia, or party at one of the clubs; city bus from Rocafuerte y Oviedo. Several *hosterías* offer lodging and meals, they are quiet midweek, there is also a campground (See Where to stay, below) and many food stalls. The beauty of the lake however, has been disfigured by the building of two motor racing circuits around its shores. The smaller one is closed to vehicles and used by cyclists. The lake is gradually drying up with totora reeds encroaching on its margins. They are woven into *esteras* (mats) and sold in huge rolls at the roadside. Reed boats can sometimes be seen. The lively weekend atmosphere at the lake hides its more somber past. Yahuarcocha means 'blood lake', and was the site of a decisive battle which the Incas won over the native Caranquis, a nation which resisted the Inca conquest for a long time. It is possible to walk along paths and back roads from Ibarra to Yahuarcocha in about 1½ hours (4 km), with nice views along the way. You can also walk from the lake to San Miguel Arcángel, on a hill to the east of the lake. Nearby is an unexplored archaeological site with tolas (mounds). To get there, take the San Miguel bus from the Mercado Mayorista, on Troya y Roldós.

About 8 km from Ibarra on the road south to Olmedo is **La Esperanza**, a pretty village in beautiful surroundings. Some 15 km further along, by Angochagua is the community of **Zuleta**. The region is known for its fine embroidery. West of La Esperanza, along a road that starts at Avenida Atahualpa, and also 8 km from Ibarra, is the community of **San Clemente**, which has a very good grassroots tourism project, **Pukyu Pamba**, www.sclemente.com; see Where to stay, below.

From either La Esperanza or San Clemente you can climb **Cubilche** volcano and **Imbabura**, more easily than from San Pablo del Lago. From the top you can walk down to Lago San Pablo (see page 116). *Guías nativos* are available for these climbs.

Ibarra to the coast

The spectacular train ride from Ibarra to San Lorenzo on the Pacific coast no longer operates. A tourist train runs on a small section of this route, see pages 123 and 137.

Some 24 km north of Ibarra is the turn-off west for **Salinas**, a mainly Afro-Ecuadorean village with a Museo de la Sal, an ethnographic cultural centre and a restaurant offering local cuisine, and the very scenic road beside the Río Mira down to San Lorenzo. At 41 km from the turn-off are the villages of **Guallupe**, **El Limonal** (see Where to stay, below), and **San Juan de Lachas**, in a lush subtropical area. Ceramic masks and figurines are produced at the latter, from where a road goes northeast 8 km to **Gualchán**. Here it divides, one branch going north to Chical, by the Colombian border, the second continuing northeast to Las Juntas, in an area with waterfalls. This is one of the access points to **Cerro Golondrinas Cloudforest** ⓘ *www.fgolondrinas.org, simple cabins 1- to 4-hr walk from Las Juntas*, a lovely cloudforest reserve near Reserva Ecológica El Angel, see below.

In **Lita**, 33 km from Guallupe, there is nice swimming in the river. Beyond is the Río Chuchubi with waterfalls and swimming holes; here is **Las Siete Cascadas resort** ⓘ *entry US$10, guide US$10 per group*, (see Where to stay, below). It is 66 km from Lita to **Calderón**, where this road meets the coastal highway coming from Esmeraldas. Two kilometres before the junction, on the Río Tululbí, is **Hostería Tunda Loma** (see Where to stay, page 282). About 7 km beyond is San Lorenzo (see page 280).

Northwest of Ibarra

Along a secondary road to the northwest of Ibarra is the town of **Urcuquí** with a basic hotel. Nearby is **Yachay**, a university and national research and technology centre, in an attractive historic hacienda. From just south of Urcuquí, a road leads via Irunguicho towards the **Lagunas de Piñán**, a beautiful, remote, high *páramo* region, part of the Reserva Ecológica Cotacachi-Cayapas. The local community of **Piñán** (3112 m) has a tourism programme (www.pinantrek.com), with a well-equipped refuge (US$12 per person, meals available), *guías nativos* (US$15 per day) and muleteers (US$12 per day, per horse). Another access to the hamlet of Piñán is via La Merced de Buenos Aires, a village reached from either Tumbabiro (see below) or San Gerónimo, near Guallupe (on the road to the coast). Along the Tumbabiro, access is via the community of Sachapamba, where muleteers and meals can be found. The nicest lakes, Donoso and Caricocha, are one-hour walk from the community. They can also be reached walking from Chachimbiro (see below), Irubí or Cuellaje in the Intag area. Otavalo agencies and hotels in Chachimbiro and Tumbabiro also offer trekking tours to Piñán. Note that a proposed irrigation and hydroelectric scheme will affect this beautiful area.

Beyond Urcuquí is the friendly town of **Tumbabiro**, with a mild climate, a good base from which to explore this region (several lodgings, see Where to stay page 135); it can also be reached from Salinas on the road to the coast. Some 8 km from Tumbabiro along a side road, set on the slopes of an extinct volcano, is **Chachimbiro**, a good area for walking and horse riding, with several resorts with thermal baths (see Where to stay, page 135). The largest one, run by the provincial government, is **Santa Agua Chachimbiro** ① *T06-264 8308, www.santagua.com.ec, 0700-2000, entry to recreational pools US$5, to medicinal pools and spa US$10,* with several hot mineral pools, lodging, restaurants, zipline and horses for riding; weekends can be crowded.

Listings Ibarra and around *map p28*

Tourist information

Ibarra

The website www.rutadelconocimiento.com (in Spanish) is also useful.

Dirección de Turismo de Imbabura
García Moreno esquina Sucre, T06-295 5225, ext 4286. Mon-Fri 0800-1645.
Provides regional information and a map, and a guide to community tourism opportunities. It also offer tours to regional attractions, see page 136.

Dirección de Turismo del Municipio
Sucre y Oviedo, T06-260 8489, www. touribarra.gob.ec. Mon-Fri 0800-1230, 1400-1730, holidays 0900-1500.
Provides a city map and pamphlets, English spoken. Free Wi-Fi.

Where to stay

Ibarra

$$$$ Hacienda Pimán
9 km northeast of town, Quito T02-256 6090, www.haciendapiman.com.
Luxuriously restored 18th-century hacienda, price includes breakfast and dinner. All-inclusive 2- and 3-day packages with a train ride and visit to El Angel Reserve.

$$$ Hacienda Chorlaví
Panamericana Sur Km 4, T06-293 2222, www.haciendachorlavi.com.
In a historical hacienda dating to 1620, comfortable rooms, very good expensive restaurant, excellent *parrillada*, pool and spa, parking, busy on weekends, folk music and crafts on Sat.

$$$ La Estelita
Km 5 Vía a Yuracrucito, T09-9811 6058.
Modern hotel 5 km from the city on a hill overlooking town and Laguna Yahuarcocha. Rooms and suites with lovely views, good restaurant, pool, spa, can arrange paragliding.

$$ Montecarlo
Av Jaime Rivadeneira 5-61 y Oviedo, near the obelisk, T06-295 8266, www. hotelmontecarloibarra.ec.
Comfortable rooms, buffet breakfast, restaurant, heated pool open at weekends, parking.

$$ Royal Ruiz
Olmedo 9-40 y P Moncayo, T06-264 4653, www.hotelroyalruiz.com.
Modern, comfortable carpeted rooms, restaurant, solar heated water, parking, long-stay discounts.

$$-$ Finca Sommerwind
Autopista Yahuarcocha Km 8, T09-3937
1177, www.finca-sommerwind.com.
A 12-ha ranch by Laguna Yahuarcocha
with cabins and campground, US$3 pp
in tent, US$5 pp for camper vans,
electricity, hot shower, laundry facilities.

$ Fran's Hostal
Gral Julio Andrade 1-58 y Rafael Larrea,
near bus terminal, T06-260 9995.
Multi-storey hotel, bright functional
rooms, no breakfast, parking.

$ Las Garzas
Flores 3-13 y Salinas, T06-295 0985.
Simple comfortable rooms, no breakfast,
sitting room.

Around Ibarra

$$$$ Hacienda Zuleta
By Angochahua, along the Ibarra–
Cayambe road, T06-266 2232/2182, Quito
T02-603 6874, www.haciendazuleta.com.
A 2000-ha working historic hacienda,
among the nicest in the country.
Superb accommodation and food,
15 rooms with fireplace, price includes
all meals (prepared with organic
vegetables, trout and dairy produced
on the farm) and excursions, advance
reservations required.

$$$ Pukyu Pamba
In San Clemente, T09-9916 1095,
www.sanclementetours.com.
Part of a community-run program.
Cottages with hot water on family
properties, cheaper in more humble
family homes, price includes 3 tasty
meals and a guided tour, you are
expected to participate in the family's
activities. Horses and *guías nativos*
available for more extended treks and
visits to other communities.

$$ Casa Aída
In La Esperanza village, T06-266 0221.
Simple rooms with good beds, includes
dinner and breakfast, restaurant, shared
bath, hot water, patios, some English
spoken, meeting place for climbing
Imbabura.

Ibarra to the coast

$$$ Las Siete Cascadas
Km 111, 15 km past Lita, T09-8261 1195,
lily_tarupi@hotmail.com.
A-frame cabins with balconies in a
204-ha reserve, price includes full
board and excursions to waterfalls
and the forest, reserve well ahead.

$$-$ Parque Bambú
*In El Limonal, about 600 m uphill from
the main square, T06-301 6606, www.
bospas.org.*
Family-run farm with splendid views of
the valley and many birds. Private rooms
with terrace, US$14 pp in dorm, good
breakfast, tasty meals available, camping
U$3 pp, trekking. Run by Belgian Piet
Sabbe, a permaculture landscape
designer, and his daughters; Piet will
share his knowledge and experience in
landscape restoration and welcomes
volunteers with a green thumb (arrange
ahead). Recommended.

Northwest of Ibarra

$$$ Aguasavia
*In Chachimbiro, 15-min walk from Santa
Agua complex, T06-304 8347, info@
aguasavia.com, on Facebook.*
Community-run modern hotel in a
beautiful setting in the crater of La Viuda
Volcano, includes 3 meals, rooms on
ground floor with jacuzzi, thermal
pools, trips.

$$$ Hacienda San Francisco
*In the community of San Francisco,
5 km past Tumbabiro on the road to
Chachimbiro, T06-304 8232, www.
hosteriasanfrancisco.com.*
Intimate family-run inn in tastefully
converted hacienda stables, includes
breakfast, expensive restaurant, full-
board packages available, small thermal
pool, nice grounds, good walking, horse
riding, tennis court, excursions to Piñán,
best Thu to Sun when owners are in.

$$$ Santa Agua Chachimbiro
*Part of the recreational complex,
T06-264 8063, in Ibarra T06-261 0250,
www.santagua.com.ec.*

Rooms and cabins (some with jacuzzi),
includes 3 meals and access to spa and
pools, restaurant, busy on weekends,
reserve ahead.

$$$-$$ Hostería Spa Pantaví
*7 km from Salinas, at the entrance
to Tumbabiro, T06-293 4185, Quito
reservations T02-234 0601, www.
hosteriapantavi.com.*
Stylish inn in a tastefully restored
hacienda. Very comfortable rooms,
decorated with the owner's original
works of art, includes nice breakfast,
good restaurant, pool, spa, jacuzzi,
pleasant gardens, attentive service,
bikes and horses for rent, tours.
Recommended.

$ Tío Lauro
*1 block from plaza, Tumbabiro,
T06-293 4148.*
Nice *residencial*, simple rooms, meals on
request, parking, friendly owner.

Restaurants

Ibarra

$$ Caribou
*Pérez Guerrero 537 entre Bolívar y
Sucre and in Yacucalle south of the bus
terminal, T06-260 5137. Mon 1700-2300,
Tue-Thu 1300-2300, Fri-Sat 1300-0030.*
Excellent meat specialities including
burgers, salads, bar, Canadian-owned.
Recommended.

$$ El Argentino
*Sucre y P Moncayo, at Plazoleta Francisco
Calderón. Tue-Sun.*
Good mixed grill and salads, small,
pleasant, outdoor seating.

$$-$ La Casona Ibarreña
Bolívar 6-47 y Oviedo. Daily.
In an attractive colonial patio,
international, seafood and local
dishes, also set lunch.

$ Casa Blanca
Bolívar 7-83. Closed Sun.
Family-run, in colonial house with
patio, good set lunches and snacks.
Recommended.

Cafés and heladerías

Café Arte
Salinas 5-43 y Oviedo. Daily from 1700.
Café-bar with character, drinks,
Mexican snacks, sandwiches, live
music Fri-Sat night.

Café Pushkin
Olmedo y Oviedo. Open 0700-1700.
For breakfast, snacks, coffee. An Ibarra
classic, very popular.

El Quinde Café
Sucre 562 y Flores.
A good place for breakfast, coffee,
cake, snacks.

Heladería Rosalía Suárez
Oviedo y Olmedo.
Excellent homemade *helados de paila*
(fruit sherbets made in large copper
basins), an Ibarra tradition since 1896.
Highly recommended.

Olor a Café
Flores y Bolívar.
Café/bar/cultural centre in an historic
home, music, library.

Bars and clubs

Ibarra
Plazoleta Francisco Calderón on Sucre
y Pedro Moncayo, has several café-bars
with outdoor seating and a pleasant
atmosphere.

Rincón de Ayer
Olmedo 9-59.
A bar with lots of character, attractively
restored.

Sambuca
Oviedo 636 y Sucre.
Bar/club, the in-place among Ibarreño
youth.

What to do

Ibarra
Paragliding
Fly Ecuador, *T06-295 3297 or T09-8487
5577, www.flyecuador.com.ec.* Tandem
flight US$67-90, course US$448,
arrange ahead.

Pelota nacional
A unique form of paddle ball, pelota
nacional, is played in the afternoon
at Yacucalle, south of the bus station.
Players have huge studded paddles for
striking the 1-kg ball.

Tour operators
EcuaHorizons, *Bolívar 4-67 y García
Moreno, T06-295 9904.* Bilingual guides
for regional tours.
Intipungo, *Rocafuerte 6-08 y Flores, T06-
295 7766.* Regional tours.
Ruta del Conocimiento, *www.
rutadelconocimiento.com (in Spanish).*
The **Dirección de Turismo de Imbabura**
(see Tourist information, page 133),
runs a choice of 6-day trips (US$25) and
a 2-day trip (US$75 including lodging

in a rural community), taking in the regional attractions.

Train rides

A tourist train runs from Ibarra to **Salinas**, 29 km away, Wed-Sun and holidays at 1030, returning 1600, US$15-20 one way, US$20-25 return. When there is high demand, there is also *ferrochiva* (open sided motorized railcar) service at 1030, US$15 one way, US$20 return. Purchase tickets in advance. Ibarra station at Espejo y Colón, T06-295 5050, daily 0800-1300,1400-1630 or through T1-800-873637; you need each passenger's passport number and date of birth to purchase tickets. The ride takes 2 hrs with stops. You can continue by bus from Salinas to **San Lorenzo**, see page 280.

see page 280.

Transport

Ibarra

Bus Terminal is at Av Teodoro Gómez y Av Eugenio Espejo, southwest of the centre, T06-264 4676. Most inter-city transport runs from here. There are no ticket counters for regional destinations, such as Otavalo, proceed directly to the platforms. City buses go from the terminal to the centre or you can walk in 15 mins. To/from **Quito**, Terminal Carcelén, every 10 mins, US$3, 2½ hrs. Shared taxis with **Taxis Lagos/ Serviquito** (Quito address under Otavalo Transport, in Ibarra at Flores 924 y Sánchez y Cifuentes, near Parque La Merced, T06-260 6858), buy ticket at least 1 day ahead, US$15 pp, 2½ hrs. To **Tulcán**, with **Expreso Turismo**, 9 daily, US$3, 2½ hrs. To **Otavalo**, platform 12, every 4 mins, US$0.50, 40 mins. To **Cotacachi**, platform 15, every 15 mins, US$0.50, 40 mins, some continue to **Quiroga**. To the coast, several companies, some go all the way to **San Lorenzo**, US$7, 4 hrs, others only as far as **Lita**, US$4.50, 2 hrs. To **Ambato**, **CITA** goes via El Quinche and the Quito airport roundabout and bypasses Quito, 10 daily, US$6.50, 5 hrs. To **Baños**, **Expreso Baños**, also by the airport and bypasses Quito, at 0500 and 1430, US$7.50, 6 hrs. To **Lago Agrio**, **Valle de Chota**, at 0900, US$11.25, via La Bonita. To **Tumbabiro** via Urcuquí, **Coop Urcuquí**, hourly, US$1, 1 hr. To **Chachimbiro, Coop Urcuquí**, at 0700, 0730 and 1200, returning Mon-Fri at 1215 (Sat-Sun at 1300), 1530 and 1630, US$1.60, 1½ hrs, taxi US$40 return. Buses to La Esperanza, Zuleta and San Clemete leave from **Parque Germán Grijalva** (east of the Terminal Terrestre, follow C Sánchez y Cifuentes, south from the centre). To **La Esperanza**, every 20 mins, US$0.30, 30 mins. To **Zuleta**, hourly, US$0.60, 1 hr. To **San Clemente**, frequent, weekdays 0650-1840, Sat-Sun 0720-1500, US$0.30, 30 mins. For nearby destinations such as **San Antonio de Ibarra**, city buses run along Pérez Guerrero.

To the north of Ibarra is a land of striking contrasts. Deep eroded canyons and warm subtropical valleys stand side by side with windswept *páramos* and potato fields. The highlight of this area is Reserva Ecológica El Angel, home of the largest stand of *frailejones* (large velvety leaved espeletia plants) in Ecuador. The Panamericana reaches the Colombian border at the busy town of Tulcán.

North of Ibarra

From Ibarra the Pan-American Highway goes past **Laguna Yahuarcocha** and then descends to the hot dry Chota Valley, a centre of Afro-Ecuadorean culture. Around the town of **Ambuquí** are many popular tourist complexes with swimming pools. Beyond the turn-off for Salinas and San Lorenzo, 30 km from Ibarra, the highway divides. The western branch follows an older route through Mira and El Angel to Tulcán on the Colombian border, the eastern route, the modern Pan-American Highway, goes to Tulcán via Bolívar, San Gabriel and Huaca. A paved road between El Angel and Bolívar connects the two branches. Off the eastern branch is the town of Pimampiro and beyond are Mariano Acosta and Nueva América. The latter has a 502-ha cloudforest reserve with trails and a community tourism project.

Western route to Tulcán

At **Mascarilla**, 1 km after the roads divide, ceramic masks are made. The women's crafts association here runs a hostel ($ El Patio de mi Casa, T09-9316 1621, meals available). Beyond by 16 km is **Mira** (2400 m), where fine woollens are made. This road is paved and in good condition as far as **El Angel** (3000 m), where the main plaza retains a few trees sculpted by José Franco (see Tulcán cemetery, page 140); market day is Monday. The road north beyond El Angel goes through beautiful *páramo*. It is poor requiring a 4WD and is a great mountain bike route.

The ★ **Reserva Ecológica El Angel** ① *T06-297 7597, office in El Angel near the Municipio; best time to visit May to Aug,* nearby protects 15,715 ha of *páramo* ranging in altitude from 3400 m to 4768 m. The reserve contains large stands of the velvet-leaved *frailejón* plant (*Espeletia hartwegiana*), also found in the Andes of Colombia and Venezuela. Also of interest are the spiny *achupallas, bromeliads* with giant compound flowers. The fauna includes *curiquingues* (caracara), deer, foxes, and a few condors. From El Angel follow the poor road north towards Tulcán for 16 km to **El Voladero** ranger station/shelter, where a self-guided trail climbs over a low ridge (30 minutes' walk) to two crystal-clear lakes. Pickups or taxis from the main plaza of El Angel charge US$25 return with one-hour wait for a day trip to El Voladero. A longer route to another area follows an equally poor road to Cerro Socabones, beginning at **La Libertad**, 3.5 km north of El Angel (transport El Angel-Cerro Socabones, US$30 return). It climbs gradually to reach the high *páramo* at the centre of the reserve and, in 40 minutes, the **El Salado** ranger station. From Socabones the road descends to the village of **Morán** (lodging and guides, transport with Sr Calderón, T09-9128 4022), the start of a nice three-day walk to Las Juntas, a warm area, off the Ibarra-San Lorenzo road.

Eastern route to Tulcán

The second branch, the Panamericana, sees much traffic, including heavy lorries. Work is in progress to widen this road and the section between Mascarilla, where the two roads divide, and Bolívar is expected to remain closed into 2016. All traffic goes on the western route to El Angel, then across to Bolívar. From Mascarilla, the Panamericana runs east through the warm Chota Valley to El Juncal, before turning northeast to **Bolívar**, a neat little town where the houses and the interior of its church are painted in lively pastel colours; there is also a huge mural by the roadside. At the **Museo Paleontológico** ⓘ *by the north entrance to town, US$2*, remains of a mammoth, found nearby, can be seen. There is a Friday market.

Some 16 km north of Bolívar is **San Gabriel**, an important commercial centre. The 60-m-high **Paluz** waterfall is 4 km north of town, beyond a smaller waterfall. To the southeast, 11 km from town on the road to Piartal is **Bosque de Arrayanes**, a 16-ha mature forest with a predominance of myrtle trees, some reaching 20 m, taxi US$5.

East of San Gabriel by 20 km is the tiny community of **Mariscal Sucre** also known as Colonia Huaqueña, the gateway to the **Guandera Reserve and Biological Station** ⓘ *the reserve is part of Fundación Jatun Sacha. Reservations should be made at the Quito office, T02-331 7163, www.jatunsacha.org.* You can see bromeliads, orchids, toucans and other wildlife in temperate forest and *frailejón páramo*. From San Gabriel, take a taxi beyond Mariscal Sucre, one hour, then walk 30 minutes to the reserve, or make arrangements with Jatun Sacha.

Between San Gabriel and Tulcán are the towns of Huaca, site of a pre-Inca settlement and Julio Andrade, with $$-$ **Hotel Naderik**, T06-220 5433, and a Saturday market (good for horses and other large animals) and, afterwards, paddleball games. This is the beginning of the road east to La Bonita, Lumbaqui and Lago Agrio. The road follows the frontier for much of the route. Make enquiries about safety before taking this beautiful route. The eastern and western roads from the south join at Las Juntas, 2 km south of Tulcán, from where a city bypass goes to the border.

Listings Ibarra to Tulcán

Where to stay

Western route to Tulcán

$$$$ Polylepis Lodge
Abutting the reserve, 14 km from El Angel along the road to Socabones, T06-263 1819, www.polylepislodgeec.com.

Rustic cabins with fireplace by a lovely 12-ha forest, includes 3 meals (vegetarian on request) and 3 guided walks, jacuzzi.

$$ Las Orquídeas
In the village of Morán, T09-8641 6936, castro503@yahoo.com.

Mountain cabin with bunk beds, shared bath, includes 3 meals, horse riding and guide, run by Carlos Castro, a local guide and conservation pioneer.

$ Blas Angel
C Espejo, facing the roundabout by the entrance to town, T06-297 7346.
Private or shared bath, parking, a good economical option.

Eastern route to Tulcán

$$ Gabrielita
Mejía y Los Andes, San Gabriel, above the agricultural supply shop, T06-229 1832.
Modern hostel, includes breakfast, parking, best in town.

Transport

Western route to Tulcán
Bus From **Ibarra** Terminal Terrestre to **Mira**, every 30 mins, US$1.25, 1 hr; to **El Angel**, hourly, US$1.75, 1½ hrs. El Angel to **Mira**, every 30 mins, US$0.50, 20 mins. El Angel to **Tulcán**, US$1.75, 1½ hrs. El Angel to **Quito**, US$5, 4 hrs.

Eastern route to the Tulcán
Bus From **San Gabriel** to **Tulcán**, vans and jeeps US$0.70, shared taxis US$0.95, 30 mins, all from the main plaza. From San Gabriel to **Ibarra**, buses, US$2, 2 hrs. From San Gabriel to **Quito**, buses, US$4.50, 3½ hrs.

Tulcán and the Colombian border *Colour map 1, A6.*
busy highland border town with fantastic cemetery topiary

The chilly city of Tulcán (population 61,900, altitude 2960 m) is the busy capital of the province of Carchi. There is a great deal of informal trade here with Colombia, a textile and dry goods fair takes place on Thursday and Sunday. Ecuador's best soccer players and cyclists come from this area.

Note Tulcán is a generally safe city, but the area around the bus terminal requires caution, especially at night. Do not travel outside town (except along the Panamericana) without advance local enquiry. There are banks in Tulcán but few places accept credit cards.

Sights
The main square is **Parque La Independencia** and five blocks to the north is **Parque Ayora**, with an amazing cantilevered statue of Abdón Calderón and his horse leaping into mid-air.

In the ★ **cemetery** ⓘ *2 blocks from Parque Ayora, daily 0800-1800*, the art of topiary is taken to beautiful extremes. Cypress bushes are trimmed into archways, fantastic figures and geometric shapes in *haut* and *bas* relief. To see the stages of this art form, go to the back of the cemetery where young bushes are being pruned. The artistry, started in 1936, is that of the late Sr José Franco, born in El Angel (see above), now buried among the splendour he created. The tradition is carried on by his sons. Around the cemetery is a promenade with fountains, souvenir and flower stalls and the tourist office. Write in advance to request a guided tour of the cemetery.

Tulcán

Where to stay 🛏
1 Florida
2 Grand Hotel Comfort
3 Los Alpes
4 Palacio Imperial
5 Sara Espíndola
6 Torres de Oro

Restaurants 🍴
1 Bocattos
2 Café Tulcán
3 Dubai

N

100 metres
100 yards

Two blocks south is the **Museo de la Casa de la Cultura** ① *Mon-Fri 0730-1300, 1500-1800*, with a collection of pre-Inca ceramics.

West of Tulcán

To the west of Tulcán, along the Colombian border, lies a scenic area of rivers, lakes and waterfalls, followed by *páramos* with geothermal activity at the foot of Volcán Chiles and, further on, tropical lowlands. The main road west is the northern border of the Reserva Ecológica El Angel, see page 138; along the way are military checkpoints. **Tufiño**, 18 km from Tulcán, is just on the border. Two blocks downhill from the main park is a museum with archaeological and ethnographic displays (free, ask around for the caretaker). By far the best hot springs of the region are **Aguas Hediondas** (stinking waters) ① *US$2, food available on weekends*, a complex of indoor and outdoor pools fed by a stream of boiling sulphurous mineral water in an impressive valley. The area around the water source is walled off because of lethal sulphur fumes; the baths are deserted on weekdays. Access is 3 km past Tufiño, from where a road goes to the right, 8 km through strange scenery, to the magnificent natural hot river. Shared taxi Tulcán–Tufiño US$0.50, you can arrange for the taxi to continue to the baths.

Past the turn-off for Aguas Hediondas the road climbs to the *páramo* on the southern slopes of **Volcán Chiles**. The border with Colombia crosses at the summit. From the baths, a path also goes towards the volcano, condors can sometimes be seen hovering above the high cliffs surrounding the valley. Chiles can be climbed in about six hours, but this border area is unsafe and in 2015 the volcano was trembling, enquire about current conditions. To the south, also within the reserve, is an area of lovely lakes, the Lagunas Verdes. The road then begins its long descent to the west. **Maldonado**, already in a subtropical area descending to the coast, is 57 km from Tufiñot and **Chical**, 12 km beyond. From Chical a road goes south to Gualchán (see page 132).

Warning The above road runs along the Colombian border and public safety is an important concern. Always enquire before travelling past Tufiño and Aguas Hediondas.

Border with Colombia: Tulcán–Ipiales

The border is at **Rumichaca** (stone bridge), 5 km from Tulcán. Border posts with immigration, customs and agriculture control are on either side of a concrete bridge over the Río Carchi, to the east of the natural stone bridge. This well-organized border is open 24 hours. On the Ecuadorean side, next to immigration (T06-298 6169), is a tourist information office. **Colombian consulate** ⓘ *Bolívar entre Ayacucho y Junín, Tulcán, T06-298 0559, Tue-Thu 0800-1300.* Visas require three days.

Pesos Colombianos can easily be changed on Parque La Independencia, the bus terminal and the border. There are money changers on both sides of the bridge; check all calculations. Ipiales, with all services, is 2 km from the border.

Listings Tulcán and the Colombian border *map p141*

Tourist information

Tulcán

Unidad de Turismo
Entrance to the cemetery, T06-298 5760, turismo@gmtulcan.gob.ec. Daily 0800-1800.
Helpful.

Where to stay

Tulcán

$$$ Palacio Imperial
Sucre y Pichincha, T06-298 0638, www.hotelpalacioimperial.com.
Modern hotel with ample rooms with wood floors, suites with jacuzzi, warm blankets, includes buffet breakfast, very popular Chinese restaurant **Chifa Pak Choy**, rooftop spa, gym, parking.

$$ Grand Hotel Comfort
Colón y Chimborazo, T06-298 1452, www.grandhotelcomfort.com.
Modern high-rise hotel with rooms and suites with jacuzzi, fridge, safety box, breakfast, restaurant with set lunch and à la carte (closed Sat-Sun evening), parking.

$$ Sara Espíndola
Sucre y Ayacucho, on plaza, T298 6209.
Comfortable rooms, with breakfast, spa, parking, helpful.

$$-$ Los Alpes
JR Arellano next to bus station, T06-298 2235.

Best option near the bus terminal, breakfast extra, restaurant, good value.

$$-$ Torres de Oro
Sucre y Rocafuerte, T06-298 0296.
Modern, comfortable, restaurant, parking.

$ Florida
Sucre y Ayacucho, T298 3849.
Simple, clean, shared bath, no breakfast, a good economy option.

Restaurants

Tulcán
Economical meals and juices at the attractively renovated and clean Mercado Central, entrances on Boyacá, Bolívar and Sucre, open 0700-1700.

$$-$ Dubai
Chimborazo. Open 1030-2200.
Set lunch, à la carte and *comida típica*, popular.

$ Bocattos
Bolívar y Panamá on Parque Ayora.
Set lunch and à la carte, Italian and Ecuadorean specialities.

$ Café Tulcán
Sucre 52-029 y Ayacucho. Open 0800-1800.
Café, snacks, desserts, juices, set lunches. A Tulcán classic.

Transport

Tulcán
Air There is an airport, but no commercial flights were operating in early 2015.

Bus The bus terminal is 1.5 km uphill from centre; best to take a taxi, US$1.25. **Note** The Panamericana from Ibarra to San Gabriel will be closed in 2015-2016 for construction. Transport will go via El Ángel, add half an hour to times indicated below (except for Lago Agrio). To **Quito**, US$5, 5 hrs, every 15 mins, service to Terminal Carcelén, some continue to Quitumbe; from Quito, service from both terminals. To **Ibarra**, 2½ hrs, US$3. **Otavalo**, US$3.75, 3 hrs (they don't go in to the Otavalo Terminal, alight at the highway turnoff where taxis are available or transfer in Ibarra). To **Guayaquil**, 20 a day, 13 hrs, US$16. To **Lago Agrio via La Bonita,** 3 a day with **Putumayo** and 2 daily with **Coop Petrolera**, US$8.75, 7 hrs, spectacular.

Border with Colombia *p1019*
Bus Minivans and shared taxis (US$1 pp) leave when full from Parque Ayora (near the cemetery); private taxi US$3.50. Taxi from the bus terminal to the border US$3, shared US$1.25 pp. **Note** These vehicles cross the international bridge and drop you off on the Colombian side, where onward transport waits. Remember to cross back over the bridge for Ecuadorean immigration. Colectivo border–Ipiales, US$1, taxi US$6-8.

Central highlands

South of Quito is some of the loveliest mountain scenery in Ecuador. This part of the country was named the 'Avenue of the Volcanoes' by the German explorer Alexander Von Humboldt, and it is easy to see why. An impressive roll call of towering peaks lines the route south: Cotopaxi, the Ilinizas, Carihuayrazo and Chimborazo, to name but a few.

This area obviously attracts its fair share of trekkers and climbers, while the less sporty tourist can browse through the many teeming markets and colonial towns that nestle among the high volcanic cones.

After you have explored the mountains to your heart's delight, rest up and pamper yourself in one of the lovely haciendas which have opened their doors to visitors, or in Baños, named and famed for its thermal baths. Situated on the main road from the central highlands to the Oriente jungle, it is also the base for activities ranging from adrenaline sports and mountain biking to café lounging and Ecuador's special attraction: volcano watching.

Best for
Climbing ▪ Markets ▪ Mountain biking ▪ Trekking

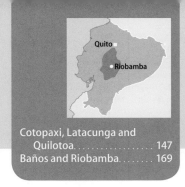

Footprint
picks

★ **Parque Nacional Cotopaxi**, page 148

The perfect cone of Cotopaxi is the second highest peak in Ecuador and one of the highest active volcanoes in the world.

★ **Quilotoa Circuit**, page 157

This popular 200-km round trip can be done in two to three days by bus and it is also a great route for biking.

★ **Thursday market in Saquisilí**, page 161

Famous for its seven plazas jam-packed with people, the great majority of them wearing red ponchos and narrow-brimmed felt hats.

★ **Pailón del Diablo**, page 172

The 'Devil's Cauldron' is probably the most spectacular of the many waterfalls in the Pastaza Basin around Baños.

★ **Reserva Faunística Chimborazo**, page 181

Visit the graceful vicuñas which inhabit the plateau at the base of Ecuador's highest summit.

★ **The Devil's Nose**, page 183

Touristy or not, this train ride takes you over an internationally acclaimed fantastic piece of railway engineering.

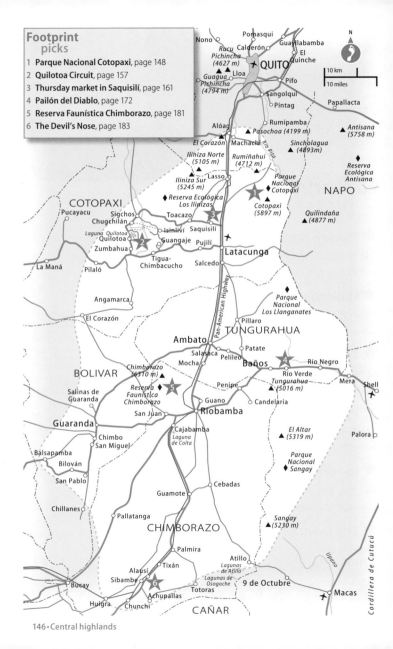

10 km
10 miles

Pomasqui
Nono
Calderón
Guayllabamba
El Quinche
Rucu Pichincha (4627 m)
QUITO
Guagua Pichincha (4794 m)
Lloa
Pifo
Sangolquí
Papallacta
Píntag
Antisana (5758 m)
Alóag
Rumipamba
Pasochoa (4199 m)
Sincholagua (4893m)
El Corazón
Machachi
Río Pita
Reserva Ecológica Antisana
Iliniza Norte (5105 m)
Rumiñahui (4712 m)
NAPO
Iliniza Sur (5245 m)
Lasso
Parque Nacional Cotopaxi
Reserva Ecológica Los Ilinizas
COTOPAXI
Sigchos
Toacazo
Saquisilí
Cotopaxi (5897 m)
Quilindaña (4877 m)
Pucayacu
Chugchilán
Isinliví
Laguna Quilotoa
Quilotoa
Guangaje
Pujilí
Latacunga
Zumbahua
Tigua-Chimbacucho
Salcedo
La Maná
Pilaló
Angamarca
El Corazón
Parque Nacional Los Llanganates
Píllaro
TUNGURAHUA
Ambato
Salasaca
Patate
Mocha
Pelileo
Baños
Río Negro
BOLIVAR
Chimborazo (6310 m)
Penipe
Río Verde
Tungurahua (5016 m)
Mera
Shell
Reserva Faunística Chimborazo
Salinas de Guaranda
San Juan
Guano
Riobamba
Candelaria
Palora
Guaranda
Chimbo
San Miguel
Cajabamba
Laguna de Colta
El Altar (5319 m)
Balsapamba
Biliván
Parque Nacional Sangay
San Pablo
Chillanes
Guamote
Cebadas
Pallatanga
CHIMBORAZO
Sangay (5230 m)
Palmira
Atillo
Lagunas de Atillo
Alausí
Tixán
Bucay
Sibambe
Lagunas de Osogoche
9 de Octubre
Macas
Huigra
Achupallas
Totoras
Chunchi
CAÑAR
Cordillera de Cutucú
Upano
Pan-American Highway

Cotopaxi, Latacunga & Quilotoa

From Quito, the six lanes of the Pan-American Highway head south towards the central highlands' hub of Ambato. The route is lined with impressive mountain scenery; the perfect cone of Cotopaxi volcano is ever-present and is one of the country's main tourist attractions. Machachi and Latacunga are good bases from which to explore the region and provide access to the beautiful Quilotoa circuit of small villages and vast expanses of open countryside.

Cotopaxi and Latacunga

some of Ecuador's most spectacular peaks and best treks

Machachi *Colour map 3, A6.*

In a valley between the summits of Pasochoa, Rumiñahui and Corazón, lies the town of **Machachi** (population 29,000, altitude 2900 m), famous for its horsemen (*chagras*), horse riding trips, mineral water springs and crystal-clear swimming pools. The water, 'Agua Güitig' or 'Tesalia', is bottled in a plant 4 km from the town, where there is also a sports/recreation complex with one warm and two cold pools, entry US$5. The annual highland 'rodeo', El Chagra, takes place in the third week in July. Tourist information office is available on the plaza. Just north of Machachi is **Alóag**, where an important road goes west to Santo Domingo and the coast.

Reserva Ecológica Los Ilinizas *Colour map 3, A5.*

Machachi is a good starting point for a visit to the northern section of the Reserva Ecológica Los Ilinizas. Below the saddle between the two peaks, at 4740 m, is the **Refugio Nuevos Horizontes** ⓘ *T09-8133 3483, office and café in El Chaupi, T02-367 4125, www.ilinizas-refuge.webs.com, US$15 per night, US$30 with dinner and breakfast, reserve ahead, take sleeping bag*, a shelter with capacity for 25.

Iliniza Norte (5105 m) although not a technical climb, should not be underestimated: a few exposed, rocky sections require utmost caution. Some climbers suggest using a rope and a helmet is recommended if other parties are there because of falling rock; allow two to four hours for the ascent from the refuge. **Iliniza Sur** (5245 m) involves ice climbing despite the deglaciation:

full climbing gear and experience are absolutely necessary. All visitors must register and be accompanied by an authorized mountain guide for both ascents; maximum three climbers per guide on Iliniza Norte; two per guide on Iliniza Sur.

Access to the reserve is through a turnoff west of the Panamericana 6 km south of Machachi, then it's 7 km to the village of El Chaupi, which is a good base for day-walks and climbing **Corazón** (4782 m, not trivial). A dirt road continues from El Chaupi 9 km to 'La Virgen' (statue), pickup US$15. Nearby are woods where you can camp. El Chaupi hotels arrange for horses with muleteer (US$25 per animal, one way).

★ **Parque Nacional Cotopaxi** *Colour map 3, A6.*
Visitors to the park must register at the entrance. Park gates are open 0800-1500, although you can stay until 1700. Visitors arriving with guides not authorized by the park are turned back at the gate. The park administration, a small museum (open daily 0800-1530) and snack bar, are 10 km from the park gates. La Rinconada shelter and camping area are 5 km beyond, just before lake Limpio Pungo. (See also Transport section below.) The museum has a 3D model of the park, information about the volcano and stuffed animals.

Cotopaxi volcano (5897 m) is at the heart of a much-visited national park. This scenic snow-covered perfect cone is the second highest peak in Ecuador and a very popular climbing destination. Cotopaxi is one of the highest active volcanoes in the world. Volcanic material from former eruptions can be seen strewn about the *páramo* surrounding Cotopaxi. The northwest flank is most often visited. Here is a high plateau with a small lake (Laguna Limpio Pungo), a lovely area for walking and admiring the delicate flora, and fauna including wild horses and native bird species such as the Andean lapwing and the Chimborazo hillstar hummingbird. The lower slopes are clad in planted pine forests, where llamas may be seen.

Breaking news
In mid-2015, after 111 years of dormancy, Cotopaxi volcano became active again and remained so when this edition went to press. The mountain and national park were closed to climbers and all other visitors although these restrictions could be lifted if volcanic activity subsides. The activity is variable and the National Geophysical Institute posts reports at www.igepn.edu.ec. Meanwhile, the sight of ash plumes being ejected from the crater of this beautiful mountain are a new and impressive attraction.

The southwest flank, or Cara Sur, has not received as much impact as the west side. Here too, there is good walking, and you can climb Morurco (4881 m) as an acclimatization hike; condors may sometimes be seen. Just north of Cotopaxi are the peaks of Rumiñahui (4722 m), Sincholagua (4873 m) and Pasochoa (4225 m). To the southeast, beyond the park boundary, are Quilindaña (4890 m) and an area of rugged *páramos* and mountains dropping down to the jungle. The area has several large haciendas which form the **Fundación Páramo** (www.fundacionparamo.org), a private reserve with restricted access.

Accessing the park The **main entrance** to Parque Nacional Cotopaxi is approached from Chasqui, 25 km south of Machachi, 6 km north of Lasso. Once through the national park gates, go past Laguna Limpio Pungo to a fork, where the right branch climbs steeply to a parking lot (4600 m). From here it's a 30-minute to one-hour walk to the José Ribas refuge, at 4800 m; beware of altitude sickness. Walking from the highway to the refuge takes an entire day or more. The **El Pedregal entrance**, from the northwest, is accessed from Machachi via Santa Ana del Pedregal (21 km from the Panamericana), or from Sangolquí via Rumipamba and the Río Pita Valley. From Pedregal to the refuge car park is 14 km. There are infrequent buses to Pedregal (two a day) then the hike in is shorter

Parque Nacional Cotopaxi

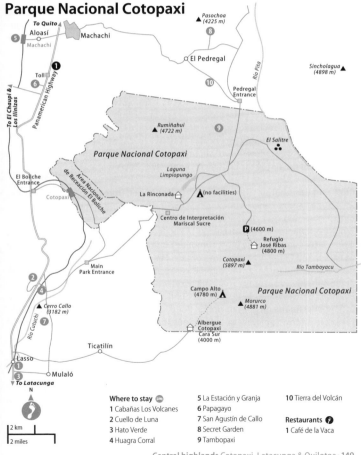

Where to stay 🛏
1 Cabañas Los Volcanes
2 Cuello de Luna
3 Hato Verde
4 Huagra Corral
5 La Estación y Granja
6 Papagayo
7 San Agustín de Callo
8 Secret Garden
9 Tambopaxi
10 Tierra del Volcán

Restaurants 🍴
1 Café de la Vaca

but still a couple of hours. The **Ticatilín access** leads to the southwest flank. Just north of Lasso, a road goes east to the village of San Ramón and on to Ticatilín (a contribution of US$2 per vehicle may be requested at the barrier here, be sure to close all gates) and Rancho María. From the south, San Ramón is accessed from Mulaló. Beyond Rancho María is the private **Albergue Cotopaxi Cara Sur** (4000 m, see Where to stay, below). Walking four hours from here you reach Campo Alto (4760 m), a climbers' tent camp.

Climbing Cotopaxi The ascent from the Ribas refuge takes five to eight hours, start climbing at 0100 as the snow deteriorates in the sun. A full moon is both practical and a magical experience. Check out snow conditions with the guardian of the refuge before climbing. The route changes from year to year due to deglaciation. Because of the altitude and weather conditions, Cotopaxi is a serious climb, equipment and experience are required. To maximize your chances of reaching the summit, make sure to be well acclimatized beforehand. Climbing with a guide is compulsory. Agencies in Quito and throughout the central highlands offer Cotopaxi climbing trips. Note that some guides encourage tourists to turn back at the first sign of tiredness: don't be bullied and insist on going at your own pace. There is no specific best season to climb Cotopaxi, weather conditions are largely a matter of luck year-round. You can also climb on the southwest flank, where the route is reported easier and safer than on the northwest face, but a little longer. To reach the summit in one day, you have to stay at Campo Alto (see above, and Where to stay below), from where it is six hours to the summit. The last hour goes around the rim of the crater with impressive views.

Climbing Rumiñahui The mountain can be climbed from the park road, starting at Laguna Limpio Pungo from where it takes about one to 1½ hours to the base of the mountain. The climb itself is straightforward and not technical, though it is quite a scramble on the rockier parts and it can be very slippery and muddy in places after rain. There are three summits: **Cima Máxima** is the highest, at 4722 m; **Cima Sur** and **Cima Central** are the others. The quickest route to Cima Máxima is via the central summit, as the climb is easier and not as steep. Note that the rock at the summits is unstable. There are excellent views of Cotopaxi and the Ilinizas. From the base to the summits takes about three to four hours. Allow around three to 3½ hours for the descent to Limpio Pungo. This is a good acclimatization climb. Take cold and wet weather gear. Even outside the rainy season there can be hail and sleet.

Lasso *Colour map 3, A6.*
Some 30 km south of Machachi is the small town of Lasso (altitude 3000 m), on the railway line and off the Panamericana. In the surrounding countryside are several *hosterías*, converted country estates, offering accommodation and meals. Intercity buses bypass Lasso.

Latacunga *Colour map 3, A6.*

Capital of Cotopaxi Province, Latacunga (population 103,000, altitude 2800 m) is a place where the abundance of light grey pumice has been artfully employed. Volcán Cotopaxi is much in evidence, though it is 29 km away. Provided they are not hidden by clouds, which unfortunately is all too often, as many as nine volcanic cones can be seen from Latacunga; the sky is usually clearest early in the morning. The colonial character of the town has been well preserved. The central plaza, **Parque Vicente León**, is a beautifully maintained garden (locked at night). There are several other gardens in the town including **Parque San Francisco** and **Lago Flores** (better known as 'La Laguna'). **Casa de los Marqueses de Miraflores** ⓘ *Sánchez de Orellana y Abel Echeverría, T02-281 1382, Mon-Fri 0800-1700, Sat 0900-1300, free*, in a restored colonial mansion has a modest museum, with exhibits on **Mama Negra** (see Festivals, page 155), colonial art, archaeology, numismatics, a library and the Jefatura de Turismo, see below.

Casa de la Cultura ⓘ *Antonia Vela 3-49 y Padre Salcedo T03-281 3247, Tue-Fri 0800-1200, 1400-1800, Sat 0800-1500, US$1*, built around the remains of a Jesuit Monastery and the old Monserrat watermill, houses a nice museum with pre-Columbian ceramics, weavings, costumes and models of festival masks; also art gallery, library and theatre. It has week-long festivals with exhibits and concerts for all the local festivities.

There is a Saturday **market** on the Plaza de San Sebastián (at Juan Abel Echeverría). Goods for sale include *shigras* (fine stitched, colourful straw bags)

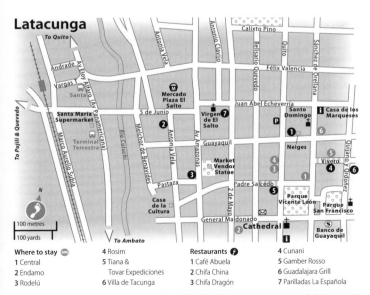

Latacunga

and homespun wool and cotton yarn. The produce market, Plaza El Salto has daily trading and larger fairs on Tuesday, Friday and Saturday.

Tourist information is available from: **Cámara de Turismo de Cotopaxi** ⓘ *Quito 14-38 y General Maldonado, T03-280 1112, www.capturcotopaxi.com/fest.htm, Mon-Fri 0900-1300, 1400-1700*, local and regional information, Spanish only; and **Jefatura de Turismo** ⓘ *Casa de los Marqueses, T03-280 8494, Mon-Fri 0800-1700*, local and regional information and maps.

Listings Cotopaxi and Latacunga *maps p149 and p151*

Where to stay

Machachi

$$$ La Estación y Granja
3 km west of the Panamericana, by railway station outside the village of Aloasí, T02-230 9246, www. hosterialaestacion.com.
Rooms in a lovely old home and newer section, also cabins, fireplaces, meals available (produce from own garden), parking, family-run, hiking access to Volcán Corazón (guides arranged), reserve ahead.

$$$ Papagayo
In Hacienda Bolívia, west of the Panamericana, take a taxi from Machachi, T02-231 0002, www.hosteria-papagayo.com.
Nicely refurbished hacienda, pleasant communal areas with fireplace and library, restaurant, jacuzzi, parking, central heating, homey atmosphere, horse riding, biking, tours, popular.

$$$ Puerta al Corazón
500 m south of the train station, T02-230 9858.
Cosy lodge, located near the rail line with good views of the mountains, small restaurant, price includes dinner and breakfast. A good base for mountain trips.

$$ Chiguac
Los Caras y Colón, 4 blocks east of the main park, T02-231 0396, amsincholagua@gmail.com.
Family-run hostel, comfortable rooms, good breakfast, other meals available, shared bath. Recommended.

Reserva Ecológica Los Ilinizas

$$$ Chuquiragua Lodge
500 m before El Chaupi, then 200 m on a cobbled road, T02-367 4046, Quito T02-603 5590, www. chuquiragualodgeandspa.com.
Inn with lovely views, a variety of rooms and prices, restaurant with roaring fireplace. US$18 pp in dorm, camping US$10 pp with hot shower (bring your own tent). Spa, horse riding, trekking, climbing, bike tours, and transport from Quito available, advance booking advised.

$$-$ La Llovizna
100 m behind the church, on the way to the mountain, T02-367 4076.
Pleasant hostel, sitting room with fireplace, includes breakfast and dinner, cheaper without meals and includes use of kitchen, private or shared bath, ping pong, horse, bike and gear rentals, helpful owner, guiding, transport to Ilinizas, book in advance.

$$-$ Nina Rumy
Near the bus stop in El Chaupi,
T02-367 4088.
Includes breakfast and supper, cheaper
without meals, simple rooms, private or
shared bath, hot water, family-run and
very friendly.

Parque Nacional Cotopaxi
All these inns are good for
acclimatization at altitudes between
3100 m and 3800 m. Just below
Limpio Pungo the **Rinconada** shelter
(US$25 pp, hot water) with 2 very basic
huts and a couple of campsites (free,
public toilets and a cooking shelter).
The **José Ribas refuge** (Quito T02-254
8072, reservas@grivari.com) was
extensively refurbished in 2015 and can
accommodate up to 80 persons with
several sleeping options, US$15-60 pp,
blankets generally not provided, bring
a warm sleeping bag; meals and snacks
for sale, supper and breakfast package
US$17-20, no public kitchen; no charge
for day visits.

$$$-$$ Tambopaxi
3 km south of the El Pedregal access (1-hr
drive from Machachi) or 4 km north of
the turn-off for the climbing shelter, T02-
600 0365 (Quito), www.tambopaxi.com.
Comfortable straw-bale mountain shelter
at 3750 m. 3 double rooms and several
dorms (US$25 pp), duvets, camping
US$7.50 pp, restaurant, excellent horse
riding with advance notice.

$$ Albergue Cotopaxi Cara Sur
At the southwestern end of the park, at
the end of the Ticatilín road, T09-8461
9264, www.cotopaxicarasur.com (see
page 150).
Very nice mountain shelter at 4000 m,
day use US$1. Includes breakfast and
dinner, use of kitchen, some cabins

with private bath, hot shower, transport
from Quito and climbing tours available,
equipment rental. **Campo Alto** is a very
basic tent camp (4780 m, US$8 pp), 4 hrs
walk from the shelter, horse to take gear
to Campo Alto US$15, muleteer US$15.

Outside the park

$$$$ Hacienda San Agustín de Callo
2 access roads from the Panamericana,
1 just north of the main park access
(6.2 km); the 2nd, just north of Lasso
(4.3 km), T03-271 9160, Quito T02-290
6157, www.incahacienda.com.
Exclusive hacienda, the only place in
Ecuador where you can sleep and dine
in an Inca building, the northernmost
imperial-style Inca structure still
standing. Rooms and suites with
fireplace and bathtub, includes breakfast
and dinner, horse rides, treks, bicycles
and fishing. Restaurant ($$$) and
buildings open to non-guests (US$5-10).

$$$$ Hacienda Santa Ana
10 mins from north entrance to Cotopaxi
National Park, T02-222 4950, www.
santaanacotopaxi.com.
17th-century former-Jesuit hacienda in
beautiful surroundings. 7 comfortable
rooms with fireplaces, central heating,
great views, horse riding, hiking,
trekking, climbing. Also run **Hotel
Sierra Madre** in Quito.

$$$$ Hacienda Yanahurco
On access road to Quilindaña, 2 hrs from
Machachi, T09-9612 7759, Quito T02-244
5248, www.haciendayanahurco.com.
Large hacienda in wild area, rooms with
fireplace or heater, includes meals, 2- to
4-day programmes, all-inclusive.

$$$ Secret Garden
T09-9357 2714,
www.secretgardencotopaxi.com.

Rooms and dorms (US$35 pp), includes 3 meals, hot drinks, nice common areas with fireplace, indoor jacuzzi with views of Cotopaxi. Offers hiking tours, horse riding and transport (US$5 from Quito). Good value for where it is.

$$$-$$ Chilcabamba
Loreto del Pedregal, by the northern access to the national park, T09-9946 0406, T02-237 7098, www.chilcabamba.com.
Cabins and rooms, US$30.50 pp in dorm, magnificent views.

$$$-$$ Cuello de Luna
2 km northwest of the park's main access on a dirt road, T09-9970 0330, www. cuellodeluna.com.
Comfortable rooms with fireplace, includes breakfast, other meals available, US$22 pp in dorm (a very low loft). Can arrange tours to Cotopaxi, horse riding and biking.

$$$-$$ Tierra del Volcán
T09-9498 0121, Quito T02-600 9533, www.tierradelvolcan.com.
3 haciendas: **Hacienda El Porvenir**, a working ranch by Rumiñahui, between El Pedregal and the northern access to the park, 3 types of rooms, includes breakfast, set meals available, horses and mountain bikes for hire, camping, zipline; **Hacienda Santa Rita**, by the Río Pita, on the Sangolquí–El Pedregal road, with ziplines, entry US$6, camping US$5 pp; and the more remote, rustic **Hacienda El Tambo** by Quilindaña, southeast of the park. Also offers many adventure activities in the park.

$$ Huagra Corral
200 m east of Panamericana along the park's main access road, T03-271 9729, Quito T02-380 8427, www.huagracorral.com.

Nicely decorated, restaurant, private or shared bath, heaters, convenient location, helpful, reserve ahead.

Lasso

$$$$ Hacienda Hato Verde
Panamericana Sur Km 55, by entry to Mulaló, southeast of Lasso, T03-271 9348, www.haciendahatoverde.com.
Lovely old hacienda and working dairy farm near the south flank of Cotopaxi, tastefully restored. 10 rooms with wood-burning stoves, includes breakfast, other meals available; horse riding (for experienced riders), trekking, trip up Cotopaxi Cara Sur, charming hosts.

$$$ Hostería La Ciénega
2 km south of Lasso, T03-271 9052, www.haciendalacienega.com.
An historic hacienda with pleasant gardens, rooms with heater or fireplace, good expensive restaurant.

$ Cabañas Los Volcanes
At the south end of Lasso, T03-271 9524, maexpediciones@yahoo.com.
Small hostel, good rooms, private or shared bath. Tours to Cotopaxi.

Latacunga

$$$ Villa de Tacunga
Sánchez de Orellana y Guayaquil, T03-281 2352.
Nicely restored colonial house built of Cotopaxi pumice stone. Comfortable rooms and suites with fireplace.

$$ Endamo
2 de Mayo 438 y Tarqui, T03-280 2678.
Modern hotel with nice rooms and a small restaurant, good value.

$$ Rodelú
Quito 16-31, T03-280 0956, www.rodelu.com.ec.

Popular hotel, restaurant, suites and rooms (some are very small, look before taking a room), breakfast included starting the 2nd day.

$$-$ Rosim
Quito 16-49 y Padre Salcedo,
T03-280 2172, www.hotelrosim.com.
Centrally located, breakfast available, some carpeted rooms, quiet and comfortable. Discounts in low season.

$$-$ Tiana
Luis F Vivero N1-31 y Sánchez de Orellana,
T03-281 0147, www.hostaltiana.com.
Includes breakfast, drinks and snacks available, private or shared bath, US$10 pp in dorm, nice patio, kitchen facilities, luggage store, popular backpackers' meeting place. Tour agency on the premises, good source of information for Quilotoa Loop.

$ Central
Sánchez de Orellana y Padre Salcedo,
T03-280 2912.
A multi-storey hotel in the centre of town, breakfast available, simple adequate rooms, a bit faded but very helpful.

Restaurants

Machachi
Not much to choose from in town.

$$$-$$ Café de la Vaca
4 km south of town on the
Panamericana. Daily 0800-1730.
Very good meals using produce from their own farm, popular.

$$-$ Pizzeria Di Ragazzo
Av Pablo Guarderas N7-107, north
of centre.
Reported good.

Latacunga
Few places are open on Sun. Many places along the Panamericana specialize in *chugchucaras*, a traditional pork dish. *Allullas* biscuits and string cheese are sold by the roadside.

$$ Chifa China
Antonia Vela 6-85 y 5 de Junio.
Daily 1030-2200.
Good Chinese food, large portions.

$$ Chifa Dragón
Amazonas y Pastaza. Daily 1100-2300.
Chinese food, large portions, popular.

$$ Gamber Rosso
Quito y Padre Salcedo, T03-281 3394.
Mon-Sat 1600-2200.
Good pizzas, antipasto and lasagne.

$$ Parilladas La Española
2 de Mayo 7-175. Mon-Sat 1230-2100.
Good grill, popular with locals.

$$-$ Guadalajara Grill
Quijano y Ordóñez y Vivero.
Economical set lunch Mon-Fri 1200-1500, good Mexican food 1800-2200.

Café Abuela
Guayaquil 6-07 y Quito, by Santo
Domingo church. Closed Sun.
Pleasant cosy café/bar, nicely decorated, drinks, sweets and sandwiches, popular with university students.

Cunani
Vivero y Sánchez de Orellana. Mon-
Fri 1300-2100.
Cosy café/restaurant serving home made ravioli, *humitas* and excellent hot chocolate. Also a handicraft store.

Festivals

Latacunga
Sep La Mama Negra is held **23-24 Sep**, in homage to the Virgen de las

Mercedes. There are 5 main characters in the parade and hundreds of dancers, some representing black slaves, others the whites. Mama Negra herself (portrayed by a man) is a slave who dared to ask for freedom in colonial times. The colourful costumes are called La Santísima Trajería.

Nov The civic festival of **Mama Negra**, with a similar parade, is on the **1st or 2nd Sat in Nov** (but not 2 Nov, Día de los Muertos). It is part of the **Fiestas de Latacunga**, **11 Nov**.

Shopping

Latacunga
Artesanía Otavalo, *Guayaquil 5-50 y Quito*. A variety of souvenirs from Otavalo.

What to do

Latacunga
All operators offer day trips to **Cotopaxi** and **Quilotoa** (US$50 pp, includes lunch and a visit to a market town if on Thu or Sat, minimum 2 people). Climbing trips to Cotopaxi are around US$200 pp for 2 days (includes one night in the *refugio*), minimum 2 people. Trekking trips US$80 pp per day. **Note** Many agencies require passport as deposit when renting gear.
Greivag, *Guayaquil y Sánchez de Orellana, Plaza Santo Domingo, L5, T03-281 0510, www.greivagturismo.com*. Day trips.
Metropolitan Touring, *Calle Guayaquil y Sánchez de Orellana, Plaza Santo Domingo, L6, T03-280 2985*. See Quito operators. Airline tickets.
Neiges, *Guayaquil 6-25, Plaza Santo Domingo, T03-281 1199, neigestours@ hotmail.com*. Day trips and climbing.
Tovar Expediciones, *at Hostal Tiana, T03-281 1333*. Climbing and trekking.

Transport

Machachi
Bus To **Quito**, from El Playón behind the stadium, every 15 mins to Terminal Quitumbe, every 30 mins to Villa Flora and El Trebol, all US$1, 1½ hrs. To **Latacunga**, from the monument to El Chagra at the Panamericana, US$0.75, 1 hr.

Reserva Ecológica Los Ilinizas
Bus From El Playón in Machachi, where buses from Quito arrive (see above), to **El Chaupi** (every 20 mins, US$0.50, 30 mins), from where you can walk to the *refugio* in 7-8 hrs. A pickup from El Chaupi to 'La Virgen' costs US$15, from Machachi US$30. It takes 3 hrs to walk with a full pack from 'La Virgen' to the *refugio*. Horses can be hired at any of the lodgings in El Chaupi.

Parque Nacional Cotopaxi
To **main park entrance** and **Refugio Ribas**, take a Latacunga bus from Quito and get off at the main access point, where there is a large overpass. Do not take an express bus as you can't get off before Latacunga. At the overpass there are usually pickup trucks which go to the park, US$20 to the parking lot before the refuge for up to 4 passengers, or US$3 to the main park entrance where other vehicles offer half-day guided tours for US$60 (also maximum 4 passengers). From **Machachi**, pickups go via the cobbled road to El Pedregal and on to Limpio Pungo and the *refugio* parking lot, US$40. From **Lasso**, full-day trip to the park, US$50 return, contact **Cabañas los Volcanes**. From **Latacunga**, arrange with tour operators.

To **Cara Sur** from Quito, **Cotopaxi Cara Sur** offer transport to the

Albergue Cara Sur, US$60 per vehicle up to 5 passengers. Alternatively take a Latacunga bound bus and get off at **Pastocalle**, and take a pickup from there, US$15 per vehicle for up to 5 passengers.

All prices subject to considerable variation; ask around and negotiate politely.

Latacunga
Air The airport is north of the centre. Two flights to **Guayaquil** and one to **Coca** with **TAME, Mon-Fri**.

Bus Buses leave from the terminal on the Panamericana just south of 5 de Junio, except **Transportes Santa**, which has its own terminal, 2 blocks away at Eloy Alfaro y Vargas Torres, T03-281 1659, serving **Cuenca**, US$11; and **Loja**, US$15; **Machala**, US$11; and **Guayaquil**, US$9.50; 4 daily to each. Other companies from main terminal: to **Quito**, every 15 mins, 2 hrs, US$2.50; also shared taxis with **Servicio Express**, T03-242 6828 (Ambato) or T09-9924 2795, US$10. To **Ambato**, 1 hr, US$1.25. To **Guayaquil**, US$8.75, 7 hrs. To **Saquisilí**, every 20 mins (see below). Through buses, which are more frequent, do not stop at Latacunga Terminal. During the day (0600-1700), they go along a bypass road 4 blocks west of the Terminal, and have small stations at Puente de San Felipe. At night they stop at the corner of Panamericana and Av 5 de Junio. To **Otavalo** and **Ibarra**, bypassing Quito, **Cita Express**, T03-280 9264, 12 daily from Puente de San Felipe, US$5; also with **Expreso Baños**. To **Baños**, US$2.25, 2 hrs, every 20 mins from Puente de San Felipe. Buses on the Zumbahua, Quilotoa, Chugchilán, Sigchos circuit are given below. **Note** On Thu most buses to nearby communities leave from Saquisilí market instead of Latacunga.

★ Quilotoa Circuit
scenic route through indigenous villages and past emerald lakes

The popular and recommended 200-km round trip from Latacunga to Pujilí, Zumbahua, Quilotoa crater, Chugchilán, Sigchos, Isinliví, Toacazo, Saquisilí, and back to Latacunga, can be done in two to three days by bus. It is also a great route for biking. Latacunga is the main city for access. Hiking from one town to another can be challenging, especially when the fog rolls in. For these longer walks hiring a guide might not be unreasonable if you don't have a proper map or enough experience.

Latacunga to Zumbahua
A fine paved road leads west from Latacunga to **Pujilí** ① *15 km, bus US$0.35*, which has a beautiful church. There's a good market on Sunday and a smaller one on Wednesday. Colourful **Corpus Christi** celebrations. Beyond Pujilí, many interesting crafts are practised by the *indígenas* in the **Tigua Valley**: paintings on leather, hand-carved wooden masks and baskets. **Chimbacucho**, also known as Tigua, is home to the Toaquiza family, most famous of the Tigua artists. The road goes on to Zumbahua, then over the Western Cordillera to La Maná and Quevedo. This is a

great paved downhill bike route. It carries very little traffic and is extremely twisty in parts but is one of the most beautiful routes connecting the highlands with the coast. Beyond Zumbahua are the pretty towns of **Pilaló** (two restaurants, small *hostal* and petrol pumps), **Esperanza de El Tingo** (two restaurants and lodging at **Carmita's**, T03-281 4657) and **La Maná** (two hotels).

Zumbahua *Colour map 3, A5.*

Zumbahua lies 800 m from the main road, 62 km from Pujilí. It has an interesting Saturday market (starts at 0600) for local produce, and some tourist items. Just below the plaza is a shop selling dairy products and cold drinks. Friday nights involve dancing and drinking. Take a fleece, as it can be windy, cold and dusty. There is a good hospital in town, Italian-funded and run. The Saturday trip to Zumbahua market and the Quilotoa crater combine to make an excellent excursion.

Quilotoa *Colour map 3, A5.*

Zumbahua is the point to turn off for a visit to Quilotoa, a volcanic crater filled by a beautiful emerald lake. From the rim of the crater (3850 m) several snowcapped volcanoes can be seen in the distance. The crater is reached by a paved road which runs north from Zumbahua (about 12 km, three- to five-hours' walk). There's a

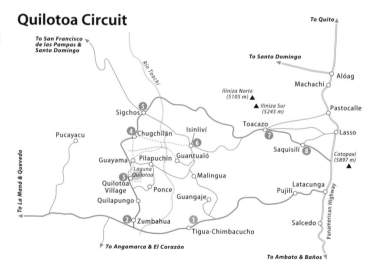

Quilotoa Circuit

To Quito

To San Francisco de las Pampas & Santo Domingo

To Santo Domingo

Río Toachi

Iliniza Norte (5105 m) ▲

▲ Iliniza Sur (5245 m)

Machachi Alóag

Pastocalle

Sigchos Isinliví Toacazo Lasso

Pucayacu Chugchilán La Quinta Colorada

Guayama Pilapuchín Guantualó Saquisilí Cotopaxi (5897 m) ▲

Laguna Quilotoa Malingua

Quilotoa Village Ponce Guangaje Latacunga

Quilapungo Pujilí Panamerican Highway

To La Maná & Quevedo

Zumbahua Salcedo

Tigua-Chimbacucho

To Angamarca & El Corazón

To Ambato & Baños

Where to stay
1 La Posada de Tigua
2 Cóndor Matzi & Richard
3 Complejo Shalalá & Quilotoa Crater Lake Lodge

4 Black Sheep Inn, El Vaquero, Mama Hilda & Hostal Cloud Forest
5 Jardín de los Andes
6 Llullu Llama & Taita Cristóbal

7 La Quinta Colorada
8 Gilocarmelo & San Carlos

N

Not to scale

300-m drop down from the crater rim to the water. The hike down takes about 30 minutes (an hour or more to climb back up, mind the altitude). The trail starts at the village of Quilotoa, up the slope from the parking area, then, down a steep canyon-like cut. You can hire a mule to ride up from the bottom of the crater (US$10), best arrange before heading down. There is a basic hostel by the lake and kayaks for rent (US$5 per hour). Everyone at the crater tries to sell the famous naïve Tigua pictures and carved wooden masks, so expect to be besieged (also by begging children). To the southeast of the crater is the village of Macapungo, which runs the Complejo Turístico Shalalá, see Where to stay, below. The Mirador Shalalá platform offers great views of the lake. To hike around the crater rim takes 4½ to six hours in clear weather. Be prepared for sudden changes in the weather, it gets very cold at night and can be foggy. Always stay on the trail as trekkers have got lost and hurt themselves. For a shorter loop (three to four hours), start on the regular circuit going right when you reach the rim by Quilotoa village and follow it to Mirador Shalalá, a great place for a picnic; then backtrack for about five minutes and take the path down to the lake. To return, follow a path near the lake until you reach the large trail which takes you back up to Quilotoa village. If you are tired, you can hire a horse to take you up.

Chugchilán, Sigchos and Isinliví *Colour map 3, A5.*
Chugchilán, a lovely scenic village, is 16 km by paved road from Quilotoa. An alternative to the road is a five- to six-hour walk around part of the Quilotoa crater rim, then down to Guayama, and across the canyon (Río Sigüi) to Chugchilán, 11 km. Outside town is a cheese factory and nearby, at Chinaló, a woodcarving shop. The area has good walking.

Continuing from Chugchilán the road, unpaved, runs to **Sigchos**, the starting point for the Toachi Valley walk, via Asache to San Francisco de las Pampas (0900 bus daily to Latacunga). There is also a vehicle road to Las Pampas, with two buses from Sigchos. Southeast of Sigchos is **Isinliví**, on the old route to Toacazo and Latacunga. It has a fine woodcarving shop and a pre-Inca *pucará*. Trek to the village of Guantualó, which has a fascinating market on Monday. You can hike to or from Chugchilán (five hours), or from Quilotoa to Isinliví in seven to nine hours.

From Sigchos, a paved road leads to **Toacazo** (**$$** La Quinta Colorada, T03-271 6122, www.quintacolorada.com, price includes breakfast and dinner) and on to Saquisilí.

Cycling around Quilotoa
This is a great area for biking and to get away from traffic, only a few sections are cobbled or rough and there is a choice of routes. Note that riding at this elevation is difficult and you should be in very good physical shape. You can make a four-day circuit or take longer to explore the beautiful surroundings along secondary roads. It's best to start on the Panamericana either from Lasso or Latacunga. On the **north** side between Toacazo and Sigchos there are two roads. The northern route is mostly paved, it hugs the canyon's edge before crossing the Río Toachi. On the older southern route via Isinliví there is a rough 4-km stretch descending

from the pass at Güingopana to Isinliví, the views along this stretch are fantastic. Between Isinliví and Sigchos is another good gravel road. From the **south** the road is paved from Latacunga to Quilotoa. Along this route you can take a turn-off to the north between Pujilí and Tigua, at about 4000 m, going to Guangaje, Guantualó and Isinliví, it is good hard-packed earth. Alternatively, you can continue on the paved road to Tigua, Zumbahua, and Quilotoa. From Quilotoa to Chugchilán and on to Sigchos is mostly downhill on gravel.

From **Saquisilí** there are a series of little lanes which take you up to Yanaurco Alto and then either over Güingopana to Isinliví or south to Cruz Blanca near Guangaje. There's no accommodation here, but with a sleeping bag you can stay overnight in the local school.

From **Zumbahua** an interesting route goes south. Take the main road towards Quevedo, turn south at Apagua on the pass and then climb to the pass above Angamarca. There is one dip on the road at a tiny village, then it is a major descent to **Angamarca**. Along the descent is **Refugio Angamarca** and in the village you will find a very basic pensión on the plaza. Below Angamarca, 3 km downhill, is the village of **Shuyo**, with a small shop with rooms used by bus drivers; if you arrive early there is usually space. The road continues to **El Corazón**. From here you can freewheel down to **Moraspungo** and **Quevedo**, or continue through the mountains to **Facundo Vela** and up to Radio Loma and into **Salinas de Guaranda** (see page 180). This latter route has a long tough uphill section from Facundo Vela, and sleeping bags are needed to sleep in village schools or churches.

Trekking around Quilotoa

There are ample opportunities for walking in the Quilotoa Circuit area. There are good day walks from all of the towns along the route and what makes the area special is the number of hostels even in some very small places. An interesting 'hostel-hopping' trek is described in the guide *Trekking in Ecuador* (www.trekkinginecuador.com).

Quilotoa crater lake is reached in a few hours if walking from Tigua, Zumbahua, Chugchilán and Isinliví (a full day is required from the latter). You can walk right round the Quilotoa crater rim in about six hours; it's very beautiful, but be sure to stick to the rim and don't head down towards the lake as there are some steep cliffs. Inexperienced or unacclimatized trekkers may need much longer for this hike and it is not unusual to be disoriented in fog, when the path can get slippery and dangerous. Enquire locally about conditions beforehand and take a stick to fend off dogs on the road.

Another beautiful walk is from Quilotoa to Chugchilán (11 km, five to six hours) following the crater rim clockwise then descending to the hamlet of **Guayama**, where there are a couple of shops with basic supplies and a hostel, and continuing across the canyon of the Río Sigüi. From Guayama you can also continue to Isinliví, which can also be reached along a road from **Pilapuchín**, on the northeast side of the lake, to **Malingua** and on to **Guantualó**. It is an eight- to nine-hour walk from Quilotoa to Isinliví on either route.

★ **Saquisilí** *Colour map 3, A5.*

Some 16 km southwest of Lasso, and 6 km west of the Panamericana is the small but very important market town of Saquisilí. Its Thursday market (0500-1400) is famous throughout Ecuador for the way in which its seven plazas and some streets become jam-packed with people, the great majority of them local *indígenas* with red ponchos and narrow-brimmed felt hats. The best time to visit the market is 0900-1200 (before 0800 for the animal market). Be sure to bargain, as there is a lot of competition. This area has colourful **Corpus Christi** processions.

Salcedo *Colour map 3, A5.*

Off the Quilotoa Circuit and 10 km south of Latacunga along the Panamericana, is Salcedo (officially San Miguel de Salcedo; population 32,000, altitude 2645 m), with a pleasant main square. The town is known for its delicious fruit ice cream, also sold in other parts of Ecuador; worth a try. The area is also known for its excellent *máchica* (roasted barley flour) and *pinol* (*máchica* with raw sugar and spices, which makes a nice drink prepared with milk). The Thursday and Sunday markets are authentic. **San Miguel** fiesta is 29 September.

From Salcedo a road goes east to Cashaloma and beyond to the northwestern edge of Parque Nacional Los Llanganates.

Listings Quilotoa Circuit *map p158*

Where to stay

Latacunga to Zumbahua
Tigua-Chimbacucho

$$ La Posada de Tigua
3 km east of Tigua–Chimbacucho,
400 m north of the road, T03-305 6103,
posadadetigua@yahoo.com.
Refurbished hacienda, part of a working dairy ranch, 6 rooms, wood-burning stove, includes tasty home-cooked breakfast and dinner, pleasant family atmosphere, horses for riding, trails, lovely views.

Zumbahua
There are only a few phone lines in town, which are shared among several people. Expect delays when calling to book a room.

$ Cóndor Matzi
Overlooking the market area, T09-8906
1572 or T03-281 2953 to leave a message.
Basic but the best in town, shared bath, hot water, dinning room with wood stove, kitchen facilities, try to reserve ahead, if it's closed when you arrive ask at **Restaurante Zumbahua** on the corner of the plaza.

$ Richard
Opposite the market on the road in to town, T09-9015 5996.
Basic shared rooms and one shower with hot water, cooking facilities, parking.

Quilotoa
Quilotoa hotels are all expensive for what they offer, and polite bargaining is appropriate. Humberto Latacunga, a good painter who also organizes

treks, runs 3 good hostels, T09-9212 5962, all include breakfast and dinner: **$$ Hostería Alpaca**, www.alpacaquilotoa.com, the most upmarket, rooms with wood stoves; **$$ Cabañas Quilotoa**, on the access road to the crater, private or shared bath, wood stoves; **$$ Hostal Pachamama**, at the top of the hill by the rim of the crater, private bath.

$$ Complejo Shalalá
In Macapungo, T09-6917 3990, http://shalala.uphero.com.
Community-run lodge in a lovely 35-ha cloudforest reserve. Nice cabins, one with wheelchair access, includes breakfast and dinner, restaurant, trails.

$$ Quilotoa Crater Lake Lodge
On the main road facing the access to Quilotoa, T03-305 5816, www.quilotoalodgeecuador.com.
Somewhat faded hacienda-style lodge, includes breakfast and dinner, dining room with fireplace, views.

Chugchilán
All the hotels listed below are recommended.

$$$$-$$$ Black Sheep Inn
Below the village on the way to Sigchos, T03-270-8077, www.blacksheepinn.com.
A lovely eco-friendly resort which has received several awards. Includes 3 excellent vegetarian meals, private and shared bath, US$35 pp in dorms, spa, water slide, zipline, arranges excursions.

$$ El Vaquero
Just outside town on the road to Quilotoa, T03-270 8003, www.hostalelvaquero.com.
Variety of rooms with private bath, great views, heaters in common areas, includes generous dinner and breakfast,

helpful owners, transport to Quilotoa available (US$20), new in 2014.

$$ Hostal Mama Hilda
On the road in to town, T03-270 8015, www.mamahilda.com.
Pleasant family-run hostel, warm atmosphere, large rooms some with wood stoves, includes good dinner and breakfast, private or shared bath, camping, parking, arranges trips.

$$ Hostal Cloud Forest
At the entrance to town, T03-270 8016, www.cloudforesthostal.com.
Simple popular family-run hostel, sitting room with wood stove, includes dinner and great breakfast, restaurant open to public for lunch, private or shared bath, also dorm, parking, very helpful, great value.

Sigchos

$ Jardín de los Andes
Ilinizas y Tungurahua, T03-271 2114.
Basic but quite clean and friendly.

Isinliví

$$$ Llullu Llama
T09-9258 0562, www.llullullama.com.
Farmhouse with cosy sitting room with wood stove, tastefully decorated rooms, shared ecological bath. Also cottages with bath, fireplace and balcony. All include good hearty dinner and breakfast. Warm and relaxing atmosphere, a lovely spot. Recommended.

$ Taita Cristóbal
T09-9137 6542, taitacristobal@gmail.com.
Simple economy hostel with rooms and dorms, includes dinner and breakfast.

Saquisilí

$$ Gilocarmelo
*By the cemetery, 800 m from town
on the road north to Guaytacama,
T09-9966 9734, T02-340 0924.*
Restored hacienda house in a 4 ha
property. Plain rooms with fireplace,
restaurant, pool, sauna, jacuzzi,
nice garden.

$ San Carlos
Bolívar opposite the Parque Central.
A multi-storey building, electric shower,
parking, good value, but watch your
valuables. Will hold luggage for US$1
while you visit the market.

Transport

Note Throughout this region, buses
leave when full, sometimes ahead of
schedule. Go to the stop well in advance.

Zumbahua
Bus Many daily on the Latacunga–
Quevedo road (0500-1900, US$1.50,
1½ hrs). Buses on Sat are packed full;
get your ticket the day before. A pickup
truck can be hired from Zumbahua
to **Quilotoa** for US$5-10 depending
on number of passengers; also to
Chugchilán for around US$30. On Sat
mornings there are many trucks leaving
the Zumbahua market for Chugchilán
which pass Quilotoa. Pickup Quilotoa–
Chugchilán, US$25.

Taxi Day trips by taxi to Zumbahua,
Quilotoa, and return to **Latacunga** cost
about US$60.

Quilotoa
Bus From the terminal terrestre in
Latacunga **Trans Vivero** daily at 1000,
1130, 1230 and 1330, US$2.50, 2 hrs. Note
that this leaves from Latacunga, not

Saquisilí market, even on Thu. Return
bus direct to Latacunga at 1300. Buses
returning at 1400 and 1500 go only as far
as Zumbahua, from where you can catch
a Latacunga bound bus at the highway.
Also, buses going through Zumbahua
bound for Chugchilán will drop you
at the turnoff, 5 mins from the crater,
where you can also pick them up on
their way to Zumbahua and Latacunga.
Taxi from Latacunga, US$40 one way. For
Shalalá, **Trans Ilinizas** from Latacunga
to **Macapungo** at 1300, US$2, or go to
Zumbahua and take a pickup from there,
US$5. From Macapungo it is a 30-min
walk to the cabins.

Chugchilán
Bus From **Latacunga**, daily at 1130
(except Thu) via Sigchos, another bus,
also at 1130, goes via Zumbahua; on
Thu from **Saquisilí market** via Sigchos
around 1130, US$3.25, 3 hrs. Buses return
to Latacunga daily at 0330 via Sigchos,
at 0400 via Zumbahua. On Sun there
are 4 extra buses to Latacunga leaving
0600, 0900, 1100 and 1200. There are
extra buses going as far as Zumbahua
Wed 0600, Fri 0600 and Sun 0900-1000;
these continue towards the coast. Milk
truck to Sigchos around 0900. On Sat
also pickups going to/from market
in Zumbahua and Latacunga. From
Sigchos, through buses as indicated
above, US$0.75, 1 hr. Pickup hire to
Sigchos US$20, up to 5 people, US$5
additional person. Pickup to **Quilotoa**
US$25, up to 5 people, US$5 additional
person. Taxi from Latacunga US$50, from
Quito US$100. To **Isinliví**, taxi US$30.

Sigchos
Bus From **Latacunga** almost every
hour, 0930-1600; returning to Latacunga
most buses leave Sigchos before

0700, then at 1430 (more service on weekends); US$2, 2 hrs. From **Quito** direct service Mon-Sat at 1400 (more frequent Sun) with **Reina de Sigchos**; also Fri 1700 with **Illinizas**; US$3.75, 3 hrs. To **La Maná** on the road to Quevedo, via Chugchilán, Quilotoa and Zumbahua, Fri at 0500 and Sun at 0830, US$4.50, 6 hrs (returns Sat at 0730 and Sun at 1530). To **Las Pampas**, at 0330 and 1400, US$3.25, 3 hrs. From Las Pampas to **Santo Domingo**, at 0300 and 0600, US$3.25, 3 hrs.

Isinliví
From **Latacunga** daily (except Thu), via Sigchos at 1215 (**14 de Octubre**) and direct at 1300 (**Trans Vivero**), on Thu both leave from Saquisilí market around

1100, on Sat the direct bus leaves at 1100 instead of 1300, US$2.25, 2½ hrs. Both buses return to Latacunga 0300-0330, except Wed at 0700 direct, Sun 1245 direct and Mon 1500 via Sigchos. buses fill quickly, be there early. Connections to Chugchilán, Quilotoa and Zumbahua can be made in Sigchos. Bus schedules are posted on www.llullullama.com.

Saquisilí
Bus Frequent service between **Latacunga** and Saquisilí, US$0.50, 20 mins; many buses daily to/from **Quito** (Quitumbe), 0530-1300, US$2.50, 2 hrs. Buses and trucks to many outlying villages leave from 1000 onwards. Bus tours from Quito cost US$45 pp, taxis charge US$80, with 2-hr wait at market.

Ambato *Colour map 3, B5.*

few sights but good services including banks, hotels and restaurants

Almost completely destroyed in the great 1949 earthquake, Ambato (population 182,000, altitude 2700 m) lacks the colonial charm of other Andean cities, though its location in the heart of fertile orchard-country has earned it the nickname of 'the city of fruits and flowers' (see Festivals, page 167). It is also a transport hub and the principal commercial city of the central highlands, with a large Monday market and smaller ones Wednesday and Friday. The town is known for its colourful festivals: a *diablada* (devils' parade) 1-6 January and Corpus Christi.

The modern cathedral faces **Parque Montalvo**, where there is a statue of the writer Juan Montalvo (1832-1889), whose **house** ⓘ *Bolívar y Montalvo, T03-282 4248, US$1, Mon-Fri 0800-1200, 1400-1800,* can be visited. The **Museo de la Provincia** in the Casa del Portal (built 1900), facing Parque Montalvo, has a photo collection.

Northeast of Ambato is the colonial town of **Píllaro**, gateway to **Parque Nacional Los Llanganates**, a beautiful rugged area (for tours see **Sachayacu Explorer**, page 178).

Ambato to Baños
To the east of Ambato, an important road leads to **Salasaca**, where the *indígenas* sell their weavings; they wear distinctive black ponchos with white trousers and broad white hats. Further east, 5 km, is **Pelileo**, the blue jean manufacturing capital of Ecuador with good views of Tungurahua. There are opportunities for cultural tourism, walking and paragliding in the area (contact Patricio Cisnero at

Blue Land Adventures ① *T03-283 0236, bluelandsalasaca@yahoo.com.ar*). From Pelileo, the road descends to Las Juntas, where the Patate and Chambo rivers meet to form the Río Pastaza. About 1 km east of Las Juntas bridge, the junction with the road to Riobamba is marked by a large sculpture of a macaw and a toucan (locally known as Los Pájaros – the lower bird was destroyed by the volcano). It is a favourite volcano watching site. The road to Baños then continues along the lower slopes of the volcano.

Eight kilometres northeast of Pelileo on a paved side-road is **Patate**, centre of the warm, fruit growing Patate valley. There are excellent views of Volcán Tungurahua from town. The fiesta of **Nuestro Señor del Terremoto** is held on the weekend leading up to 4 February, featuring a parade with floats made with fruit and flowers.

Where to stay 🛏
1 Colony
2 Florida
3 Mary Carmen
4 Pirámide Inn
5 Roka Plaza

Restaurants 🍴
1 Ali's Parillada y Pizzeria
2 Crème Brulée
3 El Alamo Chalet
4 Govinda's
5 Heladería La Fornace
6 La Fornace
7 Pastelería Quito
8 Roho Wine

Ambato to Riobamba and Guaranda

After Ambato, the Pan-American Highway runs south to Riobamba (see page 179). About half way is **Mocha**, where guinea pigs (*cuy*) are bred for the table. You can sample roast *cuy* and other typical dishes at stalls and restaurants by the roadside, **Mariadiocelina** is recommended. The highway climbs steeply south of Mocha and at the pass at **Urbina** there are fine views in the dry season of Chimborazo and Carihuayrazo.

To the west of Ambato, a paved road climbs through tilled fields, past the *páramos* of Carihuayrazo and Chimborazo to the great Arenal (a high desert at the base of the mountain), and down through the Chimbo Valley to Guaranda (see page 180). This spectacular journey reaches a height of 4380 m and vicuñas can be seen.

Listings Ambato *map p165*

Tourist information

Ministerio de Turismo
Guayaquil y Rocafuerte, Ambato,
T03-282 1800, Mon-Fri 0800-1700.
Helpful.

Where to stay

Ambato

$$$ Florida
Av Miraflores 1131, T03-242 2007,
www.hotelflorida.com.ec.
Pleasant hotel in a nice setting,
restaurant with good set meals,
weekend discounts.

$$$ Mary Carmen
Av Ceballos y Martínez, T03-242 0908,
www.hotelboutiquemc.com.
Very nice boutique hotel with gym, spa
and parking. Opened in 2014.

$$$ Roka Plaza
Bolívar 20-62 y Guayaquil, T03-242 3845,
www.hotelrokaplaza.com.
Small stylish hotel in a refurbished
colonial house in the heart of the city,
sushi restaurant.

$$-$ Colony
12 de Noviembre 124 y Av El Rey, near
the bus terminal, T03-282 5789.
A modern hotel with large rooms,
parking, spotless.

SS-$ Pirámide Inn
Cevallos y Mariano Egüez, T03-242 1920.
Comfortable hotel, cafeteria, English
spoken.

Ambato to Baños
Salasaca and Pelileo

$$-$ Runa Huasi
In Salasaca, 1 km north off main
highway, T09-9984 0125, www.
hostalrunahuasi.com.
Simple hostel, includes breakfast and
fruit, other meals on request, cooking
facilities, nice views, guided walks.

$ Hostal Pelileo
Eloy Alfaro 641, T03-287 1390.
Shared bath, hot water, simple.

Patate

$$$$ Hacienda Leito
On the road to El Triunfo, T03-306 3196,
www.haciendaleito.com.

Classy hacienda with spacious rooms and great views of Tungurahua.

$$$ Hacienda Manteles
In the Leito valley on the road to El Triunfo, T09-9213 5309, Quito T02-603 9415, www.haciendamanteles.com.
Nice converted hacienda with wonderful views of Tungurahua and Chimborazo, includes breakfast, dinner, snacks, walk to waterfalls, hiking and horse riding. Reserve ahead.

$$$ Hostería Viña del Río
3 km from town on the old road to Baños, T03-287 0314, www.hosteriavinadelrio.com.
Cabins on a 22 ha ranch, restaurant, pool, spa and mini golf, US$6.72 for day use of facilities.

$ Hostal Casa del Valle
Juan Montalvo y Ambato, 2 blocks from plaza, T09-8150 1062.
A good simple place right in town, opened in 2014.

Restaurants

Ambato

$$$-$$ Ali's Parillada y Pizzeria
Bolivar entre JL Mera y Martínez, also in Ficoa neighbourhood and opposite Mall de los Andes. Open 1030-2230.
Very good pizzas and international meat dishes.

$$$-$$ La Fornace
Cevallos 1728 y Montalvo. Open 1100-2200.
Wood oven pizza. Opposite is **Heladería La Fornace**, Cevallos y Castillo. Snacks, sandwiches, ice cream, very popular.

$$ El Alamo Chalet
Cevallos 1719 y Montalvo. Open 0800-2300 (2200 Sun).

Ecuadorean and international food. Set meals and à la carte, Swiss-owned, good quality.

$$-$ Govinda's
Cuenca y Quito. Mon-Sat 0800-2030, Sun 0800-1600.
Vegetarian set meals and à la carte, also a meditation centre (T03-282 3182).

$ Roho Wine
Quito 924 y Bolívar. Mon-Sat 1200-1530.
Good set meals.

Cafés

Crème Brulée
Juan B Vela 08-38 y Montalvo. Daily 0900-2100.
Very good coffee and pastries.

Pastelería Quito
JL Mera y Cevallos. Daily 0700-2100.
Coffee, pastries, good for breakfast.

Festivals

Ambato
Feb/Mar **Fiesta de frutas y flores**.
Ambato's famous festival during carnival when there are 4 days of festivities and parades (best Sun morning and Mon night). Must book ahead to get a hotel room.

Shopping

Ambato
Leather
Ambato is a centre for leather: stores for shoes on Bolívar; jackets, bags, belts on Vela between Lalama and Montalvo. Take a local bus up to the leather town of Quisapincha for the best deals, everyday, but big market on Sat.

What to do

Ambato
Train rides

An autoferro runs from Ambato to **Urbina** and back via **Cevallos**, Fri-Sun at 0800, US$17. The train station is at Av Gran Colombia y Chile, near the Terminal Terrestre, T03-252 2623; open Wed-Sun 0800-1630.

Transport

Ambato
Bus The main bus station is on Av Colombia y Paraguay, 2 km north of the centre. City buses go there from Plaza Cevallos in the centre, US$0.25. To **Quito**, 3 hrs, US$3.25; also door to door shared taxis with **Servicio Express**, T03-242 6828 or T09-9924 2795, US$12. To **Cuenca**, US$10, 6½ hrs. To **Guayaquil**, 6 hrs, US$7.50. To **Riobamba**, US$1.50, 1 hr. To **Guaranda**, US$2.50, 3 hrs. To **Ibarra**, via the Quito airport and bypassing Quito, **CITA**, 8 daily, 5 hrs, US$6.25. To **Santo Domingo de los Tsáchilas**, 4 hrs, US$5. To **Tena**, US$6.25, 4½ hrs. To **Puyo**, US$3.75, 2½ hrs. To **Macas**, US$8.75, 5½ hrs. To **Esmeraldas**, US$10, 8 hrs. **Note** Buses to **Baños** leave from the Mercado Mayorista and then stop at the edge of town, 1 hr, US$1.10. Through buses do not go into the terminal, they take the Paso Lateral bypass road.

Baños
& Riobamba

Baños and Riobamba are both good bases for exploring the Sierra and their close proximity to high peaks gives great opportunities for climbing, cycling and trekking (but check about Tungurahua's volcanic activity before you set out). The thermal springs at Baños are an added lure and the road east is a great way to get to the jungle lowlands. Riobamba and Alausí offer the opportunity to ride the train on the famous section of the line from the Andes to Guayaquil, around the Devil's Nose.

Baños and around *Colour map 3, B6.*

highland resort in a spectacular setting

Baños (population 18,000, altitude 1800 m) is nestled between the Río Pastaza and the Tungurahua volcano, only 8 km from its crater. Baños bursts at the seams with hotels, *residenciales*, restaurants and tour agencies. Ecuadoreans flock here on weekends and holidays for the hot springs, to visit the Basílica and enjoy the local *melcochas* (toffees), while escaping the Andean chill in a sub-tropical climate (wettest in July and August). Foreign visitors are also frequent; using Baños as a base for trekking, organizing a visit to the jungle, making local day trips on horseback or by mountain bike, or just plain hanging out.

Safety
In 1999, after over 80 years of dormancy, Tungurahua became active again and has remained so until the close of this edition. The level of activity is variable; the volcano can be quiet for weeks or months. Baños continues to be a safe and popular destination and will likely remain so unless the level of volcanic activity greatly increases. **Tungurahua is closed to climbers** but all else is normal. Since the level of volcanic activity can change, you should enquire locally before visiting Baños. The National Geophysical Institute posts reports on the web at www.igepn.edu.ec.

Sights

The **Manto de la Virgen** waterfall at the southeast end of town is a symbol of Baños. The **Basílica** attracts many pilgrims. The paintings of miracles performed by Nuestra Señora del Agua Santa are worth seeing. There are various thermal baths in town; all charge US$2 unless otherwise noted. The **Baños de la Virgen** ⓘ *0430-1700*, are by the waterfall. They get busy so it's best to visit very early in the morning. Two small hot pools are open evenings only (1800-2200, US$3). The **Piscinas Modernas** ⓘ *Fri-Sun and holidays 0900-1700*, with a water slide, are next door. **El Salado baths** ⓘ *1.5 km out of town off the Ambato road, daily 0500-1600, weekends also 1800-2100, US$3*, with several hot pools, plus icy cold river water, are repeatedly destroyed by volcanic debris (not safe when activity is high). The **Santa Ana baths** ⓘ *just east of town on the road to Puyo, Fri-Sun and holidays 0900-1700*, have hot and cold pools in a pleasant setting. All the baths can be very crowded

Baños

Where to stay
1 Alisamay *B1*
2 Apart-Hotel Napolitano *A4*
3 Casa del Molino Blanco *C1*
4 El Belén *B2*
5 El Oro *B1*
6 Finca Chamanapamba *A4*
7 Isla de Baños *C2*
8 La Casa Verde *A4*
9 La Chimenea *C4*
10 La Floresta *C2*
11 La Petite Auberge *C3*
12 Los Pinos *B4*
13 Luna Runtún *A3*
14 Plantas y Blanco *C3*
15 Posada del Arte *C4*
16 Princesa María *B1*
17 Puerta del Sol *B4*
18 Samari *A4*
19 Sangay *C4*
20 Santa Cruz *C3*
21 Transilvania *B3*
22 Villa Santa Clara *C4*
23 Volcano *C4*

Restaurants 🍴
1 Ali Cumba *C3*
2 Café Blah Blah *B2*
3 Café Hood *B2*
4 Casa Hood *C3*
5 El Castillo *C4*
6 Jota Jota *C3*
7 Mariane *C2*
8 Pancho's *C2*
9 Rico Pan *B2*
10 Sativa *C3*
11 Swiss Bistro *C3*

Bars & clubs 🎵
12 Buena Vista *B3*
13 Ferchos *B3*
14 Jack Rock *B3*
15 Leprechaun *B3*
16 Peña Ananitay *B3*

at weekends and holidays; the brown colour of the water is due to its high mineral content. The **Santa Clara baths** ⓘ *C Velasco Ibarra behind Parque Montalvo, Wed-Fri 1400-2100, Sat-Sun 1000-2100, US$4*, are not natural springs but have clean heated pools as well as a nice large cold pool for swimming laps.

As well as the medicinal baths, there are various spas, in hotels, as independent centres and massage therapists. These offer a combination of sauna, steam bath (Turkish or box), jacuzzi, clay and other types of baths, a variety of massage techniques (Shiatsu, Reiki, Scandinavian) and more.

Around Baños

There are many interesting walks in the Baños area. The **San Martín shrine** is a 45-minute easy walk from town and overlooks a deep rocky canyon with the Río Pastaza thundering below. Beyond the shrine, crossing to the north side of the Pastaza, is the **Ecozoológico San Martín** ⓘ *T03-274 0552, 0800-1700, US$2.50*, with the **Serpentario San Martín** ⓘ *daily 0900-1700, US$2*, opposite. Some 50 m beyond is a path to the **Inés María waterfall**, cascading down, but polluted. Further, a tarabita (cable-car) and ziplines span the entrance to the canyon. You can also cross the Pastaza by the **Puente San Francisco** road bridge, behind the kiosks across the main road from the bus station. From here a series of trails fans out into the hills, offering excellent views of Tungurahua from the ridge-tops in clear weather. A total of six bridges span the Pastaza near Baños, so you can make a round trip.

On the hillside behind Baños are a series of interconnecting trails with nice views. It is a pleasant 45-minute hike to the **statue of the Virgin**; go to the south end of Calle JL Mera, before the street ends, take the last street to the right (Misioneros Dominicanos) at the end of which are stairs leading to the trail. A steep narrow path continues along the ridge, past the statue. Another trail also begins at the south end of JL Mera and leads to the **Hotel Luna Runtún**, continuing on to the village of Runtún (five- to six-hour round-trip). Yet another trail starts at the south end of Calle Maldonado and leads in 45 minutes to the **Bellavista cross**, from where you can also continue to Runtún.

The scenic road to Puyo (58 km) has many waterfalls tumbling down into the Pastaza. Many *tarabitas* (cable cars) and ziplines span the canyon offering good views. By the Agoyán dam and bridge, 5 km from town, is **Parque de la Familia** ⓘ *daily 0900-1700, entry free, parking US$1*, with orchards, gardens, paths and domestic animals. Beyond, the paved road goes through seven tunnels between Agoyán and Río Negro. The older gravel road runs parallel to the paved road, directly above the Río Pastaza, and is the preferred route for cyclists who, coming from Baños, should only go through one tunnel at Agoyán and then stay to the right avoiding the other tunnels. Between tunnels there is only the paved road; cyclists must be very careful as there are many buses and lorries. The area has excellent opportunities for walking and nature observation.

At the junction of the Verde and Pastaza rivers, 17 km from Baños is the town of **Río Verde** with snack bars, restaurants and a few places to stay. The Río Verde has crystalline green water and is cold but good for bathing. The paved highway runs to the north of town, between it and the old road, the river has been dammed forming a small lake where rubber rafts are rented for paddling. Near the paved road is **Orquideario** ① *open 0900-1700, closed Wed, US$1.50*, with nice regional orchids. Before joining the Pastaza the Río Verde tumbles down several falls, the most spectacular of which is ★ **El Pailón del Diablo** (the Devil's Cauldron). Cross the Río Verde on the old road and take the path to the right after the church, then follow the trail down towards the suspension bridge over the Pastaza, for about 20 minutes. Just before the bridge take a side trail to the right (signposted) which leads you to **Paradero del Pailón**, a nice restaurant, and viewing platforms above the falls (US$1.50). The **San Miguel Falls**, smaller but also nice, are some five minutes' walk from the town along a different trail. Cross the old bridge and take the first path to the right, here is **Falls Garden** (US$1.50), with lookout platforms over both sets of falls. Cyclists can leave the bikes at one of the snack bars while visiting the falls and return to Baños by bus.

Volcano watching

This very special experience can be enjoyed from Baños, Patate, Pelileo and several other nearby locations. With clear weather and a little luck, you can take in the unforgettable sight of mushroom clouds being expelled from the crater by day, and occasionally even red-hot boulders tumbling down the flanks of the volcano at night. In town, you can see the volcano from a small bridge over the Río Bascún, accessed from the top (west) end of Calle Ambato, but this spot is dangerous when activity is high. Several operators in town may offer volcano-watching tours, both day and night, which take you to viewing spots outside town when there is sufficient activity.

Listings Baños and around *map p170*

Tourist information

There are several private 'tourist information offices' run by travel agencies near the bus station; high-pressure tour sales, maps and pamphlets available. Local artist, J Urquizo, produces an accurate pictorial map of Baños, 12 de Noviembre y Ambato, also sold in many shops. There have been reports of thefts targeting tourists on Quito-Baños buses, take extra care of your hand-luggage.

iTur
Oficina Municipal de Turismo, at the Municipio, Halflants y Rocafuerte, opposite Parque Central. Mon-Fri 0800-
1730, Sat-Sun at Pje Ermita de la Virgen next to the market 0800-1600.
Helpful, with colourful maps of the area, some English spoken.

Where to stay

Baños
Baños has plenty of accommodation but can fill during holiday weekends.

$$$$ Luna Runtún
Caserío Runtún Km 6, T03-274 0882, www.lunaruntun.com.
A classy hotel in a beautiful setting overlooking Baños. Includes dinner, breakfast and use of pools (spa extra), very comfortable rooms with balconies

and superb views, lovely gardens. Good service, English, French and German spoken, tours, nanny service.

$$$$ Samari
Vía a Puyo Km 1, T03-274 1855, www.samarispa.com.
Upmarket resort opposite the Santa Ana baths, nice grounds, tastefully decorated hacienda-style rooms and suites, pool and spa (US$24.50 for non-residents), restaurant.

$$$$-$$$ Sangay Spa Hotel
Plazoleta Isidro Ayora 100, next to waterfall and thermal baths, T03-274 0490, www.sangayspahotel.com.
A newly refurbished Baños hotel and Ayurveda spa with 3 types of room, buffet breakfast, good restaurant specializes in Ecuadorean food. Pool and spa open to non-residents 1600-2000 (US$10), parking, tennis and squash courts, games room, car hire, jungle-like ambience, live shows at weekends, midweek discounts. British/Ecuadorian-run, attentive service. Recommended.

$$$ Apart-Hotel Napolitano
C Oriente 470 y Suárez, T03-274 2464, napolitano-apart-hotel@hotmail.com.
Large comfortable apartments with kitchen, fireplace, pool and spa, garden, parking. A bit pricey, daily rentals or US$600 per month.

$$$ Finca Chamanapamba
On the east shore of the Río Ulba, a short ride from the road to Puyo, T03-274 2671, www.chamanapamba.com.
2 nicely finished wooden cabins in a spectacular location overlooking the Río Ulba and just next to the Chamanapamba waterfalls, very good café-restaurant serves German food.

$$$ Posada del Arte
Pasaje Velasco Ibarra y Montalvo, T03-274 0083, www.posadadelarte.com.
Nice cosy inn, restaurant with vegetarian options, pleasant sitting room, more expensive rooms have fireplace, terrace, US-run.

$$$ Volcano
Rafael Vieira y Montalvo, T03-274 2140, www.volcano.com.ec.
Spacious modern hotel, large rooms with fridge, some with views of the waterfall, buffet breakfast, restaurant, heated pool, massage, nice garden.

$$$-$$ Isla de Baños
Halflants 1-31 y Montalvo, T03-274 0609, www.isladebanios.com.
Nicely decorated comfortable hotel with rooms and suites, includes European breakfast and steam bath, spa operates when there are enough people, pleasant garden.

$$ Alisamay
Espejo y JL Mera, T03-2741391, www.hotelalisamay.com.
Rustic hotel, cosy rooms with balconies, includes breakfast and use of spa, gardens with pools.

$$ La Casa Verde
In Santa Ana, 1.5 km from town on Camino Real, a road parallel and north of the road to Puyo, T03-274 2671, www.lacasaverde.com.ec.
Lovely spacious hotel decorated in pine, the largest rooms in Baños, laundry and cooking facilities, very quiet, New Zealand-run.

$$ La Floresta
Halflants y Montalvo, T03-274 1824, www.laflorestahotel.com.
Lovely hotel with large comfortable rooms set around a lovely garden,

excellent buffet breakfast, wheelchair accessible, craft and book shop, parking, attentive service. Warmly recommended.

$$-$ La Petite Auberge
16 de Diciembre y Montalvo, T03-274 0936, www.lepetit.banios.com.
Rooms around a patio, some with fireplace, good upmarket French restaurant, parking, quiet.

$$-$ Los Pinos
Ricardo Zurita y C Ambato, T03-274 1825.
Large hostel with double rooms and dorms (US$8-10 pp), includes breakfast (and dinner Mon-Wed), spa, kitchen and laundry facilities, pool table, Argentine-run, great value.

$$-$ Puerta del Sol
Ambato y Arrayanes (east end of C Ambato), T03-274 2265.
Modern hotel, nicer than it looks on the outside, large well-appointed rooms, includes breakfast, pleasant dining area, laundry facilities, parking.

$ Casa del Molino Blanco
Misioneros Dominicanos y JL Mera, T03-274 1138, www.casamolinoblanco.com.
Located in a quiet area, with bath, US$11 pp in dorm, spotlessly clean, includes buffet breakfast, German spoken, opened in 2014.

$ El Belén
Reyes y Ambato, T03-274 1024, www.hotelelbelen.com.
Good-value hostel, cooking facilities, spa, parking, helpful staff.

$ El Oro
Ambato y JL Mera, T03-274 0736.
With bath, US$8 pp in dorm, laundry and cooking facilities, good value, popular. Recommended.

$ La Chimenea
Martínez y Rafael Vieira, T03-274 2725, www.hostalchimenea.com.
Pleasant hostel with terrace café, breakfast available, private or shared bath, US$8 pp in dorm, small pool, jacuzzi extra, parking for small cars, quiet, helpful and good value. Recommended.

$ Plantas y Blanco
12 de Noviembre y Martínez, T03-274 0044, www.plantasyblanco.com.
Popular hostel decorated with plants, private or shared bath, US$8-10 pp in dorm, excellent breakfast available, rooftop cafeteria, steam bath, classic films, bakery, French-owned, good value. Recommended.

$ Princesa María
Rocafuerte y Mera, T03-274 1035.
Spacious rooms, US$8 pp in dorm, laundry and cooking facilities, parking, popular budget travellers' meeting place, helpful and good value.

$ Santa Cruz
16 de Diciembre y Martínez, T03-274 3527, www.santacruzbackpackers.com.
Large rooms, US$8 pp in dorm, fireplace in lounge, small garden with hammocks, kitchen facilities, mini pool on roof.

$ Transilvania
16 de Diciembre y Oriente, T03-274 2281, www.hostal-transilvania.com.
Multi-storey building with simple rooms, includes breakfast, US$8 pp in dorm, Middle Eastern restaurant, nice views from balconies, large TV and movies in sitting room, pool table, popular meeting place.

$ Villa Santa Clara
12 de Noviembre y Velasco Ibarra, T03-274 0349, www.hotelvillasantaclara.com.

Nice cabins in a quiet location, laundry facilities, wheelchair accessible, garden, spa, parking.

Around Baños

$$$ Miramelindo
Río Verde, just north of the paved road, T03-249 3004, www.miramelindo.banios.com.
Lovely hotel and spa, nicely decorated rooms, good restaurant, pleasant gardens include an orchid collection with over 1000 plants.

$$ Hostería Río Verde
Between the paved road and town, T03-249 3007 (Ambato), www.hosteriarioverde.com.
Simple cabins in a rural setting, includes breakfast and use of spa, large pool, restaurant specializes in trout and tilapia.

Restaurants

Baños

$$$ Mariane
On a small lane by Montalvo y Halflants. Mon-Sat 1800-2300.
Excellent authentic Provençal cuisine, generous portions, lovely setting, pleasant atmosphere, popular, slow service. Highly recommended. **Hotel Mariane ($$)** at the same location, very clean and pleasant.

$$$ Swiss Bistro
Martínez y Alfaro. Daily 1200-2300, Mon 1800-2300.
International dishes and Swiss specialities, Swiss-run.

$$ Café Hood
Maldonado y Ambato, at Parque Central. Open 1000-2200, closed Wed.
Mainly vegetarian but also some meat dishes, excellent food, English spoken, always busy. Also rents rooms.

$$ Casa Hood
Martínez between Halflants and Alfaro. Open 1200-2200.
Largely vegetarian, but also some meat dishes, juices, milkshakes, varied menu including Indonesian and Thai, good set lunch and desserts. Travel books and maps sold, book exchange, repertory cinema, occasional cultural events, nice atmosphere. Popular and recommended.

$$ Sativa
Martínez y Eloy Alfaro, open 0900-2200.
Wholesome food, some organic ingredients from their own garden, try the veggie-burger.

$ El Castillo
Martínez y Rafael Vieira, in hostel. Open 0800-1000, 1200-1330.
A favourite of locals for a good filling set lunch.

Cafés

Ali Cumba
12 de Noviembre y Martínez. Daily 0800-2200.
Excellent breakfasts, salads, good coffee (filtered, espresso), muffins, cakes, homemade bread, large sandwiches, book exchange. Danish/Ecuadorean-run.

Café Blah Blah
Halflants y Matrínez. Daily 0800-2000.
Cosy café serving very good breakfasts, coffee, cakes, snacks and juices, a popular meeting place.

Jota Jota
Martínez y Halflants, Tue-Sun 1000-2200.
Great choice of coffees and cocktails, book exchange. German-run.

Pancho's

Rocafuerte y Maldonado at Parque Central. Daily 1530-2200.
Hamburgers, snacks, sandwiches, coffee, large-screen TV for sports and other events.

Rico Pan

Ambato y Maldonado at Parque Central. Mon-Sat 0700-1900, Sun 0700-1300.
Good breakfasts, hot bread (including whole wheat), fruit salads and pizzas, also meals.

Bars and clubs

Baños

Eloy Alfaro, between Ambato and Oriente has many bars including:

Buena Vista
Alfaro y Oriente.
A good place for salsa and other Latin music.

Ferchos
Alfaro y Oriente. Tue-Sun 1600-2400.
Café-bar, modern decor, snacks, cakes, good varied music, German-run.

Jack Rock
Alfaro y Ambato.
A favourite traveller hangout.

Leprechaun
Alfaro y Oriente.
Popular for dancing, bonfire on weekends, occasional live music.

Entertainment

Baños

Chivas, open-sided buses, cruise town playing music, they take you to different night spots and to a volcano lookout when Tungurahua is active.

Peña Ananitay
16 de Diciembre y Espejo.
Bar, good live music and dancing on weekends, no cover.

Festivals

Baños

During Carnival and Holy Week hotels are full and prices rise.
Oct Nuestra Señora de Agua Santa, with daily processions, bands, fireworks, sporting events and partying through the month.
Dec Week-long celebrations ending **16 Dec**, the town's anniversary, parades, fairs, sports, cultural events. The night of **15 Dec** are the **Verbenas**, when each *barrio* hires a band and parties.

Shopping

Baños

Look out for jaw-aching toffee (*melcocha*) made in ropes in shop doorways, or the less sticky *alfeñique*.

Handicrafts

Crafts stalls at Pasaje Ermita de la Vírgen, off C Ambato, by the market. Tagua (vegetable ivory made from palm nuts) crafts on Maldonado y Martínez. Leather shops on Rocafuerte between Halflants and 16 de Diciembre.
Centro Naturista, *Eloy Alfaro y Oriente.* Health foods and alternative medicine.
Latino Shop, *Ambato y Alfaro and 4 other locations.* For T-shirts.
Librería Vieira – Arte Ilusion, *Halflants y Martínez.* Bookstore with a café, Wi-Fi, good meeting place.

What to do

Baños

Various adventure sports are popular in Baños, including mountaineering, white water rafting, canyoning, canopying and bridge jumps. Safety standards vary greatly. There is seldom any recourse in the event of a mishap so these potentially hazardous activities are entirely at your own risk.

Bus tours

The *chivas* (see entertainment, above) and a **double-decker bus** (C Ambato y Halflants, T03-274 0596, US$6) visit waterfalls and other attractions. Check about their destination if you have a specific interest such as El Pailón falls.

Canopying or zipline

Involves hanging from a harness and sliding on a steel cable. Prices vary according to length, about US$10-20. Cable car, about US$1.50.

Canyoning

Many agencies offer this sport, rates US$30 half day, US$50 full day.

Climbing and trekking

There are countless possibilities for walking and nature observation near Baños and to the east. Tungurahua has been officially closed to climbers since 1999. There is nobody to stop you from entering the area, but the dangers of being hit by flying volcanic bombs are very real. Operators offer trekking and climbing tours to Cotopaxi (US$200-$220) and Chimborazo (US$200-$240). Trekking about US$45 per day.

Cycling

Many places rent bikes, quality varies, US$5-10 per day; check brakes and tyres, find out who has to pay for repairs, and insist on a helmet, puncture repair kit and pump. The following have good equipment:

Carrillo Hermanos, *16 de Diciembre y Martínez*. Rents mountain bikes and motorcycles (reliable machines with helmets, US10 per hr).

Hotel Isla de Baños, cycling tours US$15-20.

Horse riding

There are many places, but check their horses as not all are well cared for. Rates around US$8-10 per hr (minimum 2 hrs), US$40 per day. The following have been recommended:

Antonio Banderas, *Montalvo y Halflants, T03-274 2532*.

Hotel Isla de Baños, *see above*. 3½ hrs with a guide and jeep transport costs US$35 pp, English and German spoken.

Jaime Aldaz, *Martínez y Eloy Alfaro, T09-9829 2984*.

José & Two Dogs, *Maldonado y Martínez, T03-274 0746*. Flexible hours.

Ringo Horses, *12 de Noviembre y Martínez (Apart-hotel El Napolitano)*. Offers rides outside Baños.

Language schools

Spanish schools charge US$7-9 per hr, many also offer homestays.

Baños Spanish Center, *www.spanishcenter.banios.com*.

Home Stay Baños, *T03-274 0453*.

Mayra's, *www.mayraspanishschool.com*.

Raíces, *www.spanishlessons.org*.

Paragliding

See www.aeropasion.net; US$60 per day.

Puenting

Many operators offer this bungee-jumping-like activity from the bridges around Baños, US$10-20 per jump, heights and styles vary.

Whitewater rafting

Fatal accidents have occurred, but not with the agencies listed here. Rates US$30 for half day, US$70 for full day. The Chambo, Patate and Pastaza rivers are all polluted. **Geotours** and **Wonderful Ecuador** are good (see below).

Tour operators

There are many tour agencies in town, some with several offices, as well as 'independent' guides who seek out tourists on the street (the latter are generally not recommended). Quality varies considerably; to obtain a qualified guide and avoid unscrupulous operators, it is best to seek advice from other travellers who have recently returned from a tour. We have received some critical reports of tours out of Baños, but there are also highly respected and qualified operators here. Most agencies and guides offer trips to the jungle (US$50-70 per day pp). There are also volcano-watching, trekking and horse tours, in addition to the day-trips and sports mentioned above. Several companies run tours aboard a *chiva* (open-sided bus). The following agencies and guides have received positive recommendations but the list is not exhaustive and there are certainly others.
Expediciones Amazónicas, *Oriente 11-68 y Halflants*, T03-274 0506.
Geotours, *Ambato y Halflants, next to Banco Pichincha*, T03-274 1344, *www.geotoursbanios.com*. Also offer paragliding for US$60.
Imagine Ecuador, *16 de Diciembre*

y Montalvo, T03-274 3472, *www.imagineecuador.com*.
Marberktour, *Eloy Alfaro y Rocafuerte*, T03-274 1695, *www.marberktour.com*.
Sachayacu Explorer, *Bolívar 229 y Urbina, in Píllaro*, T03-287 5316 or T09-8740 3376, *www.treasureoftheincas.com*. Trekking in the Llanganates, jungle tours in Huaorani territory, Yasuní and as far as Peru, English spoken.
Wonderful Ecuador, *Maldonado y Oriente*, T03-274 1580, *www.wonderfulecuador.org*.

Baños
Bus City buses run from Alfaro y Martínez east to Agoyán and from Rocafuerte by the market, west to El Salado and the zoo. The long-distance bus station is on the Ambato–Puyo road (Av Amazonas). It gets very busy on weekends and holidays, buy tickets in advance. To **Rio Verde** take any Puyo bound bus, through buses don't go in the station, 20 mins, US$0.65. To **Quito**, US$4.25, 3 hrs, frequent service; going to Quito sit on the right for views of Cotopaxi; also shared taxis with **Autovip**, T02-600 2582 (Quito) or T09-9629 5406, US$20. Note that buses from Quito to Baños are the target of thieves, take a shared taxi or bus to Ambato and transfer there. To **Ambato**, 1 hr, US$1.10. To **Riobamba**, some buses take the direct Baños-Riobamba road but most go via Mocha, 1½ hrs, US$2.50. To **Latacunga**, 2 hrs, US$2.25. To **Otavalo** and **Ibarra** direct, bypassing Quito, **Expreso Baños**, at 0400 and 1440, US$6, 5½ hrs. To **Guayaquil**, 1 bus per day and one overnight, US$10, 6-7 hrs; or change in Riobamba. To **Puyo**, 1½ hrs, US$2.40. Sit on the right. You can cycle to Puyo

and take the bus back (passport check on the way). To **Tena**, 3½ hrs, US$6. To **Misahuallí**, change at Tena. To **Macas**, 4½ hrs, US$9 (sit on the right).

Riobamba and around
attractive colonial city with a large indigenous population and colourful markets

Guaranda and Riobamba are good bases for exploring the Sierra. Riobamba is the bigger of the two and is on the famous railway line from Quito to Guayaquil. Many indigenous people from the surrounding countryside can be seen in both cities on market days. Because of their central location Riobamba and the surrounding province are known as 'Corazón de la Patria' – the heartland of Ecuador – and the city boasts the nickname 'La Sultana de Los Andes' in honour of lofty Mount Chimborazo.

Riobamba *Colour map 3, B5. See map, page 180.*
The capital of Chimborazo Province, Riobamba (population 162,000, altitude 2754 m) has broad streets and many ageing but impressive buildings.

The main square is **Parque Maldonado** around which are the **Cathedral**, the **Municipality** and several colonial buildings with arcades. The Cathedral has a beautiful colonial stone façade and an incongruously modern interior. Four blocks northeast of the railway station is the **Parque 21 de Abril**, named after the Batalla de Tapi, 21 April 1822, the city's independence from Spain. The park, better known as **La Loma de Quito**, affords an unobstructed view of Riobamba and Chimborazo, Carihuairazo, Tungurahua, El Altar and occasionally Sangay. It also has a colourful tile tableau of the history of Ecuador; ask about safety before visiting. The **Convento de la Concepción** ① *Orozco y España, entrance at Argentinos y J Larrea, T03-296 5212, Tue-Sat, 0900-1230, 1500-1730, US$5*, has a religious art museum. **Museo de la Ciudad** ① *Primera Constituyente y Espejo, at Parque Maldonado, T03-294 4420, Mon-Fri 0800-1230, 1430-1800, free*, in a beautifully restored colonial building, has an interesting historical photograph exhibit and temporary displays.

Markets Riobamba is an important market centre where people from many communities congregate. Saturday is the main day when the city fills with colourfully dressed *indígenas* from all over Chimborazo, each wearing their distinctive costume; trading overflows the markets and buying and selling go on all over town. Wednesday is a smaller market day. The 'tourist' market is in the small **Plaza de la Concepción or Plaza Roja** ① *Orozco y Colón, Sat and Wed only, 0800-1500*, is a good place to buy local handicrafts and authentic Indian clothing. The main produce market is **San Alfonso**, Argentinos y 5 de Junio, which on Saturday spills over into the nearby streets and also sells clothing, ceramics, baskets and hats. Other markets in the colonial centre are **La Condamine** ① *Carabobo y Colombia, daily*, largest market on Fridays, **San Francisco** and **La Merced**, near the churches of the same name.

Guano

Guano is a carpet-weaving, sisal and leather working town 8 km north of Riobamba. Many shops sell rugs and you can arrange to have these woven to your own design. Buses leave from the Mercado Dávalos, García Moreno y New York, every 15 minutes, US$0.25, last bus back at 1900, taxi US$5.

Guaranda *Colour map 3, B5. See map, page 182.*

The quaint town of Guaranda (population 57,500, altitude 2650 m), capital of Bolívar Province, proudly calls itself 'the Rome of Ecuador' because it is built on seven hills. There are fine views of the mountains all around and a colourful market. Locals traditionally take an evening stroll in the palm-fringed main plaza, **Parque Libertador Simón Bolívar**, around which the Municipal buildings and a large stone **Cathedral**. Towering over the city, on one of the hills, is an impressive statue of **El Indio Guaranga**; museum (free) and art gallery. There is also a small local museum at the **Casa de la Cultura** ① *Sucre entre Manuela Cañizares y Selva Alegre.* Although not on the tourist trail, there are many sights worth visiting in the province, for which Guaranda is the ideal base. Of particular interest is the highland town of **Salinas**, with its community development projects (accommodations and tours available, see Where to stay), as well as the *subtrópico* region, the lowlands stretching west towards the coast.

Market days are Friday (till 1200) and Saturday (larger), when many indigenous people in typical dress trade at the market complex at the east end of Calle Azuay, by Plaza 15 de Mayo (9 de Abril y Maldonado), and at Plaza Roja (Avenida Gen Enríquez). Carnival in Guaranda is among the best known in the country.

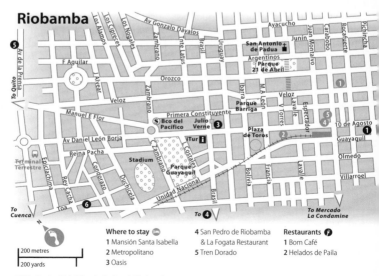

Riobamba

Where to stay 😊
1 Mansión Santa Isabella
2 Metropolitano
3 Oasis
4 San Pedro de Riobamba
& La Fogata Restaurant
5 Tren Dorado

Restaurants 🍴
1 Bom Café
2 Helados de Paila

200 metres
200 yards

Tourist office: Oficina Municipal de Turismo ⓘ *García Moreno entre 7 de Mayo y Convención de 1884, T03-298 0321, www.guaranda.gob.ec (in Spanish), Mon-Fri 0800-1200, 1400-1800.* Provides Information in Spanish and maps.

★ Reserva Faunística Chimborazo
Information from Ministerio del Ambiente, Avenida 9 de Octubre y Duchicela, Quinta Macají, Riobamba, T03-261 0029, ext110, Mon-Fri 0800-1300, 1400-1700. Ranger station T03-302 7358, daily 0800-1700. See also Riobamba tour operators.

Visitors arriving without a guide and tour operator or with services not authorized by the ministry are turned back at the gate; exceptions are made for members of alpine clubs, apply for an entry permit at the Ministerio del Ambiente in Riobamba. The most outstanding features of this reserve, created to protect the camelids (vicuñas, alpacas and llamas) which were re-introduced here, are the beautiful snowcapped volcanos of **Chimborazo** and its neighbour **Carihuayrazo**. Chimborazo, inactive, is the highest peak in Ecuador (6310 m), while Carihuayrazo, 5020 m, is dwarfed by its neighbour. Day visitors can enjoy lovely views, a glimpse of the handsome vicuñas and the rarefied air above 4800 m. There are great opportunities for trekking on the eastern slopes, accessed from **Urbina**, west of the Ambato–Riobamba road, and of course climbing Ecuador's highest peak. Horse riding and trekking tours are offered along the Mocha Valley between the two peaks and downhill cycling from Chimborazo is popular.

To the west of the reserve runs the Vía del Arenal which joins San Juan, along the Riobamba–Guaranda road, with Cruce del Arenal on the Ambato-Guaranda road. A turn-off from this road leads to the main park entrance and beyond to the **Refugio Hermanos Carrel**, a shelter at 4800 m, from where it is a 45-minute walk to **Refugio Whymper** at 5000 m. Both shelters were rebuilt in 2015. At the close of this edition the Carrel shelter had re-opened with room for 36; accommodation US$15 per person (advise rangers that you want to stay overnight when entering the reserve) and a cafeteria serving hot drinks and snacks. The access from Riobamba (51 km, paved to the park entrance) is very beautiful. Along the Vía del Arenal past San Juan are a couple of small indigenous communities which grow a few crops and raise llamas and alpacas. They offer lodging and *guías nativos*, the area is good for acclimatization The *arenal* is a large sandy plateau at about 4400 m, to the west of Chimborazo, just

3 Jamones La Andaluza & Naranjo's
4 La Abuela Rosa
5 Mónaco Pizzería
6 Zen Wei

below the main park entrance. It can be a harsh, windy place, but it is also very beautiful; take the time to admire the tiny flowers which grow here. This is the best place to see vicuñas, which hang around either in family groups, one male and its harem, or lone males which have been expelled from the group.

Climbing Chimborazo At 6310 m, this is a difficult climb owing to the altitude and variable snow conditions. No one without mountaineering experience should attempt it before doing other summits; rope, ice axe, crampon and helmet must be used, ice screws may be useful and acclimatization is essential. Climbers must go with a certified guide working for an operator who has a special permit (*patente*). Chimborazo can be climbed all year round but the weather is unpredictable. It is best to avoid late July and August, when it can be very windy and the risk of rock fall increases.

From the Whymper refuge (see above) to the summit the climb is six to eight hours and the descent about four hours. The path from the hut to the glacier is marked but difficult to follow at midnight, so it's best to check it out the day before. Parts of the route on the glacier are marked with flags, but it can be tricky in cloud or mist. There are several crevasses on the way, so you need to rope up. There are three routes depending on your experience and snow conditions. Start at 2400 or 0100. There are avalanche problems on the entire mountain and danger of falling rocks

Guaranda

Where to stay 🛏
1 Bolívar
2 El Marquez
3 La Casa de las Flores
4 La Colina
5 Oasis

Restaurants 🍴
1 Chifa Gran Cangrejo Rojo
2 La Bohemia
3 La Estancia
4 Pizza Buon Giorno
5 Salinerito

ON THE ROAD
The railway that refused to die

As you climb aboard for the *Devil's Nose*, consider the rich history of this train. What is today a popular and exhilarating tourist ride was once the country's pride and joy. Its construction was internationally acclaimed, the 11-year US$26 million project of Ecuadorean president Eloy Alfaro and US entrepreneur Archer Harman. A spectacular 464-km railway line (1.067-m gauge), which ran from Durán (outside Guayaquil) up to Riobamba, was opened in 1908. It passed through 87 km of delta lands and then, in another 80 km, climbed to 3238 m. The highest point (3619 m) was reached at Urbina, between Riobamba and Ambato. It then fell and rose before reaching Quito at 2850 m.

This was one of the great railway journeys of the world and a fantastic piece of engineering, with a maximum gradient of 5.5%. Rail lines also ran from Riobamba south to Cuenca, and from Quito north to Ibarra, then down to the coast at San Lorenzo. There were even more ambitious plans, never achieved, to push the railhead deep into the Oriente Jungle, from Ambato as far as Leticia (then Ecuador, today Colombia). Time and neglect subsequently took their toll and by the turn of the millennium only a few short segments remained in service, basically as cheap tourist rides. There was often talk of reviving the Ecuadorean railway as a whole but it never seemed to happen.

Between 2007 and 2013 however, the Ecuadorean government undertook a complete restoration of the line from Quito to Durán, which was re-opened with much fanfare. From new concrete ties to modern rolling stock, it was a formidable achievement. However, many feel disappointed that it isn't a real railway. Rather it is a series of seven short (but no longer cheap) tourist rides with cutesy names like *Tren de la Dulzura* (the 'sweetness train', because it runs through sugar cane fields), and a lavish multi-day excursion for railway buffs offered a few times a year.

We can't help but ask what happened to the dream of Eloy Alfaro and Archer Harman, which seems to have derailed along the way. Surely they envisaged a working railway to efficiently transport passengers and freight, serving the needs of Ecuador today as well as it did in the past? That vision, like the railway itself, refuses to die.

and black ice in the dry season. *Penitentes*, which are conical ice formations, may obstruct the final portion between the Veintimilla and Whymper summits.

★ **The Devil's Nose Train**

This spectacular ride is popular with both Ecuadorean and foreign tourists. In early 2015, tourist trains ran from Alausí to Sibambe, the most scenic part of the trip including the **Devil's Nose**, and from Riobamba north to Urbina and south to Colta. The route Riobamba–Alausí–Sibambe is scheduled to re-open later in 2015. For details see What to do, page 190.

Alausí *Colour map 3, C5*.

The picturesque town of Alausí (population 10,500, altitude 2350 m) perched on a hillside is where many passengers join the train for the amazing descent over *La Nariz de Diablo* to Sibambe. There is good walking, a Sunday market and a **Fiesta de San Pedro** on 29 June.

Parque Nacional Sangay

Riobamba provides access to the central highland region of **Sangay National Park** ⓘ *information from Ministerio del Ambiente, see Reserva Chimborazo above*, a beautiful wilderness area with excellent opportunities for trekking and climbing. A spectacular road, good for downhill biking, runs from Riobamba to Macas in the Oriente, cutting through the park. Near Cebadas (with a good cheese factory) a branch road joins from **Guamote**, a quiet, mainly indigenous town on the Pan-American Highway, which comes to life during its colourful Thursday market. At **Atillo**, south of Cebadas, an area of lovely *páramo* dotted with lakes, there is lodging (US$7 per person) and restaurant at **Cabaña Saskines** (T03-301 4383, atillosaskines@hotmail.com).

Climbing El Altar and Sangay

El Altar Climbs to El Altar are technical. For experienced ice climbers the Ruta Obispo offers Grade 4 and 5 mixed ice and rock. **El Obispo** is the highest and most southerly of Altar's nine summits, at 5315 m. Another technical route is to **El Canónigo** (5260 m), the northernmost of the summits, mixed ice and rock, Grade 4 and 5. Altar's seven other summits are, from north to south: **Fraile Grande** (5180 m); **Fraile Central** (5070 m); **Fraile Oriental** (5060 m); **Fraile Beato** (5050 m); **Tabernáculo** (5100 m); **Monja Chica** (5080 m); and **Monja Grande** (5160 m). One access route to El Altar is through Candelaria, see Trekking in the park, below. Rapid deglaciation is changing the climbing routes on El Altar.

Sangay This is a continuously active volcano reaching 5230 m. Access to the mountain takes at least three days and is only for those who can endure long, hard days of walking and severe weather. Climbing Sangay can be dangerous even when volcanic activity seems low and a helmet to protect against falling stones is vital, November to January is a good time to climb it. Agencies in Quito and Riobamba offer tours or you can organize an expedition independently. A guide is essential; porters can be hired in the access towns of **Alao** and **Guarguallá**. The latter has a **community tourism project** ⓘ *T03-302 6688, T09-9121 3205, accommodation in Guarguallá Chico US$15 pp, US$21 pp with dinner and breakfast (reserve in advance), kitchen facilities. Guías nativos, US$40 per day plus US$110 for ascent; porters and horses US$20 per day.*

Trekking in the park

El Altar The most popular trek is to the crater of El Altar. A well-used track (very muddy in the wet season) leads up a steep hill past **Hacienda Releche** (where there is simple accommodation), outside the little village of Candelaria (altitude 3100 m). It is about six hours from Candelaria to the Collanes plain, where there are basic thatched-roof shelters, and another two hours to the crater which is surrounded by magnificent snowcapped peaks. Horses can be hired at Hacienda Releche to carry your gear.

Sangay The access route used by climbers is also a fine trekking route; experience is required.

Lakes The Atillo and Osogoche areas offer excellent trekking and it is possible to trek from one set of lakes to the other.

Listings Riobamba and around *map p180*

Tourist information

Riobamba

iTur
Av Daniel León Borja y Brasil, T03-296 3159. Mon-Fri 0830-1230, 1430-1800.
Municipal information office, English spoken.

Where to stay

Riobamba

$$$$-$$$ Abraspungo
Km 3 on the road to Guano, T03-236 4275, www.haciendaabraspungo.com.
Good hotel in a country setting, comfortable rooms, includes buffet breakfast, excellent restaurant, parking, attentive service. Recommended.

$$$$-$$$ La Andaluza
16 km north of Riobamba along the Panamericana, T03-294 9371, www.hosteriaandaluza.com.
An old hacienda, rooms with heaters and roaring fireplaces, includes buffet breakfast, good restaurant, lovely views, good walking.

$$$ Mansión Santa Isabella
Veloz 28-48 y Carabobo, T03-296 2947, www.mansionsantaisabella.com.

Lovely restored house with pleasant patio, comfortable rooms most with bathtub, duvets, includes buffet breakfast, restaurant serves set lunches and à la carte, bar in stone basement, parking, attentive service, British/Ecuadorean-run. Recommended.

$$$ San Pedro de Riobamba
Daniel L Borja 29-50 y Montalvo, opposite the train station, T03-294 0586.
Elegant hotel in a beautifully restored house in the centre of town, ample comfortable rooms, bathtubs, cafeteria, parking, covered patio, reservations required. Recommended.

$$ Rincón Alemán
Remigio Romero y Alfredo Pareja, Ciudadela Arupos del Norte, T03-260 3540, www.hostalrinconaleman.com.
Family-run hotel in a quiet residential area north of the centre, nice ample rooms, laundry and cooking facilities, parking, fireplace, sauna, gym, garden, terrace, nice views, German spoken.

$$-$ Oasis
Veloz 15-32 y Almagro, T03-296 1210, www.oasishostelriobamba.com.
Small, pleasant, family-run hostel in a quiet location, laundry facilities, some rooms with kitchen and fridge, shared

kitchen for the others, parking, pleasant garden, Wi-Fi US$1 per day, popular with backpackers. Recommended.

$$-$ Tren Dorado
Carabobo 22-35 y 10 de Agosto, near the train station, T03-296 4890, www. hoteltrendorado.com.
Modern hotel with nice large rooms, buffet breakfast available (starting 0730, open to non-guests), restaurant, reliable hot water, good value. Recommended.

$ Metropolitano
Daniel L Borja y Lavalle, near the train station, T03-296 1714.
One of the oldest hotels in Riobamba, built in 1912 and nicely restored. Ample rooms, convenient location.

Guaranda

$$$ La Colina
Av Guayaquil 117, on the road to Ambato, T03-298 0666, www.complejolacolina.com.
Well situated on a quiet hillside overlooking the city. Bright spacious rooms, nice views, small covered swimming pool (not always open) and sauna (weekends only), gardens, parking, tours available.

$$ Bolívar
Sucre 704 y Rocafuerte, T03-298 0547, http://hotelbolivar.wordpress.com.
Pleasant hotel with courtyard, small modern rooms, best quality in the centre of town. Restaurant next door open Mon-Fri for economical breakfasts and lunches.

$$ Oasis
Gen Enriquez y Garcia Moreno, T03-298 3762.
Modern multi-storey building with large, bright and clean rooms. Opened in 2015.

$ El Marquez
10 de Agosto y Eloy Alfaro, T03-298 1053.

Pleasant hotel with family atmosphere, newer rooms with private bath are clean and modern, older ones with shared bath are cheaper, parking.

$ La Casa de las Flores
Pichincha 402 y Rocafuerte esquina, T03-298 5795.
Renovated colonial house with covered courtyard and flowers, private bath, hot water, simple economical rooms.

Salinas

$$-$ Hotel Refugio Salinas
45 min from Guaranda, T03-221 0044, www.salinerito.com.
Pleasant community-run hotel, economical meals on request, private or shared bath, dining/sitting area with fireplace, visits to community projects, walking and horse riding tours, packages available, advance booking advised.

$$-$ La Minga
By the main plaza, T09-9218 8880, www.laminga.ec.
Simple rooms with bath and dorms, meals on request, full board packages including tour available.

Reserva Faunística Chimborazo
The following are all good for acclimatization; those in Urbina can be reached by autoferro from either Riobamba or Ambato.

$$ Refugio del Tren
At the Urbina railway station 2 km west of the highway, at 3619 m, T09-9817 6400.
Converted train station, shared bath, price includes dinner and breakfast, fireplace in common areas and one room, heaters.

$ Casa Cóndor
In Pulinguí San Pablo, Vía del Arenal, T03-235 4034, T09-8650 8152.

Basic community-run hostel, dinner and breakfast available, use of cooking facilities extra, tours in the area.

$ Portal Andino
At 4200 m, 4- to 5-hr walk from Urbina, T09-9165 0788.
Simple hostel with bunk-beds, shared bath, cold water, use of cooking facilities extra, advance booking required.

$ Posada de la Estación
Opposite the Urbina railway station, T09-9969 4867.
Comfortable rooms with heaters, shared bath, meals available, wood stoves, magnificent views, trips and equipment arranged, tagua workshop, helpful. Also runs **$ Urcu Huasi**, cabins at 4150 m, 10 km (2½ hrs walking) from Urbina, in an area being reforested with polylepis trees.

Alausí

$$$ La Quinta
Eloy Alfaro 121 y M Muñoz, T03-293 0247, www.hosteria-la-quinta.com.
Nicely restored old house along the rail line to Riobamba. Pleasant atmosphere, some rooms are ample, restaurant, gardens, excellent views, not always open, reserve ahead.

$$$ Posada de las Nubes
On the north side of the Río Chanchán, 7 or 11 km from Alausí depending on the route, best with 4WD, pickup from Alausí US$7, T03-302 9362 or T09-9315 0847, www.posadadelasnubes.com.
Rustic hacienda house in cloudforest at 2600 m. Rooms are simple to basic for the price, some with bath, includes dinner and breakfast, hiking and horse riding, advance booking required.

$$ Gampala
5 de Junio 122 y Loza, T03-293 0138, www.hotelgampala.com.
Refurbished modern rooms and 1 suite with jacuzzi ($$$), restaurant and bar with pool table.

$$ La Posada del Tren
5 de Junio y Orozco, T03-293 1293.
Good, modern, parking.

$$-$ San Pedro
5 de Junio y 9 de Octubre, T03-293 0196, hostalsanpedro@hotmail.com.
Simple comfortable rooms, a few cheaper rooms in older section, restaurant downstairs, parking, amiable owner.

Parque Nacional Sangay

$ Hostal Capac Urcu
At Hacienda Releche, near the village of Candelaria, T03-301 4067.
Basic rooms in small working hacienda. Use of kitchen (US$10) or meals prepared on request, rents horses for the trek to Collanes, US$14 per horse each way, plus US$15 per muleteer each way. Also runs the *refugio* at Collanes (same price), by the crater of El Altar: thatched-roof rustic shelters with solar hot water. The *refugio* is cold, take a warm sleeping bag. Rubber boots are indispensable for the muddy trail.

Guamote

$$ Inti Sisa
Vargas Torres y García Moreno, T03-291 6529, www.intisisa.org.
Basic but nice guesthouse, part of a community development project, most rooms with bath, US$18.75 pp in dorm, includes breakfast, other meals available, dining room and communal area with fireplace, horse riding and cycling tours to highland villages, reservations necessary.

Restaurants

Riobamba
Most places closed after 2100 and on Sun.

$$ Mónaco Pizzería
Av de la Prensa y Francisco Aguilar. Mon-Fri 1500-2200, Sat-Sun 1200-2200.
Delicious pizza and pasta, nice salads, good food, service and value. Recommended.

$ La Fogata
Av Daniel L Borja y Carabobo, opposite the train station. Daily except Tue, 0700-2200.
Simple but good local food, economical set meals and breakfast.

$ Naranjo's
Daniel L Borja 36-20 y Uruguay. Tue-Sun 1200-1500.
Excellent set lunch, friendly service, popular with locals.

$ Zen Wei
Princesa Toa 43-29 y Calicuchima. Mon-Sat 1200-1500.
Oriental restaurant serving economical vegetarian set meals.

Cafés and bakeries

Bom Café
Pichincha 21-37 y 10 de Agosto. Mon-Sat 0900-1300, 1600-2100.
Very nice European-style coffee shop, with a good choice of coffee and sandwiches.

Helados de Paila
Espejo y 10 de Agosto. Daily 0900-1900.
Excellent home-made ice cream, coffee, sweets, popular.

Jamones La Andaluza
Daniel L Borja y Uruguay. Daily 0830-2300.
Indoor and outdoor seating, good set lunches, coffee, sandwiches, salads, variety of cold-cuts and cheeses, tapas.

La Abuela Rosa
Brasil y Esmeraldas. Mon-Sat 1600-2100.
Cafetería in grandmother's house serving typical Ecuadorean snacks. Nice atmosphere and good service.

Guaranda *p1045*
See also Where to stay. Most places close on Sun.

$$$-$$ Pizza Buon Giorno
Sucre at Parque Bolívar. Tue-Sun 1100-2200.
Pizza and salads.

$$ La Bohemia
Convención de 1884 y 10 de Agosto. Mon-Sat 0800-2100.
Very good economical set meals and pricier international dishes à la carte, nice decor and ambiance, very popular. Recommended.

$$ La Estancia
García Moreno y Sucre. Mon 1200-1500, Tue-Sat 1200-2100.
Excellent buffet lunch for quality, variety and value, à la carte in the evening, nicely decorated, pleasant atmosphere, popular.

$$-$ Chifa Gran Cangrejo Rojo
10 de Agosto y Convención de 1884. Open 1100-2200.
Good Chinese food.

Cafés

Cafetería 7 Santos
Convención de 1884 y Olmedo. Mon-Sat 1000-2200.
Pleasant café and bar with open courtyard. Good coffee and snacks, fireplace, live music Fri and Sat, popular.

Salinerito
Plaza Roja. Daily 0800-1300, 1430-1900.
Salinas cheese shop also serves coffee, sandwiches and pizza.

Alausí

$$ El Mesón del Tren
Ricaurte y Eloy Alfaro. Tue-Sun 0700-0930, 1200-1430.
Good restaurant, popular with tour groups, breakfast, set lunch and à la carte.

$$ Bukardia
Guatemala 107. Open 1300-2200, closed Wed.
Meat specialities, snacks and drinks.

$ Flamingo
Antonio Mora y 9 de Octubre. Open 0700-2000, closed Sat.
Good economical set meals. Also runs **$$-$ Ventura Hostal**, simple.

Riobamba

Restobar La Rayuela
Daniel L Borja 36-30 y Uruguay. Mon-Sat 1200-2200, Sun 1200-1600.
Trendy bar/restaurant, sometimes live music on Fri, sandwiches, coffee, salads, pasta.

San Valentín
Daniel L Borja y Vargas Torres. Mon-Thu 1800-2400, Fri-Sat 1800-0200.
Very popular bar, good pizzas and Mexican dishes.

Riobamba
Casa de la Cultura, *10 de Agosto y Rocafuerte, T03-296 0219.* Cultural events, cinema on Tue.
Super Cines, *at El Paseo Shopping, Vía a Guano.* 12 modern cinema halls, some films in 3D.

Riobamba
Apr Around **21 Apr** there are **independence** celebrations lasting several days, hotel prices rise.
29 Jun Fiestas Patronales in honour of San Pedro.
11 Nov The festival to celebrate the 1st attempt at independence from Spain.
Dec-Jan Fiesta del Niño Rey de Reyes, street parades, music and dancing, starts in **Dec** and culminates on **6 Jan**.

Riobamba
Camping gear
Some of the tour operators listed below hire camping and climbing gear; also **Veloz Coronado** (Chile 33-21 y Francia, T03-296 0916, after 1900). **Marathon Explorer** (at Multiplaza mall, Av Lizarzaburu near the airport). High-end outdoor equipment and clothing. **Protección Industrial** (Rocafuerte 24-51 y Orozco, T03-296 3017). Outdoor equipment, rope, fishing supplies, rain ponchos.

Handicrafts
Crafts sold at Plaza Roja on Wed and Sat. **Almacén Cacha**, *Colón y Orozco, next to the Plaza Roja.* A cooperative of indigenous people from the Cacha area, sells woven bags, wool sweaters, and other crafts, good value (closed Sun-Mon).

Riobamba and around
Mountain biking
Guided tours with support vehicle average US$50-60 pp per day.

Pro Bici, *Primera Constituyente 23-51 y Larrea, T03-295 1759, www.probici.com*. Tours and rentals.

Julio Verne, *see Tour operators*. Very good tours, equipment and routes.

Tour operators

Most companies offer climbing trips (US$220 pp for 2 days to Chimborazo or Carihuayrazo), trekking (US$100 pp per day) and day-hikes (US$50-60 pp).

Andes Trek, *Esmeraldas 21-45 y Espejo, T03-2951275, www.goandestrek.com*. Climbing and trekking, transport, equipment rental. Also runs an office and climbers' hostel in Quito.

Expediciones Andinas, *Vía a Guano, Km 3, across from Hotel Abraspungo, T03-236 4278, www.expediciones-andinas. com*. Climbing expeditions run by Marco Cruz, a guide certified by the **German Alpine Club**, operate **$$$ Estrella del Chimborazo** lodge on south flank of mountain. Recommended.

Incañán, *Brasil 20-28 y Luis A Falconí, T03-294 0508, www.incanian.com.ec*. Trekking, cycling and cultural tours.

Julio Verne, *Brasil 22-40, between Av Daniel León Borja and Primera Constituyente, T03-296 3436, www. julioverne-travel.com*. Climbing, trekking, cycling, jungle and Galápagos trips, transport, equipment rental, English spoken, Ecuadorean/Dutch-run, very conscientious and reliable. Uses official guides. Highly recommended.

The Devil's Nose Train

In early 2015 the *Devil's Nose* train departed from and returned to Alausí, Tue-Sun at 0800, 1100 and 1500 (the latter only if there are enough passengers), 2½ hrs return, US$30, includes a snack and folklore dance performance. From Riobamba, an *autoferro* (motorized rail car) ran from Riobamba to Urbina (Thu-Sun at 0800, US$13.50), where on Sat-Sun Balthazar Ushca, the last of the ice merchants, demonstrates the process of extracting glacial ice. *Autoferro* from Riobamba to Colta (Thu-Sun at 1200, US$17), dress warmly. Purchase tickets well in advance for weekends and holidays at any train station (Riobamba, T03-296 1038, Mon-Fri 0800-1630, Sat-Sun 0700-1530; Alausí, T03-293 0126, Tue-Sun 0700-1530), through the call centre (T1800-873637) or by email (reservasriobamba@ferrocarrilesdelecuador.gob.ec, then you have to make a bank deposit). Procedures change frequently, so enquire locally and check www.trenecuador.com.

Transport

Riobamba

Bus **Terminal Terrestre** on Epiclachima y Av Daniel L Borja for all long-distance buses. **Terminal Oriental**, Espejo y Cordovez, for Candelaria (access to El Altar). **Terminal Intercantonal**, Av Canónigo Ramos about 2.5 km northwest of the Terminal Terrestre, for Guamote, SanJuan and Cajabamba (Colta). Taxi from Terminal Terrestre to Oriental, US$2, from Terminal Intercantonal to the other terminals US$2. To **Quito**, US$4.75, 4 hrs, about every 30 mins; also door-to-door shared taxis with: **Montecarlo Trans Vip**, T03-301 5946 or T09-8411 4114, 7 daily, US$18 (US$5 extra for large luggage). To **Guaranda**, US$2.50, 2 hrs (sit on the right). To **Ambato**, US$1.50, 1 hr. To **Alausí**, see below. To **Cuenca**, 8 a day via Alausí, 5½ hrs, US$7.50. To **Guayaquil** via Pallatanga, frequent service, US$6, 5 hrs, spectacular for the first 2 hrs. To **Baños**, 2 hrs, US$2.50; to **Puyo** US$5, 4 hrs, to **Macas** via Parque Nacional Sangay, 8 daily, 4 hrs, US$6.25 (sit on the left).

Guaranda

Bus Terminal at Eliza Mariño Carvajal, on road to Riobamba and Babahoyo; if you are staying in town get off closer to the centre. Many daily buses to: **Ambato**, US$2.50, 2 hrs. **Riobamba**, see above. **Babahoyo**, US$3.75, 3 hrs, beautiful ride. **Guayaquil**, US$5, 5 hrs. **Quito**, US$6.25, 5 hrs.

Reserva Faunística Chimborazo

There are no buses that will take you to the shelters. You can take a tour or arrange transport with a tour operator from Riobamba (US$35 one way, US$45 return with wait). You can also take a Riobamba–Guaranda bus, alight at the turn-off for the refuges and walk the remaining steep 8 km (5 km taking short-cuts) to the first shelter. For the eastern slopes, take a trekking tour, arrange transport from an agency or take a bus between Riobamba and Ambato, get off at the turnoff for **Posada La Estación** and Urbina and walk from there.

Alausí

Bus To **Riobamba**, 1½ hrs, US$2.50, 84 km. To **Quito**, from 0600 onwards, 8 a day, 6 hrs, US$7.50 often have to change in Riobamba. To **Cuenca**, 4 hrs, US$6.25. To **Ambato** hourly, 3 hrs, US$3.75. To **Guayaquil**, 4 a day, 4 hrs, US$6.25. **Coop Patria**. Colombia y Orozco, 3 blocks up from the main street; **Trans Alausí**, 5 de Junio y Loza. Many through buses don't go into town, but have to be caught on the highway, taxi from town US$1.

Parque Nacional Sangay

To **Atillo** from Parque La Dolorosa, Puruhá y Primera Constituyente, 15 daily, US$2.50, 2 hrs Also Riobamba-**Macas** service goes through Atillo, see above. To **Alao**, from Parque La Dolorosa, hourly 0700-2300, US$1.50, 1½ hrs. To **Guarguallá Grande** from Parque La Dolorosa daily at 1345 (return to Riobamba at 0545), US$2.25 (Grande), 2 hrs; also a milk truck from La Dolorosa to Guargualla at 0530, US$2. To **Candelaria**, from Terminal Oriental, daily 0640, 1015, 1215, 1515 and 1700 US$1.50, 1½ hrs. Alternatively, take a bus from the same terminal to Penipe, every ½ hr, US$0.40, 40 mins, and hire a pickup truck from there to Candelaria, US$15, 40 mins.

Southern highlands

The convoluted topography of the southern highlands, comprising the provinces of Cañar, Azuay and Loja, reveals an ancient non-volcanic past distinct from its northern Sierra neighbours.

This region is home to many treasures. Here is Ecuador's prime Inca site, two of its most spectacular national parks, and Cuenca – the nation's most congenial city and focal point of El Austro, as southern Ecuador is called. Cuenca boasts some of the country's finest colonial architecture, and the Cuenca basin is a major artesanía centre, producing ceramics, baskets, gold and silver jewellery and textiles, as well as the famous Panama hat.

In addition to Cuenca's cultural attractions, a pleasant climate and magnificent scenery make the southern highlands prime walking country. Vilcabamba, south of Loja, is a particularly suitable base for trekking and horse riding excursions, with nearby undisturbed *páramo* and cloudforest, home to many birds and other wildlife.

The southern highlands have an extensive road network and there is access to the Peruvian border at several different points.

Best for
Crafts ▪ Relaxing ▪ Walking

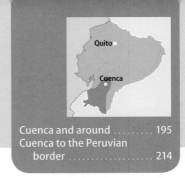

Footprint
picks

★ **Cuenca's cathedral**, page 197

One of the largest in South America, this imposing blue-domed cathedral is built on the foundations of an Inca structure.

★ **Pumapungo Museum**, page 197

The extensive holdings include a special collection of *tsantsas*, shrunken heads from the Shuar people of Oriente.

★ **Ingapirca**, page 199

Ecuador's most important archaeological site was home to the Cañari people before it was conquered by the Incas in the 15th century.

★ **Parque Nacional Cajas**, page 202

This high, cold, wet and wild natural area is easily reached from Cuenca.

★ **Parque Nacional Podocarpus**, page 216

With its broad range of altitudes and remote hinterlands, this is one of the most diverse protected areas in the world.

★ **Horse riding from Vilcabamba**, page 221

Saddle up for a ride through some of the prettiest countryside in Ecuador.

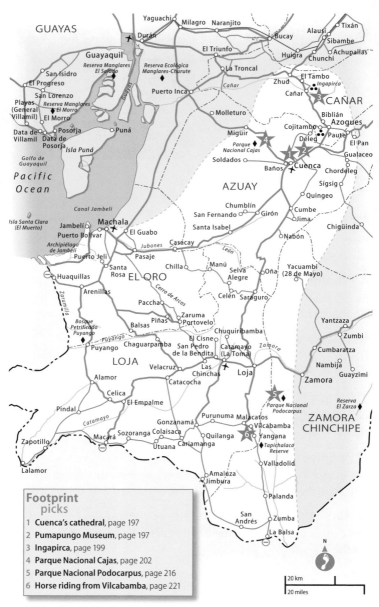

Footprint picks

Cuenca
& around

Cuenca is capital of the province of Azuay and the third largest city in Ecuador, with something of a European flavour. The city has preserved much of its colonial ambience, with many of its old buildings originally constructed from the travertine quarried nearby and elegantly renovated. Most Ecuadoreans consider this their finest city and few would disagree. Its cobble-stone streets, flowering plazas and whitewashed buildings with old wooden doors and ironwork balconies make it a pleasure to explore. In 1999 Cuenca was designated a World Heritage Site by UNESCO.

As well as being the economic centre of El Austro, as southern Ecuador is called, Cuenca is also an intellectual centre. It has a long tradition as the birthplace of notable artists, writers, poets and philosophers, earning it the title 'The Athens of Ecuador'. It remains a rather formal city, loyal to its conservative traditions. Many places close for lunch between 1300 and 1500 and on Sunday.

Cuenca is home to a growing expat retiree community. The city and surrounding areas are known for their crafts.

Essential Cuenca

Finding your feet

The **Terminal Terrestre** is on Avenida España, 15 minutes' ride northeast of the centre, T07-284 2633. The **airport**, T07-286 2203, www.aeropuertocuenca.ec, is five minutes beyond the Terminal Terrestre. Both can be reached by city bus, but best take a taxi at all hours (US$1.50-2.50 to the centre). The **Terminal Sur** for regional buses is by the Feria Libre El Arenal on Avenida Las Américas. Many city buses pass here. See Transport, page 212, for details.

The city is bounded by Río Machángara to the north and ríos Yanuncay and Tarqui to the south. The Río Tomebamba separates the colonial heart from the newer districts to the south. Avenida Las Américas is a ring road around the north and west of the city and the *autopista*, a multilane highway, bypasses the city to the south.

Getting around

The narrow streets of colonial Cuenca are clogged with cars on weekdays. Sunday is more tranquil and an excellent time to enjoy the colonial city. It is hoped that a new streetcar system projected for completion in 2017 will help alleviate the congestion.

Safety

Though safer than Quito or Guayaquil, routine precautions are advised. Outside the busy nightlife area around Calle Larga, the city centre is deserted and unsafe after 2300, taking a taxi is recommended. The river banks, the Cruz del Vado area (south end of Juan Montalvo), the Terminal Terrestre and all market areas are not safe after dark.

Best restaurants

Raymipampa, page 207
Tiestos, page 207
Good Affinity, page 208
Monte Bianco, page 208

When to go

If you're here over Christmas, Cuenca has perhaps the largest and finest Christmas parade in the country on 24 December, Pase del Niño Vlajero. five days if you include Ingapirca and Parque Nacional Cajas.

Best places to stay

La Posada Cuencana, page 204
Posada del Angel, page 204
Macondo, page 205
Posada Todos Santos, page 205

Weather Cuenca

January	February	March	April	May	June
20°C 9°C 60mm	19°C 10°C 69mm	19°C 10°C 75mm	17°C 9°C 99mm	17°C 9°C 72mm	18°C 8°C 27mm

July	August	September	October	November	December
6°C 8°C 18mm	17°C 8°C 30mm	19°C 9°C 48mm	19°C 9°C 99mm	20°C 9°C 48mm	18°C 9°C 66mm

Sights *Colour map 5, A4.*

On the main plaza, **Parque Abdón Calderón**, are the Old Cathedral, **El Sagrario** ⓘ *Mon-Fri 0900-1730, Sat-Sun 0900-1300, US$2*, begun in 1557, and the immense 'New' ★ **Catedral de la Inmaculada**, started in 1885. The latter contains a famous crowned image of the Virgin, a beautiful altar and an exceptional play of light and shade through modern stained glass. Other churches that deserve a visit are **San Blas**, **San Francisco** and **Santo Domingo**. Many churches are open at irregular hours only and for services.

The church of **El Carmen de la Asunción**, close to the southwest corner of La Inmaculada, has a flower market in the tiny **Plazoleta El Carmen** in front. There is a colourful daily market in **Plaza Rotary** where pottery, clothes, guinea pigs and local produce, especially baskets, are sold. Thursday is the busiest.

Museo del Monasterio de las Conceptas ⓘ *Hermano Miguel 6-33 entre Pdte Córdova y Juan Jaramillo, T07-283 0625, www.museodelasconceptas.org.ec, Mon-Fri 0900-1830, Sat and holidays 1000-1300, US$2.50*, in a cloistered convent founded in 1599, houses a well-displayed collection of religious and folk art, in addition to an extensive collection of lithographs by Guayasamín.

★ **Pumapungo** ⓘ *C Larga y Huayna Capac, T07-283 1521, Mon-Fri 0900-1700, Sat 0900-1300*, is a museum complex on the edge of the colonial city, at the actual site of Tomebamba excavations. Part of the area explored is seen at **Parque Arqueológico Pumapungo**. The **Sala Arqueológica** section contains all the Cañari and Inca remains and artefacts found at this site. Other halls in the premises house the **Sala Etnográfica**, with information on different Ecuadorean cultures, including a special collection of *tsantsas* (shrunken heads from Oriente), the **Sala de Arte Religioso**, the **Sala Numismática** and temporary exhibits. There are also book and music libraries, free cultural videos and music events. Three blocks west of Pumapungo, **Museo Manuel Agustín Landívar** ⓘ *C Larga 2-23 y Manuel Vega, T07-282 1177, Mon-Fri 0800-1700, Sat 0900-1300, free*, is at the site of the small Todos los Santos ruins, with Cañari, Inca and colonial remains; ceramics and artefacts found at the site are also displayed.

Museo de las Culturas Aborígenes ⓘ *C Larga 5-24 y Hermano Miguel, T07-283 9181, Mon-Fri 0900-1800, Sat 0900-1300, US$2; guided tours in English, Spanish and French, craft shop*, the private collection of Dr J Cordero Íñiguez, has an impressive selection of pre-Columbian archaeology. **Museo Remigio Crespo Toral** ⓘ *C Larga 7-25 y Borrero, T07-283 3208, Mon-Fri 1000-1730, Sat 1000-1600, Sun 1000-1300, free*, in a beautifully refurbished colonial house, has important history, archaeology and art collections. **Museo del Sombrero** ⓘ *C Larga 10-41 y Gral Torres, T07-283 1569, Mon-Fri 0900-1800, Sat 0900-1700, Sun 0930-1330*, shop with all the old factory machines for hat finishing.

On Plaza San Sebastián is **Museo Municipal de Arte Moderno** ⓘ *Sucre 1527 y Talbot, T07-282 0838, Mon-Fri 0830-1300, 1500-1830, Sat-Sun 0900-1300, free*, has a permanent contemporary art collection and art library. It holds a biennial international painting competition and other cultural activities. Across the river from the Pumapungo museum, the **Museo de Artes de Fuego** ⓘ *Las Herrerías y 10 de Agosto, T07-288 3061, Mon-Fri 0900-1300, 1500-1800, free except for special* *events*, has a display of wrought iron work and pottery. It is housed in the beautifully restored Casa de Chaguarchimbana. There is an **Orquideario** ⓘ *at the University of Cuenca, Av Víctor Manuel Albornoz, Quinta de Balzay, Mon-Fri, 0800-*

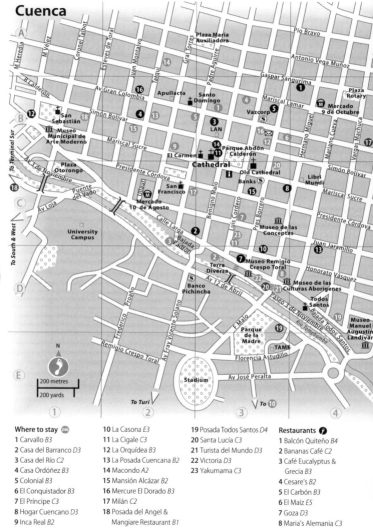

Cuenca

Where to stay 🛏
1 Carvallo *B3*
2 Casa del Barranco *D3*
3 Casa del Río *C2*
4 Casa Ordóñez *B3*
5 Colonial *B3*
6 El Conquistador *B3*
7 El Príncipe *C3*
8 Hogar Cuencano *D3*
9 Inca Real *B2*
10 La Casona *E3*
11 La Cigale *C3*
12 La Orquídea *B3*
13 La Posada Cuencana *B2*
14 Macondo *A2*
15 Mansión Alcázar *B2*
16 Mercure El Dorado *B3*
17 Milán *C2*
18 Posada del Angel & Mangiare Restaurant *B1*
19 Posada Todos Santos *D4*
20 Santa Lucía *C3*
21 Turista del Mundo *D3*
22 Victoria *D3*
23 Yakumama *C3*

Restaurants 🍴
1 Balcón Quiteño *B4*
2 Bananas Café *C2*
3 Café Eucalyptus & Grecia *B3*
4 Cesare's *B2*
5 El Carbón *B3*
6 El Maíz *E5*
7 Goza *D3*
8 Maria's Alemania *C3*

1200, 1400-1800. South of the city, accessed via Avenida Fray Vicente Solano, beyond the football stadium, is **Turi church**, orphanage and mirador. A tiled panorama explains the magnificent views.

Baños

City buses marked 'Baños' go to and from Cuenca; to walk takes 1½ hrs but is not particularly pleasant amid the heavy traffic.

There are sulphur baths, 5 km southwest of Cuenca at Baños, with its domed, blue church in a delightful landscape. Water temperatures at the source are measured at 76°C making these the hottest commercial baths in the country, but bathing pools are at various temperatures. Above **Hostería Durán** (see Where to stay) are four separate complexes of warm baths, **Merchán**, **Rodas** (www.hosteriarodas. com), **Durán** (www.novaqua.com. ec) and **Piedra de Agua** ⓘ *www. piedradeagua.com.ec, entry US$2-10.* The latter two are better maintained, more exclusive and offer a variety of treatments in their spas. The country lanes above the village offer some pleasant walks.

★ Ingapirca *Colour map 5, A4.*
Daily 0800-1800, closed public holidays, US$6, including museum and tour in Spanish; bags can be stored. Small café.

Ecuador's most important Inca ruin, at 3160 m, lies 8.5 km east of the colonial town of **Cañar** (*hostales* in **$** range). Access is from Cañar or **El Tambo**. The Inca Huayna Capac took over the site from the conquered Cañaris when his empire expanded north into Ecuador in the third quarter of the 15th century.

9 Mixx Gourmet *C5*
10 Moliendo Café *D3*
11 Raymipampa *B3*
12 San Sebas *B1*
13 Tiestos *D4*
14 Tutto Freddo *B3*
15 Viejo Rincón *C3*
16 Villa Rosa *B2*

Bars & clubs
17 La Mesa Salsoteca *B4*
18 MalAmado *C1*
19 Rue *D3*
20 Wunderbar *D3*

Ingapirca was strategically placed on the Capac Ñan, the Great Inca Road that ran from Cuzco to Quito (see Inca Trail, below).

The site, first described by the French scientist Charles-Marie de la Condamine in 1748, shows typical imperial Cuzco-style architecture, such as tightly fitting stonework and trapezoidal doorways, which can be seen on the castillo and **governor's house**. The central structure may have been a **solar observatory**. There is considerable debate as to Ingapirca's precise function. From what remains of the site, it probably consisted of storehouses, baths and dwellings for soldiers and other staff, suggesting it could have been a royal tambo, or inn. It could also have been used as a sun temple, judging by the beautiful ellipse, reminiscent of the Qoricancha in Cuzco. Furthermore, John Hemming has noted that the length of the site is exactly three times the diameter of the semi-circular ends, which may have been connected with worship of the sun in its morning, midday and afternoon positions.

A 10-minute walk from the main site is the **Cara del Inca** (face of the Inca), an immense natural formation in the rock looking over the landscape. Nearby is a throne cut into the rock, the **Sillón del Inga** (Inca's chair) and the **Ingachugana**, a large rock with carved channels. This may have been used for offerings and divination with water, chicha or the blood of various sacrificial animals. On Friday there is an interesting indigenous market at Ingapirca village.

Baños del Inca ① *Site open daily 0800-1700, US$1; 5 daily departures Wed-Sun, US$8, includes entry to El Tambo museum and Coyoctor site, excursion lasts 2 hrs.*

A tourist *autoferro* (a bus on rails) runs from El Tambo 7 km to the small Cañari-Inca archaeological site of **Baños del Inca** or **Coyoctor**, a massive rock outcrop carved to form baths, showers, water channels and seats overlooking a small amphitheatre. There is an interpretation centre with information about the site, a hall with displays about regional fiestas and an audiovisual room with tourist information about all of Ecuador.

Inca Trail to Ingapirca

The three-day hike to Ingapirca starts at **Achupallas** (lively Saturday market, one hostel), 25 km from Alausí (see page 184). The walk is covered by three 1:50,000 *IGM* sheets: Alausí, Juncal and Cañar. The Juncal sheet is most important. Note that the name Ingapirca does not appear on the latter; you may have to ask directions near the end. Also take a compass and GPS. Good camping equipment is essential. Take all food and drink with you as there is nothing along the way. A shop in Achupallas sells basic foodstuffs. There are persistent beggars the length of the hike, especially children. Tour operators in Riobamba and Cuenca offer this trek for about US$350 per person, three days, with everything included.

East of Cuenca

Northeast of Cuenca, on the paved road to Méndez in the Oriente, is **Paute**, with a pleasant park and modern church. South of Paute, **Gualaceo** is a rapidly expanding, modern town set in beautiful landscape, with a charming plaza and Sunday market. The iTur ① *at the Municipio, Gran Colombia y 3 de Noviembre, Parque Central, T07-225 5131, Mon-Fri 0800-1300, 1400-1700*, is very helpful with English-speaking staff.

A scenic road goes from Gualaceo to Limón in Oriente. Many of Ecuador's 4000 species of orchids can be seen at **Ecuagénera** ① *Km 2 on the road to Cuenca, T07-225 5237, www.ecuagenera.com, Mon-Fri 0730-1800, Sat-Sun 0930-1630, US$5 (US$3 pp for groups of 3 or more).*

South of Gualaceo is **Chordeleg**, a touristy village famous for its crafts in wood, silver and gold filigree, pottery and Panama hats. At the **Museo Municipal** ① *C 23 de Enero, Mon-Fri 0800-1300, 1400-1700, Sat-Sun 1000-1600*, is an exhibition hall with fascinating local textiles, ceramics and straw work, some of which are on sale at reasonable prices. It's a good uphill walk from Gualaceo to Chordeleg, and a pleasant hour downhill in the other direction.

Sígsig *Colour map 5, A4.*

Some 26 km south of Gualaceo and 83 km from Cuenca, is Sígsig (population 10,100, altitude 2300 m), an authentic highland town where women can be seen weaving hats 'on the move'. There are a couple of basic places to stay and eat. The main square, **Parque 3 de Noviembre** has the modern **Iglesia de San Sebastián** and a statue to Duma, the local Cañari chief who defeated the conquering Inca Tupac Yupanqui. At **Plaza Tudul** is the **Iglesia de María Auxiliadora**, with an interesting stone façade, blue domes and a Moorish tower; there are pleasant views of the surrounding hills from here. On the shore of the Río Zhingate is a recreation area. Market day is Sunday.

This area is rich in archaeology, with caves and several undeveloped ruins to explore. The magnificent gold sun with curly rays, which is the symbol of the Banco Central del Ecuador, is a Cañari piece found in Chunucari, just north of Sígsig. At the Municipio is the **Museo Cantonal** ⓘ *Parque 3 de Noviembre, T07-226 6106, Mon-Fri 0800-1600, free*, with objects from the Talcazhapa culture (700 BC-AD 1100) and information in Spanish about the area's archaeological sites.

A very scenic road (being paved in 2015) goes from Sígsig, 5 km to **Cutchil**, a hat-weavers' town, and on to a pass at 3360 m, from where it drops to **Chigüinda**, **El Aguacate** and **Gualaquiza** in southern Oriente, see page 311.

★ Parque Nacional Cajas
The park office is at Hermano Miguel y Gran Colombia, Edifico ETAPA-EP, p5, T07-237 0126, Mon-Fri 0800-1600. Entry free; overnight stay US$4 per night.

Northwest of Cuenca, Cajas is a 29,000-ha national park with over 230 lakes. The park is being diligently conserved by municipal authorities both for its environmental importance and because it is the water supply for Cuenca. The *páramo* vegetation, such as chuquiragua and lupin, is beautiful and the wildlife interesting. Cajas is very rich in birdlife; 125 species have been identified, including the condor and many varieties of hummingbird (the violet-tailed metaltail is endemic to this area). On the lakes are Andean gulls, speckled teal and yellow-billed pintails. On a clear morning the views are superb, even to Chimborazo, some 300 km away.

There are two access roads. The paved road from Cuenca to Guayaquil via Molleturo goes through the northern section and is the main route for Laguna Toreadora, the visitors' centre and Laguna Llaviuco. Skirting the southern edge of the park is a gravel secondary road, which goes from Cuenca via San Joaquín to the Soldados entrance and the community of Angas beyond (see Transport, page 213). There is nowhere to stay after the *refugio* at Laguna Toreadora (see Where to stay, below) until you reach the lowlands between Naranjal and La Troncal.

Laguna Toreadora is in a high *páramo* area at 3870 m, with some attractive polylepis (quinoa) forest fragments around the shore. Along the main road is the **Centro de Visitantes** ⓘ *Tue-Sun 0800-1630, also open Mon in high season*, the **Centro de Interpretación Ambiental**, a cafeteria with snacks and warm drinks (it also serves meals at weekends, including local trout) and the *refugio*, a basic shelter with bathrooms but no beds. **Laguna Llaviuco** is in a cloudforest area at 3150 m, on the eastern side of the park. Three kilometres off the main road is a camping area, a dock and a cafeteria. There are no facilities at **Soldados**, the southern access point into the park.

Trekking in Cajas
The park offers ideal but strenuous walking, at 3150-4450 m altitude, and the climate is cold and wet. There have been deaths from exposure so it is important to

be prepared with proper clothing and equipment. The best time to visit is August-January, when you may expect clear days, strong winds, night-time temperatures to -8°C and occasional mist. From February to July temperatures are higher but there is much more fog, rain and snow. It is best to arrive in the early morning since it can get very cloudy, wet and cool after about 1300. It is best to get the *IGM* maps in Quito (Chaucha, Cuenca, San Felipe de Molleturo, and Chiquintad 1:50,000) and take a compass and GPS. It is easy to get lost.

For day walks, there are some marked trails near the visitor centre but they tend to peter out quickly. For overnight treks, adequate experience and equipment are necessary. Open fires are not permitted, so take a stove. A very strong hiker with a good sense of direction can cross the park in two days. Independent trekkers must register with the rangers.

On the opposite side of Laguna Toreadora from the *refugio* is **Cerro San Luis** (4200 m), which may be climbed in a day; the views are excellent. From the visitor centre go anticlockwise around the lake; after crossing the outflow look for a sign 'Al San Luis', follow the yellow and black stakes to the summit and beware of a side trail to dangerous ledges.

Beyond Laguna Toreadora on a paved road is the village of **Migüir**, from where you can follow a trail past several lakes and over a pass to Soldados (two days). It is also possible to follow the **Ingañán Trail**, an old Inca road that used to connect Cuenca with the coast. It is in ill repair or lost in places but there are interesting ruins above **Laguna Mamamag**. You can access the Ingañán from the park headquarters or from Migüir, from where it is two to three days' trekking to **Laguna Llaviuco**. From Llaviuco you might get a ride with fishermen back to Cuenca or you can walk to the main road in about an hour.

Listings Cuenca and around *map p198*

Tourist information

General information from www.cuenca.com.ec. To locate an establishment see www.ubicacuenca.com. There are many banks with ATMs around Sucre y Borrero.

Cámara de Turismo
Terminal Terrestre, T07-284 5657. Mon-Sat 0830-1200, 1230-1800.
For information about the city, including city and long-distance bus routes; also at the airport.

Immigration
E Muñoz 1-42 y Gran Colombia, T07-282 1112.

Ministerio de Turismo
Sucre y Benigno Malo, on Parque Calderón next to the Municipio, T07-282 1035. Mon-Fri, 0800-2000, Sat 0830-1730, Sun 0830-1330.
Helpful.

Vazcorp
Gran Colombia 7-98 y Cordero, T07-283 3434. Mon-Fri 0830-1730, Sat 0900-1245.
Changes various currencies, fair rates.

Cuenca

$$$$ Carvallo
Gran Colombia 9-52, entre Padre Aguirre y Benigno Malo, T07-283 2063, www.hotelcarvallo.com.ec.
Combination of an elegant colonial-style hotel and art/antique gallery. Very comfortable rooms, all with bath tubs.

$$$$ Mansión Alcázar
Bolívar 12-55 y Tarqui, T07-282 3918, www.mansionalcazar.com.
Beautifully restored house, a mansion indeed, central, lovely rooms, restaurant serves gourmet international food, attractive gardens, quiet relaxed atmosphere.

$$$$ Oro Verde
Av Ordóñez Lazo, northwest of the centre towards Cajas, T07-409 0000, www.oroverdehotels.com.
Elegant hotel, buffet breakfast, excellent international restaurant (buffet Sun lunch), small pool, parking.

$$$$ Santa Lucía
Borrero 8-44 y Sucre, T07-282 8000, www.santaluciahotel.com.
An elegantly renovated colonial house, very comfortable rooms, excellent Italian restaurant, safe deposit box.

$$$ Casa Ordóñez
Lamar 8-59 y Benigno Malo, T07-282 3297, www.casa-ordonez.com.
Colonial house with wooden floors and 3 inner patios, nicely decorated rooms and common areas, down comforters, no smoking.

$$$ Inca Real
Gral Torres 8-40 entre Sucre y Bolívar, T07-282 3636, www.hotelincareal.com.ec.
Refurbished colonial house with comfortable rooms around patios, good Spanish restaurant, parking.

$$$ La Casona
Miguel Cordero 2-124, near the stadium, T07-410 3501, www.lacasonahotel.com.ec.
Lovely refurbished family home in a residential area, comfortable carpeted rooms, buffet breakfast, restaurant, parking.

$$$ La Posada Cuencana
Tarqui 9-46 y Bolívar, T07-282 6831.
Small family-run hotel with beautiful colonial-style rooms.

$$$ Mercure El Dorado
Gran Colombia 787 y Luis Cordero, T07-283 1390, www.eldoradohotel.com.ec.
Elegant modern hotel, rooms have safe and mini-bar, buffet breakfast, cafeteria, spa, gym, business centre, parking.

$$$ Posada del Angel
Bolívar 14-11 y Estévez de Toral, T07-284 0695, www.hostalposadadelangel.com.
Restored colonial house, comfortable rooms, good Italian restaurant, parking, patio with plants, some noise from restaurant, English spoken, helpful staff. Recommended.

$$$ Victoria
C Larga 6-93 y Borrero, T07-283 1120, www.grupo-santaana.net.
Elegant refurbished hotel overlooking the river, comfortable modern rooms, excellent expensive restaurant, good views.

$$ Casa del Barranco
Calle Larga 8-41 y Luis Cordero, T07-283 9763, www.casadelbarranco.com.
Restored colonial house, some rooms with lovely views over the river, cafeteria overlooking the river.

$$ Casa del Río
Bajada del Padrón 4-07 y C Larga, T07-282 9659, hostalcasadelrio@hotmail.com.
Pleasant quiet *hostal* on El Barranco overlooking the river, private or shared bath, breakfast available, good views, attentive service.

$$ Colonial
Gran Colombia 10-13 y Padre Aguirre, T07-284 1644, www.hostalcolonial.com.
Refurbished colonial house with beautiful patio, carpeted rooms.

$$ El Príncipe
J Jaramillo 7-82 y Luis Cordero, T07-284 7287, www.hotelprincipe.com.ec.
A refurbished 3-storey colonial house, comfortable rooms around an attractive patio with plants, restaurant, parking.

$$ La Orquídea
Borrero 9-31 y Bolívar, T07-282 4511.
Refurbished colonial house, bright rooms, fridge, low season and long term discounts, good value.

$$ Macondo
Tarqui 11-64 y Lamar, T07-284 0697, www.hostalmacondo.com.
Restored colonial house, large rooms, buffet breakfast, cooking facilities, pleasant patio with plants, garden, very popular, US-run. Highly recommended.

$$ Milán
Pres Córdova 989 y Padre Aguirre, T07-283 1104, www.hotelmilan.com.ec.
Multi-storey hotel with views over market, restaurant, popular.

$$ Posada Todos Santos
C Larga 3-42 y Tomás Ordóñez, near the Todos Santos Church, T07-282 4247, posadatodossantoscue@latinmail.com.
Tranquil hostel decorated with murals, very good, attentive service, English spoken, group discounts.

$ Hogar Cuencano
Hermano Miguel 436 y C Larga, T07-283 4941, celso3515@yahoo.com.
Nicely furnished family-run *hostal* in the heart of the action, private or shared bath, US$10 pp in dorm, cafeteria, cooking facilities.

$ La Cigale
Honorato Vasquez 7-80 y Cordero, T07-283 5308, lacigalecuencana@yahoo.fr.
Very popular hostel with private rooms and dorms (US$8 pp), breakfast available, very good restaurant ($$-$), hostel can be noisy until midnight.

$ Turista del Mundo
C Larga 5-79 y Hermano Miguel, T07-282 9125, esperanzab65@gmail.com.
Popular hostel with comfortable rooms, private or shared bath, cooking facilities, nice terrace, very helpful.

$ Yakumama
Cordero 5-66 y Honorato Vásquez, T07-283 4353, www.hostalyakumama.com.
Popular hostel, 2 private rooms and dorms with 2-6 beds US$7-9 pp, restaurant with Ecuadorean and Swiss dishes, bar, patio with plants and lounging area, terrace with skate ramp, can get noisy.

Baños
There are also a couple of cheap *residenciales* in town.

$$$ Caballo Campana
Vía Misicata–Baños Km 4, on an alternative road from Cuenca to Baños (2 km from Baños, taxi US$5 from the centre of Cuenca), T07-289 2360, www. caballocampana.com.
Rebuilt colonial hacienda house in 28 ha with gardens and forest, heated rooms, suites and cabins, includes buffet breakfast, Ecuadorean and international

cuisine, horse riding and lessons, sports fields, discounts for longer stays.

$$$ Hostería Durán
Km 8 Vía Baños, T07-289 2485, www.hosteriaduran.com.
Includes buffet breakfast, restaurant, parking, has well-maintained very clean pools (US$6 for non-residents), gym, steam bath, transport from Cuenca, camping.

Ingapirca
There are a couple of simple places in the village. Also good economical meals at **Intimikuna**, at the entrance to the archaeological site.

$$$ Posada Ingapirca
500 m uphill from ruins, T07-221 7116, for reservations T07-283 0064 (Cuenca), www.grupo-santaana.net.
Converted hacienda, comfortable rooms, heating, includes typical breakfast, excellent but pricey restaurant and bar with fireplace, good service, great views.

$ El Castillo
Opposite the ruins, T09-9998 3650, cab. castillo@hotmail.com.
3 simple cabins, restaurant with fireplace.

El Tambo
This is the nearest town to Ingapirca on the Pan-American Highway.

$ Chasky Wasy
Montenegro next to Banco del Austro, 1 block from the park, T09-9883 0013.
Nice hostel with ample rooms, parking nearby.

$ Sunshine
Panamericana y Ramón Borrero, at north end of town, T07-223 3394.
Simple, family-run, not always staffed,

private or shared bath, restaurant nearby, traffic noise.

Inca Trail to Ingapirca

$ Ingañán
Achupallas, T07-293 0663.
Basic, with bath, hot water, meals on request, camping.

East of Cuenca
Paute

$$$ Hostería Uzhupud
Km 32 Vía a Paute, T07-225 0329, www. uzhupud.com.
Set in the beautiful Paute valley 10 km from town, deluxe, relaxing, rooms at the back have best views, swimming pools and sauna (US$15 for non-residents), sports fields, horse riding, gardens, lots of orchids. Recommended.

$ Cutilcay
Abdón Calderón, by the river, T07-225 0133.
Older basic hostel, private or shared bath.

Gualaceo

$$ Peñón de Cuzay
Sector Bullcay El Carmen on the main road to Cuenca, T07-217 1515.
In one of the weaving communities, spa and pool. Fills on weekends, book ahead.

$ Hostal El Jardín
On the corner next to bus terminal.
Very clean ample rooms with private or shared bath, a simple decent place.

Parque Nacional Cajas
There is a *refugio* at **Laguna Toreadora**, cold, cooking facilities, and camping at **Laguna Llaviuco**. Other shelters in the park are primitive.

$$$$ Hostería Dos Chorreras
Km 21 Vía al Cajas, sector
Sayausí, T07-245 4301,
www.hosteriadoschorreras.com.
Hacienda-style inn outside the park.
Heating, restaurant serves excellent fresh
trout, reservations advised, horse rentals
with advanced notice.

Restaurants

Cuenca
There is a wide selection and fast
turnover of restaurants. Most places are
closed on Sun evening. There are cheap
comedores at the Mercados 9 de Octubre
and 10 de Agosto.

$$$ El Carbón
Borrero 10-69 y Lamar, T07-283 3711.
Mon-Wed 0700-1600, 1800-2200,
Thu-Sat until 2400.
Excellent char-grilled meat served with
a choice of fresh salads, seafood, wide
choice of dishes and breakfasts, large
portions enough for 2.

$$$ Villa Rosa
Gran Colombia 12-22 y Tarqui, T07-283
7944. Mon-Fri 1200-1430, 1900-2230.
Very elegant restaurant in the centre
of town, excellent international and
Ecuadorean food and service. A meeting
place for business people.

$$$-$$ Balcón Quiteño
Sangurima 6-49 y Borrero, and Av
Ordóñez Lazo 311 y los Pinos, T07-283
1928. Daily 0900-0100.
Good Ecuadorean and international food
and service, 1960s decor. Popular with
locals after a night's partying.

$$$-$$ Tiestos
J Jaramillo 4-89 y M Cueva, T07-283
5310. Tue-Sat 1230-1500, 1830-2200,
Sun 1230-1500.

Superb international cuisine prepared on
tiestos, shallow clay pans, comfortable
feel-at-home atmosphere, very popular,
reserve ahead.

$$ Café Eucalyptus
Gran Colombia 9-41 y Benigno
Malo. Mon-Fri 1700-2300 or later,
Sat 1900-0200.
A pleasant restaurant, café and bar in an
elegantly decorated house. Large menu
with dishes from all over the world.
British-run, popular. Recommended.

$$ Cesare's
Tarqui 9-61 y Bolívar, T07-283 2301.
Mon-Sat 1700-2200.
Mediterranean and international food,
popular with expats.

$$ El Maíz
C Larga 1-279 y C de los Molinos,
T07-284 0224. Mon-Sat 1200-2100
(variable, call ahead).
Good traditional Ecuadorean dishes with
some innovations, salads.

$$ Mangiare
Estévez de Toral 8-91 y Bolívar, at Posada
del Angel, T07-282 1360. Mon-Sat
1200-1500, 1730-2230, Sun 1200-1500.
Excellent Italian food, home-made pasta,
good value, very popular with locals.

$$ Raymipampa
Benigno Malo 8-59, at Parque Calderón.
Mon-Fri 0830-2300, Sat-Sun 0930-2230.
Good typical and international food in a
central location, economical set lunch on
weekdays, fast service, very popular, at
times it is hard to get a table.

$$-$ Viejo Rincón
Pres Córdova 7-46 y Borrero. Mon-Fri
0900-2100, Sat 0900-1500.
Tasty Ecuadorean food, very good set
lunch and à la carte, popular.

$ Good Affinity
Capulíes 1-89 y Gran Colombia. Mon-Sat 0930-1530.
Very tasty vegetarian food, vegan options, economical set lunch, pleasant garden seating.

$ Grecia
Gran Colombia y Padre Aguirre. Mon-Sat 1200-1500.
Good-quality and value set lunch.

$ Moliendo Café
Honorato Vásquez y Hermano Miguel. Mon-Sat 0900-2100.
Tasty Colombian food including set lunch, friendly service.

Cafés

Bananas Café
C Larga 9-40 y Benigno Malo. Thu-Sun 0800-1600.
Breakfast, snacks, light lunches, fruit juices, hot drinks, desserts, attentive service.

Goza
C Larga y Borrero, Plaza de la Merced. Mon-Thu 0800-2200, Fri-Sat 0800-2400, Sun 0800-2200.
Very popular café/restaurant with a varied menu; one of the few places in Cuenca with outdoor seating and open Sun evening.

Maria's Alemania
Hermano Miguel 8-09 y Sucre. Mon-Fri 0730-1800.
Excellent bakery and cafeteria, wide variety of whole-grain breads.

Mixx Gourmet
Parque San Blas 2-73 y Tomás Ordóñez.
A variety of fruit and liquor flavoured ice cream, popular. Several others nearby.

Monte Bianco
Bolívar 2-80 y Tomás Ordóñez and a couple of other locations.
Good ice cream and cream cakes, good value.

San Sebas
San Sebastián 1-94 y Sucre, Parque San Sebastián. Tue-Sun 0830-1500.
Outdoor café, popular for breakfast, good selection of giant sandwiches and salads.

Tutto Freddo
Bolívar 8-09 y Benigno Malo and several other locations. Daily 0900-2200.
Good ice cream, crêpes, pizza, sandwiches and sweets, reasonable prices, popular.

Bars and clubs

Cuenca
Calle Larga is a major destination for night life, with lots of bars with snacks and some restaurants. Av 12 de Abril, along the river near Parque de la Madre, and to the west of the centre, Plaza del Arte, Gaspar de Sangurima y Abraham Sarmiento, opposite Plazoleta El Otorongo, are also popular. Most bars open Wed-Thu until 2300, Fri-Sat until 0200.

La Mesa Salsoteca
Gran Colombia 3-36 entre Vargas Machuca y Tomás Ordóñez (no sign).
Latin music, salsa, popular among travellers and locals, young crowd.

MalAmado
C San Roque y Av 12 de Abril.
Good atmosphere, music and food. A place for dancing, US$10-15.

Rue
At Parque de la Madre, Av 12 de Abril. Tue-Sat 2200-0200.

Pleasant bar/restaurant with outdoor seating, no cover charge.

Wunderbar
Entrance from stairs on Hermano Miguel y C Larga. Mon-Fri 1100-0200, Sat 1500-0200.
A café-bar-restaurant, drinks, good coffee and food including some vegetarian. Nice atmosphere, book exchange, German-run.

Entertainment

Cuenca
Cinemas
Multicines, *Av José Peralta*. Complex of 5 theatres and food court, also at Mall del Río.

Dance classes
Cachumbambe, *Remigio Crespo 7-79 y Guayas, p2, T07-288 2023*. Salsa, merengue and a variety of other rhythms, group and individual classes.

Festivals

Cuenca
Apr **Foundation of Cuenca**, **12 Apr**. On **Good Friday** there is a fine procession through the town to the Mirador Turi.
May-Jun **Septenario**, the religious festival of Corpus Christi, lasts a week.
Nov **Independence of Cuenca**, **3 Nov**, with street theatre, art exhibitions and night-time dances all over the city. Cuenca hosts the **Bienal de Cuenca**, an internationally famous art competition The next one is due in 2017. Information from Bolivar 13-89, T07-283 1778, www.bienaldecuenca.org.
Dec **Pase del Niño Viajero**, **24 Dec**, is an outstanding parade, probably the largest and finest Christmas parade in all Ecuador. Children and adults from all the *barrios* and surrounding villages decorate donkeys, horses, cars and trucks with symbols of abundance. Little children in colourful indigenous costumes or dressed up as Biblical figures ride through the streets accompanied by musicians. The parade starts at about 1000 at San Sebastián, proceeds along C Bolívar and ends at San Blas about 5 hrs later. In the days up to, and just after Christmas, there are many smaller parades.

Shopping

Cuenca
Books
BC Carolina, *Hermano Miguel 4-46 y C Larga*. Good selection of English books for sale and exchange. Friendly service.
Librimundi, *Hermano Miguel 8-14 y Sucre, www.librimundi.com*. Nice bookshop with good selection and a café/reading area.

Camping equipment
Bermeo Hnos, *Borrero 8-35 y Sucre, T07-283 1522*.
Explorador Andino, *Av Solano y Aurelio Aguilar*.
Mono Dedo, *Av 12 de Abril y Guayas, www.monodedoecuador.com*. For climbing equipment.
Tatoo/Cikla, *Av Remigio Tamariz 2-52 y Federico Proaño, T07-288 4809, www.ec.tatoo.ws*. Good camping, hiking, climbing and biking gear. Also rent bikes. Several other shops near the university, on or near Av Remigio Crespo. Equipment rental from **Apullacta**, see Tour operators.

Handicrafts

There are many craftware shops along Gran Colombia, Benigno Malo and Juan Jaramillo alongside Las Conceptas. There are several good leather shops in the arcade off Bolívar between Benigno Malo and Luis Cordero. *Polleras*, traditional skirts worn by indigenous women are found along Gral Torres, between Sucre and Pres Córdova, and on Tarqui, between Pres Córdova and C Larga. For basketwork, take a 15-min bus ride from the Feria Libre (see Markets below) to the village of San Joaquín.

Arte, Artesanías y Antigüedades, *Borrero y Córdova*. Textiles, jewellery and antiques.

Artesa, *L Cordero 10-31 y Gran Colombia, several branches*. Modern ceramic tableware.

Centro Artesanal Municipal 'Casa de la Mujer', *Gral Torres 7-33*. Crafts market with a great variety of handicrafts.

Colecciones Jorge Moscoso, *J Jaramillo 6-80 y Borrero*. Weaving exhibitions, ethnographic museum, antiques and crafts.

El Barranco, *Hermano Miguel 3-23 y Av 3 de Noviembre*. Artisans' cooperative selling a wide variety of crafts.

El Otorongo, *3 de Noviembre by Plaza Otorongo*. Exclusive designs sold at this art gallery/café.

El Tucán, *Borrero 7-35*. Good selection. Recommended.

Galápagos, *Borrero 6-75*. Excellent selection.

La Esquina de las Artes, *12 de Abril y Agustín Cueva*. Shops with exclusive crafts including textiles; also cultural events.

Jewellery

Galería Claudio Maldonado, *Bolívar 7-75*. Has unique pre-Columbian designs in silver and precious stones.

Unicornio, *Gran Colombia y Luis Cordero*. Good jewellery, ceramics and candelabras.

Panama hats

Manufacturers have displays showing the complete hat making process, see also Museo del Sombrero, page 197.

K Dorfzaun, *Gil Ramírez Dávalos 4-34, near bus station, T07-286 1707, www.kdorfzaun.com*. Good quality and selection of hats and straw crafts, nice styles, good prices. English-speaking guides.

Homero Ortega P e Hijos, *Av Gil Ramírez Dávalos 3-86, T07-280 1288, www.homeroortega.com*. Good quality.

Markets

Feria Libre, *Av Las Américas y Av Remigio Crespo, west of the centre*. The largest market, also has dry goods and clothing, busiest Wed and Sat.

Mercado 9 de Octubre, *Sangurima y Mariano Cueva, busiest on Thu*. Nearby at **Plaza Rotary**, Sangurima y Vargas Machuca, crafts are sold, best selection on Thu. Note this area is not safe.

Mercado 10 de Agosto, *C Larga y Gral Torres*. Daily market with a prepared foods and drinks section on the 2nd floor.

Cuenca
Language courses

Rates US$6-10 per hr.

Centro de Estudios Interamericanos (CEDEI), *Gran Colombia 11-02 y General Torres, Casilla 597, T07-283 9003,* *www.cedei.org*. Spanish and Quichua lessons, immersion/volunteering programmes, also runs the attached Hostal Macondo. Recommended.

Estudio Internacional Sampere, *Hermano Miguel 3-43 y C Larga*, T07-284 2659, *www.sampere.es*. At the high end of the price range.

Sí Centro de Español e Inglés, *Bolívar 13-28 y Juan Montalvo, T07-282 0429, www.sicentrospanishschool.com*. Good teachers, competitive prices, homestays, volunteer opportunities, helpful and enthusiastic, tourist information available. Recommended.

Tours

Day tours to Ingapirca or Cajas run about US$45-50 pp. Trekking in Cajas about US$60-100 pp per day, depending on group size.

Expediciones Apullacta, *Gran Colombia 11-02 y General Torres, p 2, T07-283 7815, www.apullacta.com*. City and regional tours (Cajas, Ingapirca, Saraguro), also adventure tours (cycling, horse riding, canopy, canyoning), as well as jungle, highland and Galápagos trips; also rents camping equipment.

Metropolitan Touring, *Sucre 6-62 y Borreo, T07-284 3223, www.metropolitan-touring.com*. A branch of the Quito operator, also sells airline tickets.

Terra Diversa, *C Larga 8-41 y Luis Cordero, T07-282 3782, www.terradiversa. com*. Lots of useful information, helpful staff. Ingapirca, Cajas, community tourism in Saraguro, jungle trips, horse riding, mountain biking and other options. The more common destinations have fixed departures. Also sells Galápagos tours and flights. Recommended.

Van Service, *T07-281 6409, www. vanservice.com.ec*. City tours on a double-decker bus. The 1¾-hrs tour includes the main attractions in the colonial city and El Turi lookout. US$8, hourly departures 0900-1900 from the Old Cathedral. Also hires cars and vans with driver.

Transport

Cuenca

Air Airport is about a 20-min ride northeast of the centre. To **Quito** with **LAN** (Bolívar 9-18, T07-283 8078) and **TAME** (Florencia Astudillo 2-22, T07-288 9581). Also to **Guayaquil** with TAME.

Bus Local A new streetcar system was under construction in 2015.
City buses US$0.25. For the local **Baños**, city buses every 5-10 mins, 0600-2230, buses pass the front of the Terminal Terrestre, cross the city on Vega Muñoz and Cueva, then down Todos los Santos to the river, along 12 de Abril and onto Av Loja.

Regional Buses to nearby destinations leave from **Terminal Sur** at the Feria Libre on Av Las Américas. Many city buses pass here but it is not a safe area.

Long distance The **Terminal Terrestre** is on Av España, 15 mins by taxi northeast of centre. Take daytime buses to enjoy scenic routes. To **Riobamba**, 5½ hrs, US$7.50. To **Baños** (Tungurahua), take a bus to Riobamba and a taxi to the Terminal Oriental. To **Ambato**, 6½ hrs, US$10. To **Quito**, Terminal Quitumbe, US$12.50-15, 9 hrs. To **Alausí**, 4 hrs, US$6.25; all Riobamba-and Quito-bound buses pass by, but few enter town. To **Loja**, 4 hrs, US$9.50, see www.viajerosinternacional. com; transfer here for Vilcabamba. To **Saraguro**, US$6.25, 2½ hrs. To **Machala**, 4 hrs, US$7, sit on the left, wonderful scenery. To **Huaquillas**, 5 hrs, US$8.75. To **Guayaquil**, via Cajas and Molleturo, 4 hrs, or via Zhud, 5 hrs, both US$10. To **Macas** via Paute and Guarumales or via Gualaceo and Plan de Milagro, 7 hrs, US$10; spectacular scenery but prone to landslides, check in advance if roads are open. To **Gualaquiza**, in the southern

Oriente, via Gualaceo and Plan de Milagro or via Sígsig, 6 hrs, US$7.75.

International To **Chiclayo** (Peru) via Tumbes, **Máncora** and **Piura**, with **Super Semería**, at 2200, US$20, 11 hrs (US$15 as far as Piura or Máncora); also with **Azuay** at 2130; and **Pullman Sucre**, connecting with CIFA in Huaquillas; or go to Loja and catch a bus to Piura from there.

Long-distance taxis and vans Río Arriba, Del Batán 10-25 y Edwin Sacoto, near Feria Libre, T07-404 1790, to **Quito**, daily at 2300, US$25, 6½ hrs, from Quito, Páez N20-64 y Washington, T02-252 1336, at 1700; to **Guayaquil**, hourly 0400-2200, US$12, 3 hrs, several other companies nearby. To **Loja**, **Elite Tours**, Remigio Crespo 14-08 y Santa Cruz, T07-420 3088, also **Faisatur**, Remigio Crespo y Brazil, T07-404 4771, US$12, 3 hrs; taxi US$60. To **Vilcabamba**, van service daily at 1330 from **Hostal La Cigale**, Honorato Vásquez y Luis Cordero, US$15, 5 hrs.

Car rental Bombuscaro, España y Elia Liut, opposite the airport, T07-286 6541. **Also international companies.**

Taxi All taxis are required to use meters, approximately US$1.50 from the centre to the bus station; US$2 to airport; US$5 to Baños.

Ingapirca

Bus Direct buses **Cuenca** to Ingapirca with **Transportes Cañar** Mon-Fri at 0900 and 1220, Sat-Sun at 0900, returning 1300 and 1545, US$3.25, 2 hrs. Buses run from Cuenca to **Cañar** (US$2) and **El Tambo** (US$2.50) every 15 mins. From Cañar, corner of 24 de Mayo and Borrero, local buses leave every 15 mins for **Ingapirca**, 0600-1800, US$0.75, 30 mins; last bus returns at 1700. The same buses from Cañar go through **El Tambo**, US$0.75, 20 mins. If coming from the north, transfer in El Tambo. Pickup taxi from Cañar US$10, from El Tambo US$6.25.

Inca Trail to Ingapirca

From **Alausí to Achupallas**, small buses and pickups leave as they fill between 1100 and 1600, US$1, 1hr. Alternatively, take any bus along the Panamericana to **La Moya**, south of Alausí, at the turn-off for Achupallas, and a shared pickup from there (best on Thu and Sun), US$0.50. To hire a pickup from Alausí costs US$12-15, from La Moya US$10.

East of Cuenca

Bus From Terminal Terrestre in Cuenca: to **Paute**, every 15 mins, US$1, 1 hr; to **Gualaceo**, every 15 mins, US$0.75, 50 mins; to **Chordeleg**: every 15 mins from Gualaceo, US$0.35; 15 mins or direct bus from Cuenca, US$1, 1 hr; to **Sigsig**, every 30 mins via Gualaceo, US$1.50, 1½ hrs.

Parque Nacional Cajas

Bus From Cuenca's Terminal Terrestre take any **Guayaquil** bus that goes via Molleturo (not Zhud), US$2, 30 mins to turn-off for Llaviuco, 45 mins to Toreadora. **Coop Occidental** to Molleturo, 8 a day from the Terminal Sur/ Feria Libre, this is a slower bus and may wait to fill up. For the Soldados entrance, catch a bus from Puente del Vado in Cuenca, daily at 0600, US$1.50, 1½ hrs; the return bus passes the Soldados gate at about 1600.

Cuenca to
the Peruvian border

The province of Loja is a land of irregular topography, where the two distinct cordilleras further north give way to a maze of smaller ranges which barely reach 3000 m. Many warm valleys lie between these hills. Beautiful Parque Nacional Podocarpus is the ideal place to visit the cloudforests, which have made Loja famous since colonial days when chinchona, the bark from which quinine is extracted, was first described here.

Long isolated from the rest of the country, the far south developed its own unique character. Loja is functionally and culturally self-sufficient, home to universities, orchestras and cultural centres. The Saraguros, proud people who maintain their traditions, are today the only indigenous group in the province. The Malacatus and Palta natives disappeared long ago and many Lojanos are of European stock, dating back to early colonial times.

Vilcabamba, once an isolated village, although it is only 38 km south of the city of Loja, is today the rainbow at the end of Ecuador's gringo trail. It has an ideal climate and idyllic surroundings equally popular with Lojanos out for a weekend excursion, travellers en route between Ecuador and Peru, and with many expatriate residents.

Cuenca to Loja

The Pan-American Highway divides about 20 km south of Cuenca. One branch runs south to **Loja**, the other heads southwest through **Girón**, the **Yunguilla valley** (with a small bird reserve, see www.fjocotoco.org) and **Santa Isabel** (several hotels with pools and spas; cloudforest and waterfalls). The last stretch through sugar cane fields leads to **Pasaje** and **Machala**. The scenic road between Cuenca and Loja undulates between high, cold *páramo* passes and deep desert-like canyons.

Saraguro *Colour map 5, B3.*

On the road to Loja is the old town of Saraguro (population 9500, altitude 2500 m), where the local people, the most southerly indigenous Andean group in Ecuador, dress all in black. The men are notable for their black shorts and the women for their pleated black skirts, necklaces of coloured beads and silver *topos*, ornate pins fastening their shawls. The town has a picturesque Sunday market and interesting Mass and Easter celebrations. Traditional festivities are held during solstices and equinoxes in surrounding communities. Necklaces and other crafts are sold around the plaza. Saraguro has a community tourism programme with tours and homestay opportunities with indigenous families. Contact **Fundación Kawsay** ⓘ *18 de Noviembre y Av Loja, T07-220 0331*, or the **Oficina Municipal de Turismo** ⓘ *C José María Vivar on the main plaza, T07-220 0100 ext 18, Mon-Fri 0800-1200, 1400-1800. See also www.saraguro.org.* **Bosque Washapampa**, 6 km south, has good birdwatching.

Loja *Colour map 5, B3.*

The friendly, pleasant highland city of Loja (population 191,000, altitude 2060 m), encircled by hills, is an important transport hub, of particular interest to travellers on route to and from Peru. If spending any time in the area then the small town of Vilcabamba, 40 km to the south (see below), is a more interesting place to hang out but Loja makes a practical overnight stop with all facilities and services. **Tourist offices:** iTur ⓘ *José Antonio Eguiguren y Bolívar, Parque Central, T07-257 0407 ext 202, Mon-Fri 0800-1800, Sat-Sun 0800-1600.* Local information and map, helpful. **Ministerio de Turismo** ⓘ *Bernardo Valdivieso y 10 de Agosto, Ed Colibrí, p2, T07-257 2964, Mon-Fri 0815-1700.* Regional information for Loja, Zamora and El Oro.

Housed in a beautifully restored house on the main park is the **Centro Cultural Loja** home of the **Museo de la Cultura Lojana** ⓘ *10 de Agosto 13-30 y Bolívar, T07-257 3004, Mon-Fri 0830-1700, Sat-Sun 1000-1600, free*, with well-displayed archaeology, ethnography, art and history halls. **Parque San Sebastián** at Bolívar y Mercadillo and the adjoining **Calle Lourdes** preserve the flavour of old Loja and are worth visiting. Loja is famed for its musicians and has two symphony orchestras. Cultural evenings with music and dance are held at Plaza San Sebastián, Thursday 2000-2200. The **Museo de Música** ⓘ *Valdivieso 09-42 y Rocafuerte, T07-256 1342. Mon-Fri 0830-1300, 1500-1800, free*, honours 10 Lojano composers.

Parque Universitario Francisco Vivar Castro (Parque La Argelia) ⓘ *on the road south to Vilcabamba, Tue-Sun 0800-1700, US$1, city bus marked 'Capulí-Dos Puentes' to the park or 'Argelia' to the Universidad Nacional and walk from there*, has trails through the forest to the *páramo*. Across the road is the **Jardín Botánico Reynaldo Espinosa** ⓘ *Mon-Fri 0730-1230, 1500-1800, Sat-Sun 1300-1800, US$1*, which is nicely laid out.

★ Parque Nacional Podocarpus

Headquarters at Cajanuma entrance, T07-302 4862. Limited information from Ministerio del Ambiente in Loja, Sucre 04-55 y Quito, T07-257 9595, parquepodocarpus@gmail. com, Mon-Fri 0800-1700. In Zamora at Sevilla de Oro y Orellana, T07-260 6606. Their general map of the park is not adequate for navigation; buy topographic maps in Quito.

Podocarpus (950-3700 m) is one of the most diverse protected areas in the world. It is particularly rich in birdlife and includes one of the last major habitats for the spectacled bear. The park protects stands of *romerillo* or podocarpus, a native, slow-growing conifer. Podocarpus is divided into two areas, an upper premontane section with many lakes, spectacular walking country and lush cloudforest; and a lower subtropical section, with remote areas of virgin rainforest and unmatched quantities of flora and fauna. Both zones are wet (rubber boots recommended) but there may be periods of dry weather October to January. The upper section is also cold, so warm clothing and waterproofs are indispensable year-round.

Conservation groups working in and around the park include: **Arcoiris** ⓘ *Ciprés 12-202 y Acacias, La Pradera, T07-257 2926, www.arcoiris.org.ec;* **Naturaleza y Cultura Internacional** ⓘ *Av Pío Jaramillo y Venezuela, T07-257 3691, www.natureandculture.org.*

Access to the park Entrances to the **upper section**: at Cajanuma, 8 km south of Loja on the Vilcabamba road, from the turn-off it is a further 8 km uphill to the guard station; and at San Francisco, 24 km from Loja along the road to Zamora. Entrances to the **lower section**: Bombuscaro is 6 km from Zamora, the visitor centre is a 30-minute walk from the car park.

Hiking in the park Cajanuma is the trailhead for the demanding eight-hour hike to **Lagunas del Compadre**, a series of beautiful lakes set amid rock cliffs, camping is possible there (no services). Another trail from Cajanuma leads in one hour to a lookout with views over Loja. At **San Francisco**, the *guardianía* (ranger's station) operated by Fundación Arcoiris, offers decent accommodation (see below). This section of the park is a transition cloudforest at around 2200 m, very rich in birdlife. This is the best place to see podocarpus trees: a trail (four hours return) goes from the shelter to the trees. The **Bombuscaro** lowland section, also very rich in birdlife, has several trails leading to lovely swimming holes on the Bombuscaro River and waterfalls; see page 312.

Loja to the Peruvian border
Of all the crossings from Ecuador to Peru, by far the most efficient and relaxed is the scenic route from Loja to Piura via Macará (see below). Other routes are from Vilcabamba to La Balsa (see page 222), Huaquillas on the coast (page 248) and along the Río Napo in the Oriente (page 298). There are smaller border crossings

without immigration facilities (passports cannot be stamped) at Jimbura, southeast of Macará; and Lalamor, west of Macará.

Leaving Loja on the main paved highway going west, the airport at **La Toma** (1200 m) is reached after 35 km. La Toma is also called **Catamayo**, where there is lodging. At Catamayo, where you can catch the Loja–Macará–Piura bus, the Pan-American Highway divides: one branch runs west, the other south.

On the western road, at San Pedro de La Bendita, a road climbs to the much-venerated pilgrimage site of **El Cisne**, dominated by its large incongruous French-style Gothic church. Vendors and beggars fill the town (see page 220). Continuing on the western route, **Catacocha** is spectacularly placed on a hilltop. Visit the Shiriculapo rock for the views. There are pre-Inca ruins around the town, and the small archaeological **Museo Hermano Joaquín Liebana** ⓘ *T07-268 3201, 0800-1200, 1400-1800*. From Catacocha, the road runs south to the border at Macará.

Another route south from Catamayo to Macará is via **Gonzanamá**, a sleepy town (basic *hostales*), famed for the weaving of beautiful *alforjas* (saddlebags), and **Cariamanga**, a regional centre (various hotels and services). From here the road twists along a ridge westwards to **Colaisaca**, before descending steeply through forests to **Utuana** with a nature reserve (www.fjocotoco.org) and **Sozoranga** (one hotel), then down to the rice paddies of **Macará**, on the border. There is a choice of hotels here and good road connections to Piura in Peru.

Loja

Where to stay	Restaurants	7 Molino Café
1 Bombuscaro	1 Alivinatu	8 Pizzería Forno di Fango
2 Grand Victoria	2 Angelo's	
3 Libertad	3 Café Ruskina	
4 Londres	4 Casa Sol	
5 Real la Colón	5 El Sendero	
6 Vinarós	6 Lecka	

N

200 metres
200 yards

Border with Peru: Macará–La Tina The border is at the international bridge over the Río Macará, 2.5 km from town, taxi US$1.50. There are plans to build a border complex; in the meantime, immigration, customs and other services are housed in temporary quarters. The border is open 24 hours. Formalities are straightforward, it is a much easier crossing than at Huaquillas. In Macará, at the park where taxis leave for the border, there are money changers dealing in soles, but no changers at the bridge. On the Peruvian side, minivans and cars run to Sullana (US$5 per person) but it is much safer to take a bus from Loja or Macará directly to Piura. The **Peruvian consulate** ⓘ *Zoilo Rodríguez 03-05, T07-258 7330, Mon-Fri 0900-1300, 1500-1700*, is in Loja.

Listings Cuenca to the Peruvian border *map p217*

Where to stay

Saraguro

$$ Achik Huasi
On a hill above town, T07-220 0058, or through Fundación Kawsay, T07-220 0331.
Community-run *hostería* in a nice setting, private bath, hot water, parking, views, tours, taxi to centre US$1.

$ Saraguro
Loja 03-2 y A Castro, T07-220 0286.
Nice courtyard, electric shower, family-run, basic, good value.

Loja

$$$$ Grand Victoria
B Valdivieso 06-50 y Eguiguren, ½ a block from the Parque Central, T07-258 3500, www.grandvictoriabh.com.
Rebuilt early-20th century home with 2 patios, comfortable modern rooms and suites, restaurant, small pool, spa, gym, business centre, frigobar, safety box, parking, long-stay discounts.

$$$ Libertador
Colón 14-30 y Bolívar, T07-256 0779, www.hotellibertador.com.ec.
A very good hotel in the centre of town, comfortable rooms and suites, includes buffet breakfast, good restaurant, indoor pool (open to non-guests Sat-Sun, US$6), spa, parking.

$$ Bombuscaro
10 de Agosto y Av Universitaria, T07-257 7021, www.bombuscaro.com.ec.
Comfortable rooms and suites, includes buffet breakfast and airport transfers, restaurant, car rental. Recommended.

$$-$ Real la Colón
Colón 15-54 entre 18 de Noviembre y Sucre, T07-257 7826, hostalcolon2012@hotmail.com.
Modern centrally located multi-storey hotel, parking, decent value.

$ Londres
Sucre 07-51 y 10 de Agosto, T07-256 1936.
Economical hostel in a well-maintained old house, shared bath, hot water, basic, clean, good value.

$ Vinarós
Sucre 11-30 y Azuay, T07-258 4015, hostalvinaros@hotmail.com.
Pleasant hostel with simple rooms, private bath, electric shower, parking, good value.

Parque Nacional Podocarpus
Canjanuma
At Cajanuma, there are cabins with beds but bring a warm sleeping bag, stove and food.

San Francisco

At San Francisco, the *guardianía* (ranger's station), operated by **Fundación Arcoiris** offers rooms with shared bath, hot water and kitchen facilities, US$8 pp if you bring a sleeping bag, US$10 if they provide sheets. Ask to be let off at Arcoiris or you will be taken to Estación San Francisco, 8 km further east.

Bombuscaro

There are cabins with beds and an area for camping.

Loja to the Peruvian border
Catamayo

$$ MarcJohn's
Isidro Ayora y 24 de Mayo, at the main park, T07-267 7631, granhotelmarcjohns@hotmail.com.
Modern multi-storey hotel, rooms with fan, buffet breakfast, restaurant.

$$ Rosal del Sol
A short walk from the city on the main road west of town, T07-267 6517.
Ranch-style building, comfortable rooms with fan, restaurant not always open, small pool, parking, includes airport transfer, welcoming owner.

$ Reina del Cisne
Isidro Ayora at the park, T07-267 7414.
Simple adequate rooms, hot water, cheaper with cold water, fan, small pool, gym, parking, good value.

Macará

$ Bekalus
Valdivieso y 10 de Agosto, T07-269 4043.
Simple adequate hostel, a/c, cheaper with fan, cold water.

$ El Conquistador
Bolívar y Abdón Calderón, T07-269 4057.
Comfortable hotel, some rooms are dark, request one with balcony, includes simple breakfast, electric shower, a/c or fan, parking.

Restaurants

Saraguro

Several restaurants around the main plaza serve economical meals.

$$-$ Turu Manka
100 m uphill from Hostal Achik Huasi.
Wide selection. The food is average, but it is still one of the better choices in town.

Loja

$$ Lecka
24 de Mayo 10-51 y Riofío, T256 3878. Mon-Fri 1700-2230.
Small quaint restaurant serving German specialities, very good food, friendly.

$$-$ Casa Sol
24 de Mayo 07-04 y José Antonio Eguiguren. Daily 0830-2330.
Small place for breakfast, economical set lunches and regional dishes in the evening. Pleasant seating on balcony.

$$-$ Pizzería Forno di Fango
24 de Mayo y Azuay, T07-258 2905. Tue-Sun 1200-2230.
Excellent wood-oven pizza, salads and lasagne. Large portions, home delivery, good service and value.

$ Alivinatu
10 de Agosto 12-53 y Bernardo Valdivieso, in the health food shop. Mon-Sat 0830-1400, 1500-1900.
Very good fresh fruit or vegetable juices prepared on the spot. Also snacks and set lunches with vegetarian options.

$ Angelo's

*José Félix de Valdivieso 16-36 y Av
Universitaria. Mon-Sat 0800-1600.*
Quality set lunches, friendly service.

Cafés

Café Maracumango
*Sucre 07-48 y 10 de Agosto.
Mon-Sat 0900-1300, 1500-2000.*
Coffee, cream cakes, other sweets and
regional snacks such as *humitas*.

El Sendero
*Bolívar 13-13 y Mercadillo, upstairs.
Tue-Sat 1530-2200.*
Fruit juices, coffee and snacks, balcony
overlooking Parque San Sebastián, ping
pong and other games, library.

Molino Café
*José A Eguiguren y Sucre.
Mon-Sat 0800-2000.*
Small place, breakfast, choice of coffees,
snacks, sandwiches, set lunches.

Festivals

Loja
Aug-Sep **Fiesta de la Virgen del
Cisne**, thousands of faithful accompany
the statue of the Virgin in a 3-day
74 km pilgrimage from El Cisne to Loja
cathedral, beginning **16 Aug**. The
image remains in Loja until **1 Nov** when
the return pilgrimage starts. Town is
crowded Aug-Sep.

What to do

Loja
Exploraves, *Lourdes 14-80 y Sucre, T07-
258 2434, T09-8515 2239, www.exploraves.
com*. Specializes in birdwatching tours,
overnight trips to different types of
forest, about US$150 pp per day. Pablo
Andrade is a knowledgeable guide.

Transport

Saraguro
Bus To **Cuenca** US$6.25, 2½ hrs. To **Loja**,
US$2.25, 1½ hrs. Check if your bus leaves
from the plaza or the Panamericana.

Loja
Air The airport is at La Toma
(Catamayo), 35 km west (see Loja to
the Peruvian border, page 216): taxi
from airport to **Catamayo** town US$2,
to Loja shared taxi US$5 pp, to hire
US$20 (cheaper from Loja) eg with
Jaime González, T07-256 3714 or **Paul
Izquierdo**, T07-256 3973; to **Vilcabamba**,
US$40. There are 1-2 daily flights to
Quito and **Guayaquil** with **TAME** (24 de
Mayo y E Ortega, T07-257 0248).

Bus All buses leave from the Terminal
Terrestre at Av Gran Colombia e Isidro
Ayora, at the north of town, 10 mins by
city bus from the centre; left luggage;
US$0.10 terminal tax. Taxi from centre,
US$1. To **Cuenca**, almost every hour
(www.viajerosinternacional.com), 4 hrs,
US$9.50. Van service with **Elite Tours**,
18 de Noviembre 01-13, near Puerta de la
Ciudad, T07-256 0731, and **Faisatur**, 18 de
Noviembre y Av Universitaria, T07-258
5299, US$12, 3 hrs; taxi US$60. **Machala**,
10 a day, 5-6 hrs, US$7.50 (3 routes, all
scenic: via Piñas, for **Zaruma**, partly
unpaved and rough; via Balsas, paved;
and via Alamor, for **Puyango petrified
forest**). **Quito**, Terminal Quitumbe,
regular US$15-17.50; **Transportes Loja**
semi-cama, US$21, 12 hrs. **Guayaquil**,
US$12.50 regular, US$15 semi-cama,
8 hrs. To **Huaquillas**, US$7.50, 6 hrs
direct. To **Zumba** (for Peru), 10 daily
including **Sur Oriente** at 0500 to make
connections to Peru the same day and
Cariamanga at 0900, US$9.50, 7 hrs
but delays possible, road construction

in 2015; **Nambija** at 2400 direct to the border at La Balsa (only in the dry season), US$12.50, 8 hrs. To **Catamayo** (for airport) every 15 mins 0630-1900, US$1.25, 1 hr. To **Macará**, see below. To **Piura (Peru)**, **Loja Internacional**, via Macará, at 0700 and 2300 daily, US$15, 8-9 hrs including border formalities. Also **Unión Cariamanga** at 2400.

Parque Nacional Podocarpus
For **Cajanuma** (upper section), take a Vilcabamba-bound bus, get off at the turnoff, US$1, it is a pretty 8-km walk from there. Direct transport by taxi to Cajanuma, about US$10 (may not be feasible in the rainy season) or with a tour from Loja. You can arrange a pickup later from the guard station. Pickup from Vilcabamba, US$20. To get to **San Francisco** (upper section) take any bus between Loja and Zamora, make sure you alight by the Arcoiris *guardianía* and not at Estación Científica San Francisco which is 8 km east. **Bombuscaro** (lower section) is 6 km from Zamora, take a taxi US$6 to the entrance, then walk 1 km to the visitor centre.

Loja to the Peruvian border
Bus Transportes Loja and **Cariamanga** have frequent buses, daily from Macará to **Loja**; 6 hrs, US$7.50. Direct Loja–**Piura** buses can also be boarded in Macará, US$5 to Piura, 3 hrs. **Transportes Loja** also has service to **Quito**, US$19, 15 hrs, and **Guayaquil**, US$14, 8 hrs.

Vilcabamba to Peru
surrounded by hills and with a pleasant climate; well set up for tourism

Vilcabamba *Colour map 5, C3.*
Once an isolated village, Vilcabamba (population 4900, altitude 1520 m) is today home to a thriving and colourful expatriate community. It is popular with travellers and a good place to stop on route between Ecuador and Peru. The whole area is beautiful and tranquil, with an agreeable climate. There are many decent places to stay and good restaurants. The area offers many great day-walks and longer treks, as well as ample opportunities for ★ **horse riding** and **cycling**. A number of lovely private nature reserves are situated east of Vilcabamba, towards Parque Nacional Podocarpus. Trekkers can continue on foot through orchid-clad cloudforests to the high *páramos* of Podocarpus. Artisans sell their crafts in front of the school on weekends and there is an organic produce market by the bus terminal on Saturday morning, in addition to the regular Sunday market.

Craig's Book Exchange ① *in Yamburara, 1 km east of town, follow Diego Vaca de Vega*, has 2500 books in 12 languages and an art gallery. There are no banks, but several ATMs by iTur and the church.

Around Vilcabamba
Rumi Wilco ① *10-min walk northeast of town, take C Agua de Hierro towards C La Paz and turn left, follow signs, US$2 valid for the duration of your stay in Vilcabamba*, is a 40-ha private nature reserve with several signed trails. Many of the trees and shrubs are labelled with their scientific and common names. There are great views of town from the higher trails, and it is a very good place to go for a walk. More than 100 species of birds have been identified here. Volunteers are welcome.

Sacred Sueños ① 1½-hr walk in the hills above town, T09-8931 3698, www. sacredsuenos.wordpress.com, is a grassroots permaculture community which accepts volunteers for a minimum of two weeks.

Climbing **Mandango**, 'the sleeping woman' mountain is a scenic half-day walk. The signed access is along the highway, 250 m south of the bus terminal. Be careful on the higher sections when it is windy; enquire beforehand about public safety.

South of Vilcabamba, 45 km on the road to Zumba, is the 3500-ha bird- and orchid-rich **Reserva Tapichalaca** ① T07-250 5212, www.fjocotoco.org, entry US$15, lodge ($$$).

Border with Peru: La Balsa

Many daily buses run on the scenic road from Loja via Vilcabamba to **Zumba**, 112 km south of Vilcabamba. If you catch the bus which passes through Vilcabamba at 0600 then you can connect with the *ranchera* at 1430 from Zumba to La Balsa and

Vilcabamba

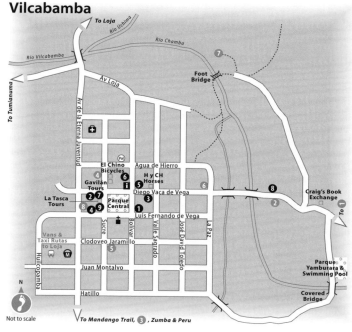

Where to stay ⊜
1 Cabañas Río Yambala
2 El Descanso del Toro
3 Izhcayluma
4 Jardín Escondido
5 Las Margaritas
6 Le Rendez-Vous
7 Rumi Wilco
8 Valle Sagrado

Restaurants ②
1 Agaveblu
2 Charlito's
3 Del Páramo
4 La Baguette
5 La Terraza
6 Natural Yogurt
7 Pura Vida
8 Shanta's
9 Vilcabamba Juice Factory

ON THE ROAD

The Vilcabamba syndrome

At the time a tiny isolated village, Vilcabamba attracted international attention in the 1960s when researchers announced that it was home to one of the oldest living populations in the world. It was said that people here often lived well over 100 years, some as old as 135.

Although doubt was subsequently cast on some of this data, there is still a high incidence of healthy, active elders in Vilcabamba. It is not unusual to find people in their 70s and 80s working in the fields and covering several miles a day on foot to get there. Such longevity and vitality has been ascribed to the area's famously healthy climate and excellent drinking water, but other factors must also be involved: perhaps physical activity, diet and lack of stress.

Attracted in part by Vilcabamba's reputation for nurturing a long and tranquil life, a number of outsiders – both Ecuadoreans and foreigners – settled in the area. Some of the earliest arrivals followed the footsteps of Doctor Johnny Lovewisdom, a California-born ascetic who arrived in 1969 to establish his Pristine Order of Paradisiacal Perfection. Others just came for a few days and never left.

For a time drugs were in vogue in Vilcabamba, especially a hallucinogenic cactus extract called San Pedro, and the flashbacks associated with its use became known as the 'Vilcabamba syndrome'. Later, the fashion turned to UFO sightings, with plans to build a large observation platform. Then people arrived to escape the impending end of the world when the Mayan calendar expired in 2012. Raw-foodists followed as did many young artisans from all over Latin America.

Through it all, more and more foreign residents, ranging from retirees to young families, have settled in Vilcabamba. Real-estate speculation has been rife and brokers' offices line the plaza alongside the cafés where the expats congregate. Catering to their needs has become the town's growth industry while, in a delightfully ironic reversal of roles, urban middle-class Ecuadoreans from Cuenca, Guayaquil and Quito come to spend their holidays and watch the colourful gringos. Today's Vilcabamba syndrome has more to do with postmodern colonialism than hallucinogenic cactus juice.

Come check it out for yourself and, if you are really interested, read the anonymously authored history: *Valley of the Rare Fruits*, available at Caballos Gavilán tour agency. Do you think the outsiders will still be able to benefit from the once famous tranquility and longevity of Vilcabamba? Or have we brought with us the seeds of our own – and Vilcabamba's – destruction?

make it as far as San Ignacio (Peru) the same day (see Loja, Transport, page 220). It is a 1½-hour rough ride by *ranchera* (open-sided bus) from Zumba to the border at La Balsa, there is a control on the way; keep your passport to hand. **La Balsa** is just a few houses on either side of the international bridge over the Río Canchis;

there are simple eateries, shops, money changers (no banks here or in Zumba), and one very basic hotel on the Peruvian side. It is a relaxed border. Ecuadorean customs and immigration are officially open 24 hours. The Peruvian border post is open 0800-1300, 1500-2000; entering Peru, visit immigration and the PNP office (see under Macará–La Tina, page 218, for Peru's consulate in Loja). On the Peruvian side mototaxis run to **Namballe**, 15 minutes away, and cars run to Namballe and **San Ignacio** when full (two hours), from where there is transport to **Jaén**. This is a faster, more direct route between Vilcabamba and **Chachapoyas** (Peru) than going via the coast. Parts are rough but it can be done in two days; best take the bus passing Vilcabamba at around 0600.

Vilcabamba - Chachapoyas (Peru)

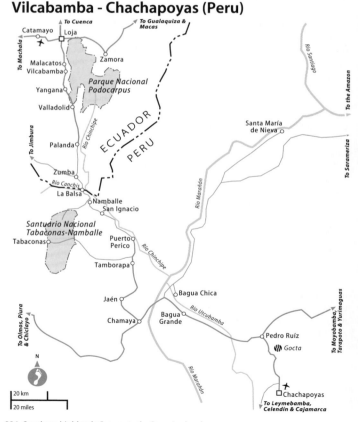

Tourist information

Vilcabamba

iTur
Diego Vaca de Vega y Bolívar, on the corner of the main plaza, T07-264 0090. Daily 0800-1300, 1400-1800.
Various pamphlets, helpful, Spanish only.

Where to stay

Vilcabamba

$$$ El Descanso del Toro
800 m from the centre on the road to Yamburara, T07-264 0007, www.descansodeltoro.com.
Tastefully decorated comfortable rooms, all with jacuzzi, pool, pleasant grounds, ample parking, attentive staff.

$$-$ Cabañas Río Yambala
Yamburara Alto, 4 km east of town (taxi US$4), T09-9106 2762, www.vilcabamba-hotel.com.
Cabins with cooking facilities in a beautiful tranquil setting on the shores of the Río Yambala, private or shared bath, hot water, sauna, monthly rates available. No shops or restaurants nearby, bring food. Tours to Las Palmas private nature reserve. English spoken.

$$-$ Izhcayluma
2 km south on road to Zumba, T07-302 5162, www.izhcayluma.com.
Popular inn with comfortable rooms and cabins with terrace and hammocks. Very good buffet breakfast available, excellent restaurant with wonderful views, private or shared bath, also dorm US$8.50 pp, pool, massage centre, yoga centre and lessons, lively bar, billiards, ping-pong, parking, bird observation platform, walking trails, map and route descriptions, English and German spoken, helpful. Highly recommended.

$$-$ Jardín Escondido
Sucre y Diego Vaca de Vega, T07-264 0281.
Refurbished old house around a lovely patio, bright comfortable rooms or a dorm, restaurant, small pool, English spoken.

$$-$ Las Margaritas
Sucre y Clodoveo Jaramillo, T07-264 0051.
Small family-run hotel with comfortable rooms, good breakfast, intermittent solar-heated water, parking, garden.

$$-$ Le Rendez-Vous
Diego Vaca de Vega 06-43 y La Paz, T09-9219 1180, www.rendezvousecuador.com.
Very comfortable rooms with terrace and hammocks around a lovely garden. Private or shared bath, pleasant atmosphere, attentive service, French and English spoken. Recommended.

$$-$ Rumi Wilco
10-min walk northeast of town, take C Agua de Hierro towards C La Paz and turn left, follow the signs from there, www.rumiwilco.com.
Cabins in the Rumi Wilco reserve. Lovely setting on the shores of the river, very tranquil, private or shared bath, laundry facilities, fully furnished kitchens, discounts for long stays and volunteers, camping US$4 pp, friendly Argentine owners, English spoken. Recommended.

$ Valle Sagrado
Av de la Eterna Juventud y Luis Fernando de Vega, T09-6843 8564.
Small basic rooms around a large scruffy garden, private or shared bath, US$5-6 pp in dorm, camping US$3.50 pp, electric shower, laundry and cooking facilities, parking.

Border with Peru
Zumba

$$-$ Emperador
Colón y Orellana, T07-230 8063.
Adequate rooms, private bath.

$ San Luis
12 de Febrero y Brasil, T07-230 8017.
Rooms on top floor are better, private or shared bath, attentive service.

Vilcabamba
Izhcayluma hotel has an excellent restaurant, see above. Around the Parque Central are many café/bar/ restaurants with pleasant sidewalk seating; too many to list, see map, page 222. Try the local microbrew, **Sol del Venado**.

$$ Shanta's
800 m from the centre on the road to Yamburara. Wed-Sun 1300-2100.
Specialities are pizza (excellent), trout, frogs legs, filet mignon and *cuy* (with advance notice). Also vegetarian options, good fruit juices and drinks. Rustic setting, pleasant atmosphere and attentive service. Recommended.

$ Charlito's
Diego Vaca de Vega y Sucre. Tue-Sun 1100-2200.
Salads, pasta, pizza, soup, sandwiches with tasty home-made bread.

$ Natural Yogurt
Bolívar y Diego Vaca de Vega. Daily 0900-2100.
Breakfast, home-made yoghurt, savoury and sweet crêpes, some pasta dishes.

$ Vilcabamba Juice Factory
Sucre y Luis Fernando de Vega, on the Parque Central. Tue-Sat 0830-1600, Sun 0830-1400.
Healthy juices, soups and salads, vegan food available, run by a naturopath.

Cafés

Del Páramo
Diego Vaca de Vega y Valle Sagrado. Wed-Fri 1530-1900, Sat-Sun 1030-1900.
Belgian chocolatier with a variety of top-quality sweets.

La Baguette
Luis Fernando de Vega y Sucre.
Closed Mon.
Small French bakery, great bread and pastries.

What to do

See Where to stay, above, for more options.

Vilcabamba
Cycling
El Chino, *Sucre y Diego Vaca de Vega*, *T09-8187 6347, chinobike@gmail.com*. Mountain bike tours (US$25-35), rentals (US$2-3 per hr, US$10-15 per day) and repairs.
Also see **La Tasca Tours**, below.

Horse riding
2-hr ride US$25, half day US$35, full day with lunch US$50, overnight trips US$70 per day, all inclusive.
Gavilán Tours, *Sucre y Diego Vaca de Vega, T07-264 0256, gavilanhorse@yahoo. com*. Run by a group of experienced horsemen.
H y CH, *Diego Vaca de Vega y Valle Sagrado, T09-9152 3118*. Alvaro León, good horses and saddles.
La Tasca Tours, *Sucre at the plaza, T09-8556 1188*. Horse and bike tours with experienced guides, René and Jaime León.

Language courses
Spanish classes with **Marta Villacrés**, T09-9751 3311.

Massage
Beauty Care, *Diego Vaca de Vega y Valle Sagrado, T09-8122 3456. Daily 1000-1200, 1400-1800*. Karina Zumba, facials, waxing, Reiki, 1 hr US$20.

Shanta's *(see Restaurants, above)*, *T09-8538 5710, Lola Encalada*. Very good 1½-hr therapeutic massage US$31, also does waxing. Recommended.

Transport

Vilcabamba
Loja to Vilcabamba, a nice 1-hr bus ride; from Loja's Terminal Terrestre, **Vilcabambaturis** minibuses, every 15-30 mins, 0545-2115, US$1.65, 1 hr; or *taxirutas* (shared taxis) from José María Peña y Venezuela, 0600-2000, US$2.25, 45 mins; taxi, US$20. To **Loja**, vans and shared taxis leave from the small terminal behind the market. For **Parque Nacional Podocarpus**, taxis charge US$20 each way, taking you right to the trailhead at **Cajanuma**. To **Cuenca** vans at 0800 from Hostería Izhcayluma, US$15, 5 hrs, Cuenca stop at **Hostal La Cigale**. To **Zumba** buses originating in Loja pass Vilcabamba about 1 hr after departure and stop along the highway in front of the market (1st around 0600, next 1000), US$8.25, 5-6 hrs, expect delays due to road construction in 2015. To **Quito** (Quitumbe) **Transportes Loja** (tickets sold for this and other routes at **Movistar** office, Av de la Eterna Juventud y Clodoveo Jaramillo) at 1900, with a stop in Loja, US$22.50, 13-14 hrs.

Vilcabamba to Peru
Zumba
Terminal Terrestre in Zumba, 1 km south of the centre. From Zumba to **La Balsa**, *rancheras* at 0800, 1430 and 1730, US$2, 1-1½ hrs. From La Balsa to Zumba at 1200, 1730 and 1930. Taxi Zumba–La Balsa, US$30. To **Loja**, see above. In Zumba, petrol is sold 0700-1700.

Guayaquil & south to Peru

Ecuador's metropolis

Guayaquil, the largest and most dynamic industrial and commercial centre in the country, is also Ecuador's chief port. The city's influence extends all along the coast and beyond.

This 'working Ecuador' is more frequently seen by business visitors than tourists, but Guayaquil has some attractions to offer. Trips to the Galápagos can be organized from here and the city is a logical starting point for travels north along the coast and south to Peru. The coastal plains nearby are the agro-industrial heartland of Ecuador. Rice, sugar, coffee, African palm, mango and other fruit, cacao and shrimp are produced in these hot and humid lowlands and processed or exported through Guayaquil.

To the south of the city, thriving banana plantations are the economic mainstay of the coastal area bordering the east flank of the Gulf of Guayaquil. Machala is the main centre here and nearby Puerto Bolívar is the port through which the oro verde (green gold) is shipped out to the world. Mangroves and islands characterize the coast leading south to Huaquillas, the main coastal border crossing to Peru. Inland from Machala, in the uplands of El Oro, is one of the best hidden treasures of Ecuador – the colonial mining town of Zaruma.

Best for
Dining ▪ Nature reserves ▪ Museums ▪ Nightlife

Footprint picks

★ **Malecón 2000 and Cerro Santa Ana**, page 233

No visit to Guayaquil is complete without a stroll along its breezy riverside promenade. Don't miss the views from Cerro Santana.

★ **MAAC Museum**, page 233

The Museo Antropológico y de Arte Contemporáneo is the place to learn about 10,000 years of Ecuadorean culture, as well as the country's modern art.

★ **Parque Histórico**, page 235

Step back into 19th-century Guayaquil to experience its urban and rural lifestyles.

★ **Isla Santay**, page 237

Ride a bicycle through this protected wetland and admire its rich birdlife and flora.

★ **Reserva Ecológica Manglares-Churute**, page 237

Mangroves and dry tropical forest are the highlights of this nature reserve, not far from Guayaquil.

★ **Zaruma**, page 247

A colonial gem, off the beaten path in the beautiful uplands of El Oro.

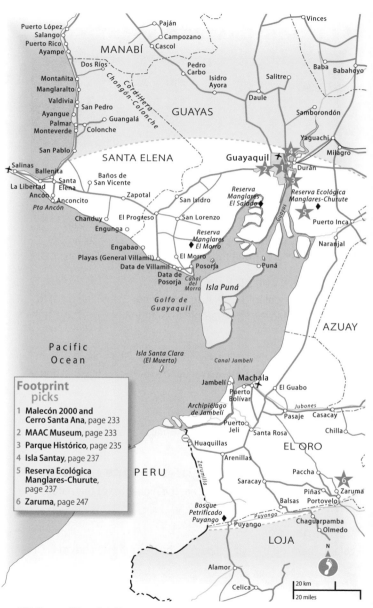

Footprint
picks

1 **Malecón 2000 and
Cerro Santa Ana**, page 233
2 **MAAC Museum**, page 233
3 **Parque Histórico**, page 235
4 **Isla Santay**, page 237
5 **Reserva Ecológica
Manglares-Churute**,
page 237
6 **Zaruma**, page 247

20 km
20 miles

Guayaquil

Guayaquil is hotter, faster and louder than the capital. Ecuador's largest city (population 2,500,000) lies on the west bank of the chocolate-brown Río Guayas, some 56 km from its outflow into the Gulf of Guayaquil. Industrial expansion and migration continually fuel the city's growth. The city has always been an intense political rival to Quito. Guayaquileños are certainly more lively, colourful and open than their Quito counterparts. Since 2000, Guayaquil has cleaned up and 'renewed' some of its most frequented downtown areas. It boasts modern airport and bus terminals, and the Metrovía transit system. In and around the city are various parks which provide its residents and visitors much needed relief from the heat.

Essential Guayaquil

Finding your feet

José Joaquín de Olmedo international airport is 15 minutes' drive north of the city centre. Not far from the airport is the Terminal Terrestre long-distance bus station. Opposite this is Terminal Río Daule, an important transfer station on the Metrovía rapid transit system. See also Transport, page 244.

Getting around

A number of hotels are centrally located in the downtown core, along the west bank of the Río Guayas, where you can get around on foot. The city's suburbs sprawl to the north and south of the centre, with middle-class neighbourhoods and some very upscale areas in the north, where some elegant hotels and restaurants are located, and poorer working-class neighbourhoods and slums to the south. Road tunnels under Cerro Santa Ana link the northern suburbs to downtown. Outside downtown, addresses are hard to find; ask for a nearby landmark to help orient your driver.

When to go

From May to December the climate is dry with often overcast days but pleasantly cool nights, whereas the hot rainy season from January to April can be oppressively humid.

Best places to stay

Grand Hotel Guayaquil, page 238
Las Peñas, page 239
Manso, page 239
Ramada, page 239

Safety

The Malecón 2000, parts of Avenida 9 de Octubre, Las Peñas and Malecón del Estero Salado are heavily patrolled and reported safe. The rest of the city requires precautions. Do not go anywhere with valuables. Parque Centenario is also patrolled, but the area around it requires caution. 'Express kidnappings' are of particular concern in Guayaquil; do not take a taxi outside the north end of the Malecón 2000 near the MAAC museum, walk south along the Malecón as far as the Hotel Ramada, where there is a taxi stand; whenever possible, call for a radio taxi.

Best restaurants

La Canoa, page 240
La Parrilla del Ñato, page 240
Lo Nuestro, page 240
California, page 242

Weather Guayaquil

January	February	March	April	May	June
31°C	30°C	31°C	31°C	30°C	29°C
24°C	24°C	24°C	24°C	23°C	22°C
160mm	257mm	252mm	113mm	65mm	69mm

July	August	September	October	November	December
28°C	29°C	29°C	29°C	30°C	31°C
21°C	20°C	21°C	21°C	22°C	23°C
111mm	135mm	84mm	75mm	93mm	116mm

Sights *Colour map 3, C3.*

Malecón 2000 and around A wide, tree-lined waterfront avenue, the Malecón Simón Bolívar runs alongside the Río Guayas for 2.5 km. Along the inland side of this avenue are the imposing **Municipal** and **Gobernación**. The riverfront along this avenue is an attractive promenade, known as ★ **Malecón 2000** ⓘ *daily 0700-2400*, where visitors and locals can enjoy the fresh river breeze and take in the views. There are gardens, fountains, children's playgrounds, monuments, walkways and an electric vehicle for the handicapped (daily 1000-2000, US$2). You can dine at upmarket restaurants, cafés and food courts.

At the north end is the **Centro Cultural Simón Bolívar**, better known as ★ **MAAC (Museo Antropológico y de Arte Contemporaneo)** ⓘ *T04-230 9400, daily 0900-1630, free,* with excellent collections of ceramics and gold objects especially from coastal cultures. This is the place to learn about 10,000 years of Ecuadorean culture. It also boasts an extensive modern art collection and shows international films year-round. Just south is an **IMAX** large-screen cinema, and downstairs the **Museo Miniatura** ⓘ *Tue-Sun 0900-2000, US$1.50*, with miniature historical exhibits. Beyond is an especially nice garden.

Towards the centre of the promenade are an information booth, the Yacht Club and several monuments. Most notable are **La Rotonda**, which marks the meeting between independence leaders Simón Bolívar and José San Martín in 1822, and a **Moorish clock tower**. Further south are the exclusive **Club de la Unión** and a monument to poet and former president José Joaquín de Olmedo. Towards the south end are souvenir shops, a shopping mall and the **Palacio de Cristal** (prefabricated by Eiffel 1905-1907), originally a market and now a gallery housing temporary exhibits.

Las Peñas North of the Malecón 2000 is the old district of **Las Peñas**, the last picturesque vestige of Guayaquil of the republican era, with its brightly painted wooden houses and narrow, cobbled main street (Numa Pompilio Llona). It is an attractive place for a walk to ★ **Cerro Santa Ana**, which offers great views of the city and the mighty Guayas. It has a bohemian feel, with bars and restaurants. A large open-air exhibition of paintings and sculpture is held here during the *fiestas julianas* (24-25 July). North of La Peñas is **Puerto Santa Ana**, with a luxury hotel, upmarket apartments, a promenade and three museums: to the romantic singer Julio Jaramillo, to beer in the old brewery, and to football.

Almost none of Guayaquil's original wooden buildings remain. Except for a few rebuilt churches, most of its colonial past is confined to the history books. **Santo Domingo**, founded in 1548, stands by Las Peñas. It was sacked and burned by pirates in 1624. Its present form was built in 1938, replacing the wooden structure with concrete in classical style.

West of Las Peñas, below **Cerro El Carmen**, the huge, sprawling **cemetery**, with its dazzling, high-rise tombs and the ostentatious mausoleums of the rich, is worth a visit. A flower market over the road sells the best blooms in the city. Go on a Sunday when there are plenty of people about.

Cathedral and around Back in the centre, by the pleasant shady **Parque Bolívar** or **Seminario**, stands the **Cathedral** (Chimborazo y 10 de Agosto), in Gothic style, inaugurated in the 1950s. In the park are many iguanas and it is popularly referred to as Parque de las Iguanas. The nearby **Museo Municipal** ⓘ *in the Biblioteca Municipal, Sucre y Chile, Tue-Sat 0900-1700, free,* has paintings, gold and archaeological collections, shrunken heads, a section on the history of Guayaquil and a good newspaper library. Two other notable churches in the city centre are **San Francisco**, with its restored colonial interior, at Parque Rocafuerte, 9 de Octubre y Pedro Carbo, and the beautiful **La Merced**, on Parque Pedro Carbo, Pedro Carbo y Victor Manuel Rendón.

Between the Parque Bolívar and the Malecón is **Plaza de la Administración**, with a statue of Sucre. Here is the **Museo Nahim Isaías** ⓘ *Pichincha y Clemente Ballén, T04-232 4283, Tue-Fri 0830-1630, Sat-Sun 0900-1600, free*, a colonial art museum with a permanent religious art collection and temporary exhibits.

Along Avenida 9 de Octubre The busy Avenida 9 de Octubre, the city's main artery, runs west from the Malecón. Halfway along it is **Parque Centenario** with a

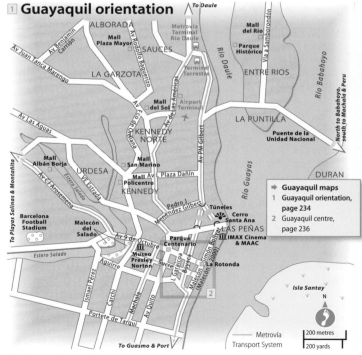

1 Guayaquil orientation

➡ **Guayaquil maps**
1 Guayaquil orientation, page 234
2 Guayaquil centre, page 236

— Metrovía Transport System

BACKGROUND

Guayaquil

Santiago de Guayaquil had a complicated start. It was founded as Santiago de Quito (sic) in 1534 by Diego de Almagro up in the Sierra, by the chilly shores of Laguna de Colta. It was subsequently moved four times until, in 1547, it found its definitive location near the native settlement of Chief Guayaquile. Colonial Guayaquil with its bamboo and wood houses was repeatedly sacked and burnt by pirates. Throughout the colonial and republican periods, Guayaquil always retained its strategic importance as Ecuador's main port. The current Puerto Marítimo, opened in 1964, handles three-quarters of the country's imports and almost half of its exports. It has been a frequent bone of contention between costeños and serranos that Guayaquil is not given better recognition of its importance in the form of greater local authority and more central government funds. The city's mayor, Jaime Nebot, currently in his third term of office, is a leading national figure who has at times challenged the authority of the Quito government.

towering monument to the liberation of the city erected in 1920. Overlooking the park is the museum of the **Casa de la Cultura** ⓘ *9 de Octubre 1200 y P Moncayo, T04-230 0500, Mon-Fri 0900-1800, Sat 0900-1500, free, English-speaking guides available,* which houses an impressive collection of prehispanic gold items in its archaeological museum; and a photo collection of old Guayaquil.

West of Parque Centenario, the **Museo Presley Norton** ⓘ *Av 9 de Octubre y Carchi, T04-229 3423, Tue-Sat 0900-1700, free,* has a nice collection of coastal archeology in a beautifully restored house. At the west end of 9 de Octubre are **Plaza Baquerizo Moreno** and the **Malecón del Estero Salado**, another pleasant waterfront promenade along a brackish estuary. It has various monuments, eateries specializing in seafood, and rowing boats and pedal-boats for hire.

Outside the city

★ **Parque Histórico Guayaquil** ⓘ *Vía Samborondón, near Entreríos, T04-283 2958, Wed-Sun 0900-1630, free; CISA buses to Samborondón leave from the Terminal Terrestre every 20 mins, US$0.25.* The park recreates Guayaquil and its rural surroundings at the end of the 19th century. There is a natural area with native flora and fauna, a traditions section where you can learn about rural life, an urban section with old wooden architecture, and eateries. A pleasant place for a family outing.

Botanical Gardens ⓘ *Northwest of the centre, Av Francisco de Orellana, in Ciudadela Las Orquídeas (bus line 63), T04-289 9689, daily 0800-1600, US$3, guiding service for up to 5 visitors US$10 (English available).* There are over 3000 plants, including 150 species of Ecuadorean and foreign orchids (most flower August to December). One area emulates the Amazon rainforest and has monkeys and other animals.

Bosque Protector Cerro Blanco ⓘ *Vía a la Costa, Km 16, T09-8622 5077 (Spanish), fundacionprobosque@ymail.com, US$4, additional guiding fee US$10-15 depending on trails visited, camping US$20 for group of 8, lodge available.*

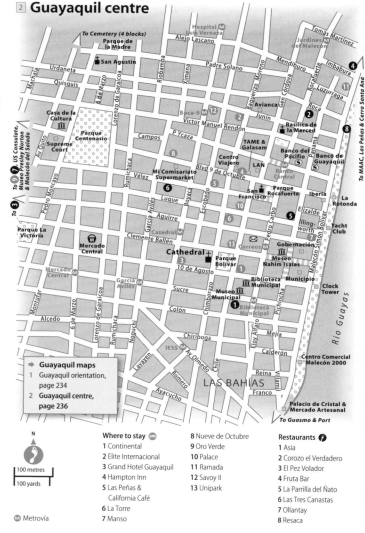

Guayaquil maps
1 Guayaquil orientation, page 234
2 Guayaquil centre, page 236

N

100 metres
100 yards

Ⓜ Metrovía

Where to stay 🛏
1 Continental
2 Elite Internacional
3 Grand Hotel Guayaquil
4 Hampton Inn
5 Las Peñas & California Café
6 La Torre
7 Manso
8 Nueve de Octubre
9 Oro Verde
10 Palace
11 Ramada
12 Savoy II
13 Unipark

Restaurants 🍴
1 Asia
2 Corozo el Verdadero
3 El Pez Volador
4 Fruta Bar
5 La Parrilla del Ñato
6 Las Tres Canastas
7 Ollantay
8 Resaca

The reserve, run by **Fundación Pro-Bosque**, is set in tropical dry forest with an impressive variety of birds (over 200 species), many reptiles and with sightings of monkeys and other mammals. Unfortunately it is getting harder to see the animals due to human encroachment in the area. Reservations required during weekdays, for groups larger than eight at weekends, and for birders wishing to arrive before or stay after normal opening hours (0800-1600). Take a **CLP** bus from the Terminal Terrestre, a **Cooperativa Chongón** bus from Antepara y 10 de Agosto (hourly) or a taxi (US$8-10).

On the other side of the road, at Km 18, is **Puerto Hondo**, where **rowboat trips** ⓘ *through the mangroves are offered, T09-9140 0186, US$15 for a group of 7, 1hr, reserve ahead.*

★ **Area Nacional de Recreación Isla Santay** ⓘ *On the Río Guayas, opposite downtown Guayaquil, www.turismo.guayaquil.gob.ec, click on Atractivos Turísticos, Afuera de Guayaquil, free entry, open 0600-1800, bicycle rental US$4.* This is a Ramsar wetland rich in fauna and flora. Two pedestrian draw bridges (open 0600-2100) link the island with the mainland, one from Calle El Oro, south of Malecón 2000, the second from the city of Durán; a boardwalk/cycle path joins the two.

By the local village, 2.8 km from the Guayaquil bridge and 5.3 km from the Durán bridge, is the **Eco Aldea**, with a crocodile breeding centre (open 0600-1700), a cabin and restaurant run by the local community. The paths are made of recycled plastic and wood, so it gets very warm, take something to drink. Boat service to the Eco Aldea from **Cooperativa las Palmeras** ⓘ *T09-8654 7034, US$4 pp return, minimum 10 passengers, depart from the Yacht Club.*

★ **Isla Puná** The largest and outermost island in Guayaquil Bay, Isla Puná also has a community tourism programme with hostels in the towns of Subida Alta and Cauchiche. Access is by boat; dolphins may be seen in the bay.

★ **Reserva Ecológica Manglares-Churute** ⓘ *Head east then south from Guayaquil, 22 km beyond the main crossroads, at Km 50 on the road to Machala. Free entry, camping and use of basic cabins; boat tour US$20-40, depending on group size (2-4 hrs recommended to appreciate the area); arrange several days ahead through the Dirección Regional, Ministerio del Ambiente in Guayaquil, Parque de los Samanes, Bloque 7, in the north of the city, T04-372 9066. Buses (CIFA, Ecuatoriano Pullman, 16 de Junio) leave the Terminal Terrestre every 30 mins, going to Naranjal or Machala; ask to be let off at the Churute information centre. The reserve can also be reached by river.* This rich natural area, with five different ecosystems, was created to preserve mangroves in the Gulf of Guayaquil and forests of the Cordillera Churute. Many waterbirds, monkeys, dolphins and other wildlife can be seen. There is a trail through the dry tropical forest (1½ hours' walk) and you can also walk (one hour) to Laguna Canclón or Churute, a large lake where ducks nest. Near the park is **Monoloco Lodge** ($), www.monoloco.ec; tours available.

Tourist information

There are also information booths at the Malecón 2000 by the clock tower (irregular hours), and at the Terminal Terrestre.

Centro de Información Turística del Municipio
Clemente Ballén y Pichincha, at Museo Nahim Isaías, T04-232 4182, ext 26. Mon-Fri 0830-1630, turismo.guayaquil.gob.ec (in Spanish).
Has pamphlets and city maps.

Ministerio de Turismo, Subsecretaría del Litoral
Av Francisco de Orellana y Justino Cornejo, Edif Gobierno del Litoral, p 8 and counter on the ground floor, Ciudadela Kennedy, T04-268 4274, www.ecuador. travel. Mon-Fri 0900-1700.
Information about the coastal provinces of Ecuador and whale watching regulations.

Immigration
Av Río Daule, near the bus terminal, T04-214 0002.

Where to stay

Guayaquil has some of the best high-end accommodation in Ecuador. For major chain hotels see: www.hilton. com (**Hilton Colón** and **Hampton Inn**, both excellent), www.oroverdehotels. com (**Oro Verde** and **Unipark**), www. hotelcontinental.com.ec, www. hojo.com (**Howard Johnson**), www. hdoral.com (**Best Western**), www. marriott.com, www.sheraton.com www.sonesta.com/guayaquil and www.wyndham.com (with excellent location and views of the river). There are several refurbished mid-range (**$$**) hotels on Junín between Gen Córdova and Escobedo but decent economy places are few and far between; the latter are concentrated around Parque Centenario, not a safe area.

$$$$ Mansión del Río
Numa Pompilio Llona 120, Las Peñas, T04-256 6044, www.mansiondelrio-ec.com.
Elegant boutique hotel in a 1926 mansion, period European style, river view, buffet breakfast, airport transfers, 10 mins from city centre.

$$$ Castell
Av Miguel H Alcivar y Ulloa, by Parque Japonés, Kennedy Norte, T04-268 0190, www.hotelcastell.com.
Modern comfortable hotel in a quiet location in the north of the city, includes buffet breakfast, restaurant, a/c, convenient for the airport (taxi US$2.50).

$$$ Grand Hotel Guayaquil
Boyacá 1600 y 10 de Agosto, T04-232 9690, www.grandhotelguayaquil.com.
A traditional Guayaquil hotel, central, includes buffet breakfast, good restaurants, pool, gym and sauna.

$$$ Nazú B&B
Ciudadela La Cogra, Manzana 1, Villa 2, off Av Carlos Julio Arosemena Km 3.5 (taxi from bus terminal or airport US$6-8, Metrovía '28 de Mayo' stop, best without luggage), T04-220 1143, www.nazuhouse.com.
Lovely suburban guesthouse with a variety of rooms and suites with a/c, includes dinner and breakfast, pool, parking, terrace with views of the city, English and German spoken, refurbished and under new management in 2014.

If your budget is up to it, Guayaquil has one of the best selections of upmarket accommodation in Ecuador. They include various international chains as well as excellent local hotels. The **Grand Hotel Guayaquil**, the **Ramada**, the **Wyndham** and the smaller, more economical, **Manso**, are all worth mentioning in this price category. The latter three have especially good locations near the Malecón 2000.

The majority of Guayaquil hotels are in our $$$ range, offering comfortable rooms and attentive service in varied surroundings. Las Peñas and La Torre are good options downtown, around the east end of Avenida 9 de Octubre.

Those seeking some peace and quiet, plus gardens and swimming pools, can do very well in a number of suburban hostels in this same price range. They include Nazú B&B and Tangara Guest House (a bit more economical but mind the proximity to the airport flight path). The suburban hotels would be ideal were they not so hard to find. Best call to book in advance and try to get precise instructions for the taxi driver or arrange to be picked up on arrival.

The downtown core also has some decent economy hotels in our $$-$ range, such as Elite Internacional, Savoy II and Nueve de Octubre.

The cheapest hotels are concentrated around Parque Centenario. This area is not recommended however, since it is unsafe at all hours and travellers have been mugged. Many hotels here are used by short-stay couples, and they are noisy and run-down.

$$$ Palace
Chile 214 y Luque, T04-232 1080, www.hotelpalaceguayaquil.com.ec.
Modern hotel, includes buffet breakfast, restaurant, 24-hr cafeteria, traffic noise on Av Chile side, good value for business travellers.

$$$ Ramada
Malecón 606 e Imbabura, T04-256 5555, www.hotelramada.com.
Excellent location right on the Malecón, rooms facing the river are more expensive, includes buffet breakfast, restaurant, a/c, pool, spa.

$$ La Torre
Chile 303 y Luque, p 13-15, T04-253 1316.
Popular hotel in a downtown office tower, long flight of stairs to get into the building, comfortable rooms, cafeteria,

a/c, nice views, reasonably quiet for where it is, popular, advance booking advised, good value.

$$ Las Peñas
Escobedo 1215 y Vélez, T04-232 3355.
Good hotel in an attractive part of downtown, ample modern rooms, cafeteria, a/c, quiet despite being in the centre of town, good value. Recommended.

$$ Manso
Malecón 1406 y Aguirre, upstairs, T04-252 6644, www.manso.ec.
Refurbished hostel in a great location opposite the Malecón. Rooms vary from fancy with a/c, private bath and river view, to simpler with shared bath and fan, and 3-4-bed dorms (US$17 pp), English spoken.

$$ Tangara Guest House
Manuela Sáenz y O'Leary, Manzana F,
Villa 1, Ciudadela Bolivariana, T04-228
4445, www.tangara-ecuador.com.
Comfortable hotel in a nice area by the
university and near the Estero Salado, a/c,
fridge, low season discounts, convenient
for airport and bus terminal but also
along the flight path, so it is noisy.

$$-$ Elite Internacional
Baquerizo Moreno 902 y Junín,
T04-256 5385.
Completely refurbished old downtown
hotel, comfortable rooms with a/c and
hot water, some rooms remodeled in
2015, parking.

$$-$ Savoy II
Junín 627 y Boyacá, T04-231 0206.
Central location, simple rooms with a/c
and hot water.

$ Nueve de Octubre
9 de Octubre 736 y García Avilés,
T04-256 4222.
Busy 8-storey hotel in a central location.
Simple functional rooms, those
facing the street are larger but noisy,
restaurant, private bath, cold water, a/c,
cheaper with fan, parking extra. Fills
early and does not accept reservations.
Good value.

Restaurants

Main areas for restaurants are the
centre with many in the larger hotels,
around Urdesa and the residential
and commercial neighbourhoods to
the north.

$$$ Cangrejo Criollo
Av Rolando Pareja, Villa 9, La Garzota,
T04-262 6708. Mon-Sat 0900-0100,
Sun 0900-2300.
Excellent, varied seafood menu.

$$$ Lo Nuestro
VE Estrada 903 e Higueras, Urdesa,
T04-238 6398. Daily 1200-2300.
Luxury restaurant with typical coastal
cooking, good seafood platters and
stuffed crabs, colonial decor.

$$$ Manny's
Av Miraflores 112 y C Primera, Miraflores,
T04-220 2754; also in Urdesa and
Kennedy. Daily 1000-2400.
Well-known crab house with specialities
such as *cangrejo al ajillo* (crab in garlic
butter), good quality and value.

$$$-$$ La Canoa
At Hotel Continental, Chile y 10 de
Agosto. Open 24 hrs.
Regional dishes rarely found these days,
with different specials during the week,
a Guayaquil tradition.

$$$-$$ La Parrilla del Ñato
VE Estrada 1219 y Laureles in Urdesa; Av
Francisco de Orellana opposite the Hilton
Colón; Luque y Pichincha downtown; and
several other locations, T04-268 2338.
Daily 1200-2300.
Large variety of dishes, salad bar, also
pizza by the metre, good quality,
generous portions. Try the *parrillada de*
mariscos, available only at the Urdesa
and Kennedy locations. Recommended.

$$$-$$ Piccolo Mondo
Bálsamos 504 y las Monjas, Urdesa,
T04-238 7079. Mon-Sat 1230-2330, Sun
1230-2200.
Very exclusive Italian restaurant since
1980, the best in food and surroundings,
good antipasto.

$$$-$$ Riviera
VE Estrada 707y Ficus, Urdesa, and Mall
del Sol, T04-288 3790. Daily 1230-2330.

Dining out in Guayaquil

Dining out can be the highlight of a visit to Guayaquil. The city's unique culinary traditions go back to the days when typical foods were sold from wooden carts along the Malecón. They made up in flavour for whatever they may have lacked in hygiene but the carts were eventually banned by municipal authorities. Undeterred, their owners found simple locales for their establishments which became known as *huecas*, the quintessential hole-in-the-wall eateries. *Huecas* have always been popular but in recent years they have even become fashionable and attract diners from all walks of life.

Given the city's coastal location, it is not surprising that many typical dishes offered by the *huecas* feature seafood. These include *encebollado*, a tasty fish and *yuca* chowder served with pickled onions, and of course the ubiquitous *ceviche*. Another speciality is *carne asada con arroz, menestra y patacones* (grilled meat with rice, beans and fried bananas), also a perennial favourite.

Drawing on the same local gastronomic traditions as the *huecas*, but in an entirely different price category, many upmarket Guayaquil restaurants offer their delicacies in elegant air-conditioned surroundings. Some are located in the city's best hotels while others have become traditions in their own right. They are generally worth the price, perhaps for a special last night out on the town.

Juice bars are understandably popular in Guayaquil's warm climate and often serve typical snacks like *empanadas de verde* (a fried ground plantain shell filled with cheese, meat or shrimp) as well as a wide variety of refreshing fresh fruit juices.

For additional details about Guayaquil's gastronomy and dining, see http://turismo.guayaquil.gob.ec/en/gastronomy.

Extensive Italian menu, good pasta, antipasto, salads, bright surroundings, good service.

$$$-$$ Sion Lung
VE Estrada 621 y Ficus, Urdesa, also Av Principal, Entre Ríos, T04-288 8213. Daily 1200-2230.
Chinese food, a variety of rice (*chaulafán*) and noodle (*tallarín*) dishes.

$$ Asia
Sucre 321 y Chile, downtown, also VE Estrada 508 y Las Monjas, Urdesa and in shopping centres in the north. Daily 1100-2130.
Chinese food, large portions, popular.

$$-$ Manso
Malecón 1406 y Aguirre, at the hotel. Mon-Fri 1230-2200, Sat 1830-2200.
Small dining area serving innovative set lunches, à la carte dishes and snacks. Tables overlooking the river.

$ Corozo el Verdadero
Rocafuerte y Roca. Mon-Sat 0730-1600.
Traditional *hueca* specializing in *encocado* and other dishes typical the province of Esmeraldas.

$ El Pez Volador
Aguirre 1800 entre Esmeralda y José Mascote, west of downtown. Daily 0900-1500.

Traditional *hueca* specializing in *encebollado*, *bollos* as well as other typical fish and seafood dishes.

$ Ollantay
Tungurahua 508 y 9 de Octubre, west of downtown.
Good vegetarian food.

Cafés and snacks

Aroma Café
Malecón 2000 by Tomás Martínez. Daily 1200-2300.
Café, also serves regional food, pleasant garden setting.

California
Escobedo 1215 y Vélez, below Hotel Las Peñas. Mon-Sat 0700-2000, Sun 0800-1500.
Good and popular for breakfast, snacks, drinks, sweets and à la carte meals.

Fruta Bar
Malecón e Imbabura, VE Estrada 608 y Monjas, Urdesa.
Excellent fruit juices and snacks, unusual African decor, good music.

Las Tres Canastas
Vélez y García Avilés and several other locations.
Breakfast, snacks, safe fruit juices and smoothies.

Bars and clubs

Guayaquil nightlife is not cheap. Most discos charge a cover of around US$5-10 on weekdays, US$10-15 at weekends, and drinks are expensive. There are clubs and bars in most of the major hotels, as well as in the northern suburbs, especially at the Kennedy Mall. Also in vogue are the Las Peñas area and the Zona Rosa, bounded by the Malecón Simón Bolívar and Rocafuerte, C Loja and C Roca. Both these areas are considered reasonably safe but take a radio taxi back to your hotel. Yellow street cabs have been involved in holdups here. Note that alcohol is not sold on Sun.

La Paleta
Escalón 176, Las Peñas. Tue-Sat from 2000.
Good music, great drinks and snacks. US$10-15 cover Fri and Sat, popular, reserve.

Praga
Rocafuerte 636 y Mendiburo. Tue-Sat from 1830.
US$10-16 cover, live music Fri-Sat. Pleasant atmosphere, several halls, varied music.

Resaca
Malecón 2000, at the level of Junín. Daily 1130-2400.
Lovely setting, live tropical music Fri-Sat night. Also serves set lunches on weekdays, regional dishes and pricey drinks.

Vulcano
Rocafuerte 419 y Padre Aguirre. Fri-Sat from 2230.
Cover US$7-8. Popular gay bar which attracts a mixed crowd, varied modern music.

Entertainment

Party boats
See What to do, below.

Cinemas
These are found at the main shopping centres and cost US$4-8. The IMAX Cinema, Malecón 2000, projects impressive films on its oversize screen.

The MAAC museum regularly features films from different countries, US$3-4.

Theatre
Centro Cívico, *Quito y Venezuela*. Excellent theatre/concert facility, home to the Guayaquil Symphony which gives free concerts.

Festivals

The foundation of Guayaquil is celebrated on **24-25 Jul**, and the **city's independence** on **9-12 Oct**. Both holidays are lively and there are many public events; cultural happenings are prolonged throughout Oct.

Shopping

There are many shopping malls, noisy but air conditioned for cooling off on hot days.

Camping equipment
Casa Maspons, *Ballén 517 y Boyacá*. For camping gas.

Handicrafts
Mercado Artesanal del Malecón 2000, *at the south end of the Malecón*. Has many kiosks selling varied crafts.
Mercado Artesanal, *Baquerizo Moreno between Loja and J Montalvo*. Greatest variety, almost a whole block of stalls with good prices.
In Albán Borja Mall are: **El Telar** with a good variety of *artesanías* and **Ramayana**, with nice ceramics.

Malls
Centro Comercial Malecón 2000, *at the south end of the Malecón*.
Centro Comercial San Marino, *Av Francisco de Orellana y L Plaza Dañín*.

Huge, one of the largest in South America.
Mall del Sol, *near the airport on Av Constitución y Juan Tanca Marengo*. Has craft shops.

What to do

Boat tours
The gulf islands and mangroves can be visited on tours from Guayaquil, Puerto Hondo or Puerto El Morro. Isla Puná, the largest of the islands has a community tourism programme.
Capitan Morgan, *Muelle Malecón y Sucre*. 1-hr tours on the river with good city views, Tue-Fri at 1600, 1800 and 1930, Sat and Sun at 1230, 1400, 1600, 1800 and 1930, Fri and Sat also at 2130; US$7. Also 2-hr party cruises, Thu 2130-2330, Fri-Sat from 2330-0200, US$15, with live music, open bar and dancing.
Cruceros Discovery, *Muelle Malecón y Tomás Martínez*. 1-hr river cruises, US$7, Tue-Fri from 1600, Sat-Sun from 1300, and party trips.

Tour operators
A 3-hr city tour costs about US$14 pp in a group. See **Guayaquil Visión** (below) for bus tours of the city. Tours to coastal haciendas, offer a glimpse of rural life.

Centro Viajero, *Baquerizo Moreno 1119 y 9 de Octubre, of 805, T04-256 4064, T09-235 7745 for 24-hr service, www.centroviajero.com*. Custom-designed tours to all regions, travel information and bookings, flight tickets, car and driver service, well informed about options for Galápagos, helpful, English, French and Italian spoken. Recommended.
Galasam, *Edif Gran Pasaje, 9 Octubre 424, ground floor, T04-230 4488, www.galapagos-islands.com*. Galápagos

cruises, city tours, tours to reserves near Guayaquil, diving trips, also runs highland and jungle tours and sell flight tickets.

Guayaquil Visión, *ticket booth at Olmedo y Malecón, T04-292 5332, www.guayaquilvision.com*. City tours on a double-decker bus, US$6-17 depending on route, departs from Plaza Olmedo and the Rotonda, Malecón at the bottom of 9 de Octubre. Also tours to attractions outside the city and night-time party tours.

La Moneda, *Av de las Américas 406, Centro de Convenciones Simón Bolívar, of 2, T04-292 5660, www.lamoneda. com.ec*. City and coastal tours, whale watching, also other regions.

Metropolitan Touring, *Francisco De Orellana, Edif. World Trade Center, CC Millenium Galery, PB, T04-263 0900, www.metropolitan-touring.com*. High-end land tours and Galápagos cruises.

Train rides

The train station is in Durán, across the river from Guayaquil, T04-215 4254, reservations T1800-873637, www. trenecuador.com, Mon-Fri 0800-1630, Sat-Sun 0730-1530. For information on the luxury *Tren Crucero* from Durán to Quito, see page 79. Combined train/

bus day trips to Bucay, 88 km away, cost US$25. Two similar itineraries depart Thu-Sun and holidays at 0800 and return at 1800; snack included. Tickets are also sold at the railcar in Malecón 2000, Malecón y Aguirre, Wed-Fri 1000-1600, Sat-Sun 1000-1530.

Transport

Air **José Joaquín de Olmedo** is a modern airport with all services including banks (change only cash euros at poor rates) and luggage storage. The information booth outside international arrivals (T04-216 9000, open 24 hrs) has flight, hotel and transport information. It is 15 mins to the city centre by taxi, US$5, and 5-10 mins to the bus terminal, US$3. Fares from the airport to other areas are posted at exit doors and on www.taxiecuadorairport.com. Official airport taxis are more expensive but safer than those out on the street. It is along line 2 of the Metrovía, but neither the Metrovía nor buses to the centre (eg Línea 130 'Full 2') are safe or practical with luggage. For groups, there are van services such as **M&M**, T04-216 9294, US$15 to centre.

Many flights daily to **Quito** (sit on the right for the best views) and the **Galápagos**, with **Avianca** (Junín 440 y

Córdova, T04-231 1028, T1-800-003434), **LAN** (Gen Córdova 1042 y 9 de Octubre, and in Mall del Sol, T1-800-101075) and **TAME** (9 de Octubre 424 y Chile, T04-268 9127 and Galerías Hilton Colón, T04-268 9135 or T1-700-500800). **TAME** also flies to **Esmeraldas**, **Latacunga**, **Loja** and **Coca**.

Bus Metrovía (T04-213 0402, www. metrovia-gye.com.ec, US$0.25) is an integrated transport system of articulated buses running on exclusive lanes and *alimentadores* (feeder buses) serving suburbs from the terminuses. **Line 1** runs from the Terminal Río Daule, opposite the Terminal Terrestre, in the north, to the Terminal El Guasmo in the south. In the city centre it runs along Boyacá southbound and Pedro Carbo northbound. **Line 2** goes from the Terminal Río Daule along Avenida de las Américas past the airport, then through the centre and on to Integración Pradera in the southern suburbs. **Line 3** goes from the centre (transfer points to line 1at Biblioteca Municipal and IESS; to line 2 at Plaza La Victoria) along C Sucre to the northwest as far as Bastión Popular and provides access to neighbourhoods such as Urdesa, Miraflores, and Los Ceibos. The Metrovía is a good way of getting around without luggage or valuables. It is very crowded at peak hours.

City buses These cost US$0.25 and are only permitted on a few streets in the centre; northbound buses go along Rumichaca or the *Malecón*, southbound along Lorenzo de Garaicoa or García Avilés. They get very crowded at rush hour.

Taxis Using a radio taxi, such as **Samboroncar**, T04-284 3883, or **Vipcar**, T04-239 3000, is recommended. Short

trips costs US$2.50, fares from the centre to Urdesa, Policentro or Alborada are around US$4-5. Taxis are supposed to use a meter, but in mid-2015, not all drivers where using them.

Long distance The **Terminal Terrestre**, just north of the airport, is off the road to the Guayas bridge. The Metrovía, opposite the bus station, and many city buses (eg Línea 84 to Parque Centenario) go from to the city centre but these are not safe with luggage; take a taxi (US$3-4). The bus station doubles as a shopping centre with supermarket, shops, banks, post office, calling centres, internet, food courts, etc. Incoming buses arrive on the ground floor, where the ticket offices are also located. Regional buses depart from the 2nd level and long-distance (interprovincial) buses depart from the 3rd level. The terminal is very large, so you need to allow extra time to get to your bus. Check the board at the entrance for the location of the ticket counters for your destination, they are colour-coded by region.

Several companies to **Quito**, 8 hrs, US$12.50, US$15for express buses which go at night; also non-stop, a/c services, eg **Transportes Ecuador**, Av de las Américas y Hermano Miguel, opposite the airport terminal, T04-292 5139. To **Cuenca**, 4 hrs via Molleturo/Cajas, 5 hrs via Zhud, both US$10, both scenic; also hourly van service, 0500-2100, with **Río Arriba**, Centro de Negocios El Terminal, Bloque C, of 38, Av de las Américas y entrada a Bahía Norte, T09-8488 9269, US$12, 3 hrs, reserve ahead; several others at the same address, departures every 30-40 mins. **Riobamba**, 5 hrs, US$6.25. To **Santo Domingo de los Tsáchilas**, 5 hrs, US$6.25. **Manta**, 4 hrs, US$5. **Esmeraldas**, 8 hrs, US$10. To

Bahía de Caráquez, 6 hrs, US$6.25. To **Ambato**, 6 hrs, US$7.50. Frequent buses to **Playas**, 2 hrs, US$3.25; and to **Salinas**, 2½ hrs, US$4.75. To **Santa Elena**, 2 hrs, US$3.25, change here for **Puerto López**. To **Montañita** and **Olón**, CLP, at 0520, 0620, 0900, 1300, 1500 and 1640, 3¼ hrs, US$7.25. For the Peruvian border, to **Huaquillas** direct, 4½-5 hrs, US$7.50; van service with **Transfrosur**, Chile 616 y Sucre, T04-232 6387, hourly 0500-2000, Sun 0700-2000, 4 hrs, US$13.50; to **Machala**, 3 hrs, US$5, also hourly vans with **Oro Guayas**, Luque y García Avilés, T04-252 3297, US$12, 3 hrs. To **Zaruma**, 8 buses daily, US$8.25, 6 hrs. To **Loja**, with **Trans Loja**, 8 daily, US$12.50, 9-10 hrs.

International CIFA, T04-213 0379, www.cifainternacional.com, from Terminal Terrestre to **Tumbes** (Peru) 8 daily, 6 hrs, US$10 *ejecutivo*, US$15 *bus cama*; to **Piura** (Peru) via **Máncora** (9 hrs, same price as Piura), *ejecutivo* service at 0720, and 2100, 10-11 hrs, US$15; and *bus-cama* at 1950 and 2330, US$20; also with **CIVA**, daily at 2130, *semi-cama* US$17, *cama* US$20. To **Chiclayo** (Peru) with **Super Semería**, at 2200 daily, US$25, 12 hrs. To **Lima** with **Cruz del Sur**, of 88, T04-213 0179, www.cruzdelsur.com.pe, Tue, Wed, Fri, Sun at 1400, US$85 *semi-cama*, US$120 *cama* (including meals), 27 hrs (stops in Trujillo). With **Ormeño**, Centro de Negocios El Terminal (near Terminal Terrestre), Of C34, T04-213 0847, Tue, Thu, Sun at 1200 to **Lima**, US$60; Tue, Wed, Sat to **Bogotá**, US$100, 38 hrs; Tue at 0200 to **Caracas**, US$190, 3½ days.

South to Peru

old gold-mining towns and a petrified forest

Machala and around *Colour map 5, B2.*

Machala (population 249,000, altitude 4 m), capital of the province of El Oro, is a booming agricultural town in a major banana producing and exporting region. It is unsafe, somewhat dirty and oppressively hot. For the tourist, the only reasons for stopping here are to go to the beautiful tranquil uplands of El Oro (see Zaruma and Piñas, below), and to catch a through CIFA bus to Peru (also runs from Guayaquil) for the beaches around Máncora. **Tourist office** ⓘ *25 de Junio y 9 de Mayo, Municipio, iturmachala@hotmail.com, Mon-Fri 0800-1300, 1430-1730, Spanish only.* Some 30 km south along the road to Peru is **Santa Rosa** with the regional airport.

Puerto Bolívar, on the Estero Jambelí among mangroves, is a major export outlet for over two million tonnes of bananas annually. From the old pier canoes cross to the beaches of **Jambelí** (every 30 minutes, 0730-1500, US$4 return) on the far side of the mangrove islands which shelter Puerto Bolívar from the Pacific. The beaches are crowded at weekends, deserted during the week and not very clean. Boats can be rented for excursions to the **Archipiélago de Jambelí**, a maze of islands and channels just offshore, stretching south between Puerto Bolívar and the Peruvian border. These mangrove islands are rich in birdlife (and insects for them to feed on, take repellent), the water is very clear and you may also see fish and reefs.

★ Zaruma *Colour map 5, B2.*

Some 118 km southeast of Machala is the lovely old gold-mining town of Zaruma (population 10,800, altitude 1300 m). It is reached from Machala by paved road via Piñas, by a smaller scenic road off the main Loja–Machala road, or via Pasaje and Paccha on another scenic road off the Machala–Cuenca road.

Founded in 1549 on the orders of Felipe II to try to control the gold extraction, Zaruma is characterized by steep, twisting streets and painted wooden buildings. The beautiful main plaza is marred by the cement municipality, facing one of Ecuador's largest and loveliest wooden churches. A preservation order now protects the town centre from similar acts of architectural vandalism.

Many of the noticeably white-skinned inhabitants of direct Spanish stock still work as independent gold miners. On the outskirts of town you can see large chancadoras, primitive rock-crushing operations, where miners take their gold-bearing rocks to be crushed then passed through sluices to wash off the mud. It is possible to visit some of the small roadside mining operations and watch the whole process. **Mina del Sexmo** ⓘ *access at the end of Calle El Sexmo, an easy walk from the centre, daily 0800-1800, free*, one of the oldest mines in the area (exploited by the Spanish since 1539 and by local inhabitants before that), is now a museum. Other mines are in Portovelo (see below). Agricultural production in this area includes coffee (some of the best in Ecuador), citrus and cattle ranching.

Zaruma is also known for its excellent Arabica coffee. **El Cafetal** shop in Zaruma roasts its own and the proud owner will show you around if the store isn't busy.

The **tourist office** ⓘ *in the Municipio, at the plaza, T07-297 3533, Mon-Fri 0800-1200, 1400-1800, Sat 0900-1600*, is very friendly and helpful. They can arrange for guides and accommodation with local families. Next door is the small **Museo Municipal** ⓘ *Wed-Fri 0800-1200, 1400-1800, Sat 0900-1600, Sun 0900-1300, free*. It has a collection of local historical artefacts. The Zaruma area has a number of prehispanic archaeological sites and petroglyphs are also found in the region. Tours with **Oroadventure** ⓘ *at the Parque Central, T07-297 2761*, or with English-speaking guide **Ramiro Rodríguez** ⓘ *T07-297 2523, kazan_rodríguez@yahoo.com*.

On top of the small hill beyond the market is a public swimming pool (US$1), from where there are amazing views over the hot, dry valleys. For even grander views, walk up **Cerro del Calvario** (follow Calle San Francisco); go early in the morning as it gets very hot.

Around Zaruma

South of Zaruma and in the lower valley of the Río Amarillo, **Portovelo** (altitude 600 m) is the site of the largest gold mine in the area. It was exploited by French and British companies in the early 1800s, followed by American companies until 1949. The huge gold mine took many hundreds of tonnes of gold out of the country but allegedly never paid any taxes. The mine continues to be exploited by several medium-sized companies. Portovelo was deemed too hot and unhealthy so the miners' families were moved to Zaruma. The **Museo Magner Turner** ⓘ *at the old Campamento Americano, in the hills above town, T07-294 9345, daily 0900-1730, US$2*, run by the grandson of one of the early US geologists, is set inside a mine shaft. It has an interesting, eclectic collection of minerals, archaeological pieces, historical documents and paraphernalia.

Piñas, 19 km west of Zaruma, along the road to Machala is a pleasant town which conserves just a few of its older wooden buildings.

Northwest of Piñas, 20 minutes along the road to Saracay and Machala, is **Buenaventura**, to the north of which lies an important area for bird conservation, with over 310 bird species recorded, including many rare ones. The Jocotoco Foundation (www.fjocotoco.org) protects a 1500-ha forest in this region, with 13 km of trails, entry US$15, $$$$ category lodge, advance booking required.

Bosque Petrificado Puyango
110 km south of Machala, west of the Arenillas–Alamor road, T07-293 2106 (Machala), bosquepuyango@hotmail.com, 0900-1700, US$1.

A great number of petrified trees, ferns, fruits and molluscs, 65 to 120 million years old, have been found in this 2659-ha protected area. A deciduous dry tropical forest at elevations between 270 m and 750 m covers the area. Over 120 species of birds can be seen here, including several endemics. There are good Spanish-speaking guides who do an interesting tour of a small segment of the reserve.

The village of Puyango is 5 km from the Arenillas road; the reserve's information centre and a small museum with interesting fossils are 250 m past the village; the mirador, a gazebo at the entrance to the trails, is 1 km beyond. There is no accommodation in the village and nowhere to eat in the park. Camping is permitted by the mirador, where there are toilets and water, and by the trail to the pleasant Las Pailas swimming holes, in a small stream; note that there are snakes in the area, stay on the trails and cleared areas. Basic accommodation is available in **Las Lajas**, 20 minutes north (one residencial) and **Alamor**, 20 km south (several hotels, eg $ **Rey Plaza**, T07-268 0256).

Huaquillas *Colour map 5, B1.*
The stiflingly hot Ecuadorean border town of Huaquillas (population 50,400, altitude 12 m) is something of a shopping arcade for Peruvians. The border runs along the Canal de Zarumilla and is crossed by two international bridges, one at the western end of Avenida La República in Huaquillas and a second newer one further south.

Border with Peru: Huaquillas–Tumbes
By far the best way to cross this border is on one of the international buses that run between Ecuador and Peru. Border formalities are only carried out at the new bridge, far outside the towns of Huaquillas (Ecuador) and Aguas Verdes (Peru). There are two border complexes called CEBAF (**Centro Binacional de Atención Fronteriza**), open 24 hours, on either side of the bridge; they are about 4 km apart. Both complexes have Ecuadorean and Peruvian customs and immigration officers so you get your exit and entry stamps in the same place. There is a **Peruvian**

Consulate ⓘ *Urb Unioro, Mz 14, V 11, near Hotel Oro Verde, Machala, T07-298 5379, Mon-Fri 0830-1300, 1500-1730.*

If crossing with your own vehicle, you have to stop at both border complexes for customs and, on the Ecuadorean side, you also have to stop at the customs (*aduana*) post at Chacras, 7 km from the Ecuadorean CEBAF, on the road to Machala. If you do not take one of the international buses, the crossing is inconvenient. A taxi from Huaquillas to the Ecuadorean CEBAF costs US$2.50, to the Peruvian CEBAF US$5.

Banks do not change money in Huaquillas. Many street changers deal in soles and US dollars cash. Do not change more US dollars than you need to get to Tumbes, where there are reliable cambios, but get rid of all your soles here as they are difficult to exchange further inside Ecuador. Only clean, crisp US dollar bills are accepted in Peru. Those seeking a more relaxed crossing to or from Peru should consider Macará (see page 217) or La Balsa (see page 222).

Listings South to Peru

Where to stay

Machala

$$$$ Oro Verde
Circunvalación Norte in Urbanización Unioro, T07-298 5444, www.oroverdehotels.com.
Includes buffet breakfast, 2 restaurants, pool (US$13 for non-guests), beautiful gardens, tennis courts, full luxury. Best in town.

$$ Oro Hotel
Sucre y Juan Montalvo, T07-293 0032, www.orohotel.com.
Includes breakfast, pricey restaurant, a/c, fridge, parking, nice comfortable rooms but those to the street are noisy, helpful staff. Recommended.

$ San Miguel
9 de Mayo y Sucre, T07-292 0474.
Good quality and value, some rooms without windows, hot water (request), no meals, a/c, cheaper with fan, fridge, helpful staff.

Zaruma

$$ Hostería El Jardín
Barrio Limoncito, 10-min walk from centre (taxi US$1.50), T07-297 2706.
Lovely palm garden and terrace with views, internet, parking, comfortable rooms, breakfast extra, family-run. Recommended.

$$-$ Roland
At entrance to town on road from Portovelo, T07-297 2800.
Comfortable rooms (some are dark) and nicer more expensive cabins around pool, no breakfast, parking.

$$-$ Zaruma Colonial
Sucre y Sesmo, T07-297 2742, on Facebook.
Colonial-style hotel, ample rooms, those to the back have mountain views, no meals, new in 2014.

$ Blacio
C Sucre, T07-297 2045.
Modern, ask for rooms with balcony, no meals.

$ Romería
On the plaza facing the church,
T07-297 3618.
Old wooden house with balcony, a treat,
restaurant downstairs.

Huaquillas

$$-$ Hernancor
1 de Mayo y 10 de Agostso, T07-299 5467,
grandhotelhernancor@gmail.com.
Decent rooms with a/c, includes
breakfast, parking.

$$-$ Sol del Sur
Av La República y Chiriboga, T07-251
0898, www.soldelsurhotel.com.
Nice rooms, includes breakfast, a/c, small
bathrooms, parking.

$ Vanessa
1 de Mayo y Hualtaco, T07-299 6263.
A/c, internet, fridge, parking, pleasant.

Restaurants

Machala
The best food is found in the better hotels.

$$ Mesón Hispano
Av Las Palmeras y Sucre.
Very good grill, attentive service,
outstanding for Machala.

$ Chifa Gran Oriental
25 de Junio entre Guayas y Ayacucho.
Good food and service, clean place.
Recommended.

Zaruma

$$ Amalsi
C Pichincha s/n. Mon-Sat 1100-2100.
Good pizzas, hamburgers and meals.

$$-$ 200 Millas
Av Honorato Márquez, uphill from
bus station.
Good seafood.

$ Cafetería Uno
C Sucre.
Good for breakfast and Zaruma
specialities, best *tigrillo* in town.

Transport

There may be military checkpoints on
the roads in this border area; keep your
passport to hand.

Machala
Air The regional airport is at Santa Rosa,
32 km from Machala. No commercial
flights were operating in mid-2015.

Bus There is no Terminal Terrestre.
Do not take night buses into or out of
Machala as they are prone to hold-ups.
To **Quito**, with **Occidental** (Buenavista
entre Sucre y Olmedo), 10 hrs, US$10,
8 daily, with **Panamericana** (Colón y
Bolívar), 7 daily. To **Guayaquil**, 3 hrs,
US$6, hourly with **Ecuatoriano Pullman**
(Colón y Rocafuerte), **CIFA** (Bolívar y
Guayas) and **Rutas Orenses** (Tarqui y
Rocafuerte), half-hourly; also hourly vans
with **Oro Guayas**, Guayas y Pichincha,
T07-293 4382, US$15, 3 hrs. There are
3 different scenic routes to **Loja**, each
with bus service. They are, from north
to south: via **Piñas** and **Zaruma**, partly
paved and rough; via **Balsas**, fully paved;
and via **Arenillas** and **Alamor**, for
Puyango petrified forest. Fare to **Loja**,
6 hrs, US$7, several daily with **Trans Loja**
(Tarqui y Bolívar). To **Zaruma**, see below.
To **Cuenca**, half-hourly with **Trans
Azuay** (Sucre y Junín), 4 hrs, US$6.25. To
Huaquillas, with **CIFA**, direct, 1½ hrs,
US$2.50, every 20 mins. To **Piura**, in
Peru, with **CIFA**, at 1100, 2300 and 2400,
US$10-15, 6 hrs, via **Máncora**, US$9-14,
5 hrs and **Tumbes**, 6 daily, US$5, 3 hrs.

Zaruma

Bus To/from **Machala** with **Trans Piñas** or **TAC**, half-hourly, US$4.50, 3 hrs. To **Piñas**, take a Machala-bound bus, US$1.25, 1 hr. To **Guayaquil**, 8 buses daily US$8.25, 6 hrs. To **Quito**, 5 daily, US$13.75, 12 hrs; to **Cuenca**, 3 daily (**Trans Azuay** at 0730, US$8.75, 6 hrs and **Loja**, 4 daily, US$6.25, 5 hrs (may have to change at Portovelo).

Puyango

Puyango is west of the Arenillas–Alamor highway: alight from bus at turn-off at the bridge over the Río Puyango. Bus from **Machala**, **Trans Loja** at 0930 and 1300, **CIFA** at 0600, US$3.50, 2½ hrs. From **Loja**, **Trans Loja** 0900, 1400 and 1930, US$7, 5 hrs. From **Alamor**, **Trans Loja** at 0730, 1000 and 1300, US$1.50, 1 hr. From **Huaquillas**, CIFA at 0500, **Trans Loja** at 0740 and **Unión Cariamanga** at 1130, US$2.50, 1½ hrs. You might be able to hire a pickup from the main road to the park, US$3. Pickup from Alamor to Puyango US$25 return, including wait.

Huaquillas

Bus There is no Terminal Terrestre, each bus company has its own office, many on Teniente Cordovez. If you are in a hurry, it can be quicker to change buses in Machala or Guayaquil. To **Machala**, with **CIFA** (Santa Rosa y Machala), direct, 1½ hrs, US$2.50, every 20 mins; via Arenillas and Santa Rosa, 2 hrs, every 10 mins. To **Quito**, with **Occidental**, every 2 hrs, 12 hrs, US$12.50; with **Panamericana**, 11½ hrs, 3 daily via Santo Domingo; 2 daily via **Riobamba** and **Ambato,** 12 hrs. To **Guayaquil**, frequent service with **CIFA** and **Ecuatoriano Pullman**, 4½-5 hrs, US$7.50, take a direct bus; van service to downtown Guayaquil with **Transfrosur**, C Santa Rosa y Machala, T07-299 5288, hourly 0500-2000, Sun 0700-2000, 4 hrs, US$13.50. To **Cuenca**, 8 daily, 5 hrs, US$7.50. To **Loja**, 6 daily, 6 hrs, US$7.

Northern Pacific lowlands

sun, surf and ceviche

This vast tract of Ecuador covers everything west of the Andes and north of the Guayas delta. Although overlooked by some foreign visitors, this area offers great natural beauty, diversity and a rich cultural heritage. Quiteños and Guayaquileños come here in droves for weekends and holidays.

You can surf, watch whales at play, visit ancient archaeological sites or enjoy some of the country's best cuisine. The jewel in the coastal crown, Parque Nacional Machalilla, protects an important area of primary tropical dry forest, pre-Columbian ruins, coral reef and a wide variety of wildlife. Further north, in the province of Esmeraldas, are unique ecosystems and the Afro-Ecuadorean way of life.

Even if your time is limited, the coast is easily accessible from Quito, making it an ideal short break from the Andean chill. The water is warm for bathing and there are a number of attractive beaches. Coastal resorts are busy and more expensive from December to April, the *temporada de playa*.

Best for
Beaches ▪ Seafood ▪ Surfing ▪ Whale watching

Footprint
picks

★ **The Montañita surf scene**, page 256

A major resort, packed with everything for surfers and their entourage.

★ **Parque Nacional Machalilla**, page 258

This beautiful park preserves marine ecosystems as well as the dry tropical forest and archaeological sites on shore.

★ **Whale watching from Puerto López**, page 258

From mid-June to September, this is the place to spot humpback whales.

★ **Air sports at Crucita**, page 268

A popular beach with ideal conditions for paragliding, hang-gliding and kitesurfing.

★ **Canoa on a weekday**, page 270

Once a quiet fishing village with a splendid 200-m-wide beach, Canoa has grown rapidly but is still very pleasant during the week.

★ **Surfing at Mompiche**, page 277

The town combines great waves with a laid-back atmosphere.

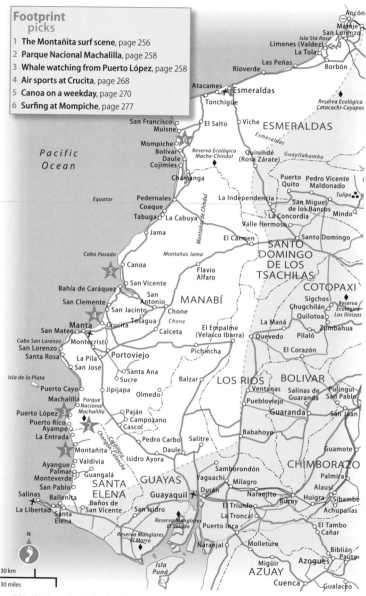

Footprint picks

Pacific Ocean

Equator

ESMERALDAS

SANTO DOMINGO DE LOS TSÁCHILAS

COTOPAXI

MANABÍ

LOS RIOS

BOLIVAR

CHIMBORAZO

GUAYAS

SANTA ELENA

AZUAY

N

30 km
30 miles

Southwest of Guayaquil is the beach resort of Playas and, west of it, the Santa Elena peninsula, with Salinas at its tip. From the town of Santa Elena, capital of the province of the same name, the coastal road stretches north for 737 km to Mataje on the Colombian border; along the way are countless beaches and fishing villages, and a few cities. Puerto López is the perfect base for whale watching and from which to explore the beautiful Parque Nacional Machalilla.

Playas and Salinas *Colour map 3, C1/C2.*

The beach resorts of Playas (population 45,600) and Salinas (population 36,300) remain as popular as ever with vacationing Guayaquileños. The paved toll highway from Guayaquil divides after 63 km at El Progreso (Gómez Rendón). One branch leads to **Playas** (General Villamil), the nearest seaside resort to Guayaquil. Bottle-shaped ceibo (kapok) trees characterize the landscape as it turns into dry, tropical thorn scrub. In Playas a few single-sailed balsa rafts, very simple but highly ingenious, can still be seen among the motor launches returning laden with fish. In high season (*temporada* – December to April), and at weekends, Playas is prone to severe crowding, although the authorities are trying to keep the packed beaches clean and safe (thieving is rampant during busy times). Out of season or midweek, the beaches are almost empty especially north towards Punta Pelado (5 km). Playas has six good surf breaks. There are showers, toilets and changing rooms along the beach, with fresh water, for a fee. Many hotels in our $$-$ ranges. Excellent seafood and typical dishes from over 50 beach cafés (all numbered and named). Many close out of season. **Tourist office** ⓘ *on the malecón, Tue-Fri 0800-1200, 1400-1800, Sat-Sun 0900-1600.*

Salinas, surrounded by miles of salt flats, is Ecuador's answer to Miami Beach. **Turismo Municipal** ⓘ *Eloy Alfaro y Mercedes de Jesús Molina, Chipipe, T04-293 0004, Tue-Fri 0800-1700, Sat 0800-1400.* There is safe swimming in the bay and high-rise blocks of holiday flats and hotels line the seafront. More appealing is the (still urban) beach of **Chipipe**, west of the exclusive Salinas Yacht Club. From December to April it is overcrowded; its services stretched to the limit. Even in the off season it is not that quiet. On the south shore of the Santa Elena peninsula, 8 km south of La Libertad, built on high cliffs is **Punta Carnero**, with hotels in the $$$-$$ range. To the south is a magnificent 15-km beach with wild surf and heavy undertow, there is whale watching in season.

North to Puerto López

The '**Ruta del Spondylus**' north to Puerto López in the province of Manabí parallels the coastline and crosses the Chongón–Colonche coastal range. Most of the numerous small fishing villages along the way have good beaches and are slowly being developed for tourism. Beware of rip currents and undertow.

Valdivia *Colour map 3, B1.*

San Pedro and Valdivia are two unattractive villages which merge together. There are many fish stalls. This is the site of the 5000-year-old Valdivia culture. Many houses offer 'genuine' artefacts (it is illegal to export pre-Columbian artefacts from Ecuador). Juan Orrala, who makes excellent copies, lives up the hill from the **Ecomuseo Valdivia** ⓘ *open daily, US$1.50*, which has displays of original artefacts from Valdivia and other coastal cultures. There is also a handicraft section, where artisans may be seen at work, and lots of local information. At the museum is a restaurant and five rooms with bath to let. Most of the genuine artefacts discovered at the site are in museums in Quito and Guayaquil.

Manglaralto *Colour map 3, B1.*

Located 180 km northwest of Guayaquil, Manglaralto (population 30,800) is the main centre of the region north of Santa Elena. There is a tagua nursery; ask to see examples of worked 'vegetable ivory' nuts. It is a pleasant place, with a quiet beach and good surf, but little shade. **Pro-pueblo** ⓘ *office in San Antonio south of Manglaralto, T04-278 0230, and headquarters in Guayaquil, T04-268 3569, www.propueblo.com*, is an organization working with local communities to foster family-run orchards and cottage craft industry, using tagua nuts, *paja toquilla* (the fibre Panama hats are made from), and other local products. It has a craft shop in town (opposite the park). **Proyecto de Desarrollo Ecoturístico Comunitario** ⓘ *contact Paquita Jara T09-9174 0143*, has a network of simple lodgings with local families (US$9 per person), many interesting routes into the Cordillera Chongón Colonche and whale-watching and island tours.

Montañita and Olón *Colour map 3, B1.*

About 3 km north of Manglaralto, ★ **Montañita** has mushroomed into a major surf resort, packed with hotels, restaurants, surf-board rentals, tattoo parlours and craft/jewellery vendors. There's an ATM at **Banco Bolivariano** and one other (not always working, take cash). At the north end of the bay, 1 km away, is another hotel area with more elbow-room, **Baja Montañita** (or Montañita Punta, Surf Point). Between the two is a lovely beach where you'll find some of the best surfing in Ecuador. Various competitions are held during the year. At weekends in season, the town is full of Guayaquileños. Beyond an impressive headland and a few minutes north of Montañita is **Olón**, with a spectacular long beach, still tranquil but starting to get some of the overflow from Montañita. Nearby is **El Cangrejal**, a 7-ha dry tropical forest with mangroves.

Ayampe to Salango *Colour map 3, B1.*

North of Montañita, by **La Entrada**, the road winds up and inland through lush forest before continuing to the small, tranquil village of **Ayampe**. Tourism is growing here, with many popular places to stay at south end of the beach, but the village retains an especially peaceful atmosphere, carefully safeguarded by the local community. The surfing here is very good. North of Ayampe are the villages of **Las Tunas**, **Puerto Rico** and **Río Chico**. There are places to stay all along this stretch

ON THE ROAD
Valdivia culture

The village of Valdivia gave its name to one of the earliest of Ecuador's cultures, famed for its ceramics and dating back to 3300 BC. In the 1950s and 1960s these were the earliest ceramics known in the Americas. The superficial similarities between Valdivia ceramics and those of the Jomon Culture of Japan led many archaeologists to the conclusion that the Valdivia ceramics were first introduced to the Americas by Japanese fishermen.

However, subsequent discoveries showed that ceramic manufacture in the Americas has its own long path of development and that the idea of a Japanese contribution to pre-European cultures in South America should be discarded.

A much more compelling notion is that ceramic production in Ecuador had its origins in the eastern Amazon basin. Findings at Brazilian sites place early pottery there at between 6000-5000 BC. It is possible that ceramic technology was transmitted from the Amazon basin through commerce or movement of people.

The third alternative is that the development of pottery occurred locally and may have accompanied the development of a more sedentary lifestyle on the Colombian, Venezuelan and Ecuadorean coasts.

The impressive Valdivia figurines are, in most cases, female representations and are nude and display breasts and a prominent pubic area. Some show pregnancy and in the womb of these are placed one or more seeds or small stones. Others have infants in their hands and some have two heads.

These figurines fill museum cases throughout the country (notably the excellent museums of the Ministerio de Cultura in Guayaquil, Quito and Cuenca). They are still being produced by artisans in the fishing village of Valdivia today and can be purchased here or at the museum in Salango, further north near Puerto López. In fact, according to the research of several Ecuadorean archaeologists, many of the figurines housed in the museum collections were made in the 1950s and 1960s because the archaeologists working at that time would pay for any figurines that were found.

(Jonathan D Kent, PhD, Associate Professor, Metropolitan State College of Denver).

of coast. Just north of Río Chico is **Salango**, with an ill-smelling fish-processing plant, but worth visiting for the excellent **Salango archaeological museum** ① *at the north end of town, daily 0900-1200, 1300-1700, US$1*, housing artefacts from excavations right in town. It also has a craft shop and, at the back, nice rooms with bath in the $ range. There is a place for snorkelling offshore, by Isla Salango.

⭐ **Puerto López** *Colour map 3, B1.*

The pleasant fishing town of Puerto López (population 11,600) is beautifully set in a horseshoe bay. The beach is best for swimming at the far north and south ends, away from the fleet of small fishing boats moored offshore. The town is popular with tourists for watching humpback whales from approximately mid-June to September, and for visiting Parque Nacional Machalilla and Isla de la Plata. **Banco Pichincha**, large building at south end of Malecón, has the only ATM in town, best take some cash.

⭐ **Parque Nacional Machalilla**
Park office in Puerto Lópe, C Eloy Alfaro y García Moreno, daily 0800-1200, 1400-1600.

The park extends over 55,000 ha, including Isla de la Plata, Isla Salango, and the magnificent beach of **Los Frailes** and preserves marine ecosystems as well as the dry tropical forest and archaeological sites on shore. The beach is clean and well cared for, but gets busy with Ecuadorean families on weekends and holidays. At the north end of Los Frailes beach is a trail through the forest leading to a lookout with great views and on to the town of Machalilla (don't take valuables). The land-based part of the park is divided into three sections which are separated by private land, including the town of Machalilla. The park is recommended for birdwatching, especially in the cloudforest of Cerro San Sebastián (see below); there are also howler monkeys, several other species of mammals and reptiles.

About 5 km north of Puerto López, at Buena Vista, a dirt road to the east leads to **Agua Blanca** (park kiosk at entry). Here, 5 km from the main road, in the national park, amid hot, arid scrub, is a small village and a fine, small **archaeological museum** ① *0800-1800, US$5 for a 2-hr guided tour of the museum, ruins (a 45-min walk), funerary urns and*

Puerto López

To Machalilla & Manta
To ❸❺❼ & Fish Market
Río Pital
Abdón Calderón
González Suárez
Lascano
Machalilla
Atahualpa
Machalilla Nat Park Office
iTUR
Eloy Alfaro
General Córdova
García Moreno
To 2
Banco Pichincha
Mariscal Sucre
To Pier
To Montañita & Guayaquil

N
Not to scale

Where to stay 🛏
1 Itapoa
2 La Terraza
3 Mandála
4 Máxima
5 Nantu
6 Sol Inn
7 Victor Hugo

Restaurants 🍴
1 Bellitalia
2 Carmita
3 Patacón Pisao
4 Whale Café

ON THE ROAD
A whale of a time

Whale watching is a major tourist attraction along Ecuador's coast. A prime site to see these massive mammals is around Isla de La Plata but whales travel the entire length of Ecuador's shores and well beyond.

Between June and September, each year, groups of up to 10 individuals of this gregarious species make the 7200-km-long trip from their Antarctic feeding grounds to the equator. They head for these warmer waters to mate and calve. Inspired by love – we presume – the humpbacks become real acrobats. Watching them breach (jump almost completely out of the water) is the most exciting moment of any tour. Not far behind, though, is listening to them 'sing'. Chirrups, snores, purrs and haunting moans are all emitted by solitary males eager to use their chat-up techniques on a prospective mating partner. These vocal performances can last half an hour or more.

Adult humpbacks reach a length of over 15 m and can exceed 30 tonnes in weight. The gestation period is about one year and newborn calves are 5-6 m long. The ventral side of the tail has a distinctive series of stripes which allows scientists to identify and track individual whales.

Humpbacks got their English name from their humped dorsal fins and the way they arch when diving. Their scientific name, *Megaptera novaeangliae*, which translates roughly as 'large-winged New Englanders', comes from the fact that they were first identified off the coast of New England, and from their very large wing-like pectoral fins. In Spanish they are called *ballena jorobada* or *yubarta*.

These whales have blubber up to 20 cm thick. Combined with their slow swimming, this made them all too attractive for whalers during the 19th and 20th centuries. During that period their numbers are estimated to have fallen from 100,000 to 2500 worldwide. Protected by international whaling treaties since 1966, the humpbacks are making a gradual recovery. Ironically, the same behaviour that once allowed them to be harpooned so easily makes the humpbacks particularly appealing to whale watchers today. The difference is that each sighting is now greeted with the shooting of cameras instead of lethal harpoons.

sulphur lake, horses can be hired for the visit, camping is possible and there's a cabin and 1 very basic room for rent above the museum for US$5 per person; pickup from Puerto López US$8, containing some fascinating ceramics from the Manteño civilization.

San Sebastián, 9 km from Agua Blanca, is in tropical moist forest at 800 m; orchids and birds can be seen and possibly Howler Monkeys. Although part of the national park, this area is administered by the Comuna of Agua Blanca, which charges an entry fee; you cannot go independently. It's five hours on foot or by horse. A tour to the forest costs US$40 per day including guide, horses and camping (minimum two people), otherwise lodging is with a family at extra cost.

About 24 km offshore is **Isla de la Plata**. Trips are popular because of the similarities with the Galápagos but your expectations should be reasonable – this is a lovely spot but it is not Galápagos. Wildlife includes nesting colonies of waved albatross (April to November), frigates and three different booby species. Whales can be seen from June to September, as well as sea lions. It is also a pre-Columbian site with substantial pottery finds, and there is good diving and snorkelling, as well as walks. Take a change of clothes, water, precautions against sun and seasickness (most agencies provide snorkelling equipment). You can only visit with a tour and staying overnight is not permitted.

Puerto López to Manta

North of Machalilla, the road forks at **Puerto Cayo**, where whale-watching tours may be organized July-August. One road follows the coast, partly through forested hills, passing **Cabo San Lorenzo** with its lighthouse. The other route heads inland through the trading centre of **Jipijapa** to Montecristi, below an imposing hill, 16 km before Manta. **Montecristi** is renowned as the centre of the Panama hat industry. Also produced are varied straw- and basketware, and wooden barrels which are strapped to donkeys for carrying water. Ask for José Chávez Franco, Rocafuerte 203, where you can see Panama hats being made.

Portoviejo

Some 23 km east of Montecristi, 40 km inland from Manta and 65 km northeast from Jipijapa, Portoviejo (population 218,000) is the capital of Manabí province and a major commercial centre. It is one of the hottest cities in Ecuador and less than safe at all hours.

Lortoviejo is one of the main places where kapok mattresses and pillows are made from the fluffy fibre of the seed capsule of the ceibo. In **Calle Alajuela** you can buy montubio hammocks, bags, hats, etc, made by the coastal farmers (or montubios, as they are known). The **Jardín Botánico** is along Avenida Universitaria in the north of the city. About 10 minutes from town, on the road that later branches to Bahía, is the village of **Sosote**; its main street is lined with workshops where figurines are carved out of tagua nuts (vegetable ivory) into innumerable shapes.

Listings Guayaquil to Puerto López *map p258*

Where to stay

Salinas

$$$ El Carruaje
Malecón 517, T04-277 4282.
Comfortable rooms, some with ocean view, all facilities, good restaurant, electric shower, a/c, fridge, parking.

$$ Francisco I and II
Enríquez Gallo y Rumiñahui,
T04-277 4106; Malecón y Las Palmeras,
T04-277 3751.
Both are good with comfortable rooms, restaurant, a/c, fridge pool.

$$ Travel Suites
Av 5 Y C 13, T04-277 2856,
miltoninnhotel@hotmail.com.
Modern, a/c, kitchenette with fridge, very good value in low season.

$$-$ Porto Rapallo
Av Edmundo Azpiazu y 24 de Mayo,
T04-277 1822.
Modern place in a quiet area, hot water, a/c, cheaper with fan, good value.

Valdivia

$$ Valdivia Ecolodge
At Km 40, just south of San Pedro.
Screened cabins without walls in an attractive location above the ocean; fresh and interesting. Restaurant, pool and access to a good bathing beach.

Manglaralto

See also **Proyecto de Desarrollo Ecoturístico Comunitario**, page 256.

$$-$ Manglaralto Sunset
1 block from the plaza, T09-9440 9687,
manglaralto_beach@yahoo.com.
Modern, comfortable rooms with a/c, hammocks, cafeteria bar, electric shower, parking.

Montañita

There are many places to stay in town; the quieter ones are at Montañita Punta. Prices are negotiable in low season.

$$$-$$ Balsa Surf Camp
50 m from the beach in Montanita Punta,
T09-8971 4685.
Lovely spacious cabins with terrace, hammocks in garden, fan, parking, surf classes and rentals, small well-designed spa, French/Ecuadorean-run. Recommended.

$$ La Casa del Sol
In Montañita Punta, T09-6863 4956,
www.casadelsolmontanita.com.
A/c, some rooms are dark, fan, restaurant/bar, surf classes and rentals, yoga drop-in (US$8).

$$ Pakaloro
In town at the end of C Guido Chiriboga,
T04-206 0092.
Modern 4-storey building with lots of wood, ample rooms with balcony and hammock, fan, shared kitchen, lovely setting by the river, good value.

$$ Rosa Mística
Montañita Punta, T09-9798 8383,
www.hostalrosamistica.net.
Tranquil place, small rooms, cheaper ones away from beach, a/c, garden.

$$-$ La Casa Blanca
C Guido Chiriboga, T09-9918 2501.
Wooden house, rooms with bath, mosquito nets, hammocks, good restaurant and bar. A Montañita clasic, in the heart of the action.

$$-$ Las Palmeras
*Malecón at south end of town,
T09-8541 9938.*
Reasonably quiet, fan, laundry, family-run, English spoken.

$$-$ Sole Mare
*On the beach at the north end of
Montañita Punta, T04-206 0119.*
In a lovely setting on the beach,
fan, garden, parking, run by an
attentive father and son, both called
Carlos, English spoken, good value.
Recommended.

Olón

$$$ Samai
*10 mins from town by taxi (US$5),
T09-462 1316, www.samailodge.
com.* Rustic cabins in a natural setting,
great views, restaurant/bar, pool, jacuzzi,
advance booking required.

$$ Isramar
*Av Sta Lucia, ½ block from the beach,
T04-278 8096.*
Rooms with bath and fan, small
garden, restaurant/bar, friendly
owner Doris Cevallos.

$$-$ La Mariposa
*A block from the beach, near church, T09-
8017 8357, www.la mariposahostal.com.*
3-storey building, ocean views from top
floor, Italian-run, English and French also
spoken, good value.

Ayampe to Salango
Ayampe

$$ Finca Punta Ayampe
*South of other Ayampe hotels, Quito T09-
9189 0982, www.fincapuntaayampe.com.*
Bamboo structure high on a hill with
great ocean views, restaurant, hot water,
mosquito nets, helpful staff.

$$-$ Cabañas de la Iguana
*Ayampe, T05-257 5165,
www.hotelayampe.com.*
Cabins for 4, mosquito nets, cooking
facilities, quiet, relaxed family
atmosphere, knowledgeable and helpful,
organizes excursions, good choice.

Las Tunas–Puerto Rico

$$$-$$ La Barquita
*By Las Tunas, 4 km north of Ayampe, T05-
234 7051, www.hosterialabarquita.com.*
Restaurant and bar are in a boat on
the beach with good ocean views,
rooms with fan and mosquito nets,
pool, attractive garden, games, tours,
Swiss-run.

Salango

$$ Islamar
*On a hilltop south of Salango, T09-9385
7580, www.islamarsalango.com.*
Ample comfortable cabins, restaurant,
lovely views of Isla Salango, camping
in your own tent US$10 pp, parking for
motorhomes. Offers paragliding and
diving, Swiss/Ecuadorean-run, advance
booking advised.

Puerto López

$$$ La Terraza
*On hill overlooking town (moto-taxi
US$0.50), T09-8855 4887,
www.laterraza.de.*
Spacious cabins, great views over the
bay, gardens, restaurant (only for guests),
crystal-clear pool and jacuzzi, parking,
German-run.

$$$ Victor Hugo
*North along the beach, T05-230 0054,
www.victorhugohotel.com.ec.*
Ample rooms with bamboo decor,
balconies.

$$ Mandála

Malecón at north end of the beach, T05-230 0181, www.hosteriamandala.info.
Nice cabins decorated with art, fully wheelchair accessible, gorgeous tropical garden, good restaurant only for guests, fan, mosquito nets, games, music room, Swiss/Italian-run, English spoken, knowledgeable owners. Highly recommended.

$$ Nantu

Malecón at north end of the beach, T05-230 0040, www.hosterianantu.com.
Ample modern well-maintained rooms, a/c, small pool and garden, restaurant and bar overlooking the beach.

$$-$ Itapoa

On a lane off Abdón Calderón, between the malecón and Montalvo, T09-9314 5894.
Thatched cabins around large garden, hot water, cheaper in dorm, includes breakfast on a lovely terrace overlooking the sea, family-run, English spoken.

$ Máxima

González Suárez y Machalilla, T05-230 0310, www.hotelmaxima.org.
Cheaper with shared bath, mosquito nets, laundry and cooking facilities, parking, modern, English spoken, good value.

$ Sol Inn

Montalvo entre Eloy Alfaro y Lascano, T05-230 0248, hostal_solinn@hotmail.com.
Bamboo and wood construction, private or shared bath, hot water, fan, laundry and cooking facilities, garden, pool table, popular, relaxed atmosphere.

Puerto López to Manta
There are other places to stay but many close out of season.

$$ Luz de Luna

5 km north of Puerto Cayo on the coastal road, T09-9708 8613 Quito T02-249 3825, www.hosterialuzdeluna.com.
On a clean beach, comfortable spacious rooms with balcony, a/c, cheaper with fan, cold water in cabins, shared hot showers available, mosquito nets, pool.

$$ Puerto Cayo

South end of beach, Puerto Cayo, T05-238 7119, T09-9752 1538.
Good restaurant, a/c or fan, comfortable rooms with hammocks and terrace overlooking the sea.

Restaurants

Salinas
A couple of blocks inland from the malecón are food stalls serving good *ceviches* and freshly cooked seafood.

$$$ La Bella Italia

Malecón y C 17, near Hotel El Carruaje.
Good pizza and international food.

$$$-$$ Amazon

Malecón near Banco de Guayaquil, T04-277 3671.
Elegant upmarket eatery, grill and seafood specialities, good wine list.

$$ Oyster Catcher

Enríquez Gallo entre C 47 y C 50. Oct-May.
Restaurant and bar, friendly place, safe oysters, enquire here about birdwatching tours with local expert Ben Haase.

$ El Mayquito

Av 2 y C 12.
Simple place with very good food and friendly service.

Montañita

$$$-$$ Tikilimbo
Opposite Hotel Casa Blanca.
Good quality, vegetarian dishes available.

$$ Hola Ola
In the centre of town.
Good international food and bar with some live music and dancing, popular.

$$ Marea Pizzeria Bar
10 de Agosto y Av 2. Open evenings only.
Real wood-oven pizza, very tasty. Recommended.

$$ Rocío
10 de Agosto y Av 2, inside the eponymous hotel.
Good Mediterranean food.

Salango

$$ El Delfín Mágico.
Excellent, order meal before visiting museum because all food is cooked from scratch, very fresh and safe.

Puerto López

$$$ Bellitalia
North toward the river, T09-9617 5183. Mon-Sat 1800-2100.
Excellent authentic Italian food, home-made pasta, attentive owners Vittorio and Elena. Reservations required. Recommended.

$$ Carmita
Malecón y General Córdova.
Tasty fish and seafood, a Puerto López tradition. Try the *camarones en salsa de maní* (prawns in peanut sauce).

$$ Patacón Pisao
Gen Córdova, half a block from the malecón.

Colombian food, giant *patacones* and *arepas*.

$$ Whale Café
Towards the south end of the malecón.
High season only. Good pizza, stir-fried Asian dishes, Thai specialities, sandwiches, vegetarian salads, cakes and pies. Great breakfast, famous for pancakes. US-run, open irregular hours.

What to do

Salinas
Ben Haase, *at Museo de Ballenas, Av Enríquez Gallo 1109 entre C47 y C50*, T04-277 7335, T09-8674 7607. Expert English-speaking naturalist guide runs birdwatching tours to the Ecuasal salt ponds, US$50 for a small group. Also whale watching and trips to a sea lion colony.
Fernando Félix, *T04-238 4560, T09-7915 8079.* English-speaking marine biologist, can guide for whale-watching and other nature trips, arrange in advance.

Montañita
Surfboard rentals all over town from US$4 per hr, US$15 per day.

Language courses
Montañita Spanish School, *on the main road 50 m uphill outside the village, T04-206 0116, www.montanitaspanishschool.com.*

Ayampe
Otra Ola, *beside Cabañas de la Iguana, www.otraola.com.* Surf lessons and board rental, Yoga and Spanish classes. Very nice enthusiastic owners, Vanessa and Ryan from Canada.

Puerto López

Diving

Exploramar Diving, *Malecón y Gral Córdova, T05-230 0123, www. exploradiving.com. Quito based, T02-256 3905.* Have 2 boats for 8-16 people and their own compressor to fill dive tanks. PADI Dive Master accompanies qualified divers to various sites, but advance notice is required, US$120 pp for all-inclusive diving day tour (2 tanks). Also offers diving lessons. Recommended.

Language courses

La Lengua, *Abdón Calderón y García Moreno, east of the highway, T09-233 9316 or Quito T02-250 1271,* www.la-lengua.com.

Tour operators

Aventuras La Plata, *on the malecón, T05-230 0189, www.aventuraslaplata.com.* Whale-watching tours.

Cercapez, *at the Centro Comercial on the highway, T05-230 0173.* All-inclusive trips to San Sebastián, with camping, local guide and food cost US$40 pp per day.

Palo Santo, *Malecón y Abdón Calderón, T05-230 0312, palosanto22@gmail.com.* Whale-watching tours.

Whale watching

Puerto López is a major centre for trips from Jun to Sep, with many more agencies than we can list; avoid touts on the street. Whales can also be seen elsewhere, but most reliably in Puerto López. There is a good fleet of small boats (16-20 passengers) running excursions, all have life jackets and a toilet; those with 2 engines are safer. All agencies offer the same tours for the same price. Beware touts offering cheap tours to "La Isla", they take you to Isla Salango not Isla de la Plata. In high season: US$40 pp for whale watching, Isla de la Plata and snorkelling, with a snack and drinks, US$25 for whale watching only (available Jun and Sep). Outside whale season, tours to Isla de la Plata and snorkelling cost US$40. Trips depart from the pier (US$1 entry fee) around 0800 and return around 1700. Agencies also offer tours to the mainland sites of the national park. A day tour combining Agua Blanca and Los Frailes costs US$25 pp plus US$5 entry fee. There are also hiking, birdwatching, kayaking, diving (be sure to use a reputable agency, there have been accidents) and other trips.

Transport

Playas

Bus Trans Posorja and Trans Villamil to **Guayaquil**, frequent, 2 hrs, US$3.25; taxi US$25.

Salinas

Bus To **Guayaquil**, Coop Libertad Peninsular (CLP), María González y León Avilés, every 5 mins, US$4.75, 2½ hrs. For **Montañita**, **Puerto López** and points north, transfer at La Libertad (not safe, take a taxi between terminals) or Santa Elena. From La Libertad, every 30 mins to Puerto López, US$5, 2½ hrs; or catch a Guayaquil–Olón bus in Santa Elena.

Manglaralto

Bus To **Santa Elena** and **La Libertad**, US$1.50, 1 hr. Transfer in Santa Elena for Guayaquil. To **Guayaquil** direct, see Olón schedule below. To **Puerto López**, 1 hr, US$2.

Montañita and Olón

Bus Montañita is just a few mins south of Olón, from where **CLP** has direct buses to **Guayaquil** at 0445, 0545, 1000, 1300, 1500, 1700 (same schedule from Guayaquil), US$7.50, 3 hrs; taxi US$90; or transfer in Santa Elena, US$2, 1½ hrs. To **Puerto López**, **Cooperativa Manglaralto** every 30 mins, US$2.50, 45 mins.

Puerto López
Mototaxis all over town, US$0.50 pp.

Bus Modern bus terminal 2 km north of town. To **Santa Elena** or **La Libertad**, every 30 mins, US$5, 2½ hrs. To **Montañita** and **Manglaralto**, US$3.25, 1 hr. To **Guayaquil**, direct with **Cooperativa Jipijapa** via Jipijapa, 10 daily, US$5.75, 4 hrs; or transfer in Olón or Santa Elena. Pickups for hire to nearby sites are by the market, east of

the highway. To/from **Manta**, direct, hourly, US$3.75, 2½ hrs; or transfer in Jipijapa. To **Quito** with **Reina del Camino**, office in front of market, daily 0800 and 2000; and **CA Aray** at 0500, 0900 and 1900, 9 hrs, US$16. To **Jipijapa**, **Cooperativa Jipijapa**, every 45 mins, US$2, 1 hr.

Parque Nacional Machalilla
Bus To **Los Frailes**: take a bus towards Jipijapa (US$0.75), mototaxi (US$5), or a pickup (US$8), and alight at the turn-off just south of the town of Machalilla, then walk for 30 mins. No transport back to Puerto López after 2000 (but check in advance). To **Agua Blanca**: take tour, a pickup (US$7), mototaxi (US$10 return with 2 hrs wait) or a bus bound for Jipijapa (US$0.75); it is a hot walk of more

Manta

To Piers

PLAYA MURCIELAGO

Malecón Escénico

Malecón Jaime Chávez Gutiérrez

Museo del Banco Central

Aduana

Autoridad Portuaria

Manta Yacht Club

Tunafish Monument

AV 3

Banco d Guayaqu

AV 6

AV 7

Velboni Supermarket

AV 11

AV 8

AV 10

Perpetuo Socorro

Manicentro

Av Flavio Reyes

AV 13

AV 15

AV 21

AV 17

AV 16

AV 18

AV 20

AV 23

AV 24

AV 25

AV 26

Where to stay
1 Centenario *B4*
2 Chávez Inn *C6*
3 Manakin *B2*
4 Oro Verde *B1*
5 Vistalmar *B1*
6 YorMar *B2*

than 1 hr from the turning to the village.
To **Isla de la Plata**: the island can only
be visited on a day trip. Many agencies
offer tours, see Puerto López above.

Puerto López to Manta
Bus From Jipijapa (terminal on the
outskirts) to **Manglaralto** (2 hrs,
US$2.50), to **Puerto López** (1 hr, US$1.25,
these go by Puerto Cayo), to **Manta** (1 hr,
US$1.25), to **Quito** (10 hrs, US$9).

Manta and Bahía de Caráquez

surfing, air sports and some of Ecuador's best beaches

Two quite different seaside places: Manta a rapidly growing port city, prospering
on fishing and trade; Bahía de Caráquez a relaxed resort town and a pleasant
place to spend a few days. It is proud of its 'eco' credentials. Just beyond Bahía,
on the other side of the Río Chone estuary, is the popular resort village of Canoa,
boasting some of the finest beaches in Ecuador.

Manta and around *Colour map 3, A1.*

Ecuador's second port after Guayaquil, Manta (population 230,000) is a busy
town that sweeps round a bay filled with all sorts of boats. A constant sea breeze

Restaurants 🍴
1 Café Trovador *B4*
2 Club Ejecutivo *B4*

3 El Marino *B6*
4 Peberes *B4*

tempers the intense sun and makes the city's *malecones* pleasant places to stroll. At the gentrified west end of town is **Playa Murciélago**, a popular beach with wild surf (flags indicate whether it is safe to bathe), with good surfing from December to April. Here, the **Malecón Escénico** has a cluster of bars and seafood restaurants. It is a lively place especially at weekends, when there is good music, free beach aerobics and lots of action. Beyond El Murciélago, along the coastal road are **San Mateo**, **Santa Marianita**, **San Lorenzo** and **Puerto Cayo**, before reaching Machalilla and Puerto López.

The **Museo Centro Cultural Manta** ① *Malecón y C 19, T05-262 6998, Mon-Fri 0900-1630, Sat-Sun 1000-1500, free,* has a small but excellent collection of archaeological pieces from seven different civilizations which flourished on the coast of Manabí between 3500 BC and AD 1530. Three bridges join the main town with its seedy neighbour, **Tarqui**.

★ **Crucita** *Colour map 3, A2.*

A rapidly growing resort, 45 minutes by road from either Manta or Portoviejo, Crucita (population 14,900) is busy at weekends and holidays when people flock here to enjoy ideal conditions for paragliding, hang-gliding and kitesurfing. The best season for flights is July to December. There is also an abundance of sea birds in the area. There are many restaurants serving fish and seafood along the seafront. A good one is **Motumbo**, try their *viche*; they also offer interesting tours and rent bikes.

North to Bahía

About 60 km northeast of Manta (30 km south of Bahía de Caráquez) are **San Clemente** and, 3 km south, **San Jacinto**. The ocean is magnificent but be wary of the strong undertow. Both get crowded during the holiday season and have a selection of *cabañas* and hotels. Some 3 km north of San Clemente is **Punta Charapotó**, a high promontory clad in dry tropical forest, above a lovely beach. Here are some nice out-of-the way accommodations and an out-of-place upmarket property development.

Bahía de Caráquez and around *Colour map 3, A2.*

Set on the southern shore at the seaward end of the Chone estuary, Bahía (population 26,400) has an attractive riverfront laid out with parks along the malecón which goes right around the point to the ocean side. The beaches in town are nothing special, but there are excellent beaches nearby between San Vicente and Canoa and at Punta Bellaca (the town is busiest July-August). Bahía has declared itself an 'eco-city', with recycling projects, organic gardens and eco-clubs. Tricycle rickshaws called 'eco-taxis' are a popular form of local transport and keep the streets blissfully quiet. Information about the eco-city concept can be obtained from **Río Muchacho Organic Farm** in Canoa (page 270) or the **Planet Drum Foundation**, www.planetdrum.org. The **Museo Bahía de Caráquez** ① *Malecón Alberto Santos y Aguilera, T05-269 2285, Tue-Sat 0830-1630, free,* has an interesting collection of archaeological artefacts from prehispanic coastal cultures, a life-size balsa raft and modern sculpture. Bahía is a port for international yachts, with good service at **Puerto Amistad** ① *T05-269 3112*. There are ATMs at **Banco de Guayaquil**, Avenida Bolívar y Riofrío, and Banco Pichincha, Bolívar y Azcazubi.

The Río Chone estuary has several islands with mangrove forest. The area is rich in birdlife, and dolphins may also be seen. **Isla Corazón** has a boardwalk through an area of protected mangrove forest and there are bird colonies at the end of the island which can only be accessed by boat. The village of **Puerto Portovelo** is involved in mangrove reforestation and runs an eco-tourism project (tour with

Bahía de Caráquez

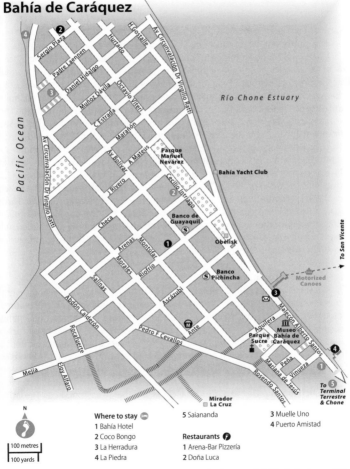

Where to stay 🛏
1 Bahía Hotel
2 Coco Bongo
3 La Herradura
4 La Piedra

5 Saiananda

Restaurants 🍴
1 Arena-Bar Pizzería
2 Doña Luca

3 Muelle Uno
4 Puerto Amistad

guía nativo US$6 per person). You can visit independently, taking a Chone-bound bus from San Vicente or with an agency. Visits here are tide-sensitive, so if you go independently, it is best to check about the best time to visit.

Inland near Chone is **La Segua** wetland, very rich in birds; Bahía agencies offer tours here. **Saiananda** ⓘ *5 km from Bahía along the bay, T05-239 8331, owner Alfredo Harmsen, biologist, reached by taxi or any bus heading out of town, US$2*, is a private park with extensive areas of reforestation and a large collection of animals, a cactus garden and spiritual centre. There is first-class accommodation on offer ($$ including breakfast) and vegetarian meals served in an exquisite dining area over the water.

San Vicente and Canoa *Colour map 3, A2.*

On the north side of the Río Chone, **San Vicente** is reached from Bahía de Caráquez by the longest bridge in Ecuador. Some 17 km beyond, ★ **Canoa**, once a quiet fishing village with a splendid 200-m-wide beach, has grown rapidly and is increasingly popular with Ecuadorean and foreign tourists. It has lost some of its charm along the way, but it is still pleasant enough on weekdays, crowded, noisy and dirty on weekends and especially holidays. The choice of accommodation and restaurants is very good. There is no ATM in Canoa, but you can find one in San Vicente at Banco Pichincha. The beautiful beach between San Vicente and Canoa is a good walk, horse or bike ride. Horses and bicycles can be hired through several hotels. Surfing is good, particularly during the wet season, December to April. In the dry season there is good wind for windsurfing. Canoa is also a good place for hang-gliding and paragliding. Tents for shade and chairs are rented at the beach for US$3 a day. About 10 km north of Canoa, the **Río Muchacho Organic Farm** accepts visitors and volunteers, it's an eye-opener to rural coastal (*montubio*) culture and to organic farming ($$ with activities and mostly vegetarian full board, family-run, English spoken, www.riomuchacho.com, for their Canoa office see What to do, page 275).

North to Pedernales *Colour map 1, B1.*

The coastal road cuts across Cabo Pasado to **Jama** (1½ hours; cabins and several *hostales*), then runs parallel to the beach past coconut groves and shrimp hatcheries, inland across some low hills and across the equator to **Pedernales** (population 35,600), a market town and crossroads with nice undeveloped beaches to the north. In town, where beaches are less attractive, they cater to the *quiteño* holiday market. A poor unpaved road goes north along the shore to Cojimíes. The main coastal road, fully paved, goes north to Chamanga, El Salto and Esmeraldas. Another important road goes inland to El Carmen, where it divides: one branch to Santo Domingo de los Tsáchilas, another to La Concordia. The latter is the most direct route to Quito.

Santo Domingo de los Tsáchilas *Colour map 1, C3.*

In the hills above the western lowlands, Santo Domingo (population 500,000), 129 km from Quito, is an important commercial centre and transport hub. It is capital of the eponymous province. The city is big, noisy and unsafe, caution is recommended at all times in the market areas, including the pedestrian walkway along 3 de Julio and in peripheral neighbourhoods. Sunday is market day, shops and banks close Monday instead. It was known as 'Santo Domingo de los Colorados', a reference to the traditional red hair dye, made with *achiote* (annatto), worn by the indigenous Tsáchila men. Today the Tsáchila only wear their indigenous dress on special occasions. There are less than 2000 Tsáchilas left, living in eight communities off the roads leading from Santo Domingo towards the coast. Their lands make up a reserve of some 8000 ha. Visitors interested in their culture are welcome at the **Complejo Turístico Huapilú**, in the Comunidad Chigüilpe, where there is a small but interesting museum (contributions expected). Access is via the turn-off east at Km 7 on the road to Quevedo, from where it is 4 km. Tours are run by travel agencies in town. The Santo Domingo area also offers opportunities for nature trips and sports activities, such as rafting.

Listings Manta and Bahía de Caráquez *maps p266 and p269*

Tourist information

Manta and around
Ministerio de Turismo (Paseo José María Egas 1034 (Av 3) y C 11, T05-262 2944, Mon-Fri 0900-1230, 1400-1700); **Dirección Municipal de Turismo** (C9 y Av 4, T05-261 0171, Mon-Fri 0800-1700); and **Oficina de Información ULEAM** (Malecón Escénico, T05-262 4099, daily 0900-1700); all helpful and speak some English. Manta has public safety problems, enquire locally about the current situation.

Where to stay

Manta and around
All streets have numbers; those above 100 are in Tarqui (those above C110 are not safe).

$$$$ Oro Verde
Malecón y C 23, T05-262 9200, www.oroverdehotels.com.
Includes buffet breakfast, restaurant, pool, all luxuries.

$$$ Vistalmar
C M1 y Av 24B, at Playa Murciélago, T05-262 1671.
Exclusive hotel overlooking the ocean. Ample cabins and suites tastefully decorated with art, a/c, pool, cabins have kitchenettes, gardens by the sea. A place for a honeymoon.

$$ Manakin
C 20 y Av 12, T05-262 0413.
A/c, comfortable rooms, small patio, nice common areas.

$$ YorMar
Av 14 entre C 19 y C 20, T05-262 4375, www.hostalyormar.com.ec.
Nice rooms with small kitchenette and patio, a/c, parking.

$$-$ Donkey Den
In Santa Marianita, 20 mins south of Manta, T09-9723 2026, www.donkeydenguesthouse.com.
Nice rooms right on the beach where kitesurfing is popular, private or shared bath, dorm for 5 US$15 pp, cooking

facilities, breakfast available, popular with US expats, taxi from Manta US$10.

$ Centenario
C 11 #602 y Av 5, enquire at nearby Lavamatic Laundry, T05-262 9245, josesanmartin@hotmail.com.
Pleasant hostel in a nicely refurbished old home in the centre of town. Shared bath, hot water, fan, cooking facilities, great views, quiet location, good value.

Tarqui

$$-$ Chávez Inn
Av 106 y C 106, T05-262 1019.
Modern hotel, a/c, fridge, small bright rooms.

Crucita

$$-$ Cruzita
Towards the south end of beach, T05-234 0068.
Attractive hostel right on the beach with great views, meals on request, cold water, fan, small pool, use of kitchen in the evening, parking, good value. Owner Raul Tobar offers paragliding flights and lessons. Recommended.

$$-$ Hostal Voladores
At south end of beach, T05-234 0200, www.parapentecrucita.com.
Simple but decent, restaurant, private bath, cheaper with shared bath, hot water, small pool, sea kayaks available. Owner Luis Tobar offers paragliding flights and lessons.

North to Bahía
San Jacinto and San Clemente

$$ Hotel San Jacinto
On the beach between San Jacinto and San Clemente, T05-267 2516, www.hotelsanjacinto.com.

Older refurbished place with a good location right by the ocean, restaurant, hot water, fan.

Punta Charapotó

$$-$ Peñón del Sol
On the hillside near Punta Charapotó, T09-9941 4149, penondelsol@hotmail.com.
Located on a 250-ha dry tropical forest reserve, meals on request, shared bath, cold water, great views, camping possible.

$ Sabor de Bamboo
On the ocean side of the road to Punta Charapotó, T09-8024 3562.
Simple wooden cabins with sea breeze, cold water, restaurant and bar, music on weekends, wonderfully relaxed place, friendly owner Meier, German and English spoken.

Bahía de Caráquez

$$$ La Piedra
Circunvalación near Bolívar, T05-269 0154, www.hotellapiedra.com.
Modern hotel with access to the beach and lovely views, good expensive restaurant, a/c, pool, good service, bicycle rentals for guests.

$$-$ La Herradura
Bolívar e Hidalgo, T05-269 0446, www.laherradurahotel.com.
Older well-maintained hotel, restaurant, a/c, cheaper with fan and cold water, nice common areas, cheaper rooms are good value.

$ Bahía Hotel
Malecón y Vinueza.
A variety of different rooms, those at the back are nicer, a/c, cheaper with fan, parking.

$ Coco Bongo
Cecilio Intriago y Arenas, T09-8544 0978,
www.cocobongohostel.com.
Popular hostel with a good atmosphere,
private bath, cheaper in dorm, breakfast
available, electric shower, ceiling fan,
US-run, renovated in 2015.

Canoa
There are over 60 hotels in Canoa.

$$$ Hostería Canoa
1 km south of town, T09-9995 5401,
www.hosteriacanoa.com.
Comfortable cabins and rooms, good
restaurant and bar, a/c, pool, sauna,
whirlpool.

$$-$ Baloo
On the beach at south end of the village,
T05-261 6355, www.baloo-canoa.com.
Wood and bamboo cabins, restaurant,
private or shared bath, British-run. Quiet
location but a little run-down.

$$-$ Bambú
On the beach just north of
C Principal, T09-9926 3365,
www.hotelbambuecuador.com.
Pleasant location and atmosphere.
A variety of rooms and prices, good
restaurant including vegetarian options,
private or shared bath, also dorm,
camping possible (US$5 pp with your
own tent), fan. Dutch/Ecuadorean-
owned, very popular. Recommended.

$$-$ La Vista
On the beach towards the south end of
town, T09-9228 8995.
All rooms have balconies to the sea,
palm garden with hammocks, good
value. Recommended.

$ Casa Shangrila
On main road 200 m north of bridge,
T09-9146 8470.

Inland, away from the buzz of the
centre but only 5 mins' walk from a
quiet stretch of beach. Rooms with fan
and private bath, hot water, attractive
garden, small pool, attentive service,
good value.

$ Coco Loco
On the beach toward the south
end of town, T09-8764 6459,
www.hostalcocoloco.weebly.com.
Pleasant breezy hotel with good views,
café serves breakfast and snacks, bar,
private or shared bath, also dorm, hot
showers, cooking facilities, surfboard
rentals, party atmosphere, excellent
horse riding, English spoken, popular.

North to Pedernales
Jama

$$$$-$$$ Punta Prieta Guest House
By Punta Prieta, T09-8640 1298, Quito
T02-286 2986, www.puntaprieta.com.
Gorgeous setting on a headland high
above the ocean with access to pristine
beaches. Meals available, comfortable
cabins and suites with fridge, balcony
with hammocks, nice grounds.

$ Palo Santo
C Melchor Cevallos, by the river in Jama
town, T09-9363 0521, luchincevallos@
hotmail.com.
Cabins on pleasant grounds, cold water,
ceiling fan.

Pedernales
There are many other hotels in all price
ranges.

$$ Agua Marina
Jaime Roldós 413 y Velasco Ibarra,
T05-268 0491.
Modern hotel, cafeteria, a/c, pool,
parking.

$$ Cocosolo
On a secluded beach 20 km north of Pedernales (pickups from main park US$1, 30 mins), T09-9921 5078.
A lovely hideaway set among palms. Cabins and rooms, camping possible, restaurant, horses for hire, French and English spoken.

$ Mr John
Plaza Acosta y Malecón, 1 block from the beach, T05-268 0235.
Modern hotel, cold water, fan, parking, rooms facing the beach can be noisy at weekends. Good value.

Santo Domingo de los Tsáchilas

$$$$ Tinalandia
16 km from Santo Domingo, on the road to Quito, poorly signposted, look for a large rock painted white; T09-9946 7741, Quito T02-244 9028, www.tinalandia.com.
Includes full board, chalets in cloud-forest reserve bordering on Bosque Protector Tanti, great food, spring-fed pool, good birdwatching, advance booking required.

$$$ Zaracay
Av Quito 1639, 1.5 km from the centre, T02-275 0316, www.hotelzaracay.com.
Restaurant, gardens and swimming pool (US$5 for non-guests), parking, good rooms and service. Advance booking advised, especially on weekends.

$$-$ Royal Class
Cadmo Zambrano y César López, near the bus station, T02-274 3348.
Multi-storey modern hotel, a/c, cheaper with fan, parking, the best choice near the bus station, reasonably quiet location, good value.

$ Safiro Internacional
29 de Mayo 800 y Loja, T02-276 0706.
Comfortable modern hotel, cafeteria, hot water, a/c, good value.

Restaurants

Manta and around
Restaurants on Malecón Escénico serve local seafood.

$$ Club Ejecutivo
Av 2 y C 12, top of Banco Pichincha building.
First-class food and service, great view.

$$ El Marino
Malecón y C 110, Tarqui. Open for lunch only.
Classic fish and seafood restaurant, for *ceviches*, *sopa marinera* and other delicacies.

$ Café Trovador
Av 3 y C 11, Paseo José María Egas. Closes 2100.
Very good coffee, snacks, sandwiches and economical set lunches.

$ Peberes
Av 1 entre C 13 y C 14.
Good quality, set lunch, popular with locals.

Bahía de Caráquez

$$ Puerto Amistad
On the pier at Malecón y Vinueza. Mon-Sat 1200-2400.
Attractive setting over the water, international food and atmosphere, popular with yachties.

$$-$ Arena-Bar Pizzería
Riofrío entre Bolívar y Montúfar, T05-269 2024. Daily 1700-2330.
Restaurant/bar serving good pizza, salads and other dishes, good

atmosphere, also takeaway and delivery service. Recommended.

$$-$ Muelle Uno
By the pier where canoes leave for San Vicente. Daily 1000-2400.
Good grill and seafood, lovely setting over the water.

$ Doña Luca
Cecilio Intriago y Sergio Plaza, towards the tip of the peninsula. Daily 0800-1800.
Simple little place serving excellent local fare, *ceviches, desayuno manabita* (a wholesome breakfast), and set lunches. Friendly service, recommended.

Canoa

$$ Amalur
Behind the soccer field. Daily 1200-2100.
Fresh seafood and authentic Spanish specialities, attentive service.

$$ Bambú
At the hotel (see above).
Good food in an unbeatable location with great ocean views.

$$-$ Surf Shak
At the beach. Daily 0800-2400.
Good for pizza, burgers and breakfast, best coffee in town, Wi-Fi, popular hangout for surfers, English spoken.

$ Lolita
C Principal, 2 blocks from the beach.
Good set meals, tasty and abundant.

What to do

Manta and around
Language courses
Academia Sur Pacífico, *Av 24 y C 15, Edif Barre, p3, T05-261 0838, www.surpacifico.k12.ec.*

Tour operators
Delgado Travel, *Av 6 y C 13, T05-262 2813, vtdelgad@hotmail.com.* City and regional tours, whale-watching trips, Parque Nacional Machalilla, runs **Hostería San Antonio** at El Aromo, 15 km south of Manta.

Bahía de Caráquez
Language courses
Sundown, *at Sundown Inn, in Canoa, on the beach, 3 km toward San Vicente, contact Juan Carlos, T09-9364 5470, www. ecuadorbeach.com.* US$7 per hr.

Canoa
Surfboard rentals US$3 per hr.
Alas y Olas, *ask around for Greg, T09-9857 1144, www.alasyolasecuador. com.* Paragliding flights and lessons, kitesurfing Jul-Dec.
Canoa Thrills, *at the beach next to Surf Shak.* Surfing tours and lessons, sea kayaking. Also rent boards and bikes. English spoken.
Kiki, *bamboo shack along the beach, ask around.* Popular for surf lessons, US$20 per hr.
Río Muchacho Organic Farm, *J Santos y Av 3 de Noviembre, T05-258 8184, www. riomuchacho.com.* Bookings for the organic farm and eco-city tours. Hikes from Canoa to Río Muchacho and around Río Muchacho. Knowledgeable and helpful with local information. Recommended.

Transport

Manta and around
Air Eloy Alfaro airport. **TAME** (T05-390 5052), **Avianca** (T05-262 8899) and **LAN** to **Quito**, several daily.

Bus Most buses leave from the terminal on C 7 y Av 8 in the centre. A couple of companies have their own private terminals nearby. To **Quito** Terminal Quitumbe, 9 hrs, US$10. **Guayaquil**, 4 hrs, US$5, hourly. **Esmeraldas**, 3 daily, 10 hrs, US$10. **Santo Domingo**, 7 hrs, US$7.50. **Portoviejo**, 45 mins, US$1, every 10 mins. **Jipijapa**, 1 hr, US$1.25, every 20 mins. **Bahía de Caráquez**, 3 hrs, US$3.75, hourly.

Crucita
Bus Buses run along the malecón. There are frequent services to **Portoviejo**, US$1.25, 1 hr, and **Manta**, US$1.50, 1½ hrs.

North to Bahía
Bus From San Clemente to **Portoviejo**, every 15 mins, US$1.50, 1¼ hrs. To **Bahía de Caráquez**, US$0.75, 30 mins; a few start in San Clemente in the morning or wait for a through bus at the highway. Mototaxis from San Clemente to **Punta Charapotó**, US$0.75.

Bahía de Caráquez
Boat Motorized canoes (*lanchas* or *pangas*) cross the estuary to **San Vicente**, from the dock opposite C Ante, US$0.50.

Bus The Terminal Terrestre is at the entrance to town, 3 km from centre, taxi US$2. To **Quito** Terminal Quitumbe, **Reina del Camino** at 0620, 0800, 2145 and 2220, 8 hrs, US$12.50. To **Santo Domingo**, 5 hrs, US$7.50. To **Guayaquil**, hourly, 6 hrs, US$8.75. To **Portoviejo**, 2 hrs, US$2.50. To **Manta**, 3 hrs. US$3.75. To **Puerto López**, change in Manta, Portoviejo or Jipijapa.

Canoa
Bus To/from **San Vicente**, every 30 mins, 0600-1900, 30 mins, US$0.75;

taxi US$5. Taxi to/from Bahía de Caráquez, US$7. To **Pedernales**, every 30 mins 0600-1800, 2 hrs, US$3.25. To **Quevedo**, 4 daily, where you can get a bus to **Quilotoa** and **Latacunga**. To **Quito**, direct with **Reina del Camino** at 2145, US$12.50, 6 hrs; or transfer in Pedernales or Bahía.

Pedernales
Bus To **Santo Domingo**, every 15 mins, 3½ hrs, US$5, transfer to Quito. To **Quito** (Quitumbe) direct **Trans Vencedores**, 7 daily via Santo Domingo, US$7.75, 5 hrs; also starting in Jama at 0815 and 2300. To **Chamanga**, hourly 0600-1700, 1½ hrs, US$2.50, change there for **Esmeraldas**, 3½ hrs, US$4.50. To **Bahía de Caráquez**, shared vans from Plaza Acosta 121 y Robles, T05-268 1019, 7 daily, US$5.75.

Santo Domingo de los Tsáchilas
Bus The bus terminal is on Av Abraham Calazacón, at the north end of town, along the city's bypass. Long distance buses do not enter the city. Taxi downtown, US$1, bus US$0.25. A major hub with service throughout Ecuador. To **Quito** via Alóag US$3.75, 3 hrs; via San Miguel de los Bancos, 5 hrs; also **Sudamericana Taxis**, Cocaniguas y Río Toachi, p 2, T02-275 2567, door to door shared taxi service, frequent departures via Alóag or Los Bancos, 0400-1900, US$15-17, 3-4 hrs. To **Ambato** US$5, 4 hrs. To **Loja** US$16.25, 11 hrs. To **Guayaquil** US$6.25, 5 hrs. To **Esmeraldas** US$3.75, 3 hrs. To **Atacames**, US$5, 4 hrs. To **Manta** US$7.50, 7 hrs. To **Bahía de Caráquez** US$6.25, 6 hrs. To **Pedernales** US$5, 3½ hrs.

A mixture of palm-lined beaches, mangroves (where not destroyed for shrimp production), tropical rainforests, Afro-Ecuadorean and Cayapa Indian communities characterize this part of Ecuador's Pacific lowlands as they stretch north to the Colombian border.

North to Atacames

North of Pedernales the coastal highway veers northeast, going slightly inland, then crosses into the province of Esmeraldas near **Chamanga** (San José de Chamanga; population 4400), a village with houses built on stilts on the freshwater estuary. This is a good spot from which to explore the nearby mangroves; there is one basic *residencial* and frequent buses north and south. The town is 1 km from the highway.

Inland, and spanning the provincial border is the **Reserva Ecológica Mache-Chindul**, a dry forest reserve. North of Chamanga by 31 km and 7 km from the main road along a paved side road is ★ **Mompiche** with a lovely beach and one of Ecuador's best surfing spots. There is an international resort complex and holiday real-estate development 2 km south at Punta Portete. The beach is being gradually eroded by the sea and a break-water has been built near the town. The nearest banks and ATMs are far away in Atacames and Pedernales. Take sufficient cash. The main road continues through El Salto (reported unsafe), the crossroads for **Muisne**, a town on an island with a beach (strong underow), a selection of hostels and a mangrove protection group which offers tours.

The fishing village of **Tonchigüe** is 25 km north of El Salto. South of it, a paved road goes west and follows the shore to **Punta Galera**, along the way is the secluded beach of **Playa Escondida** (see Where to stay, below). Northeast of Tonchigüe by 3 km is Playa de **Same**, with a beautiful, long, clean, grey sandy beach, safe for swimming. The accommodation here is mostly upmarket, intended for wealthy Quiteños, but it is wonderfully quiet in the low season. There is good birdwatching in the lagoon behind the beach and some of the hotels offer whale-watching tours in season. Ten kilometres east of Same and 4 km west of Atacames, is **Súa**, a friendly little beach resort, set in a beautiful bay. It gets noisy on weekends and in the July to September high season, but is otherwise tranquil.

Atacames *Colour map 1, A2.*

One of the main resorts on the Ecuadorean coast, Atacames (population 18,700), 30 km southwest of Esmeraldas, is a real 24-hour party town during the high season (July-September), at weekends and national holidays. Head instead for Súa or Playa Escondida (see above) if you want peace and quiet. Most hotels are on a peninsula between the Río Atacames and the ocean. The main park, most services and the bus stops are south of the river. Information from **Oficina Municipal de Turismo** ⓘ *on the road into town from Esmeraldas, T06-273 1912, Mon-Fri 0800-*

1230, 1330-1600. **Banco Pichincha** ⓘ *Espejo y Calderón by the plaza*, has an ATM and there are a few other ATMs in town and along the beach.

Camping on the beach is unsafe. Do not walk along the beach from Atacames to Súa, as there is a risk of mugging. Also the sea can be very dangerous, there is a powerful undertow and people have drowned.

Esmeraldas *Colour map 1, A2.*

Capital of the eponymous province, Esmeraldas (population 186,000) is a place to learn about Afro-Ecuadorean culture and some visitors enjoy its very relaxed swinging atmosphere. Marimba groups can be seen practising in town; enquire about schedules at the tourist office. Ceramics from La Tolita culture (see below) are found at the **Museo y Centro Cultural Esmeraldas** ⓘ *Bolívar y Piedrahita, US$1, English explanations*. At the **Centro Cultural Afro** ⓘ *Malecón y J Montalvo, T06-272 7076, Tue-Sun 0900-1630, free, English explanations*, you can see 'La Ruta del Esclavo', an exhibit showing the harsh history of Afro-Ecuadoreans brought as slaves to Ecuador (some English explanations). Despite its wealth in natural resources, Esmeraldas is among the poorest provinces in the country. Shrimp farming has destroyed much mangrove, and timber exports are decimating Ecuador's last Pacific rainforest.

Tourist office: Ministerio de Turismo ⓘ *Bolívar y Ricaurte, Edif Cámara de Turismo, p3, T06-271 1370, Mon-Fri 0900-1200, 1500-1700*. Mosquitoes and malaria are a serious problem throughout Esmeraldas province, especially in the rainy season (January to May). Most *residenciales* provide mosquito nets (*toldos* or *mosquiteros*), or buy one in the market near the bus station. The town also suffers from public safety problems, water shortages and erratic phone service. There are ATMs at several banks on Calle Bolívar in the centre.

North of Esmeraldas

From Esmeraldas, the coastal road goes northeast to Camarones and Río Verde, which has a good beach. From here it goes east to **Las Peñas**, once a sleepy seaside village with a nice wide beach, now a holiday resort. With a paved highway from Ibarra, Las Peñas is the closest beach to any highland capital, only four hours by bus. Ibarreños pack the place on weekends and holidays. From Las Peñas, a secondary road follows the shore north to **La Tola** (122 km from Esmeraldas) where you can catch a launch to Limones. Here the shoreline changes from sandy beaches to mangrove swamp; the wildlife is varied and spectacular, especially the birds. The tallest mangrove trees in the world (63.7 m) are found by **Majagual** to the south. In the village of **Olmedo**, just northwest of La Tola, the Unión de Mujeres runs an ecotourism project; accommodation, cheap meals and tours are available. La Tola itself is not a pleasant place to stay, women especially may be harassed; Olmedo is a better option, ask for Catalina Montes or her son Edwin. To the northeast of La Tola and on an island on the northern shore of the Río Cayapas is **La Tolita**, a small, poor village, where the culture of the same name thrived between 300 BC and AD 700. Many remains have been found here, several burial mounds remain to be explored and looters continue to take out artefacts to sell.

Limones (also known as Valdez) is the focus of traffic downriver from much of northern Esmeraldas Province, where bananas from the Río Santiago are sent to Esmeraldas for export. The Cayapa Indians live up the Río Cayapas and can sometimes be seen in Limones, especially during the crowded weekend market, but they are more frequently seen at Borbón (see below). Two shops in Limones sell the very attractive Cayapa basketry. There has been a great deal of migration from neighbouring Colombia to the Limones, Borbón and San Lorenzo areas. Smuggling, including drugs, is big business and there are occasional searches by the authorities. Mosquito-borne diseases are another hazard, always take a net. Accommodation is basic.

Borbón *Colour map 1, A3.*

From Las Peñas, the coastal highway runs inland to **Borbón** (population 8100), upriver from La Tola, at the confluence of the Cayapas and Santiago rivers, a lively, dirty, busy and somewhat dangerous place, with a high rate of malaria. It is a centre of the timber industry that is destroying the last rainforests of the Ecuadorean coast. Ask for Papá Roncón, the King of Marimba, who, for a beer or two, will put on a one-man show. Cayapa handicrafts are sold in town and at the road junction outside town, Afro musical instruments are found at **Artesanía** on 5 de Agosto y Valdez. The local fiestas with marimba music and other Afro-Ecuadorean traditions are held the first week of September. The bakery across from the church is good for breakfast. Sra Marcia, one block from the malecón serves good regional food.

Upriver from Borbón are Cayapa or Chachi Indian villages and Afro-Ecuadorean communities, you will see the Chachis passing in their canoes and in their open longhouses on the shore. To visit these villages, arrangements can be made through **Hostal Brisas del Río**. Alternatively, around 0700, canoes arrive at the malecón in Borbón and return to their homes around 1000. You can arrange to go with them. For any independent travel in this area take a mosquito net, insect repellent, food and a means of water purification. Upriver along the Río Cayapas, above its confluence with the Río Onzole, are the villages of **Pichiyacu** and **Santa María** (two hours). Beyond is **Zapallo Grande**, a friendly place with many gardens (3½ hours) and **San Miguel**, beautifully situated on a hill at the confluence of the San Miguel and Cayapas rivers (four hours). Along this river are a couple of lodges, the ride is not comfortable but it is an interesting trip. San Miguel is the access to the lowland section of **Reserva Ecológica Cotacachi-Cayapas**, about 30 minutes upriver. The community also runs its own 1200-ha forest reserve, bordering on the national reserve, and has an ecotourism project with accommodation and guiding service.

From Borbón, the coastal road goes northeast towards **Calderón** where it meets the Ibarra–San Lorenzo road. Along the way, by the Río Santiago, are the nature reserves of **Humedales de Yalare**, accessed from **Maldonado**, and Playa de Oro (see below). From Calderón, the two roads run together for a few kilometres before the coastal road turns north and ends at **Mataje** on the border with Colombia. The road from Ibarra continues to San Lorenzo.

San Lorenzo *Colour map 1, A4.*

The hot, humid town of San Lorenzo (population 28,500) stands on the Bahía del Pailón, which is characterized by a maze of canals. It is a good place to experience the Afro-Ecuadorean culture including marimba music and dances. There is a local festival 6-10 August and groups practise throughout the year; ask around. At the seaward end of the bay are several beaches without facilities, including San Pedro (one hour away) and Palma Real (1¾ hours). On weekends canoes go to the beaches around 0700-0800 and 1400-1500, US$3. **Banco Pichincha** ⓘ *C Ponce y Garcés*, has the only ATM in town; take some cash. Note that this is an unsafe border area, enquire about current conditions with the police or Navy (Marina). From San Lorenzo you can visit several natural areas; launches can be hired for excursions, see Transport, page 284.

There are mangroves at **Reserva Ecológica Cayapas-Mataje**, which protects islands in the estuary northwest of town. **Reserva Playa de Oro** ⓘ *www. touchthejungle.org, see Where to stay, page 282*, has 10,406 ha of Chocó rainforest, rich in wildlife, along the Río Santiago. Access is from **Selva Alegre** (a couple of basic *residenciales*), off the road to Borbón.

Border with Colombia: San Lorenzo–Tumaco

The Río Mataje is the border with Colombia. From San Lorenzo, the port of Tumaco in Colombia can be reached by a combination of boat and land transport. Because this is a most unsafe region, travellers are advised not to enter Colombia at this border. Go to Tulcán and Ipiales instead.

Listings Northern lowlands

Where to stay

North to Atacames
Mompiche
There are several economical places in town. Camping on the beach is not safe.

$$-$ Iruña
East along the beach, vehicle access only at low tide, T09-9497 5846, teremompiche@yahoo.com.
A lovely secluded hideaway with cabins of different sizes and prices. Large terraces and hammocks, meals on request, fan, nice gardens.

$ Gabeal
300 m east of town, T09-9969 6543.
Lovely quiet place with ample grounds

and beachfront. Bamboo construction with ocean views, balconies, small rooms, cabins and dorms (U$10 pp), camping (US$5 pp) breakfast available, discounts in low season. Rooms 6-10 are good choices.

Tonchigüe to Punta Galera

$$ Playa Escondida
10 km west of Tonchigüe and 6 km east of Punta Galera, T06-273 3106, T09-9650 6812, www.playaescondida.com.ec.
A charming beach hideaway set in 100 ha with 500-m beachfront stretching back to dry tropical forest. Run by Canadian Judith Barett on an ecologically sound basis. Rustic cabins

overlooking a lovely little bay, excellent restaurant, private showers, shared composting toilets, camping US$10 pp, good birdwatching, swimming and walking along the beach at low tide. Also offers volunteer opportunities.

$$$-$$ Cabañas Isla del Sol
At south end of beach, T06-273 3470, www.cabanasisladelsol.com.
Comfortable cabins, meals available in high season, electric shower, a/c, cheaper with fan, pool, boat tours and whale watching in season.

$$ Casa de Amigos
By the entrance to the beach, T06-247 0102.
Restaurant, electric shower, a/c, rooms with balconies, use of kayaks and surfboards included, English and German spoken.

$$-$ La Terraza
On the beach, T06-247 0320, pepo@hotmail.es.
Rooms and cabins for 3-4 with balconies, hammocks and large terrace, spacious, hot water, a/c, fan, mosquito net, some rooms have fridge, good restaurant open in season, Spanish-run.

Súa

$ Buganvillas
On the beach.
Nice, room 10 has the best views, pool, helpful owners.

$ Chagra Ramos
On the beach, T06-273 1006.
Ageing hotel with balconies overlooking the beach, restaurant, cold water, fan, parking, good service.

$ Sol de Súa
Across from beach towards west end of town, T06-273 1021.

Cold water, ceiling fan, mosquito net, simple cabins on ample grounds with palm trees, camping possible.

Atacames
Prices rise on holiday weekends, discounts may be available in low season. There are many more hotels than we can list.

$$$ Juan Sebastián
Towards the east end of the beach, T06-273 1049.
Large upmarket hotel with cabins and suites, restaurant, a/c, 3 pools and small spa (US$5 for non-guests), fridge, parking, popular with Quiteños.

$$ Carluz
Behind the stadium, T06-273 1456.
Decent hotel in a good, quiet location. Comfortable suites for 4 and apartments for 6, good restaurant, a/c, fan, pool, fridge, parking.

$$ Cielo Azul
Towards the west end of the beach, near the stadium, T06-273 1813, www.hotelcieloazul.com.
Restaurant, fan, pool, fridge, rooms with balconies and hammocks, comfortable and very good.

$$-$ Tahiti
Towards the east end of the beach, T06-276 0085, lucybritogarcia@yahoo.com.ar.
Rooms and cabins with fan, cheaper with cold water, good restaurant, pool, parking, ample grounds.

$ Chill Inn
Los Ostiones y Malecón, T06-276 0477, www.chillinnecuador.com.
Small backpacker hostel with bar, good beds, fan, parking, balcony with hammocks, breakfast available, Swiss-run, helpful.

Esmeraldas

Hotels in the centre are poor; better to stay in the outskirts.

$$ Apart Hotel Esmeraldas
Libertad 407 y Ramón Tello, T06-272 8700.
Good restaurant, a/c, fridge, parking, excellent quality.

$$ Perla Verde
Piedrahita 330 y Olmedo, T06-272 3820.
Good rooms with a/c and fridge.

$ Andrés
Sucre 812 y Piedrahita, T06-272 2975.
Simple hostel in a multi-storey building, cold water, fan.

$ Zulema 2
Malecón y Rocafuerte.
Modern concrete hostel with large rooms, cold water, fan, parking.

North of Esmeraldas
Las Peñas

$ Mikey
By the beach, T06-278 6031.
Cabins with kitchenettes, private bath, hot water, pool.

Limones

$ Colón
Next to the church at the main park, T06-278 9311.
A good hostel for where it is, with bath, cold water, fan.

Borbón

$ Brisas del Río Santiago
Malecón y 23 de Noviembre, T06-278 6211.
Basic concrete hostel with good air circulation, private bath, cold water, fan, mosquito net, meeting point for travellers going upriver. Owner Sr

Betancourt can arrange canoes for excursions.

San Miguel

In villages like **Pichiyacu** (ethnic Chachi) and Santa María (Afro-Ecuadorean), local families can provide accommodation.

$$$ Eco San Miguel
Above the village of San Miguel, contact Soyander Oravio, T09-9223 6338, or Gustavo Boboy, T09-8299 8056.
Community-run lodge, price includes transport from Borbón, meals and excursion to the forest. Advance booking advised.

San Lorenzo

Expect to be mobbed by children wanting a tip to show you to a hotel or restaurant. Also take insect repellent.

$$$ Playa de Oro
On the Río Santiago, upriver from Borbón, contact Ramiro Buitrón at Hotel Valle del Amanecer in Otavalo, T06-292 0990, www.touchthejungle.org.
Basic cabins with shared bath, includes 3 meals and guided excursion. Advance booking required.

$$ Tunda Loma
Km 17 on the road to Ibarra (taxi from San Lorenzo US$5), T06-278 0367.
Beautifully located on a hill overlooking the Río Tululbí. Wood cabins, includes breakfast, restaurant, warm water, fan, organizes tubing trips on the river and hikes in the forest.

$ Pampa de Oro
C 26 de Agosto y Tácito Ortiz, T06-278 0214.
Adequate family run hotel, with bath, cold water, fan, mosquito net.

$ San Carlos
C Imbabura near the train station,
T06-278 0284.
Simple concrete hotel, private or shared
bath, a/c or fan, cold water, mosquito nets.

Restaurants

North to Atacames
Mompiche

$$ La Facha
Between the main street and
Hotel Gabeal.
Great seafood and vegetarian (try their
veggie burgers), very creative and
recommended. Argentine chef.

$ Comedor Margarita
On main street, 2 blocks from the beach.
Daily from 0730.
Basic *comedor* serving tasty local fare,
mostly fish and seafood. Several other
places serve cheap set meals.

Same

$$$ Seaflower
By the beach at the entrance road.
Excellent international food.

Súa

$ Churuco's
Diagonally across from the park, 100 m
from the beach. Wed-Sun 0900-2100.
Simple *comedor* serving good set meals
and local snacks, generous portions,
good value.

Atacames
The beach is packed with bars and
restaurants offering seafood.

$$ Da Giulio
Malecón y Cedros. Weekdays 1700-2300,
weekends from 1100.
Spanish and Italian cuisine, good pasta.

$$-$ El Tiburón
Malecón y Súa.
Good seafood.

$$-$ Le Cocotier
Malecón y Camarones.
Very good pizza.

Esmeraldas
There are restaurants and bars by Las
Palmas beach offering regional specialities.

$$ Chifa Asiático
Cañizares y Bolívar.
Chinese and seafood, a/c, excellent.

$$-$ El Manglar
Quito y Olmedo.
Good *comida esmeraldeña*.

$ Tapao.con
6 de Diciembre 1717 y Piedrahita.
A popular place for typical dishes such
as *tapado*, *encocado* and *ceviche*.

San Lorenzo

$ El Chocó
C Imbabura.
Good fish and local specialities. Also
economical set lunches and the best
batido de borojó (milkshake) in town.

Transport

North to Atacames
Bus Hourly from **Chamanga** to
Esmeraldas, US$4.50, 3½ hrs, and
to **Pedernales**, US$2.50, 1½ hrs.
Mompiche to/from **Esmeraldas**, 8 a
day, US$3.75, 3 hrs, the last one from
Esmeraldas about 1630. To **Playa
Escondida**: take a ranchera or bus from
Esmeraldas or Atacames for Punta Galera
or Cabo San Francisco, 5 a day, US$2.50,
2 hrs. A taxi from Atacames costs US$15
and a pickup from Tonchigüe US$6.25.
To **Súa** and **Same**: Buses every 30 mins

to and from **Atacames**, 15 mins, US$0.50. Make sure it drops you at Same and not at Club Casablanca.

Atacames

Bus To **Esmeraldas**, every 15 mins, US$1, 1 hr. To **Guayaquil**, US$11.25, 8 hrs, **Trans Esmeraldas** at 0830 and 2245. To **Quito**, various companies, about 10 daily, US$10, 7 hrs. To **Pedernales**, **Coop G Zambrano**, 4 daily, US$5, 4 hrs or change in Chamanga.

Esmeraldas

Air Gen Rivadeneira Airport is along the coastal road heading north. A taxi to the city centre (30 km) costs US$6, buses to the Terminal Terrestre from the road outside the airport pass about every 30 mins. If headed north towards San Lorenzo, you can catch a bus outside the airport. **TAME** (Bolívar y 9 de Octubre, T06-272 6863), 1-2 daily flights to **Quito**, continuing to **Cali** (Colombia) Mon, Wed, Fri; to **Guayaquil**, 1 daily Mon, Wed, Fri.

Bus Trans-Esmeraldas (10 de Agosto at Parque Central, recommended) and **Panamericana** (Colón y Salinas) have *servicio directo* or *ejecutivo* to Quito and Guayaquil, a better choice as they are faster buses and don't stop for passengers along the way. Frequent service to **Quito** via Santo Domingo or via Calacalí, US$8.75, 6 hrs; ask which terminal they go to before purchasing ticket; also shared vans via Los Bancos with **Esmetur Express**, Espejo y Eloy Alfaro, T06-271 3488 or T09-9226 0857, 4 vehicles daily, 5 hrs, US$30, US$10-20 extra to/from the beaches. To **Ibarra**, 9 hrs, US$12.50, via Borbón. To **Santo Domingo**, US$3.75, 3 hrs. To **Ambato**, 6 a day, US$10, 8 hrs. To **Guayaquil**, hourly, US$10, *directo*, 8 hrs. To **Bahía**

de Caráquez, via Santo Domingo, US$10, 9 hrs. To **Manta**, US$10, 10 hrs. **La Costeñita** and **El Pacífico**, both on Malecón, to/from **La Tola**, 8 daily, US$4.75, 3 hrs. To **Borbón**, frequent service, US$4.50, 3 hrs. To **San Lorenzo**, 8 daily, US$5.75, 4 hrs. To **Súa**, **Same** and **Atacames**, every 15 mins from 0630-2030, to Atacames US$1, 1 hr. To **Chamanga**, hourly 0500-1900, US$4.50, 3½ hrs, change here for points south.

North of Esmeraldas

Ferry There are launches between **La Tola** and **Limones** which connect with the buses arriving from Esmeraldas, US$3.75, 1 hr, and 3 daily Limones–**San Lorenzo**, 2 hrs US$3. You can also hire a launch to **Borbón**, a fascinating trip through mangrove islands, passing hunting pelicans, approximately US$10 per hr.

Borbón

Bus To **Esmeraldas**, US$4.50, 3 hrs. To **San Lorenzo**, US$2, 1 hr.

Ferry 4 launches a day run to communities upriver, 1030-1100. Check how far each one is going as only one goes as far as **San Miguel**, US$8, 4-5 hrs.

San Lorenzo

Bus Buses leave from the train station or environs. To **Ibarra**, 10 daily, US$5, 4 hrs. To **Esmeraldas**, via Borbón, 8 daily, US$5.75, 4 hrs.

Ferry Launch service with **Coopseturi**, T06-278 0161; and **Costeñita**, both near the pier. All services are subject to change and cancellation. To **Limones**, 4 daily, US$3, 2 hrs. To **La Tola**, US$6, 4 hrs. To **Palma Real**, for beaches, 2 daily, US$3, 2 hrs. To hire a boat for 5 passengers costs US$20 per hr.

The Oriente

the vast green carpet of Amazonia

East of the Andes the hills fall away to El Oriente, the vast green carpet of Amazonia. Some of this beautiful wilderness remains unspoiled and sparsely populated, with indigenous settlements along the tributaries of the Amazon.

For the visitor, the Ecuadorean jungle, especially northern Oriente, has the advantage of being relatively accessible and tourist infrastructure here is well developed.

Most tourists love the exotic feeling of El Oriente, and El Oriente needs tourists. Large tracts of jungle are under threat; colonists have cleared many areas for agriculture, while others are laid waste by petroleum exploration or mining. The region's irreplaceable biodiversity and traditional ways of life can only be protected if sustainable ecotourism provides a viable economic alternative.

The eastern foothills of the Andes, where the jungle begins, offer a good introduction to the rainforest for those with limited time or money. Further east lie the remaining tracts of primary rainforest, teeming with life, which can be visited from several excellent (and generally expensive) jungle lodges. Southern Oriente is as yet less developed for tourism, it offers good opportunities off the beaten path but is threatened by large mining projects.

Best for
Ethno-tourism ▪ Jungle lodges ▪ Whitewater sports

Footprint
picks

⭐ **Rafting and kayaking from Baeza or Tena**,
pages 289 and 306
Both of these pleasant towns provide access to excellent white water
tumbling down the eastern slopes of the Andes.

⭐ **San Rafael Falls**, page 289
This beautiful and impressive 145-m cascade is believed to be the highest
in Ecuador. See it before the hydroelectric project starts operating.

⭐ **Cuyabeno Wildlife Reserve**, page 297
This is among the best places in Ecuador to see Amazon wildlife and
offers a more economical jungle experience than many other areas
of the Oriente.

⭐ **Río Napo Jungle Lodges**, pages 297, 302 and 314
Along the upper and lower reaches of the Napo River are some of the
finest jungle lodges in the country, offering top-notch facilities
surrounded by pristine rainforest.

⭐ **Río Nangaritza Gorge**, page 311
In the far south of Oriente, the upper Río Nangaritza flows through
Shuar territory and a magnificent jungle-covered gorge with
200-m-high walls.

Footprint
picks

1 **Rafting and kayaking from Baeza or Tena**, pages 289 and 306

2 **San Rafael Falls**, page 289

3 **Cuyabeno Wildlife Reserve**, page 297

4 **Río Napo Jungle Lodges**, pages 297, 302 and 314

5 **Río Nangaritza Gorge**, page 311

Much of the northern Oriente is taken up by the Parque Nacional Yasuní, the Cuyabeno Wildlife Reserve and most of Parque Nacional Cayambe Coca. The main towns for access are Baeza, Lago Agrio and Coca.

Quito to the Oriente

From Quito to Baeza, a paved road goes via the **Guamaní pass** (4064 m). It crosses the Eastern Cordillera just north of **Volcán Antisana** (5705 m), and then descends via the small village of **Papallacta** (hot springs, see page 88) to the old mission settlement of Baeza. The trip between the pass and Baeza has beautiful views of the glaciers of Antisana (clouds permitting), high waterfalls, *páramo*, cloudforest and a lake contained by an old lava flow.

Baeza *Colour map 2, B1.*

The mountainous landscape and high rainfall have created spectacular waterfalls and dense vegetation. Orchids and bromeliads abound. Baeza (population 8000, altitude 1900 m), in the beautiful Quijos valley, is about 1 km from the main junction of roads from Lago Agrio and Tena. The town itself is divided in two parts: a faded but pleasant **Baeza Colonial** (Old Baeza) and **Baeza Nueva** (New Baeza), where most shops and services are located. The trail/road from Baeza Vieja to Las Antennas has nice views, two hours return. There are excellent ★ **kayaking** and **rafting** opportunities in the area. Tours are offered by Casa de Rodrigo (see Where to stay, below) and operators in Quito and Tena.

Beyond Baeza

From Baeza a road heads south to Tena, with a branch going east via Loreto to Coca, all paved. Another paved road goes northeast from Baeza to Lago Agrio, following the Río Quijos past the villages of **Borja** (8 km from Baeza, very good *comedor* Doña Cleo along the highway, closed Sundays) and **El Chaco** (12 km further, basic accommodation) to the slopes of Reventador volcano.

Volcán Reventador (3560 m) is an active volcano which lies on the edge of the Parque Nacional Cayambe Coca, poking up from the Oriente rainforest. A sudden eruption in 2002 produced impressive lava flows and a 20-km-high cloud which covered Quito – 100 km away – in ash. The area is beautiful for trekking but conditions change unexpectedly. Always check volcanic activity updates (on www.igepn.edu.ec) and also enquire locally. It is a full day of hard hiking through lovely forest on frequently muddy trails up to the rim of the volcanic caldera and back. From the rim, views of the immense caldera filled with steaming blocks of lava are breathtaking. The trailhead is hard to find, ask at Hostería El Reventador. From Quito, tours are offered by **Ecuador Journeys** (page 77).

Half a kilometre south of the bridge over the Río Reventador is signed access to the impressive 145-m ★ **San Rafael Falls** (also part of Parque Nacional Cayambe

Essential Oriente

Finding your feet

There are commercial flights from Quito to Lago Agrio, Coca and Macas; and from Guayaquil to Coca via Latacunga. From Quito, Macas and Shell, light aircraft can be chartered to any jungle village with a landing strip. Western Oriente is also accessible by scenic roads which wind their way down from the highlands. Quito, via Baeza, to Lago Agrio and Coca, Baños to Puyo, and Loja to Zamora are fully paved, as is the entire lowland road from Lago Agrio south to Zamora. Other access roads to Oriente (many are paved or in the process of being paved) include: Tulcán to Lago Agrio via Lumbaqui, Riobamba to Macas, and three different roads from Cuenca to Macas and Gualaquiza.

Tip...

There may be police and military checkpoints in the Oriente, so always have your passport handy.

Getting around

Some roads are narrow and tortuous and subject to landslides in the rainy season, but all have a regular bus service and all can be travelled in a 4WD or in an ordinary car with good ground clearance. Deeper into the rainforest, motorized canoes provide the only alternative to air travel.

Jungle lodges

These complexes are normally located in natural settings away from towns and villages and are in most cases built to blend into the environment through the use of local materials and elements of indigenous design. Some are owned by urban-based nationals or foreigners, have offices in Quito and often deal with national or international travel agencies. Others are joint ventures or owned outright by local communities.

Experiencing the jungle in this way usually involves the purchase of an all-inclusive package in Quito or abroad, including reasonably comfortable accommodation, three good meals a day, and a leisurely programme of guided activities suited to special interests such as birdwatching. Getting to the lodge may involve a long canoe ride, with a longer return journey upstream and perhaps a pre-dawn start. Standards of service are generally high. Most lodges employ well-qualified personnel and claim a high degree of environmental awareness. Many have made some sort of arrangement with neighbouring indigenous communities but their contribution to local employment and the local economy varies.

When staying at a jungle lodge, you will need to take a torch (flashlight), insect repellent, protection against the sun and a rain poncho. Rubber boots are usually provided, but very large sizes may not be available so ask in advance. Note that most lodges count travel days as part of their package, which means that a 'four-day/three-night tour' often spends only two days actually in the rainforest. Most lodges have fixed departure days and it may not be possible to arrange a special departure on another day; check before planning your trip. Advance bookings are mandatory at most jungle lodges and can usually be made on the internet and through most Quito agencies. For lists of jungle lodges, see pages 300, 302, 314 and 316.

lists of jungle lodges, see pages 300, 302, 314 and 316.

River cruises

The river cruise experience is substantially different from that of a jungle lodge. It offers a better appreciation of the grandeur of Amazonia, but less intimate contact with life in the rainforest. Passengers sleep and take their meals onboard comfortable river boats designed specifically for tourism, stopping en route to visit local communities and make excursions into the jungle. At present two such vessels sail the Río Napo downstream from Coca. When the water level is low, however, they may only be able to cover part of their usual routes. For further details about these cruise boats, see page 305.

Yet another experience may be had using public river transport along the lower Napo, from Coca to Nuevo Rocafuerte, with connections to Iquitos (Peru). This is much cheaper and less

Oriente Jungle Lodges

COLOMBIA

To La Bonita & Tulcán

To Quito

Papallacta

Baeza

Narupa

Puerto Misahuallí

Tena

Puerto Napo

Ahuano

Puyo

Macas

To Baños & Ambato

To Riobamba

To Gualaquiza, Zamora & Loja

Lago Agrio

Río Coca

La Joya de los Sachas

Coca

Shushufindi

Pompeya

Limoncocha

Tarapoa

Puerto El Carmen del Putumayo

Río Cuyabeno

Río Aguarico

Pañacocha

Río Napo

Añangu

Mondaña

Río Napo

Río Tiputini

Río Shiripuno

Río Tiguino

Río Curaray

Río Capahuari

Río Pastaza

Río Cononaco

Tiputini

Nuevo Rocafuerte

Pantoja

Pantoja

PERU

N

Not to scale

Lodges		
1 Amazon Dolphin	6 Jatun Sacha Biological Station	11 Nicky
2 Casa del Suizo	7 Kapawi	12 Sacha
3 Cotococha	8 La Selva	13 Sani
4 Cuyabeno Lodges	9 Liana	14 Shiripuno
5 Huaorani Ecolodge	10 Napo Wildlife Center	15 Yachana

comfortable than a river cruise, and touring opportunities are limited. You can stop at communities along the way but facilities are basic at best. Plenty of time and patience are needed to travel the river in this way. For details of river travel to Peru, see page 298.

Guided tours

Guided tours of varying length are offered by tour operators, who should be licensed by the Ecuadorean **Ministerio de Turismo**. Tour companies are mainly concentrated in Quito, Baños, Puyo, Tena, Misahuallí and Coca, and, to a lesser extent in Macas and Zamora. When shopping around for a guided tour ensure that the agency specifies the details of the programme, the services to be provided and whether payments to indigenous communities are included. Be especially prudent with cheaper tour agencies, some are good but we have also received negative reports. If possible, try to get a personal recommendation from a previous customer. Serious breaches of contract can be reported to the **Ministerio de Turismo**, but you should be reasonable about minor details. Most guided tours involve sleeping in simple shelters (open-sided raised platforms) or camping in tents or under plastic sheets.

Community ecotourism

A number of indigenous communities and families offer ecotourism programmes in their territories. These are either community-controlled and operated, or organized as joint ventures between the indigenous community or family and a non-indigenous partner. These programmes usually involve guides who are licensed as *guías nativos* with the right to guide within their communities. Accommodation is typically in simple native shelters of varying quality. Local food may be quite good, but keep an eye on hygiene. You should be prepared to be more self-sufficient on such a trip than on a visit to a jungle lodge or a tour with a high-end operator. Bring a light sleeping bag, rain jacket, trousers (not only shorts), long-sleeved shirt for mosquitoes, binoculars, torch (flashlight), insect repellent, sunscreen, hat, water-purifying tablets, and a first aid kit. Keep everything in waterproof stuff-sacks or several plastic bags to keep it dry. Ask if rubber books are provided.

Tours without a guide

Jungle travel without a guide is not recommended. Access to national parks and reserves is controlled, some indigenous groups prohibit the entry of outsiders to their territory, navigation in the jungle is difficult, and there is a variety of dangerous animals. For your own safety as well as to be a responsible tourist, the jungle is not a place to wander off on your own.

Choosing a rainforest

A tropical rainforest is one of the most exciting things to see in Ecuador, but it isn't easy to find a good one. The key is to have realistic expectations and choose accordingly. Think carefully about your interests. If you simply want to relax in nature and see some interesting plants, insects, small birds and mammals, you have many choices, including some that are quite economical and easily accessible. If you want to experience something of the cultures of rainforest people, you must go further. If you want the full experience, with large mammals and birds, you will have to go further still and spend more money, because large creatures have been hunted or driven out of settled areas.

A visit to a rainforest is not like a visit to the Galápagos. The diversity of life in a good rainforest far exceeds that of the Galápagos, but creatures don't sit around and let themselves be seen. Even in the best forests, your experiences will be unpredictable – none of this 'today is Wednesday, time to see iguanas'. A rainforest trip is a real adventure; the only guarantee is that the surprises will be genuine, and hence all the more unforgettable.

There are things that can increase the odds of really special surprises. One of the most important is the presence of a canopy tower or walkway. Even the most colourful rainforest birds are mere specks up in the branches against a glaring sky, unless you are above them looking down. Towers and walkways add an important dimension to bird and mammal watching. A good guide is another necessity. Avoid places that emphasize medicinal plants over everything else – this usually means that there isn't anything else around to show. If you are interested in exploring indigenous cultures, give preference to a guide from the same ethnic group as the village you will visit.

If you want to see real wilderness, with big birds and mammals, there are not many lodges you can drive to. Expect to travel at least a couple of hours in a motorized canoe, or pay extra to arrive in a small aircraft (when this option is available). Don't stay near villages even if they are in the middle of nowhere. In remote villages people hunt a lot for food, and animals will be scarce. Indigenous villages are no different in this regard; most indigenous groups (except for a very few that now specialize in ecotourism) are ruthlessly efficient hunters.

Responsible jungle tourism

A few guides or their boatmen may try to hunt meat for your dinner – don't let them, and report such practices to the Ministerio del Ambiente. Don't buy anything made with animal or bird parts. Avoid making a pest of yourself in indigenous villages; don't take photographs or videos without permission, and don't insist. Try to minimize your impact on the forest and its people. Also remember when choosing a tour agency, that the cheapest is not the best. What happens is that agencies undercut each other and offer services that are unsafe or harm local communities and the environment. Do not encourage this practice.

A number of *centros de rescate* (wild animal rescue centres) exist in Oriente, ostensibly to prepare captive animals to return to their natural habitats. While this may seem laudable, it is not clear whether such efforts can in fact succeed. The *centros de rescate* are convenient for observing fauna close-up but, while some may have genuinely good intentions, others are really just zoos with small cages.

Health and safety

A yellow fever vaccination is required. Anti-malarial tablets are recommended, as is an effective insect repellent. There may be police and military checkpoints in the Oriente, so always have your passport handy. In the province of Sucumbíos, enquire about public safety before visiting sites near the Colombian border.

When to go

Heavy rain can fall at any time, but it is usually wettest from March to September.

ON THE ROAD
Orellana's River

The legends of the Incas fuelled the greed and ambition of the Spanish invaders, dreaming of untold riches buried deep in the Amazon jungle. The most famous and enduring of these was the legend of El Dorado, which inspired a spate of ill-fated expeditions deep into this mysterious and inhospitable world.

Francisco Pizarro, conqueror of the Incas, had appointed his younger brother, Gonzalo, as governor of Quito. Lured by tales of fresh lands to be conquered to the east and riches in cinnamon and gold, an expedition under the command of Gonzalo Pizarro left Quito at the end of February 1541. It was made up of 220 Spanish soldiers, 4000 indigenous slaves, 150 horses and 900 dogs, as well as a great many llamas and other livestock. They headed across the Andes not far from Papallacta and down through the cloudforest until they reached a place they called Zumaco. Here Pizarro was joined by Francisco de Orellana, founder of Guayaquil, accompanied by 23 more *conquistadors* who had left Quito a few weeks after the main expedition.

After proceeding to the shores of the Río Coca, the Spaniards began to run out of food and built a small ship, the *San Pedro*. Rumours that they would find food once they reached the Río Napo led Pizarro to dispatch Orellana and his men to look for this river and bring back provisions. Orellana and his party sailed down river in the San Pedro but found nothing for many days, and claimed they could not return against the current. Pizarro, for his part, was convinced that he had been betrayed and abandoned by Orellana.

On 12 February 1542, Orellana reached the confluence of the Napo and the Amazon – so called by him because he said he had been attacked by the legendary women warriors of the same name. Another name for the mighty new river, but one which never caught on, was *El Río de Orellana*.

On 26 August 1542, 559 days after he had left Guayaquil, Orellana and his men arrived at the mouth of the Amazon, having become the first Europeans to cross the breadth of South America and follow the world's greatest river from the Andes to the Atlantic. Totally lost, they then followed the coastline north and managed to reach the port of Cubagua in Venezuela. In the meantime, Gonzalo Pizarro had suffered enormous losses and limped back to Quito at about the same time, with only 80 starving survivors.

Orellana returned to Spain and, with great difficulty, organized a second expedition which sailed up the Amazon in 1544 only to meet with disaster. Three of his four vessels were shipwrecked and many of the survivors, including Orellana himself, died of fever.

Dominican friar Gaspar de Carvajal, who accompanied Orellana on his first voyage, penned a 31-page chronicle of this odyssey. Carvajal's manuscript survives to this day and the story has been retold countless times. Orellana is a national hero in Ecuador and his journey is a pillar of the country's assertion that it "is, was, and will be" an Amazonian nation.

Coca), believed to be the highest in Ecuador. It is a pleasant 45-minute hike through cloudforest to a *mirador* with stunning views of the thundering cascade. Many birds can be spotted along the trail, including cock-of-the-rock, also monkeys and coatimundis. A large hydroelectric project was under construction here in 2015. Although access to the falls will not be restricted, the turbines will use up to 70% of the water in the Río Quijos, leaving only 30% to go over the falls – the sooner you go the better.

Lago Agrio *Colour map 2, B3.*

The capital of Sucumbíos province, Lago Agrio (population 63,500, altitude 300 m) is an old oil town which now lives mainly from commerce with neighbouring Colombia. The name comes from Sour Lake, the US headquarters of Texaco, the first oil company to exploit the Ecuadorean Amazon in the 1970s. It is also called Nueva Loja or just 'Lago'. If taking a Cuyabeno tour from Lago Agrio, it is worth leaving Quito a couple of days early, stopping en route at Papallacta, Baeza and San Rafael falls (see above). There are various ATMs in town and casas de cambio on Quito between Colombia and Pasaje Gonzanamá, change Colombian pesos. Lago Agrio is 30 km from the Colombian border, the crossing here is not safe and routine precautions are advised in town as well; it's best to return to your hotel by 2200.

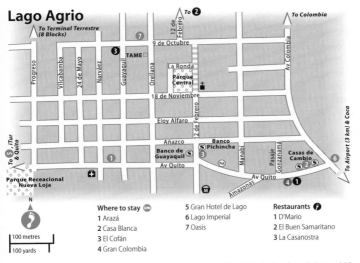

Lago Agrio

Where to stay
1 Arazá
2 Casa Blanca
3 El Cofán
4 Gran Colombia
5 Gran Hotel de Lago
6 Lago Imperial
7 Oasis

Restaurants
1 D'Mario
2 El Buen Samaritano
3 La Casanostra

ON THE ROAD
The high price of petroleum

Coca and Lago Agrio are the main towns serving the petroleum industry operating in Oriente. Starting with Texaco from the USA, oil companies and their subcontractors have come from all over the world; today they are mostly from China. Large and powerful, they have turned the Ecuadorean Amazon into a place where barrels of oil mean more than biodiversity or human rights. Neither drawn-out international litigation by indigenous communities, nor protests by environmental groups, nor innovative but half-hearted attempts by the Ecuadorean government, have been able to halt their relentless advance.

Hundreds of thousands of barrels of oil flow out of the jungle every day through two pipelines that snake over the Andes and down to the coast for export. In their wake, feeder pipes crisscross the devastated terrain, toxic waste sumps contaminate watersheds and cancer rates run high among the local population. Oil spills have on occasion contaminated the Cuyabeno Wildlife Reserve or so badly polluted the Río Coca that they left the city of Coca without drinking water for weeks.

The natural habitat around Lago Agrio was the first to be decimated, followed by that along the Vía Auca, an oil company road running south from Coca into Huaorani territory. More recently the primary rainforest south of the upper Río Napo, between Coca and Misahuallí, has come under threat. Next in line are parts of Parque Nacional Yasuní.

Yet all the direct damage caused by the petroleum industry pales in comparison to that inflicted by the colonists who inevitably follow in its wake. The oil companies build access roads to their wells, and these become corridors of deforestation as settlers take out timber and introduce cattle and crops. Their agricultural practices are unsuited to the poor soils of the rainforest and are not sustainable. At the same time, the way of life of the native lowland people has been permanently altered. These issues are not unique to Ecuador but since the country's slice of the Amazon is among the smallest and biologically richest in South America, the prospect of catastrophe is all the more imminent. See www.sosyasuni.org and www.accionecologica.org; *Amazon Crude*, and other works by Judith Kimerling; and *Savages*, by Joe Kane.

Despite it all, the ongoing international demand for fossil fuels will continue to foster new exploration. And whatever the future price of a barrel of crude in London or New York, the price paid by the Ecuadorean Amazon has already been too high.

★ Cuyabeno Wildlife Reserve

This large tract of rainforest, covering 603,000 ha, is located about 100 km east of Lago Agrio along the Río Cuyabeno, which eventually drains into the Aguarico. In the reserve are many lagoons and a great variety of wildlife, including river dolphins, tapirs, three species of caimans, ocelots, 11 species of monkeys and some 680 species of birds. This is among the best places in Ecuador to see jungle birds and animals. The reserve is deservedly popular and offers a more economical jungle experience than many other areas in Oriente.

Access to most lodges is by paved road from Lago Agrio via Tarapoa as far as the bridge over the Río Cuyabeno, where there is a ranger station and visitors must register. Nobody is allowed to enter the reserve without a tour. From the bridge, transport is mainly by motorized canoe; **Magic River** also offers a worthwhile paddling alternative (see Cuyabeno jungle lodges, below). Most tours include a visit to a local Siona community.

The reserve can be visited year-round but the dry season (January-February) can bring low water levels and generally less wildlife, although certain species may be easier to see at this time. In order to see as many animals as possible and minimally impact their habitat, seek out a small tour group which scrupulously adheres to responsible tourism practices. Cuyabeno is close to the Colombian border and there have been occasional armed robberies of tour groups. Do not take unnecessary valuables. No incidents were reported from 2013 to the close of this edition. Most Cuyabeno tours are booked through Quito agencies or online (see Cuyabeno jungle lodges, below).

Coca *Colour map 2, B3. See map, page 298.*

Officially named **Puerto Francisco de Orellana**, Coca (population 52,400, altitude 250 m) is a hot, noisy, bustling city at the junction of the Río Payamino and Río Napo, which has experienced exceptionally rapid growth from petroleum development. It is the capital of the province of Orellana and, for tourists, a launch pad to visit the lower Río Napo and jungle areas accessed from the Vía Auca, a road running south from the city. The view over the water is nice, and the riverfront **Malecón** can be a pleasant place to spend time around sunset; various indigenous groups have craft shops here. Hotel and restaurant provision is adequate but heavily booked and – ironically for an oil-producing centre – petrol supplies are erratic.

Jungle tours from Coca The ★ **Lower Río Napo**, **Parque Nacional Yasuní** and **Huaorani Reserve**, all accessed from Coca, offer some of the finest jungle facilities and experiences in Ecuador. Wildlife in this area is none-the-less under threat, insist that guides and fellow tourists take all litter back and ban all hunting. Many tours out of Coca are booked through agencies in Quito but there are also a few local operators (see below).

The paved road to Coca via Loreto passes through **Wawa Sumaco**, where a rough road heads north to **Sumaco National Park**; 7 km along it is $$$$ **Wildsumaco** ① T06-301 8343, Quito office T02-333 1633, www.wildsumaco.com, reservations required, a comfortable birdwatching lodge with full board, excellent trails and over 500 birds including many rare species. Just beyond is the village of **Pacto Sumaco** from where a trail runs through the park to the *páramo*-clad summit of **Volcán Sumaco** (3732 m), a six-to seven-day round-trip. Local guides must be hired; there are three nice shelters along the route and a community-run hostel in the village (T06-301 8324, www.sumacobirdwatching.com).

Coca to Nuevo Rocafuerte and Iquitos (Peru)

Pañacocha is halfway between Coca and Nuevo Rocafuerte, near a magnificent lagoon. Here are a couple of lodges (see Lodges on the Lower Napo listings, below) and Coca agencies also run tours to the area (see Tour operators, below). Entry to Pañacocha reserve US$10. There are basic places to stay and eat in Pañacocha village.

Following the Río Napo to Peru is rough, adventurous and requires plenty of time and patience. There are two options: by far the more economical is to take a motorized canoe from Coca to **Nuevo Rocafuerte** on the border. This tranquil

Coca

Where to stay
1 Amazonas
2 El Auca
3 Heliconias
4 La Misión
5 Omaguas
6 Río Napo
7 San Fermín
8 Santa María

Restaurants
1 Fuego y Carne
2 La Casa del Maito
3 Media Noche
4 Ocaso
5 Pizza Choza

Bars & clubs
6 Papa Dan's

100 metres
100 yards
N

riverside town has simple hotels, eateries, a phone office and basic shops. It can be a base for exploring the endangered southeastern section of **Parque Nacional Yasuní**; local guides are available.

Ecuadorean immigration is two blocks from the pier, next to the Municipio. Peruvian entry stamps are given in **Pantoja**, where there is a decent municipal *hospedaje*, $ **Napuruna**. Shopkeepers in Nuevo Rocafuerte and Pantoja change money at poor rates; soles cannot be changed in Coca. In addition to immigration, you may have to register with the navy on either side of the border so have your passport at hand. See Transport, page 306, for boat services Coca–Nuevo Rocafuerte and onward to Pantoja and Iquitos.

The second option for river travel to Iquitos is to take a tour with a Coca agency, taking in various attractions on route, and continuing to Iquitos or closer Peruvian ports from which you can catch onward public river transport. These tours are expensive and may involve many hours of sitting in a small, cramped boat; confirm all details in advance.

Listings Northern Oriente *maps p295 and p298*

Tourist information

Lago Agrio

iTur
Av Quito y 20 de Junio, in the Parque Recreacional, T06-283 3951, iturlagoagrio@hotmail.com. Mon-Fri 0800-1700.

Coca

iTur
Chimborazo y Amazonas, by the malecón, T06-288 0532, www.orellanaturistica.gob.ec. Mon-Sat 0730-1630.

Ministerio de Turismo
Quito y Chimborazo, Ed Azriel Shopping, T06-288 1583.
The place to file any complaints regarding a jungle lodge or tour.

Where to stay

Baeza

$$-$ Gina
Jumandy y Batallón Chimborazo, just off the highway in the old town, T06-232 0471, restaurantgina@hotmail.com.
Hot water, parking, pleasant, popular restaurant.

$$-$ Quinde Huayco
By the park in the old town, T06-232 0649.
Ample rooms, garden, restaurant, quiet location away from the main road.

$ La Casa de Rodrigo
In the old town, T09-232 0467, rodrigobaeza1@yahoo.com.
Modern and comfortable, hot water, cheaper with shared bath, kitchen facilities, friendly owner offers rafting trips, kayak rentals and birdwatching. Good value and recommended.

$ Samay
Av de los Quijos, in the new town,
T06-232 0170.
Very well-maintained older place with
private or shared bath, hot water,
friendly, family-run, good value.

Around Baeza

$$$$ Cabañas San Isidro
Near Cosanga, 19 km south of
Baeza, T02-289 1880 (Quito),
www.cabanasanisidro.com.
A 1200-ha private nature reserve
with rich bird life, comfortable
accommodation and warm hospitality.
Includes 3 excellent meals, reservations
required.

$$ Hostería El Reventador
On the main highway next to
bridge over the Río Reventador,
turismovolcanreventador@yahoo.com.
Meals on request, hot water, pool,
simple rooms, busy at weekends, a bit
run-down and mediocre service but well
located for San Rafael Falls and Volcán
Reventador.

Lago Agrio

$$$ Gran Hotel de Lago
Km 1.5 Vía Quito, T06-283 2415,
granhoteldelago@grupodelago.com.
Restaurant, a/c, pool, parking, cabins
with nice gardens, quiet. Recommended
and often full.

$$ Arazá
Quito 536 y Narváez, T06-283 1287,
www.hotel-araza.com.
Comfortable rooms, restaurant, a/c, pool,
fridge, parking. Recommended.

$$ El Cofán
12 de Febrero 3915 y Quito, T06-283 0526,
elcofanhotel@yahoo.es.

Restaurant, a/c, fridge, parking, older
place but well maintained.

$$ Lago Imperial
Colombia y Quito, T06-283 0453,
hotellagoimperial@hotmail.com.
A/c, some rooms with hot water, ample
common areas, pool, patio, restaurant,
central location, good value.

$$-$ Gran Colombia
Quito y Pasaje Gonzanamá, T06-283
1032, hgrancolombia@yahoo.es.
With a/c, cheaper with fan and cold
water, more expensive rooms in back are
quieter and better, front rooms musty,
indoor parking, centrally located.

$$-$ Oasis
9 de Octubre y Orellana, T06-283 0879.
Modern multi-storey hotel away from
centre, a/c, cheaper with fan, very clean,
includes breakfast.

$ Casa Blanca
Quito 228 y Colombia, T06-283 0181.
Simple adequate rooms with electric
shower and fan.

Cuyabeno Wildlife Reserve
Lodges

There were over a dozen lodges
operating in Cuyabeno in 2015, more
than we can list. The following are
all recommended. Prices range from
US$250-400 pp for 5 days/4 nights,
including transport from Lago Agrio,
accommodation, all meals and guiding.
A small community fee is charged
separately.

Caiman Lodge
T09-9161 0922, www.caimanlodge.com.
On Quebrada La Hormiga near the
lagoon. Well-maintained lodge with an
observation tower.

Cuyabeno Lodge
Operated by Neotropic Turis, Quito
T02-292 6153, www.neotropicturis.com
(see map, page 291).
On the lagoon. This was the first lodge in the reserve, operating since 1988. Very well organized and professional. Ample grounds, comfortable accommodation in several price categories, observation tower and paddle canoes for use of guests.

Guacamayo Ecolodge
Operated by Ara Expeditions,
Quito T02-290 4765,
www.guacamayoecolodge.com.
On the Río Cuyabeno near the lagoon. Well-maintained lodge with an observation tower.

Magic River
Quito T02-262 9303, www.
magicrivertours.com.
On the Río Cuyabeno downstream from the lagoon. Specializes in paddling trips (great fun and wildlife watching without engine noise) which spend the 1st night in a tent camp in the jungle. Friendly atmosphere at the lodge, good food and service.

Nicky Lodge
Operated by Dracaena, Quito T02-290
6644, www.amazondracaena.com
(see map, page 291).
On the lower Río Cuyabeno near it's confluence with the Aguarico, far from all the other lodges. Good wildlife including some species not easily seen elsewhere.

Siona Lodge
Booked through Galasam, Quito
T02-290 3909, www.galasam.net.
On the lagoon. Comfortable lodge with very good infrastructure.

Tapir Lodge
Quito T02-380 1567, www.tapirlodge.com.
On the Río Cuyabeno downstream from the lagoon. Known for high-quality guiding.

Coca
Coca hotels are often full, best to book in advance.

$$$ Heliconias
Cuenca y Amazonas, T06-288 2010,
heliconiaslady@yahoo.com.
Spotless rooms, ample grounds, upmarket restaurant, includes buffet breakfast, pool (US$8 for non-guests). Large new section under construction in 2015. Recommended.

$$$-$$ El Auca
Napo y García Moreno, T06-288 1554,
www.hotelelauca.com.
Restaurant, a/c, parking, a variety of different rooms and mini-suites. Comfortable, nice garden with hammocks, English spoken. Popular and centrally located but can get noisy.

$$$-$$ Río Napo
Bolívar entre Napo y Quito, T06-288 0872,
www.hotelrionapo.com.
Modern rooms with a/c, good but a bit overpriced.

$$ La Misión
By riverfront 100 m downriver
from the bridge, T06-288 0260,
hotelamision@hotmail.com.
A larger hotel, restaurant, disco on weekends, a/c and fridge, pool (US$3 for non-guests), parking, a bit faded but still adequate.

$$ Omaguas
Quito y Cuenca, T06-288 2436,
h_omaguas@hotmail.com.

Very clean rooms with tile floors, a/c, restaurant, parking, attentive service.

$$-$ Amazonas
12 de Febrero y Espejo, T06-288 0444, hosteriacoca@hotmail.com.
Nice quiet setting by the river, away from centre, restaurant, electric shower, a/c, cheaper with fan, parking.

$$-$ San Fermín
Quito 75-04 y Bolívar, T06-288 0802, alexandragalarza@amazonwildlife.ec.
Variety of different rooms, some with a/c, cheaper with fan, ample parking, popular and busy, good value, owner organizes tours. Recommended.

$ Santa María
Rocafuerte entre Quito y Napo, T09-9761 7034.
Small adequate rooms with a/c or fan, private bath, cold water, good economy option.

Jungle tours from Coca
Lodges on the Lower Río Napo
See map, page 291.

All Napo lodges count travel days as part of their package, which means that a '3-day tour' spends only 1 day actually in the jungle. All prices given below are per person based on double occupancy, including transport from Coca. Most lodges have fixed departure days from Coca (eg Mon and Fri) and it is very expensive to get a special departure on another day. For lodges in Cuyabeno, see page 300; for lodges on the Upper Napo, see page 314, for southern Oriente lodges see page 316.

Amazon Dolphin Lodge
Quito T02-250 4037, www.amazondolphinlodge.com.
On Laguna de Pañacocha, 4½ hrs downriver from Coca. Special wildlife

here includes Amazon river dolphins and giant river otters as well as over 500 species of birds. May be closed in dry season (Jan-Feb). Cabins with private bath, US$600 for 4 days.

Napo Wildlife Center
Quito T02-600-5893, USA T1-866-750-0830, UK T0-800-032-5771, www.ecoecuador.org.
Operated by and for the local Añangu community, 2½ hrs downstream from Coca. This area of hilly forest is rather different from the low flat forest of some other lodges, and the diversity is slightly higher. There are big caimans and good mammals, including giant otters, and the birdwatching is excellent with 2 parrot clay-licks and a 32-m canopy tower. US$1110 for 4 days. Recommended.

La Selva
Quito T02-255 0995, www.laselvajunglelodge.com.
An upmarket lodge and spa, 2½ hrs downstream from Coca on a picturesque lake. Surrounded by excellent forest, especially on the far side of Mandicocha. Bird and animal life is exceptionally diverse. Many species of monkey are seen regularly. A total of 580 bird species have been found, one of the highest totals in the world for a single elevation. Comfortable cabins, excellent meals, massage treatments available at extra cost. High standards, most guides are biologists. New canopy tower under construction in 2015. US$1115 for 4 days.

Sacha
Quito T02-256 6090, www.sachalodge.com.
An upmarket lodge 2½ hrs downstream from Coca. Very comfortable cabins, excellent meals. The bird list is outstanding; the local bird expert, Oscar

Tapuy (Coca T06-288 1486), can be requested in advance. Canopy tower and 275-m canopy walkway. Several species of monkey are commonly seen. Nearby river islands provide access to a distinct habitat. US$950 for 4 days.

Sani
Quito T02-243 5939, www.sanilodge.com.
All proceeds go to the Sani Isla community, who run the lodge with the help of outside experts. It is located on a remote lagoon which has 4- to 5-m-long black caiman. This area is rich in wildlife and birds, including many species such as the scarlet macaw which have disappeared from most other Napo area lodges. There is good accommodation and a 35-m canopy tower. An effort has been made to make the lodge accessible to people who have difficulty walking; the lodge can be reached by canoe (total 3½ hrs from Coca) without a walk. US$858 for 4 days. Good value, recommended.

Lodges in the Reserva Huaorani
See map, page 291.

Huaorani Ecolodge
Operated by Tropic Journeys in Nature in Quito (see page 79), a joint venture with several Huaorani communities who staff the lodge.
Winner of sustainable tourism awards. It's small (10 guests) with wooden cabins and solar lighting – a spontaneous, rewarding and, at times, challenging experience. Includes much community involvement, rainforest hikes, conservation area, kayaking (US$40 per day), dug-out canoe trips. Tours arrive by small plane from Shell and leave on the Vía Auca to Coca. River journeys are non-motorized except the last stretch from Nenquepare Camp (cabins, kitchen and bathrooms) where the last night is spent, to the road. US$730 for 4 days, plus US$150 airfare.

Otobo's Amazon Safari
www.rainforestcamping.com.
8-day/7-night camping expeditions in Huaorani territory, access by road from Coca then 2-day motorized canoe journey on the Ríos Shiripuno and Cononaco. All meals and guiding included. Excellent jungle with plenty of wildlife. US$200 pp per night.

Shiripuno
Quito T02-227 1094, www. shiripunolodge.com.
A lodge with capacity for 20 people, very good location on the Río Shiripuno, a 4-hr canoe ride downriver from the Vía Auca. Cabins have private bath. The surrounding area has seen relatively little human impact to date. US$400 for 4 days, plus US$20 entry to Huaorani territory.

Coca to Nuevo Rocafuerte and Iquitos

$ Casa Blanca
Malecón y Nicolás Torres, T06-238 2184.
Rooms with a/c or fan, nice, simple, welcoming. There are a couple of other basic places to stay in town.

Restaurants

Baeza

$$-$ Kopal
50 m off the main road opposite the old town.
Good pizza, nice atmosphere, closes early.

$ El Viejo
East end of Av de los Quijos, the road to Tena in the new town. Daily 0700-2100.
Good set meals and à la carte.

Lago Agrio

There are good restaurants at the larger hotels (see above).

$$-$ D'Mario
Av Quito 2-63. Daily 0630-2200.
Set meals and à la carte, generous portions, popular, meeting place for Cuyabeno groups.

$$-$ La Casanostra
Guayaquil 500 y 9 de Octubre. Mon 1200-1500. Tue-Sat 1200-1500, 1830-2230.
Quiet place with open-air seating, good set lunch, à la carte at night.

$ El Buen Samaritano
12 de Febrero y Venezuela. Sun-Fri 0700-1930.
Cheap and simple vegetarian restaurant.

Coca

$$ Fuego y Carne
Fernando Roy y Amazonas.
Upmarket for Coca, good grill and Italian dishes.

$$-$ Pizza Choza
Rocafuerte entre Napo y Quito. Daily 1800-2200.
Good pizza, nice atmosphere.

$ La Casa del Maito
Espejo entre Quito y Napo. Daily 0700- 2300.
Simple place serving *maitos* and other local specialities, good food, hopelessly chaotic service, go early before it gets crowded.

$ Media Noche
Napo y Rocafuerte (no sign). Daily 1700-2400.
Only chicken in various dishes, large portions, quick service, very popular, a Coca institution.

$ Ocaso
Eloy Alfaro entre Napo y Amazonas. Mon-Sat 0630-2030, Sun 0630-1400.
Simple set meals and à la carte.

Bars and clubs

Papa Dan's Bar
Napo y Chimborazo.
A landmark watering-hole by the malecón. Several other bars nearby.

What to do

Cuyabeno Wildlife Reserve
Magic River Tours, *T03-288 6449, www.magicrivertours.com.* Specializes in canoeing tours into the Cuyabeno Wildlife Reserve, also accommodation at **Magic River Ecolodge** (see Where to stay, above).

Canoeing Tours into the Cuyabeno Wildlife Reserve

Magic River

T~O~U~R~S

Accommodation at Magic River Ecolodge. Excellent wildlife observations and birding.

www.magicrivertours.com / Lago Agrio / Ecuador

Coca

Jungle tours from Coca

See also page 297.

Amazon Travel, *Amazonas y Espejo, in Hotel Safari, T06-288 1805, www. ecuadortravelamazon.com*. Patricio Juanka runs jungle tours throughout the region, very knowledgeable and helpful.

Luis Duarte, *at Casa del Maito (see Restaurants above), T06-288 2285, cocaselva@hotmail.com*. Regional tours and trips to Iquitos.

Sachayacu Explorer, *in Píllaro near Baños (see page 178), T03-287 5316, www. treasureoftheincas.com*. Although not based in Coca, experienced jungle guide Juan Medina offers recommended jungle tours and trips to Iquitos. Advance arrangements required.

Wildlife Amazon, *Robert Vaca at Hotel San Fermín (see Where to stay), T06-288 0802, www.amazonwildlife.ec*. Jungle tours and trips to Iquitos.

River cruises on the Lower Río Napo

Manatee, *operated by Advantage Travel, Quito T02-336 0887, www. manateeamazonexplorer.com*. This 30-passenger vessel sails between Pompeya and Pañacocha, US$986 for 4 days. First-class guides, excellent food, en suite cabins. They also operate similar cruises onboard the 40-passenger luxury vessel *Anakonda* (www. anakondaamazoncruises.com), US$1800 for 4 days.

Coca to Nuevo Rocafuerte and Iquitos

Juan Carlos Cuenca, *Nuevo Rocafuerte, T06-238 2257*. Is a *guía nativo* who offers tours to Parque Nacional Yasuní, about US$60 per day.

Transport

Baeza

Bus Buses to and from **Tena** pass right through town. If arriving on a **Lago Agrio** bus, get off at the crossroads (La "Y") and walk or take a pickup for US$0.25. From **Quito**, Mon-Sat at 1130, 1245, 1520, 1645, with **Trans Quijos**, T02-295 0842, from Chile E3-22 y Pedro Fermín Cevallos (near La Marín, an unsafe area), US$4, 3 hrs. These continue to Borja and El Chaco. To Quito from El Chaco Mon-Sat at 0330, 0430, 0600, 0800, buses pass Baeza about 20 mins later.

Lago Agrio

Air The airport is 3 km southeast of the centre, taxi US$1.50. **TAME** (Orellana y 9 de Octubre, T06-283 0113) flies once or twice a day to **Quito**. Book several days in advance. If there is no space available to **Lago Agrio** then you can fly to **Coca** instead, from where it is only 2 hrs by bus on a good road.

Bus Terminal terrestre, Manuela Sáenz y Progreso, 8 blocks north of Av Quito, taxi US$1.25. To **Quito** Terminal Quitumbe, frequent service with several companies (**Trans Baños** is good), US$10, 7-8 hrs; most buses go via Reventador and El Chaco, but may take the slightly longer route via Coca if there are disruptions. To **Baeza** 5 hrs, pay fare to Quito. To **Tena**, US$8.75, 6 hrs. **To Tulcán** via La Bonita, US$8.75, 7 hrs. Several companies offer service direct to **Guayaquil**, without stopping in Quito, US$17.50, 14 hrs, as well as various other cities on the coast. To **Coca**, every 15 mins 0800-1830, US$3.75, 2 hrs.

Coca

Air Flights to **Quito** with **TAME** (C Quito y Enrique Castillo, T06-288 0768) and **Avianca** (at the airport T06-288 1742), several daily, fewer on weekends, reserve as far in advance as possible. Also one daily to **Latacunga** and **Guayaquil** with TAME.

Bus All long-distance buses, including those to Lago Agrio, depart from the modern Terminal Terrestre, 3 km north of centre, taxi US$1.50. A small terminal on 9 de Octubre serves only regional destinations. **Hotel San Fermin** (T06-288 0802, see above) will purchase bus tickets from Coca for a small commission. To **Quito** Terminal Quitumbe, US$12.50, 7 hrs via Loreto, 9 hrs via Lago Agrio, several daily. To **Baeza**, pay fare to Quito, 5 hrs. To **Tena**, US$8.75, 4 hrs. To **Baños**, US$12.50, 7 hrs. To **Riobamba**, US$13.50, 9 hrs. To **Guayaquil**, US$20, 15-16 hrs.

River Down the Río Napo to **Nuevo Rocafuerte** on the Peruvian border, 50-passenger motorized canoes leave Coca daily except Sat, 0700, 10-12 hrs; returning at 0500, 12-14 hrs; US$15. Details change, enquire locally, buy tickets at the dock a day in advance and arrive early for boarding. **Transportes Fluvial Orellana**, T06-288 2582, cfluvialorellana@yahoo.es, and 2 other companies.

From Nuevo Rocafuerte boats can be hired for the 30-km trip downriver to the Peruvian border town of **Pantoja**, US$60 per boat, try to share the ride. Departure dates of riverboats from Pantoja to **Iquitos** are irregular, about once a month; be prepared for a long wait. Try to call Iquitos or Pantoja from Coca, or check with Luis Duarte at **Casa del Maito** restaurant (see above), to enquire about the next sailing. For the journey, take a hammock, cup, bowl, cutlery, extra food and snacks, drinking water or purification, insect repellent, toilet paper, soap, towel, cash dollars and soles in small notes; soles cannot be purchased in Coca.

Central and southern Oriente

easily accessible jungle and ethno-tourism

Quito, Baños, Puyo, Tena and Puerto Misahuallí are all starting points for cental Oriente. Further south, Macas, Gualaquiza and Zamora are the main gateways. All have good road connections.

Archidona *Colour map 2, C1.*

Archidona (population 12,700, altitude 550 m), 65 km south of Baeza and 10 km north of Tena, has a striking, small painted church and not much else. Tours can be arranged to a private reserve on **Galeras mountain** where there is easy walking as well as a tougher trek; the forest is wonderful. Contact Elias Mamallacha, T09-8045 6942, mamallacha@yahoo.com.

Tena and around *Colour map 2, C1.*

Relaxed and friendly, Tena (population 37,500, altitude 500 m) is the capital of Napo Province. It occupies a hill above the confluence of the Río Tena and Río

Pano, there are nice views of the Andean foothills often shrouded in mist. Tena is Ecuador's most important centre for ★ **whitewater rafting** and also offers ethnotourism. It makes a good stop en route from Quito to points deeper in Oriente. The road from the north passes the old airstrip and market and heads through the town centre as Avenida 15 de Noviembre on its way to the bus station, nearly 1 km south of the river. Tena is quite spread out. A couple of pedestrian bridges and a vehicle bridge link the two halves of town.

Misahuallí *Colour map 2, C1.*

The small port of Misahuallí (population 5300, altitude 400), at the junction of the Napo and Misahuallí rivers, is perhaps the best place in Ecuador from which to visit the 'near Oriente', but your expectations should be realistic. The area has been colonized for many years and there is no extensive virgin forest nearby (except at **Jatun Sacha** and **Liana Lodge**, see Lodges on the Upper Río Napo,

Tena

Where to stay 🛏
1 Austria
2 Christian's Palace
3 Gran Sumaco
4 La Casa del Abuelo
5 Limoncocha
6 Los Yutzos

Restaurants 🍴
1 Café Tortuga
2 Chuquitos
3 Guayusa Lounge
4 La Fogata
5 Pizzería Bella Selva
6 The Marquis

ON THE ROAD
Monkey business in Misahuallí

"Get out the camera, George. The plaza is full of monkeys!" "Sure, Mabel, what are they doing here?"

Misahuallí's experience with white-fronted capuchin monkeys (*Cebus albifrons*) apparently dates back to the 1980s. At the time, the story goes, a pet male monkey named Octavio escaped from his owner, who then tried to lure him back with a female. Instead, she also escaped and the young couple took up residence in a tree by the river.

Among their progeny was Peco, another male who became famous for his mischievous antics with tourists. Peco and his family eventually moved from the outskirts to an abandoned house right on the plaza, where he came to an untimely end in the jaws of a local great Dane. Peco's troop, however, not only multiplied but also thoroughly integrated themselves into Misahuallí society.

The monkeys' interaction with humans is a subtle and unusual one, in which both sides appear to benefit. The monkeys have gained a steady source of food and shelter from the town's shops and tourists, and the townspeople have gained an important tourist attraction.

The capuchins have proven amazingly adaptable due to their ability to consume a wide variety of foods, as well as their behavioural complexity which has enabled them to learn how to unscrew the tops off of bottles, unzip tourist luggage, turn doorknobs to get into houses and open refrigerators for a snack.

The commensal relationship of Misahuallí's two species of urban primates (those with and those without a camera) has also attracted serious scientific attention. An anthropology student did her PhD research here, comparing the town monkeys with their country cousins.

In 2015, the Ministério del Ambiente became the latest challenge to Peco's tribe, threatening to forcibly evict them from Misahuallí. It will be interesting to see who gains the upper hand in the forthcoming battle of wits.

page 314). Access is very easy however, prices are reasonable, and while you will not encounter large animals in the wild, you can still see birds, butterflies and exuberant vegetation – enough to get a taste for the jungle. Beware the troop of urban monkeys by the plaza, who snatch food, sunglasses, cameras, etc (see box, above, Monkey business in Misahuallí). There is a fine, sandy beach on the Río Misahuallí, but don't camp on it as the river can rise unexpectedly. A narrow suspension bridge crosses the Río Napo at Misahuallí and joins the road along the south shore. At Chichicorumi, outside Misahuallí, is **Kamak Maki** ⓘ *US$2.50, T09-9982 7618, www.museokamakmaki.com*, an ethno-cultural museum run by the local Kichwa community.

Puyo *Colour map 4, A2.*

The capital of the province of Pastaza, Puyo (population 40,000, altitude 950 m) feels more like a lowland city anywhere in Ecuador rather than a typical jungle town. Visits can nonetheless be made to nearby forest reserves and tours deeper into the jungle can also be arranged from Puyo. It is the junction for road travel into the northern and southern Oriente (80 km south of Tena, 130 km north of Macas), and for traffic heading to or from Ambato and Riobamba via Baños; all on paved roads. The Sangay and Altar volcanoes can occasionally be seen from town.

Omaere ⓘ *T06-288 3174, Tue-Sun 0900-1700, US$3, access by footbridge off the Paseo Turístico, Barrio Obrero,* is a 15.6-ha ethnobotanical reserve located in the north of Puyo. It has three trails with a variety of plants, an orchidarium and traditional indigenous homes. There are other private reserves of varying quality in the Puyo area and visits are arranged by local tour operators (see page 319). You cannot however expect to see large tracts of undisturbed primary jungle here.

Macas *Colour map 4, B1.*

Capital of Morona-Santiago province, Macas (population 20,700, altitude 1050 m) is situated high above the broad Río Upano valley. It is a pleasant tranquil place, established by missionaries in 1563. **Sangay volcano** (5230 m) can be seen on clear mornings from the plaza, creating an amazing backdrop to the tropical jungle surrounding the town. The modern cathedral, with beautiful stained-glass windows, houses the much-venerated image of La Purísima de Macas. Five blocks north of the cathedral, at Don Bosco y Riobamba, the **Parque Recreacional,** which also affords great views of the Upano valley, has a small orchid collection. The

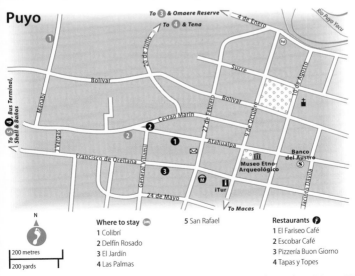

Puyo

Where to stay
1 Colibrí
2 Delfín Rosado
3 El Jardín
4 Las Palmas
5 San Rafael

Restaurants
1 El Fariseo Café
2 Escobar Café
3 Pizzería Buon Giorno
4 Tapas y Topes

Sunday market on 27 de Febrero is worth a visit. **Fundación Chankuap** ⓘ *Soasti y Bolívar, T07-270 1176, www.chankuap.org*, sells a nice variety of locally produced crafts and food products. **Ministerio de Turismo** ⓘ *Bolívar y 24 de Mayo, T07-270 1480, Mon-Fri 0800-1700.* Macas provides access to **Parque Nacional Sangay** ⓘ *Macas office, Juan de la Cruz y Guamote, T07-270 2368, Mon-Fri 0800-1300, 1400-1700.* The lowland area of the park has interesting walking with many rivers and waterfalls. See also Sangay Transport (page 191) for notes on the road from Macas to Riobamba.

Macas to Gualaquiza

South of Macas lies one of Ecuador's least touristed areas, promising much to explore. **Sucúa**, 23 km from Macas, is the administrative centre of the Shuar indigenous people who inhabit much of southern Oriente. The town has most services and some attractions nearby; enquire at the **tourist office** in the Municipio. **Logroño**, 24 km further south, has a large limestone cave nearby (to visit contact Mario Crespo, T07-391 1013). It is another 31 km to (Santiago de) **Méndez**, a crossroads with a modern church. A paved road descends from Cuenca

Macas

Where to stay	Sol de Oriente **6**	Pagoda China **4**
Casa Blanca **1**		Sports Café **5**
Esmeralda **2**	**Restaurants**
Heliconia **3**	La Italiana **1**	**Bars & clubs**
La Orquídea **4**	La Napolitana **2**	Antojitos **6**
Plaza **5**	Lo Nuestro **3**	La Maravilla **7**

via Paute and Guarumales to Méndez, and another road heads east from Méndez via Patuca to Santiago and San José de Morona, near the Peruvian border. Some 26 km south of Méndez is **Limón** (official name General Leónidas Plaza Gutiérrez), a busy, friendly place, surrounded by impressive hills. From Limón the road climbs steeply 10 km to **Plan de Milagro**, another crossroads, where a great road for birdwatching (being paved in 2015), descends from Cuenca via Gualaceo. Next are **Indanza**, 5 km south, then **San Juan Bosco**, 16 km further, with striking views of Cerro Pan de Azucar (2958 m) rising abruptly out of the jungle, before the road reaches Gualaquiza, 55 km ahead.

Gualaquiza *Colour map 5, B5.*

A pleasant town (population 9500 m, altitude 850 m) with an imposing church on a hilltop, Gualaquiza's 'pioneer settlement' charm is threatened by large mining projects in the area. Fortunately, tourism offers an alternative as there are also lovely waterfalls, good rivers for tubing, caves, and undeveloped archaeological sites nearby.

At Gualaquiza, a road (being paved in 2015) forks northwest to climb steeply to Cuenca via **Sígsig**. The road south from Gualaquiza passes El Pangui and Yantzaza (55 km), 8 km south of which is **Zumbi**, with basic hotels on the plaza. At Zumbi, a bridge crosses the Río Zamora and a side road goes southeast to Guayzimi and the beautiful ★ **Alto Nangaritza** region, with **Reserva El Zarza**. The upper Río Nangaritza flows through Shuar territory and a magnificent jungle-covered gorge with 200-m-high walls. There are also oilbird caves and other natural attractions. There is bus service to the area from Zamora, and tours are available form **Cabañas Yankuam** (see Where to stay, page 317) and Zamora tour operators. South of Zumbi, the broad valley of the Río Zamora becomes progressively narrower, with forested mountains and lovely views. It is 35 km to Zamora.

Zamora *Colour map 5, B4.*

The colonial mission settlement of Zamora (population 14,000, altitude 950 m), at the confluence of the Río Zamora and Río Bombuscaro, today has a boom-town feeling due to large mining and hydroelectric projects in the area. It is reached by road from Gualaquiza (see above) or Loja, 64 km away. The road from Loja is beautiful as it wanders from *páramo* down to high jungle, crossing mountain ranges of cloudforest, weaving high above narrow gorges as it runs alongside the Río Zamora. The town itself is hilly, with a pleasant climate. It gives access to the **Alto Nangaritza** (see above) and is the gateway to the lowland portion of **Parque Nacional Podocarpus** (see page 216). Between town and the park is **Copalinga**, a bird-rich private reserve (see Where to stay, page 317). There are two *orquidearios*, **Tzanka** ⓘ *José Luis Tamayo y Jorge Mosquera, T07-260 5692, US$2, 0830-1630,* and **Pafinia** ⓘ *Av del Ejército Km 2.* For information about the town: **Unidad de Turismo** ⓘ *Municipio, Diego de Vaca y 24 de Mayo, by the plaza, T07-260 5316, ext 425, Mon-Fri 0800-1230, 1400-1730.*

Around Zamora

Zamora's most important attraction is the easy access it provides to the subtropical part of **Parque Nacional Podocarpus** via the **Bombuscaro** entrance. To get there, take a pickup from the Terminal Terrestre to the park entrance (US$6 each way). If driving or walking, take the road east out of Zamora and turn right when you reach the Río Bombuscaro. Do not cross the river; take the road that follows the river upstream. The road ends in 6 km at a car park, where the trail begins.

About 30 minutes' walk from the car park takes you to the visitor centre and more trails, including one to La Poderosa waterfall. There are simple facilities at the visitor centre where you can arrange to stay or camp, but you must bring your own food, sleeping bag, mosquito protection, etc. The entrance trail along the Bombuscaro river is very pleasant and full of subtropical birds hard to find elsewhere in Ecuador (such as coppery-chested jacamar, white-breasted parakeet, highland motmot and many more). The area is highly recommended for nature lovers.

Halfway from Zamora to the park entrance is **Copalinga**, a 100-ha private reserve with forest, good trails (some very steep) and excellent birdwatching. There are comfortable cabins on the site and delicious meals are available if arranged in advance (see Zamora, Where to stay, page 317). They also offer volunteer opportunities for qualified naturalists (minimum three-month commitment).

Listings Central and southern Oriente *maps p307, p309 and p310*

Tourist information

Tena

iTur and Ministerio de Turismo
Malecón, sector El Balnerio, T06-288 8046. Mon-Fri 0730-1230, 1400-1700.
Has several information offices under one roof.

Puyo

iTur
Francisco de Orellana y 9 de Octubre, T06-288 5122. Daily 0800-1700; also at Treminal Terrestre, T06-288 5122, Wed-Sun 0900-1600.

Gualaquiza
Oficina Municipal de Turismo
García Moreno y Gonzalo Pesántez. Mon-Fri 0730-1230, 1330-1630.

Information and tours, and from
Leonardo Matoche (Canela y Café).

Zamora

Ministerio de Turismo
José Luis Tamayo y Amazonas. Mon-Fri 0815-1700.
English spoken.

Where to stay

Archidona

$$$$ Hakuna Matata
Vía Shungu Km 3.9, off the road between Tena and Archidona, T06-288 9617, www.hakunamat.com.
Comfortable cabins in a lovely setting by the Río Inchillaqui. Includes 3 meals, walks, river bathing and horse riding.

$$$ Huasquila
Vía Huasquila, Km 3.5, Cotundo,
T06-237 7430, www.huasquila.com.
Wheelchair-accessible bungalows
and Kichwa-style cabins, includes
breakfast and dinner, jungle walks,
caving, rock art.

$$$ Orchid Paradise
2 km north of town, T06-288 9232.
Cabins in secondary forest with lots of
birds. Full board or cheaper with only
breakfast, owner organizes tours in
the area.

$ Regina
Rocafuerte 44, opposite the hospital,
T06-288 9144.
Private or shared bath, cold water, ample
parking (car campers welcome, US$7),
very friendly, family-run. New rooms
under construction in 2015.

Tena

$$ Christian's Palace
JL Mera y Sucre, T06-288 6047.
Restaurant, a/c, cheaper with fan, pool,
parking, modern and comfortable.

$$ La Casa del Abuelo
JL Mera 628, T06-288 6318,
www.tomas-lodge.com.
Quiet place, comfortable rooms, small
garden, hot water, ceiling fan, parking,
tours. Recommended.

$$ Los Yutzos
Augusto Rueda 190 y 15 de Noviembre,
T09-9567 0160, www.uchutican.com/
yutzos.
Comfortable rooms and beautiful
grounds overlooking the Río Pano,
quiet and family-run. A/c, cheaper
with fan, parking.

$$-$ Austria
Tarqui y Díaz de Pineda, T06-288 7205.
Spacious rooms, with a/c, cheaper with
fan, ample parking, quiet, good value.

$$-$ Gran Sumaco
Augusto Rueda y 15 de Nov, T06-288
8434, www.hostalgransumaco.net.
Pleasant hotel in a good location, quiet,
spotlessly clean, bright, ample rooms,
many with balcony and river views. A/c,
cheaper with fan, very good value.

$ Limoncocha
Sangay 533, Sector Corazón de Jesús, on
a hillside 4 blocks from the bus station,
ask for directions, T06-284 6303, www.
hostallimoncocha.com.
Concrete house with terrace and
hammocks, some rooms with a/c,
private or shared bath, hot water, fan,
laundry and cooking facilities, breakfast
available, parking, German/Ecuadorean-
run, enthusiastic owners organize
tours. Out of the way in a humble
neighbourhood, nice views, pleasant
atmosphere, good value.

Misahuallí

$$$$ El Jardin Aleman
Jungle lodge on shores of Río Mishualli,
3 km from town, T06-289 0122, www.
eljardinaleman.com.
Comfortable rooms with bath, hot water.
Price includes 3 meals and river tour, set
in protected rainforest.

$$$$ Hamadryade
Behind the Mariposario, 4 km from town,
T09-8590 9992, www.hamadryade-
lodge.com.
Luxury lodge in a 64-ha forest reserve,
5 designer wood cabins, packages
include breakfast, dinner and excursions,
French chef, pool, lovely views down to
the river.

$$$ Hostería Misahuallí
Across the river from town, T06-289 0063,
www.hosteriamisahualli.com.
Cabins for up to 6 in an attractive
setting, includes breakfast, other meals
on request, electric shower, fan, pool
and tennis court, lovely sunsets.

$$ Cabañas Río Napo
Cross the suspension bridge, then 100 m
on the left-hand side, T06-289 0071,
www.cabanasrionapo.com.
Rustic cabins with thatch roof, private
bath, hot water, ample grounds along
the river, run by a local Kichwa family,
enthusiastic and friendly.

$$-$ Banana Lodge
500 m from town on road to Pununo,
T06-289 0190, www.bananalodge.com.
Nicely decorated hostel, ample rooms,
US$9 pp in dorm, huge garden with
hammocks, breakfast available,
cooking facilities, parking, US$4 pp
for campervans, Russian/
Ecuadorean-run.

$$-$ El Paisano
Rivadeneyra y Tandalia, T06-289 0027,
www.hostalelpaisano.com.
Restaurant, hot water, mosquito nets,
small pool, helpful.

$ Shaw
Santander on the Plaza, T06-289 0163,
hostalshaw@hotmail.com.
Good restaurant, hot water, fan, simple
rooms, annexe with kitchen facilities
and small pool, operate their own tours,
English spoken, very knowledgeable.
Good value. Recommended.

Lodges on the Upper Río Napo
See map, page 291.

Casa del Suizo
Quito T02-256 6090,
www.casadelsuizo.com.
On the north shore at Ahuano. Resort
with a capacity for 200. Comfortable
rooms, well-tended grounds, pool,
gift shop, great river views. Swiss/
Ecuadorean-owned. US$135 per night.

Cotococha Amazon Lodge
Km 10 along the road from Puerto
Napo to Ahuano, at the shore of the
Napo River; Quito office: Muros N27-94
y González Suárez, T02-223 4336,
www.cotococha.com.
Comfortable well-screened cabins.
Jungle walks, tubing, waterfalls and
community visits. Packages including
all meals, excursions by dug-out canoe,
local guides and entrance fees start
from US$99 pp. Popular 3-day/2-night
package US$195 pp.

Jatun Sacha Biological Station
Quito T02-331 7163,
www.jatunsacha.org.
East of Ahuano and easily accessible by
bus. A 2500-ha reserve for education,
research and tourism. 507 birds, 2500
plants and 765 butterfly species have
been identified. Basic cabins with shared
bath, cold water, good self-guided trails,
canopy tower. US$30 per night, day
visit US$6, guiding US$30 per group.
Good value.

Liana Lodge
*On Río Arajuno near its confluence
with the Napo, Tena T06-301 7702,
www.amazoonico.org.*
Comfortable cabins with terraces and
river views on a 1700-ha reserve. *Centro
de rescate* has animals on site. US$265 for
4 days. Also arranges stays at **Runa Wasi**,
next door; basic cabins run by the local
Kichwa community, US$25 per night
with 3 meals, guiding extra.

Yachana
Quito T02-252 3777, www.yachana.com.
6 km upstream from the village of
Mondaña, 2 hrs downstream from
Misahuallí and 2½ hrs upstream from
Coca, also accessible by road (about
6 hrs from Quito). New facilities opened
in 2014 in a 2500-ha reserve on the
north shore of the Río Napo, 14 cabins
on a bluff overlooking the river.
Proceeds help support community
development projects. US$915 for
4 days. Recommended.

Yacuma Eco Lodge
*Parroquia Chontayacu, northeast
of San Pedro, T02-222 6038,
www.yacuma.travel.*
Real natural experience in one of the
most ecologically friendly lodges in
South America, a joint ecotourism

initiative of the rainforect community
of Chontayacu and Ecuahotel.

Puyo

$$$$ Altos del Pastaza Lodge
*Access from Km 16 of Puyo–Macas road,
Quito T09-9767 4686.*
Attractive lodge in 65-ha reserve
overlooking the Río Pastaza, pool. Don't
expect much wildlife, but a nice place to
relax, 1- to 4-day packages include meals
and walking tours.

$$$$ Las Cascadas Lodge
Quito T02-250 0530, www.surtrek.com.
First-class lodge 40 km east of Puyo,
8 rooms with terraces, includes full
board, activities and transport from/to
Quito, waterfalls; 3- and 4-day packages
available.

$$$ El Jardín
*Paseo Turístico, Barrio Obrero,
T03-288 6101, www.eljardinrelax.com.ec.*
Nice rooms and garden, good upmarket
restaurant.

$$ Delfín Rosado
Ceslao Marín y Atahualpa, T03-288 8757.
Pool, modern rooms with a/c, parking.

$$ Las Palmas
*20 de Julio y 4 de Enero, 5 blocks from
centre, T03-288 4832, hostal_laspalmas_
puyo@yahoo.com.*
Comfortable modern rooms with a/c
and fridge, older ones with fan are
cheaper (best upstairs), parking.

$ Colibrí
*Av Manabí entre Bolívar y Galápagos,
T03-288 3054.*
Hot water, private bath, parking, away
from centre, simple but nice, good value,
offers tours. Recommended.

$ San Rafael
Tte Hugo Ortiz y Juan de Velazco,
1½ blocks from bus station, T03-288 7275.
Good choice for late arrivals or early
departures. Clean rooms with private
bath, hot water, good value.

Southern Oriente jungle lodges
See map, page 291.

Kapawi
Quito T02-600 9333, www.kapawi.com.
A top-of-the-line lodge located on
the Río Capahuari near its confluence
with the Pastaza, not far from the
Peruvian border. Run by the local
Achuar community and accessible only
by small aircraft and motor canoe. The
biodiversity is good, but more emphasis
is placed on ethno-tourism here than at
other upmarket jungle lodges. US$1420
for 4 days includes land and air transport
from Quito.

Macas

$$$ Arrayán y Piedra
Km 7 Vía a Puno, T07-304 5949,
arrayanypiedra@hotmail.com.
Large resort-style lodging, nice rooms,
pool, ample grounds, restaurant with
very good food, but variable service.

$$$ Casa Upano
Av La Ciudad, Barrio La Barranca,
1 km from centre, T07-270 2674,
www.realnaturetravel.com.
A family-run B&B in a private home,
other meals available with advance
notice, excellent food, parking, ample
comfortable rooms, huge garden with
many birds, day visits US$5 with advance
notice. Very helpful, English spoken,
organize birdwatching tours. Warmly
recommended.

$$ Casa Blanca
Soasti 14-29 y Sucre, T07-270 0195.
Hot water, small pool, modern and
comfortable, very helpful, good value,
often full, book in advance.

$$-$ Nivel 5
Juan de la Cruz y Amazonas,
T07-270 1240.
Nice modern multi-storey hotel, hot
water, fan, pool, parking, helpful staff.

Macas to Gualaquiza
Sucúa
Several other hotels ($) in town.

$$ Lucelinda
1 km vía a Cuenca, T07-274 2118.
Comfortable rooms with fans, large
clean pool, good restaurant.

$$ Arutam
Vía a Macas Km 1, north of town,
T07-274 0851.
Restaurant, pool and sauna, parking,
modern comfortable rooms, nice grounds,
sports fields, well suited to families.

Méndez

$ Interoceánico
C Quito on the plaza, T07-276 0245.
Hot water, parking, smart and modern,
good value.

Limón

$ Dream House
Quito y Bolívar, T07-277 0166.
With restaurant, shared bath, hot
water, adequate.

San Juan Bosco

$ Antares
On the plaza, T07-304 2128.
Restaurant, hot water, indoor pool,
simple functional rooms, helpful owner.

Gualaquiza

$ Gran Hotel
Orellana y Gran Pasaje, T07-278 0722.
Modern concrete building, hot water, fan, parking, small rooms, some without windows.

$ Wakis
Orellana 08-52 y Domingo Comín, T07-278 0138.
Older simple place with small rooms, private or shared bath, hot water, parking, enthusiastic owner speaks English.

Alto Nangaritza

$$ Cabañas Yankuam
3 km south of Las Orquideas, T07-260 5739 (Zamora), www.lindoecuadortours.com.
Rustic cabins, includes breakfast, other tasty meals on request, private or shared bath, good walking in surrounding jungle-clad hills, organizes trips up the Río Nangaritza. Family-run. Reservations required.

Zamora

With the ongoing mining boom, there are many new hotels in town.

$$$ Copalinga
Km 3 on the road to the Bombuscaro entrance of Parque Nacional Podocarpus, T09-9347 7013, www.copalinga.com.
Nice comfortable cabins with balcony in a lovely setting, includes very good breakfast, other delicious meals available if arranged in advance, more rustic cabins with shared bath are cheaper, excellent birdwatching, walking trails. Belgian-run, English, French and Dutch spoken, attentive, reserve 3 days ahead. Highly recommended.

$$ Samuria
24 de Mayo y Diego de Vaca, T07-260 7801, hotelsamuria@hotmail.com.
Modern bright hotel, comfortable well-furnished rooms, a/c, cheaper with fan, restaurant, parking.

$$ Wampushkar
Diego de Vaca y Pasaje Vicente Aldeán, T07-260 7800.
Modern hotel, ample rooms, a/c, cheaper with fan, hot water, parking, good value.

$ Betania
Francisco de Orellana entre Diego de Vaca y Amazonas, T07-260 7030, hotel-betania@hotmail.com.
Modern, functional, breakfast available, private bath, hot water.

Restaurants

Tena

$$$ The Marquis
Amazonas entre Calderón y Olmedo. Daily 1200-1600, 1800-2200.
Upmarket restaurant serving good steaks.

$$ Chuquitos
García Moreno by the plaza. Mon-Sat 0700-2100, Sun 1100-2100.
Good food, à la carte only, seating on a balcony overlooking the river. Pleasant atmosphere, attentive service and good views. Popular and recommended.
Araña Bar downstairs, Mon-Thu 1700-2400, weekends until 0200.

$$ Pizzería Bella Selva
Malecón south of the footbridge; 2nd location on east side. Daily 1100-2300.
Pizza and pasta.

$$-$ Guayusa Lounge
Juan Montalvo y Olmedo. Tue-Sat 1500-2300.
Light meals, snacks and cocktails, good meeting place, US-run.

$ La Fogata
Serafín Guetiérrez entre Rafaela Segala and Av Napo. Daily 1200-2200.
Tasty set meals, large portions, good value.

Café Tortuga
Malecón south of the footbridge. Mon-Sat 0700-1930, Sun 0700-1300.
Juices, snacks and sweets, book exchange, handy bus timetable, Wi-Fi, good location, spotless, friendly Swiss owner. Recommended.

Misahuallí

$$$ El Jardín
300 m past bridge to Ahuano. Daily 1200-1600, 1800-2200.
Variety of dishes, beautiful garden setting.

$$-$ Bijao
On the plaza. Wed-Sun 0900-2200.
Good set meals and *comida típica* à la carte.

Puyo
There are several cheap *comedores* serving local dishes on C San Francisco near 10 de Agosto.

$$$-$$ Tapas y Topes
Opposite Parque Acuático near bus terminal. Mon-Sat 1000-1530, 1800-2400.
Wide variety of tasty dishes.

$$ Pizzería Buon Giorno
Orellana entre Villamil y 27 de Febrero. Mon-Sat 1200-2300, Sun 1400-2300.
Good pizza, lasagne and salads,

pleasant atmosphere, very popular. Recommended.

El Fariseo Café
Atahualpa entre 27 de Febrero y General Villamil. Mon-Sat 0700-2200.
Good cakes and the best coffee in town.

Escobar Café
Atahualpa y Ceslao Marín. Mon-Sat 0630-2400.
Good for early breakfast, sandwiches, bar at night, attractive bamboo decor.

Macas

$$ Junglab
Bolívar entre Guamote y Amazonas, T07-270 2448. Daily 1200-2230.
Delicious creative meals using local produce.

$$-$ La Italiana
Soasti y Sucre. Mon-Sat 1200-2300.
Great pizzas, pasta and salads.

$ La Choza de Mama Sara
24 de Mayo y Domingo Comín. Mon-Sat 0830-2100.
Traditional Macabeo cuisine such as *ayampacos* and yuca and palm *tamales*, served for breakfast. Also a choice of set lunches, good value.

$ Rincón Manabita
Amazonas y 29 de Mayo. Mon-Fri 0700-2200, Sat-Sun 0700-1600.
Good breakfasts and a choice of set meals which are delicious and filling. Also à la carte.

Zamora

$ Las Gemelitas
Amazonas across from the market (near bus station). Mon-Sat 0600-2030, Sun 0600-1500
Good variety of set meals.

Spiga Pan
24 de Mayo, Av del Maestro y Pío Jaramillo.
Great bakery with a variety of hot bread, cream cakes and fresh fruit yoghurt. A very good option in this otherwise un-gastronomic town.

What to do

Tena
Rafting tours cost US$40-80 per day, safety standards vary between operators. Avoid touts selling tours on the street.
Caveman Tours, *Malecón y 9 de Octubre, T06-288 8394, www.cavemanecuador.com.* Water sports and tours.
Limoncocha, *at Hostal Limoncocha (see Where to stay, above).* Rafting, kayaking and jungle, English and German spoken.
Ríos Ecuador, *Tarqui 230 y Díaz de Pineda, T06-288 6727, www.riosecuador. com.* Highly recommended whitewater rafting and kayak trips, and a 4-day kayaking school. Also offers jungle tours.
River People, *15 de Noviembre y 9 de Octubre, T06-288 7887, www. riverpeopleecuador.com.* Rafting and kayaking.

Misahuallí
Jungle tours (US$45-80 pp per day) can be arranged by most hotels as well as the following:
Ecoselva, *Santander on the plaza, T06-289 0019, www.ecoselvapepetapia.com.* Recommended guide Pepe Tapia speaks English and has a biology background. Well organized and reliable. Bike rentals, US$10 per day.
Runawa Tours, *in La Posada hotel, on the plaza, T09-9818 1961, www. misahualliamazon.com.* Owner Carlos Santander, tubing, kayak and jungle tours.

Teorumi, *on the plaza, T06-289 0203, www.teorumi.com.* Offers tours to the Shiripuno Kichwa community.

Puyo
All of the following offer jungle tours of varying lengths, US$25-50 pp per day.
Coka Tours, *27 de Febrero y Ceslao Marín, T03-288 6108, denisecoka@gmail.com.*
Naveda Santos, *at the Terminal Terrestre, upstairs, T03-288 3974.* Owner, Marco Naveda.
Selvavida Travel, *Ceslao Marín y Atahualpa, T03-288 9729, www. selvavidatravel.com.* Specializes in rafting and Parque Nacional Yasuní.

Macas
Tours to indigenous communities and lowland portions of Parque Nacional Sangay, cost about US$50 per day.
Insondu, *Bolívar y Soasti, T07-270 2533.*
Planeta Tours, *Domingo Comín 7-35 y Soasti, T07-270 1328.*
Real Nature Travel Company, *at Casa Upano, see Where to stay, above.* Run by RhoAnn Wallace and professional birdwatching guide Galo Real, English spoken.

Zamora
BioAventura, *at Orquideario Tzanka (see page 311), T09-9381 4472.* Fernado Ortega offers downhill bike rides along the old road Loja–Zamora.
Cabañas Yankuam, *see page 317.* Offer tours to the Alto Nangaritza.
Wellington Valdiviezo, *T09-9380 2211, lindozamoraturistico@yahoo.es.* Tours to the Alto Nangaritza, Shuar communities, adventure sports, visits to shamans. Contact in advance.

Transport

Tena

Air Airport at Ahuano. **TAME** to **Quito** on Mon, Wed and Fri.

Bus Rundown Terminal Terrestre on 15 de Noviembre, 1 km from the centre (taxi US$1). To **Quito**, US$7.50, 5 hrs. To **Ambato**, via Baños, US$6.25, 4½ hrs. To **Baños**, US$6, 3½ hrs. To **Riobamba**, US$7.50, 5½ hrs. To **Puyo**, US$3.75, 2 hrs. To **Coca** and **Lago Agrio**, see page 295. To **Misahuallí**, see below. To **Archidona**, from Amazonas y Bolívar by market, every 20 mins, US$0.35, 15 mins.

Misahuallí

Bus Local buses run from the plaza. To **Tena**, hourly 0600-1900, US$1.25, 45 mins. Make long-distance connections in Tena. To **Quito**, 1 direct bus a day at 0830, US$8.75, 5 hrs.

River No scheduled passenger service, but motorized canoes for 8-10 passengers can be chartered for touring.

Puyo

Air The nearest airport to Puyo is at Shell, 13 km. Military flights to jungle villages are not open to foreigners, but light aircraft can be chartered starting around US$300 per hr.

Bus Terminal Terrestre on the outskirts of town, a 10- to 15-min walk from the centre; taxi US$1. To **Baños**, US$2.50, 1½ hrs. To **Ambato**, US$3.75, 2½ hrs. To **Quito**, US$6.25, 5 hrs via Ambato; shared taxis with **Autovip**, T02-600 2582 or T09-9629 5406, US$30-40, 8 daily, fewer on weekends. To **Riobamba**, US$5, 3½ hrs. To **Tena**, see above. To **Macas**, US$6.25, 2½ hrs. To **Coca**, US$11.25, 8hrs. To **Lago Agrio**, US$15, 11 hrs.

Macas

Air Small modern airport within walking distance at Cuenca y Amazonas. To **Quito**, Mon, Wed and Fri with **TAME** (office at airport T07-270 4940) Sit on left for best views of Volcán Sangay. Air taxis available to jungle villages, US$600 per hr for 9 passengers.

Bus Terminal Terrestre by the market. To **Puyo**, see above. To **Baños**, US$9, 4½ hrs. To **Quito**, via Puyo, Baños and Ambato, US$10, 8 hrs. To **Riobamba** through Parque Nacional Sangay, a beautiful ride, 6 daily, US$6.25, 4 hrs. To **Cuenca**, US$10, 8 hrs, via Guarumales and Paute or via Plan de Milagro and Gualaceo. To **Gualaquiza**, US$8, 8 hrs, where you can get a bus to Zamora and Loja (see below). To **Sucúa**, hourly, US$1.25, 30 mins. To 9 de Octubre, for **PN Sangay**, US$2, 45 mins.

Gualaquiza

Bus To **Macas**, see above. To **Cuenca**; via Sígsig, 4 daily, US$7.75, 6 hrs; or via Plan de Milagro and Gualaceo. To **Zamora**, US$4.50, 3½ hrs. To **Loja**, US$7.50, 5½ hrs.

Alto Nangaritza

To **Las Orquídeas**, with **Trans Zamora**, from Zamora at 0400, 0645, 1115 and 1230, US$4.75, 3½ hrs; from Yantzaza at 0440, 0740, 1150 and 1310, US$3.25, 3½ hrs; with **Unión Yantzaza**, from Yantzaza at 0430, 0930, 1130, 1430 and 1630; from Loja at 1415, 1510, US$7.75, 5½ hrs.

Zamora

Bus Leave from Terminal Terrestre. To **Loja**, frequent, 1½-2 hrs, US$3; to **Gualaquiza**, US$4.50, 3½ hrs, where you transfer for Macas.

FEEL *MYSTERY* AGAIN

ALL YOU NEED IS ECUADOR

COMUNIDAD KICHWA AÑANGU - NAPO
AMAZON

This is
Galápagos

A trip to the Galápagos is an unforgettable experience. As Charles Darwin put it: 'the natural history of this archipelago is very remarkable: it seems to be a little world within itself'. The islands are world renowned for their fearless wildlife but no amount of hype can prepare you for such a close encounter with nature.

Lying right on the equator, this ancient achipelago of harsh volcanic landscapes is ruled by animals, and human vistors are reduced to the role of voyeur. Here, you can snorkel with penguins and sea lions, watch 200-kg tortoises lumbering through giant cactus forest, and enjoy the courtship display of the blue-footed booby and frigate bird, all at startlingly close range. Both above and below water, sit back, wait patiently and allow the anilmals to come to you. They nearly always do.

On land, immerse yourself in another world. Sit beside newborn sea lion pups and their parents will simply lift their heads and give you a cursory glance. Marine iguanas bask by your toes, while birds pause on their backs doing daily clean-up duty.

Biodiversity figures are not as high as in some other places, yet the number of endemic species is unparalleled. Beneath the incessant waves, there are vast numbers of sharks, from the sleek silky to gentle whale sharks. Huge schools of hammerheads are the most common, yet they can also appear solo, sitting by your shoulder.

The Galápagos consist of six main islands: San Cristóbal, Santa Cruz, Isabela, Floreana, Santiago and Fernandina (Santiago and Fernandina are uninhabited). There are also 12 smaller islands as well as over 40 small islets, which can only be visited on cruises.

Despite their relative isolation and the cost of getting there, these islands are ever popular. A steady stream of people flies in daily, passing along well-trodden routes to witness the spectacular wildlife.

① North Seymour A good introduction to Galápagos wildlife, this small, flat island has sea lions, marine and land iguanas, blue-footed boobies and frigate birds. Dry landing on black basalt lava.

② South Plaza The jetty on South Plaza is often taken over by sea lions. Land iguanas are common. A trail leads across the island to seabird cliffs.

③ Santa Fe From a sea lion-strewn bay on the northeast of Santa Fe, a trail winds through cactus forest home to land iguanas. Spot rays and turtles in the bay.

④ Punta Pitt (San Cristóbal) A cliff trail provides encounters with all three species of booby: blue-footed, red-footed and Nazca.

⑤ Gardner Bay (Española) Wade ashore on a dazzling 2-km-long coral-sand beach smothered in sea lions. Snorkelling around the offshore islet is excellent.

⑥ Punta Suárez (Española) Spectacular rocky headland, often pounded by surf and the site of a blowhole on the southern coast. Wildlife is outstanding: marine iguanas, lava lizards, Nazca and blue-footed boobies, swallow-tailed gulls red-billed tropicbirds, three species of Darwin's finch, Galápagos hawks and (from April to December) a colony of waved albatross.

Galápagos landing sites

❼ Punta Cormorant (Floreana) Wet landing on olivine beach (you may see Galápagos penguins in the bay), followed by a trail that heads inland past a brackish lagoon (flamingos, stilts and other waders) to a sandy beach that's used as a nesting ground by green turtles. Look for stingrays in the shallows and lava lizards on the rocky headlands.

❽ Bartolomé A small island off the east coast of Santiago, Bartolomé has a boardwalk that climbs through a volcanic landscape of ash fields, lava tubes and cinder cones to a viewpoint overlooking Pinnacle Rock. You can snorkel at the Pinnacle, often with penguins and reef sharks.

❾ Genovesa Remote and spectacular, the flooded caldera of Genovesa has over a million nesting seabirds. Great frigate birds, red-footed boobies, lava and swallow-tailed gulls and yellow-crowned night herons are best seen around the sandy beach at Darwin Bay. At Prince Philip Steps a short climb leads onto basalt cliffs where daytime-hunting short-eared owls can be observed snatching white-vented storm petrels as they return to their nesting burrows. The trail also leads through dry woodland with nesting Nazca and red-footed boobies. Mockingbirds are common. Snorkel along the base of the cliffs near Prince Philip Steps to see large numbers of king angelfish, Moorish idols, yellow-tail surgeonfish and, possibly, a few Galápagos sharks and fur seals.

❿ Puerto Egas (James Bay, Santiago) Snorkelling from the black-sand beach is good, while a walking trail follows the coast to a series of tide pools teeming with marine iguanas and Sally Lightfoot crabs. Don't miss the fur seal grottoes.

⓫ Punta Espinosa The shield volcano of La Cumbre looms over black lava fields where the Galápagos' biggest concentration of marine iguanas can be found. Pioneer cactus, lava lizards and sally lightfoot crabs have also claimed the ropy coils of lava, while sea lions lounge on coves of crushed shell and pencil urchin spines. Look out for whales and dolphins in the Canal Bolívar.

⓬ Tagus Cove (Isabela) This sheltered, steep-sided bay is excellent for snorkelling – green turtles are abundant and you should also see flightless cormorants, penguins, sea lions, marine iguanas, large shoals of fish and even giant manta rays, sharks and dolphins. A *panga* ride along the shore will get you close to penguins and flightless cormorants, while a short hike above the bay has wonderful views across a flooded crater known as Darwin's Lake. Look for finches, flycatchers and yellow warblers in the surrounding woodland.

⓭ Urbina Bay (Isabela) Wet landing on a steep beach. Giant tortoise, land and marine iguanas, plus flightless cormorants.

⓮ Punta Moreno (Isabela) After navigating a maze of mangrove channels, you make a dry landing on pahoehoe lava before following a scant trail to a series of brackish lagoons – home to flamingos, pintail ducks and brown pelicans.

novesa
9
ia
win

Note Cruise itineraries are strictly controlled to avoid overcrowding or damaging the islands. As a result these landing sites are subject to change.

Pacific Ocean

San Cristóbal
Bahía Hobbs
Cabo Norte
Caleta Tortuga
Punta Dedo (Finger)
4 Punta Pitt
Kicker Rock (Léon Dormido)
Bahía Stephens
Punta Bassa
Cerro San Joaquín
Cerro Brujo
Canal de Santa Fé
I Lobos
Bahía Wreck
Bahía Rosa Blanca
Puerto Baquerizo Moreno
El Progreso
El Junco
Roca Este
Punta Wreck
Puerto Chino
Roca Ballena (Whale)
Bahía Agua Dulce (Freshwater)

Arrecife Macgowen

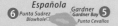

Española
6 Punta Suárez
Blowhole
Gardner **5**
Gardner Bay
Punta Cevallos

January As the rainy season starts, marine iguanas become brightly coloured and land birds begin nesting. Green turtles start egg laying and warming sea temperatures are ideal for snorkelling.

February Galápagos dove courtship is in full swing; flamingos and pintail ducks are also breeding, along with marine iguanas on Santa Cruz. Sea temperatures reach 25°C.

March Expect frequent downpours this month. Marine iguanas are nesting on Fernandina, but the big event in late March is the mass arrival of waved albatross to Española.

April Waved albatross waste no time in practising their courtship dances. Frigatebirds are also engaged in frenzied mating rituals. Green turtle and Isabela land iguana eggs hatch. As the rains come to an end, the islands are at their greenest.

May As North Seymour's blue-footed boobies begin their courtship, waved albatross are laying eggs on Española and turtle hatchlings are emerging. Marine iguana eggs are also hatching on Santa Cruz.

June The *garua* (mist) season begins as giant tortoises descend from the Santa Cruz highlands to find a nest. Seas can be choppy. This is a good month to spot migratory birds and humpback whales.

July Sea temperatures will drop to around 21°C this month. Everywhere you go, seabird colonies are a riot of courtship, egg-brooding and chick-feeding. It's another good month for whale watching.

August Sea temperatures fall to around 18°C. Sea lions begin to pup, and it's a good time to look for courting Galápagos hawks, nesting Nazca boobies and swallow-tailed gulls. Migrant shore birds arrive, while giant tortoises head back to the highlands.

September It's a good month to brave the waters around Bartolomé where Galápagos penguins are usually active. Most seabirds are also still busy nesting and rearing chicks. Male beachmaster sea lions start fighting over females.

October The *garúa* period is coming to an end. Galápagos fur seals start mating, lava herons begin nesting and blue-footed boobies have chicks on Española and Isabela.

November Seas are calmer and water temperatures start rising. Snorkellers can enjoy encounters with sea lion pups. Storm petrels are busy nesting on Genovesa and dodging the island's short-eared owls.

December Giant tortoise eggs hatch between now and April; green turtles are mating in offshore waters, while the first waved albatross chicks fledge.

Essential Galápagos

Finding your feet

There are no international flights to the Galápagos. Flights from Quito or Guayaquil arrive at two main airports: **Baltra**, across a narrow strait from Santa Cruz (the most populated island), and **Puerto Baquerizo Moreno**, on San Cristóbal. The two islands are 96 km apart and on most days there are flights between them, as well as to **Puerto Villamil** on Isabela. There is also a *lancha* (speedboat) service between **Puerto Ayora** (Santa Cruz) and the other populated islands. See Transport, page 372

Tour options

Live-aboard cruise The traditional and best way to visit the Galápagos is on a live-aboard cruise (*tour navegable*), where you travel and sleep on a yacht, tour boat or cruise ship. These vessels travel at night, arriving at a new landing site each day. Cruises range from three to 14 nights; seven is recommended. Itineraries are controlled by the national park to distribute cruise boats evenly throughout the islands. There is a vast range of options from economy to luxury and standards and prices vary considerably. See page 372 for more information.

Island-hopping This is an alternative option for visiting Galápagos whereby you spend a night or two at hotels on the four populated islands, travelling between them in speedboats. You cover less ground than on a cruise, see fewer wildlife sites, and cannot visit the more distant islands. Island-hopping is sold in organized packages but visitors in no rush can also travel between

and explore the populated islands independently at their leisure.

Day tours Day tours (*tour diario*) are based mostly out of Puerto Ayora. Some take you for day visits to national park landing sites on nearby unpopulated islands, such as Bartolomé, Seymour, Plazas and Santa Fe, and can be quite good. Others go for the day to the populated islands of Isabela or Floreana, with no stops permitted along the way. The latter require at least four hours of speedboat travel and generally leave insufficient time to enjoy visitor sites; they are not recommended.

When to go

The Galápagos climate can be divided into a hot season (December-May), when there is a possibility of heavy showers, and the cooler *garúa* (mist) season (June to November), when the days are generally more cloudy and there is often rain or drizzle. July and August can be windy, force four or five. The sea is cold July-October; underwater visibility is best January-March. Ocean temperatures are usually higher to the east and lower at the western end of the archipelago. Despite all these climatic variations, conditions are generally favourable for visiting Galápagos throughout the year.

High season for tourism is June-August and December-January, when last-minute arrangements are generally not possible. Some boats may be heavily booked throughout the year and you should plan well in advance if you want to travel on a specific vessel at a specific time.

Responsible tourism and safety

- Never touch any of the animals, birds or plants.

- Keep your distance from the male 'beach-master' sea lions, they have been known to bite.

- Do not transfer sand, seeds or soil from one island to another.

- Do not leave litter anywhere or take food onto the islands.

- All areas of the national park are non-smoking.

Wildife of
the Galápagos

Over many hundreds of thousands of years, animals and plants migrated to the islands from across the sea and adapted themselves to the islands' conditions. Thus many of them are unique: a quarter of the species of shore fish, half of the plants and almost all the reptiles are found nowhere else. Plant and animal species in the Galápagos are grouped into three categories – endemic, native and introduced – terms you will hear often during your visit.

Reptiles

The reptiles found on the Galápagos islands are represented by five groups: iguana, lava lizards, geckos, snakes and, of course, the giant tortoise. Of the 27 species of reptile on the islands, 17 are endemic.

❶ Giant tortoise
Geochelone elephantopus

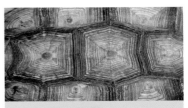

Species specifics

Endemic species Species which occur only in the Galápagos and nowhere else on earth.
Native species Species that are found in the Galápagos as well as other parts of the world. Although not unique to the islands, these native species have been an integral part of the Galápagos ecosystems for a very long time.
Introduced species These are very recent arrivals, brought by man, and inevitably the cause of much damage (see Tourists and settlers, page 377).

Sighting *In captivity on San Cristóbal, Isabela and Floreana, or in the wild at the tortoise reserve on Santa Cruz.*

The Galápagos are named after the saddle-back tortoise (*galápago* means saddle), one of 14 species of giant tortoise that have been discovered on the islands, although now only 10 survive (the famous Lonesome George – thought to be a subspecies all of hid own – sadly died in 2012). Much prized by 17th- and 18th-century sailors as a source of fresh meat on long voyages, their eggs make a tasty snack for introduced species such as black rats, feral dogs and pigs. Numbers dwindled from an estimated 250,000 to just 15,000 in 1980. These days there are between 20,000 and 25,000 on the islands. The Darwin Research Station in Santa Cruz rears young for reintroduction to the wild, giving visitors the opportunity to see them close up. The tortoises mate during the wet season (January to March). Later, between February and May, the females amble down the coast where they bury up to 16 eggs in a nest about 30 cm deep. Three to eight months later, the eggs hatch, usually between mid-January and March.

■ *The oldest inhabitant of the Darwin Research Station may be 180 years old – old enough to have met Darwin himself.*

❷ Marine turtle
Chelonia mydas

Sighting *Caleta Tortuga Negra, at the northern tip of Santa Cruz, and the white-sand beach on Floreana.*

Of the eight species of marine turtle in the world only one is found on the islands: the Pacific green turtle. Mating turtles are a common sight in December and January. Egg-laying usually takes place between January and June, when the female comes ashore to dig a hole and lay 80 to 120 eggs under cover of darkness. After about two months the hatchlings emerge from their shells and scramble across the beach to the sea.

■ *Baby turtles always hatch at night to avoid crabs, herons, frigates and lava gulls on the lookout for a midnight feast as they make their perilous journey to the sea.*

❸ Marine iguana
Amblyrhynchus cristatus

Sighting *In the water or wandering around on most of the islands.*

The only sea-going lizard in the world, marine iguanas gather in huge herds on the coastal lava rocks. They vary in size, from 60 cm for the smallest variety (Isla Genovesa) up to 1 m for the largest (Isla Isabela). Their black skin acts as camouflage and allows them to absorb heat from the fierce equatorial sun, although those on Española have red and green coloration. The marine iguana's flat tail is ideal for swimming but, although they can dive to depths of 20 m and stay underwater for up to an hour at a time, they prefer to feed on the seaweed on exposed rocks at low tide.

■ *This prehistoric-looking endemic species could be as much as nine million years old, making it even older than the islands themselves.*

❹ Land iguana
Conolophus subcristatus, pallidus and rosada

Sighting *Conolophus subcristatus inhabits Santa Cruz, Plaza, Isabela and Fernandina; Conolophus pallidus is found only on Santa Fe; Conolophus rosada lives on Isabela.*

There are three endemic species of land iguana on the islands: *Conolophus subcristatus* is yellow-orange, *Conolophus pallidus* is whitish to chocolate brown and *Conolophus rosada* is pink. The biggest land iguanas weigh 6-7 kg and measure over 1 m in length. Their numbers have been greatly reduced over the years, as the young often fall prey to rats and feral animals; the chances of survival for a land iguana in the wild is less than 10%. It feeds mainly on the fruits and flowers of the prickly pear cactus.

■ *The land iguana is a friendly chap and can often be seen at close quarters.*

Sea birds were probably the first animals to colonize the archipelago. Half of the resident population of birds is endemic to the Galápagos, but only five of the 19 species of sea bird found on the Galápagos are unique to the islands. They are: the Galápagos penguin, the flightless cormorant, the lava gull, the swallowtail gull and the waved albatross. The endemism rate of land birds is much higher, owing to the fact that they are less often migratory. There are 29 species of land bird in the Galápagos, 22 of which are endemic, among them the 14 species of finch made famous by Darwin.

❺ Galápagos penguin
Spheniscus mendiculus

Sighting *In the water and around Fernandina and Isabela.*

The penguin population is small and fluctuates in response to the El Niño cycle. Breeding takes place on Fernandina and Isabela, where upwelling of the Cromwell Current cools the sea. These birds may appear ungraceful on land, hopping clumsily from rock to rock, but underwater they are fast and agile swimmers and can be seen breaking the surface, like dolphins.

■ *This is the world's most northerly species of penguin.*

❻ Flightless cormorant
Phalacrocorax harrisi

Sighting *Fernandina and Isabela*

This is one of the world's rarest birds, with an estimated population of 700 pairs. It is found only on Isla Fernandina and the west coast of Isla Isabela, where the nutrient-rich Cromwell Current brings a plentiful supply of fish from the central Pacific.

■ *Despite having lost the ability to fly, the cormorant still spreads its stunted wings to dry in the wind, proving that old habits die hard.*

❼ Waved albatross
Phoebastria irrorata

Sighting *Across the islands.*

The largest bird in the Galápagos, with a wingspan of 2.5 m, is a cousin of the petrels and puffins. It was not only endemic to the archipelago but also to Isla Española, until a few breeding pairs were found on Isla de la Plata off the Ecuadorean mainland (see page 260). Outside the April-December breeding season, the albatross glides majestically across the Pacific Ocean, sometimes as far as Japan. It returns after six months to begin a spectacular courtship display, a cross between an exotic dance and a fencing duel, which is repeated over and over.

■ *Not surprisingly, given the effort they put into their mating ritual, albatrosses stay faithful to their mate for life.*

❽ Frigate bird
Fregata minor and magnificens

Sighting *San Cristóbal, Genovesa and North Seymour.*

Both the great frigate bird and the magnificent frigate bird are found on the Galápagos. These 'avian pirates' have a wingspan to rival the albatross and spend much of their time gliding in circles with their distinctive long forked tail and angled wings. During the courtship display the males inflate a huge red sac under their throats, like a heart-shaped scarlet balloon, and flutter their spread wings. This seduces and attracts females to the nest, which the males have already prepared for mating. This amazing ritual can be seen in March and April on San Cristóbal and Genovesa, or throughout the year on North Seymour.

Unlike the great frigate bird, the magnificent frigate bird is an 'inshore feeder' and feeds near the islands. It is very similar in appearance, but the male has a purple sheen on its plumage and the female has a black triangle on the white patch on her throat.

■ *Having lost the waterproofing of their black plumage, the frigate never lands on sea; instead it pursues other birds and harasses them for food, or catches small fish on the surface of the water with its hooked beak.*

Boobies
Sula nebouxii, Sula sula and Sula Granti

hting *Common throughout the ápagos.*

ee species of booby are found in the ápagos. Most common is the blue-ted booby, *Sula nebouxii*. It can lay up three eggs at a time, though if food nsufficient the stronger firstborn will k its siblings out of the nest. Unlike its -footed relative, the blue-footed booby es inshore, dropping on its prey like an ow from the sky. It is best known for its nical and complicated courtship dance. The red-footed booby, *Sula sula*, is the y Galápagos booby to nest in trees, nks to feet that are adapted to gripping branches. Many are light brown in colour, although there is also a less common white variety. The largest colony of red-footed boobies is found on Isla Genovesa.

The Nazca booby, *Sula granti* (formerly called the masked booby), is the heaviest of the three boobies and has white plumage with a distinctive black mask on the eyes. Like its blue-footed cousin, the white or masked booby nests on the ground and surrounds its nest with waste. It chooses to fish between the other two boobies, thus providing an excellent illustration of the idea of the 'ecological niche'.

■ *The name 'booby' is thought to derive from pájaro bobo (silly bird); their extreme tameness once led to many being killed for sport.*

337

The number of native mammals in the archipelago is limited to two species of bat, a few species of rat and, of course, sea lions and seals. This is explained by the fact that the islands were never connected to the mainland. Since the arrival of man, however, goats, dogs, donkeys, horses and the black rat have been introduced and threaten the fragile ecological balance of the islands.

❿ Sea lion
Zalophus wollebaeki

Sighting *Colonies on South Plaza, Santa Fe, Rábida, James Bay (Isla Santiago), Española, San Cristóbal and Isabela.*

Galápagos sea lions are common throughout the archipelago, gathering in large colonies on beaches or on the rocks. The male, distinguished from the female by its huge size and domed forehead, is very territorial, especially at the beginning of the May to January mating season. He patrols a territory of 40-100 sq m with a group of up to 30 females, chasing off intruders and keeping an eye on the young, who may wander too far from the safety of the beach. Males that are too tired or too old to hold a territory gather in bachelor clubs. The friendly, inquisitive females are one of the main tourist attractions, especially when cavorting with swimmers.

■ *The sea lions' favourite games are surfing the waves and playing 'water polo', using a marine iguana instead of a ball.*

⓫ Fur seal
Arctocephalus galapagoensis

Sighting *Santiago.*

Fur seals and sea lions both belong to the *otaridae* or eared seal family. Fortunately, these *lobos de dos pelos* (double-fur sea wolves), as they are known locally, survived and can be seen most easily in Puerto Egas on Santiago island, usually hiding from the sun under rocks or lava cracks. The fur seal is distinguished from the sea lion by its smaller size, its pointed nose, big round sad moist eyes, larger front flippers and more prominent ears.

■ *The fur seal's dense, luxuriant pelt attracted great interest and the creature was hunted almost to extinction at the beginning of the 20th century by whalers and other skin hunters.*

Marine life

The Galápagos Islands are washed by three currents: the cold Humboldt and Cromwell currents, and the warm El Niño current. This provides the islands with diverse and unusual underwater fauna.

The number of species of fish could exceed 400, of which about 20% are endemic. Among the huge number of fish found in the islands' waters, there are 18 species of moray, five species of ray (stingrays, golden ray, marbled ray, spotted eagle ray and manta ray) and about 12 species of shark.

The most common sharks are the white-tip reef shark, the black-tip reef shark, two species of hammerhead, the Galápagos shark, the grey reef shark, the tiger shark, the hornshark and the whale shark. Among the marine mammals, at least 16 species of whale and seven species of dolphin have been identified.

The most common dolphins are the bottle-nosed dolphin, *Tursiops truncatus*, and the common dolphin.

Whales include the sperm whale, humpback whale, pilot whale, the orca and the false killer whale, sei whale, minke whale, Bryde's whale, Cuvier's beaked whale and the blue whale. These whales can be seen around all the islands, but most easily to the west of Isabela and Fernandina. The waters are also rich in starfish, sea urchins, sea cucumbers and crustaceans, including the ubiquitous and distinctive Sally Lightfoot crab.

A Galápagos cruise

William Gray, author of Footprint's *Wildlife Travel*, gives a flavour of his encounters with the animals.

On the island of Española, surf blooms white on the cliffs at Punta Suárez – a relentless procession of sinewy waves hurling themselves onto the rocks and filling the air with the salty sweat of their exertions. Anywhere else in the world and you would be spellbound by such a vibrant seascape. But this is the Galápagos and the boulder beach below us is twitching with sea lions and marine iguanas. Sally Lightfoot crabs daub the rocks with splashes of red and gold; waved albatross cartwheel overhead and Nazca boobies stand sentinel on rocky pedestals, their fluffy white chicks crouched in crevices like snagged cotton wool. The sea can flex its muscles all it likes, but it will never upstage the wildlife on Darwin's 'Enchanted Isles'.

Many places in the world have amazing wildlife. Some of them boast extraordinary biodiversity or a superabundance of animals. Others are renowned for endemic species, or allow intimate close-up encounters. It's a rare place, though, that combines all these attributes, and the Galápagos archipelago is one of them.

Punta Suárez on Española is only the third shore excursion on our week-long Galápagos cruise, but already we have seen several of the island's trademark wildlife highlights: blue-footed boobies dancing on North Seymour, hundreds of sea lions dozing on the beach at Gardner Bay, a Galápagos hawk feeding on one of Darwin's

finches – evidence for the theory of natural selection ripped apart before our very eyes.

Over the next few days, our small expedition ship (with just 24 passengers onboard) loops through the archipelago. Each morning, we wake to find a new island. Zodiacs (or *pangas*) shuttle us ashore and we spend the next few hours walking slowly along trails that grapple with old lava flows or thread through forests of palo santo trees.

There is no need to walk far. At Punta Cormorant on Floreana Island (our fourth landing), we have barely strolled a dozen metres before our guide delivers a double whammy of Galápagos penguin and Caribbean flamingo. It's probably the only place in the world where the two can be seen together in the wild.

On Genovesa, there's another incongruous spectacle as we watch short-eared owls hunting storm petrels in broad daylight – the raptors waiting in ambush, perfectly camouflaged in clifftop lava fields, as swarms of the dainty seabirds return to their nesting burrows.

Then there are the Galápagos icons: flightless cormorants preening stubby wings; male frigate birds shaking bright red, party-balloon throat pouches in courtship frenzies; marine iguanas snorting salt from their nostrils and, of course, the high-stepping, head-bowing courtship dances of blue-footed boobies.

Then, just when you think the Galápagos has exhausted its cache of surprises, someone suggests you go snorkelling.

During an hour's drift along the rocky coast of Targus Bay on Isabela Island, we count 26 green turtles, sometimes in twos and threes, grazing on algae or drifting in watery space. Anywhere else in the world, this would be exceptional, but turtles are so common here they almost become part of the background. Sea lions steal the show in surging swim-pasts; penguins zip along at the surface like overwound bath toys, and flightless cormorants dive alongside you, their plumage wrapped in silver cocoons of trapped air.

And as if all this wasn't enough, the sea is squirming with fish – stately king angelfish parading from cover, vast shoals of yellowtail surgeonfish, wrasse, damselfish, parrotfish and even a brief encounter with an octopus.

Climbing into the zodiac and heading back to ship, I feel a warm glow of satisfaction. It's been another exceptional day of wildlife. I can't help but wonder whether the cruise will end in anticlimax, but early the next morning, the ship anchored in another pristine bay, I glance down and there, cruising off the stern, is an enormous manta ray...

www.**ECUADOR**.travel

FEEL ALIVE AGAIN

ALL YOU NEED IS ECUADOR

SAN CRISTÓBAL
GALÁPAGOS

The archipelago populated islands

'a little world within itself'

Santa Cruz: Puerto Ayora

Santa Cruz (population 16,600) is the most central of the Galápagos Islands and the main town is Puerto Ayora.

★**Charles Darwin Research Station** ⓘ *about 1.5 km from the pier is the at Academy Bay, www.darwinfoundation. org, office Mon-Fri 0730-1700, visitor areas 0600-1800 daily, free.* A visit to the station is a good introduction to the islands. Collections of several of the rare species of giant tortoise are maintained on the station as breeding nuclei, together with tortoise-rearing pens for the young.

The **Centro Comunitario de Educación Ambiental** ⓘ *west end of Charles Binford, Mon-Fri 0730-1200, 1400-1700, Sat morning only, free,* has an aquarium and exhibits about the Galápagos Marine Reserve.

★**Tortuga Bay** There is a beautiful beach at Tortuga Bay, 45 minutes' easy walk (2.5 km each way) west from Puerto Ayora on an excellent cobbled path through cactus forest. Start at the west end of Calle Charles Binford; further on there is a gate where you must register (open daily 0600-1700, free). Make sure you take a hat, sunscreen and drinking water; and beware of the very

Santa Cruz best for ...

■ *visitor facilities: shops, hotels, restaurants, banks and tour operators*
■ *Charles Darwin Research Centre*
■ *beautiful Tortuga Bay*
■ *100-year-old wild giant tortoises*

strong undertow. Do not walk on the dunes above the beach, which are a marine tortoise nesting area. At the west end of Tortuga Bay is a trail to a lovely mangrove-fringed lagoon, with calmer warmer water, shade, and sometimes a kayak for rent.

Las Grietas is a lovely gorge with a natural pool at the bottom which is popular (crowded on weekends) and splendid for bathing (open daily 0600-1700, free). Take a water taxi from the port to the dock at Punta Estrada (five minutes, US$0.60). It is a 10-minute walk from here to the **Finch Bay** hotel and 20 minutes further over lava boulders to Las Grietas – well worth the trip.

Puerto Ayora–Baltra The Puerto Ayora–Baltra road goes through the agricultural zone in the highlands. The community of **Bellavista** is 7 km from the port, and **Santa Rosa** is 15 km beyond. The area has national park visitor sites, walking possibilities and upmarket lodgings. **Los Gemelos** are a pair of large sinkholes, formed by collapse of the ground above empty magma chambers. They straddle the road to Baltra, beyond Santa Rosa. You can take a taxi or airport bus all the way; otherwise take a bus to Santa Rosa, then walk one hour uphill. There are several **lava tubes** (natural tunnels) on the island. Some are at **El Mirador**, 3 km from Puerto Ayora on the road to Bellavista. Two more lava tubes are 1 km from Bellavista. They are on private land, it costs US$3-5 (US$10 with torch – or bring your own) to enter the tunnels and it takes about 30 minutes to walk through them. Tours to the lava tubes can be arranged in Puerto Ayora.

Cerro Crocker The highest point on Santa Cruz Island is Cerro Crocker at 864 m. You can hike here and to two other nearby 'peaks' called **Media Luna** and **Puntudo**. The

trail starts at Bellavista where a rough trail map is painted as a mural on the wall of the school. The round trip from Bellavista takes six to eight hours. A permit and guide are not required, but a guide may be helpful. Always take food, water and a compass or GPS.

El Chato Tortoise Reserve Another worthwhile trip is to the El Chato Tortoise Reserve, where giant tortoises can be seen in the wild during the dry season (June to February). In the wet season the tortoises are breeding down in the arid zone. Follow the road that goes past the Santa Rosa school to 'La Reserva'. At the end of the road (about 3 km) you reach a faded wooden memorial to an Israeli tourist who got lost here. Take the trail to the right (west) for about 45 minutes. There are many confusing trails in the reserve itself; take food, water and a compass or GPS. If you have no hiking experience, horses can sometimes be hired at Santa Rosa or arrange a tour from Puerto Ayora.

Tortoises can also be seen at **Cerro Mesa** and at several private ranches, some of which have camping facilities; eg **Butterfly Ranch** ① *Hacienda Mariposa, entry US$3, camping US$25 pp including breakfast, access at Km 16, just before Santa Rosa, walk 1 km from here, make previous arrangements at Moonrise Travel.*

San Cristóbal: Puerto Baquerizo Moreno

Puerto Baquerizo Moreno, on San Cristóbal island (population 7900), is the capital of the archipelago. Electrical energy here is provided by wind generators in the highlands, see www.eolicsa.com.ec.

The town's attractive *malecón* has many shaded seats shared by tourists, residents and sea lions. The **cathedral** ① *on Av Northía y Cobos, 0900-1200, 1600-1800*, has interesting artwork combining religious and Galápagos motifs.

To the north of town, opposite **Playa Mann** (suitable for swimming), is the Galápagos National Park visitor centre or

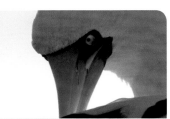

San Cristóbal best for ...

■ *Intrepretation Centre*
■ *sailing or diving through Kicker Rock*
■ *spotting three species of booby at Punta Pitt*

★**Centro de Interpretación** ① *T05-252 0138, ext 123, daily 0700-1700, free.* It has excellent displays of the natural and human history of the islands including contemporary issues,

recommended. A good trail goes from the Centro de Interpretación to the northeast through scrub forest to **Cerro Tijeretas**, a hill overlooking town and the ocean, 30 minutes away. From here a rougher trail continues 45 minutes to **Playa Baquerizo**. Frigate birds nest in this area and can be observed gliding overhead; there are sea lions on the beaches below. To go back from Cerro Tijeretas, if you take the trail which follows the coast, you will end up at **Playa Punta Carola**, a popular surfing beach, too rough for swimming. To the south of Puerto Baquerizo Moreno, 30 minutes' walk past the stadium and high school (ask for directions), is **La Lobería**, a rocky shore with sea lions, marine iguanas, and a rough trail leading to beautiful cliffs with many birds, overlooking the sea.

Four buses a day run the 6 km inland from Puerto Baquerizo Moreno to **El Progreso**, US$0.50, 15 minutes, then it's a 2½-hour walk to **El Junco lake**, the largest body of fresh water in Galápagos. Pickup trucks to El Progreso charge US$3, or you can hire them for touring: US$25 to El Junco (return with wait), US$50 continuing to the beaches at **Puerto Chino** on the other side of the island, past a man-made tortoise reserve. Camping is possible at Puerto Chino with a permit from the national park; take food and drinking water. At El Junco there is a path to walk around the lake in 20 minutes. The views are lovely in clear weather but it is cool and wet in the *garúa* season, so take adequate clothing. Various small roads fan out from El Progreso and make for pleasant walking. Jatun Sacha (www.jatunsacha.org) has a volunteer centre on an old hacienda in the highlands beyond El Progreso, working on eradication of invasive species and a native plant nursery; US$15 taxi ride from town, take repellent.

Boats go to **Punta Pitt** at the northeast end of San Cristóbal where you can see all three species of booby. Off the northwest coast is **Kicker Rock** (León Dormido), the basalt remains of a volcanic plug; many seabirds, including Nazca and blue-footed boobies, can be seen around its cliffs (five-hour trip, including snorkelling, recommended).

Isabela: Puerto Villamil

Isabela (population 2500) is the largest island in the archipelago; at 120 km long it forms over half the total land area of the archipelago. It was formed by the coalesced lava flows of six volcanoes. Five are active and each has (or had) its own separate sub-species of giant tortoise. Isabela is also the island which is changing most rapidly, driven by growing land-based tourism. It remains a charming place but is at risk from uncontrolled development. Most residents live in Puerto Villamil. In the highlands, there is a cluster of farms at Santo Tomás. There are several lovely beaches right by town, but mind the strong undertow and ask locally about the best spots for swimming and surfing.

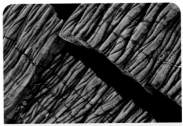

Isabela best for ...

- *volcanic landscape of black lava fields*
- *hiking to the caldera of Sierra Negra volcano*
- *visiting massive colonies of marine iguanas and seabirds*

It is 8 km west to **Muro de las Lágrimas**, built by convict labour under hideous conditions. These days it makes a great day-hike or hire a bicycle (always take water). Short side-trails branch off the road to various attractions along the way, and a trail continues from the Muro to nearby hills with lovely views. Along the same road, 30 minutes from town, is the **Centro de Crianza**, a breeding centre for giant tortoises surrounded by lagoons with flamingos and other birds. In the opposite direction, 30 minutes east toward the *embarcadero* (pier) is **Concha de Perla Lagoon**, with a nice access trail through mangroves and a small dock from which you can go swimming with sea lions and other creatures. Tours go to **Las Tintoreras**, a set of small islets in

the harbour where white-tipped reef sharks and penguins may be seen in the still crystalline water (US$30 per person). There are also boat tours to **Los Túneles** at Cabo Rosa (US$65 per person, a tricky entrance from the open sea), where fish, rays and turtles can be seen in submerged lava tunnels.

★ **Sierra Negra Volcano** has the second-largest basaltic caldera in the world, 9 km by 10 km. It is 19 km (30 minutes) by pickup truck to the park entrance (take passport and national park entry receipt), where you start the 1½-hour hike to the crater rim at 1000 m. It is a further 1½ hours' walk along bare brittle lava rock to **Volcán Chico**, with several fumaroles and more stunning views. You can camp on the crater rim but must take all supplies, including water, and obtain a permit the day before from the national park office in Puerto Villamil. A tour including transport and lunch costs about US$80 per person. Highland tours are also available to **La Cueva de Sucre**, a large lava tube with many chambers; be sure to take a torch if visiting on your own. A bus to the highlands leaves the market in Puerto Villamil at 0700 daily, US$0.50, ask the driver for directions to the cave and return times.

Floreana (population 160) is the island with the richest human history and the fewest inhabitants, most living in Puerto Velasco Ibarra. You can easily reach the island with a day-tour boat from Puerto Ayora, but these do not leave enough time to enjoy the visit. A couple of days' stay is recommended, however note that there may not always be space on boats returning to Puerto Ayora, so you must be flexible.

Floreana best for ...

■ *Post Office Bay*
■ *snorkelling at Devil's Crown*
■ *pink flamingos and green sea turtles*

Community tourism is getting underway on Floreana but services are limited. One shop has basic supplies and there are a handful of places to eat and sleep, none is cheap (see Where to stay, page 365). Margaret Wittmer, one of the first settlers on Floreana, died in 2000, but you can meet her daughter and granddaughter.

La Lobería is a beautiful little peninsula (which becomes an island at high tide), 15 minutes' walk from town, where sea lions, sea turtles, marine iguanas and various birds can be seen. The climate in the highlands is fresh and comfortable, good for walking and birdwatching. A *ranchera* runs up to **Asilo de La Paz**, with a natural spring and tortoise area (Monday to Saturday 0600 and 1500, returning 0700 and 1600; Sunday 0700 returning 1000). Or you can walk down in three to four hours, detouring to climb **Cerro Allieri** along the way.

★Post Office Bay, on the north side of Floreana, is visited by tour boats. There is a custom (since 1792) for visitors here to place unstamped letters and cards in a barrel, and deliver, free of charge, any addressed to their own destinations. An interesting trail has been re-opened from Puerto Velasco Ibarra to Post Office Bay, but was not yet open to visitors at the close of this edition.

The archipelago
unpopulated
islands

It is not the strongest of the species that survives, nor the most intelligent, but the one most responsive to change

Baltra

Once a US Airforce base, Baltra is now a small military base for Ecuador and also the main airport into the islands. Also known as South Seymour, this is the island most affected by human presence. **Mosquera** is a small sandy bank just north of Baltra, home to a large colony of sea lions.

★ Bartolomé

Bartolomé is a small island located in Sullivan Bay off the eastern shore of Santiago. It is probably the most easily recognized, the most visited and most photographed of all the islands in the Galápagos with its distinctive **Pinnacle Rock**. The trail leads steeply up to the summit, taking 30-40 minutes, from where there are panoramic views. At the second visitor site on the island there is a lovely beach from which you can snorkel or swim and usually see penguins

Bartolomé best for ...

- *coloured rock formations, lava fields and craters*
- *views from Pinnacle Rock or Cerro Bartolomé*
- *excellent snorkelling*
- *tropical fish, penguins, reef sharks*

Daphne Major

West of Baltra, Daphne Island has very rich birdlife, in particular the nesting boobies. Because of the possible problems of erosion, only small boats may land here and are limited to one visit each month.

Española best for ...

- *white-sand beaches of Gardner Bay*
- *large colony of waved albatross and other seabirds*
- *dramatic kleef landscapes*

Española

This is the southernmost island of the Galápagos and, following a successful programme to remove all the feral species, is now the most pristine of the islands with many migrant, resident and endemic seabirds. **Gardner Bay**, on the north coast, is a beautiful white-sand beach with excellent swimming and snorkelling. **Punta Suárez**, on the western tip of the island, has a trail through a rookery. As well as a wide range of seabirds (including blue-footed and Nazca boobies) there is a great selection of wildlife including sea lions and the largest and most colourful marine iguanas of the Galápagos plus the original home of the waved albatrosses.

Fernandina

Fernandina is the youngest of the islands, at about 700,000 years old, and also the most volcanically active, with eruptions every few years. The visitor site of **Punta Espinosa** is on the northeast coast of Fernandina. The trail goes up through a sandy nesting site for huge colonies of marine iguanas. The nests appear as small hollows in the sand. You can also see flightless cormorants drying their atrophied wings in the sun and go snorkelling in the bay.

Fernandina best for ...

■ *dramatic coastline*
■ *impressive lava flows*
■ *penguins, marina iguanas, flightless cormorants*

Genovesa

Genovesa best for ...

■ *Prince Phillip's Steps*
■ *snorkelling with marine iguanas*
■ *the largest nesting colonies of red-footed boobies and frigate birds*

Located in the northeast of the archipelago, this is an outpost for many sea birds. It is an eight- to 10-hour all-night sail from Puerto Ayora. Like Fernandina, Genovesa is best visited on longer cruises or ships with larger range.

One of the most famous sites is **Prince Phillip's Steps**, an amazing walk through a seabird rookery that is full of life. You will see tropic birds, all three boobies, frigates, petrels, swallow-tailed and lava gulls, and many others. There is also good snorkelling at the foot of the steps, with lots of marine iguanas. The entrance to **Darwin Bay**, on the eastern side of the island, is very narrow and shallow and the anchorage in the lagoon is surrounded by mangroves, home to a large breeding colony of frigates and other seabirds.

Plaza Sur

One of the closest islands to Puerto Ayora is Plaza Sur. It's an example of a geological uplift and the southern part of the island has formed cliffs with spectacular views. It has a combination of both dry and coastal vegetation zones. Walking along the sea cliffs is a pleasant experience as swallowtail gulls, shearwaters and red-billed tropic birds nest here. This is the home of the **Men's Club**, a rather sad-looking colony of bachelor sea lions who are too old to mate and who get together to console each other. There are also lots of blue-footed boobies and a large population of land iguanas on the island.

Rábida

This island is just to the south of Santiago. The trail leads to a salt-water lagoon with an area of mangroves which are best explored by panga. The marshy lake is full of flamingos. This island is said to have the most diversified volcanic rocks of all the islands. It is a mating spot for green Pacific turtles and white-tipped sharks and mustard rays are found in the waters around the island. You can snorkel and swim from the dark red-sand beach populated with sea lions.

Santa Fe

This island is located on the southeastern part of Galápagos, between Santa Cruz and San Cristóbal, and was formed by volcanic uplift. The lagoon is home to a large colony of sea lions which are happy to join you for a swim. From the beach the trail goes inland, through a semi-arid landscape of cactus. This little island has its own species of land iguana.

Santiago

This large island, also known as James, is to the east of Isla Isabela. It has a volcanic landscape full of cliffs and pinnacles, and is home to several species of marine birds. **James Bay** is on the western side of the island, where there is a wet landing on the dark sands of **Puerto Egas**. The trail leads to the remains of an unsuccessful salt mining operation. Fur seals are seen nearby. **Espumilla Beach** is another famous visitor site. After landing on a large beach, walk through a mangrove forest that leads to a lake usually inhabited by flamingos, pintail ducks and stilts. There are nesting and feeding sites for flamingos. Sea turtles dig their nests at the edge of the mangroves. **Buccaneer**

Santiago best for ...

■ *marine iguanas sunbathing on black volcanic rocks*
■ *swimming with fur seals*
■ *hidden snorkelling spots and white-sand beaches*

Cove, on the northwest part of the island, was a haven for pirates during the 1600s and 1700s. **Sullivan Bay** is on the eastern coast of Santiago, opposite Bartolomé Island. The visitor trail leads across an impressive lunar landscape of lava fields formed during eruptions in 1890.

Seymour Norte

Just north of Baltra, Seymour Norte is home to sea lions, marine iguanas, swallow-tailed gulls, magnificent frigate birds and blue-footed boobies. The trail leads through mangroves in one of the main nesting sites for blue-footed boobies and frigates in this part of the archipelago.

Seymour Norte best for ...

■ *swimming with sea lions*

Sombrero Chino

This is just off the southeastern tip of Santiago, and its name refers to its shape. It is most noted for the volcanic landscape including sharp outcrops, cracked lava formations, lava tubes and volcanic rubble. This site is only accessible to smaller vessels.

Galápagos
cruises & tours

A visit to the islands doesn't come cheap. The return flight from Quito and national park fees add up to about US$600; plus around US$200 per person per day for sailing on an economy-class boat. There are few such inexpensive vessels and even fewer good inexpensive ones. Since you are already spending so much money, it is worth spending a bit more to make sure you sign up with a reputable agency on a better cruise, the quality of which is generally excellent.

Land-based and independent travel on the populated islands are alternatives, but there is simply no way to enjoy Galápagos on a shoestring. For those with a passion for nature, the once-in-a-lifetime Galápagos experience is well worth saving for. At the same time, high prices might be one way of keeping the number of visitors within sustainable levels. The islands have already suffered the impact of rapidly growing tourism and a viable mechanism is urgently needed to ensure their survival as the world's foremost wildlife sanctuary.

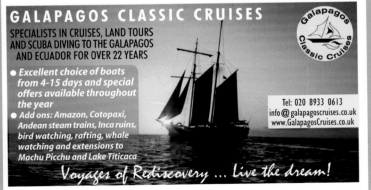

Choosing a boat *See also page 372.*

Most international visitors explore the islands on pre-arranged boat tours where you sleep on board overnight. Prices and standards vary substantially from small yachts with basic facilities to luxury cruise ships; both have their advantages and disadvantages. Captains, crews and guides regularly change on all boats. These factors, as well as the sea, weather and your fellow passengers will all influence the quality of your experience

The **least expensive boats** (economy class) cost up to US$200 per person per day and a few of these vessels are dodgy. The boats are normally smaller and less powerful so you see less and spend more time travelling; also the guiding may be mostly in Spanish. There may be limitations for vegetarians on the cheaper boats.

The **more expensive boats** have air conditioning, hot water and private baths. Tourist and tourist superior class cost around US$250-600 per day and you will be on a better, faster boat which can travel more quickly between visitor sites, leaving more time to spend ashore.

Over US$600 per day are the first-class and luxury brackets, with far more comfortable and spacious cabins, as well as a superior level of service and cuisine.

Other considerations All cruises begin with a morning flight from the mainland on the first day and end on the last day with a midday flight back to the mainland. No boat may sail without a park-trained guide. All boats have to conform to certain minimum safety standards; more expensive boats are better equipped. Boats with over 20 passengers take quite a time to disembark and re-embark people, while the smaller boats have a more lively motion, which is important if you are prone to seasickness.

Time required

A seven-day cruise will allow time to get a good idea of the diversity of life and landscapes of the Galápagos and visit some of the outlying islands such as Genovesa, Española or Fernandina. Bear in mind that with any tour from the mainland, the first and last days will be spent travelling, which means that you

should book a nine- or 10-day tour to allow enough time on the boat. Study the itinerary carefully. As a general rule, the better trips spend less time on the populated islands and more time further afield.

Fees and inspections

The islands are a national park. A US$20 fee is collected at Quito or Guayaquil airport, where a registration form must be completed. It is best to pre-register online at **www.gobiernogalapagos.gob.ec**, or ask your tour operator to do so for you. Bags are checked prior to flights to Galápagos. No live animals, meat, dairy products, fresh fruit or vegetables may be taken to the islands. On arrival, every foreign visitor must pay a US$100 national park fee. All fees are cash only. Be sure to have your passport to hand at the airport and keep all fee receipts throughout your stay in the islands. Bags are checked again on departure, as nothing may be taken off the islands. Puerto Villamil charges a US$5 port fee on arrival in Isabela.

Booking a tour

Galápagos is such a special destination for nature-lovers that most agree it is worth saving for and spending on a quality tour. You can book a Galápagos cruise in several different ways:

- Over the internet
- From either a travel agency or directly though a Galápagos wholesaler in your home country (many are listed on page 372)
- From one of the very many agencies found throughout Ecuador, especially in Quito (see page 76) but also in other tourist centres and Guayaquil (page 243)
- From local agencies, mostly in Puerto Ayora but also in Puerto Baquerizo Moreno (page 370)

The trade-off is always between time and money: booking from home is most efficient and expensive, last-minute arrangements in Galápagos are cheapest but most time-consuming (and the cost of staying in Puerto Ayora while you wait is high), while Quito and Guayaquil are intermediate. It is not possible to obtain discounts or make last-minute arrangements in high

ENCHANTED EXPEDITIONS

www.enchantedexpeditions.com

Cruise the Galapagos Islands aboard our exclusive small-group yachts and experience Ecuador on a custom-made adventure with Enchanted Expeditions. Join us for a trip of a lifetime!

GALAPAGOS & ECUADOR

Whether you wish to explore the Amazon, Andean Highlands, or sail on one of our all-inclusive cruises to the Enchanted Galapagos Islands in Ecuador or extend your trip to Peru; Zenith Travel is more than qualified to meet all your holiday and adventure travel needs.

ZENITH Travel

Travel Agency, Tour Operator & Destination Management

WWW. ZENITHECUADOR.COM

PBX: **(593-2) 252-9993** (593-9) 995377773 / US: **1-516-9261530**
E-mail: **info@zenithecuador.com** Skype: zenith.travel
Juan Leon Mera N24-264 y Cordero / Quito - Ecuador

season (see When to go, page 17). Surcharges may apply when using a credit card to purchase tours on the islands, there are limits to ATM withdrawals and no cash advances in Galápagos, so take sufficient cash if looking for a last-minute cruise. Also, if looking for a last-minute sailing, it is best to pay your hotel one night at a time since hoteliers may not refund advance payments. Especially on cheaper boats, check carefully about what is and is not included (eg drinking water, snorkelling equipment, etc). Below is a selection of vessels which will give a good idea of the price category, what facilities to expect and the islands usually visited.

Making the most of your trip

■ Always bring some US dollars cash to Galápagos. There are only a handful of ATMs in Puerto Ayora and **Puerto Baquerizo Moreno**, and they may not work with all cards. ATM withdrawals are limited to US$300-500 per day and cash advances on credit cards cannot be obtained in Galápagos.

■ Daytime clothing should be lightweight and even on luxury cruises should be casual and comfortable. At night, particularly at sea and at higher altitudes, temperatures fall below 15°C and warm clothing is required.

The following are examples of vessels and not necessarily recommendations:

Cachalote
Type Two-masted schooner
Length 21 m
Berths 16 passengers in seven double/twin cabins, each with private shower and toilet.
Facilities Bar, saloon, dining area, three wooden decks, including sundeck, air conditioning throughout, sea kayaks onboard.
Crew Six crew and one naturalist guide.
Price category First class.
Islands usually visited Baltra, Santa Cruz, Santa Fe, San Cristóbal, Española, Floreana, Santiago and Genovesa.

Isabela II
Type Motor yacht
Length 53 m
Berths 40 passengers in en suite double/twin cabins.
Facilities Lounge, bar, restaurant, library, gift shop, sundeck, jacuzzi, sea kayaks, glass-bottom boat, snorkelling gear, lecture areas, air conditioning throughout.
Crew 24 crew, one doctor and three naturalist guides.
Price category Luxury.
Islands usually visited Baltra, North Seymour, Española, Floreana, Santa Cruz, Genovesa, Isabela, Fernandina, Santiago and Bartolomé.

La Pinta
Type Motor yacht
Length 63 m
Berths 48 passengers in en suite cabins, some interconnecting for families.
Facilities Lounge, bar, restaurant, library, gift shop, sundeck, jacuzzi, outside bar, sea kayaks, glass-bottom boat, snorkelling gear, children's activities, air conditioning.
Crew 25 crew, one doctor and three naturalist guides.
Price category Luxury.
Islands usually visited Baltra, San Cristóbal, North Seymour, Rábida, Santa Cruz, Floreana, Isabela, Fernandina and Bartolomé.

- Bring good footwear, soles soon wear out on the abrasive lava terrain.
- A remedy for seasickness is recommended.
- A good supply of sun block and skin cream to prevent wind-burn and chapped lips is essential, as are a hat and good sunglasses.
- Be prepared for dry and wet landings. The latter involves wading ashore.
- Take plenty of memory cards for your camera. The animals are so tame that you will use far more than you expected. A telephoto lens is not essential, but bring it if you have one. An underwater camera is also an excellent idea.
- Snorkelling equipment is particularly useful as much of the sealife is only visible underwater. Few of the cheaper boats provide good snorkelling gear. If in doubt, bring your own, rent in Puerto Ayora or buy it in Quito.
- On most cruises a ship's crew and guides are usually tipped separately. The amount is a very personal matter; you may be guided by suggestions made onboard or in the agency's brochures, but the key factors should always be the quality of service received and your own resources.
- Raise any issues first with your guide or ship's captain. Additional complaints may be filed with the Ministerio de Turismo in Puerto Ayora orPuerto Baquerizo Moreno, see page 361.

Nemo II
Type Motor sail catamaran

Length 22 m

Berths 12 passengers in seven en suite air-conditioned double or single cabins.

Facilities Salon, bar, sundeck air conditioning, kayaks and snorkellng gear.

Crew Seven crew and one naturalist guide.

Price category First class.

Islands usually visited Baltra, Santa Cruz, San Cristóbal, Española, Floreana, Santa Fe, Santiago, Isabela, Fernandina and Genovesa.

Samba
Type Steel-hulled motor-sailor with stabilizing sail

Length 24 m

Berths 14 passengers in seven en suite air-conditioned cabins.

Facilities Salon, large foreward deck, aft dining deck area, air conditioning, mini library and large-screen TV lecture area, two pangas.

Crew Six crew and one naturalist guide.

Price category Tourist class.

Islands usually visited Baltra, North Seymour, Santa Cruz, Genovesa, Marchena, Floreana, Fernandina, Isabela, Bartolomé and Española.

Santa Cruz
Type Motor-cruiser

Length 72 m

Berths 90 passengers in 48 en suite cabins, including spacious suites.

Facilities Lounge, bar, dance floor, restaurant, library, gift shop, sundeck, stargazing program, jacuzzi, glass-bottom boat, snorkelling gear, air conditioning.

Crew 52 crew, one doctor and six naturalist guides.

Price category Luxury.

Islands usually visited Baltra, Santa Fe, North Seymour, Santa Cruz, San Cristóbal, Española, Fernandina and Isabela.

Listings Galápagos Islands

Tourist information

Santa Cruz
Puerto Ayora

iTur
*Av Charles Darwin y 12 de Febrero,
T05 252 6153 ext 22, Mon-Fri 0730-1230,
1400-1730, Sat-Sun 1600-1930.*
Has information about Puerto Ayora
and Santa Cruz Island.

Ministerio de Turismo
*Charles Binford y 12 de Febrero,
T05-252 6174, Mon-Fri 0830-1300,
1430-1730.*
Mostly an administrative office but also
receives complaints about agencies
and vessels.

San Cristóbal
Puerto Baquerizo Moreno

Municipal tourist office
*Malecón Charles Darwin y 12 de Febrero,
T05-252 0119 ext 120, Mon-Fri 0730-1230,
1400-1800.*
Downstairs at the Municipio.

Ministerio de Turismo
*12 de Febrero e Ignacio Hernández,
T05-252 0704, Mon-Fri 0830-1230,
1400-1730.*
Operates as in Santa Cruz, above.

Isabela
Puerto Villamil

Municipal tourist office
*By the park, T05-252 9002, ext 113,
Mon-Fri 0730-1230, 1400-1700*
Has local information.

Where to stay

Santa Cruz
Puerto Ayora
Reservations are advised in high season.

$$$$ Angemeyer Waterfront Inn
*by the dock at Punta Estrada,
T05-252 6561, www.angermeyer-
waterfront-inn.com.*
Gorgeous location overlooking the bay.
Includes buffet breakfast, restaurant,
very comfortable modern rooms and
apartments, some with kitchenettes,
a/c, attentive service. Spa, pool and gym
under construction in 2015.

$$$$ Silberstein
*Darwin y Piqueros, T05-252 6277, Quito
T02-225 0553, www.hotelsilberstein.com.*
Modern and comfortable with lovely
grounds, pool in tropical garden, a/c,
buffet breakfast, restaurant, bar, spacious
rooms and common areas, very nice.

$$$$ Sol y Mar
*Darwin y Binford, T05-252 6281,
www.hotelsolymar.com.ec.*
Right in town but with a privileged
location overlooking the bay. Includes
buffet breakfast, restaurant, bar, pool,
jacuzzi and use of bicycles.

$$$ España
*Berlanga y 12 de Febrero, T05-252 6108,
www.hotelespanagalapagos.com.*
Pleasant and quiet, spacious rooms,
a/c, small courtyard with hammocks,
good value.

$$ Jean's Home
*Punta Estrada, T05-252 6446,
T09-9296 0347, gundisg@hotmail.es.*
Comfortably refurbished home in a
lovely out-of-the-way location (short

Puerto Ayora

50 metres

50 yards

Where to stay
1 España & Gardner
2 Estrella de Mar
3 Lobo de Mar
4 Los Amigos
5 Peregrina
6 Silberstein
7 Sol y Mar

Restaurants
1 El Descanso del Guía
2 Il Giardino
3 Isla Grill
4 La Dolce Italia
5 La Garrapata
6 Pizza Eat

water taxi ride from town), a/c, family-run, English and German spoken.

$$$ Lobo de Mar
12 de Febrero y Darwin, T05-252 6188, Quito T02-250 2089, www.lobodemar.com.ec.
Modern building with balconies and rooftop terrace, great views over the harbour. A/c, small pool, fridge, modern and comfortable, attentive service.

$$$ Peregrina
Darwin e Indefatigable, T05-252 6323, peregrinagalapagos@yahoo.com.
Away from the centre of town, a/c, nice rooms and common areas, small garden, family-run, homey atmosphere.

$$ Estrella de Mar
by the water on a lane off 12 de Febrero, T05-252 6427.
Quiet location with views over the bay. A/c, fan, fridge, spacious rooms, sitting area.

$$-$ Gardner
Berlanga y 12 de Febrero, T05-252 6979, hotelgardner@yahoo.com.
Clean comfortable rooms with a/c, cheaper with fan, private bath, kitchen facilities, breakfast available, good value.

$$-$ Los Amigos
Darwin y 12 de Febrero, T05-252 6265.
Small place, basic rooms with shared bath, cold water, fan, laundry facilities, good value.

Highlands of Santa Cruz

$$$$ Galápagos Safari Camp
T09-8296 8228, www.galapagossafaricamp.com.
Luxury resort with a central lodge and accommodation in comfortable, en suite tents. Includes breakfast and

dinner, swimming pool, organizes tours and activities.

$$$$ Semilla Verde
T05-301-3079, www.gps.ec.
Located on a 5-ha property being reforested with native plants. Comfortable rooms and common areas, includes breakfast, other meals available or use of kitchen facilities, British/ Ecuadorean-run, family atmosphere.

San Cristóbal
Puerto Baquerizo Moreno

$$$$ Miconia
Darwin e Isabela, T05-252 0608, www.hotelmiconia.com.
Restaurant, a/c, small pool, large well-equipped gym, modern if somewhat small rooms, some with fridge.

$$$ Blue Marlin
Española y Northía, T05-252 0253, www.bluemarlingalapagos.ec.

Puerto Baquerizo Moreno

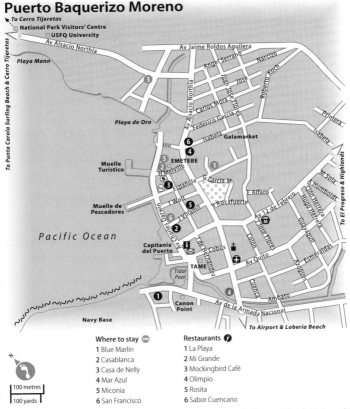

Where to stay 🛏
1 Blue Marlin
2 Casablanca
3 Casa de Nelly
4 Mar Azul
5 Miconia
6 San Francisco

Restaurants 🍴
1 La Playa
2 Mi Grande
3 Mockingbird Café
4 Olimpio
5 Rosita
6 Sabor Cuencano

Ample modern rooms are mostly wheelchair accessible, bathtubs, a/c, pool, fridge.

$$ Casablanca
Mellville y Darwin, T05-252 0392, www.casablancagalapagos.com.
Large white house with lovely terrace and views of the harbour. Each room is individually decorated by the owner who has an art gallery on the premises.

$$ Casa de Nelly
Tijeretas y Northía, T05-252 0112, www.casadenellygalapagos.com.ec.
3-storey building in a quiet location, bright comfortable rooms, a/c, kitchen facilities, family-run.

$$ Mar Azul
Northía y Esmeraldas, T05-252 0139, www.marazulgalapagos.com.
Comfortable lodgings, electric shower, a/c and fan, fridge, kitchen facilities, pleasant. Same family runs 2 more expensive hotels nearby.

$ San Francisco
Darwin y Villamil, T05-252 0304.
Simple rooms with private bath, cold water, fan, kitchen facilities, good value.

El Progreso

$$ Casa del Ceibo
Pto Baquerizo Moreno T05-252 0248.
A single unique room in the branches of a huge kapok tree. Private bath, hot water, ingenious design, US$1.50 to visit, advance booking required.

Isabela
Puerto Villamil
Many hotels have opened in recent years, more than we can list below.

$$$$ Albemarle
on the beachfront in town, T05-252 9489, www.hotelalbemarle.com.
Attractive Mediterranean-style construction, restaurant, bright comfortable rooms with wonderful ocean views, a/c, small pool.

$$$$ La Casa de Marita
at east end of beach, T05-252 9238, www.galapagosisabela.com.
Tastefully chic, includes breakfast, other meals on request, a/c and fridge, very comfortable, each room is slightly different, some have balconies. A little gem and recommended.

$$$ Caleta Iguana
Antonio Gil at west end of the beach, T05-301 6612, www.caletaiguana.com.
Comfortable rooms with fridge and fan, terrace overlooking the ocean, nice views, popular with upmarket surfers.

$$$ Casa Isabela on the Beach
on the beachfront in town, T05-252 9103, casitadelaplaya@hotmail.com, Quito office: Galacruises, www.islasgalapagos. travel.
Pleasant house on the beach, rooms with a/c, some have balconies, good ocean views.

$$$ La Laguna
Los Flamencos y Los Petreles, T05-349 7940, www.gruposanvicentegalapagos.com.
Pleasant rooms with a/c, attractive balconies and common areas, jacuzzi.

$$$ San Vicente
Cormoranes y Pinzón Artesano, T05-252 9140,www.gruposanvicentegalapagos.com.
Very popular and well-organized hotel which also offers tours and kayak rentals, includes breakfast, other meals on request or use of cooking facilities,

a/c, jacuzzi, rooms a bit small but nice, family-run.

$$ Hostal Villamil
10 de Marzo y Antonio Gil, T05-252 9180, www.gruposanvicentegalapagos.com.
A/c, kitchen and laundry facilities, small patio with hammocks, family-run and very friendly, good value. Recommended.

$$ The Jungle
off Antonio Gil at the west edge of town, T05-301 6690.
Good rooms with a/c, beach views, meals on request, secluded location away from the centre.

Highlands of Isabela

$$ Campo Duro
T09-8545 3045, refugiodetortugasgigantes@hotmail. com.
Camping (tents provided), includes breakfast and dinner, nice ample grounds, giant tortoises may be seen (US$2 to visit), friendly owner. Taxi from Pto Villamil, US$7.

Floreana
Puerto Velasco Ibarra

$$$$ Lava Lodge
book through **Tropic Journeys in Nature***, www.destinationecuador.com.*
Wooden cabins on the beach a short distance outside town, family-owned, full board, kayak, snorkel and SUP equipment, guided tours to wildlife and historic sites, popular with groups.

$$$ Hostal Santa María
opposite the school, T05-253 5022.
Modern rooms with private bath, hot water, fan, fridge, screened windows, friendly owner Sr Claudio Cruz.

$$$ Hotel Wittmer
right on Black Beach, T05-253 5013.
Lovely location with beautiful sunsets, simple comfortable rooms, electric shower, fan, very good meals available, family-run, German spoken, reservations required.

Restaurants

Santa Cruz
Puerto Ayora

$$$ Il Giardino
Charles Darwin y Charles Binford, T05-252 6627. Open 0800-2230, closed Tue.
Very good international food, service and atmosphere, excellent ice cream, very popular.

$$$ Isla Grill
Charles Darwin y Tomás de Berlanga, T05-252 4461. Tue-Sun 1200-2200.
Upmarket grill, seafood and pizza.

$$$ La Dolce Italia
Charles Darwin y 12 de Febrero. Daily 1100-1500, 1800-2200.
Italian and seafood, wine list, a/c, pleasant atmosphere, attentive owner.

$$$-$$ La Garrapata
Charles Darwin between 12 de Febrero and Tomás de Berlanga. Mon-Sat 0900-2200.
Good food, attractive setting and nice music.

$$ Kiosks
along Charles Binford between Padre Herrera and Rodríguez Lara.
Many kiosks serving tasty local fare, including a variety of seafood, outdoor seating, lively informal atmosphere, busy at night. Also beside the fishermen's dock at Pelican Bay, evenings only.

$$ Pizza Eat
Darwin y Berlanga.
A popular place for pizza and salads.

El Descanso del Guía
*Charles Darwin y Los Colonos. Daily
0645-1945.*
Good set meals, very popular with locals.

San Cristóbal
Puerto Baquerizo Moreno

$$$-$$ La Playa
*Av de la Armada Nacional, by the navy
base. Daily 0930-2330.*
Varied menu, fish and seafood.

$$$-$$ Olimpio
Northía y Isabela.
Closed Sun. Attractive restaurant
serving international food.

$$$-$$ Rosita
*Ignacio de Hernández y General Villamil.
Daily 0930-1430, 1700-2230.*
Old-time yachtie hangout, good food,
large portions, nice atmosphere, à
la carte and economical set meals.
Recommended.

$$ Descanso del Marinero
*Northia y Española. Open 0800-2100,
closed Tue.*
Ceviches and seafood, pleasant
outdoor seating.

$ Mi Grande
Villamil y Darwin, upstairs.
Popular for set meals and
good breakfast.

$ Several simple places serving
economical set meals on Northia
between Española and 12 de Febrero.
Also Sunday lunch up at El Progreso
good *comida del campo.*

Mockingbird Café
*Española y Hernández. Mon-Sat
0730-2330, Sun from 0930.*
Fruit juices, brownies, snacks, internet.

Sabor Cuencano
Northía y Isabela.
Good popular bakery. Closed Sun.

Isabela
Puerto Villamil

$$-$$ There are various outdoor
restaurants around the plaza all with
similar menus featuring seafood:
Cesar's, Los Delfines and Pepa's
are reported good.

$$-$ Isabela Grill
16 de Marzo y Flamencos.
Good choice for set lunch, dinner and
à la carte.

$ El Faro
*Las Fragatas ½ block from Plaza.
Daily 1200-1400, 1800-1930.*
Simple set lunch, grill at night, popular
with locals.

Floreana
Puerto Velasco Ibarra

$$-$$ Meals available at hotels or from
a couple of restaurants catering to tour
groups all require advance notice.

$$ Lelia Restaurante
opposite the school, T05-253 5041.
Good home cooking. Friendly owner
also has two rooms for rent.

$ The Devil's Crown
*100 m from the dock on the road to
the highlands.*
Set lunch and dinner on most days, ask
in advance.

ACTIVITY

Dive boats

Name	Type	Capacity	Website	Class
Aggressor III	MY	16	www.aggressor.com	L
Astrea	MY	16	various	TS
Deep Blue	MY	16	various	F
Galapagos Sky	MY	16	www.galapagossky.com	L
Humbolt Explorer	MY	16	www.galasam.net	F
Pingüino Explorer	MY	16	www.galacruises.com	TS
Encantada	2mSch	12	www.scubagalapagos.com	T
Nortada	MY	8	www.galapagosnortada.com	F

MY = motor yacht   **L** = luxury   **F** = first class
2mSch = 2-masted schooner   **TS** = tourist superior   **T** = tourist

Shopping

Most items can be purchased on the islands but cost more than in mainland Ecuador. Do not buy anything made of black coral as it is an endangered species.

Santa Cruz
Puerto Ayora
There is an attractive little **Mercado Artesanal** (craft market) at Charles Darwin y Tomás de Berlanga. **Proinsular**, opposite the pier, is the largest and best-stocked supermarket in Galápagos.

San Cristóbal
Puerto Baquerizo Moreno
Galamarket, Isabela y Juan José Flores, is a modern well-stocked supermarket.

What to do

Santa Cruz: Puerto Ayora
Cycling
Mountain bikes can be hired from travel agencies in Puerto Ayora. Prices and quality vary, about US$15-20 for 3 hrs.

Diving
See diving box, page 368:
Dive Center Silberstein, opposite Hotel Silberstein, T05-252 6028, www.divingalapagos.com. Day tours in nice comfortable boat for up to 8 guests, English-speaking guides, good service, dive courses and trips for all levels of experience. Island-hopping dive tours and 8-day diving cruises also organized.
Nautidiving, Av Charles Darwin, T05-252 7004. Offers day-trips to central islands as well as longer trips.
Scuba Iguana, Charles Darwin near the research station, T05-252 6497, www.scubaiguana.com. Matías Espinoza runs this reliable and recommended dive operator. Courses up to PADI Dive Master.

Horse riding
For riding at ranches in the highlands, enquire at **Moonrise Travel** (see below).

Snorkelling
Masks, snorkels and fins can be rented from travel agencies and dive shops, US$5 a day, deposit required. Las Grietas is a popular place to snorkel near Puerto Ayora.

ACTIVITY
Scuba diving

The Galápagos are among the most desirable scuba diving destinations in the world. At first look you might wonder why, with cold water, strong currents, difficult conditions and limited visibility (15 m or less). So what is the attraction?

Marine life
There is a profusion and variety of animals here that you won't find anywhere else, and so close up that you won't mind the low visibility. Not just reef fish and schooling fish and pelagic fish, but also sea lions, turtles, whalesharks, schools of hammerheads, flocks of several species of rays, diving birds, whales and dolphins; an exuberant diversity including many endemic species. You could be with a Galápagos marine iguana, the world's only lizard that dives and feeds in the sea, or perhaps meet a glittering man-sized sailfish. Make no mistake, this is no tame theme park: Galápagos is adventure diving, where any moment could surprise you.

Dive options
There are basically two options for diving in the Galápagos: live-aboard dive cruises and hotel-based day trips. Live-aboard operations usually expect the divers to bring their own equipment, and supply only lead and tanks. The day trip dive operators supply everything. Day trip diving is mostly offered by boats operating out of Puerto Ayora, as well as a couple of operators in Puerto Baquerizo Moreno and Puerto Villamil.

Live-aboard dive cruises (typically 10 days) can only be done on specialized boats, of which there are few and usually reserved far in advance. You cannot dive as part of an ordinary Galápagos cruise.

Day trip diving is more economical and spontaneous, often arranged at the dive shop the evening before. The distances between islands limit the range of the day trip boats to the central islands. Nevertheless, day boats can offer reliable service and superb dive locations including Gordon Rocks, world-famous for schooling hammerheads. The day trip dive boats cannot take passengers ashore at the usual visitors' sites but you can always do some diving day trips before or after a regular Galápagos cruise. A few live-aboard diving vessels may operate as dive boats for one week then as regular cruise boats the next, allowing for a combined experience.

See page 370 for details of companies offering diving tours and services. For a list of live-aboard dive boats see table, page 367. Live-aboard diving cruises currently cost about US$800 per person per day.

General advice
Visitors should be aware of some of the special conditions in Galápagos. The national park includes practically all of the land and the surrounding waters. The national park prohibits collecting samples or souvenirs, spear-fishing,

touching animals, or other environmental disruptions. Guides apply the national park rules, and they can stop your participation if you do not cooperate. The experienced dive guides can help visitors have the most spectacular opportunities to enjoy the wildlife.

Nonetheless, diving requires self reliance and divers are encouraged to refresh their skills and have equipment serviced before the trip. Though the day-trip operators can offer introductory dives and complete certification training, this is not a place for a complete novice to come for a diving vacation. On many dives you could meet any combination of current, surge, cold water, poor visibility, deep bottom and big animals.

Like many exotic dive destinations, medical care is limited. There is a hyperbaric chamber in Puerto Ayora, the cost is high so you must carry adequate insurance or confirm with your tour operator whether they have coverage. To avoid the risk of decompression sickness, divers are advised to stay an extra day on the islands after their last dive before flying to the mainland, especially to Quito at 2840 m above sea level.

Dive sites
Santa Fe This site offers wall dives, rock reefs, shallow caves, fantastic scenery and usually has clear calm water. You can dive with sea lions, schooling fish, pelagic fish, moray eels, rays and Galápagos sharks. Like everywhere in Galápagos, you should expect the unexpected.

Seymour Norte You can see sea lions, reef fish, hammerhead sharks, giant manta rays and white tip reef sharks. Occasionally whalesharks, humpback whale and porpoises.

Floreana Island The dive sites are offshore islets, each with its own character and scenery. Devil's Crown is a fractured ring of spiked lava around coral reefs. Champion is a little crater with a nesting colony of boobies, sea lion beaches and underwater rocky shelves of coral and reef fish. Enderby is an eroded tuff cone where you often meet large pelagics: rays, turtles, tunas and sharks. Gardner has a huge natural arch like a cathedral's flying buttress. These and other islets offer diving with reef fish, schooling fish, sea lions, invertebrates, rays, moray eels, white tip reef sharks, turtles, big fish including amberjack, red snapper, and grouper. Sometimes you can see giant mantas, hammerheads, Galápagos sharks, whales, seahorses, and the bizarre red-lipped batfish.

Gordon Rocks Just north of the Plazas are two large rocks that are all that remains of the rim of a long-extinct volcano. On the inner side of the collapsed caldera rim the seabed is a mass of rocks jumbled over each other, while on the outer wall the sea drops away into thousands of feet of water. Currents here are exceptionally strong and the local name for the dive site is *La Lavadora* (washing machine). Here you can see schools of hammerheads, amberjacks and pompano, eagle rays, golden cowrays, whitetips and turtles.

Surfing
There is surfing at Tortuga Bay and at other more distant beaches accessed by boat. Look for the surf club office at Pelican Bay. There is better surfing near Puerto Baquerizo Moreno on San Cristóbal. The **Lonesome George** agency rents surfboards, see below.

Tour operators
Avoid touts offering cheap tours at the airport or in the street. Also be wary of agencies that specialize in cut-rate cruises. **Lonesome George**, Av Baltra y Enrique Fuentes, T05-252 6245, lonesomegrg@ yahoo.com. Run by Victor Vaca. Sells tours and rents: bicycles (US$3 per hr), surfboards (US$30 per day) snorkelling equipment and motorcycles.
Moonrise Travel, Av Charles Darwin y Charles Binford, T05-252 6348, www. galapagosmoonrise.com. Last-minute cruise bookings, day-tours, bay tours, airline reservations, run guesthouse in Punta Estrada and rent chalets by Playa de los Alemanes. Owner Jenny Devine is knowledgeable and helpful.

San Cristóbal: Puerto Baquerizo Moreno
Cycling
Bike rentals US$3 per hr, US$15 per day.

Diving
See scuba diving box, page 368. There are several dive sites around San Cristóbal, most popular being Kicker Rock, Roca Ballena and Punta Pitt, full day about US$200, see Tour operators below.

Kayaking
Rentals US$10 per hr; from **Islander's Store**, Av J Roldós, above cargo pier, T05-252 0348; and **Galápagos Eco**

Expedition, Av de la Armada, next to La Playa restaurant.

Surfing
There is good surfing in San Cristóbal, the best season is Dec-Mar. Punta Carola near town is the closest surfing beach; other spots are Canon and Tongo Reef, past the navy base. There is a championship during the local *fiesta*, the 2nd week of Feb.

Tour operators
Canon Point, Armada Nacional y Darwin. Rents bikes, skate boards and surfboards.
Chalo Tours, Darwin y Villamil, T05-252 0953, chalotours@hotmail.com. Specializes in diving and snorkelling.
Sharksky, Darwin y Villamil, T05-252 1188, www.sharksky.com. Highlands, diving, snorkelling, island-hopping, last-minute cruise bookings and gear rental. Also has an office on Isabela. Swiss/ Ecuadorean-run, English, German and French spoken, helpful.
Wreck Bay Dive Center, Darwin y Wolf, T05-252 1663, www.wreckbay.com. Reported friendly and respectful of the environment.

Isabela: Puerto Villamil
Tour operators
Hotels also arrange tours. Kayak rentals at **Hotel San Vicente**. For diving, see box, page 368.
Galápagos Dive Center, 16 de Marzo y Cormoranes, T05-301 6570. Dive trips, diving gear sale and rental.
Galapagos Native, Cormoranes y 16 de Marzo, T05-252 9140, www. gruposanvicentegalapagos.com. Mountain biking downhill from Sierra Negra, full day including lunch, US$42. Also rentals: good bikes US$3 per hr,

ACTIVITY

Galápagos tourist vessels

Name	Type	Capacity	Website	Class
Galapagos Legend	CS	100	kleintours.com	L
Silver Galapagos	CS	100	silversea.com	L
Xpedition	CS	100	galapagosxpedition.co.uk	L
Santa Cruz	CS	90	metropolitan-touring.com	L
Eclipse	CS	48	oagalapagos.com	L
Isabela II	CS	40	metropolitan-touring.com	L
Evolution	MV	32	galapagosxpeditions.com	L
La Pinta	CS	32	metropolitan-touring.com	L
Integrity	MY	16	inca1.com	L
Queen Beatriz	MC	16	peakdmc.com	L
Coral I	MY	36	kleintours.com	F
Flamingo I	MY	20	ecoventura.com	F
Anahi	MC	16	andandotours.com	F
Archipel II	MC	16	galacruises.com	F
Beluga	MY	16	enchantedexpeditions.com	F
Cachalote	2mSch	16	enchantedexpeditions.com	F
Grand Odyssey	MY	16	galapagosgrandodyssey.com	F
Mary Anne	3mBarq	16	andandotours.com	F
Seaman Journey	MC	16	galapagosjourneycruises.com	F
Stellamaris	MY	16	galasam.net	F
Tip Top IV	MY	16	rwittmer.com	F
Treasure of Galapagos	MC	16	treasureofgalapagos.com	F
Beagle	2mSch	13	galapagosexperience.net	F
Nemo II	MC	12	nemogalapagoscruises.com	F
Monserrat	MY	20	monserrat-cruise.info	TS
Aída María	MY	16	aidamariatravel.com	TS
Archipel I	MY	16	galacruises.com	TS
Cormorant Evolution	MC	16	haugancruises.com	TS
Floreana	MY	16	yatefloreana.com	TS
Fragata	MY	16	yatefragata.com	TS
Samba	SV	14	galapagosexperience.net	TS
Galaxy I	MC	16	galagents.com	T
Golondrina	MY	16	golondrinaturismo.com	T
Guantanamera	MY	16	ecuadortierradefuego.com	T
Nemo III	MC	16	nemogalapagoscruises.com	T
Petrel	MC	16	haugancruises.com	T

CS = cruise ship
MY = motor yacht
MV = motor vessel
MC = motor catamaran

2mSch = 2-masted schooner
3mSch = 3-masted schooner
3mBarq = 3-masted barquentine
SV = sailing vessel

L = luxury
F = first
TS = tourist superior
T = tourist class

US$20 per day; snorkelling gear US$5 per day; surf boards US$4 per hr.
Isabela Dive Center, Escalecias y Alberto Gil, T05-252 9418, www.isabeladivecenter. com.ec. Diving, land and boat tours.

Transport

Air

Avianca, LAN and **TAME** all fly from **Quito** and **Guayaquil** to Baltra or San Cristóbal. Baltra receives more flights but there is at least one daily to each destination. You can arrive at one and return from the other. You can also depart from Quito and return to Guayaquil or vice versa, but you may not buy a one-way ticket. The return airfare varies considerably, starting at about US$500 from Quito, US$400 from Guayaquil (2015 prices); slightly lower fares may be available if you purchase in advance. See also Fees and inspections, page 357.

Buses meet flights from the mainland at **Baltra**: some run to the port or muelle (10 mins, no charge) where the cruise boats wait; others go to Canal de Itabaca, the narrow channel which separates Baltra from Santa Cruz. It is 15 mins to the Canal (free), then you cross on a small ferry (US$1). On the other side, buses (US$2, may involve a long wait while they fill) and pickup truck taxis (US$18 for up to 4 passengers) run to **Puerto Ayora**, 45 mins. For the return trip to the airport, buses leave the Terminal Terrestre on Avenida Baltra in Puerto Ayora (2 km from the pier, taxi US$1) at 0700, 0730 and 0830 daily.

Inter-island flights in light aircraft are available with **Emetebe Avionetas**, www.emetebe.com.ec. There are 2 daily flights (except Sun) between **Puerto Baquerizo Moreno** (San Cristóbal), **Baltra** and **Puerto Villamil**

(Isabela). All fares US$165 one way; baggage allowance 25 lbs.

Sea

Lanchas (speedboats with 3 large engines and capacity for about 20 passengers) run daily from **Puerto Ayora** on Santa Cruz (from the pier near the volleyball courts, see map) to each of the following: **Puerto Baquerizo Moreno (San Cristóbal)** at 1400; **Puerto Villamil (Isabela)** at 0730 and 1400; **Puerto Velasco Ibarra (Floreana)** at 0700; all fares US$30, 2 hrs or more depending on the weather and sea conditions. Tickets are sold by several agencies in, Puerto Ayora, and Puerto Villamil; purchase a day before travelling. This can be a wild ride in rough seas, life vests provided, take drinking water.

Pickup truck taxis

These may be hired for transport throughout Puerto Ayora (Santa Cruz), US$1. A *ranchera* runs up to the highlands from the **Tropidurus** store, Av Baltra y Jaime Roldóss, 2 blocks past the market: to **Bellavista** US$0.50, 10 mins; **Santa Rosa** US$1, 20 mins.

Water taxis

Water taxis (*taxis acuáticos*) run from the pier in Puerto Ayora (Santa Cruz) to Punta Estrada or anchored boats, US$0.60 during the day, US$2 at night.

Yacht agents

All yachts must use an agent, regulations are strictly enforced. **Galápagos Ocean Services** (Peter Schiess), Charles Darwin next to Garrapata restaurant, Puerto Ayora, Santa Cruz, T09-9477 0804, www.gos.ec. **Naugala Yacht Services** (Jhonny Romero), Puerto Ayora, Santa Cruz, T05-252 7403, www.naugala.com.

Background Galápagos Islands

Geography and geology

Lying on the equator, 970 km west of the Ecuadorean coast, the Galápagos are not structurally connected to the mainland and, so far as is known, were never part of the South American Plate. They lie near the boundary between the Nazca Plate and the Cocos Plate to the north. A line of weakness, evidenced by a ridge of undersea lava flows, stretches southwest from the coast of Panama. This meets another undersea ridge running along the equator from Ecuador but separated from the continental shelf by a deep trench. At this conjuncture appear the Galápagos. Volcanic activity here has been particularly intense and the islands are the peaks of structures that rise over 7000 m from the deepest parts of the adjacent ocean floor. The oldest islands are San Cristóbal and Española in the east of the archipelago: three to 3½ million years old. The youngest ones, Fernandina and Isabela, lie to the west, and are between 700,000 and 800,000 years old. In geological terms, therefore, the Galápagos Islands have only recently appeared from the ocean and volcanic activity continues on at least five of them.

Evolution and wildlife

Galápagos has unique marine and terrestrial environments. This is due to the continuing volcanic formation of the islands in the west of the archipelago and its location at the nexus of several major marine currents, among other factors. Their interaction has created laboratory-type conditions where only certain species have been allowed access. Others have been excluded, and the resulting ecology has evolved in a unique direction, with many of the ecological niches being filled from some unexpected angles. A highly evolved sunflower, for instance, has in some areas taken over the niche left vacant by the absence of trees. There are also formidable barriers which prevent many species from travelling within the islands, hence a very high level of endemism. For example, each of the five main volcanoes on Isabela has evolved its own subspecies of giant tortoise.

Charles Darwin recognized this speciation within the archipelago when he visited the Galápagos on the Beagle in 1835 and his observations played a substantial part in his formulation of the theory of evolution. Since no large land mammals reached the islands (until they were recently introduced by man), reptiles were dominant just as they had been all over the world in the very distant past. Another extraordinary feature of the islands is the tameness of the animals. The islands were uninhabited when they were discovered in 1535 and the animals still have little instinctive fear of man.

Galápagos National Park and Marine Reserve

The Galápagos are a UNESCO World Heritage Site and 97% of the land area and 100% of the surrounding ocean are part of the Galápagos National Park and Marine Reserve. Within the park there are some 70 visitor sites, each with defined trails, so the impact of visitors to this fragile environment is minimized. There are

Difficult choices for Galápagos

As you enjoy your unforgettable Galápagos experience, consider the future of the islands. Are they first and foremost a sanctuary, a treasure so unique and precious for all mankind as to merit the strictest conservation in the sovereign custody of Ecuador? Or is Galápagos primarily a province of a developing South American republic, with natural resources to be exploited for the enjoyment of visitors and to satisfy the economic needs of residents? And who decides?

also designated dive site in the marine reserve. These sites can only be visited with a national park guide as part of a cruise or tour.

Each of the visitor sites has been carefully chosen to show the different flora and fauna and, due to the high level of endemism, nearly every trail has flora and fauna that can be seen nowhere else in the world. The itineraries of tourist boats are strictly regulated in order to avoid crowding at the visitor sites and some sites are periodically closed by the park authorities in order to allow them to recover from the impact of tourism. Certain sites are only open to smaller boats and, additionally, limited to a maximum number of visits per month.

The 3% of Galápagos which is not national park is made up of towns and agricultural zones on four populated islands: Santa Cruz, San Cristóbal, Isabela and Floreana. However, there are also large restricted areas of national park land on these islands.

History of human settlement

The finding of fragments of ceramics suggests that the islands might have been visited by pre-Columbian sailors from the coast of Ecuador. They were uninhabited, however, when discovered accidentally by Tomás de Berlanga, the Bishop of Panama, in 1535. He was on his way to Peru when his ship was becalmed and swept 800 km off course by the currents. Like most of the early arrivals, Bishop Tomás and his crew arrived thirsty and disappointed at the dryness of the place. He did not even give the islands a name, although he did dub the giant tortoises *galápagos*.

The islands first appeared on a map in 1574, as Islands of Galápagos, which has remained in common use ever since. The individual islands, though, have had several names, both Spanish and English. The latter names come from visits by English buccaneers who used the Galápagos as a hideout, in particular a spot North of James Bay on Santiago Island, still known as Buccaneers' Cove. The pirates were the first to visit many of the islands and they named them after English kings and aristocracy or famous captains of the day.

The Spanish called the islands Las Encantadas, 'enchanted' or 'bewitched', owing to the fact that for much of the year they are surrounded by mists giving the impression that they appear and disappear as if by magic. Also, the tides and currents were so confusing that they thought the islands were floating and not real islands.

BACKGROUND
Charles Darwin and the Galápagos

Without a doubt, the most famous visitor to the islands is Charles Darwin and his brief stay on the archipelago proved hugely significant.

In September 1835, Darwin sailed into Galápagos waters on board the HMS Beagle, captained by the aristocratic Robert FitzRoy whose job was to chart lesser-known parts of the world. FitzRoy had wanted on board a companion of his own social status and a naturalist, to study the strange new animals and plants they would find en route. He chose Charles Darwin to fill both roles.

Darwin was only 22 years old when he set sail from England in 1831 and it would be five years before he saw home again. They were to sail around the world, but most of the voyage was devoted to surveying the shores of South America, giving Darwin the chance to explore a great deal of the continent. The visit to the Galápagos was just a short stop on the return journey, by which time Darwin had become an experienced observer.

During the six weeks that the Beagle spent in the Galápagos, Darwin went ashore to collect plants, rocks, insects and birds. The unusual life forms and their adaptations to the harsh surroundings made a deep impression on him and eventually inspired his revolutionary theory on the evolution of species. The Galápagos provided a kind of model of the world in miniature. Darwin realized that these recently created volcanoes were young in comparison with the age of the Earth, and that life on the islands showed special adaptations. Yet the plants and animals also showed similarities to those from the South American mainland, where he guessed they had originally come from.

Darwin concluded that the life on the islands had probably arrived there by chance drifting, swimming or flying from the mainland and had not been created on the spot. Once the plants and animals had arrived, they evolved into forms better suited to the strange environment in which they found themselves. Darwin also noted that the animals were extremely tame, because of the lack of predators. The islands' isolation also meant that the giant tortoises did not face competition from more agile mammals and could survive.

On his return to England, Darwin in effect spent the rest of his life developing the ideas inspired by the Galápagos. It was, however, only when another scientist, named Alfred Russel Wallace, arrived at a similar conclusion to his own that he dared to publish a paper on his theory of evolution. Then followed his all-embracing The Origin of Species by means of natural selection, in 1859. It was to cause a major storm of controversy and to earn Charles Darwin recognition as the man who "provided a foundation for the entire structure of modern biology".

Between 1780 and 1860, the waters around the Galápagos became a favourite place for British and American whaling ships. At the beginning of the whaling

One of the more bizarre and notorious periods of human life on the Galápagos began on Floreana Island in 1929 with the arrival of German doctor and philosopher, Friedrich Ritter, and his mistress, Dore Strauch. Three years later, the Wittmer family, attracted in part by Ritter's writings, also decided to settle there. Floreana soon became so fashionable that luxury yachts used to call. One visitor was Baroness von Wagner de Bosquet, an Austrian woman who settled on the island with her two lovers and grandiose plans to build a hotel for millionaires.

Soon after landing in 1932, the Baroness proclaimed herself Empress of Floreana, which was not to the liking of Dr Ritter or the Wittmer family, and tensions rose. There followed several years of mysterious and unsavoury goings-on, during which everyone either died or disappeared, except Dore Strauch and the Wittmer family. The longest survivor of this still unexplained drama was Margret Wittmer, who lived at Black Beach on Floreana until her death in 2000, at age 95. Her account of life there, entitled *Floreana, Poste Restante*, was published in 1961 and became a bestseller, but she took the story of what really happened on the island in the 1930s with her to the grave. A fascinating and impartial account is given in *The Galápagos Affair*, by John Treherne.

era, in 1793, a British naval captain erected a barrel on Floreana Island to facilitate communication between boats and the land. It is still in Post Office Bay to this day.

The first island to be inhabited was Floreana, in 1807, by a lone Irishman named Patrick Watkins, who grew vegetables to trade for rum with passing ships. After two years he commandeered a lifeboat and a handful of sailors but later arrived in Guayaquil without his companions, who were never seen again. After his departure the Galápagos were again uninhabited for 25 years, but the bizarre episode set the tone for many more unusual colonists and nefarious events. Their story is told in The Curse of the Tortoise, by Octavio Latorre.

In 1832, Ecuadorean General José Villamil founded a colony on Floreana, mainly composed of convicts and political prisoners, who traded meat and vegetables with whalers. The same year, following the creation of the young republic, Colonel Ignacio Hernández took official possession of the archipelago for Ecuador. Spanish names were given to the islands, in addition to the existing English ones, and both remain in use.

From 1880 to 1904 Manuel J Cobos ran a large sugar cane plantation and cattle ranch on San Cristóbal, notorious for mistreatment of its workers who eventually mutinied and killed him. The cruelty of prison colonies and slave farms like Cobos' cast a dark shadow over human presence in the archipelago.

There followed Norwegian fishermen and German philosophers, among others, many of whom met with some strange and tragic fate. Among the earliest colonists to endure were the Wittmer family on Floreana and the Angermeyers on Santa Cruz, whose story is beautifully told in My Father's Island, by Johanna Angermeyer.

From these small and erratic beginnings, Galápagos became the fastest growing province in Ecuador. In an attempt to protect the islands, controls on migration from the mainland were imposed in 2000 but these are frequently circumvented. Residents of the islands, now into their third and fourth generation, still call themselves *colonos* (colonists).

Tourists and settlers

The most devastating of the newly introduced species are human beings, both tourists and settlers. To a large degree, the two groups are connected, one supporting the other economically, but there is also a sizeable proportion who make an income independent of tourism by working the land or at sea.

While no great wealth has accumulated to those who farm, fortunes have been made by exporters and fishermen in a series of particularly destructive fisheries: black coral, lobster, shark fin, sea cucumber and sea horse. It is, however, farmers who are responsible for the largest number of introduced species. These include cattle, goats, donkeys, pigs, dogs, rats and ani (used to eat parasites living on cattle – although in the Galápagos it prefers baby finches when it can get them), and over 500 species of plants such as elephant grass (to provide pastures), guava trees (which have become a plague on Isabela) and tilapia in El Junco lake on San Cristóbal. The unchecked expansion of these introduced species has upset the natural balance of the archipelago. There are now quarantine programs and any domestic animals must be neutered before they can be brought to the islands. There have also been campaigns to eradicate introduced species on some islands, but this is inevitably a very slow, expensive and difficult process.

Galápagos is also a victim of its success as a tourist destination. The number of tourists has grown steadily: from 11,800 in 1979, to 68,900 in 2000, to approximately 210,000 in 2014. The prosperity achieved through tourism has created a strong demand for workers from the poorer mainland and hence fuelled rapid population growth. The rising number of inhabitants need more and more infrastructure: services such as drinking water, sewage systems, electricity, transportation, schools, hospitals, etc, all of which place a growing burden on the unique and fragile natural environment. The islands and tour boats need fuel and there have been minor oil spills which, through good fortune alone, did not cause irreparable damage. With generous international financing, a wind-powered electric generating system was implemented on San Cristóbal, but even this is not without its environmental consequences, interfering as it does with the local petrel population.

From 2007 to 2010, Galápagos was on the UNESCO list of endangered World Heritage Sites. Although it is now off the list, promoting environmental conservation and sustainable development in the face of growing tourism and population remains a substantial challenge.

Background
Ecuador

History & politics

Earliest civilizations

The oldest archaeological artefacts that have been uncovered in Ecuador date back to approximately 10,000 BC. They include obsidian spear tips and belong to a pre-ceramic period during which the region's inhabitants are thought to have been nomadic hunters, fishers and gatherers. A subsequent formative period (4000-500 BC) saw the development of pottery, presumably alongside agriculture and fixed settlements. One of these settlements, known as Valdivia, existed along the coast of Ecuador and remains of buildings and earthenware figures have been found dating from 3500-1500 BC (see box, page 257).

Between 500 BC and AD 500, many different cultures evolved in all the geographic regions of what is today Ecuador. Among these were the Bahía, Guangalá, Jambelí and Duale-Tejar of the coast; Narrío, Tuncahuán and Panzaleo in the highlands; and Upano, Cosanga and Yasuní in Oriente. The period AD 500-1480 was an era of integration, during which dominant or amalgamated groups emerged. These included, from north to south in the Sierra, the Imbayas, Shyris, Quitus, Puruhaes and Cañaris; and the Caras, Manteños and Huancavilcas along the coast.

This rich and varied mosaic of ancient cultures is today considered the bedrock of Ecuador's national identity. It was confronted, in the mid-15th century, with the relentless northward expansion of the most powerful prehispanic empire on the continent: the Incas.

The Inca Empire

The Inca Kingdom already existed in southern Peru from the 11th century. It was not until the mid-15th century, however, that the empire began to expand northwards. Pachacuti Yupanqui became ruler of the Incas in 1428 and, along with his son **Túpac Yupanqui**, led the conquest of the Andean highlands north into present-day Ecuador. The Cañaris fiercely resisted for many years but were defeated around 1470. Their northern counterparts fought on for some decades, defeating various Inca armies.

Huayna Capac, Túpac Yupanqui's son, was probably born in Tomebamba (present-day Cuenca), although some claim he was born in Cuzco. Tomebamba eventually became one of the most important centres of the Inca Empire. Quito was finally captured in 1492 (a rather significant year) and became the base from which the Incas extended their territory even further north. A great road was built between Cuzco and Quito, but the empire was eventually divided; it was ruled after the death of Huayna Capac by his two sons, **Huáscar** at Cuzco and **Atahualpa** at Quito.

BACKGROUND
Ecuador fact file

Population: 14.5 million (2010 census)
Urban population: 64%
Population density: 56.4 inhabitants per sq km
Population growth rate: 1.5% per year (2001-2010)
Infant mortality: 17 per 1000 live births
Life expectancy at birth: 76 years
Literacy: 91%
Minimum wage: US$354 a month
Gross Domestic Product per capita: US$6270

Conquest and colonial rule

Civil war broke out between the two halves of the empire, and in 1532 Atahualpa secured victory over Huáscar and established his capital in Cajamarca, in northern Peru. In the same year, conquistador **Francisco Pizarro** set out from Tumbes, on the Peru-Ecuador border, finally reaching Cajamarca. There, he captured the Inca leader and put him to death in 1533. This effectively ended Inca resistance and their empire collapsed.

Pizarro claimed the northern kingdom of Quito, and his lieutenants **Sebastián de Benalcázar** and **Diego de Almagro** took the city in 1534. Pizarro founded Lima in 1535 as capital of the whole region and four years later replaced Benalcázar at Quito with Gonzalo, his brother. **Gonzalo Pizarro** later set out on the exploration of the Oriente. He moved down the Napo river, and sent **Francisco de Orellana** ahead to prospect. Orellana did not return. He drifted down the river finally to reach the mouth of the Amazon, thus becoming the first white man to cross the continent in this way; an event which is still considered significant in the history of Ecuador (see box, page 294).

Quito became a *real audiencia* under the viceroyalty of Peru. For the next 280 years Ecuador reluctantly accepted the new ways brought by the conquerors. Gonzalo Pizarro had already introduced pigs and cattle; wheat was now added. The native people were Christianized and colonial laws, customs and ideas were introduced. The marriage of the arts of Spain to those of the Inca led to a remarkable efflorescence of painting, sculpture and building in Quito, one of the very few positive effects of conquest, which otherwise effectively enslaved the natives. In the 18th century, the production and export of cacao began and black slave labour was brought in to work cacao and sugar plantations.

Independence and the 19th century

Ecuadorean independence came about in several stages beginning in 1809, but was not completed until royalist forces were defeated by **Antonio José de Sucre** in the Battle of Pichincha in 1822. For the next eight years Ecuador was a province of Gran Colombia under the leadership of **Simón Bolívar**. As Gran Colombia collapsed in 1830, Ecuador at last became a fully independent nation.

Following independence, Ecuadorean politics were dominated by various elites. They were sometimes divided along regional lines (Quito and the highlands versus Guayaquil and the coast) and frequently fought among each other. Rule by rival oligarchies under the cloak of constitutional democracy or military dictatorship, has proved to be an enduring theme in Ecuadorean history.

Ecuador has had a great many presidents, but two diametrically opposed leaders are emblematic of their times. **Gabriel García Moreno** (president 1860-1865 and 1869-1875) was an arch-conservative, renowned for his cruel dictatorship and attempts to force Catholicism on the entire population; he denied citizenship to non-Catholics. He was eventually hacked to death by machete at the entrance of the presidential palace in Quito. **Eloy Alfaro** (1895-1901 and 1906-1911), was precisely the opposite, a liberal who sought to bring Ecuador into the modern world, based on revenues from the cacao boom. He introduced secular education, civil marriage and divorce, confiscated church lands and abolished capital punishment. Assassinated by his opponents, Alfaro's body was dragged through the streets of Quito before being publicly burned. García Moreno and Alfaro had more in common than their gruesome fate, both were *caudillos* (strong-men) who ruled by force of arms, as well as charisma. *Caudillismo* also remains an enduring feature of Ecuadorean public life.

The 20th century

Ecuadorean politics have long kept time with the country's fragile economy, with greater stability during occasional periods of prosperity and chaos during the more frequent lean years. The Great Depression exemplified the latter. Between 1931 and 1948 there were 21 governments, none of which succeeded in completing its term of office. "There were ministers who lasted hours, presidents who lasted for days, and dictators who lasted for weeks." (G Abad, *El proceso de lucha por el poder en el Ecuador*, Mexico 1970.) Political stability was only restored with the growth of coastal banana plantations created a fresh source of national revenue after the cacao boom had gone bust. The country's next larger-than-life president was **José María Velasco Ibarra**, a fiery orator who was elected four times in the 1950s and 1960s, and ousted each time by a military coup.

Like most other South American countries Ecuador experienced several periods of military rule during the 1960s and 1970s, but it did not suffer the widespread human rights abuses which took places in some other nations. Since 1979, Ecuador has enjoyed its longest period of civilian constitutional government since independence. In 1978 a young and charismatic **Jaime Roldós** was elected president, but died three years later in a still-mysterious plane crash. The following twenty years saw a series of governments which ostensibly alternated between the political right and left but, in practice, were little different from one another.

One of the outstanding personalities of this period was **León Febres Cordero** of the right-wing **Partido Social Cristiano**, strong-armed president 1984-1988, then twice popular mayor of Guayaquil and twice member of Congress. Equally newsworthy was **Abdalá Bucaram** of the populist **Partido Roldosista Ecuatoriano**, who was swept to power in 1996, but lasted barely six months. In 1997, following mass demonstrations, Congress voted to remove him on the grounds of 'mental incapacity'. Febres Cordero and Bucaram were Ecuador's late 20th century caudillos par excellence.

Jamil Mahuad of the **Democracia Popular** was narrowly elected president in 1998, amid border tensions with Peru. He diffused this explosive situation and signed a definitive peace treaty, putting an end to decades – even centuries – of conflict (see Peru, below). This early success was Mahuad's last, as a series of bank failures sent the country into an economic and political tailspin. In a desperate bid for stability, Mahuad decreed the adoption of the US dollar as the national currency in 1999. Less than a month later, in January 2000, he was forced out of office by Ecuador's indigenous peoples and disgruntled members of the armed forces. The coup lasted barely three hours before power was transferred to vice-president **Gustavo Noboa** and Mahuad joined the ranks of other Ecuadorean politicians in exile. Noboa, with assistance from the USA and the International Monetary Fund (IMF), was left to flesh out and implement the dollarization scheme.

Modern Ecuador

21st-century politics

In 2002 **Colonel Lucio Gutiérrez**, leader of the **Partido Sociedad Patriótica** (PSP) and leader of the 2000 coup, was elected president. He had run on a populist platform in alliance with the indigenous movement and labour unions, but began to change his stripes soon after taking office. In 2005, he became the third Ecuadorean president in eight years to be deposed by popular unrest. The colonel briefly took asylum in Brazil but soon returned home to again become an active political player.

In 2006, with disenchantment in the democratic process at an understandable high after so much political tragicomedy, **Rafael Correa**, a 43-year-old economics professor and leader of the **Alianza País (AP)** movement, was elected president. He came to office with a well-defined social and economic agenda and immediately convened a constituent assembly. The assembly drew up Ecuador's 19th constitution, which espouses *sumak kawsay* – a Quichua term roughly meaning 'quality of life' – as the fundamental goal of society. The new socially oriented charter was approved by nationwide referendum in 2008, and Correa was re-elected president in 2009 with a 52% majority and again in 2013 with 57%.

The Correa administration's affinity with other so called '21st-century socialist' governments (such as Venezuela, Bolivia and Nicaragua) has drawn international attention but there have been no expropriations of property nor other drastic measures in Ecuador. Rather, the country entered another boom phase of it's cyclic development due mostly to high petroleum prices and even cocao exports once again flourished. The resulting revenues along with heavy borrowing from China allowed the Correa government to focus on long-neglected social issues. Heavy spending and an impressive growth of government bureaucracy are among the criticisms of Correa's opponents but he retains a strong following nationwide. The constitution does not allow the president to run for a third consecutive term of office, but there has been talk of an amendment which would permit Correa to do so in 2017.

Ecuador's neighbours

Peru

After the dissolution of Gran Colombia in 1830 (largely present-day Venezuela, Colombia and Ecuador), repeated attempts to determine the extent of Ecuador's eastern jungle territory failed. While Ecuador claimed that its territory has been reduced from that of the old Real Audiencia de Quito by gradual Colombian and especially Peruvian infiltration, Peru insisted that its Amazonian territory was established in law and in fact before the foundation of Ecuador as an independent state.

The dispute reached an acute phase in 1941 when war broke out between the two countries. The war ended with military defeat for Ecuador and the signing of the Rio de Janeiro Protocol of 1942 which allotted most of the disputed territory to Peru. Since 1960 Ecuador denounced the Protocol as unjust (because it was imposed by force of arms) and as technically flawed (because it refers to certain non-existent geographic features). According to Peru, the Protocol adequately demarcated the entire boundary.

Sporadic border skirmishes continued throughout subsequent decades. In January 1995 these escalated into an undeclared war over control of the headwaters of the Río Cenepa. Argentina, Brazil, Chile and the USA (guarantors of the Rio de Janeiro Protocol) intervened diplomatically and a cease-fire took effect. Negotiations followed and a definitive peace treaty was signed on 26 October 1998, finally ending the seemingly interminable dispute.

Under the terms of the agreement, Ecuador gained access to two Peruvian ports on the Amazon, Ecuador's navigation rights on the river were confirmed and, in the area of the most recent conflict, it was given a symbolic square kilometre of Peruvian territory as private property. In practice, Ecuador has yet to avail itself of any of the above. More significantly, however, relations have at last improved between the two former adversaries. New border crossings were opened and new international bus routes established. Adventurous travellers can now sail from the Ecuadorean Amazon to Peru (and beyond), and tour operators offer a variety of packages involving both countries.

Colombia

Ecuador and Colombia have traditionally enjoyed excellent relations. Their larger, more progressive neighbour to the north was for many decades a role model for Ecuadoreans. With escalating crime and violence in Colombia, however, that admiration gradually turned to fear. At the same time, commercial ties have always remained very strong.

Following the election of the Correa government, left-wing politics in Quito did not mesh well with the right-wing Uribe administration in Bogotá. Relations deteriorated dramatically in 2008, when the Colombian armed forces first bombed and then attacked with ground troops a group of Colombian insurgents (including an important guerilla leader) camped three kilometres inside Ecuadorean territory. Outraged by the violation of its sovereignty, Ecuador severed diplomatic ties which were re-established the following year. The two countries have since resumed excellent relations.

Over the years, hundreds of thousands of Colombians came to live in Ecuador, either as refugees or economic migrants. They have an economic and cultural presence important presence in places like Lago Agrio and Santo Domingo de los Tsáchilas.

Government

There are 24 provinces, including the Galápagos Islands. Provinces are divided into *cantones* which are subdivided into *parroquias* for administration.

Under the 2008 constitution, all citizens over the age of 16 are entitled to vote. Between ages 18 and 65 voting is obligatory. The president and vice-president are elected for a four-year term and may be re-elected once. The president appoints cabinet ministers and provincial governors. The unicameral *Asamblea Nacional* (National Assembly) has 137 members who are elected for a four-year term at the same time as the president.

Culture

People

According to the latest census (2010, see www.ecuadorencifras.gob.ec), almost 72% of Ecuador's 14.5 million people consider themselves mestizos, descendants of *indígenas* and Spaniards. *Cholo* is another (mildly derogatory) term for this group, although infrequently used in Ecuador. Rural coastal dwellers are referred to as *montubios* and represent about 7.5% of the population. Roughly 7% of all Ecuadoreans today identify themselves as belonging to one of 14 different indigenous peoples.

Andean peoples

The largest indigenous group are the **Andean Quichuas**. The common language, Quichua, is closely related to the Quechua spoken in parts of Peru and Bolivia. Once thought to have been imposed on conquered peoples by the Incas, Quechua/Quichua is now considered to have developed as a common trading language in the central Andes, long before the advent of the Inca Empire. Though Ecuador's highland natives all speak a similar language, indigenous dress differs from region to region. In the north, **Otavaleño** women are very distinctive with their blue skirts and embroidered blouses, while in the south the **Saraguros** traditionally wear black. A very important part of indigenous dress is the hat, which also varies from region to region.

Rainforest peoples

The largest indigenous groups in the Oriente are the **Kichwas**, in the north, and the **Shuar**, in the south. The Amazonian Kichwas speak a different dialect to their highland Quichua counterparts and their way of life is markedly distinct. Other Amazonian peoples of Ecuador include the **Achuar** and **Huaorani** as well as the **Cofán**, **Secoya**, **Shiwiar**, **Siona** and **Zápara**, all of whom are very few in number and in danger of disappearing.

Those very few jungle peoples who still maintain a traditional lifestyle, hunt and practise a form of itinerant farming which requires large areas of land, in order to allow the jungle to recover. Their way of life is under dire threat and many Amazonian indigenous communities are fighting for land rights in the face of oil exploration and colonization from the highlands.

There are also small groups of *indígenas* on the coastal plain. **Awas** live in Esmeraldas and Carchi provinces; **Chachis** and **Eperas** live nearer the coast and a little further south; **Tsáchilas**, formerly known as Colorados, live in the lowlands around Santo Domingo. These groups of coastal *indígenas* are also in danger of disappearing.

Afro-Ecuadoreans

The black population is estimated at about 7% of all Ecuadoreans. They live mostly in the coastal province of Esmeraldas and in neighbouring Imbabura and are descended from slaves who were brought from Africa in the 18th century to work on coastal plantations. Although the slave trade was abolished in 1821, slavery itself continued until 1852. Even then, freedom was not guaranteed until the system of debt tenancy was ended in 1881 and slaves could at last leave the plantations. However, the social status of Ecuador's black population remains low. They suffer from poor education and the racism endemic in all levels of society.

Indigenous cultures

COLOMBIA

Pacific Ocean

ESMERALDAS
Ch E N

CARCHI
Qs

IMBABURA
N O Qs

SUCUMBIOS
C K Se Si

PICHINCHA
A Qs T

NAPO
K

MANABI

ORELLANA
H K

COTOPAXI
Qs

LOS RIOS

TUNGURAHUA
Qs S

BOLIVAR
Qs

PASTAZA
Ac H K Sh Z

GUAYAS

CHIMB-ORAZO
Qs

CAÑAR
Qs

MORONA SANTIAGO
Ac Sh

AZUAY
Qs

EL ORO

ZAMORA-CHINCHIPE
Sh

LOJA
Qs Sa

PERU

N
Not to scale

Cultural groups

A Awa
Ac Achuar
Ch Chachi
C Cofán
E Epera
H Huaorani
K Kichwa of the Oriente
N Negro-afroecuatoriano

O Otavaleño
Qs Quichua of the Sierra
S Salasaca
Sa Saraguro
Se Secoya
Sh Shuar
Si Siona
T Tsachila
Z Zápara

Religion

According to 2012 statistics, about 80% of the population belongs to the Roman Catholic faith. In recent decades a variety of Evangelical Protestant groups from the USA, Seventh-Day Adventists, Mormons and Jehovah's Witnesses have increased their influence. Freedom of worship is guaranteed by the Ecuadorean constitution.

Just as many of the great colonial churches of Ecuador are built over Inca and pre-Inca temples, the nation's impressive edifice of Roman Catholic faith rests firmly on pre-Christian foundations. The syncretism (mixing) of Catholic and earlier beliefs can be seen in many traditions and practices. One example is *fanesca*, a traditional soup eaten during Holy Week, made with salt fish and many different grains. The Catholic component is the lack of meat, which was not consumed during Lent, while the many grains came from native traditions to celebrate the beginning of the harvest at this time of year. The original native *fanesca* might have been made with *cuy*.

Arts and crafts

Ecuador is a shopper's paradise. Everywhere you turn there's some particularly seductive piece of *artesanía* being offered. This word loosely translates as handicrafts, but that doesn't really do them justice. The indigenous peoples make no distinction between fine arts and crafts, so *artesanía* is valued as much for its practical use as its beauty. See also Shopping tips, page 26.

Panama hats

Most people don't even know that the Panama hat, Ecuador's most famous export, comes from Ecuador. The confusion over the origin of this natty piece of headwear dates back over 100 years.

Until the 20th century, the Isthmus of Panama was the quickest and safest seafaring route to Europe and North America and the major trading post for South American goods, including the straw hats from Ecuador. In the mid-19th century, at the height of the California gold rush, would-be prospectors heading west to seek their fortune picked up the straw hats. Half a century later, when work on the Panama Canal was in full swing, labourers found the hats provided ideal protection against the fierce tropical sun and, like the gold-diggers before them, named them after the place they were sold rather than where they originated. The name stuck and, to Ecuador's eternal chagrin, the name of the Panama hat was born.

The plant from which these stylish titfers is made – *Carludovica palmata* – grows best in the low hills of the province of Manabí. The hats are woven from the very fine fronds of the plant, which are boiled, then dried in the sun before being taken to the various weaving centres – Montecristi and Jipijapa in Manabí and Azogues, Biblián and Sigsig in Azuay. Montecristi, though, enjoys the reputation of producing the best *superfinos*. These are Panama hats of the highest quality, requiring many months' work. They are tightly woven, using the thinnest, lightest straw. When turned upside down they should hold water as surely as a glass, and when rolled up, should be able to pass through a wedding ring like silk.

From the weaver, the hat passes to a middleman, who then sells it on to the factory. The loose ends are trimmed, the hat is bleached and the brim ironed into shape and then softened with a mallet. The hat is then rolled into a cone and wrapped in paper in a balsawood box ready for exporting. The main export centre, and site of most of the factories, is Cuenca, where countless shops also sell the *sombreros de paja toquilla*, as they are known locally, direct to tourists.

Weavers of Otavalo

During Inca times, textiles held pride of place, and things are no different today. Throughout the highlands, beautiful woven textiles are still produced, often using techniques unchanged for centuries. One of the main weaving centres is Otavalo, which is a nucleus of trade for more than 75 scattered Otavaleño communities, and home of the famous handicrafts market which attracts tourists in their thousands.

The history of weaving in Otavalo goes back to the time of conquest when the Spanish exploited the country's human resources through the feudal system of *encomiendas*. A textile workshop (*obraje*) was soon established in Otavalo using forced indigenous labour. *Obrajes* were also set up elsewhere in the region, for example in Peguche and Cotacachi, using technology exported from Europe: the spinning wheel and treadle loom. These are still in use today.

Though the *encomiendas* were eventually abolished, they were replaced by the equally infamous *huasipungo* system, which rendered the indigenous people virtual serfs on the large haciendas that were created. Many of these estates continued to operate weaving workshops, producing cloth in large quantities.

The Otavalo textile industry as it is known today was started in 1917 when weaving techniques and styles from Scotland were introduced to the native workers on Hacienda Cusín. These proved successful in the national market and soon spread to other families and villages in the surrounding area. The development of the industry received a further boost with the ending of the *huasipungo* system in 1964. The *indígenas* were granted title to their plots of land, allowing them to weave at home.

Today, weaving in Otavalo is almost exclusively for the tourist and export trades by which it is quite naturally influenced. Alongside traditional local motifs, are found many designs from as far afield as Argentina and Guatemala. The Otavaleños are not only renowned for their skilled weaving, but also for their considerable success as traders. They travel extensively, to Colombia, Venezuela, North America and Europe, in search of new markets for their products. As these begin to saturate, Otavaleños are now peddling their wares in Asia.

Woodcarving

During the colonial era, uses of woodcarving were extended to provide the church with carved pieces to adorn the interiors of its many fine edifices. Wealthy families also commissioned work such as benches and chairs, mirrors and huge *barqueños* (chests) to decorate their salons.

In the 16th and 17th centuries woodcarvers from Spain settled north of Quito, where San Antonio de Ibarra has become the largest and most important woodcarving centre in South America. Initially the *mudéjar*, or Spanish-Moorish styles, were imported to the New World, but as the workshops of San Antonio spread north to Colombia and south to Chile and Argentina, they evolved their own styles. Today, everyone in San Antonio is involved with woodcarving and almost every shop sells carved wooden figures, or will make items to order.

Bags

Plant fibre is used not only for weaving but is also sewn into fabric for bags and other articles. In Cotopaxi province, *shigras*, bags made from sisal, were originally used to store dry foodstuffs around the home. It is said that very finely woven ones were even used to carry water from the wells, the fibres swelling when wet to make the bags impermeable. These bags almost died out with the arrival of plastic containers, until tourist demand ensured that the art survived. *Shigras* can be found at the market in Salcedo (early in the morning) and are also re-sold at tourist shops throughout the country.

Like the small backstrap looms and drop spindles of the Andes, the bags are portable and can be sewn while women are herding animals in the fields. Today, women's production is often organized by suppliers who provide dyed fibres for sewing and later buy the bags to resell. A large, blunt needle is used to sew the strong fibres and the finished article is likely to last a lot longer than the user.

Bread figures

The inhabitants of the town of Calderón, northeast of Quito, know how to make dough. The main street is lined with shops selling the vibrantly coloured figures made of flour and water which have become hugely popular in recent years.

The origins of this practice are traced back to the small dolls made of bread for the annual celebrations of Día de los Difuntos (Day of the Dead, 2 November). The original edible figures, made in wooden moulds in the village bakery, were decorated with a simple cross over the chest in red, green and black, and were placed in cemeteries as offerings to the hungry souls of the dead. Gradually, different types of figures appeared and people started giving them as gifts for children and friends.

Primitivist paintings

In the province of Cotopaxi, near Zumbahua and the Quilotoa crater, a regional craft has developed specifically in response to tourist demand. It is the production of 'primitivist' paintings on leather, now carried out by many of the area's residents, depicting typical rural or village scenes and even current events. Following the 1999 volcanic eruptions of Tungurahua, these began to figure prominently in the Tigua paintings – named after the town where the work originated. The paintings vary in price and quality and are now also widely available in Quito, Otavalo and other tourist destinations.

Music and dance

Culturally, ethnically and geographically, Ecuador is very much two countries – the Andean highlands with their centre in Quito and the Northern Pacific Lowlands behind Guayaquil. In spite of this, the music is relatively homogeneous and it is the Andean music that would be regarded as 'typically Ecuadorean'.

The principal highland rhythms are the Sanjuanito, Cachullapi, Albaza, Yumbo and Danzante, danced by *indígenas* and *mestizos* alike. These may be played by brass bands, guitar trios or groups of wind instruments, but it is the *rondador*, a small panpipe, that provides the classic Ecuadorean sound, although of late the Peruvian *quena* has been making heavy inroads via pan-Andean groups and has become a threat to the local instrument.

The coastal region has its own song form, the *Amorfino*, but the most genuinely 'national' song and dance genres, both of European origin, are the *Pasillo* (shared with Colombia) in waltz time and the *Pasacalle*, similar to the Spanish *Pasodoble*.

Music of the highland indigenous communities is, as elsewhere in the region, related to religious feasts and ceremonies and geared to wind instruments such as the *rondador*, the *pinkullo* and *pifano* flutes and the long *guarumo* horn with its mournful note. The guitar is also usually present and brass bands with well-worn instruments can be found in even the smallest villages.

There is one totally different cultural area, that of the black inhabitants of the Province of Esmeraldas and the highland valley of the Río Chota in Imbabura. The former is a southern extension of the Colombian Pacific coast negro culture, centred round the marimba, a huge wooden xylophone. The musical genres are also shared with black Colombians, including the *Bunde*, *Bambuco*, *Caderona*, *Torbellino* and *Currulao* dances and this music is some of the most African sounding in the whole of South America. The Chota Valley is an inverted oasis of desert in the Andes and here the black people dance the *Bomba*. It is also home to the unique Bandas Mochas, whose primitive instruments include leaves that are doubled over and blown through.

Literature
www.literaturaecuatoriana.com and www.diccionariobiograficoecuador.com.

Much Ecuadorean literature has reflected political issues such as the rivalry between liberals and conservatives and between Costa and Sierra, and the position of the *indígenas* and other marginalized members of society, and many of the country's writers have adopted a strongly political line. Among the earliest were Francisco Eugenio de Santa Cruz y Espejo, who led a rebellion against Spain in 1795, José Joaquín de Olmedo, Federico González Suárez (archbishop of Quito) and Juan Montalvo.

The 19th century
José Joaquín de Olmedo (1780-1847) was a disciple of Espejo and was heavily involved first in the independence movement and then the formative years of the

young republic. In 1825 he published *La Victoria de Junín, Canto a Bolívar*, a heroic poem glorifying the Liberator. His second famous poem was the *Canto al General Flores, Al Vencedor de Miñarica* (Juan José Flores was the Venezuelan appointed by Bolívar to govern Ecuador). He also wrote political works.

Juan Montalvo (1832-1889) was an essayist who was influenced by French Romantics such as Victor Hugo and Lamartine. One of his main objectives as a writer was to attack what he saw as the failings of Ecuador's rulers, but his position as a liberal, in opposition to conservatism such as García Moreno's, encompassed a passionate opposition to all injustice. His *Capítulos que se le olvidaron a Cervantes* (1895) was an attempt to imitate the creator of Don Quijote, translating him into an Ecuadorean setting.

Montalvo's contemporary and enemy, **Juan León Mera** (1832-1894), did write a book about the *indígena, Cumandá*. This dealt with the unsubjugated Amazonians, *los errantes y salvajes hijos de las selvas* (the wandering and savage sons of the jungles), a book which created much debate.

The 20th century and beyond

In 1904 **Luis A Martínez** (1869-1909) published *A la costa*, which attempts to present two very different sides of the country (the coast and the highlands) and the different customs and problems in each. *Plata y bronce* (1927) and *La embrujada* (1923), both by **Fernando Chávez** (1902-1999), portray the gulf between the white and the indigenous communities.

For the next 15 to 20 years, novelists in Ecuador produced a realist literature which was heavily influenced by writers like Zola and Sinclair Lewis. This was realism at the expense of beauty. The novelists in this period wrote politically committed stories about marginalized people in crude language and stripped-down prose. Among the more prominent writers in this era are José de la Cuadra (1903-1941), Alfredo Pareja D (1908-1993) and Demetrio Aguilera M (1909-1981). Continuing the realist literature and with a predominately indigenous theme are authors like Humberto Mata (1904-1988) and Jorge Icaza (1906-1978). Icaza's novel *Huasipungo* (1934) has been described as "the most contoversial novel in the history of Latin American narrative". Unlike some indigenist fiction, there is no attempt to portray the life on the Indians as anything other than brutal, inhuman, violent and hopeless.

The 1960s ushered in the so-called boom, with writers such as Gabriel García Márquez and Mario Vargas Llosa, gaining international recognition for the Latin American novel. At the same time, the Ecuadorean poet, essayist and novelist **Jorge Enrique Adoum** (1923-2009) wrote *Entre Marx y una mujer desnuda* (1976). This extraordinary novel is a dense investigation of itself, of novel-writing, of Marxism and politics, sex, love and Ecuador. Adoum has also written *Ciudad sin angel* (1995), plays (eg *El sol bajo las patas de los caballos* – 1972) and several collections of poetry, which is also intense and inventive (eg *No son todos los que están, 1949-1979*); his essay, *Ecuador: señales particulares* (1998), is a profound reflection on the Ecuadorean identity.

Among contemporary authors, **Alicia Yánez Cossío** (born 1929), in a long and productive career has delved into all aspects of Ecuadorean society. Her twelfth novel, *Memorias de la Pivihuarmi Cuxirimay Ocllo* (2008), is based on the life and tribulations of an Inca princess married to Atahualpa. Other prominent writers and their recent works include: **Jorge Dávila Vásquez** (born 1952), *María Joaquina en la vida y en la muerte* (1976) and *Este mundo es el camino* (1980); **Modesto Ponce** (born 1938), *El palacio de los espejos* (2005) and *La casa del desván* (2008); **Gabriela Alemán** (born 1968), *Fuga permanente* (2002) and *Pozo Wells* (2007); and **Javier Vásconez** (born 1946), *El viajero de Praga* (1996), *La sombra del apostador* (1999) and *Jardín Capelo* (2007).

Poetry
The major figure, perhaps of all Ecuadorean poetry, was **Jorge Carrera Andrade** (1903-1978). He was involved in socialist politics in the 1920s before going to Europe. In the 1930s and 1940s, Carrera Andrade moved beyond the socialist realist, revolutionary stance of his contemporaries and of his own earlier views, seeking instead to explore universal themes. His first goal was to write beautiful poetry. He published many volumes, including the haiku-like *Microgramas* (see *Registro del mundo: antología poética*; 1922-1939), *El alba llama a la puerta* (1965-1966), *Misterios naturales* and others. Contemporary poets include: **Juan Carlos Morales M** (born, 1967), *Mitologías de Imbabura* and *Los dioses mágicos del Amazonas*; **María Fernanda Espinosa** (born 1964), *Antología* (2005); **Francisco Granizo** (born 1928), *Poesía Junta* (2005); **Edwin Madrid** (born 1961), *Mordiendo el frío* (2004); **Xavier Oquendo** (1972), *Salvados del naufragio* (2005); and **Cristóbal Zapata** (1968), *No hay naves para Lesbos* (2004).

Many schools and workshops continue to promote poetry in Ecuador, notably the **Centro Internacional de Estudios Poéticos del Ecuador** (CIEPE), which has published collections like *Poemas de luz y ternura* (Quito 1993).

Fine art and sculpture

The 16th and 17th centuries
Colonial Quito was a flourishing centre of artistic production, exporting works to many other regions of Spanish South America. The origins of this trade date back to the year of the Spanish foundation of Quito, 1534, when the Franciscans established a college to train *indígenas* in European arts and crafts. Two Flemish friars, Jodoco Ricke and Pedro Gosseal, are credited with teaching a generation how to paint the pictures and carve the sculptures and altarpieces that were so urgently needed by the many newly founded churches and monasteries in the region. As well as the initial Flemish bias of the first Franciscans, stylistic influences on the Quito school came from Spain, particularly from the strong Andalucían sculptural tradition.

Colonial painting was as much influenced by Italy as by Spain. An important early figure in this was the Quito-born mestizo Pedro Bedón (1556-1621). Educated in Lima where he probably had contact with the Italian painter Bernardo Bitti,

Bedón returned home to combine the duties of Dominican priest with work as a painter. He is best-known for his illuminated manuscripts.

Indigenous influence is not immediately apparent in painting or sculpture despite the fact that so much of it was produced by natives. The features of Christ, the Virgin and saints are European, but in sculpture the proportions of the bodies are often distinctly Andean: broad-chested and short-legged. In both painting and sculpture the taste – so characteristic of colonial art in the Andes – for patterns in gold applied over the surface of garments may perhaps be related to the high value accorded to textiles in pre-conquest times.

The 18th century

Representations of the Virgin are very common, especially that of the Virgin Immaculate, patron of the Franciscans and of the city of Quito. This curious local version of the Immaculate Conception represents the Virgin standing on a serpent and crescent moon as tradition dictates, but unconventionally supplied with wings.

In the later 18th century the sculptor Manuel Chili, known to his contemporaries as *Caspicara* 'the pockmarked', continued the tradition of polychrome images with powerful emotional appeal ranging from the dead Christ to sweet-faced Virgins and chubby infant Christs. Outside Quito the best-known sculptor was Gaspar Sangurima of Cuenca who was still producing vividly realistic polychrome crucifixions in the early 19th century.

Painting in the later 18th century is dominated by the much lighter, brighter palette of Manuel Samaniego (c 1766-1824), author of a treatise on painting which includes instructions on the correct human proportions and Christian iconography, as well as details of technical procedures and recipes for paint.

Independence and after

As elsewhere in Latin America, the struggle for Independence created a demand for subjects of local and national significance and portraits of local heroes. **Antonio Salas** (1795-1860) became the unofficial portrait painter of the Independence movement. His paintings of heroes, military leaders and notable churchmen can be seen in Quito's Museo Jijón y Caamaño. Antonio's son, **Rafael Salas** (1828-1906), was among those to make the Ecuadorean landscape a subject of nationalist pride, as in his famous bird's-eye view of Quito sheltering below its distinctive family of mountain peaks (private collection).

Rafael Salas and other promising young artists of the later 19th century studied in Europe, returning to develop a style of portraiture which brings together both the European rediscovery of 17th-century Dutch and Spanish art and Ecuador's own conservative artistic tradition. They also brought back from their travels a new appreciation of the customs and costumes of their own country. The best-known exponent of this new range of subject matter was **Joaquín Pinto** (1842-1906). Although he did not travel to Europe and received little formal training, his affectionate, often humorous paintings and sketches present an unrivalled panorama of Ecuadorean landscape and peoples.

The 20th century and beyond

Pinto's documentation of the plight of the *indígena*, particularly the urban *indígena*, presaged the 20th-century indigenist tendency in painting whose exponents include **Camilo Egas** (1899-1962), **Eduardo Kingman** (1913-1997) and most famously **Oswaldo Guayasamín** (1919-1999, see the front cover of this book). Their brand of social realism, while influenced by the Mexican muralists, has a peculiarly bitter hopelessness of its own. Their work can be seen in Quito at **Museo Camilo Egas**, **Museo La Casa de Kingman** and **Posada de las Artes Kingman**, and Museo Guayasamín and **Capilla del Hombre** (the Chapel of Man).

The civic authorities in Ecuador, particularly during the middle years of the 20th century, have been energetic in peopling their public spaces with monuments to commemorate local and national heroes and events. Inevitably such sculpture is representational and often conservative in style, but within these constraints there are powerful examples in most major town plazas and public buildings are generously adorned with sculptural friezes, such as in the work of **Jaime Andrade** (1913-1989) on the **Central University** and **Social Security** buildings in Quito. **Estuardo Maldonado** (born 1930) works in an abstract mode using coloured stainless steel to create dramatic works for public and private spaces. **Milton Barragán** (born 1958) sculpts metal in dialogue with wood; he designed el *Templo a la Patria* on Cima de la Libertad in Quito. **Gonzalo Endara Crow's** (1936-1998) mosaic-tiled sculptures adorn plazas in several cities.

In recent years there have been many interesting artistic experiments which can be appreciated in museums and especially the galleries of the **Casa de la Cultura** across the country. Information on some contemporary artists is found in www.latinartmuseum.com. **Cuenca** hosts an important biennial and Ecuador is unusual among the smaller Latin American countries for its lively international art scene. Among prominent contemporary artists are: **Oswaldo Viteri** (born 1931, www.viteri.com.ec), **Nicolás Svistoonoff** (born 1945), **Marcelo Aguirre** (born 1956), **Jaime Zapata** (born 1957), **Luigi Stornaiolo** (born 1957), **Miguel Betancourt** (born 1958), **Jorge Velarde** (born 1960), and **Mario Tapia** (born 1967).

Land & environment

Ecuador, named for its position on the equator, is the smallest country of South America (256,370 sq km) after Uruguay and the Guianas. It is bounded by Colombia in the north, by Peru to the east and south, and by the Pacific Ocean to the west. Its population of 14.5 million (in 2010) is also small, but it has the highest population density of any of the South American republics, at 56.4 inhabitants per sq km. The border had been a source of conflict with its neighbours and Ecuador lost a significant part of its former territory towards the Amazon to Peru in 1941-1942 (see Ecuador's neighbours, page 383).

The Galápagos Islands became part of Ecuador in 1832. They lie in the Pacific, 970 km west of the mainland, on the equator, and consist of six principal islands and numerous smaller islands and rocks totalling about 8000 sq km and scattered over 60,000 sq km of ocean. They are the most significant island group in the eastern Pacific Ocean.

Geology

Geologically, Ecuador is the creation of the Andean mountain-building process, caused in turn by the South American Plate moving west, meeting the Nazca plate which is moving east and sinking beneath the continent. This process began in the late Cretaceous Period around 80 million years ago and has continued to the present day. Before this, and until as late as perhaps 25 million years ago, the Amazon basin tilted west and the Amazon river drained into the Pacific through what is now southern Ecuador.

The Andes between Peru and Colombia are at their narrowest (apart from their extremities in Venezuela and southern Chile), ranging from 100-200 km in width. Nevertheless, they are comparatively high with one point, Chimborazo, over 6000 m and several others not much lower. Unlike Peru to the south, most of the peaks in Ecuador are volcanoes, and Cotopaxi is one of the highest active volcanoes in the world, at 5897 m. The 55 volcanic craters that dot the landscape of the northern highlands suggest a fractured and unstable area beneath the surface. A dramatic example of volcanic activity was an eruption of Cotopaxi in 1877 which was followed by a pyroclastic flow or *nuée ardente* (literally, a burning cloud) which flowed down the side of the volcano engulfing many settlements. Snow and ice at the summit melted to create another volcanic phenomenon called a *lahar*, or mud flow, which reached Esmeraldas (150 km away) in only 18 hours. The most recently volcanic episodes began in 1999, with eruptions of Guagua Pichincha, Tungurahua and Reventador. For detailed information about Ecuador's volcanoes, see the website of the **National Geophysical Institute**, www.igepn.edu.ec.

The eastern third of the country is part of the Amazon basin filled with sedimentary deposits from the mountains to the west. The coastlands rise up to

1000 m and are mainly remnants of Tertiary basalts, similar to the base rocks of the Amazon basin on the other side of the Andes.

The Galápagos are not structurally connected to the mainland and, so far as is known, were never part of the South American Plate. They lie near the boundary between the Nazca Plate and the Cocos Plate to the north. A line of weakness, evidenced by a ridge of undersea lava flows, stretches southwest from the coast of Panama. This meets another undersea ridge running along the equator from Ecuador but separated from the continental shelf by a deep trench. At this conjuncture appear the Galápagos. Volcanic activity here has been particularly intense and the islands are the peaks of structures that rise over 7000 m from the deepest parts of the adjacent ocean floor. The oldest islands are San Cristóbal and Española in the east of the archipelago: three to 3½ million years old. The youngest ones, Fernandina and Isabela, lie to the west, and are between 700,000 and 800,000 years old. In geological terms, therefore, the Galápagos Islands have only recently appeared from the ocean and volcanic activity continues on at least five of them.

The Andes

The Andes form the backbone of the country. In Colombia to the north, three distinct ranges come together near Pasto, with three volcanoes overlooking the border near Tulcán. Although it is essentially one range through Ecuador, there is a trough of between 1800 m and 3000 m above sea level running south for over 400 km with volcanoes, many active, on either side. The snowline is at about 5000 m and rising due to global climate change, with 10 peaks over that height, making for a dramatic landscape.

Overlooking Quito to the west is **Pichincha**, which was climbed by Charles-Marie de La Condamine in 1742 and, in 1802, by Alexander Von Humboldt. Humboldt climbed many other Ecuadorean volcanoes, including Chimborazo. Although he did not make it to the summit, he reached over 6000 m, the first recorded climb to this height. He christened the road through the central Andes the 'Avenue of the Volcanoes'.

Further south, near Riobamba, is **Volcán Sangay**, 5230 m, which today is the most continuously active of Ecuador's volcanoes. There are fewer volcanoes towards in the southern highlands and the scenery is less dramatic. Here, the mountains rarely exceed 4000 m and the passes are as low as 2200 m. Although active volcanoes are concentrated in the northern half of the country, there are many places where there are sulphur baths or hot springs and the whole Andean area is seismically active with severe earthquakes from time to time.

The central trough is crossed by several transverse ranges called *nudos*, made up of extruded volcanic material, creating separate basins or *hoyas*. South of Quito, the basins are lower, the climate hotter and drier with semi-desert stretches. The lack of surface water is aggravated by large quantities of volcanic dust which is easily eroded by wind and water and can produce dry 'badland' topography. Landslides in this unstable and precipitous terrain are common.

The coast

West of the Andes there are 100-200 km of lowlands with some hilly ground up to 1000 m. The greater part is drained by the Daule, Vinces and Babahoyo rivers that run north to south to form the Guayas, the largest river on the Pacific coast of South America, which meets the sea near Guayaquil. There are several shorter rivers in the north including the Esmeraldas, whose headwaters include the Río Machángara which unfortunately is the open sewer of Quito. Another system reaches the ocean at La Tola. All of these rivers have created fertile lowlands which are used for banana, cacao and rice production, and there are good cattle lands in the Guayas basin. This is one of the best agricultural areas of South America.

Mangrove swamps thrived on coastal mudflats in tropical rainforest zones and were typical of parts of Esmeraldas, Manabí and Guayas provinces. Many have been destroyed to make way for shrimp farms.

Amazonia

The eastern foothills of the Andes are mainly older granite (Mesozoic) rocks, more typical of Brazil than the Pacific coast countries. As with most of the western Amazon basin, it has a heavy rainfall coming in from the east and much is covered with tropical forest along a dozen or so significant tributaries of the Amazon.

With good water flow and easy gradients, many of the rivers of this region are navigable at least to small craft. The Napo in particular is a significant potential communications route from Coca to Iquitos in Peru and the Brazilian Amazon beyond.

Climate

In spite of its small size, the range of tropical climates in Ecuador is large. The meeting of the north-flowing Humboldt current with warm Pacific equatorial water takes place normally off Ecuador, giving the contrast between high rainfall to the north and desert conditions further south in Peru. Periodic changes in the balance between these huge bodies of water, known as the El Niño phenomenon, can lead to heavy rains and flooding (see box, opposite).

The Coast

The climate along the Pacific coast is a transition area between the heavy tropical rainfall of Colombia and the deserts of Peru. The rainfall is progressively less from north to south, with lush tropical rainforests in Esmeraldas and semi-desert conditions by the peruvian border.

The Andes and Oriente

Inland, the size of the Andean peaks and volcanoes create many different microclimates, from the permanent snows over about 5000 m to the semi-desert hollows in the central trough. Most of the basins and the adjoining slopes have a moderate climate, though at altitude daily temperature fluctuations can be considerable. In the north, the basins are higher and temperatures are warm

BACKGROUND
El Niño

Among the early European scientists to visit South America, Alexander von Humboldt observed a cold ocean current flowing from south to north along the coast of Peru; it was later given his name. The Humboldt current follows South America s Pacific coastline northward as far as the equator, causing very low precipitation (because of low evaporation from its cool waters) and creating deserts in northern Chile, Peru and southern Ecuador. At the equator it turns due west, sweeping past the Galápagos Islands into the central Pacific.

North of the equator, a warm countercurrent flows in the opposite direction, eastward towards Panama and then south along the Pacific coast (where it is called the Panama current) until it meets the Humboldt current at the equator. This warm current brings warm moist air and high precipitation to the Pacific coasts of Panama, Colombia and northern Ecuador. The relative strength of these two currents, warm and cold, varies with the time of year. The warm Panama current can be stronger around Christmas and hence was dubbed the *Corriente del Niño*, the current of the (Christ) child. Under certain circumstances, which tend to recur in an irregular five- to 10-year cycle, this warm current can be exceptionally strong and sweep as far south as Chile, causing very heavy rains and associated calamities in these normally desert areas. This is the El Niño phenomenon.

A more global outlook notes that under normal conditions the trade winds, which blow westward across the tropical Pacific Ocean, pile up warm sea surface water in the west. Consequently, the sea level by Indonesia is normally about 50 cm higher than it is by Ecuador. This movement of warm water to the west causes an up-welling of deeper cold water in the east (the Humboldt current) resulting in a temperature difference of about 8°C at the same latitude, between the water by the coast of South America and that by Southeast Asia.

When the trade winds diminish in intensity, there is a gradual eastward-moving warming of surface water in the Pacific. Heavy rainfall follows the warmer water east to the Pacific coast of South America (the El Niño phenomenon) and is accompanied by simultaneous drought in Southeast Asia and Australia. The ocean level rises along the west coast of South America causing *marejadas*, exceptionally high tides which can destroy beaches and seaside property.

Very strong El Niños took place in 1992-1993 and 1997-1998, and both were devastating for the Ecuadorean coast. Since then the phenomenon has been weak to moderate but scientists are forecasting a stronger El Niño for 2015-2016. For more details see www.elnino.noaa.gov.

by day and cool at night. It rains mostly between October and May; Quito has an average of 1300 mm per year. Near the border with Peru, the mountain climate can be very pleasant. Vilcabamba in Loja province is reputed to have a most favourable climate for a long and healthy life. In the Oriente the climate is indistinguishable from the hot, very humid lands of the western Amazon basin. There is heavy rainfall all year round, particularly May to December.

Galápagos
Although lying on the equator, there is considerable variation in the weather of the Galápagos Islands. The islands are affected by the cool water from the southeast Pacific which turns west near the equator. Surface water temperatures can fall to 20°C in July to September, causing *garúa* (mist) and cool air. Temperatures are highest from January to May and brief tropical downpours occur frequently at this time.

Wildlife and vegetation

No country in the world has as much biological diversity in as little space as Ecuador. The geologically recent uplift of the Andes has caused this diversity by dividing the country into two parts, west and east, and by creating a complex topography that fosters the evolution of new species. It is an exciting thing to experience this diversity first hand, and Ecuador's extensive road system makes it easy. Our brief survey of this diversity, from west to east, gives an idea of the enormous range of Ecuador's life forms. For the Galápagos wildlife, see pages 330-339.

Northwestern lowlands
The westernmost part of mainland Ecuador is a broad rolling plain covered in the north by some of the wettest rainforest in the world. (There are some low coastal mountains but they do not reach significant elevations.) The biological centre of this region is the Chocó forest of neighbouring Colombia, so Ecuador's northwest shares many species with that area. Among the so-called Chocó endemics that reach Ecuador are some very fancy birds like the **long-wattled umbrellabird**, **banded ground-cuckoo** and **scarlet-breasted dacnis**. Many other birds, mammals and plants of this region are found all along the wet Pacific lowlands from northwest Ecuador to Central America. Visitors familiar with Central American wildlife will feel at home here amongst the **mantled howler monkeys**, **chestnut-mandibled toucans** and **red-capped manakins**. Unfortunately this forest is severely endangered by commercial logging, cattle ranching and farming, and good examples of it are now hard to find.

Southwestern lowlands
The cold Humboldt ocean current creates a completely different environment in the southwestern lowlands. Here the forest is deciduous (driest in July and August), and the southernmost parts of this area are desert-like. The birds and

plants of this region are very different from those of the wet northwest; they belong to the Tumbesian bioregion and many are restricted to this small corner of Ecuador and adjacent northwest Peru. Some of the Tumbesian endemic birds are the **El Oro parakeet**, **rufous-headed chachalaca** and **elegant crescentchest**. This is a densely populated region, however, and many of the species endemic to it are threatened with extinction.

Western slopes

Rising suddenly from these flat lowlands are the western Andes, very steep and irregular. Here the constant mists keep the forest wet all the way from north to south. In southern Ecuador it is therefore possible to go from desert to cloudforest in the space of a few hundred metres of elevation. This cloudforest is thick, tall and dark, and every branch is loaded with bromeliads, orchids and mosses. Orchids reach their maximum diversity in Ecuadorean cloudforests, and many spectacular varieties are found in the west, especially the weird Draculas. Many of the birds in these mountains are restricted to western Ecuador and western Colombia, including spectacular species like the gaudy **plate-billed mountain-toucan**. At higher elevations there are more similarities with the eastern slope of the Andes. Among the highlights of these forests are the mixed foraging flocks of colourful **tanagers**, with exotic names like Glistening-green, Beryl-spangled and Flame-faced tanagers. Mammals are scarce; lower elevations have capuchin, **spider** and **howler monkeys**, while high elevations have the elusive **spectacled bear**. Insects too diminish as elevation increases and their role as flower pollinators is taken over by the many hummingbirds, including the **violet-tailed sylph**, **velvet-purple coronet** and **gorgeted sunangel**, to name but a few.

Western páramo

The cloudforest becomes low and stunted above about 3300 m, and at higher elevations the forest is replaced by the grassland environment called *páramo*. Here, in contrast to the lower forests, the plants are largely from familiar temperate-zone families like the daisy and blueberry. They take on increasingly bizarre forms as the altitude increases, and the species of the highest elevations look like cushions of moss. Mammals are scarce but include **spectacled bear**, which feeds on the terrestrial bromeliads called *puyas* or *achupallas* (which look a lot like pineapple plants); and **rabbits**, which can be so numerous that they make broad trails in the vegetation. Preying on the rabbits are a form of **great horned owl** and the **Andean fox**. The birds and insects of these elevations are mostly drab, and many of the families represented here have their origins in North America or temperate southern South America. Forming islands of high forest in the *páramos* are the polylepis trees, in the rose family; their distinctive flaky reddish bark is the favorite foraging substrate for the **giant conebill**.

Inter-Andean basins

Between the western and eastern Andes lies the Inter-Andean basin, really a series of basins formed by various river valleys. This region is in the rain shadows of both the western and eastern Andes, so it is relatively dry all year. Much of the original vegetation was destroyed centuries ago, replaced with grasses and more recently with introduced pine and eucalyptus trees. Only on high mountains like Chimborazo or Cotopaxi do relatively undisturbed habitats remain. Here a desolate zone of volcanic ash and bare rock marks the upper end of the *páramo*. There is little vegetation beyond, apart from the colonization of lichens, which grow right up to the 5000 m snow line.

Eastern páramo

To the east of the Inter-Andean basins are the high eastern *páramos*, very much like the western ones but wetter. Here **mountain tapirs** are the largest animal, but they, like all big chunks of meat in Ecuador, survive only in remote regions. **spectacled bears** are here too, along with **white-tailed deer** and its faithful predator the **mountain lion**. A miniature deer, the **pudu**, also lives here but is rarely seen. **Andean condors**, one of the largest flying birds in the world, can be seen soaring majestically overhead. Condors are scavengers and clean up the larger animals after they die.

Eastern slopes

The eastern slope of the Andes is clothed in cloudforest like the western slope, but this cloudforest is much less seasonal, and has a higher diversity. Many west slope species of plants and birds have east slope sister species; the plate-billed mountain-toucan, for example, is here replaced by the **black-billed mountain-toucan**. The lower elevations have some Amazonian species like **woolly monkey**, and there are a few birds that have no western or Amazonian counterparts, like the strange **white-capped tanager**. Plant diversity is very high here; orchids are especially diverse, even more so than in the west. The eastern cloudforests are much less damaged by man than the western ones, and there are still a few wildernesses that are virtually unknown biologically.

Eastern lowlands

The eastern Amazonian lowland rainforest is the most diverse habitat in Ecuador for birds and mammals, with up to 14 primate species and 550 bird species at a single site. This is as diverse as life gets on this planet. Here is the home of the biggest snake in the world, the semiaquatic **anaconda**, and various species of alligator-like caimans. The birds are very impressive, like the multicoloured **macaws**, the monkey-eating **harpy eagle**, the comical **hoatzin** and the elusive **nocturnal curassow**. Mammals include five species of cats, three anteaters, a couple of sloths, two dolphins and an endless variety of bats – bats that troll for fish, bats that suck nectar, bats that catch sleeping birds by smelling them, bats that eat fruit, bats that catch insects, and even vampire bats that really drink blood. The variety of fish is even greater than the variety of birds and bats, and include piranhas, stingrays, giant catfish and electric eels. There are fewer epiphytes here than in cloudforests, but many more species of trees: 1 ha can have over 300 species of trees! Insect life reflects the diversity of plants; for example, there can be over 700 species of butterflies at a single site, including several species of huge shining **blue morphos**.

National parks

Ecuador has an outstanding array of 50 protected natural areas. National parks and other government reserves cover almost five million hectares of land plus another 14 million hectares of marine reserves. These are distributed throughout the country and include many unique tracts of wilderness. But the term 'protected' may not mean what it does in other parts of the world; native communities, settlements, haciendas, and even oil drilling camps can be found in the heart of some Ecuadorean national parks. Park boundaries are seldom clearly defined, and less often respected. What park facilities exist, along with most park rangers, are concentrated at the access points to a few frequently visited areas. Elsewhere, infrastructure ranges from very basic to nonexistent.

National parks are administered by the **Ministerio del Ambiente** ⓘ *Madrid E12-102 y Andalucía, T02-398 7600, www.ambiente.gob.ec*. Entry to all national protected areas is free except for Parque Nacional Galápagos. Some parks can only be visited with authorized guides. For information on specific protected areas, contact park offices in the cities nearest the parks, they have more information than the ministry in Quito.

For further details see the map and table, pages 404 and 406, which list those parks mentioned in the travelling text.

Private reserves

In addition to national parks, there are many private or NGO-run nature reserves throughout Ecuador. Most cater to birdwatchers but are also of interest to hikers or anyone with an interest in nature. In healthy forest where birds abound, chances are that you can also find orchids, frogs, butterflies and many other fascinating plants and animals.

Below, we list some of the best national parks, private reserves, lodges and roads for birding according to their biological region; within each region the sites are listed from north to south. The number of bird species is approximate and usually a lower bound. Both sites and regions are more fully described in the main text.

Birdwatching areas

Western lowlands and lower foothills
Bilsa (400-700 m, 305 species, access from Santo Domingo de los Tsáchilas, page 270), a virgin site in Esmeraldas province, contains even the rarest foothill birds (such as banded ground-cuckoo and long-wattled umbrellabird), though access can be an ordeal in the wet season.
Tinalandia (700-900 m, 360 species, page 97), near Alluriquín on the

National parks & reserves

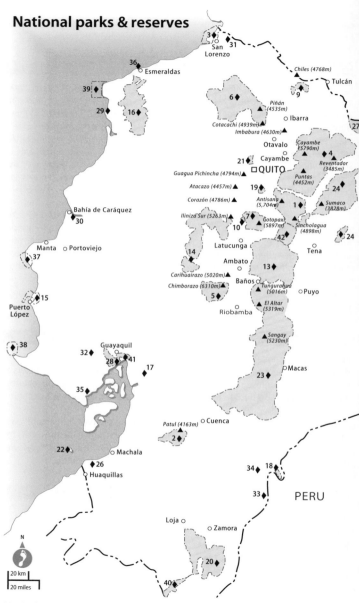

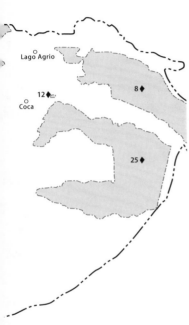

COLOMBIA

Lago Agrio

Coca

12 ◆

8 ◆

25 ◆

Galápagos

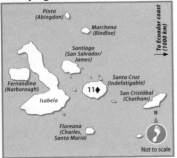

Pinta
(Abingdon)

Marchena
(Bindloe)

Santiago
(San Salvador/
James)

Fernandina
(Narborough)

Isabela

Santa Cruz
(Indefatigable)

11 ◆

San Cristóbal
(Chatham)

Floreana
(Charles,
Santa María)

To Ecuador coast
(1000 km)

N

Not to scale

Alóag–Santo Domingo road, is a great introduction to the world of tropical birds. There are lots of colourful species and they are easier to observe here than at most other places, but some of the larger species have been lost from this area. The lodge itself is easily accessible.

Río Palenque (200 m, 370 species, access from Santo Domingo de los Tsáchilas, page 270) between Santo Domingo and Quevedo is one of the last islands of western lowland forest. It is a very rich birding area although it has begun to lose some species because of its isolation from other forests.

Parque Nacional Machalilla (0-850 m, 115 species, page 258), on the coast near Puerto López, has lightly disturbed dry forest and cloudforest, with many dry-forest specialities. The higher areas are slightly difficult to access.

Ecuasal Ponds (0 m), on the Santa Elena peninsula (page 255), hold a variety of seabirds and shorebirds; famous for their Chilean flamingos and other migratory species.

Cerro Blanco (250-300 m, 190 species, page 236), just outside Guayaquil, is one of the best remaining examples of dry forest. There have on occasion been breeding great green macaws, and even jaguars have been spotted.

Manglares Churute (50-650 m, 65 species, page 237), southeast of Guayaquil, contains a dry-to-moist forest and a mangrove forest. The bird list is short but the area has not been well studied.

Lalo Loor (200-600 m 171 species, access from Pedernales, page 270) about 20 km southwest of Pedernales, is in the rich and highly endangered transition zone between dry and wet

BACKGROUND
National parks and reserves

	Map	Name	Created	Size (ha)
Coast	26	Arenillas	2001	17,082
	3	Cayapas-Mataje	1995	51,300
	32	Parque-Lago	2002	2283
	28	Manglares El Salado	2002	5217
	30	Isla Corazón	2002	700
	22	Isla Santa Clara	1999	5
	31	La Chiquita	2002	809
	15	Machalilla	1979	56,184
	16	Mache-Chindul	1996	119,172
	17	Manglares Churute	1979	49,894
	29	Río Muisne	2003	3173
	35	Manglares El Morro	2007	10,030
	36	Estuario Río Esmeraldas	2008	242
	37	Pacoche	2008	13,630
	38	Puntilla Santa Elena	2008	47,455
	39	Galera San Francisco	2008	54,604
	41	Isla Santay	2010	2179
Highlands	1	Antisana	1993	120,000
	2	Cajas	1977	28,808
	5	Chimborazo	1987	58,530
	7	Cotopaxi	1975	33,396
	9	El Angel	1992	15,715
	10	El Boliche	1979	400
	14	Ilinizas	1996	149,900
	19	Pasochoa	1996	500
	21	Pululahua	1966	3383
	40	Yacuri	2009	43,090
Highlands to coast	6	Cotacachi-Cayapas	1968	204,420
Highlands to Oriente	4	Cayambe-Coca	1970	403,103
	13	Llanganates	1996	219,707
	20	Podocarpus	1982	146,280
	23	Sangay	1975	517,765
	42	Colonso Chalupas	2014	93,246
Oriente	27	Cofán Bermeo	2002	55,451
	8	Cuyabeno	1979	603,380
	18	El Cóndor	1999	2440
	12	Limoncocha	1985	4613
	24	Sumaco	1994	205,249
	25	Yasuní	1979	982,000
	33	El Zarza	2006	3643
	34	El Quimi	2006	9071
Galápagos	11	Galápagos	1936	693,700
		Galápagos Marine Reserve	1996	14,110,000

Habitats/features	Access	Page
dry forest, restricted access	Arenillas	404
mangrove	San Lorenzo	280
recreation area	Guayaquil	404
mangrove	Guayaquil	404
mangrove, nesting frigate birds	Bahía de Caráquez	269
island	Puerto Bolívar	404
jungle	San Lorenzo	404
beach, dry forest, Isla de la Plata	Puerto López	258
dry forest	Esmeraldas	277
mangrove, dry forest	Guayaquil	237, 405
mangrove	Muisne	277
mangrove	Guayaquil	404
mangrove	Esmeraldas	404
ocean, seashore	Manta	404
ocean	Salinas	404
ocean	Esmeraldas	404
river estuary, wetland	Guayauquil	237
glacier, *páramo*	Quito	86
páramo	Cuenca	202
glacier, *páramo*, vicuñas	Riobamba	181
glacier, *páramo*	Machachi, Latacunga	148
páramo, frailejones	El Angel	138
planted pine forest, recreation area	Quito	404
glacier, *páramo*	Machachi	147
páramo, cloudforest, recreation area	Quito	86
agricultural, extinct volcanic crater	Quito	57
lakes, cloudforest	Loja	405
páramo to jungle	Cotacachi, Borbón	127
glacier to jungle	Cayambe, Papallacta	87
páramo, cloudforest	Píllaro, Baños	164
páramo to jungle	Loja, Zamora	216
glacier to jungle, active volcanoes	Baños, Riobamba, Macas	184
páramo, cloudforest, rainforest	Tena	405
jungle	Lago Agrio	405
jungle	Lago Agrio	297
jungle, international park	Gualaquiza	405
jungle	Coca	405
jungle to *páramo*	Coca, Baeza, Tena	297
jungle	Coca	297
jungle, river gorge	Zamora	405
jungle	Gualaquiza	405
island	Quito, Guayaquil	322
ocean	Quito, Guayaquil	373

forest in the largely deforested province of Manabí. In addition to birds, it has monkeys and other wildlife.

Puyango (300-400 m, 130 species, acess from Loja, page 215, or Machala page 246), a pertified forest in the far south, which also has live trees and typical dry forest birds.

Jorupe (500-2000 m, access from Macará, page 217) is a beautiful dry forest reserve with almost all the rare southwestern endemic birds. A lodge is operated here by the **Jocotoco Foundation**.

Western Andes

Reserva Ecológica El Angel (2500-4500 m, 160 species, page 138) south of Tulcán, is a spectacular grassland dotted with tall tree-like herbs called *frailejones*.

Intag Cloud Forest Reserve (1800-2800 m), **Junín Cloud Forest Reserve** (1500-2200 m) and **Reserva Alto Chocó** are all in the Intag region (page 125), with a full set of cloudforest birds. Access is via Otavalo, page 112.

Los Cedros Reserve (1000-2700 m, page 127), near the Cotacachi-Cayapas Ecological Reserve, has excellent forest over an interesting range of elevations. Populations of many bird species are higher here than in more accessible places.

Yanacocha (3300-4000 m, page 116) is a surprisingly well preserved high-elevation forest on the west side of the Pichincha volcano. Access is from Quito.

Ecoruta (the Nono–Mindo road, 1500-3400 m, page 92) is a famous birding route starting from Quito and passing through a wide variety of forest types. It is somewhat disturbed in its higher sections but quite good in its lower half, where there are several excellent lodges.

Tandayapa Lodge (1700 m, 318 species, page 96) on the Nono–Mindo road is well done, easily accessible and comfortable. Serious birders seeking rarities will benefit from the knowledgeable guides who can show practically any species they are asked to find.

Bellavista (1800-2300 m, page 94) on the Nono–Mindo road is a perfectly situated lodge with colourful easy-to-see birds, and plenty of rarities for hard-core birders.

El Pahuma (1600-2600 m, 139 species, page 95) is an easy day trip from Quito (about 1 hr) on the Calicali–La Independencia road. There is a large orchid garden and a visitor centre offering lodging.

Maquipucuna (1200-2800 m, 300 species, page 94) north of the Calacalí–La Independencia road has extensive good forest and cabins for guests.

Mindo (1300-2400 m, 400 species, page 97), has many good lodges. Mindo has repeatedly won the **American Birding Association's** (www.aba.org) Christmas bird count. Even the road into town (easily reached from Quito in 2 hrs) is excellent for good views of beautiful birds like quetzals and tanagers.

Chiriboga road (900-3200 m, page 92) from the south of Quito to near Santo Domingo is good for birds in its middle and lower sections, but it can be very muddy; a 4WD vehicle is recommended.

Otonga (800-2300 m, page 97) is a private reserve rising into the mountains south of the Alóag–Santo Domingo road. The birdlife here is known for not being shy, especially the dark-backed wood-quails.

Chilla, Guanazán, Manú and **Selva Alegre** (2800-3000 m, access from Saraguro, page 215), on the road from

Saraguro to the coast, have remnant forests and good birds.

Buenaventura (800-1000 m, 310 species, page 248) 24 km north of the road from Loja to the coast is a **Jocotoco Foundation** bird reserve, particularly important because there are few remaining tracts in the area. Piñas has many rare birds.

Guachanamá Ridge (2000-2800 m, access from Alamor) between Celica and Alamor in extreme southwest Ecuador contains many rare southwestern endemic birds.

Sozoranga–Nueva Fátima road (1300-2600 m, 190 species, access from Sozoranga, page 217) near the Peruvian border in Loja has remnants of a wide variety of mid-elevation forests, and has many southwest endemics.

Inter-Andean forests and páramos

Guandera Reserve (3100-3800 m, page 139), near the Colombian border, has beautiful temperate forest with Espeletia *páramo* and many rare birds.

Pasochoa (2700-4200 m, about 120 species, page 86) provides a very easy cloudforest to visit just south of Quito. Not virgin, but lots of birds.

Parque Nacional Cotopaxi (3700-6000 m, 90 species, page 148), 1½ hrs south of Quito, is a spectacular setting in which to find birds of the high arid *páramo*. There is also a birdy lake and marsh, Limpiopungo.

Parque Nacional Cajas (3000-4500 m, 125 species, page 202) has extensive *páramo* and high-elevation forest, accessible from Cuenca. Birds include condor and the violet-throated metaltail, an endemic hummingbird.

Eastern Andes

Papallacta (3000-4400 m, page 88), 1½ hrs east of Quito, has a dramatic cold wet landscape of grassland and high elevation forest. Condors are regular here, along with many other highland birds.

Guango (2700 m, 95 species) is a lodge with good birding in temperate forest below Papallacta.

Baeza (1900-2400 m, page 289), about 2 hrs east of Quito, has forest remnants near town which can be surprisingly birdy. The road to the antenna above town is especially rich.

San Isidro (2000 m, 260 species, page 300), 30 mins from Baeza just off the Baeza–Tena road, is a comfortable lodge with bird-rich forests all around, and wonderful hospitality.

San Rafael Falls (1400 m, 200 species, page 289) on the Baeza–Lago Agrio road is a good place to see cock-of-the-rocks and other subtropical birds. Access is an easy walk. A massive hydroelectric project was under construction here in 2015.

Guacamayos Ridge (1700-2300 m, access from Baeza, page 289) on the Baeza–Tena road has excellent roadside forest rich in birdlife.

Wildsumaco Lodge (1300-1600 m, 432 species, page 297) off the road from Tena to Coca via Loreto, and near Parque Nacional Sumaco. A very comfortable lodge with nice trails. Birds include coppery-chested jacamar and military macaws as well as various other rare species.

Baños–Puyo corridor (900-5000 m) offers an interesting mix of Amazonian and highland birds. The San Antonio area (2400-3300 m) above the Río Ulba is the most accessible place to see high cloudforest birds. Machay (1700-2200 m) is the most accessible good mid-elevation cloudforest, and the Topo–Zuñac area (1300-1600 m) is the most accessible good forest for foothill birds.

Gualaceo–Limón road (1400-3350 m, 200-300 species, page 201) northeast of Cuenca has perhaps the best roadside birding on the east slope, in a spectacular natural setting.

Parque Nacional Podocarpus (950-3700 m, 800 species, page 216), near Loja, is one of the most diverse protected areas in the world. There are several easy access points at different elevations. The park is very rich in birds, including many rarities.

Loja–Zamora road (1000-2850 m, 375 species, page 311), segments of the old road (parallel to the current one) are good for birds.

Tapichalaca Reserve (1800-3100 m, page 222) south of Loja between Yangana and Valladolid protects the cloudforest home of the Jocotoco Antpitta. A fine lodge has been built here by the **Jocotoco Foundation**.

Oriente jungle

Reserva Faunística Cuyabeno (200-300 m, 400 species, page 297) in the northern Oriente has seasonally flooded forests not found elsewhere and lots of wildlife.

Lower Río Napo lodges (200-300 m, 550 species, page 302) in the north and central Oriente provide a wide spectrum of facilities and prices, in forest ranging from moderately disturbed to absolutely pristine. Some of these lodges are among the most bird-rich single-elevation sites in the world.

Upper Río Napo lodges (300-600 m, page 314) in west-central Oriente are much easier and cheaper to reach than other sites, and the lodges are especially comfortable. The forest in this area is somewhat disturbed, however, so larger birds and mammals are scarce or absent.

Gareno Lodge, further from Tena but still accessible by vehicle, has virgin forest and a full set of wildlife including occasional nesting harpy eagles.

Kapawi Lodge (200-300 m, page 316) in the southern Oriente has a slightly different set of birds than the other areas, and a different cultural environment.

Galápagos

See the Galápagos chapter, page 322.

Hot springs

Ecuador is located on the 'Ring of Fire' and has many volcanoes: active, dormant and non-active (dead). Hot springs are associated with all three, although they are mostly found near the older volcanoes where sufficient time has elapsed since the last eruption for water systems to become established. Below is a selection of Ecuador's best thermal springs. Some are inside protected natural areas, others are in towns or part of private hotels and spas.

Aguas Hediondas About 1½ hrs west of Tulcán (page 140). Geothermal activity increased here in 2015 and they may not be safe for bathing.

Baños (Tungurahua) The hot springs of Baños in the province of Tungurahua are the best known in Ecuador. There are 6 separate bathing complexes here, and the town of Baños is overflowing with accommodation, restaurants and activities. See page 169.

Baños (Cuenca) This is another Baños, near the city of Cuenca, which has the hottest commercial springs in the country. It is only 10 mins by bus from the city centre. See page 199.

Baños de San Vicente These springs are not far from Salinas on the coast. They are not all that attractive but they are famed for the curative properties of the warm mud lake which people slide into before baking themselves dry.

Chachimbiro A thermal area with several places to stay and an upmarket resort/spa. Access is from Ibarra. See page 133.

Nangulví These small and simple baths are reached from Otavalo. See page 126.

Oyacachi There are 4 simple but clean hot pools. Also several small places to stay, or you can camp at the springs. See page 110.

Papallacta These are the best-developed hot springs in the country, and can be visited on a day trip from Quito. You can also stay overnight at the luxury hotel and spa on the site, or at one of several more economical places nearby. See page 88.

Books

See also Literature, page 391.

Birdwatching

Canaday, C and Jost, L *Common Birds of Amazonian Ecuador* (Ediciones Libri Mundi, Quito, 1997).

Cooper, M and Gellis, R *Plumas* (Latin Web, 2006).

Hilty, S *Birds of Tropical America* (Chapters Publishing, Shelburne, VT, USA).

Hilty, S and Brown, W *A Guide to the Birds of Colombia* (Princeton University Press, USA, 1986).

Moore, J *CDs of Ecuadorean birdsongs.* Available at **Libri Mundi** in Quito.

Ridgely, R and Greenfield, P *Birds of Ecuador* (Cornell University Press, Ithaca, NY, USA, 2001).

Williams, R, Best, B and Heijnen, T *A Guide to Birdwatching in Ecuador and the Galápagos* (Biosphere Publications, UK, 1996).

Climbing

Brain, Y *Ecuador: A Climbing Guide* (The Mountaineers, Seattle, 2000).

Cruz, M *Montañas del Ecuador* (Dinediciones, Quito, 1993) and *Die Schneeberge Ecuador.*

Schmudlach, G *Bergfürer Ecuador* (Panico Alpinverlag, 2nd ed, 2009).

Coffee-table books

There are a great many gorgeous photo collections of Ecuador. Among the most original and beautiful are:

Anhalzer, J *Ecuador as Seen from Space* (and Guevara Nogales, M, Imprenta Mariscal, Quito, 2003); and *The High Andes of Ecuador* (Imprenta Mariscal, Quito, 2008).

de Roy, T *Los Andes a Vuelo de Cóndor* (Ediciones Libri Mundi, 2005).

Oxford, P and Bish, R *Ecuador* (Imprenta Mariscal, 3rd ed, Quito, 2008); and Chagras (Dinediciones, Quito, 2004).

Travelogues

Barrera Valverde, A *El País de Manuelito* (Editorial El Conejo, Quito, 1981).

Condamine, C *Diario del viaje al Ecuador* (1745; N Gómez ed, Ediguias, Quito, 1994).

Hassaurek, F *Four Years among the Ecuadorians* (1867; Southern Illinois University Press, 1967; Cuatro Años Entre Los Ecuatorianos, Abya-Yala, Quito, 1997).

Honigsbaum, M *Valverde's Gold* (Macmillan, London, 2004).

Lafond de Lurcy, G *Viajero y testigo de la historia ecuatoriana* (Banco Central del Ecuador, Quito, 1988).

Lara, D *Viajeros franceses al Ecuador en el siglo XIX* (Casa de la Cultura Ecuatoriana, Quito, 1972).

Lourie, P *Sweat of the Sun, Tears of the Moon* (Antheneum, New York, 1991).

Michaux, H *Ecuador* (1929; OUP, 1952).

Miller, T *The PanamaHat Trail* (Abacus, 1986).

Thomsen, M *Living Poor* (University of Washington Press, Seattle, 1969); and *Farm on the River of Emeralds* (Houghton Mifflin, Boston, 1978).

Whymper, E *Travels Amongst the Great Andes of the Equator* (1891; Gibbs M Smith, Salt Lake City, UT, USA, 1987; *Viajes a través de los majestuosos Andes del Ecuador*, Abya-Yala, Quito, 1994).

Trekking

Kunstaetter, R and D *Trekking in Ecuador* (The Mountaineers, Seattle, 2002, www.trekkinginecuador.com).
Rachoweicki, R and Thurber, M *Ecuador: Climbing and Hiking Guide* (Viva Travel Guides, 2009).

Galápagos Islands

General
Angermeyer, J *My Father's Island* (Anthony Nelson, 1998).
Darwin, C *Voyage of the Beagle* (1839; Penguin, London, 1989).
Latorre, O *The Curse of the Tortoise* (Quito, 2001).
Melville, H *The Encantadas* (1854; in Billy Bud, Sailor and Other Stories, Penguin, 1971).
Treherne, J *The Galápagos Affair* (Jonathan Cape, 1983).
Wittmer, M *Floreana* (Michael Joseph, 1961).

Field guides
Castro, I and Phillips, A *A Guide to the Birds of the Galápagos Islands* (Christopher Helm, 1996).
Constant, P *Galápagos: A Natural History Guide* (Odyssey, 7th ed, 2007), and *Marine Life of the Galapagos* (Calao Life Experience, 2003).
Horwell, D *Galápagos: the Enchanted Isles* (Dryad Press, 1988).
Hickman, J *The Enchanted Isles* (Anthony Nelson, 1985).
Hickman, P and Zimmerman, T *Galapagos Marine Life Series* (Sugar Spring Press, 2000).
Humann, P *Reef Fish Identification* (Libri Mundi, 1993).
Jackson, M *H, Galápagos: A Natural History Guide* (University of Calgary Press, 1985).

Merlen, G *A Field Guide to the Fishes of Galápagos* (Libri Mundi, 1988).
Schofield, E *Plants of the Galápagos Islands* (Universe Books, New York, 1984).

Coffee-table books
De Roy, T *Galapagos: Islands Born of Fire* (Swan Hill Press, 2001).
There are a great many others.

Oriente jungle

Kane, J *Savages* (Vintage Books, New York, 1996).
Kimerling, J *Amazon Crude* (Natural Resource Defense Council, 1991; Spanish translation, Abya-Yala, 2006).
Latorre, O *La Expedicióna laCanela y el Descubrimiento del Amazonas* (1995).
Perkins, J *Confessions of an Economic Hit Man* (Berrett-Koehler, 2004).
Smith, A *The Lost Lady of the Amazon* (Constable, UK, 2003).
Smith, R *Crisis Under the Canopy* (Abya-Yala, Quito).
Whitaker, R *The Mapmaker's Wife* (Basic Books, New York, 2004).

Practicalities
Ecuador

Getting there

Air

International flights into Ecuador arrive either at **Quito** (UIO) or **Guayaquil** (GYE); there are frequent domestic flights between the two, as well as ample bus services. International airfares from North America and Europe to Ecuador may vary with low and high season. High season is generally July to September and December. International flights to Ecuador from other South or Central American countries, however, usually have one price year-round. See also Tour operators, page 433.

From Europe
KLM, Iberia and LAN offer direct flights from Europe to Ecuador, the former originating in Amsterdam, the latter two in Madrid. Connections on several other European carriers can be made in Bogotá and Caracas. US carriers offer connections from Europe through their respective North American hubs, see below.

From North America
Miami's busy international airport is the most important air transport gateway linking Ecuador with North America. **American** has two daily non-stop flights from Miami to both Quito and Guayaquil. **LAN** flies daily from Miami to Quito and from New York City (JFK) to Guayaquil. **United** flies daily from Houston to Quito, and **Delta** flies daily from Atlanta to Quito.

From Australia and New Zealand
There are three options: 1) To Los Angeles, USA, with **Qantas**, **Air New Zealand** or **United**, continuing to Ecuador via Houston or Miami (see above); 2) From Auckland to Santiago, Chile, continuing to Ecuador, all with **LAN**; 3) To Buenos Aires, Argentina, from Sydney with **Aerolíneas Argentinas**, continuing to Ecuador with various South American carriers. These are all expensive long-haul routes. Round-the-World and Circle Pacific fares may be convenient alternatives.

From Latin America
There are flights to Quito and/or Guayaquil from Bogotá, Buenos Aires, Cali, Caracas, Lima, Mexico City, Panama City, San Salvador, Santiago and São Paulo. Connections can easily be made from other South American cities. **Copa** and **Avianca** offer connections between Ecuador and various destinations in Central America, Mexico and the Caribbean.

TRAVEL TIP

Packing for Ecuador

Everybody has their own list, below are a few things which are particularly useful for travelling in Ecuador. Try to think light and compact. All but the most specialized products are available in Quito and Guayaquil, while most basic commodities are readily purchased throughout the country.

A **moneybelt** or **pouch** is absolutely indispensable. Be sure to bring an adequate supply of any **medications** you take on a regular basis, plus two weeks' spare supply, as these may not be available in Ecuador. Sturdy comfortable **footwear** is a must for travels anywhere. **Sun protection** is very important in all regions of the country and for visitors of all complexions. This should include a sun hat, sunglasses and sunscreen for both skin and lips. Take **insect repellent** if you plan to visit the coast or jungle. Also recommended are **flip-flops** for use on the beach, at hot springs and in hotel showers. If you use **contact lenses**, be sure also to bring a pair of glasses. A small lightweight **towel** is an asset, as is a short length of **clothesline**. A compact **torch** (flashlight), **alarm**, **watch** and **pocket knife** may all be useful. Always carry some **toilet paper**, as this is seldom found in public washrooms unless it is sold at the entrance.

A good general principle is to take half the clothes and twice the money you think you will need. You should pack spring **clothing** for the highlands (mornings and evenings are cool), but on the coast tropical or lightweight clothes are needed. In general, clothing is less formal in the lowlands, both on the coast and in Oriente, where men and women wear shorts. In the highlands, people are more conservative; wearing shorts is acceptable for sports and on hiking trails, but long trousers or skirts are needed for churches or cemeteries. Nude bathing is generally unacceptable in Ecuador, so a swimsuit is essential.

Road and river

There are roads and international bus services to Ecuador from neighbouring Colombia and Peru as well as South American countries further afield, but no vehicle road connecting with Central America. The most advisable border crossings are at Tulcán in the north and Macará in the south.

Peru For land borders with Peru, see pages 218, 222 and 248; for river travel to and from Peru, see Coca, page 298. For details of immigration procedures at these borders, see under the relevant sections of respective towns.

Except for the Ecuadorean bus companies with routes from Guayaquil, Cuenca and Loja to cities in northern Peru, it is usually much cheaper to buy bus tickets only as far as the nearest border town, cross on foot or by taxi, and then purchase tickets locally in the country you have just entered. If entering Ecuador by car, customs procedures are given on page 419.

Getting around

Air

Ecuador is a small country and flying times are typically under one hour to all destinations, with the exception of Galápagos. Most flights originate in Quito but Guayaquil also has direct service to Coca, Cuenca, Latacunga, Loja and Galápagos, and there are frequent flights between the Guayaquil and Quito. Domestic airfares (except to Galápagos) are generally less than US$120 one way. Foreigners pay more than Ecuadoreans for flights to Galápagos. Seats are not assigned on domestic flights.

TAME is the most established Ecuadorean carrier and several other airlines also operate domestic routes, see below for details. The routes covered by domestic carries and their itineraries change frequently. For Galápagos flight details see page 372.

Domestic airlines

Avianca, T1-800-003434 or Quito T02-294 2800, www.avianca.com. Serving Quito, Guayaquil, Coca, Manta and Galápagos and international routes to Bogotá and Lima.
LAN, T1-800-842526, www.lan.com. Quito, Guayaquil, Cuenca and Galápagos and international routes to Miami, New York, Madrid, Lima and Santiago.

TAME, T1-700-500800 or Quito T02-397 7100, www.tame.com.ec. Quito, Guayaquil, Cuenca, Latacunga, Loja, Coca, Lago Agrio, Tena, Macas, Esmeraldas, Manta and Galápagos and international routes to Bogotá, Buenos Aires, Cali, Caracas, Lima, New York and São Paulo.

Rail

A series of mostly short tourist rides (some combining train and bus travel) have replaced regular passenger service along the spectacular Ecuadorean railway system, extensively restored in recent years. Some trains have two classes of service, standard and plus; carriages are fancier in the latter and a snack is included. On some routes, an *autoferro* (a motorized railcar) runs instead of the train. The following routes are on offer: **Quito to El Boliche** (Cotopaxi); **Alausí to Sibambe** via the Devil's Nose; **Ambato to Urbina**; **Riobamba to Urbina** or **Colta**; **Otavalo** and **Ibarra to Salinas**; **El Tambo to Coyoctor** near Ingapirca; **Durán** (outside Guayaquil) **to Bucay**; and the **Tren Crucero**, an upmarket all-inclusive tour of up to four days along the entire line from Quito to Durán. Details are given under What to do, in the corresponding city listings. Further details area aviable from **Empresa de Ferrocarriles Ecuatorianos** ⓘ *T1-800-873637, www.trenecuador.com.*

River

Few of Ecuador's jungle rivers are navigable by larger craft but a couple of tourist vessels operate on the lower Río Napo out of Coca (see page 297). Large motorized canoes provide local services downstream from Coca to the Peruvian border at Nuevo Rocafuerte and riverside towns en route.

Road

An excellent network of paved roads runs throughout most of the country. Maintenance of major highways is franchised to private firms, who charge tolls of around US$1. Roads are subject to damage during heavy rainy seasons. Always check road conditions before setting out. Unfortunately, better roads have meant higher speeds and more serious accidents. Bus and truck drivers, in particular, are known for their speed and recklessness. Driving is safer during the daytime, especially on mountain roads, and it is best to stay off the road altogether at the beginning and end of busy national holidays.

Highlands to the coast Several important roads, almost all paved, link the highlands and the Pacific coast. These include from north to south: Ibarra to San Lorenzo; Quito to Esmeraldas via Calacalí and La Independencia; Quito to Guayaquil via Alóag and Santo Domingo de los Tsáchilas (the busiest highway in Ecuador); Latacunga to Quevedo via La Maná; Ambato to Babahoyo via Guaranda; Riobamba to Guayaquil via Pallatanga and Bucay; Cuenca to Guayaquil via Zhud and La Troncal; Cuenca to Guayaquil via Molleturo; Cuenca to Machala via Girón and Pasaje; Loja to Machala or Huaquillas.

Coastal roads Santo Domingo de los Tsáchilas is the hub of most roads on the coast of Ecuador. From Guayaquil, the coastal route south to Peru is a major artery, with four lanes from Machala to the border. From Guayaquil north, there are coastal roads all the way to Mataje on the Colombian frontier.

East of the Andes On the eastern side of the Andes, roads from Quito, via Baeza, to Lago Agrio and Coca, Baños to Puyo, and Loja to Zamora are fully paved, as is the entire lowland road from Lago Agrio south to Zamora. Other access roads to Oriente (many are paved or in the process of being paved) include: Tulcán to Lago Agrio via Lumbaqui, Riobamba to Macas, and three different roads from Cuenca to Macas and Gualaquiza. Some roads are narrow and tortuous and subject to landslides in the rainy season, but all have regular bus service and all can be travelled in a 4WD or in an ordinary car with good ground clearance.

TRAVEL TIP

Driving in Ecuador

Bringing a vehicle to Ecuador To bring a foreign car or motorcycle into the country, its original registration document (title) in the name of the driver is required. If the driver is not the owner, a notarized letter of authorization is required. All documents must be accompanied by a Spanish translation. A 90-day permit is granted on arrival, extensions are only granted if the vehicle is in the garage for repairs. No security deposit is required and you can enter and leave at different land borders. Procedures are generally straightforward but it can be a matter of luck. Shipping a vehicle requires more paperwork and hiring a customs broker. The port of Guayaquil is prone to theft and particularly officious. Manta and Esmeraldas are smaller and more relaxed, but receive fewer ships. A valid driver's licence from your home country is generally sufficient to drive in Ecuador and rent a car, but an international licence is helpful.

Car hire To rent a car you must be at least 21 and have an international credit card. Surcharges apply to drivers aged 21-25. You will be asked to sign two blank credit card vouchers, one for the rental fee and the other as a security deposit for the vehicle, and authorization for a charge of as much as US$5000 may be requested against your credit card account if you do not purchase full insurance. The uncashed vouchers will be returned to you when you return the vehicle. Make sure the car is parked securely at night. A small car suitable for city driving costs around US$550 per week including unlimited mileage, tax and full insurance. A 4WD or pickup truck (recommended for unpaved roads) costs about US$1400 a week. Drop-off charges are about US$125.

Fuel There are two grades of petrol, 'Extra' (82 octane, US$1.48 per US gallon) and 'Super' (92 Octane, US$1.98-2.30). Both are unleaded. Extra is available everywhere, while Super may not be available in more remote areas. Diesel fuel (US$1.03) is notoriously dirty and available everywhere.

Buses, vans and shared taxis

Most destinations in Ecuador have frequent bus service and bus travel is generally convenient except for the location of Quito's terminals very far from the city centre. Many itineraries are listed on **http://latinbus.com**, where tickets for some major routes can be purchased online (for a fee). Bus fare increases were being implemented in 2015 as this edition went to press. The fares given in the text are approximate; confirm locally for exact amounts. **Note** Throughout Ecuador, travel by bus is safest during the daytime.

Vans and shared taxis operate between major cities and offer a faster, more comfortable and more expensive alternative to buses. Some provide pickup and drop-off at your hotel.

TRAVEL TIP

Bus travel tips

Bus travel in Ecuador can be a great way to get to know the country and its people. A few simple precautions should help you enjoy a safe trip.

Travel only by daylight. The risks are highest after dark, both for traffic accidents and for hold-ups. In the event of an assault, never resist or hold back your valuables, they are not worth getting hurt. Considering the risks, travelling overnight to save on accommodation is a poor strategy, besides you miss the views and arrive too tired to enjoy the next day's touring.

Some bus lines take precautions against hold-ups on their longer routes, like not stopping to pick up passengers between towns or photographing passengers when they first board the bus. You should also take your own precautions. Politely refuse any food, drink, sweets or cigarettes offered by strangers on a bus. These may be drugged as a way of robbing you. Two tourists travelling together in adjacent seats are at less risk.

Always carry money and valuable documents in your money-belt with you on the bus, but also have some spare cash at hand. Keep a separate stash of cash in your luggage. Never use the overhead rack for your belongings nor place them under your seat. A daypack can be slashed from the seat behind you, best keep it on your lap and ignore anyone who insists on you doing otherwise. If you want to hold your seat at a stop, leave a newspaper or other insignificant item on it, not your bag.

Luggage can be checked with the larger bus companies and will be stowed in a locked compartment. On smaller buses it usually rides on the roof, in which case you should make sure it is covered with a tarpaulin to protect against dust and rain. In all cases it is your own responsibility to keep an eye on your gear, never leave it unattended at bus stations.

Some buses have toilets on board but neither these nor the sanitary facilities at rest stops are likely to be very clean. Avoid the very back of the bus if you can, as you will be right next to the toilet. Take warm clothing when travelling in the highlands.

It is possible to buy food and drinks on the roadside, but keep an eye out for hygiene and make sure you have small change on hand. Bus drivers usually know the best places for meal stops and some roadside *comedores* can be quite good. On a longer journey, take snacks and a bottle of water just in case.

Cycling

Given ample time and reasonable energy, a bicycle is one of the best modes of transport for exploring Ecuador. It can be ridden, carried by almost every form of transport from an aeroplane to a jungle canoe, and can even be lifted across one's shoulders over short distances. Also see Mountain biking, page 23.

Tips Strong and waterproof front and back panniers are a must. When packed these are likely to be heavy and should be carried on the strongest racks available.

Everything should be packed in plastic bags for protection against dust and rain. Take care to avoid dehydration; drink regularly. In hot, dry areas with limited water, be sure to carry an ample supply.

Security When sightseeing, try to leave your bicycle with someone such as a café owner or shopkeeper. Always see that your bicycle is secure (most hotels will allow bikes to be kept in rooms). A good bike lock is essential equipment.

Dogs Dogs are ubiquitous in Ecuadorean towns and the countryside; they love to chase bikes and have been known to bite riders.

Traffic Main roads and highways are a nightmare; it is far more rewarding to keep to the smaller country roads. When riding in big cities, Ecuadorean cyclists recommend behaving like a car and occupying the entire lane; this is safer and drivers usually respect you. Quito and Cuenca have bike lanes on some streets. Make yourself conspicuous by wearing bright clothing and always use a helmet. A rearview mirror is indispensable.

Repairs Most towns have a bicycle shop of some description, but it is best to do your own repairs and adjustments whenever possible. Big city bike shops may also have boxes/cartons in which to send bicycles home. The **Expedition Advisory Centre**, administered by the **Royal Geographical Society**, www.rgs.org, has a useful monograph entitled *Bicycle Expeditions*, by Paul Vickers, which can be downloaded free from their website. In the UK there is also the **Cyclist's Touring Club (CTC)**, www.ctc.org.uk, for touring and technical information.

Transporting a bike Check with airlines about their policy regarding bicycles before purchasing tickets. Most Ecuadorean bus lines will carry bicycles on the roof racks for little or no extra charge. It is advisable to supervise the loading and assure that the derailleur is not jammed up against luggage which might damage it. If you can, take some cardboard to protect the bike while it's on the bus. If you take a long bus journey with major altitude changes let a little air out of the tyres especially when going from lower to higher altitudes.

Hitchhiking

Public transport in Ecuador is so abundant that there is seldom any need to hitchhike along the major highways. On small out-of-the-way country roads however, the situation can be quite different, and giving passers-by a ride is common practice and safe. A small fee is usually charged, check in advance. For obvious reasons women should not hitch alone. Besides, you are more likely to get a lift if you are with a partner, be they male or female.

Taxis

In major cities, all taxis must in principle use meters. At especially busy times or at night drivers may nonetheless refuse to so, in which case you should always agree on the fare before you get in.

Maps and city guides

Instituto Geográfico Militar (IGM) ⓘ *Senierges y Telmo Paz y Miño, east of Parque El Ejido, Quito, T02-397 5100, ext 2502, www.geoportaligm.gob.ec, Mon-Thu 0730-1600, Fri 0700-1430, take ID.* Country and topographic maps are available in a variety of printed and digital formats. Prices range from US$3 to US$7. Maps of border and sensitive areas are 'reservado' (classified) and not available for sale without a permit. It's best to buy all your maps here as they are rarely available outside Quito.

Essentials A-Z

Accident and emergency

For all emergencies nationwide, T911.

Children

Travel with children can bring you into closer contact with Ecuadorean families and, generally, presents no special problems – in fact the path may even be smoother for family groups. Officials are sometimes more amenable where children are concerned and they are pleased if your child knows a little Spanish. For more detailed advice, see Footprint's *Travel with Kids* by William Gray.

Bus travel Remember that a lot of time can be spent waiting for and riding buses. You should take reading material with you as it is difficult to find and expensive. Also look for the locally available comic strip *Condorito*, which is quite popular and a good way for older children to learn a bit of Spanish. Reading on the bus itself, especially on winding mountain roads, is not recommended. On long-distance buses you pay for each seat, and there are no half fares. For shorter trips it is cheaper, if less comfortable, to seat small children on your knee. Sometimes there are spare seats which children can occupy after tickets have been collected. Make sure that children accompanying you are fully covered by your travel insurance policy.

Food This can be a problem if the children are not adaptable. It is easier to take food with you on longer journeys than to rely on meal stops where the food may not be to taste. Avocados are safe, readily available, easy to eat and nutritious; they can be fed to babies as young as 6 months and most older children like them. Best stick to simple things like bread, bananas and tangerines while you are actually on the road. Biscuits, packaged junk food and bottled drinks abound. In restaurants, you can try to buy a *media porción* (half portion), or divide a full-sized helping between 2 children.

Customs and duty free

On arrival

Customs inspection is carried out at airports after you clear immigration. When travelling by land, customs authorities may also set up checkpoints along the country's highways. Tourists seldom encounter any difficulties but if you are planning to bring any particularly unusual or valuable items to Ecuador then you should enquire beforehand with an Ecuadorean diplomatic representative (see Embassies and consulates, page 424) and obtain any necessary permits, or be prepared to pay the prevailing customs duties. Reasonable amounts of climbing gear, personal photo/video equipment and one laptop are generally not a problem. For details on bringing a vehicle into Ecuador, see box, page 419.

Shipping goods to Ecuador

Except for documents, customs duties must be paid on all goods shipped to Ecuador. Enforcement is strict, duties are high and procedures are slow and complicated. You are therefore advised to bring anything you think you will need with you when you travel, rather than having it sent to you once you are in the country.

On departure

Your airline baggage will be inspected by security personnel and sniffed by dogs looking for drugs. Never transport anything you have not packed yourself, you will be held responsible for the contents.

No export duties are charged on souvenirs you take home from Ecuador, but there are various items for which you require special permits. These include specimens of wild plants and animals, original archaeological artefacts, certain works of art and any objects considered part of the country's national heritage. When in doubt, enquire well in advance.

Disabled travellers

Disabled Ecuadoreans have finally been receiving a little more attention since Lenin Moreno, who is paraplegic, served as vice-president (2007-2013). As with most Latin American countries however, facilities for the disabled traveller are still sadly lacking. Wheelchair ramps are a rare luxury in most of the country, but they are present in the resort town of **Baños**, see page 169. Getting a wheelchair into a bathroom or toilet is well nigh impossible, except for some of the more upmarket hotels (for example **Swissôtel** in Quito and **Blue Marlin** in Galápgaos as well as the more affordable **La Floresta** in Baños). Quito's trolley system has wheelchair access in principle, but it is much too crowded to make this practical. Disabled Ecuadoreans obviously have to cope with these problems and mainly rely

on the help of others to move around; fortunately most bystanders are very helpful.

Some travel companies specialize in exciting holidays, tailor-made for individuals with a variety of disabilities. For further information, consult the **Disabled Travel Network**, www.disabledtravelers.com.

Electricity

110 v AC, 60 cycles, US-type flat-pin plugs.

Embassies and consulates

For all Ecuadorean embassies and consulates abroad and for all foreign embassies and consulates in Ecuador, see http://embassy.goabroad.com and http://cancilleria.gob.ec.

Health

Health care in Ecuador is varied: there are some excellent clinics and hospitals, which usually follow the North American style of medicine (where you are referred straight to a specialist), but as with all medical care, first impressions count. If a facility looks grubby, then be wary of the general standard of medicine and hygiene. The best medical facilities and physicians who speak languages other than Spanish are located in Quito, Guayaquil and Cuenca, and are generally expensive. Your embassy or consulate can usually make recommendations.

Medical services in Ecuador
The following hospitals and clinics are recommended.

Cuenca
Hospital Monte Sinaí, Miguel Cordero

6-111 y Av Solano, near the stadium, T07-288 5595, several English-speaking physicians.

Hospital Santa Inés, Av Toral 2-113, T07-281 7888; Dr Jaime Moreno Aguilar speaks English.

Galápagos Islands
Public Hospital, Av Baltra, Pto Ayora, Santa Cruz.

Public Hospital, Av Northía y Quito, Pto Baquerizo Moreno, San Cristóbal.

Guayaquil
Clínica Alcívar, Coronel 2301 y Azuay, T04-258 0030.

Clínica Guayaquil, Padre Aguirre 401 y General Córdova, T04-256 3555 (Dr Roberto Gilbert speaks English and German).

Clínica Kennedy, Av San Jorge y la 9na, T04-228 9666. Reliable; also has branches in Ciudadela La Alborada XIII, Mz-1227 and Entre Ríos. It has many specialists (Dr Roberto Morla speaks German) and a very competent emergency department.

Ibarra
Instituto Médico de Especialidades, Egas 1-83 y Av Teodoro Gómez de La Torre, northern highlands, T06-295 5612.

Latacunga
Clínica Latacunga, Sánchez de Orellana 11-79 y Marqués de Maenza, central highlands, T03-281 0260, 24 hrs.

Loja
Clínica San Agustín, 18 de Noviembre 10-72 y Azuay, T07-257 3002.

Quito
Clínica Pichincha, Veintimilla E3-30 y Páez, T02-256 2296, ambulance T02-250 1565. Good but expensive.

Metropolitano, Mariana de Jesús y Occidental, T02-226 1520, ambulance T02-226 5020. Very professional and recommended, but expensive.

Voz Andes, Villalengua Oe 2-37 y Av 10 de Agosto, T02-226 2142, quick and efficient, fee based on ability to pay, a good place to get vaccines.

Before you go
See your GP/practice nurse or travel clinic at least 6 weeks before your departure for general advice on travel risks, malaria prevention and recommended vaccinations. Make sure you have travel insurance, get a dental check (especially if you are going to be away for more than a month), know your own blood group and if you suffer a long-term condition such as diabetes or epilepsy make sure someone knows or that you have a **Medic Alert** bracelet/necklace with this information on it.

Vaccinations
Vaccinations for yellow fever and rabies (if travelling to jungle and/or remote areas), as well as hepatitis B are commonly recommended for Ecuador. The final decision, however, should be based on a consultation with your GP or travel clinic. You should also confirm your primary courses and boosters are up to date (diphtheria, tetanus, poliomyelitis, hepatitis A, typhoid). A yellow fever certificate is required by visitors over one year old who are entering from an infected area. **Malaria** precautions are important for the Oriente jungle and far northern Pacific coast (below 1500 m) all year round, see below. Specialist advice should be taken on the best anti-malarial to use.

Health risks

Altitude sickness is a common but usually mild affliction for most visitors to Ecuador. Flying into Quito (2840 m) from sea level is likely to leave you feeling a bit lightheaded for the first few days, so give yourself a chance to acclimatize before heading off on trips and treks. Smokers and those with underlying heart or lung disease are often hardest hit. Take it easy for a few days, rest from your trip and drink plenty of water; you will feel better soon. It is essential to get acclimatized before undertaking long treks or arduous activities. No one should attempt to climb over 5000 m until they have spent at least a week at the height of Quito and then a couple of nights around 4000 m. Agencies who offer 2-day climbs without adequate acclimatization are not to be trusted.

Because you are so close to the equator, **sun protection** is a must throughout Ecuador, especially on the beach and in the highlands regardless of how cool it may feel; always use sun block and a hat. All travellers, especially mountaineers, should use sunglasses that provide 100% UV protection.

The major health risks in lower parts of the country are those **diseases carried by insects** such as mosquitoes and sandflies. These include malaria, dengue fever, chikungunya, and less frequently Chagas disease and leishmaniasis. Because insects bite at different times of day, repellent application and covered limbs are a 24-hr issue. Long trousers, a long-sleeved shirt and insect repellent all offer protection. Mosquito nets dipped in permethrin provide a good physical and chemical barrier at night.

A bout of **stomach upset** is almost inevitable on a longer visit to Ecuador. Consider it part of the travel experience and don't get scared or overreact. The standard advice to avoid diarrhoea is to be careful with water and ice for drinking. If you have any doubts then boil it, filter it or treat it. There are many filter/treatment devices available on the market. Food can also transmit disease. Be wary of salads, reheated foods or food that has been left out in the sun having been previously cooked. There is a simple adage that says wash it, peel it, boil it or forget it. Also be wary of raw salads and undercooked meat. The key treatment with all diarrhoea is rehydration. Try to keep hydrated by taking the right mixture of salt and water. This is available in Ecuadorean pharmacies as an oral rehydration solution (*suero oral)* or can be made up by adding a teaspoon of sugar and a half teaspoon of salt to a litre of clean water. If diarrhoea persists for several days or you develop additional symptoms, then see a physician.

Road accidents are an often overlooked threat to travellers' health. You can reduce the likelihood of accidents by not travelling at night, avoiding overcrowded buses, not drinking and driving, wearing a seatbelt in cars and a helmet on bicycles and motorbikes (even if some Ecuadoreans do not).

If you go **diving** make sure that you are fit do so. The **British Sub-Aqua Club** (**BSAC**), www.bsac.com, can put you in touch with doctors who do medical examinations. Protect your feet and keep an eye out for secondary infection. Check that the dive company has appropriate certification from **BSAC** or **PADI**, www.padi.com, and that the equipment is well maintained. In case of emergency, there is a hyperbaric chamber in Puerto Ayora. Make sure you allow plenty of time after diving before taking a flight (see box, page 368).

Useful websites

www.btha.org British Travel Health Association.

www.cdc.gov US government site that gives excellent advice on travel health and details of disease outbreaks.

www.gov.uk/foreign-travel-advice British Foreign and Commonwealth Office travel site has useful information on eachcountry, people, climate and a list of UK embassies/consulates abroad.

www.fitfortravel.scot.nhs.uk A-Z of vaccine/health advice for each country.

www.travelhealth.co.uk Independent travel health site with advice on vaccination, travel insurance and health risks.

www.who.int World Health Organization.

Identification

You are required by Ecuadorean law to carry your passport at all times. Whether or not a photocopy is an acceptable substitute is at the discretion of the individual police officer, having it notarized can help.

Insurance

Travel insurance is a must for all visitors to Ecuador. Always take out insurance that covers both medical expenses and baggage loss, and read the small print carefully before you set off. Check that all the activities you may end up doing are covered. Mountaineering and scuba diving, for example, as well as 'adrenalin sports' like bridge jumps and canyoning are excluded from many policies. Also check if medical coverage includes air ambulance and emergency flights back home. Be aware of the payment protocol: in Ecuador you are likely to have to pay out-of-pocket and later request reimbursement from the insurance company. Have the receipts for expensive personal effects like cameras and laptops on file, take photos of these items and note the serial numbers.

Internet

Cyber cafés are common in the cities and towns of Ecuador but are gradually being replaced by widespread Wi-Fi access. Wi-Fi is available in most hotels, at many cafés and in some public places.

Language

The official languages of Ecuador are **Spanish** and **Quichua**. English and a few other European languages may be spoken in some establishments catering to tourists in Quito and the most popular tourist destinations. Away from these places, knowledge of Spanish is essential, so it's a good idea to learn some before you go, or begin your travels in Ecuador with a period of language study. Language training opportunities abound; see box, Language schools in Quito, page 75. Schools in Cuenca, Otavalo, Baños, Montañita, Puerto López, Manta and Canoa can be found in the 'What to do' listings for each town. The following USA-based companies can also organize language training in Ecuador: **AmeriSpan**, T1-800-511 0179, www.amerispan.com and **Spanish Abroad**, T1-888-722 7623, www.spanishabroad.com.

There may be opportunities to learn Quichua at the **Universidad Católica** in Quito (see box, page 75), at the

Universidad de Otavalo, T06-292 3850, ext 113, and at **CEDEI** in Cuenca (see page 210); enquire well in advance.

Living in Ecuador

Since 2005 a growing number of foreigners, many of them retirees, have settled in Ecuador. Cuenca has the largest expatriate community in the country, numbering in the thousands, and colonies have also sprung up in Cotacachi, Jama, Manta and Vilcabamba, among other locations. 'Colonies' is an unfortunately accurate term, as many expats have chosen to isolate themselves physically and culturally from Ecuadoreans by living in gated communities and not learning Spanish. Real estate prices have soared in expat areas and this, alongside cultural insensitivity on the part of the foreigners, has led to local resentment. If considering a move to Ecuador, you are strongly advised to come for an extended visit first, to get to know the country, blemishes and all. Note the public safety situation (see below), and remember that you are undertaking a major life-change, not merely looking for a place with lower prices and a better climate than your current home. Be cautious with the many real-estate agents, attorneys, middle-men and facilitators, be they foreign or Ecuadorean, who have made a growth industry of catering to expatriates.

LGBT travellers

The Ecuadorean constitution prohibits discrimination on the basis of sexual orientation and attitudes have gradually become more liberal in big cities including Quito, Guayaquil and Cuenca. In small towns, however, values are still conservative. In order to avoid offending local sensibilities, discretion is advised to same-sex couples travelling in Ecuador. **Zenith Travel**, www.zenithecuador.com. Has a department that caters to gay and lesbian travellers, English and French spoken. See also www.quitogay.net.

Media

The main national newspapers include *El Comercio* (Quito, **www.elcomercio.com**), *El Hoy* (Quito, **www.hoy.com.ec**), *El Mercurio* (Cuenca, **www.elmercurio.com.ec**), *El Universo* (Guayaquil, **www.eluniverso.com**) and *La Hora* (various regional editions, good for local news, **www.lahora.com.ec**). They all offer reasonably accurate reporting without any strong political bias.

Ecuadorean television tends to be more sensationalist than the print media, and radio is best reserved for music. Among the major television broadcasters are **Ecuavisa** (www.ecuavisa.com), **TC Televisión** (www.tctelevision.com) and **Teleamazonas** (www.teleamazonas.com). A smaller highly regarded TV station is **Telerama** (www.telerama.ec) from Cuenca. **Ecuador TV** (www.ecuadortv.ec) is public broadcasting; some of their programs feature the tourist attractions of the country.

International satellite or cable television is common even in inexpensive hotels and streaming video from anywhere in the world can be had wherever there is Wi-Fi. Foreign newspapers and magazines are available in luxury hotels and a few speciality shops in Quito and Guayaquil.

Money

The **US dollar** (US$) is the official currency of Ecuador. Only US$ bills circulate. US coins are used alongside the equivalent size and value Ecuadorean coins. Ecuadorean coins have no value outside the country. Many establishments are reluctant to accept bills larger than US$20 because of counterfeit notes or lack of change. There is no substitute for cash-in-hand when travelling in Ecuador; US$ cash in small denominations is by far the simplest and the only universally accepted option. Other currencies are difficult to exchange outside large cities and fetch a poor rate. Some of the US$ banknotes circulating in Ecuador are tattered and grubby. If travelling on to Peru try to exchange these for crisper cleaner bills, as the scruffy ones will not be accepter there.

Credit cards, ATMs and banks

The most commonly accepted **credit cards** are Visa, MasterCard, Diners and, to a lesser extent, American Express. Paying by credit card may incur a surcharge, bargaining and obtaining discounts is easier if you pay cash. Cash advances on credit cards can be obtained through many ATMs (only Banco de Guayaquil for Amex), but daily limits apply. Larger advances on Visa, MasterCard and less frequently Amex are available from several banks. Their fees, procedures and the time required vary considerably and are subject to change, confirm all details locally. Among the more efficient banks for cash advances in Ecuador are: **Banco del Austro** (www. bancodelaustro.com), up to US$2000 a day on Visa or MC, 4% commission; **Banco Bolivariano** (www.bolivariano.

com.ec), up to US$1000 a day on Visa or MC, no commission.

Internationally linked **ATMs** are common, although not all machines work with all cards. Credit cards are generally easier to use in Ecuadorean ATMs than debit cards. ATMs are a focus for scams and robberies, use them judiciously. Funds may be rapidly wired to Ecuador by **Western Union** (www.westernunion.com) or **MoneyGram** (www.moneygram.com), fees and taxes apply, enquire in advance. With very few exceptions, travellers' cheques are of no use in Ecuador.

Cost of living/travelling

A budget of US$60-75 pp a day, including transport, will allow you to travel fairly comfortably. Your budget will be higher if you are staying in big cities, Galápagos and resort areas (especially in high season) and depending on how many internal flights you take. Bus travel is about US$1.25 per hr; flights cost almost 10 times as much for the same route. Rooms range from about US$10-15 pp for basic accommodation to about US$30-40 for mid-range places, to more than US$100 for upmarket hotels.

Opening hours

Banks Mon-Fri 0900-1700.
Government offices Variable hours Mon-Fri, some close for lunch. **Other offices** 0900-1230, 1430-1800.
Shops 0900-1900; close at midday in smaller towns, open till 2100 on the coast.

Post and courier

The Ecuadorean post office is known as **Correos del Ecuador** (www. correosdelecuador.gob.ec).

Opening hours for post offices may vary from town to town and from branch to branch. In Quito they are generally Mon-Fri 0800-1800, Sat 0800-1200. Postal branches in small towns may not be familiar with all rates and procedures. Your chances are better at the main branches in provincial capitals, also in Otavalo, and better yet in Quito: at Colón corner Almagro in La Mariscal district, at the main sorting centre on Japón N36-153 y Naciones Unidas (behind the CCI shopping centre), or at Ulloa 273 y Ramírez Dávalos for very large parcels.

EMS (Express Mail) is the fastest and most expensive service. Registered mail is a slower and more economical option for important items. Both can be tracked on line.

For international courier service, **DHL** (www.dhl.com.ec) has offices in the larger cities. For courier service within Ecuador, **Servientrega** (www. servientrega.com.ec) has offices throughout the country; a reliable 1- to 2-day service is available to all areas and costs about US$4 for up to 2 kg. There are also other courier companies operating in Ecuador, but quality of service and reliability vary greatly.

Public holidays

The following are national public holidays. Other local holidays are listed under the corresponding cities and towns. There is no hard and fast rule for public holidays which fall on a weekday. They are sometimes moved at the last moment to make a long weekend (*un puente*), ask around in advance.

1 Jan   **New Year's Day**.
Feb/Mar   **Carnival**, Mon and Tue before Lent.
Mar/Apr   **Easter**, **Maundy Thu** and **Good Fri**.
1 May   **Labour Day**.
24 May   **Battle of Pichincha** (Independence Day).
10 Aug   **1st attempt at independence**.
9 Oct   **Independence of Guayaquil**.
2 Nov   **Day of the Dead**.
3 Nov   **Independence of Cuenca**.
25 Dec   **Christmas Day**.

Punctuality

Ecuadoreans, like most Latin Americans, have a fairly relaxed attitude towards time. They will think nothing of arriving an hour or so late on social occasions. If you expect to meet someone at an exact time, you can tell them that you want to meet at such and such an hour *'en punto'*.

Safety

Public safety is an important concern throughout mainland Ecuador; Galápagos is generally safe. Armed robbery, bag snatching and slashing, and holdups along the country's highways are among the most significant hazards. 'Express kidnapping', whereby victims are taken from ATM to ATM and forced to withdraw money, is a threat in major cities, and fake taxis are often involved. Radio taxis are usually safer.

Secure your belongings at all times, be wary of con tricks, avoid crowds and congested urban transport, and travel during the daytime. It is the larger cities, especially Guayaquil, Quito, Cuenca, Manta, Machala, Esmeraldas and Santo Domingo which call for the greatest care. Small towns and the countryside in the highlands are generally safer than on the coast or in the jungle. The entire border with Colombia calls for precautions; enquire locally before travelling off the beaten path there.

Although currently uncommon, sporadic social unrest remains part of life in Ecuador and you should not overreact. Strikes and protests are usually announced days or weeks in advance, and their most significant impact on tourists is the restriction of overland travel. It is usually best to wait it out rather than insisting on keeping to your original itinerary.

Drugs

Almost all foreigners serving long sentences in Ecuador's squalid jails are there on drug charges. The authorities carry out sporadic raids in bars and clubs, anti-narcotics police set up checkpoints along the country's roads, and drug searches may be conducted at international departures areas of airports.

Anyone found carrying even the smallest amount of drugs may be automatically considered a trafficker. If arrested, the wait for trial in prison can take several years. Your foreign passport will not shield you in this situation, indeed you may be dealt with more harshly because of it. If you are unconvinced, then visit an Ecuadorean prison to see for yourself. Your embassy can give you the names of citizens of your country serving sentences who would appreciate a visitor.

Hotel security

The cheapest hotels are usually found near markets and bus stations but these are also the least safe areas of most Ecuadorean towns. Look for something

a little better if you can afford it, and if you must stay in a suspect area, try to return to your hotel before dark. If you trust your hotel, then you can leave any valuables you don't need in their safe deposit box, but always keep an inventory of what you have deposited.

An alternative to leaving valuables with the hotel administration is to lock everything in your luggage and secure that in your room; a light bicycle cable and a small padlock will provide at least a psychological deterrent for would-be thieves. Even in the safest hotels, never leave valuables strewn about your room.

Protecting money and valuables

Make photocopies of important documents and give them to your family or travelling companion, this may speed up replacement if documents are lost or stolen and will allow you to have some ID while getting replacements. Keep all documents (including your passport, credit and debit cards) secure and hide your main cash supply in several different places. If one stash is lost or stolen, you will still have the others to fall back on.

The following means of concealing cash and documents have all been recommended: extra pockets sewn inside shirts and trousers, pockets closed with a zip or safety pin, money-belts (best worn below the waist and never within sight) and neck or leg pouches. Never carry valuables in an ordinary pocket, purse or daypack. Keep fancy cameras in bags or daypacks and generally out of sight. Do not wear expensive wrist watches or jewellery. If you are wearing a shoulder bag in a crowd, carry it in front of you. In crowded places wear your daypack on your chest with both straps looped over your shoulders. Whenever visiting an area which is considered unsafe, take the bare minimum of valuables with you.

Street crime and scams
Pickpockets, bag snatchers and slashers are always a hazard for tourists, especially in crowded areas such as markets. Keep alert and avoid swarms of people. Crowded city buses and the various Quito and Guayaquil mass transit lines are notorious for thieves. Likewise avoid deserted areas, such as parks or plazas after hours. If someone follows you when you're in the street, slip into a nearby shop or hail a cab. If you are the victim of an armed assault, never resist or hold back your valuables; they can always be replaced.

The old scam of smearing tourists with mustard, ketchup, shaving cream and almost anything else, in order to distract and rob them, is alive and well in Ecuador. It happens on the street and in cybercafés. An apparently well-meaning bystander usually helps clean you up, while their accomplice expertly cleans you out. If you are smeared, move along quickly to a secure location or hail a cab.

More sinister but fortunately less frequent is drugging people in order to rob them. The drugs can be added to food, drink or cigarettes. Politely refuse these and keep an eye on your drink in bars. Victims usually awaken hours or days after the fact with a splitting headache and without their belongings.

Volcanoes
Ecuador's active volcanoes are spectacular, but have occasionally threatened nearby communities. The **National Geophysics Institute** provides daily updates at www.igepn.edu.ec.

Smoking

Smoking is not permitted on buses and is not appropriate in restaurants. A few better hotels have non-smoking rooms or are entirely non-smoking.

Student travellers

An **International Student Identity Card (ISIC)** may help you obtain some discounts when travelling in Ecuador. ISIC cards are sold by **Grupo Idiomas**, Roca 130 y 12 de Octubre, p 2, Quito, T02-250 0264; Junín 203 y Panamá, p 2, Guayaquil, T04-256 6939. They need proof of full-time enrolment in Ecuador or abroad (minimum 20 hrs per week), 2 photos, passport, US$20 and the application form found in www.isic.com.ec.

Tax

Airport tax International and domestic departure tax is included in the ticket price.
VAT/IVA 12%, may be reclaimed on departure if you show official invoices with your name and passport number; don't bother with amounts under US$50. High surtaxes applied to various imported items make them expensive to purchase in Ecuador.

Telephone

Country code +593.
There are independent phone offices, *cabinas*, in most cities and towns, but mobile (cellular) phones are by far the most common form of telecommunication. You can purchase a SIM card (*un chip*) for US$5 for either of the 2 main mobile carriers: **Claro** and **Movistar**; in principle an Ecuadorean *cédula* (national ID card) is required but

a passport is sometimes accepted or ask an Ecuadorean friend to buy a chip for you. The chips work with many foreign mobile phones, but enquire about your unit before purchasing. Mobile phone shops are everywhere, look for the carrier's logo. You get an Ecuadorean mobile phone number and can purchase credit (*recarga*) anywhere for as much or as little as you like. Calls cost about US$0.20 per min and only the caller pays. Mobile phone numbers have 10 digits starting with 09, landlines (*fijos*) have 7 digits plus an area code (eg 02 for Quito, 04 for Guayaquil). When calling a landline from a mobile, you must include the area code. Skype and similar services on Wi-Fi-enabled devices are the most economical form of international communication from Ecuador.

Time

GMT-5 on the Ecuadorean mainland, GMT-6 in Galápagos.

Tipping

In most of the better restaurants a 10% service charge is included in the bill, but you can give a modest additional tip if the service is especially good. Many simpler restaurants, especially those serving set meals, do not include service in the bill and tips are not expected. Taxi drivers are not usually tipped, but you can always round up the fare for particularly good service. Tipping for all other services is entirely discretionary, how much depends on the quality of service received.

Tour operators

For local operators see Quito (page 76), Guayaquil (page 243), Galápagos (page 370), and cities throughout the text.

UK and Ireland
For further information on specialist travel firms, contact the **Latin American Travel Association**, www.lata.org.
Amazing Ecuador, 9 Alma Rd, Manchester M19 2FG, T0808-234 6805 (freephone) www.amazingdestinations. net. Adventure, cultural and ecological tours including land-based tour to the Galápagos. Offices in Quito and in the Galápagos.
Austral Tours, 20 Upper Tachbrook St, London SW1V 1SH, T020-7233 5384, www.latinamerica.co.uk. Tailor-made itineraries, including flights and accommodation.
Chimu Adventures, 15 Theed St, London SE1 8ST, T020-7403 8265, www.chimuadventures.com. Offers

tailor-made itineraries throughout South America and expedition cruises to Antarctica.

Condor Journeys and Adventures, 2 Ferry Bank, Colintraive, Argyll PA22 3AR, T01700-841 318, www.condorjourneys-adventures.com. Ecuador and Galápagos specialist tour operator; tailor-made and activity holidays.

Cox & Kings Travel, 6th floor, 30 Millbank, London SW1P 4EE, T020-7873 5000, www.coxandkings.co.uk. Quality group tours and tailor-made holidays to many of the world's most fascinating regions; from the lavish to the adventurous, planned by experts.

Explore, 1 Frederick St, Aldershot, Hants GU11 1LQ, T0870-333 4002, www.explore.co.uk. Highly respected operator with offices in Ireland, Australia, New Zealand, USA and Canada, running 2- to 5-week tours in more than 90 countries worldwide, including Ecuador.

Equatorial Travel, 3a Victoria Sq, Ashbourne, Derbyshire DE6 1GG, T01335-348770, www.equatorialtravel.co.uk. Fair Trade tours to Ecuador as well as other parts of the world.

Galapagos Classic Cruises, 6 Keyes Rd, London NW2 3XA, T020-8933 0613, www.galapagoscruises.co.uk. An experienced company providing specialist cruises, diving holidays and adventure tours for individuals and groups.

Geodyssey, 116 Tollington Park, London N4 3RB, T020-7281 7788, www.geodyssey.co.uk. In-depth travel service for Ecuador and the Galápagos, with specialist itineraries and tailor-made tours available.

Journey Latin America, 401 King St, London W6 9NJ, T020-3432 5923, www.journeylatinamerica.co.uk. Specialist in tailor-made holidays in Latin America; offers a wide range of flight options.

Last Frontiers, Fleet Marston Farm, Aylesbury, Buckinghamshire HP18 0QT, T01296-653000, www.lastfrontiers.com. South American specialists offering tailor-made itineraries to Ecuador including the Galápagos, plus specialist themed tours.

Select Latin America (incorporating **Galapagos Adventure Tours**), 3.51 Canterbury Court, 1-3 Brixton Rd, Kennington Park Business Centre, London SW9 6DE, T020-7407 1478, www.selectlatinamerica.co.uk. Tailor-made holidays and small group tours. Specialist in cruises around the Galápagos Islands.

South American Experience, 47 Causton St, Pimlico, London SW1P 4AT, T020-7976 5511, www.southamericanexperience.co.uk. Flights, accommodation and tailor-made trips.

Steppes Travel, 51 Castle St, Cirencester

GL7 1QD, T01285-885333, www.
steppestravel.co.uk. Ecuador mainland
and Galápagos tours. Tailor-made
itineraries for destinations throughout
Latin America.

Sunvil Latin America, Sunvil House,
Upper Sq, Old Isleworth, Middlesex TW7
7BJ, T020-8758 4774, www.sunvil.co.uk.
Fly/drive and small group holidays for
adventurous travellers.

Trips Worldwide, 14 Frederick Pl,
Clifton, Bristol BS8 1AS, T0117-311
4400, www.trips worldwide.co.uk.
Broad range of travel options and
tours across Latin America.

North America

Ecoventura-Galapagos Network,
5805 Blue Lagoon Dr, Suite 160, Miami,
FL 33126, T1-800-633 7972, T1-305-262
6264, www.ecoventura.com. Galápagos
cruises and mainland tours.

**eXito Latin American Travel
Specialists**, 712 Bancroft Rd 455, Walnut
Creek, CA 94598, USA, T1-800-655 4053,
www.exitotravel.com. Latin America
experts.

**International Nature & Cultural
Adventures (INCA)**, 1311 63rd St,
Emeryville CA94608, T1-510-420
1550, www.inca1.com. Tailor-made
itineraries in the Galápagos aboard their
16-passenger luxury yacht *Integrity*.

Ladatco Tours, 2200 South Dixie
Highway, Suite 704, Coconut Grove, FL
33133, T1-800-327 6162, www.ladatco.
com. South American specialists,
operate explorer tours.

Myths and Mountains, 976 Tee
Ct, Incline Village, Nevada 89451,
USA, T1-800-670 6984, www.
mythsandmountains.com. Cultural and
natural tours of Galápagos and Ecuador.

Tambo Tours, 4405 Spring Cypress Rd,
Suite 210, Spring, TX 77388, USA, T1-888-
2-GO-PERU (246-7378), T1-281-528 9448,
www.2GOPERU.com. Long-established
adventure and tour specialist with
offices in Peru and USA. Customized trips
to the Amazon and archaeological sites
of Peru and Ecuador.

Tropical Nature Travel, PO Box 5276,
Gainsville, FL 32627-5276, USA, T1-877-
827 8350, www.tropicalnaturetravel.
com. Eco-tour operator offering wildlife,
culture and nature tours of Ecuador and
Galápagos.

Australia and New Zealand

Contours Travel, Level 6, 310 King St,
Melbourne, Vic 3000, T3-9670 6900,
www.contourstravel.com.au. Specializes
in Latin American destinations.

Tourist information

Tourist information and promotion
is handled at the national level by
the **Ministerio de Turismo**, Av Gran
Colombia y Briceño, Quito, T02-399 9333
or T1-800-887476, www.ecuador.travel,
www.turismo.gob.ec. The *ministerio* has
regional offices in the larger provincial
capitals and there are **municipal tourist
offices** in almost every town; details
are given in the text. The quality of
service and information provided vary
considerably, if your expectations are
modest then you may be pleasantly
surprised. Some tourist offices are
identified by signs marked '**iTur**'.

South American Explorers (www.
saexplorers.org) is a USA-based non-
profit organization which provides its
members with travel information about
Ecuador and South America. For details
of their Quito clubhouse see page 58.

Useful websites

www.ecuador.travel A good general introduction to the country.
www.ecuador.com; **www. ecuadortravelmag.com**; **www. quitoadventure.com**; **www. paisturistico.com** and **www. explored.com.ec** General guides with information about services, activities and national parks.
www.ecuadorexplorer.com; **www.ecuador-travel-guide.org**; **www.ecuadortravelsite.org**; **www.ecuaworld.com** and **www. thebestofecuador.com** Are all travel guides; the latter includes volunteering options.
www.trekkinginecuador.com for hiking information.
www.paginasamarillas.info.ec, **www.edina.com.ec** and **www. guiatelefonica.com.ec** Telephone directories.

Visas and immigration

All visitors to Ecuador must have a passport valid for at least 6 months and an onward or return ticket, but the latter is seldom asked for. Citizens of Afghanistan, Bangladesh, China, Eritrea, Ethiopia, Kenya, Nepal, Nigeria, Pakistan and Somalia require a visa to visit Ecuador; other tourists do not require a visa unless they wish to stay more than 90 days. Upon entry all visitors must complete an international embarkation/disembarkation card. Keep your copy, you will be asked for it when you leave, and keep this and your passport to hand when travelling in Ecuador, see ID above.

Tourists are granted 90 days upon arrival and there are no extensions except for citizens of the Andean Community of Nations. Visitors are not allowed back in the country if they have already stayed 90 days during the past 12 months. If you want to spend more time studying, volunteering, etc, you may be able to get a purpose-specific visa at the end of your 90 days as a tourist. Purpose-specific visas are issued by the **Ministerio de Relaciones Exteriores** (Foreign Office, http://cancilleria.gob.ec); ask for category '12-IX', about US$200 and paperwork, and allow extra time. There is no fine at present for overstaying but if you do so then you must obtain an exit permit form an immigration office 48 hrs before departure and you may be barred from returning to Ecuador.

There are immigration offices in all provincial capitals (see www.ministeriointerior.gob.ec/migracion). If your passport is lost or stolen then, after it has been replaced by your embassy, you will have go to an immigration office to obtain a *movimiento migratorio* (a certificate indicating the date you entered Ecuador) in order to be able to leave the country.

Tourists are not permitted to work under any circumstances. Visas for work, study and longer stays are issued by the Ministerio de Relaciones Exteriores (see above) through Ecuador's diplomatic representatives abroad. All of the foregoing regulations are subject to change.

Volunteering

'Voluntourism' is very popular in Ecuador, attracting many visitors, from students to retirees. It is a good way to become more intimately acquainted with the country (blemishes and all) and, at the same time, to try and lend a hand to its people. If you are seriously interested in volunteering, you should research both local and international organizations well before you leave home. Try to choose a position that matches your individual skills. Think carefully about the kind of work that you would find most satisfying but remember that you may also be assigned menial tasks. Likewise be realistic about how much you might be able to achieve. The shorter your stay, the more limited should be your expectations in all regards. One month is a reasonable minimum. You must speak at least basic Spanish, and preferably a good deal more, in order to work effectively in a local community setting.

You always have to pay your own airfare, and generally also contribute toward your room and board. There are many different areas where voluntary work is possible, of which we list but a few. Many nature reserves in and around Mindo and on the Western slopes of Pichincha currently offer volunteer opportunities, see page 97. Note that the following categories often overlap with each other and with conventional tourism.

Community work
Centro de la Niña Trabajadora (CENIT), Huacho E2-63 y José Peralta, Quito, T02-265-2861 ext 4, www.cenitecuador.org. This local organization helps working children (girls). US$100 one-off fee (does not provide accommodation or meals), minimum 6 months.

New Era Galápagos Foundation, Charles Darwin y 12 de Febrero, Puerto Baquerizo Moreno, T09-9964 0929, www.neweragalapagos.org. A small NGO that works with local youth. Volunteers teach foreign languages and run environmental projects. No charge (does not provide accommodation or meals), minimum 1 month.

Tierra del Volcán, Quito office: Vía Lactea 350 y Chimborazo, vía al Colegio Menor, Cumbayá, Quito, T02-204 1520, www.tierradelvolcan.com. Conservation, tourism and community projects in and around Parque Nacional Cotopaxi. US$300 per month, minimum 1 month.

Environmental conservation
Fundación Jatun Sacha, Pasaje Eugenio de Santillán N34-248 y Maurián, Quito, T02-331 7163, www.jatunsacha. org. A large Ecuadorean NGO running 8 biological research stations, all in exceptional natural areas. Fees and conditions vary from reserve to reserve.

Fundación Maquipuicuna, Baquerizo Moreno E9-153 y Tamayo, Quito, T02-250 7200, www.maqui.org. This NGO works with ecotourism, reforestation and environmental education at their reserve northwest of Quito. US$26 application fee, US$1000 per month, minimum 1 month.

Los Cedros Research Station, in the Intag region, T02-361 2546, www. reservaloscedros.org. A cloudforest reserve protecting many bird and orchid species. US$500 per month, minimum 2 weeks.

Rumi Wilco, contact Orlando or Alicia Falco, Vilcabamba, rumiwilco@yahoo. com, www.rumiwilco.com. A family-run 40-ha private nature reserve. Volunteers receive a discount on accommodation (see page 221), minimum 1 week.

Santa Lucía, Nanegal, outside Quto, T02-215 7242, www.santaluciaecuador. com. A community-based conservation and ecotourism project which protects a 730-ha tract of cloudforest. US$18 per day, minimum 2 weeks.

Yunguilla, Calacalí, outside Quto, T09-8021 5476, www.yunguilla.org.ec. This community of 50 local families combines environmental conservation with sustainable agriculture. US$15 per day.

Permaculture

Parque Bambú, El Limonal, along the road from Ibarra to San Lorenzo, contact Piet Sabbe, T06-301 6606, www.bospas.org. A small family-run reserve and centre for permaculture and reforestation. US$245 per month or US$18 per day.

Río Muchacho Organic Farm, contact Nicola Mears or Darío Proaño, J Santos y 3 de Noviembre, Canoa, T05-258 8184, www.riomuchacho.com. A small organization working with sustainable agriculture, local education and community development. US$105 for the first week, US$10 per day thereafter, minimum 1 week.

Sacred Sueños, contact Yves Zehnder, Vilcabamba, T09-8931 3698, www. sacredsuenos.wordpress.com. A small young 'intentional community' involved with permaculture, 1½ hrs' walk from town. About US$50 per week depending on length of stay, minimum 2 weeks.

Weights and measures

Officially metric, some English measures are used for hardware, some Spanish measures for produce.

Women travellers

See www.journeywoman.com.
Generally women travellers should find visiting Ecuador an enjoyable experience. Gender stereotyping has diminished, however machismo lives on. You should be prepared for this and try not to overreact. When you set out, err on the side of caution until your instincts have adjusted to the customs of a new culture. If, as a single woman, you can befriend an Ecuadorean woman, you will learn more about the country and its current norms.

Note that tampons may be hard to find in smaller towns; sanitary towels are available everywhere.

Join us online...

Follow **@FootprintBooks** on **Twitter**, like **Footprint Books** on **Facebook** and talk travel with us! Ask us questions, speak to our authors, swap stories and be kept up-to-date with travel news, exclusive discounts and fantastic competitions.

Upload your travel pics to our **Flickr** site and inspire others on where to go next.

And don't forget to visit us at **footprint**travelguides.com

Footnotes
Ecuador

Basic Spanish for travellers

Learning Spanish is a useful part of the preparation for a trip to Latin America and no volumes of dictionaries, phrase books or word lists will provide the same enjoyment as being able to communicate directly with the people of the country you are visiting. It is a good idea to make an effort to grasp the basics before you go. As you travel you will pick up more of the language and the more you know, the more you will benefit from your stay.

General pronunciation

Whether you have been taught the 'Castilian' pronunciation (z and c followed by i or e are pronounced as the th in think) or the 'American' pronunciation (they are pronounced as s), you will encounter little difficulty in understanding either. Regional accents and usages vary, but the basic language is essentially the same everywhere.

Vowels

a	as in English *cat*
e	as in English *best*
i	as the *ee* in English *feet*
o	as in English *shop*
u	as the *oo* in English *food*
ai	as the *i* in English *ride*
ei	as *ey* in English *they*
oi	as *oy* in English *toy*

Consonants

Most consonants can be pronounced more or less as they are in English. The exceptions are:

g	before e or i is the same as *j*
h	is always silent (except in *ch* as in *chair*)
j	as the *ch* in Scottish *loch*
ll	as the *y* in *yellow*
ñ	as the *ni* in English *onion*
rr	trilled much more than in English
x	depending on its location, pronounced *x*, *s*, *sh* or *j*

Spanish words and phrases

Greetings, courtesies

hello	*hola*	what is your name?	*¿cómo se llama?*
good morning	*buenos días*		*¿cómo te llamas?*
good afternoon/	*buena stardes/*	yes/no	*sí/no*
evening/night	*noches*	please	*por favor*
goodbye	*adiós/chao*	thank you (very much)	*(muchas) gracias*
pleased to meet	*you mucho gusto*	I speak Spanish	*hablo español*
see you later	*hasta luego*	I don't speak Spanish	*no hablo español*
how are you?	*¿cómo está?/*	do you speak English?	*¿habla inglés?*
	¿cómo estás?	I don't understand	*no entiendo/*
I'm fine, thanks	*estoymuy bien, gracias*		*no comprendo*
I'm called...	*me llamo...*	please speak slowly	*hable despacio*
			por favor

I am very sorry	lo sientomucho/ disculpe	I don't want it	no lo quiero
what do you want?	¿qué quiere? ¿qué quieres?	leave me alone	déjeme en paz/ no me moleste
I want	quiero	good/bad	bueno/malo

Questions and requests

Have you got a room for two people?
  ¿Tiene una habitación para dos personas?
How do I get to_? *¿Cómo llego a_?*
How much does it cost?
  ¿Cuánto cuesta? ¿cuánto es?
I'd like tomake a long-distance phone call
  Quisiera hacer una llamada de larga distancia
Is service included?
  ¿Está incluido el servicio?

Is tax included?
  ¿Están incluidos los impuestos?
When does the bus leave (arrive)?
  ¿A qué hora sale (llega) el bus?
When? *¿cuándo?*
Where is_? *¿dónde está_?*
Where can I buy tickets?
  ¿Dónde puedo comprar boletos?
Where is the nearest petrol station?
  ¿Dónde está la gasolinera más cercana?
Why? *¿por qué?*

Basics

bank	el banco	market	el mercado
bathroom/toilet	el baño	note/coin	le billete/la moneda
bill	la factura/la cuenta	police (policeman)	la policía (el policía)
cash	el efectivo	post office	el correo
cheap	barato/a	public telephone	el teléfono público
credit card	la tarjeta de crédito	supermarket	el supermercado
exchange house	la casa de cambio	ticket office	la taquilla
exchange rate	el tipo de cambio	traveller's cheques	los cheques de viajero/los travelers
expensive	caro/a		

Getting around

aeroplane	el avión	first/second class	primera/segunda clase
airport	el aeropuerto		
arrival/departure	la llegada/salida	left/right	izquierda/derecha
avenue	la avenida	ticket	el boleto
block	la cuadra	empty/full	vacío/lleno
border	la frontera	highway, main road	la carretera
bus station	la terminal de buses/ la terminal terrestre	immigration	la inmigración/ migración
bus	el bus/el autobús collective	insurance	el seguro
		insured person	el/la asegurado/a
fixed-route taxi	el taxi rutas	to insure yourself against	
corner	la esquina	asegurarse contra	
customs	la aduana	luggage	el equipaje

motorway, freeway	la autopista/	puncture	el pinchazo
	la carretera	street	la calle
north, south,	norte, sur,	that way	por allí/por allá
west, east	oeste (occidente),	this way	por aquí/por acá
	este (oriente)	tourist card/visa	la tarjeta de turista
oil	el aceite	tyre	la llanta
to park	estacionarse	unleaded	sin plomo
passport	el pasaporte	to walk	caminar/andar
petrol/gasoline	la gasolina		

Accommodation

air conditioning	el aire acondicionado	power cut	el apagón/corte
all-inclusive	todo incluido	restaurant	el restaurante
bathroom, private	el baño privado	room/bedroom	el cuarto/
bed, double/single	la cama		la habitación
	matrimonial/sencilla	sheets	las sábanas
blankets	las cobijas/mantas	shower	la ducha/regadera
to clean	limpiar	soap	el jabón
dining room	el comedor	toilet	el sanitario/excusado
guesthouse	la casa de huéspedes	toilet paper	el papel higiénico
hotel	el hotel	towels, clean/dirty	las toallas limpias/
noisy	ruidoso		sucias
pillows	las almohadas	water, hot/cold	el agua caliente/fría

Health

aspirin	la aspirina	diarrhoea	la diarrea
blood	la sangre	doctor	el médico
chemist	la farmacia	fever/sweat	la fiebre/el sudor
condoms	los preservativos,	pain	el dolor
	los condones	head	la cabeza
contact lenses	los lentes de contacto	period/	la regla/
contraceptives	los anticonceptivos	sanitary towels	las toallas sanitarias
contraceptive pill	la píldora	stomach	el estómago
	anticonceptiva	altitude sickness	el soroche

Family

family	la familia	married	casado/a
brother/sister	el hermano/	single/unmarried	soltero/a
	la hermana		
daughter/son	la hija/el hijo		
father/mother	el padre/la madre		
husband/wife	el esposo (marido)/		
	la esposa		
boyfriend/girlfriend	el novio/la novia		
friend	el amigo/la amiga		

Months, days and time

January	*enero*	Saturday	*sábado*
February	*febrero*	Sunday	*domingo*
March	*marzo*		
April	*abril*	at one o'clock	*a launa*
May	*mayo*	at half past two	*a las dos y media*
June	*junio*	at a quarter to three	*a cuartopara las*
July	*julio*		*tres/a las tres*
August	*agosto*		*menos quince*
September	*septiembre*	it's one o'clock	*es la una*
October	*octubre*	it's seven o'clock	*son las siete*
November	*noviembre*	it's six twenty	*son las seis y*
December	*diciembre*		*veinte*
		it's five to nine	*son las*
Monday	*lunes*		*nuevemenos*
Tuesday	*martes*		*cinco*
Wednesday	*miércoles*	in ten minutes	*en diez minutos*
Thursday	*jueves*	five hours	*cinco horas*
Friday	*viernes*	does it take long?	*¿tarda mucho?*

Numbers

one	*uno/una*	sixteen	*dieciséis*
two	*dos*	seventeen	*diecisiete*
three	*tres*	eighteen	*dieciocho*
four	*cuatro*	nineteen	*diecinueve*
five	*cinco*	twenty	*veinte*
six	*seis*	twenty-one	*veintiuno*
seven	*siete*	thirty	*treinta*
eight	*ocho*	forty	*cuarenta*
nine	*nueve*	fifty	*cincuenta*
ten	*diez*	sixty	*sesenta*
eleven	*once*	seventy	*setenta*
twelve	*doce*	eighty	*ochenta*
thirteen	*trece*	ninety	*noventa*
fourteen	*catorce*	hundred	*cien/ciento*
fifteen	*quince*	thousand	*mil*

Food

avocado	*el aguacate*	beef steak or pork fillet	*el bistec*
baked	*al horno*	boiled rice	*el arroz blanco*
bakery	*la panadería*	bread	*el pan*
banana	*el plátano*	breakfast	*el desayuno*
beans	*los fréjoles/*	butter	*la mantequilla*
	los porotos	cake	*el pastel*
beef	*la carne de res*	chewing	*gum el chicle*

chicken	el pollo	pepper (ground)	la pimienta
chilli or green pepper	el ají/pimiento	pasty, turnover	la empanada/
clear soup, stock	el caldo		el pastelito
cooked	cocido	pork	el cerdo
dining room	el comedor	potato	la papa
egg	el huevo	prawns	los camarones
fish	el pescado	raw	crudo
fork	el tenedor	restaurant	el restaurante
fried	frito	salad	la ensalada
garlic	el ajo	salt	la sal
goat	el chivo	sandwich	el sánduche
grapefruit	la toronja	sauce	la salsa
grill	la parrilla	sausage	la longaniza/el
grilled/griddled	a laplancha		chorizo
guava	la guayaba	scrambled eggs	los huevos revueltos
ham	el jamón	seafood	losmariscos
hamburger	la hamburguesa	soup	la sopa
hot, spicy	picante	spoon	la cuchara
ice cream	el helado	squash	la calabaza
jam	la mermelada	squid	los calamares
knife	el cuchillo	supper	la cena
lime	el limón	sweet	dulce
lobster	la langosta	to eat	comer
lunch	el almuerzo/	toasted	tostado
	la comida	turkey	el pavo
		vegetables	las legumbres/
meal	la comida		los vegetales
meat	la carne		
minced meat	la carne molida	without meat	sin carne
onion	la cebolla	yam	el camote
orange	la naranja		

Drink

beer	la cerveza	glass	el vaso
boiled	hervido/a	hot	caliente
bottled	en botella	ice/without ice	el hielo/sin hielo
camomile tea	la manzanilla	juice	el jugo
canned	en lata	lemonade	la limonada
coffee	el café	milk	la leche
coffee, white	el café con leche	mint	la menta
cold	frío	rum	el ron
cup	la taza	soft drink	la cola
drink	la bebida	sugar	el azúcar
drunk	borracho/a	tea	el té
firewater	el aguardiente	to drink	beber/tomar
fruit milkshake	el batido/licuado	water	el agua

| water, carbonated | el agua mineral con gas | wine, red | el vino tinto |
| water, still | mineral el agua mineral sin gas | wine, white | el vino blanco |

Key verbs

to go	**ir**
I go	voy
you go (familiar)	vas
he, she, it goes, you (formal) go	va
we go	vamos
they, you (plural) go	van

to have (possess)	**tener**
I have	tengo
you (familiar) have	tienes
he, she, it, you (formal) have	tiene
we have	tenemos
they, you (plural) have	tienen
there is/are	hay
there isn't/aren't no	hay

to be	**ser** (permanent state) **estar** (positional or temporary state)		
I am	soy	estoy
you are	eres	estás
he, she, it is, you (formal) are	es	está
we are	somos	estamos
they, you (plural) are	son	están

This section has been assembled on the basis of glossaries compiled by André de Mendonça and David Gilmour of South American Experience, London, and the Latin American Travel Advisor, No 9, March 1996.

Index

Entries in bold refer to maps

FOOTPRINT

Features

About the authors & correspondents

Robert and Daisy Kunstaetter

As a little girl growing up in Quito, toward the end of each school year Daisy Isacovici would stare out her classroom window at the snow-covered slopes of Cotopaxi and dream of holidays and travel. It was destiny, perhaps, that her dreams of travelling throughout Ecuador were not fulfilled until after she met Robert. He hails from Canada, where they met, and shortly thereafter he suggested they travel around South America for a "year or so". That was in 1986 and the year proved to be elastic, they have since lived or travelled in every country on the continent.

Over the years and miles, Robert and Daisy became regular correspondents for Footprint, helping to update annual editions of the *South American Handbook*. Based back in Ecuador since 1993, they have been closely involved with tourism here as well as in Peru and Bolivia. They are authors, co-authors, contributors to and cartographers for numerous Footprint guidebooks. They are also authors of a trekking guide to Ecuador and are currently writing one for Peru.

Robert and Daisy usually enjoy the company of their friends as well as the tranquility of their hammock, but all that changes when they are preparing a new edition. When not travelling, writing or out for morning walks during this period, they are usually sound asleep.

Correspondents

Jeaneth Barrionuevo hails from Baños and teaches Spanish and English in Cuenca. Jeaneth's enthusiasm is as contagious as her handwriting is neat.

Jean Brown came to Ecuador from England to teach in 1976, and has been studying the country ever since. She ran an archaeology field school in Salango and a very successful tour agency in Quito. The depth and breadth of Jean's knowledge is matched only by her generosity in sharing it.

Michael Resch set out from Austria to tour the world for 17 years, before settling near Baños in 1996. Along the way he mastered the art and science of travel. He is also a master of *sumak kawsay*.

Peter Schramm hails from Germany and sailed with the navy before moving to Vilcabamba in 2002. He is a successful hotelier with the heart of a *mochilero* and yogi.

Popkje van der Ploeg was a journalist in the Netherlands before moving to Ecuador in 1994. She runs a successful tour agency in Riobamba.

Acknowledgements

Ecuador is our home. We are passionate about its many joys and wonders, and like nothing better than talking about them. On the other side of the same coin, we get upset when we learn of another block of Oriente jungle being opened to petroleum depredation or San Rafael falls threatened by a massive hydro-electric project. Perhaps these sentiments, both our pride and our frustration, can be felt through the pages of this book. They are by and large shared by our team of correspondents, all of whom have, like us, chosen to make their lives here. This diverse dedicated team of travel professionals and professional travellers has worked hard to share their intimate knowledge of Ecuador, and we thank them warmly. They are listed above.

Additional valuable contributions to this edition were made by Douglas Chang, Darcy Gaechter, Fernando Guales, Harry Jonitz, Lou Jost, Iván Suárez and Delia María Torres. We would also like to thank all of the following for their assistance, including those readers who wrote about their experiences in Ecuador: Baruch & Aviva Aziza, Jessica Belfield, Gwen Burton, Angie Chang, Miles Drury, Vilma Durán, Henry Guillén, Luis Hernández, Alexandra Lozano, Esteban Ludeña, Rodrigo Morales, Hubert Olbrich, Richard Parsons, Eliana Rhor, Katja Saubert, Nikki Sevel, Liliana Tarupi, Carla Valarezo, María Viteri, Gwen von Bargen and Roger and Pat Wagstaff.

This edition is built on the hard work of several generations of Footprint travel writers and editors. We thank the entire Footprint editorial and production team, in particular Ben Box, our editors Nicola Gibbs, Jo Williams and Felicity Laughton.

Picture credits: Galápagos Islands
Page 323: farbled / Shutterstock.com. **Page 326**: Alan Brookstone / Shutterstock.com. **Page 328**: Fotos593/Shutterstock.com. **Page 330**: Jess Kraft/Shutterstock.com. **Page 331**: roroto12p/Shutterstock.com; Shaun Jeffers/Shutterstock.com. **Page 332**: Longjourneys/Shutterstock.com. **Page 333**: Roland Spiegler/Shutterstock.com; DigitalMagus/Shutterstock.com. **Page 334**: Watchtheworld/Shutterstock.com; Thomas O'Neil/Shutterstock.com. **Page 335**: Gail Johnson/Shutterstock.com. **Page 336**: Frank Wasserfuehrer/Shutterstock.com; photoiconix/Shutterstock.com. **Page 337**: Anna Azimi/Shutterstock.com. Page Anastasia Koro/Shutterstock.com; Mr. Tobin/Shutterstock.com. **Page 339**: Amanda Nicholls/Shutterstock.com; Stephen Frink/SuperStock.com; Minden Pictures /SuperStock.com; National Geographic/SuperStock.com. **Page 340**: Steve Allen/Shutterstock.com. **Page 341**: Minden Pictures/Superstock.com. **Page 343**: Minden Pictures/Superstock.com. **Page 344**: Marisa Estivill/Shutterstock.com. **Page 345**: foxie/Shutterstock.com;

RHIMAGE/Shutterstock.com. **Page 346**: Stacy Funderburke/Shutterstock.com; Marisa Estivill/Shutterstock.com. **Page 347**: Fotos593/Shutterstock.com; Jess Kraft/Shutterstock.com. **Page 348**: Mint Image/SuperStock.com. **Page 349**: Ecuadorpostales/Shutterstock.com; sunsinger/Shutterstock.com; Guido Vermeulen-Perdaen/Shutterstock.com. **Page 350**: Fotos593/Shutterstock.com. **Page 351**: Ingram Publishing/SuperStock.com; Steve Allen/Shutterstock.com; Alberto Loyo/Shutterstock.com. **Page 352**: David Thyberg/Shutterstock.com; farbled/Shutterstock.com. **Page 353**: Ammit Jack/Shutterstock.com. **Page 354**: Erkki & Hanna/Shutterstock.com; Alfie Photography/Shutterstock.com.

Duotones Page Pages 38 and 106: Anton_Ivanov/Shutterstock.com. **Page 144**: Ecuadorpostales/Shutterstock.com. **Page 192**: onairda/Shutterstock.com. **Page 228**: Fotos593 / Shutterstock.com. **Page 252**: Fotos593/Shutterstock.com. **Page 286**: Ksenia Ragozina/Shutterstock.com.

Credits

Footprint credits

Editors: Nicola Gibbs, Jo Williams
Production and layout: Emma Bryers
Maps: Robert Kunstaetter, Kevin Feeney
Colour sections: Angus Dawson, Patrick Dawson

Publisher: Patrick Dawson
Managing Editor: Felicity Laughton
Administration: Elizabeth Taylor
Advertising sales and marketing:
John Sadler, Kirsty Holmes,
Debbie Wylde

Photography credits

Front cover: BlueOrange Studio/
Shutterstock.com
Back cover: Top Anton_Ivanov/Shutterstock.
com. **Bottom** James Harrison/Shutterstock.
com

Colour section

Inside front cover: Ecuadorpostales/
Shutterstock, NaturePL/Shutterstock,
KalypsoWorldPhotography/Shutterstock.
Page 1: Justin Black/Shutterstock. **Page
2**: kongsak sumano/Shutterstock. **Page
4**: Stefano Paterna/Superstock, Noradoa/
Shutterstock. **Page 5**: Fotos593/Shutterstock,
Ksenia Ragozina/Shutterstock, Santiago
Cornejo/Shutterstock, Jess Kraft/Shutterstock.
Page 6: Kunstatters, Robert Francis/
South American Pictures, Paul S. Wolf/
Shutterstock. **Page 7**: Michael Hanson/
Superstock, Marcelina Zygula/Shutterstock,
Sergey Uryadnikov/Shutterstock. **Page 10**:
Fotos593/Shutterstock. **Page 11**: Ksenia
Ragozina/Shutterstock. **Page 12**: Ammit Jack/
Shutterstock, Jess Kraft/Shutterstock. **Page
13**: Vladimir Korostyshevskiy/Shutterstock.
Page 14: steve100/Shutterstock, Rafal
Cichawa/Shutterstock. **Page 15**: Hemis.fr/
Superstock, RobHamm/Shutterstock, Ivan
Smuk/Shutterstock, Gabrielle & Michel Th/
Superstock. **Page 16**: Fotos593/Shutterstock.

Printed in Spain by GraphyCems

Publishing information

Footprint Ecuador
8th edition
© Footprint Handbooks Ltd
November 2015

ISBN: 978 1 910120 39 2
CIP DATA: A catalogue record for this
book is available from the British Library

® Footprint Handbooks and the
Footprint mark are a registered
trademark of Footprint Handbooks Ltd

Published by Footprint
6 Riverside Court
Lower Bristol Road
Bath BA2 3DZ, UK
T +44 (0)1225 469141
F +44 (0)1225 469461
footprinttravelguides.com

Distributed in the USA by
National Book Network, Inc.

Every effort has been made to ensure
that the facts in this guidebook are
accurate. However, travellers should still
obtain advice from consulates, airlines,
etc about travel and visa requirements
before travelling. The authors and
publishers cannot accept responsibility
for any loss, injury or inconvenience
however caused.

Colour map index

Distance table

Ambato																		
40	**Baños**																	
306	309	**Cuenca**																
390	430	667	**Esmeraldas**															
288	288	250	472	**Guayaquil**														
251	291	557	433	535	**Ibarra**													
397	388	700	579	674	365	**Lago Agrio**												
47	87	353	343	335	204	350	**Latacunga**											
511	514	205	832	415	764	904	558	**Loja**										
230	190	231	620	432	479	456	277	436	**Macas**									
382	383	188	608	191	633	766	429	235	419	**Machala**								
404	444	446	442	196	505	649	355	611	628	387	**Manta**							
231	271	537	413	515	20	345	184	742	459	613	485	**Otavalo**						
101	61	370	491	349	350	327	148	519	129	444	505	330	**Puyo**					
136	176	442	318	420	115	259	89	647	366	518	390	95	237	**Quito**				
52	55	254	442	233	303	440	99	459	245	328	456	283	116	188	**Riobamba**			
451	451	413	622	163	685	803	498	578	595	354	225	665	512	570	396	**Salinas**		
205	245	482	185	287	248	394	158	647	435	423	257	228	306	133	257	437	**Santo Domingo**	
185	140	449	497	428	271	248	227	598	208	523	584	251	79	186	195	591	312	**Tena**

Distances in kilometres 1 kilometre = 0.62 miles

Footprint Mini Atlas
Ecuador &
Galápagos

San Lorenzo
La Tola
Esmeraldas
Atacames
ESMERALDAS
Muisne
Quinindé
IMBABURA
Ibarra
Otavalo
Cojimíes
Pedernales
Mindo
Equator
QUITO
El Carmen
Santo
Domingo
NAPO
Baeza
Canoa
MANABI
Bahía de
Caráque
COTOPAXI
Manta
Quevedo
Latacunga
Cotopaxi
Tena
Portoviejo
Jipijapa
LOS
RIOS
BOLIVAR
Ambato
Baños
Puyo
Puerto López
Chimborazo
Guaranda
Tungurahua
Babahoyo
Riobamba
GUAYAS
CHIMBORAZO
Salinas
Guayaquil
SANTA
ELENA
El Triunfo
Alausí
Macas
La Troncal
Cañar Ingapirca
Playas
Puerto Inca
CAÑAR
MORONA
SANTIAGO
Azogues
Cuenca
Machala
AZUAY
Tumbes
Huaquillas
Gualaquiza
EL ORO
Zaruma
LOJA
Zamora
Loja
Vilcabamba
ZAMORA
Macará
CHINCHIPE
Zumba

Ipiales
Tulcan
CARCHI
COLOMBIA
Lago Agrio
Río Putumayo
Río Aguarico
Río Napo
Coca
ORELLANA
Nuevo
Rocafuerte
PASTAZA
Río Pastaza
PERU

Panamerican Highway

Altitude in metres
4000
3000
2000
1000
500
200
0
Neighbouring
country

——— Primary road
——— Secondary road
——— Railway

N

50 km
50 miles

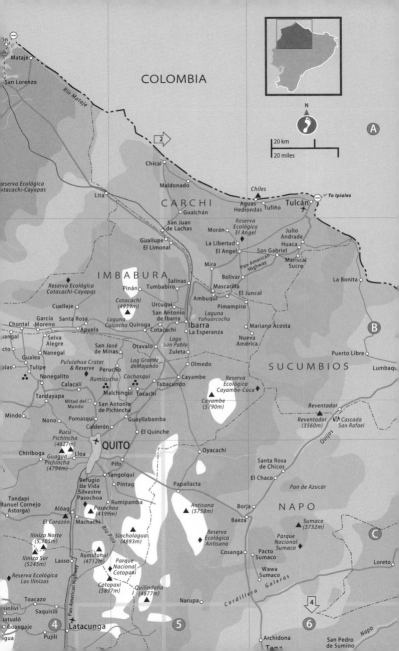

Map 2

Map 4

Chontapunta

Salcedo

Parque
Nacional
Los Llanganates

Pillaro

NAPO · Nopo

Archidona
Tena ✈
Misahuallí
Ahuano
San Pedro
de Sumino

Puerto Napo

⬆1

asaca Patate
lileo

A

Baños
Río Negro

Río Verde

Arajuno

Tungurahua
(5016m)

Mera

Candelaria

Shell
Puyo

Villano

El Altar
(5315m)

Porvenir

Canelos

PASTAZA

Parque
Nacional
Sangay

Palora

Sarayacu

Bobonaza

Chuitayo

las

Sangay
(5230m)

unas
Atillo

B

Atillo

MORONA
SANTIAGO

Pastaza

unas de
goche

9 de Octubre

Upano

Cordillera de Cutucú

Macas ✈

⬇5

Taisha

Sucúa

Logroño

Méndez

⬅3

Patuca

Yaupi

San José
de Morona

Morona

Puerto
Morona

Limón (Gral Leónidas
Plaza Gutiérrez)

C

Zamora

Plan de Milagro

Santiago

Santiago

Indanza

PERU

Parque
Binacional
El Cóndor ①

②

③

ORELLANA

Nashiño

Cononaco

Conanaco ○

A

Pavacachi ○

Curaray

↑2

Pintoyacu

Conambo ○

Conambo

atalvo

B

Corrientes

Río Corientes ○

Ishpingo ○

C

N

20 km
20 miles

④ ⑤ ⑥

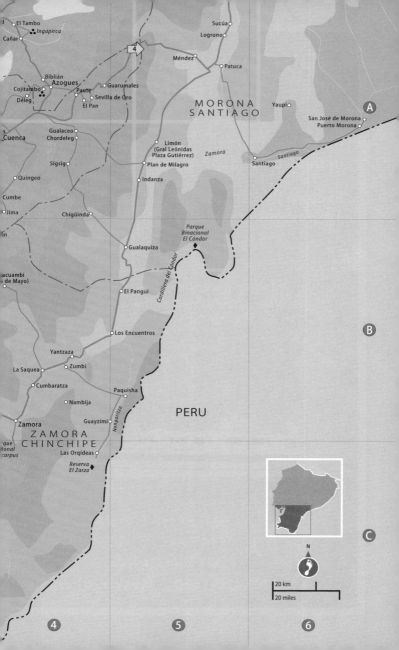